Microsoft®
OFFICE 2010
BRIEF

Gary B. Shelly
Misty E. Vermaat

Contributing Authors
Raymond E. Enger
Steven M. Freund
Mary Z. Last
Philip J. Pratt
Jeffrey J. Quasney
Susan L. Sebok

COURSE TECHNOLOGY
CENGAGE Learning™

SHELLY
CASHMAN
SERIES®

Australia • Brazil • Japan • Korea • Mexico • Singapore • Spain • United Kingdom • United States

COURSE TECHNOLOGY
CENGAGE Learning

Microsoft Office 2010: Brief
Gary B. Shelly, Misty E. Vermaat

Vice President, Publisher: Nicole Pinard

Executive Editor: Kathleen McMahon

Senior Product Manager: Mali Jones

Associate Product Manager: Aimee Poirier

Editorial Assistant: Lauren Brody

Director of Marketing: Cheryl Costantini

Marketing Manager: Tristen Kendall

Marketing Coordinator: Stacey Leasca

Print Buyer: Julio Esperas

Director of Production: Patty Stephan

Content Project Manager: Matthew Hutchinson

Development Editors: Jill Batistick, Amanda Brodkin, Deb Kaufmann, Lyn Markowicz

Copyeditors: Foxxe Editorial and Troy Lilly

Proofreaders: Chris Clark and Karen Annett

Indexer: Rich Carlson

QA Manuscript Reviewers: Chris Scriver, John Freitas, Serge Palladino, Susan Pedicini, Danielle Shaw, Susan Whalen

Art Director: Marissa Falco

Cover Designer: Lisa Kuhn, Curio Press, LLC

Cover Photo: Tom Kates Photography

Text Design: Joel Sadagursky

Compositor: PreMediaGlobal

For product information and technology assistance, contact us at
Cengage Learning Customer & Sales Support, 1-800-354-9706

For permission to use material from this text or product, submit all requests online at **cengage.com/permissions**
Further permissions questions can be emailed to
permissionrequest@cengage.com

Library of Congress Control Number: 2010929673

softcover binding:
ISBN-13: 978-1-4390-7842-6
ISBN-10: 1-4390-7842-4

softcover spiral binding:
ISBN-13: 978-1-4390-7843-3
ISBN-10: 1-4390-7843-2

Course Technology
20 Channel Center Street
Boston, MA 02210
USA

Cengage Learning is a leading provider of customized learning solutions with office locations around the globe, including Singapore, the United Kingdom, Australia, Mexico, Brazil, and Japan. Locate your local office at:
international.cengage.com/region

Cengage Learning products are represented in Canada by Nelson Education, Ltd.

Visit our website **www.cengage.com/ct/shellycashman** to share and gain ideas on our textbooks!

To learn more about Course Technology, visit **www.cengage.com/coursetechnology**

Purchase any of our products at your local college store or at our preferred online store **www.CengageBrain.com**

We dedicate this book to the memory of James S. Quasney (1940 – 2009), who for 18 years co-authored numerous books with Tom Cashman and Gary Shelly and provided extraordinary leadership to the Shelly Cashman Series editorial team. As series editor, Jim skillfully coordinated, organized, and managed the many aspects of our editorial development processes and provided unending direction, guidance, inspiration, support, and advice to the Shelly Cashman Series authors and support team members. He was a trusted, dependable, loyal, and well-respected leader, mentor, and friend. We are forever grateful to Jim for his faithful devotion to our team and eternal contributions to our series.

The Shelly Cashman Series Team

Printed in the United States of America
2 3 4 5 6 7 15 14 13 12 11

Microsoft® OFFICE 2010
BRIEF

Contents

Microsoft **Word 2010**

CHAPTER ONE
Creating, Formatting, and Editing a Word Document with Pictures

CHAPTER TWO
Creating a Research Paper with Citations and References

Microsoft PowerPoint 2010

CHAPTER ONE

Creating and Editing a Presentation with Clip Art

CHAPTER TWO

Enhancing a Presentation with Pictures, Shapes, and WordArt

Microsoft **Excel 2010**

CHAPTER ONE
Creating a Worksheet and an Embedded Chart

CHAPTER TWO
Formulas, Functions, and Formatting

Microsoft Access 2010

CHAPTER ONE

Databases and Database Objects: An Introduction

CHAPTER TWO

Querying a Database

Appendices

Preface

The Shelly Cashman Series® offers the finest textbooks in computer education. We are proud that since Mircosoft Office 4.3, our series of Microsoft Office textbooks have been the most widely used books in education. With each new edition of our Office books, we make significant improvements based on the software and comments made by instructors and students. For this Microsoft Office 2010 text, the Shelly Cashman Series development team carefully reviewed our pedagogy and analyzed its effectiveness in teaching today's Office student. Students today read less, but need to retain more. They need not only to be able to perform skills, but to retain those skills and know how to apply them to different settings. Today's students need to be continually engaged and challenged to retain what they're learning.

With this Microsoft Office 2010 text, we continue our commitment to focusing on the user and how they learn best.

Objectives of This Textbook

Microsoft Office 2010: Brief is intended for a course that includes a brief introduction to Office 2010. No experience with a computer is assumed, and no mathematics beyond the high school freshman level is required. The objectives of this book are:

- To teach the fundamentals of, Microsoft Word 2010, Microsoft PowerPoint 2010, Microsoft Excel 2010, Microsoft Access 2010, and Microsoft Windows 7

- To expose students to practical examples of the computer as a useful tool

- To acquaint students with the proper procedures to create documents, worksheets, databases, and presentations suitable for coursework, professional purposes, and personal use

- To help students discover the underlying functionality of Office 2010 so they can become more productive

- To develop an exercise-oriented approach that allows learning by doing

New to This Edition

Microsoft Office 2010: Brief offers a number of new features and approaches, which improve student understanding, retention, transference, and skill in using Office 2010 programs. The following enhancements will enrich the learning experience:

- Office 2010 and Windows 7: Essential Concepts and Skills chapter prevents repetitive coverage of basic skills in the application chapters.

- Streamlined first chapters for each application allow the ability to cover more advanced skills earlier.

- Chapter topic redistribution offers concise chapters that ensure complete skill coverage.

- Expanded coverage of PowerPoint gives exposure to the numerous enhancements made to this application.

- New pedagogical elements enrich material creating an accessible and user-friendly approach.

  - Break Points, a new boxed element, identify logical stopping points and give students instructions regarding what they should do before taking a break.

  - Within step instructions, Tab | Group Identifiers, such as (Home tab | Bold button), help students more easily locate elements in the groups and on the tabs on the Ribbon.

  - Modified step-by-step instructions tell the student what to do and provide the generic reason why they are completing a specific task, which helps students easily transfer given skills to different settings.

The Shelly Cashman Approach

A Proven Pedagogy with an Emphasis on Project Planning

Each chapter presents a practical problem to be solved, within a project planning framework. The project orientation is strengthened by the use of Plan Ahead boxes, which encourage critical thinking about how to proceed at various points in the project. Step-by-step instructions with supporting screens guide students through the steps. Instructional steps are supported by the Q&A, Experimental Step, and BTW features.

A Visually Engaging Book that Maintains Student Interest

The step-by-step tasks, with supporting figures, provide a rich visual experience for the student. Call-outs on the screens that present both explanatory and navigational information provide students with information they need when they need to know it.

Supporting Reference Materials (Appendices, Quick Reference)

The appendices provide additional information about the Application at hand and include such topics and project planning guidelines and certification. With the Quick Reference, students can quickly look up information about a single task, such as keyboard shortcuts, and find page references of where in the book the task is illustrated.

Integration of the World Wide Web

The World Wide Web is integrated into the Office 2010 learning experience by (1) BTW annotations; (2) BTW, Q&A, and Quick Reference Summary Web pages; and (3) the Learn It Online section for each chapter.

End-of-Chapter Student Activities

Extensive end-of-chapter activities provide a variety of reinforcement opportunities for students where they can apply and expand their skills.

Instructor Resources

The Instructor Resources include both teaching and testing aids and can be accessed via CD-ROM or at www.cengage.com/login.

Instructor's Manual Includes lecture notes summarizing the chapter sections, figures and boxed elements found in every chapter, teacher tips, classroom activities, lab activities, and quick quizzes in Microsoft Word files.

Syllabus Easily customizable sample syllabi that cover policies, assignments, exams, and other course information.

Figure Files Illustrations for every figure in the textbook in electronic form.

Powerpoint Presentations A multimedia lecture presentation system that provides slides for each chapter. Presentations are based on chapter objectives.

Solutions to Exercises Includes solutions for all end-of-chapter and chapter reinforcement exercises.

Test Bank & Test Engine Test Banks include 112 questions for every chapter, featuring objective-based and critical thinking question types, and including page number references and figure references, when appropriate. Also included is the test engine, ExamView, the ultimate tool for your objective-based testing needs.

Data Files for Students Includes all the files that are required by students to complete the exercises.

Additional Activities for Students Consists of Chapter Reinforcement Exercises, which are true/false, multiple-choice, and short answer questions that help students gain confidence in the material learned.

SAM: Skills Assessment Manager

SAM 2010 is designed to help bring students from the classroom to the real world. It allows students to train on and test important computer skills in an active, hands-on environment.

SAM's easy-to-use system includes powerful interactive exams, training, and projects on the most commonly used Microsoft Office applications. SAM simulates the Microsoft Office 2010 application environment, allowing students to demonstrate their knowledge and think through the skills by performing real-world tasks such as bolding word text or setting up slide transitions. Add in live-in-the-application projects, and students are on their way to truly learning and applying skills to business-centric documents.

Designed to be used with the Shelly Cashman Series, SAM includes handy page references so that students can print helpful study guides that match the Shelly Cashman textbooks used in class. For instructors, SAM also includes robust scheduling and reporting features.

Content for Online Learning
Course Technology has partnered with the leading distance learning solution providers and class-management platforms today. To access this material, instructors will visit our password-protected instructor resources available at www.cengage.com/coursetechnology. Instructor resources include the following: additional case projects, sample syllabi, PowerPoint presentations per chapter, and more. For additional information or for an instructor user name and password, please contact your sales representative. For students to access this material, they must have purchased a WebTutor PIN-code specific to this title and your campus platform. The resources for students may include (based on instructor preferences), but are not limited to: topic review, review questions, and practice tests.

Workbook for Microsoft Office 2010: Introductory Concepts and Techniques
This highly popular supplement (ISBN 1-4390-7844-0) includes a variety of activities that help students recall, review, and master the concepts presented. The Workbook complements the end-of-chapter material with an outline; a self-test consisting of true/false, multiple-choice, short answer, and matching questions; and activities calculated to help students develop a deeper understanding of the information presented.

CourseNotes
Course Technology's CourseNotes are six-panel quick reference cards that reinforce the most important and widely used features of a software application in a visual and user-friendly format. CourseNotes serve as a great reference tool during and after the student completes the course. CourseNotes are available for software applications such as Microsoft Office 2010, Word 2010, PowerPoint 2010, Excel 2010, Access 2010, and Windows 7. Topic-based CourseNotes are available for Best Practices in Social Networking, Hot Topics in Technology, and Web 2.0. Visit www.cengage.com/ct/coursenotes to learn more!

A Guided Tour
Add excitement and interactivity to your classroom with "*A Guided Tour*" product line. Play one of the brief mini-movies to spice up your lecture and spark classroom discussion. Or, assign a movie for homework and ask students to complete the correlated assignment that accompanies each topic. "*A Guided Tour*" product line takes the prep work out of providing your students with information about new technologies and applications and helps keep students engaged with content relevant to their lives; all in under an hour!

About Our Covers
The Shelly Cashman Series is continually updating our approach and content to reflect the way today's students learn and experience new technology. This focus on student success is reflected on our covers, which feature real students from Bentley University using the Shelly Cashman Series in their courses, and reflect the varied ages and backgrounds of the students learning with our books. When you use the Shelly Cashman Series, you can be assured that you are learning computer skills using the most effective courseware available.

Textbook Walk-Through

The Shelly Cashman Series Pedagogy: Project-Based — Step-by-Step — Variety of Assessments

Plan Ahead boxes prepare students to create successful projects by encouraging them to think strategically about what they are trying to accomplish before they begin working.

Step-by-step instructions now provide a context beyond the point-and-click. Each step provides information on why students are performing each task, or what will occur as a result.

Q&A boxes offer questions students may have when working through the steps and provide additional information about what they are doing right where they need it.

Experiment Steps within our step-by-step instructions, encourage students to explore, experiment, and take advantage of the features of the Office 2010 user interface. These steps are not necessary to complete the projects, but are designed to increase the confidence with the software and build problem-solving skills.

Explanatory callouts summarize what is happening on screen.

Navigational callouts in red show students where to click.

General Project Decisions

While creating an Excel worksheet, you need to make several decisions that will determine the appearance and characteristics of the finished worksheet. As you create the worksheet necessary to meet the requirements shown in Figure 2–2, you should follow these general guidelines:

1. **Plan the layout of the worksheet.** Rows typically contain items analogous to items in a list. A name could serve as an item in a list, and, therefore, each name could be placed in a row. As a list grows, such as a list of employees, the number of rows in the worksheet will increase. Information about each item in the list and associated calculations should appear in columns.

2. **Determine the necessary formulas and functions needed.** Calculations result from known values. Formulas for such calculations should be known in advance of creating a worksheet. Values such as the average, highest, and lowest values can be calculated using Excel functions as opposed to relying on complex formulas.

3. **Identify how to format various elements of the worksheet.** The appearance of the worksheet affects its ability to express information clearly. Numeric data should be formatted in generally accepted formats, such as using commas as thousands separators and parentheses for negative values.

4. **Establish rules for conditional formatting.** Conditional formatting allows you to format a cell based on the contents of the cell. Decide under which circumstances you would like a cell to stand out from related cells and determine in what way the cell will stand out.

5. **Specify how the hard copy of a worksheet should appear.** When it is possible that a person will want to create a hard copy of a worksheet, care should be taken in the development of the worksheet to ensure that the contents can be presented in a readable manner. Excel prints worksheets in landscape or portrait orientation, and margins can be adjusted to fit more or less data on each page. Headers and footers add an additional level of customization to the printed page.

When necessary, more specific details concerning the above guidelines are presented at appropriate points in the chapter. The chapter also will identify the actions performed and decisions made regarding these guidelines during the creation of the worksheet shown in Figure 2–1 on page EX 67.

Plan
Ahead

Excel Chapter 2

To Change the Font of Selected Text

The default theme font for headings is Cambria and for all other text, called body text in Word, is Calibri. Many other fonts are available, however, so that you can add variety to documents.

To draw more attention to the headline, you change its font so that it differs from the font of other text in the flyer. The following steps change the font of the headline from Calibri to Arial Rounded MT Bold.

Word Chapter 1

BTW

Aesthetics versus Function
The function, or purpose, of a worksheet is to provide a user with direct ways to accomplish tasks. In designing a worksheet, functional considerations should come before visual aesthetics. Avoid the temptation to use flashy or confusing visual elements within the worksheet. One exception to this guideline occurs when you may need to draw the user's attention to an area of a worksheet that will help the user more easily complete a task.

❶
- With the text selected, click the Font box arrow (Home tab | Font group) to display the Font gallery (Figure 1–18).

Q&A — Will the fonts in my Font gallery be the same as those in Figure 1–18?
Your list of available fonts may differ, depending on the type of printer you are using and other settings.

Q&A — What if the text is no longer selected?
Follow the steps on page WD 15 to select a line.

Figure 1–18

❷
- Scroll through the Font gallery, if necessary, and then point to Arial Rounded MT Bold (or a similar font) to display a live preview of the selected text in the selected font (Figure 1–19).

🄴 **Experiment**
- Point to various fonts in the Font gallery and watch the font of the selected text change in the document window.

❸
- Click Arial Rounded MT Bold (or a similar font) to change the font of the selected text.

Figure 1–19

Other Ways			
1. Click Font box arrow on Mini toolbar, click desired font in Font gallery	box), select desired font in Font list, click OK button	font in Font list, click OK button	
2. Right-click selected text, click Font on shortcut menu, click Font tab (Font dialog	3. Click Font Dialog Box Launcher (Home tab | Font group), click Font tab (Font dialog box), select desired	4. Press CTRL+D, click Font tab (Font dialog box), select desired font in the Font list, click OK button	

Textbook Walk-Through

Chapter Summary A concluding paragraph, followed by a listing of the tasks completed within a chapter together with the pages on which the step-by-step, screen-by-screen explanations appear.

To Quit PowerPoint

The project now is complete. The following steps quit PowerPoint. For a detailed example of the procedure summarized below, refer to the Office 2010 and Windows 7 chapter at the beginning of this book.

1 If you have one PowerPoint document open, click the Close button on the right side of the title bar to close the document and quit PowerPoint; or if you have multiple PowerPoint documents open, click File on the Ribbon to open the Backstage view and then click Exit in the Backstage view to close all open documents and quit PowerPoint.

2 If a Microsoft Office PowerPoint dialog box appears, click the Save button to save any changes made to the document since the last save.

Chapter Summary

In this chapter you have learned how to apply a document theme, create a title slide and text slides with a bulleted list, clip art, and a photograph, size and move clip art and a photograph, format and edit text, add a slide transition, view the presentation in Slide Show view, and print slides as handouts. The items listed below include all the new PowerPoint skills you have learned in this chapter.

1. Start PowerPoint (PPT 4)
2. Choose a Document Theme (PPT 5)
3. Enter the Presentation Title (PPT 7)
4. Enter the Presentation Subtitle Paragraph (PPT 9)
5. Select a Paragraph (PPT 10)
6. Italicize Text (PPT 11)
7. Increase Font Size (PPT 11)
8. Select a Word (PPT 12)
9. Change the Text Color (PPT 13)

20. Insert a Clip from the Clip Organizer into the Title Slide (PPT 27)
21. Insert a Clip from the Clip Organizer into a Content Placeholder (PPT 30)
22. Insert a Photograph from the Clip Organizer into a Slide without a Content Placeholder (PPT 32)
23. Resize Clip Art (PPT 33)
24. Move Clips (PPT 36)
25. Duplicate a Slide (PPT 38)
26. Arrange a Slide (PPT 39)
27. Delete Text in a Placeholder (PPT 41)
28. Add a Transition between Slides (PPT 43)
29. Change Document Properties (PPT 46)
30. Save an Existing Presentation with the Same File Name (PPT 47)
31. Start Slide Show View (PPT 47)
32. Move Manually through Slides in a Slide Show (PPT 49)
33. Quit PowerPoint (PPT 50)
34. Open a Document from PowerPoint (PPT 50)
35. Print a Presentation (PPT 51)

r profile, your instructor may have assigned an autogradable
so, log into the SAM 2010 Web site at www.cengage.com/sam2010
and start files.

STUDENT ASSIGNMENTS

Learn It Online

Test your knowledge of chapter content and key terms.

Instructions: To complete the Learn It Online exercises, start your browser, click the Address bar, and then enter the Web address **scsite.com/wd2010/learn**.   When the Word 2010 Learn It Online page is displayed, click the link for the exercise you want to complete and then read the instructions.

Chapter Reinforcement TF, MC, and SA
A series of true/false, multiple choice, and short answer questions that test your knowledge of the chapter content.

Flash Cards
An interactive learning environment where you identify chapter key terms associated with displayed definitions.

Practice Test
A series of multiple choice questions that test your knowledge of chapter content and key terms.

Who Wants To Be a Computer Genius?
An interactive game that challenges your knowledge of chapter content in the style of a television quiz show.

Wheel of Terms
An interactive game that challenges your knowledge of chapter key terms in the style of the television show *Wheel of Fortune*.

Crossword Puzzle Challenge
A crossword puzzle that challenges your knowledge of key terms presented in the chapter.

Apply Your Knowledge

Reinforce the skills and apply the concepts you learned in this chapter.

Modifying Text and Formatting a Document
Note: To complete this assignment, you will be required to use the Data Files for Students. See the inside back cover of this book for instructions on downloading the Data Files for Students, or contact your instructor for information about accessing the required files.

Instructions: Start Word. Open the document, Apply 1-1 Buffalo Photo Shoot Flyer Unformatted, from the Data Files for Students. The document you open is an unformatted flyer. You are to modify text, format paragraphs and characters, and insert a picture in the flyer.

Perform the following tasks:
1. Delete the word, single, in the sentence of body copy below the headline.
2. Insert the word, Creeks, between the words, Twin Buffalo, in the sentence of body copy below the headline.
3. At the end of the signature line, change the period to an exclamation point.
4. Center the headline and the signature line.
5. Change the theme colors to the Aspect color scheme.
6. Change the font and font size of the headline to 48-point Impact, or a similar font. Change the case of the headline text to all capital letters. Apply the text effect called Gradient Fill – Orange, Accent 1, Outline – White to the headline.
7. Change the font size of body copy between the headline and the signature line to 20 point.
8. Use the Mini toolbar to change the font size of the signature line to 26 point.
9. Select the words, hundreds of buffalo, in the paragraph below the headline and underline them.

Learn It Online Every chapter features a Learn It Online section that is comprised of six exercises. These exercises include True/False, Multiple Choice, Short Answer, Flash Cards, Practice Test, and Learning Games.

Apply Your Knowledge This exercise usually requires students to open and manipulate a file from the Data Files that parallels the activities learned in the chapter. To obtain a copy of the Data Files for Students, follow the instructions on the inside back cover of this text.

Extend Your Knowledge

Extend the skills you learned in this chapter and experiment with new skills. You may need to use Help to complete the assignment.

Modifying Text and Picture Formats and Adding Page Borders

Note: To complete this assignment, you will be required to use the Data Files for Students. See the inside back cover of this book for instructions on downloading the Data Files for Students, or contact your instructor for information about accessing the required files.

Instructions: Start Word. Open the document, Extend 1-1 TVC Cruises Flyer, from the Data Files for Students. You will enhance the look of the flyer shown in Figure 1–76. *Hint:* Remember, if you make a mistake while formatting the picture, you can reset it by clicking the Reset Picture button or Reset Picture button arrow (Picture Tools Format tab | Adjust group).

Perform the following tasks:

1. Use Help to learn about the following formats: remove bullets, grow font, shrink font, art page borders, decorative underline(s), picture bullets, picture border shading, shadow picture effects, and color saturation and tone.

2. Remove the bullet from the paragraph below the picture.

3. Select the text, 10 percent, and use the Grow Font button to increase its font size.

4. Add an art page border to the flyer. If the border is not in color, add color to it.

5. Change the solid underline below the word, cruises, to a decorative underline. Change

NEED AN ESCAPE?

change border color and add shadow effect; change color saturation and color tone

remove bullet

use Grow Font button to increase font size

change to picture bullets

change style an

• **Tango Vacation Club members receive a 10 percent discount for _cruises_ booked during May. Select from a variety of destinations.**

An experience of a lifetime awaits you!

• **Ultimate relaxation**
• **Endless fun and entertainment**
• **Breathtaking scenery**
• **Friendly, attentive staff**
• **Clean facilities**

Interested? Call TVC at 555-1029.

Figure 1–76

add art page border

Make It Right

Analyze a document and correct all errors and/or improve the design.

Correcting Spelling and Grammar Errors

Note: To complete this assignment, you will be required to use the Data Files for Students. See the inside back cover of this book for downloading the Data Files for Students, or contact your instructor for information about accessing the required files.

Instructions: Start Word. Open the document, Make It Right 1-1 Karate Academy Flyer Unchecked, from the Data Files for Students. The document is a flyer that contains spelling and grammar errors, as shown in Figure 1–77. You are to correct each spelling (red wavy underline) and grammar error (green and blue wavy underlines) by right-clicking the flagged text and then clicking the appropriate correction on the shortcut menu.

If your screen does not display the wavy underlines, click File on the Ribbon and then click Options in the Backstage view. When the Word Options dialog box is displayed, click Proofing in the left pane, be sure the 'Hide spelling errors in this document only' and 'Hide grammar errors in this document only' check boxes do not contain check marks, and then click the OK button. If your screen still does not display the wavy underlines, redisplay the Word Options dialog box, click Proofing, and then click the Recheck Document button.

Change the document properties, including keywords, as specified by your instructor. Save the revised document with the name, Make It Right 1-1 Karate Academy Flyer, and then submit it in the format specified by your instructor.

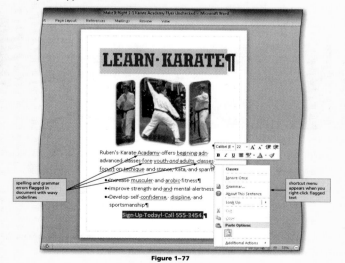

Figure 1–77

STUDENT ASSIGNMENTS

Word Chapter 1

STUDENT ASSIGNMENTS

Textbook Walk-Through

STUDENT ASSIGNMENTS

In the Lab

Design and/or create a document using the guidelines, concepts, and skills presented in this chapter. Labs are listed in order of increasing difficulty.

Lab 1: Creating a Flyer with a Picture

Problem: As a part-time employee in the Student Services Center at school, you have been asked to prepare a flyer that advertises study habits classes. First, you prepare the unformatted flyer shown in Figure 1–78a, and then you format it so that it looks like Figure 1–78b. *Hint:* Remember, if you make a mistake while formatting the flyer, you can click the Undo button on the Quick Access Toolbar to undo your last action.

Note: To complete this assignment, you will be required to use the Data Files for Students. See the inside back cover of this book for instructions on downloading the Data Files for Students, or contact your instructor for information about accessing the required files.

Instructions: Perform the following tasks:

1. Start Word. Display formatting marks on the screen.

2. Type the flyer text, unformatted, as shown in Figure 1–78a, inserting a blank line between the headline and the body copy. If Word flags any misspelled words as you type, check their spelling and correct them.

3. Save the document using the file name, Lab 1-1 Study Habits Flyer.

4. Center the headline and the signature line.

5. Change the theme colors to Concourse.

6. Change the font size of the headline to 36 point and the font to Ravie, or a similar font. Apply the text effect called Gradient Fill – Dark Red, Accent 6, Inner Shadow.

7. Change the font size of body copy between the headline and the signature line to 20 point.

8. Change the font size of the signature line to 22 point. Bold the text in the signature line.

> **In the Lab** Three all new in-depth assignments per chapter require students to utilize the chapter concepts and techniques to solve problems on a computer.

Studying All Night?

`blank line`

Let us help you! Our expert instructors teach effective stu... energy-building techniques.

Classes are $15.00 per session

Sessions last four weeks

Classes meet in the Student Services Center twice a week

Call 555-2838 or stop by to sign up today!

Figure 1–78 (a) Unform...

Word Chapter 3

STUDENT ASSIGNMENTS

create a building block for Fair Grove Elementary School and insert the building block whenever you have to enter the school name. Resize table columns to fit contents. Check the spelling of the letter. Change the document properties, as specified by your instructor. Save the letter with Lab 3-3 Education Board Letter as the file name.

Cases and Places

Apply your creative thinking and problem solving skills to design and implement a solution.

Note: To complete these assignments, you may be required to use the Data Files for Students. See the inside back cover of this book for instructions on downloading the Data Files for Students, or contact your instructor for information about accessing the required files.

1: Create a Letter to a Potential Employer

Academic

As a student about to graduate, you are actively seeking employment in your field and have located an advertisement for a job in which you are interested. You decide to write a letter to the potential employer: Ms. Janice Tremont at Home Health Associates, 554 Mountain View Lane, Blue Dust, MO 64319.

The draft wording for the letter is as follows: I am responding to your advertisement for the nursing position in the *Blue Dust Press*. I have tailored my activities and education for a career in geriatric medicine. This month, I will graduate with concentrations in Geriatric Medicine (24 hours), Osteopathic Medicine (12 hours), and Holistic Nursing (9 hours). In addition to receiving my bachelor degree in nursing, I have enhanced my education by participating in the following activities: volunteered at Blue Dust's free health care clinic; attended several continuing education and career-specific seminars, including An Aging Populace, Care of the Homebound, and Special Needs of the Elderly; completed one-semester internship at Blue Dust Community Hospital in spring semester of 2012; completed Certified Nursing Assistant (CNA) program at Blue Dust Community College; and worked as nurse's aide for two years during college. I look forward to an interview so that we can discuss the position you offer and my qualifications. With my background and education, I am confident that I will make a positive contribution to Home Health Associates.

The letter should contain a letterhead that uses a shape and clip art, a table (use a table to present the areas of concentration), and a bulleted list (use a bulleted list to present the activities). Insert nonbreaking spaces in the newspaper name. Use the concepts and techniques presented in this chapter to create and format a letter according to the modified block style, creating appropriate paragraph breaks and rewording the draft as necessary. Use your personal information for contact information in the letter. Be sure to check the spelling and grammar of the finished letter. Submit your assignment in the format specified by your instructor.

2: Create a Letter Requesting Donations

Personal

As an alumnus of your historic high school, you are concerned that the building is being considered for demolition. You decide to write a letter to another graduate: Mr. Jim Lemon, 87 Travis Parkway, Vigil, CT 06802.

The draft wording for the letter is as follows: As a member of the class of 1988, you, like many others, probably have many fond memories of our alma mater, Vigil East High School. I recently learned that the building is being considered for demolition because of its age and structural integrity.

> **Cases & Places** exercises call on students to create open-ended projects that reflect academic, personal, and business settings.

Continued >

Office 2010 and Windows 7: Essential Concepts and Skills

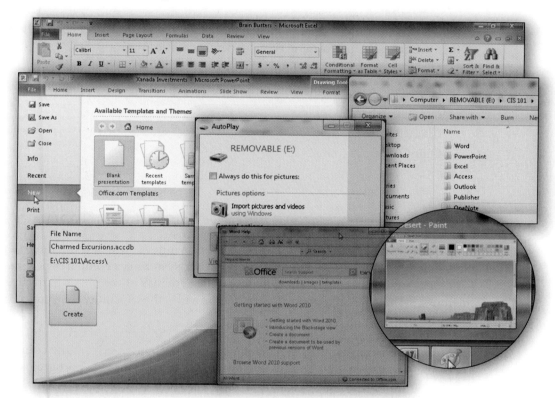

Objectives

You will have mastered the material in this chapter when you can:

- Perform basic mouse operations
- Start Windows and log on to the computer
- Identify the objects on the Windows 7 desktop
- Identify the programs in and versions of Microsoft Office
- Start a program
- Identify the components of the Microsoft Office Ribbon

- Create folders
- Save files
- Change screen resolution
- Perform basic tasks in Microsoft Office programs
- Manage files
- Use Microsoft Office Help and Windows Help

Office 2010 and Windows 7: Essential Concepts and Skills

Office 2010 and Windows 7

This introductory chapter covers features and functions common to Office 2010 programs, as well as the basics of Windows 7.

Overview

As you read this chapter, you will learn how to perform basic tasks in Windows and Office programs by performing these general activities:

- Start programs using Windows.
- Use features common across Office programs.
- Organize files and folders.
- Change screen resolution.
- Quit Office programs.

Introduction to the Windows 7 Operating System

Windows 7 is the newest version of Microsoft Windows, which is the most popular and widely used operating system. An **operating system** is a computer program (set of computer instructions) that coordinates all the activities of computer hardware such as memory, storage devices, and printers, and provides the capability for you to communicate with the computer.

The Windows 7 operating system simplifies the process of working with documents and programs by organizing the manner in which you interact with the computer. Windows 7 is used to run **application software**, which consists of programs designed to make users more productive and/or assist them with personal tasks, such as word processing.

Windows 7 has two interface variations, Windows 7 Basic and Windows 7 Aero. Computers with up to 1 GB of RAM display the Windows 7 Basic interface (Figure 1a). Computers with more than 1 GB of RAM also can display the Windows Aero interface (Figure 1b), which provides an enhanced visual appearance. The Windows 7 Professional, Windows 7 Enterprise, Windows 7 Home Premium, and Windows 7 Ultimate editions have the capability to use Windows Aero.

Using a Mouse

Windows users work with a mouse that has at least two buttons. For a right-handed user, the left button usually is the primary mouse button, and the right mouse button is the secondary mouse button. Left-handed people, however, can reverse the function of these buttons.

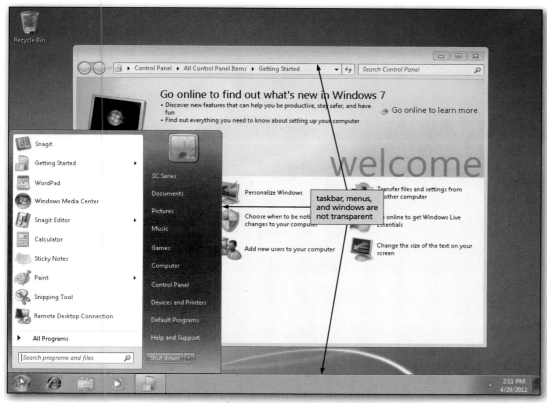

Figure 1 (a) Windows 7 Basic interface

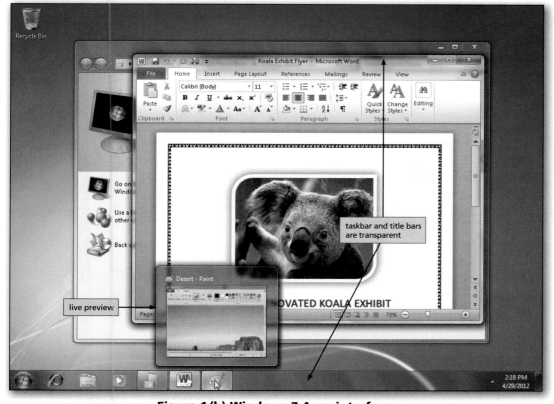

Figure 1 (b) Windows 7 Aero interface

Table 1 explains how to perform a variety of mouse operations. Some programs also use keys in combination with the mouse to perform certain actions. For example, when you hold down the CTRL key while rolling the mouse wheel, text on the screen becomes larger or smaller based on the direction you roll the wheel. The function of the mouse buttons and the wheel varies depending on the program.

Table 1 Mouse Operations		
Operation	**Mouse Action**	**Example***
Point	Move the mouse until the pointer on the desktop is positioned on the item of choice.	Position the pointer on the screen.
Click	Press and release the primary mouse button, which usually is the left mouse button.	Select or deselect items on the screen or start a program or program feature.
Right-click	Press and release the secondary mouse button, which usually is the right mouse button.	Display a shortcut menu.
Double-click	Quickly press and release the left mouse button twice without moving the mouse.	Start a program or program feature.
Triple-click	Quickly press and release the left mouse button three times without moving the mouse.	Select a paragraph.
Drag	Point to an item, hold down the left mouse button, move the item to the desired location on the screen, and then release the left mouse button.	Move an object from one location to another or draw pictures.
Right-drag	Point to an item, hold down the right mouse button, move the item to the desired location on the screen, and then release the right mouse button.	Display a shortcut menu after moving an object from one location to another.
Rotate wheel	Roll the wheel forward or backward.	Scroll vertically (up and down).
Free-spin wheel	Whirl the wheel forward or backward so that it spins freely on its own.	Scroll through many pages in seconds.
Press wheel	Press the wheel button while moving the mouse.	Scroll continuously.
Tilt wheel	Press the wheel toward the right or left.	Scroll horizontally (left and right).
Press thumb button	Press the button on the side of the mouse with your thumb.	Move forward or backward through Web pages and/or control media, games, etc.

*Note: the examples presented in this column are discussed as they are demonstrated in this chapter.

Scrolling

A **scroll bar** is a horizontal or vertical bar that appears when the contents of an area may not be visible completely on the screen (Figure 2). A scroll bar contains **scroll arrows** and a **scroll box** that enable you to view areas that currently cannot be seen. Clicking the up and down scroll arrows moves the screen content up or down one line. You also can click above or below the scroll box to move up or down a section, or drag the scroll box up or down to move up or down to move to a specific location.

Shortcut Keys

In many cases, you can use the keyboard instead of the mouse to accomplish a task. To perform tasks using the keyboard, you press one or more keyboard keys, sometimes identified as

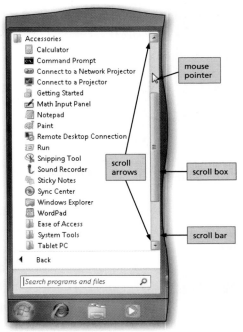

Figure 2

a **shortcut key** or **keyboard shortcut**. Some shortcut keys consist of a single key, such as the F1 key. For example, to obtain help about Windows 7, you can press the F1 key. Other shortcut keys consist of multiple keys, in which case a plus sign separates the key names, such as CTRL+ESC. This notation means to press and hold down the first key listed, press one or more additional keys, and then release all keys. For example, to display the Start menu, press CTRL+ESC, that is, hold down the CTRL key, press the ESC key, and then release both keys.

Starting Windows 7

It is not unusual for multiple people to use the same computer in a work, educational, recreational, or home setting. Windows 7 enables each user to establish a **user account**, which identifies to Windows 7 the resources, such as programs and storage locations, a user can access when working with a computer.

Each user account has a user name and may have a password and an icon, as well. A **user name** is a unique combination of letters or numbers that identifies a specific user to Windows 7. A **password** is a private combination of letters, numbers, and special characters associated with the user name that allows access to a user's account resources. A **user icon** is a picture associated with a user name.

When you turn on a computer, an introductory screen consisting of the Windows logo and copyright messages is displayed. The Windows logo is animated and glows as the Windows 7 operating system is loaded. After the Windows logo appears, depending on your computer's settings, you may or may not be required to log on to the computer. **Logging on** to a computer opens your user account and makes the computer available for use. If you are required to log on to the computer, the **Welcome screen** is displayed, which shows the user names of users on the computer (Figure 3). Clicking the user name or picture begins the process of logging on to the computer.

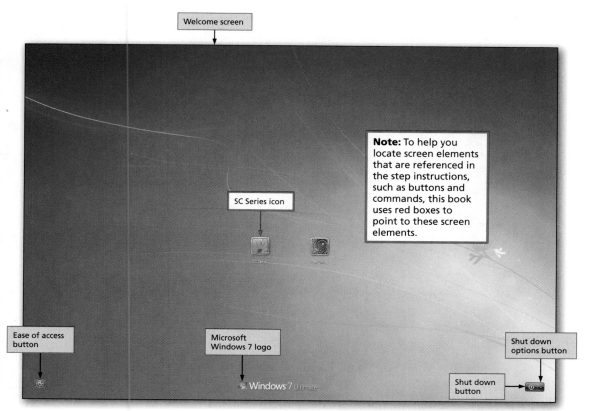

Figure 3

At the bottom of the Welcome screen is the 'Ease of access' button, Windows 7 logo, a Shut down button, and a 'Shut down options' button. The following list identifies the functions of the buttons and commands that typically appear on the Welcome screen:

- Clicking the 'Ease of access' button displays the Ease of Access Center, which provides tools to optimize your computer to accommodate the needs of the mobility, hearing, and vision impaired users.
- Clicking the Shut down button shuts down Windows 7 and the computer.
- Clicking the 'Shut down options' button, located to the right of the Shut down button, provides access to a menu containing commands that perform actions such as restarting the computer, putting the computer in a low-powered state, and shutting down the computer. The commands available on your computer may differ.
  - The **Restart command** closes open programs, shuts down Windows 7, and then restarts Windows 7 and displays the Welcome screen.
  - The **Sleep command** waits for Windows 7 to save your work and then turns off the computer fans and hard disk. To wake the computer from the Sleep state, press the power button or lift a notebook computer's cover, and log on to the computer.
  - The **Shut down command** shuts down and turns off the computer.

To Log On to the Computer

After starting Windows 7, you might need to log on to the computer. The following steps log on to the computer based on a typical installation. You may need to ask your instructor how to log on to your computer. This set of steps uses SC Series as the user name. The list of user names on your computer will be different.

- Click the user icon (SC Series, in this case) on the Welcome screen (shown in Figure 3 on the previous page); depending on settings, this either will display a password text box (Figure 4) or will log on to the computer and display the Windows 7 desktop.

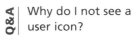 Why do I not see a user icon?

Your computer may require you to type a user name instead of clicking an icon.

Q&A What is a text box?

A text box is a rectangular box in which you type text.

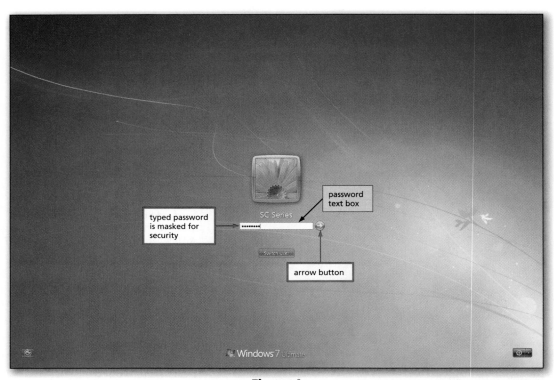

Figure 4

Q&A Why does my screen not show a password text box?

Your account does not require a password.

2

- If Windows 7 displays a password text box, type your password in the text box and then click the arrow button to log on to the computer and display the Windows 7 desktop (Figure 5).

Q&A

Why does my desktop look different from the one in Figure 5?

The Windows 7 desktop is customizable, and your school or employer may have modified the desktop to meet its needs. Also, your screen resolution, which affects the size of the elements on the screen, may differ from the screen resolution used in this book. Later in this chapter, you learn how to change screen resolution.

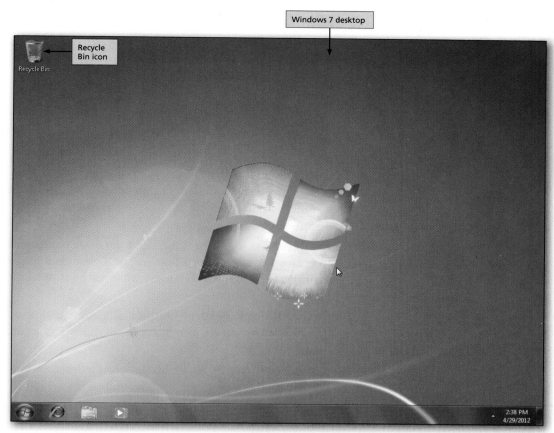

Figure 5

The Windows 7 Desktop

The Windows 7 desktop (Figure 5) and the objects on the desktop emulate a work area in an office. Think of the Windows desktop as an electronic version of the top of your desk. You can perform tasks such as placing objects on the desktop, moving the objects around the desktop, and removing items from the desktop.

When you start a program in Windows 7, it appears on the desktop. Some icons also may be displayed on the desktop. For instance, the icon for the **Recycle Bin**, the location of files that have been deleted, appears on the desktop by default. A **file** is a named unit of storage. Files can contain text, images, audio, and video. You can customize your desktop so that icons representing programs and files you use often appear on your desktop.

Introduction to Microsoft Office 2010

Microsoft Office 2010 is the newest version of Microsoft Office, offering features that provide users with better functionality and easier ways to work with the various files they create. These features include enhanced design tools, such as improved picture formatting tools and new themes, shared notebooks for working in groups, mobile versions of Office programs, broadcast presentation for the Web, and a digital notebook for managing and sharing multimedia information.

Microsoft Office 2010 Programs

Microsoft Office 2010 includes a wide variety of programs such as Word, PowerPoint, Excel, Access, Outlook, Publisher, OneNote, InfoPath, SharePoint Workspace, Communicator, and Web Apps:

- **Microsoft Word 2010**, or Word, is a full-featured word processing program that allows you to create professional-looking documents and revise them easily.
- **Microsoft PowerPoint 2010**, or PowerPoint, is a complete presentation program that allows you to produce professional-looking presentations.
- **Microsoft Excel 2010**, or Excel, is a powerful spreadsheet program that allows you to organize data, complete calculations, make decisions, graph data, develop professional-looking reports, publish organized data to the Web, and access real-time data from Web sites.
- **Microsoft Access 2010**, or Access, is a database management system that allows you to create a database; add, change, and delete data in the database; ask questions concerning the data in the database; and create forms and reports using the data in the database.
- **Microsoft Outlook 2010**, or Outlook, is a communications and scheduling program that allows you to manage e-mail accounts, calendars, contacts, and access to other Internet content.
- **Microsoft Publisher 2010**, or Publisher, is a desktop publishing program that helps you create professional-quality publications and marketing materials that can be shared easily.
- **Microsoft OneNote 2010**, or OneNote, is a note taking program that allows you to store and share information in notebooks with other people.
- **Microsoft InfoPath 2010**, or InfoPath, is a form development program that helps you create forms for use on the Web and gather data from these forms.
- **Microsoft SharePoint Workspace 2010**, or SharePoint, is collaboration software that allows you access and revise files stored on your computer from other locations.
- **Microsoft Communicator** is communications software that allows you to use different modes of communications such as instant messaging, video conferencing, and sharing files and programs.
- **Microsoft Web Apps** is a Web application that allows you to edit and share files on the Web using the familiar Office interface.

Microsoft Office 2010 Suites

A **suite** is a collection of individual programs available together as a unit. Microsoft offers a variety of Office suites. Table 2 lists the Office 2010 suites and their components.

Programs in a suite, such as Microsoft Office, typically use a similar interface and share features. In addition, Microsoft Office programs use **common dialog boxes** for performing actions such as opening and saving files. Once you are comfortable working with these elements and this interface and performing tasks in one program, the similarity can help you apply the knowledge and skills you have learned to another Office program(s). For example, the process for saving a file in Word is the same in PowerPoint, Excel, and the other Office programs. While briefly showing how to use several Office programs, this chapter illustrates some of the common functions across the programs and also identifies the characteristics unique to these programs.

Table 2 Microsoft Office 2010 Suites	Microsoft Office Professional Plus 2010	Microsoft Office Professional 2010	Microsoft Office Home and Business 2010	Microsoft Office Standard 2010	Microsoft Office Home and Student 2010
Microsoft Word 2010	✔	✔	✔	✔	✔
Microsoft PowerPoint 2010	✔	✔	✔	✔	✔
Microsoft Excel 2010	✔	✔	✔	✔	✔
Microsoft Access 2010	✔	✔	✗	✗	✗
Microsoft Outlook 2010	✔	✔	✔	✔	✗
Microsoft Publisher 2010	✔	✔	✗	✔	✗
Microsoft OneNote 2010	✔	✔	✔	✔	✔
Microsoft InfoPath 2010	✔	✗	✗	✗	✗
Microsoft SharePoint Workspace 2010	✔	✗	✗	✗	✗
Microsoft Communicator	✔	✗	✗	✗	✗

Starting and Using a Program

To use a program, you must instruct the operating system to start the program. Windows 7 provides many different ways to start a program, one of which is presented in this section (other ways to start a program are presented throughout this chapter). After starting a program, you can use it to perform a variety of tasks. The following pages use Word to discuss some elements of the Office interface and to perform tasks that are common to other Office programs.

Word

Word is a full-featured word processing program that allows you to create many types of personal and business documents, including flyers, letters, memos, resumes, reports, fax cover sheets, mailing labels, and newsletters. Word also provides tools that enable you to create Web pages and save these Web pages directly on a Web server. Word has many features designed to simplify the production of documents and add visual appeal. Using Word, you easily can change the shape, size, and color of text. You also can include borders, shading, tables, images, pictures, charts, and Web addresses in documents.

To Start a Program Using the Start Menu

Across the bottom of the Windows 7 desktop is the taskbar. The taskbar contains the **Start button**, which you use to access programs, files, folders, and settings on a computer. A **folder** is a named location on a storage medium that usually contains related documents. The taskbar also displays a button for each program currently running on a computer.

Clicking the Start button displays the Start menu. The **Start menu** allows you to access programs, folders, and files on the computer and contains commands that allow you to start programs, store and search for documents, customize the computer, and obtain help about thousands of topics. A **menu** is a list of related items, including folders, programs, and commands. Each **command** on a menu performs a specific action, such as saving a file or obtaining help.

The following steps, which assume Windows 7 is running, use the Start menu to start an Office program based on a typical installation. You may need to ask your instructor how to start Office programs for your computer. Although the steps illustrate starting the Word program, the steps to start any Office program are similar.

1

- Click the Start button on the Windows 7 taskbar to display the Start menu (Figure 6).

Q&A Why does my Start menu look different?

It may look different depending on your computer's configuration. The Start menu may be customized for several reasons, such as usage requirements or security restrictions.

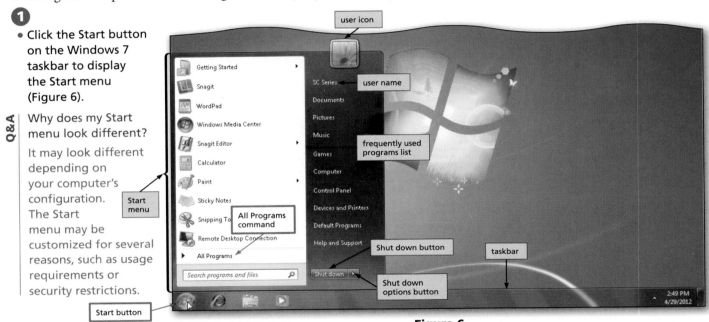

Figure 6

2

- Click All Programs at the bottom of the left pane on the Start menu to display the All Programs list (Figure 7).

Q&A What is a pane?

A **pane** is an area of a window that displays related content. For example, the left pane on the Start menu contains a list of frequently used programs, as well as the All Programs command.

Q&A Why might my All Programs list look different?

Most likely, the programs installed on your computer will differ from those shown in Figure 7. Your All Programs list will show the programs that are installed on your computer.

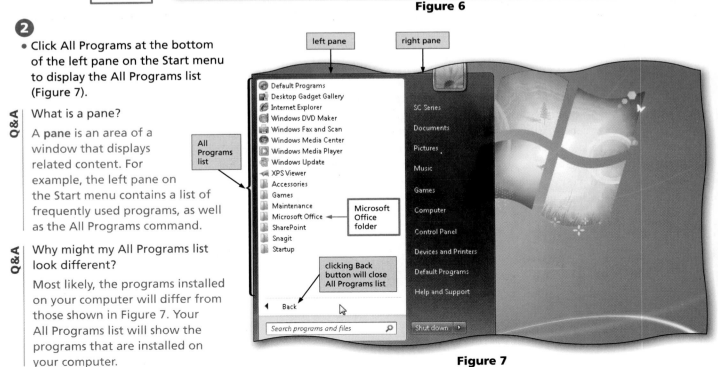

Figure 7

3

- If the program you wish to start is located in a folder, click or scroll to and then click the folder (Microsoft Office, in this case) in the All Programs list to display a list of the folder's contents (Figure 8).

Q&A Why is the Microsoft Office folder on my computer?

During installation of Microsoft Office 2010, the Microsoft Office folder was added to the All Programs list.

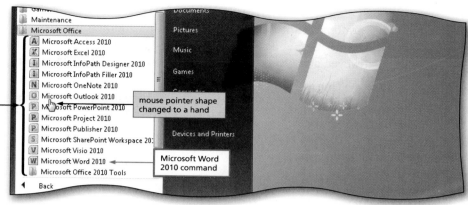

Figure 8

4

- Click, or scroll to and then click, the program name (Microsoft Word 2010, in this case) in the list to start the selected program (Figure 9).

Q&A What happens when you start a program?

Many programs initially display a blank document in a program window, as shown in the Word window in Figure 9; others provide a means for you to create a blank document. A **window** is a rectangular area that displays data and information. The top of a window has a **title bar**, which is a horizontal space that contains the window's name.

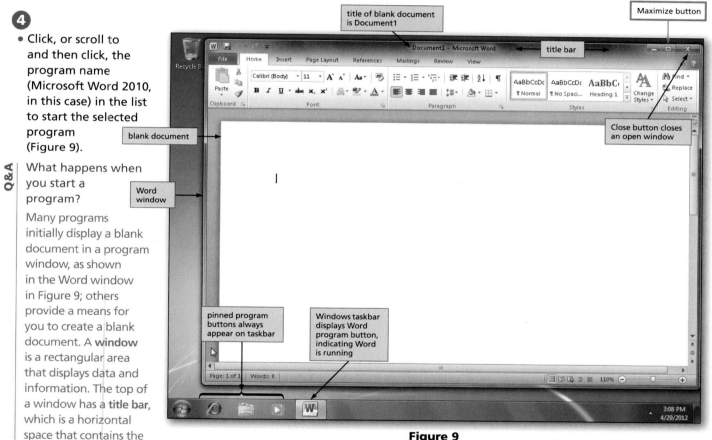

Figure 9

Q&A Why is my program window a different size?

The Word window shown in Figure 9 is not maximized. Your Word window already may be maximized. The next steps maximize a window.

Other Ways

1. Double-click program icon on desktop, if one is present
2. Click program name in left pane of Start menu, if present
3. Display Start menu, type program name in search box, click program name
4. Double-click file created using program you want to start

To Maximize a Window

Sometimes content is not visible completely in a window. One method of displaying the entire contents of a window is to **maximize** it, or enlarge the window so that it fills the entire screen. The following step maximizes the Word window; however, any Office program's window can be maximized using this step.

- If the program window is not maximized already, click the Maximize button (shown in Figure 9 on the previous page) next to the Close button on the window's title bar (the Word window title bar, in this case) to maximize the window (Figure 10).

 Q&A What happened to the Maximize button?

It changed to a Restore Down button, which you can use to return a window to its size and location before you maximized it.

Q&A How do I know whether a window is maximized?

A window is maximized if it fills the entire display area and the Restore Down button is displayed on the title bar.

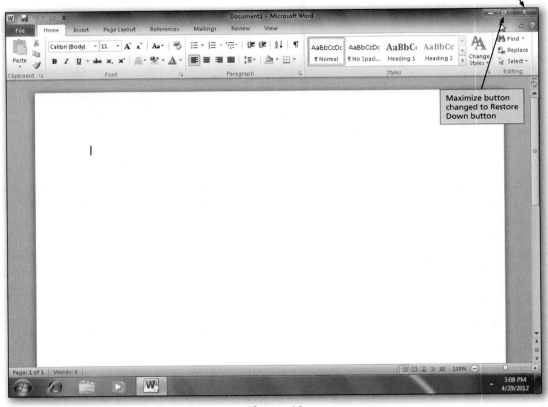

Figure 10

Other Ways
1. Double-click title bar
2. Drag title bar to top of screen

The Word Document Window, Ribbon, and Elements Common to Office Programs

The Word window consists of a variety of components to make your work more efficient and documents more professional. These include the document window, Ribbon, Mini toolbar, shortcut menus, and Quick Access Toolbar. Most of these components are common to other Microsoft Office 2010 programs; others are unique to Word.

You view a portion of a document on the screen through a **document window** (Figure 11). The default (preset) view is **Print Layout view**, which shows the document on a mock sheet of paper in the document window.

Scroll Bars   You use a scroll bar to display different portions of a document in the document window. At the right edge of the document window is a vertical scroll bar. If a document is too wide to fit in the document window, a horizontal scroll bar also appears at the bottom of the document window. On a scroll bar, the position of the scroll box reflects the location of the portion of the document that is displayed in the document window.

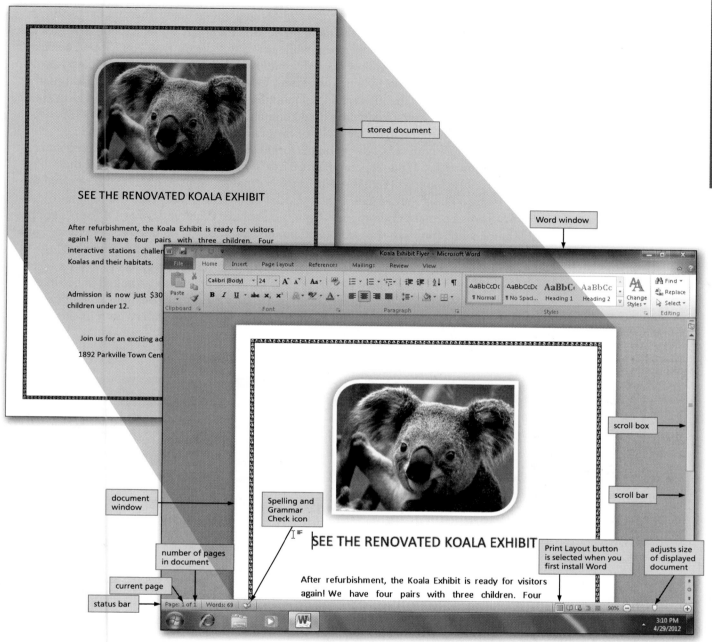

Figure 11

Status Bar   The **status bar**, located at the bottom of the document window above the Windows 7 taskbar, presents information about the document, the progress of current tasks, and the status of certain commands and keys; it also provides controls for viewing the document. As you type text or perform certain tasks, various indicators and buttons may appear on the status bar.

The left side of the status bar in Figure 11 shows the current page followed by the total number of pages in the document, the number of words in the document, and an icon to check spelling and grammar. The right side of the status bar includes buttons and controls you can use to change the view of a document and adjust the size of the displayed document.

Ribbon The Ribbon, located near the top of the window below the title bar, is the control center in Word and other Office programs (Figure 12). The Ribbon provides easy, central access to the tasks you perform while creating a document. The Ribbon consists of tabs, groups, and commands. Each **tab** contains a collection of groups, and each **group** contains related functions. When you start an Office program, such as Word, it initially displays several main tabs, also called default tabs. All Office programs have a **Home tab**, which contains the more frequently used commands.

In addition to the main tabs, Office programs display **tool tabs**, also called contextual tabs (Figure 13), when you perform certain tasks or work with objects such as pictures or tables. If you insert a picture in a Word document, for example, the Picture Tools tab and its related subordinate Format tab appear, collectively referred to as the Picture Tools Format tab. When you are finished working with the picture, the Picture Tools Format tab disappears from the Ribbon. Word and other Office programs determine when tool tabs should appear and disappear based on tasks you perform. Some tool tabs, such as the Table Tools tab, have more than one related subordinate tab.

Items on the Ribbon include buttons, boxes (text boxes, check boxes, etc.), and galleries (Figure 12). A **gallery** is a set of choices, often graphical, arranged in a grid or in a list. You can scroll through choices in an in-Ribbon gallery by clicking the gallery's scroll arrows. Or, you can click a gallery's More button to view more gallery options on the screen at a time.

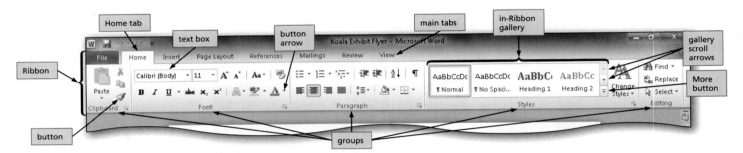

Figure 12

Some buttons and boxes have arrows that, when clicked, also display a gallery; others always cause a gallery to be displayed when clicked. Most galleries support **live preview**, which is a feature that allows you to point to a gallery choice and see its effect in the document — without actually selecting the choice (Figure 13).

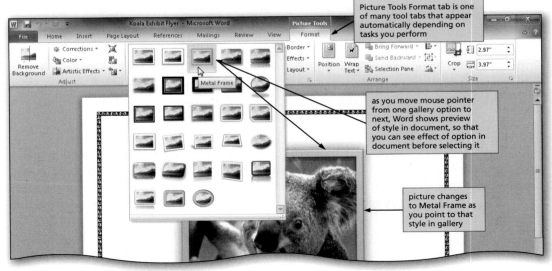

Figure 13

Some commands on the Ribbon display an image to help you remember their function. When you point to a command on the Ribbon, all or part of the command glows in shades of yellow and orange, and an Enhanced ScreenTip appears on the screen. An **Enhanced ScreenTip** is an on-screen note that provides the name of the command, available keyboard shortcut(s), a description of the command, and sometimes instructions for how to obtain help about the command (Figure 14). Enhanced ScreenTips are more detailed than a typical ScreenTip, which usually displays only the name of the command.

Some groups on the Ribbon have a small arrow in the lower-right corner, called a **Dialog Box Launcher**, that when clicked, displays a dialog box or a task pane with additional options for the group (Figure 15). When presented with a dialog box, you make selections and must close the dialog box before returning to the document. A **task pane**, in contrast to a dialog box, is a window that can remain open and visible while you work in the document.

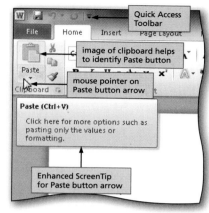

Figure 14

Mini Toolbar   The **Mini toolbar**, which appears automatically based on tasks you perform, contains commands related to changing the appearance of text in a document. All commands on the Mini toolbar also exist on the Ribbon. The purpose of the Mini toolbar is to minimize mouse movement.

When the Mini toolbar appears, it initially is transparent (Figure 16a). If you do not use the transparent Mini toolbar, it disappears from the screen. To use the Mini toolbar, move the mouse pointer into the toolbar, which causes the Mini toolbar to change from a transparent to bright appearance (Figure 16b). If you right-click an item in the document window, Word displays both the Mini toolbar and a shortcut menu, which is discussed in a later section in this chapter.

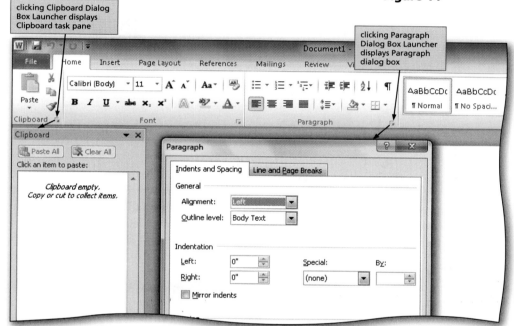

Figure 15

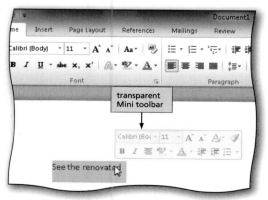

(a) transparent Mini toolbar

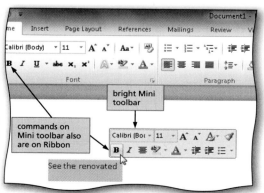

(b) bright Mini toolbar

Figure 16

BTW

Turning Off the Mini Toolbar
If you do not want the Mini toolbar to appear, click File on the Ribbon to open the Backstage view, click Options in the Backstage view, click General (Options dialog box), remove the check mark from the Show Mini Toolbar on selection check box, and then click the OK button.

Quick Access Toolbar   The **Quick Access Toolbar**, located initially (by default) above the Ribbon at the left edge of the title bar, provides convenient, one-click access to frequently used commands (Figure 14 on the previous page). The commands on the Quick Access Toolbar always are available, regardless of the task you are performing. The Quick Access Toolbar is discussed in more depth later in the chapter.

KeyTips   If you prefer using the keyboard instead of the mouse, you can press the ALT key on the keyboard to display **KeyTips**, or keyboard code icons, for certain commands (Figure 17). To select a command using the keyboard, press the letter or number displayed in the KeyTip, which may cause additional KeyTips related to the selected command to appear. To remove KeyTips from the screen, press the ALT key or the ESC key until all KeyTips disappear, or click the mouse anywhere in the program window.

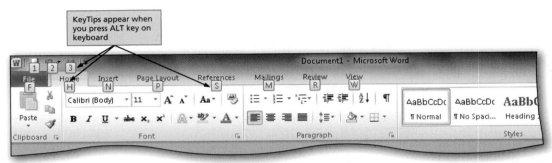

Figure 17

To Display a Different Tab on the Ribbon

When you start Word, the Ribbon displays eight main tabs: File, Home, Insert, Page Layout, References, Mailings, Review, and View. The tab currently displayed is called the **active tab**.

The following step displays the Insert tab, that is, makes it the active tab.

1

- Click Insert on the Ribbon to display the Insert tab (Figure 18).

(P) **Experiment**

- Click the other tabs on the Ribbon to view their contents. When you are finished, click the Insert tab to redisplay the Insert tab.

Q&A

If I am working in a different Office program, such as PowerPoint or Access, how do I display a different tab on the Ribbon?

Follow this same procedure; that is, click the desired tab on the Ribbon.

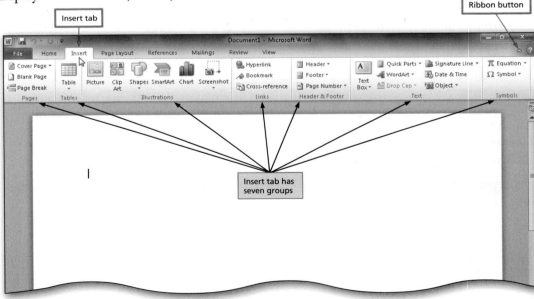

Figure 18

To Minimize, Display, and Restore the Ribbon

To display more of a document or other item in the window of an Office program, some users prefer to minimize the Ribbon, which hides the groups on the Ribbon and displays only the main tabs. Each time you start an Office program, the Ribbon appears the same way it did the last time you used that Office program. The chapters in this book, however, begin with the Ribbon appearing as it did at the initial installation of the software.

The following steps minimize, display, and restore the Ribbon in an Office program.

• Click the Minimize the Ribbon button on the Ribbon (shown in Figure 18) to minimize the Ribbon (Figure 19).

Q&A What happened to the groups on the Ribbon?

When you minimize the Ribbon, the groups disappear so that the Ribbon does not take up as much space on the screen.

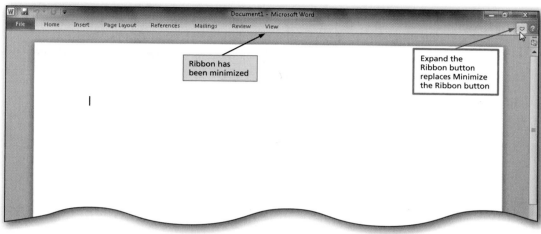

Figure 19

Q&A What happened to the Minimize the Ribbon button?

The Expand the Ribbon button replaces the Minimize the Ribbon button when the Ribbon is minimized.

• Click Home on the Ribbon to display the Home tab (Figure 20).

Q&A Why would I click the Home tab?

If you want to use a command on a minimized Ribbon, click the main tab to display the groups for that tab. After you select a command on the Ribbon, the groups will be hidden once again. If you decide not to use a command on the Ribbon, you can hide the groups by clicking the same main tab or clicking in the program window.

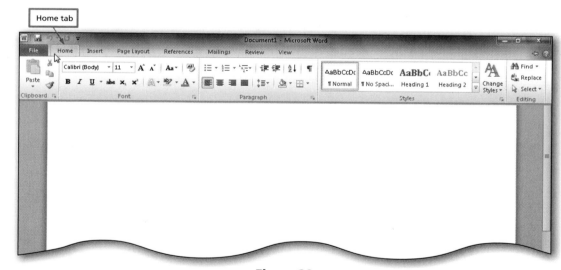

Figure 20

• Click Home on the Ribbon to hide the groups again (shown in Figure 19).

• Click the Expand the Ribbon button on the Ribbon (shown in Figure 19) to restore the Ribbon.

Other Ways

1. Double-click Home on the Ribbon
2. Press CTRL+F1

To Display and Use a Shortcut Menu

When you right-click certain areas of the Word and other program windows, a shortcut menu will appear. A **shortcut menu** is a list of frequently used commands that relate to the right-clicked object. When you right-click a scroll bar, for example, a shortcut menu appears with commands related to the scroll bar. When you right-click the Quick Access Toolbar, a shortcut menu appears with commands related to the Quick Access Toolbar. You can use shortcut menus to access common commands quickly. The following steps use a shortcut menu to move the Quick Access Toolbar, which by default is located on the title bar.

- Right-click the Quick Access Toolbar to display a shortcut menu that presents a list of commands related to the Quick Access Toolbar (Figure 21).

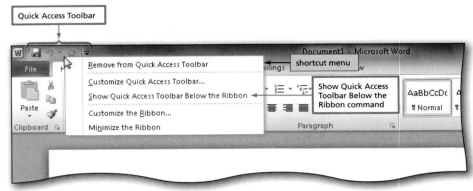

Figure 21

- Click Show Quick Access Toolbar Below the Ribbon on the shortcut menu to display the Quick Access Toolbar below the Ribbon (Figure 22).

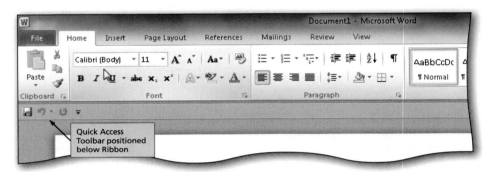

Figure 22

- Right-click the Quick Access Toolbar to display a shortcut menu (Figure 23).

- Click Show Quick Access Toolbar Above the Ribbon on the shortcut menu to return the Quick Access Toolbar to its original position (shown in Figure 21).

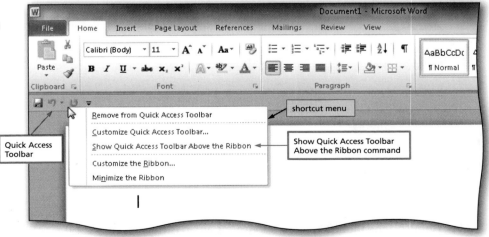

Figure 23

To Customize the Quick Access Toolbar

The Quick Access Toolbar provides easy access to some of the more frequently used commands in Office programs. By default, the Quick Access Toolbar contains buttons for the Save, Undo, and Redo commands. You can customize the Quick Access Toolbar by changing its location in the window, as shown in the previous steps, and by adding more buttons to reflect commands you would like to access easily. The following steps add the Quick Print button to the Quick Access Toolbar.

1

- Click the Customize Quick Access Toolbar button to display the Customize Quick Access Toolbar menu (Figure 24).

Q&A

Which commands are listed on the Customize Quick Access Toolbar menu?

It lists commands that commonly are added to the Quick Access Toolbar.

Q&A

What do the check marks next to some commands signify?

Check marks appear next to commands that already are on the Quick Access Toolbar. When you add a button to the Quick Access Toolbar, a check mark will be displayed next to its command name.

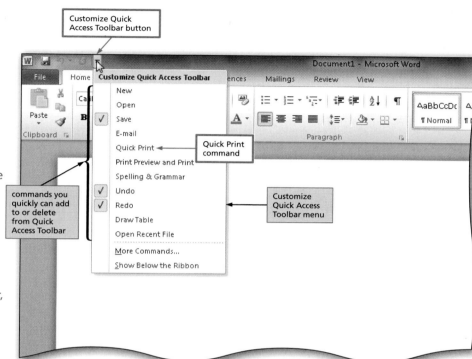

Figure 24

2

- Click Quick Print on the Customize Quick Access Toolbar menu to add the Quick Print button to the Quick Access Toolbar (Figure 25).

Q&A

How would I remove a button from the Quick Access Toolbar?

You would right-click the button you wish to remove and then click Remove from Quick Access Toolbar on the shortcut menu.

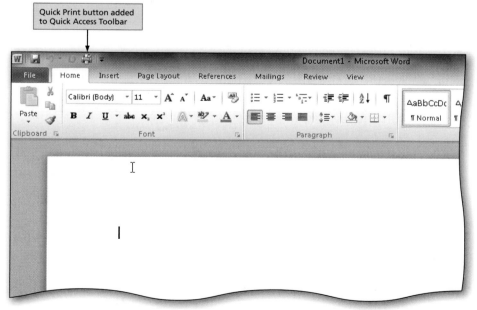

Figure 25

To Enter Text in a Document

The first step in creating a document is to enter its text by typing on the keyboard. By default, Word positions text at the left margin as you type. To begin creating a flyer, for example, you type the headline in the document window. The following steps type this first line of text, a headline, in a document.

1

- Type **SEE THE RENOVATED KOALA EXHIBIT** as the text (Figure 26).

What is the blinking vertical bar to the right of the text?

The insertion point. It indicates where text, graphics, and other items will be inserted in the document. As you type, the insertion point moves to the right, and when you reach the end of a line, it moves downward to the beginning of the next line.

What if I make an error while typing?

You can press the BACKSPACE key until you have deleted the text in error and then retype the text correctly.

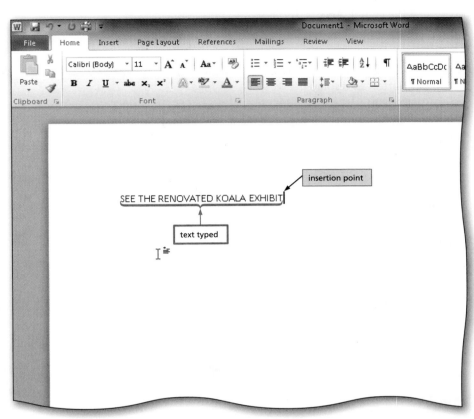

Figure 26

2

- Press the ENTER key to move the insertion point to the beginning of the next line (Figure 27).

Why did blank space appear between the entered text and the insertion point?

Each time you press the ENTER key, Word creates a new paragraph and inserts blank space between the two paragraphs.

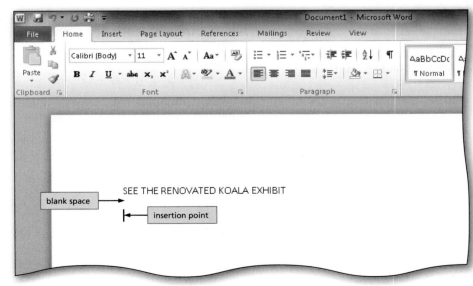

Figure 27

Saving and Organizing Files

While you are creating a document, the computer stores it in memory. When you save a document, the computer places it on a storage medium such as a hard disk, USB flash drive, or optical disc. A saved document is referred to as a file. A **file name** is the name assigned to a file when it is saved. It is important to save a document frequently for the following reasons:

- The document in memory might be lost if the computer is turned off or you lose electrical power while a program is running.
- If you run out of time before completing a project, you may finish it at a future time without starting over.

When saving files, you should organize them so that you easily can find them later. Windows 7 provides tools to help you organize files.

Organizing Files and Folders

A file contains data. This data can range from a research paper to an accounting spreadsheet to an electronic math quiz. You should organize and store these files in folders to avoid misplacing a file and to help you find a file quickly.

If you are a freshman taking an introductory computer class (CIS 101, for example), you may want to design a series of folders for the different subjects covered in the class. To accomplish this, you can arrange the folders in a hierarchy for the class, as shown in Figure 28.

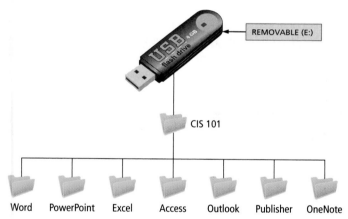

Figure 28

The hierarchy contains three levels. The first level contains the storage device, in this case a USB flash drive. Windows 7 identifies the storage device with a letter, and, in some cases, a name. In Figure 28, the USB flash drive is identified as REMOVABLE (E:). The second level contains the class folder (CIS 101, in this case), and the third level contains seven folders, one each for a different Office program that will be covered in the class (Word, PowerPoint, Excel, Access, Outlook, Publisher, and OneNote).

When the hierarchy in Figure 28 is created, the USB flash drive is said to contain the CIS 101 folder, and the CIS 101 folder is said to contain the separate Office folders (i.e., Word, PowerPoint, Excel, etc.). In addition, this hierarchy easily can be expanded to include folders from other classes taken during additional semesters.

The vertical and horizontal lines in Figure 28 form a pathway that allows you to navigate to a drive or folder on a computer or network. A **path** consists of a drive letter (preceded by a drive name when necessary) and colon, to identify the storage device, and one or more folder names. Each drive or folder in the hierarchy has a corresponding path.

BTW

File Type
Depending on your Windows 7 settings, the file type .docx may be displayed immediately to the right of the file name after you save the file. The file type .docx is a Word 2010 document.

BTW

Saving Online
Instead of saving files on a USB flash drive, some people prefer to save them online so that they can access the files from any computer with an Internet connection. For more information, read Appendix C.

Table 3 shows examples of paths and their corresponding drives and folders.

Table 3 Paths and Corresponding Drives and Folders	
Path	**Drive and Folder**
Computer ▶ REMOVABLE (E:)	Drive E (REMOVABLE (E:))
Computer ▶ REMOVABLE (E:) ▶ CIS 101	CIS 101 folder on drive E
Computer ▶ REMOVABLE (E:) ▶ CIS 101 ▶ Word	Word folder in CIS 101 folder on drive E

The following pages illustrate the steps to organize the folders for this class and save a file in one of those folders:

1. Create the folder identifying your class.
2. Create the Word folder in the folder identifying your class.
3. Create the remaining folders in the folder identifying your class (one each for PowerPoint, Excel, Access, Outlook, Publisher, and OneNote).
4. Save a file in the Word folder.
5. Verify the location of the saved file.

To Create a Folder

When you create a folder, such as the CIS 101 folder shown in Figure 28 on the previous page, you must name the folder. A folder name should describe the folder and its contents. A folder name can contain spaces and any uppercase or lowercase characters, except a backslash (\), slash (/), colon (:), asterisk (*), question mark (?), quotation marks ("), less than symbol (<), greater than symbol (>), or vertical bar (|). Folder names cannot be CON, AUX, COM1, COM2, COM3, COM4, LPT1, LPT2, LPT3, PRN, or NUL. The same rules for naming folders also apply to naming files.

To store files and folders on a USB flash drive, you must connect the USB flash drive to an available USB port on a computer. The following steps create your class folder (CIS 101, in this case) on a USB flash drive.

1

- Connect the USB flash drive to an available USB port on the computer to open the AutoPlay window (Figure 29).

Q&A Why does the AutoPlay window not open?

Some computers are not configured to open an AutoPlay window. Instead, they might display the contents of the USB flash drive automatically, or you might need to access contents of the USB flash drive using the Computer window. To use the Computer window to display the USB flash drive's contents, click the Start button, click Computer on the Start menu, and then click the icon representing the USB flash drive.

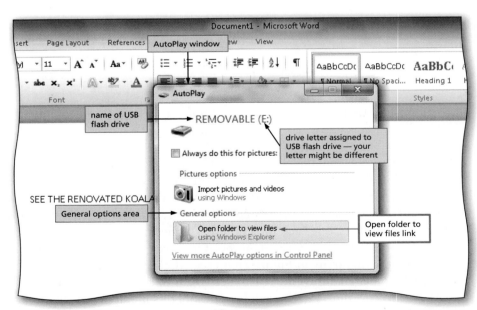

Figure 29

Q&A Why does the AutoPlay window look different from the one in Figure 29?

The AutoPlay window that opens on your computer might display different options. The type of USB flash drive, its contents, and the next available drive letter on your computer all will determine which options are displayed in the AutoPlay window.

2

- Click the 'Open folder to view files' link in the AutoPlay window to open the USB flash drive window (Figure 30).

Q&A

Why does Figure 30 show REMOVABLE (E:) for the USB flash drive?

REMOVABLE is the name of the USB flash drive used to illustrate these steps. The (E:) refers to the drive letter assigned by Windows 7 to the USB flash drive. The name and drive letter of your USB flash drive probably will be different.

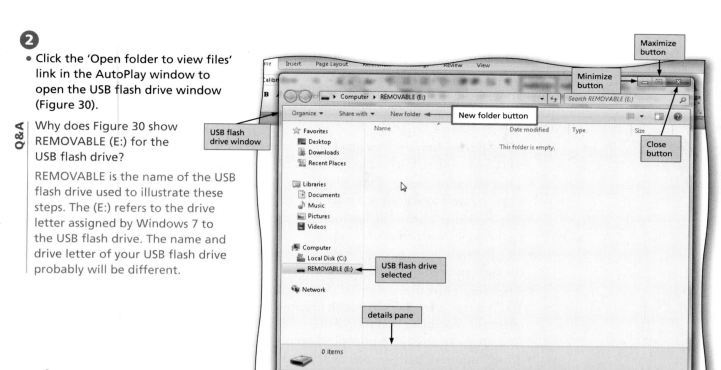

Figure 30

3

- Click the New folder button on the toolbar to display a new folder icon with the name, New folder, selected in a text box.

- Type **CIS 101** (or your class code) in the text box to name the folder.

- Press the ENTER key to create a folder identifying your class on the selected drive (Figure 31). If the CIS 101 folder does not appear in the navigation pane, double-click REMOVABLE (E:) in the navigation pane to display the folder just added.

Q&A

What happens when I press the ENTER key?

The class folder (CIS 101, in this case) is displayed in the File list, which contains the folder name, date modified, type, and size.

Q&A

Why is the folder icon displayed differently on my computer?

Windows might be configured to display contents differently on your computer.

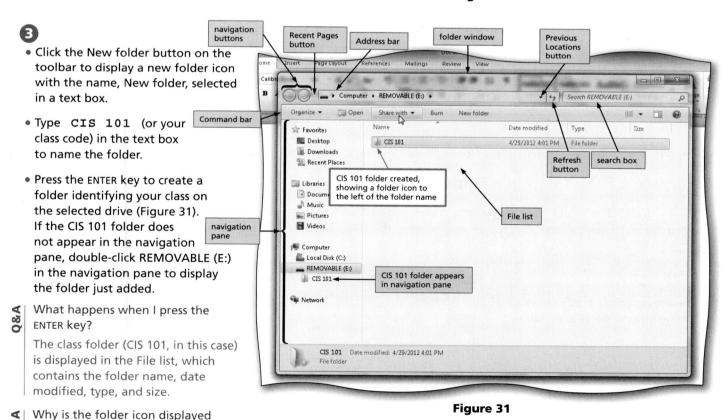

Figure 31

Folder Windows

The USB flash drive window (shown in Figure 31 on the previous page) is called a folder window. Recall that a folder is a specific named location on a storage medium that contains related files. Most users rely on **folder windows** for finding, viewing, and managing information on their computer. Folder windows have common design elements, including the following (Figure 31).

- The **Address bar** provides quick navigation options. The arrows on the Address bar allow you to visit different locations on the computer.
- The buttons to the left of the Address bar allow you to navigate the contents of the left pane and view recent pages. Other buttons allow you to specify the size of the window.
- The **Previous Locations button** saves the locations you have visited and displays the locations when clicked.
- The **Refresh button** on the right side of the Address bar refreshes the contents of the right pane of the folder window.
- The **search box** to the right of the Address bar contains the dimmed word, Search. You can type a term in the search box for a list of files, folders, shortcuts, and elements containing that term within the location you are searching. A **shortcut** is an icon on the desktop that provides a user with immediate access to a program or file.
- The **Command bar** contains five buttons used to accomplish various tasks on the computer related to organizing and managing the contents of the open window.
- The **navigation pane** on the left contains the Favorites area, Libraries area, Computer area, and Network area.
- The **Favorites area** contains links to your favorite locations. By default, this list contains only links to your Desktop, Downloads, and Recent Places.
- The **Libraries area** shows links to files and folders that have been included in a library.

A **library** helps you manage multiple folders and files stored in various locations on a computer. It does not store the files and folders; rather, it displays links to them so that you can access them quickly. For example, you can save pictures from a digital camera in any folder on any storage location on a computer. Normally, this would make organizing the different folders difficult; however, if you add the folders to a library, you can access all the pictures from one location regardless of where they are stored.

To Create a Folder within a Folder

With the class folder created, you can create folders that will store the files you create using each Office program. The following steps create a Word folder in the CIS 101 folder (or the folder identifying your class).

- Double-click the icon or folder name for the CIS 101 folder (or the folder identifying your class) in the File list to open the folder (Figure 32).

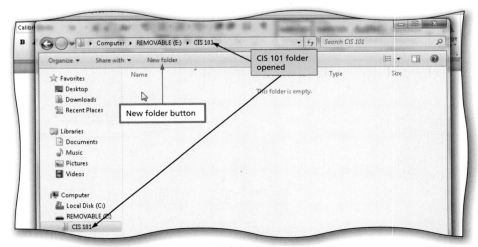

Figure 32

2

- Click the New folder button on the toolbar to display a new folder icon and text box for the folder.

- Type **Word** in the text box to name the folder.

- Press the ENTER key to create the folder (Figure 33).

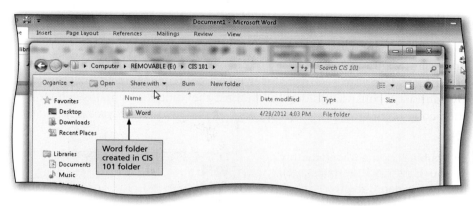

Figure 33

To Create the Remaining Folders

The following steps create the remaining folders in the folder identifying your class (in this case, CIS 101).

1 Click the New folder button on the toolbar to display a new folder icon and text box.

2 Type **PowerPoint** in the text box to name the folder.

3 Repeat Steps 1 and 2 to create each of the remaining folders, using the names Excel, Access, Outlook, Publisher, and OneNote as the folder names (Figure 34).

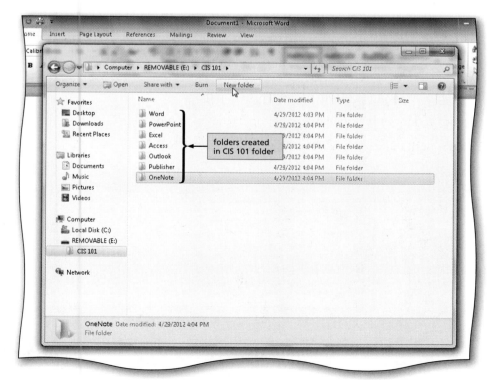

Figure 34

To Expand a Folder, Scroll through Folder Contents, and Collapse a Folder

Folder windows display the hierarchy of items and the contents of drives and folders in the right pane. You might want to expand a drive in the navigation pane to view its contents, scroll through its contents, and collapse it when you are finished viewing its contents. When a folder is expanded, it lists all the folders it contains. By contrast, a collapsed folder does not list the folders it contains. The following steps expand, scroll through, and then collapse the folder identifying your class (CIS 101, in this case).

• Double-click the folder identifying your class (CIS 101, in this case), which expands the folder to display its contents and displays a black arrow to the left of the folder icon (Figure 35).

Q&A Why are the subject folders indented below the CIS 101 folder in the navigation pane?

It shows that the folders are contained within the CIS 101 folder.

Q&A Why did a scroll bar appear in the navigation pane?

When all contents cannot fit in a window or pane, a scroll bar appears. As described earlier, you can view areas currently not visible by (1) clicking the scroll arrows, (2) clicking above or below the scroll bar, and (3) dragging the scroll box.

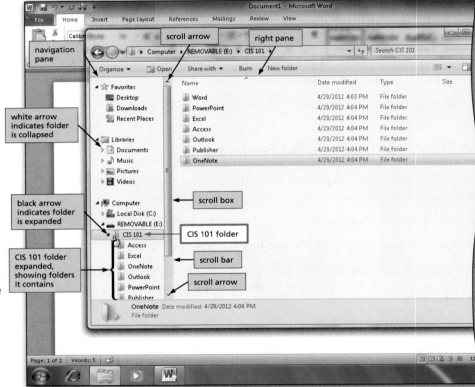

Figure 35

🔎 **Experiment**

• Click the down scroll arrow on the vertical scroll bar to display additional folders at the bottom of the navigation pane.

• Click the scroll bar above the scroll box to move the scroll box to the top of the navigation pane.

• Drag the scroll box down the scroll bar until the scroll box is halfway down the scroll bar.

2

• Double-click the folder identifying your class (CIS 101, in this case) to collapse the folder (Figure 36).

Other Ways

1. Point in navigation pane to display arrows, click white arrow to expand or click black arrow to collapse

2. Select folder to expand or collapse using arrow keys, press RIGHT ARROW to expand; press LEFT ARROW to collapse.

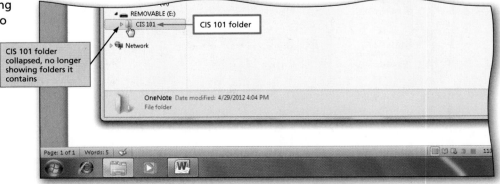

Figure 36

To Switch from One Program to Another

The next step is to save the Word file containing the headline you typed earlier. Word, however, currently is not the active window. You can use the program button on the taskbar and live preview to switch to Word and then save the document in the Word document window.

If Windows Aero is active on your computer, Windows displays a live preview window whenever you move your mouse on a button or click a button on the taskbar. If Aero is not supported or enabled on your computer, you will see a window title instead of a live preview. The steps below use the Word program; however, the steps are the same for any active Office program currently displayed as a program button on the taskbar.

The following steps switch to the Word window.

- Point to the Word program button on the taskbar to see a live preview of the open document(s) or the window title(s) of the open document(s), depending on your computer's configuration (Figure 37).

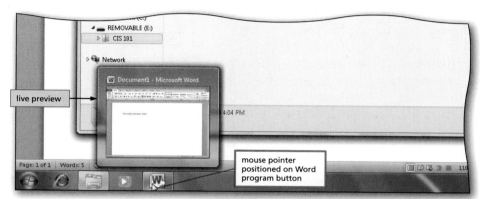

Figure 37

- Click the program button or the live preview to make the program associated with the program button the active window (shown in Figure 27 on page OFF 20).

Q&A What if multiple documents are open in a program?

If Aero is enabled on your computer, click the desired live preview. If Aero is not supported or not enabled, click the window title.

To Save a File in a Folder

Now that you have created the folders for storing files, you can save the Word document. The following steps save a file on a USB flash drive in the Word folder contained in your class folder (CIS 101, in this case) using the file name, Koala Exhibit.

- With a USB flash drive connected to one of the computer's USB ports, click the Save button on the Quick Access Toolbar to display the Save As dialog box (Figure 38).

Q&A Why does a file name already appear in the File name text box?

Word automatically suggests a file name the first time you save a document. The file name normally consists of the first few words contained in the document. Because the suggested file name is selected, you do not need to delete it; as soon as you begin typing, the new file name replaces the selected text.

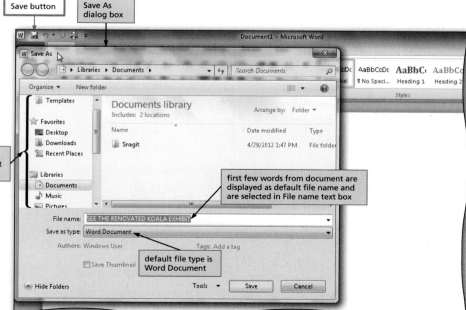

Figure 38

2

- Type **Koala Exhibit** in the File name text box (Save As dialog box) to change the file name. Do not press the ENTER key after typing the file name because you do not want to close the dialog box at this time (Figure 39).

Q&A

What characters can I use in a file name?

The only invalid characters are the backslash (\), slash (/), colon (:), asterisk (*), question mark (?), quotation mark ("), less than symbol (<), greater than symbol (>), and vertical bar (|).

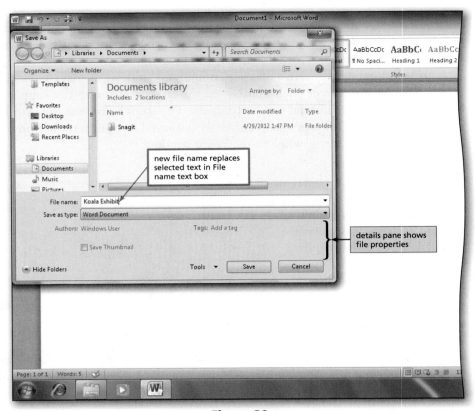

Figure 39

3

- Navigate to the desired save location (in this case, the Word folder in the CIS 101 folder [or your class folder] on the USB flash drive) by performing the tasks in Steps 3a, 3b, and 3c.

- If the navigation pane is not displayed in the dialog box, click the Browse Folders button to expand the dialog box.

- If Computer is not displayed in the navigation pane, drag the navigation pane scroll bar until Computer appears.

- If Computer is not expanded in the navigation pane, double-click Computer to display a list of available storage devices in the navigation pane.

- If necessary, scroll through the dialog box until your USB flash drive appears in the list of available storage devices in the navigation pane (Figure 40).

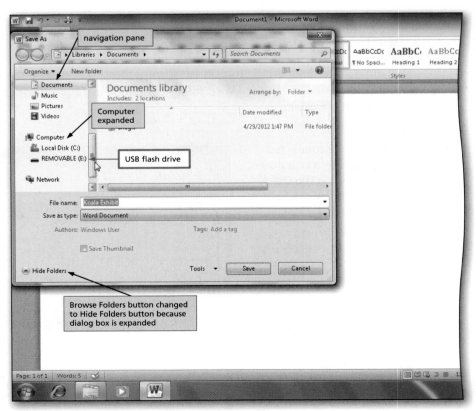

Figure 40

- If your USB flash drive is not expanded, double-click the USB flash drive in the list of available storage devices in the navigation pane to select that drive as the new save location and display its contents in the right pane.

- If your class folder (CIS 101, in this case) is not expanded, double-click the CIS 101 folder to select the folder and display its contents in the right pane.

Q&A What if I do not want to save in a folder?

Although storing files in folders is an effective technique for organizing files, some users prefer not to store files in folders. If you prefer not to save this file in a folder, skip all instructions in Step 3c and proceed to Step 4.

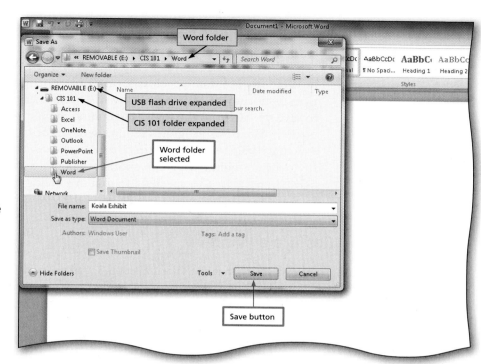

Figure 41

- Click the Word folder to select the folder and display its contents in the right pane (Figure 41).

4

- Click the Save button (Save As dialog box) to save the document in the selected folder on the selected drive with the entered file name (Figure 42).

Q&A How do I know that the file is saved?

While an Office program is saving a file, it briefly displays a message on the status bar indicating the amount of the file saved. In addition, the USB flash drive may have a light that flashes during the save process.

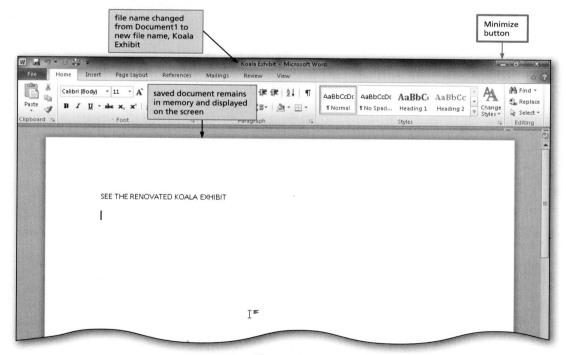

Figure 42

Other Ways
1. Click File on Ribbon, click Save, type file name, navigate to desired save location, click Save button
2. Press CTRL+S or press SHIFT+F12, type file name, navigate to desired save location, click Save button

Navigating in Dialog Boxes

Navigating is the process of finding a location on a storage device. While saving the Koala Exhibit file, for example, Steps 3a – 3c in the previous set of steps navigated to the Word folder located in the CIS 101 folder. When performing certain functions in Windows programs, such as saving a file, opening a file, or inserting a picture in an existing document, you most likely will have to navigate to the location where you want to save the file or to the folder containing the file you want to open or insert. Most dialog boxes in Windows programs requiring navigation follow a similar procedure; that is, the way you navigate to a folder in one dialog box, such as the Save As dialog box, is similar to how you might navigate in another dialog box, such as the Open dialog box. If you chose to navigate to a specific location in a dialog box, you would follow the instructions in Steps 3a – 3c on pages OFF 28 and OFF 29.

To Minimize and Restore a Window

Before continuing, you can verify that the Word file was saved properly. To do this, you will minimize the Word window and then open the USB flash drive window so that you can verify the file is stored on the USB flash drive. A **minimized window** is an open window hidden from view but that can be displayed quickly by clicking the window's program button on the taskbar.

In the following example, Word is used to illustrate minimizing and restoring windows; however, you would follow the same steps regardless of the Office program you are using.

The following steps minimize the Word window, verify that the file is saved, and then restore the minimized window.

- Click the Minimize button on the program's title bar (shown in Figure 42 on the previous page) to minimize the window (Figure 43).

Q&A

Is the minimized window still available?

The minimized window, Word in this case, remains available but no longer is the active window. It is minimized as a program button on the taskbar.

- If necessary, click the Windows Explorer program button on the taskbar to open the USB flash drive window.

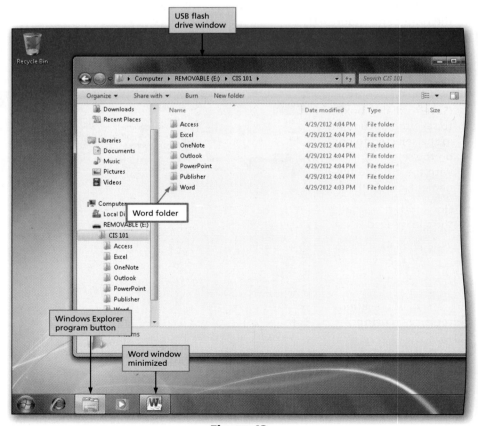

Figure 43

②

- Double-click the Word folder to select the folder and display its contents (Figure 44).

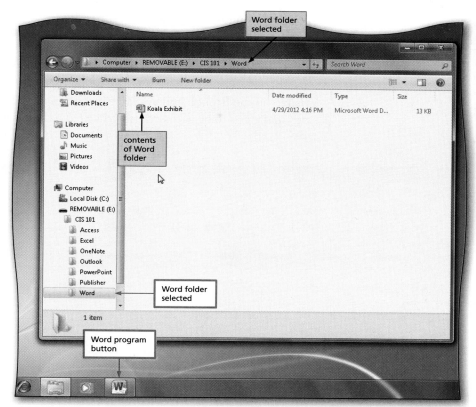

Figure 44

Q&A

Why does the Windows Explorer button on the taskbar change?

The button changes to reflect the status of the folder window (in this case, the USB flash drive window). A selected button indicates that the folder window is active on the screen. When the button is not selected, the window is open but not active.

③

- After viewing the contents of the selected folder, click the Word program button on the taskbar to restore the minimized window (as shown in Figure 42 on page OFF 29).

Other Ways
1. Right-click title bar, click Minimize on shortcut menu, click taskbar button in taskbar button area   2. Press WINDOWS+M, press WINDOWS+SHIFT+M

Screen Resolution

Screen resolution indicates the number of pixels (dots) that the computer uses to display the letters, numbers, graphics, and background you see on the screen. When you increase the screen resolution, Windows displays more information on the screen, but the information decreases in size. The reverse also is true: as you decrease the screen resolution, Windows displays less information on the screen, but the information increases in size.

Screen resolution usually is stated as the product of two numbers, such as 1024 × 768 (pronounced "ten twenty-four by seven sixty-eight"). A 1024 × 768 screen resolution results in a display of 1,024 distinct pixels on each of 768 lines, or about

786,432 pixels. Changing the screen resolution affects how the Ribbon appears in Office programs. Figure 45 shows the Word Ribbon at screen resolutions of 1024 × 768 and 1280 × 800. All of the same commands are available regardless of screen resolution. Word, however, makes changes to the groups and the buttons within the groups to accommodate the various screen resolutions. The result is that certain commands may need to be accessed differently depending on the resolution chosen. A command that is visible on the Ribbon and available by clicking a button at one resolution may not be visible and may need to be accessed using its Dialog Box Launcher at a different resolution.

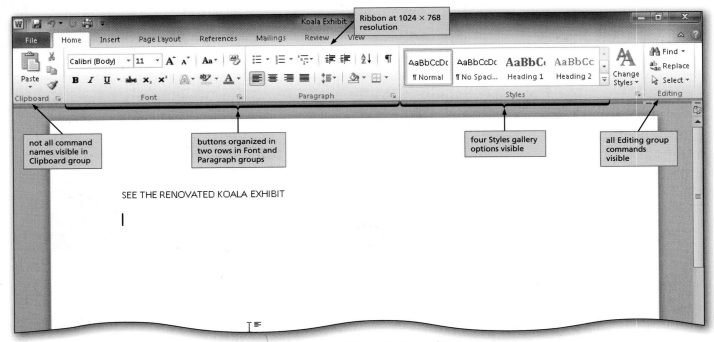

Figure 45 (a) Ribbon at Resolution of 1024 x 768

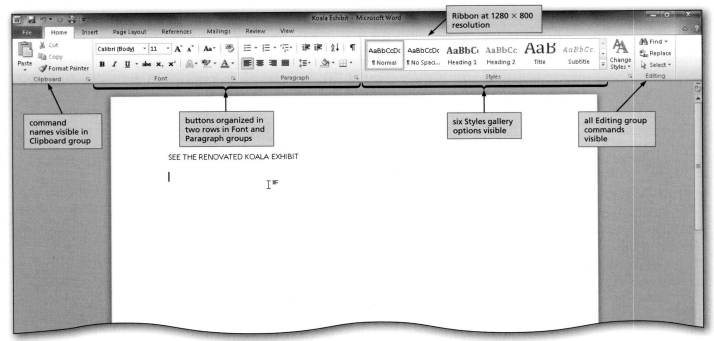

Figure 45 (b) Ribbon at Resolution of 1280 x 800

Comparing the two Ribbons in Figure 45, notice the changes in content and layout of the groups and galleries. In some cases, the content of a group is the same in each resolution, but the layout of the group differs. For example, the same gallery and buttons appear in the Styles groups in the two resolutions, but the layouts differ. In other cases, the content and layout are the same across the resolution, but the level of detail differs with the resolution. In the Clipboard group, when the resolution increases to 1280×800, the names of all the buttons in the group appear in addition to the buttons themselves. At the lower resolution, only the buttons appear.

To Change the Screen Resolution

If you are using a computer to step through the chapters in this book and you want your screen to match the figures, you may need to change your screen's resolution. The figures in this book use a screen resolution of 1024×768. The following steps change the screen resolution to 1024×768. Your computer already may be set to 1024×768 or some other resolution. Keep in mind that many computer labs prevent users from changing the screen resolution; in that case, read the following steps for illustration purposes.

1
- Click the Show desktop button on the taskbar to display the Windows 7 desktop.

- Right-click an empty area on the Windows 7 desktop to display a shortcut menu that displays a list of commands related to the desktop (Figure 46).

Q&A

Why does my shortcut menu display different commands?

Depending on your computer's hardware and configuration, different commands might appear on the shortcut menu.

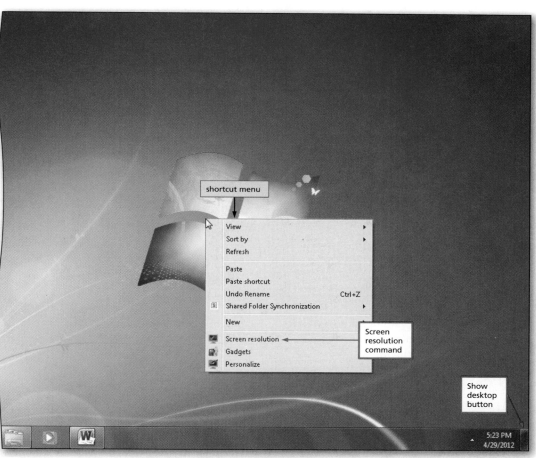

Figure 46

2

- Click Screen resolution on the shortcut menu to open the Screen Resolution window (Figure 47).

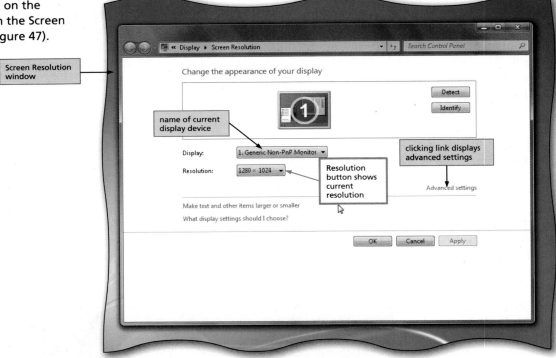

Figure 47

3

- Click the Resolution button in the Screen Resolution window to display the resolution slider.

Q&A

What is a slider?

A **slider** is an object that allows users to choose from multiple predetermined options. In most cases, these options represent some type of numeric value. In most cases, one end of the slider (usually the left or bottom) represents the lowest of available values, and the opposite end (usually the right or top) represents the highest available value.

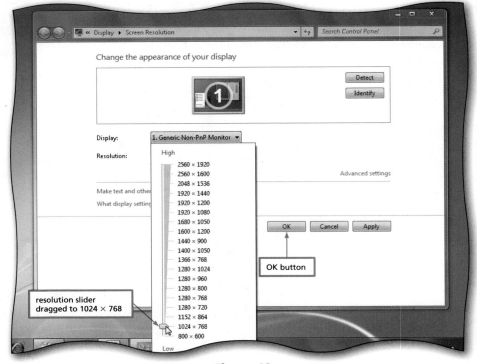

4

- If necessary, drag the resolution slider until the desired screen resolution (in this case, 1024 × 768) is selected (Figure 48).

Q&A

What if my computer does not support the 1024 × 768 resolution?

Figure 48

Some computers do not support the 1024 × 768 resolution. In this case, select a resolution that is close to the 1024 × 768 resolution.

- Click an empty area of the Screen Resolution window to close the resolution slider.

- Click the OK button to change the screen resolution and display the Display Settings dialog box (Figure 49).

- Click the Keep changes button (Display Settings dialog box) to accept the new screen resolution.

Q&A Why does a message display stating that the image quality can be improved?

Some computer monitors are designed to display contents better at a certain screen resolution, sometimes referred to as an optimal resolution.

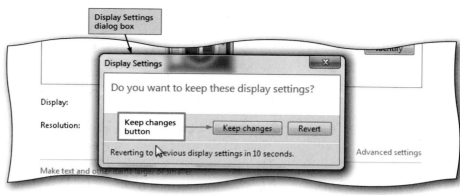

Figure 49

To Quit an Office Program with One Document Open

When you quit an Office program, such as Word, if you have made changes to a file since the last time the file was saved, the Office program displays a dialog box asking if you want save the changes you made to the file before it closes the program window. The dialog box contains three buttons with these resulting actions: the Save button saves the changes and then quits the Office program, the Don't Save button quits the Office program without saving changes, and the Cancel button closes the dialog box and redisplays the file without saving the changes.

If no changes have been made to an open document since the last time the file was saved, the Office program will close the window without displaying a dialog box.

The following steps quit an Office program. In the following example, Word is used to illustrate quitting an Office program; however, you would follow the same steps regardless of the Office program you were using.

1

- If necessary, click the Word program button on the taskbar to display the Word window on the desktop.

- Point to the Close button on the right side of the program's title bar, Word in this case (Figure 50).

Figure 50

2

- Click the Close button to close the document and quit Word.

Q&A What if I have more than one document open in an Office program?

You would click the Close button for each open document. When you click the last open document's Close button, the Office program also quits. As an alternative, you could click File on the Ribbon to open the Backstage view and then click Exit in the Backstage view to close all open documents and quit the Office program.

Q&A What is the Backstage view?

The **Backstage view** contains a set of commands that enable you to manage documents and data about the documents. The Backstage view is discussed in more depth later in this chapter.

3

- If a Microsoft Word dialog box appears, click the Save button to save any changes made to the document since the last save.

Other Ways
1. Right-click the Office program button on Windows 7 taskbar, click Close window or 'Close all windows' on shortcut menu
2. Press ALT + F4

Break Point: If you wish to take a break, this is a good place to do so. To resume at a later time, continue to follow the steps from this location forward.

Additional Microsoft Office Programs

The previous section used Word to illustrate common features of Office and some basic elements unique to Word. The following sections present elements unique to PowerPoint, Excel, and Access, as well as illustrate additional common features of Office.

In the following pages, you will learn how to do the following:

1. Start an Office program (PowerPoint) using the search box.
2. Create two small documents in the same Office program (PowerPoint).
3. Close one of the documents.
4. Reopen the document just closed.
5. Create a document in a different Office program (Excel).
6. Save the document with a new file name.
7. Create a file in a different Office program (Access).
8. Close the file and then open the file.

PowerPoint

PowerPoint is a complete presentation program that allows you to produce professional-looking presentations (Figure 51). A PowerPoint **presentation** also is called a **slide show**. PowerPoint contains several features to simplify creating a slide show. To make presentations more impressive, you can add diagrams, tables, pictures, video, sound, and animation effects. Additional PowerPoint features include the following:

- **Word processing** — Create bulleted lists, combine words and images, find and replace text, and use multiple fonts and font sizes.
- **Outlining** — Develop a presentation using an outline format. You also can import outlines from Microsoft Word or other word processing programs, including single-level and multilevel lists.
- **Charting** — Create and insert charts into presentations and then add effects and chart elements.
- **Drawing** — Create and modify diagrams using shapes such as arcs, arrows, cubes, rectangles, stars, and triangles. Then, customize and add effects to the diagrams, and arrange these objects by sizing, scaling, and rotating them.
- **Inserting multimedia** — Insert artwork and multimedia effects into a slide show. The Microsoft Clip Organizer, included with Office programs, contains hundreds of media files, including pictures, sounds, and movies.
- **Saving to the Web** — Save presentations or parts of a presentation so that they can be viewed in a Web browser. You can publish your slide show to the Internet or to an intranet.
- **E-mailing** — Send an entire slide show as an attachment to an e-mail message.
- **Collaborating** — Share a presentation with friends and coworkers. Ask them to review the slides and then insert comments that offer suggestions to enhance the presentation.
- **Preparing delivery** — Rehearse integrating PowerPoint slides into your speech by setting timings, using presentation tools, showing only selected slides in a presentation, and packaging the presentation for an optical disc.

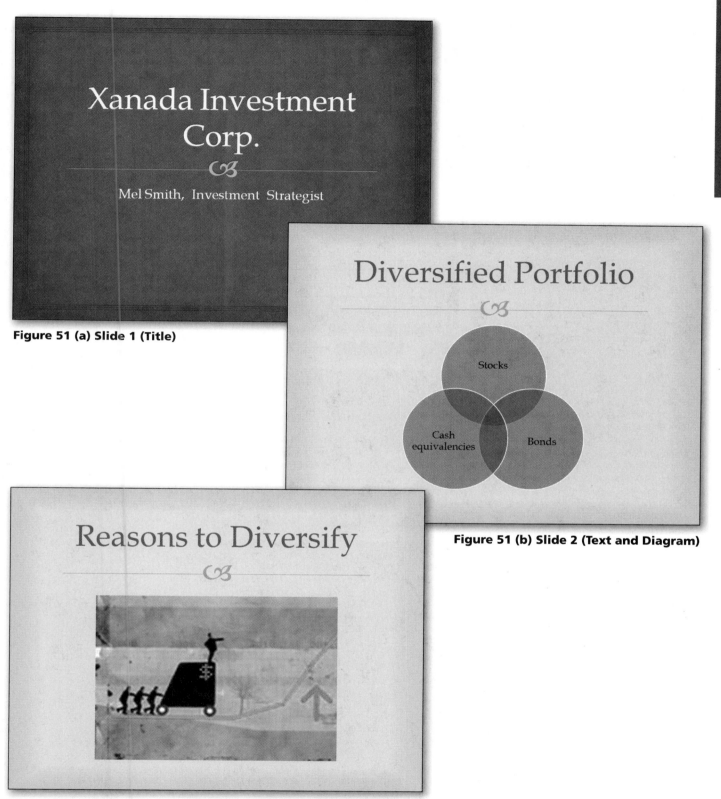

Figure 51 (a) Slide 1 (Title)

Figure 51 (b) Slide 2 (Text and Diagram)

Figure 51 (c) Slide 3 (Text and Picture)

To Start a Program Using the Search Box

The steps on the next page, which assume Windows 7 is running, use the search box to start the PowerPoint Office program based on a typical installation; however, you would follow similar steps to start any Office program. You may need to ask your instructor how to start programs for your computer.

1

- Click the Start button on the Windows 7 taskbar to display the Start menu.

2

- Type **Microsoft PowerPoint** as the search text in the 'Search programs and files' text box and watch the search results appear on the Start menu (Figure 52).

Do I need to type the complete program name or correct capitalization?

No, just enough of it for the program name to appear on the Start menu. For example, you may be able to type PowerPoint or powerpoint, instead of Microsoft PowerPoint.

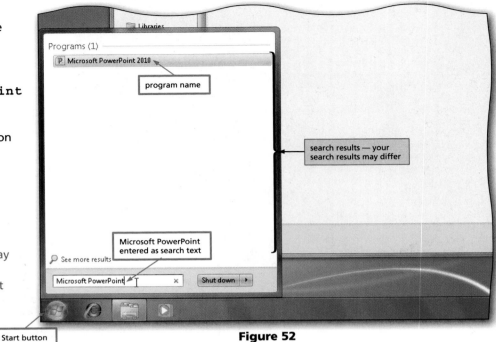

Figure 52

3

- Click the program name, Microsoft PowerPoint 2010 in this case, in the search results on the Start menu to start PowerPoint and display a new blank presentation in the PowerPoint window.

- If the program window is not maximized, click the Maximize button on its title bar to maximize the window (Figure 53).

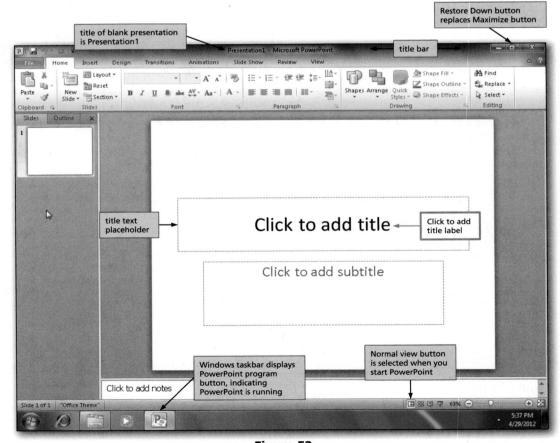

Figure 53

The PowerPoint Window and Ribbon

The PowerPoint window consists of a variety of components to make your work more efficient and documents more professional: the window, Ribbon, Mini toolbar, shortcut menus, and Quick Access Toolbar. Many of these components are common to other Office programs and have been discussed earlier in this chapter. Other components, discussed in the following paragraphs and later in subsequent chapters, are unique to PowerPoint.

The basic unit of a PowerPoint presentation is a **slide**. A slide may contain text and objects, such as graphics, tables, charts, and drawings. **Layouts** are used to position this content on the slide. When you create a new presentation, the default **Title Slide** layout appears (Figure 54). The purpose of this layout is to introduce the presentation to the audience. PowerPoint includes eight other built-in standard layouts.

The default slide layouts are set up in **landscape orientation**, where the slide width is greater than its height. In landscape orientation, the slide size is preset to 10 inches wide and 7.5 inches high when printed on a standard sheet of paper measuring 11 inches wide and 8.5 inches high.

BTW

Portrait Orientation
If your slide content is dominantly vertical, such as a skyscraper or a person, consider changing the slide layout to a portrait orientation. To change the orientation to portrait, click the Slide Orientation button (Design tab | Page Setup group) and then click Portrait. You can use both landscape and portrait orientation in the same slide show.

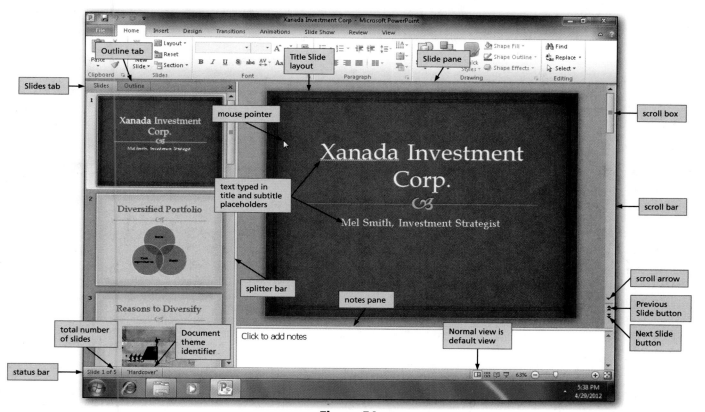

Figure 54

Placeholders   **Placeholders** are boxes with dotted or hatch-marked borders that are displayed when you create a new slide. All layouts except the Blank slide layout contain placeholders. Depending on the particular slide layout selected, title and subtitle placeholders are displayed for the slide title and subtitle; a content text placeholder is displayed for text, art, or a table, chart, picture, graphic, or movie. The title slide in Figure 53 has two text placeholders for the main heading, or title, of a new slide and the subtitle.

Ribbon   The Ribbon in PowerPoint is similar to the one in Word and the other Microsoft Office programs. When you start PowerPoint, the Ribbon displays nine main tabs: File, Home, Insert, Design, Transitions, Animations, Slide Show, Review, and View.

To Enter Content in a Title Slide

With the exception of a blank slide and a slide with a picture and caption, PowerPoint assumes every new slide has a title. Many of PowerPoint's layouts have both a title text placeholder and at least one content placeholder. To make creating a presentation easier, any text you type after a new slide appears becomes title text in the title text placeholder. As you begin typing text in the title text placeholder, the title text also is displayed in the Slide 1 thumbnail in the Slides tab. The presentation title for this presentation is Xanada Investments. The following steps enter a presentation title on the title slide.

1

- Click the label 'Click to add title' located inside the title text placeholder (shown in Figure 53 on page OFF 38) to select the placeholder (Figure 55).

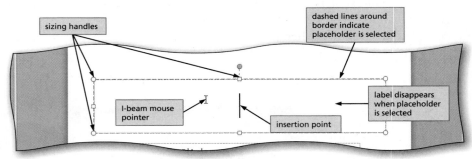

Figure 55

2

- Type **Xanada Investments** in the title text placeholder. Do not press the ENTER key because you do not want to create a new line of text (Figure 56).

Q&A

What are the white squares and circles that appear around the title text placeholder as I type the presentation title?

The white squares and circles are sizing handles, which you can drag to change the size of the title text placeholder. Sizing handles also can be found around other placeholders and objects within a presentation.

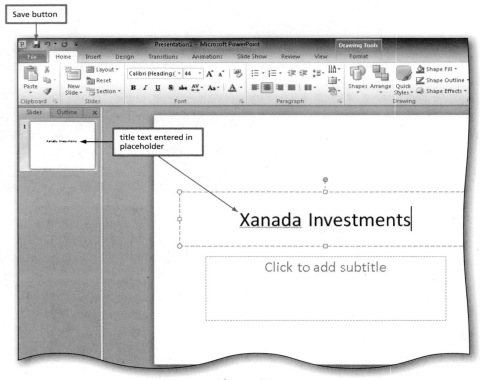

Figure 56

To Save a File in a Folder

The following steps save the presentation in the PowerPoint folder in the class folder (CIS 101, in this case) on a USB flash drive using the file name, Xanada Investments.

1 With a USB flash drive connected to one of the computer's USB ports, click the Save button on the Quick Access Toolbar to display the Save As dialog box.

2 If necessary, type `Xanada Investments` in the File name text box to change the file name. Do not press the ENTER key after typing the file name because you do not want to close the dialog box at this time.

3 Navigate to the desired save location (in this case, the PowerPoint folder in the CIS 101 folder [or your class folder] on the USB flash drive). For specific instructions, perform the tasks in Steps 3a through 3g.

3a If a navigation pane is not displayed in the Save As dialog box, click the Browse Folders button to expand the dialog box.

3b If Computer is not displayed in the navigation pane, drag the navigation pane scroll bar (Save As dialog box) until Computer appears.

3c If Computer is not expanded in the navigation pane, double-click Computer to display a list of available storage devices in the navigation pane.

3d If necessary, scroll through the Save As dialog box until your USB flash drive appears in the list of available storage devices in the navigation pane.

3e If your USB flash drive is not expanded, double-click the USB flash drive in the list of available storage devices in the navigation pane to select that drive as the new save location and display its contents in the right pane.

3f If your class folder (CIS 101, in this case) is not expanded, double-click the CIS 101 folder to select the folder and display its contents.

3g Click the PowerPoint folder to select it as the new save location and display its contents in the right pane.

4 Click the Save button (Save As dialog box) to save the presentation in the selected folder on the selected drive with the entered file name.

To Create a New Office Document from the Backstage View

As discussed earlier, the Backstage view contains a set of commands that enable you to manage documents and data about the documents. From the Backstage view in PowerPoint, for example, you can create, open, print, and save presentations. You also can share documents, manage versions, set permissions, and modify document properties. In other Office 2010 programs, the Backstage view may contain features specific to those programs. The steps on the following pages create a file, a blank presentation in this case, from the Backstage view.

1

• Click File on the Ribbon to open the Backstage view (Figure 57).

Q&A

What is the purpose of the File tab?

The **File** tab is used to display the Backstage view for each Office program.

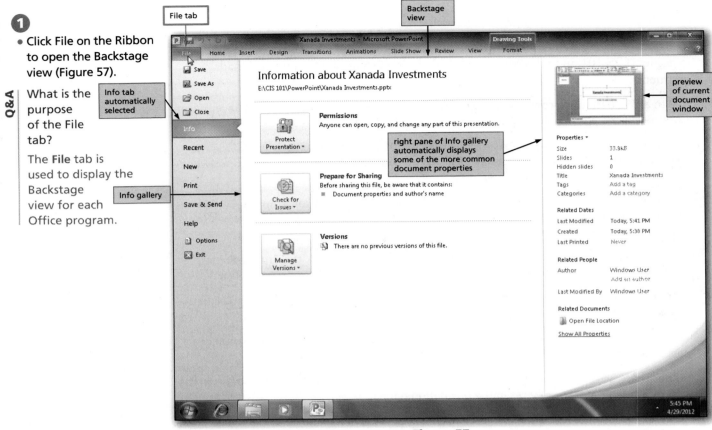

Figure 57

2

• Click the New tab in the Backstage view to display the New gallery (Figure 58).

Q&A

Can I create documents through the Backstage view in other Office programs?

Yes. If the Office program has a New tab in the Backstage view, the New gallery displays various options for creating a new file.

Figure 58

3

- Click the Create button in the New gallery to create a new presentation (Figure 59).

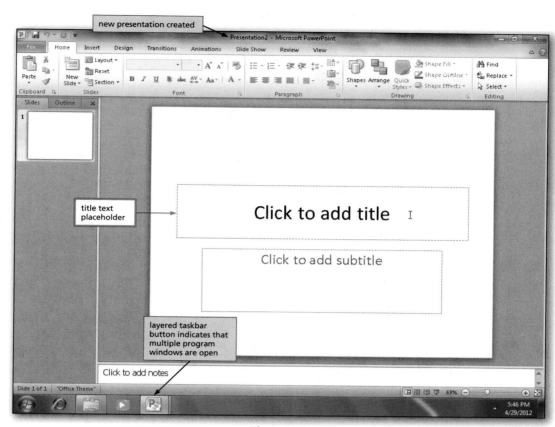

Figure 59

Other Ways

1. Press CTRL+N

To Enter Content in a Title Slide of a Second PowerPoint Presentation

The presentation title for this presentation is Koala Exhibit Gala. The following steps enter a presentation title on the title slide.

1 Click the title text placeholder (shown in Figure 59) to select it.

2 Type **Koala Exhibit Gala** in the title text placeholder. Do not press the ENTER key (Figure 60).

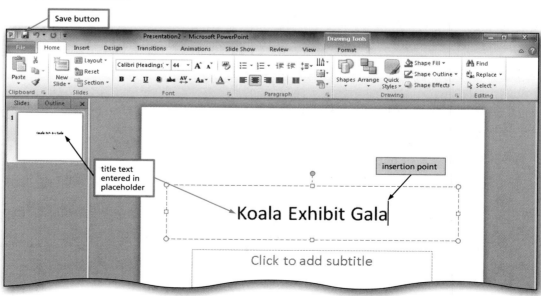

Figure 60

To Save a File in a Folder

The following steps save the second presentation in the PowerPoint folder in the class folder (CIS 101, in this case) on a USB flash drive using the file name, Koala Exhibit Gala.

1 With a USB flash drive connected to one of the computer's USB ports, click the Save button on the Quick Access Toolbar to display the Save As dialog box.

2 If necessary, type **Koala Exhibit Gala** in the File name text box to change the file name. Do not press the ENTER key after typing the file name because you do not want to close the dialog box at this time.

3 If necessary, navigate to the desired save location (in this case, the PowerPoint folder in the CIS 101 folder [or your class folder] on the USB flash drive).

4 Click the Save button (Save As dialog box) to save the presentation in the selected folder on the selected drive with the entered file name.

To Close an Office File Using the Backstage View

Sometimes, you may want to close an Office file, such as a PowerPoint presentation, entirely and start over with a new file. You also may want to close a file when you are finished working with it so that you can begin a new file. The following steps close the current active Office file, that is, the Koala Exhibit Gala presentation, without quitting the active program (PowerPoint in this case).

1
- Click File on the Ribbon to open the Backstage view (Figure 61).

2
- Click Close in the Backstage view to close the open file (Koala Exhibit Gala, in this case) without quitting the active program.

Q&A What if the Office program displays a dialog box about saving?

Click the Save button if you want to save the changes, click the Don't Save button if you want to ignore the changes since the last time you saved, and click the Cancel button if you do not want to close the document.

Q&A Can I use the Backstage view to close an open file in other Office programs, such as Word and Excel?

Yes.

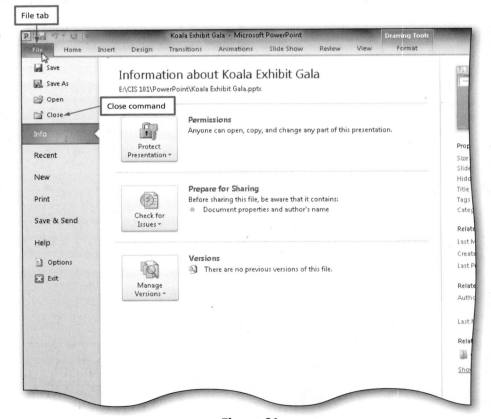

Figure 61

To Open a Recent Office File Using the Backstage View

You sometimes need to open a file that you recently modified. You may have more changes to make such as adding more content or correcting errors. The Backstage view allows you to access recent files easily. The following steps reopen the Koala Exhibit Gala file just closed.

1

- Click File on the Ribbon to open the Backstage view.

- Click the Recent tab in the Backstage view to display the Recent gallery (Figure 62).

2

- Click the desired file name in the Recent gallery, Koala Exhibit Gala in this case, to open the file (shown in Figure 60 on page OFF 43).

Q&A

Can I use the Backstage view to open a recent file in other Office programs, such as Word and Excel?

Yes, as long as the file name appears in the list of recent files in the Recent gallery.

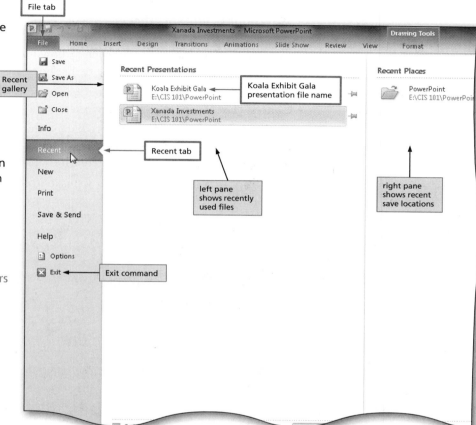

Figure 62

Other Ways

1. Click Start button, point to program name, click file name on submenu

2. Click File on Ribbon, click Open in Backstage view, navigate to file (Open dialog box), click Open button

To Quit an Office Program

You are finished using PowerPoint. Thus, you should quit this Office program. The following steps quit PowerPoint.

1 If you have one Office document open, click the Close button on the right side of the title bar to close the document and quit the Office program; or if you have multiple Office documents open, click File on the Ribbon to open the Backstage view and then click Exit in the Backstage view to close all open documents and quit the Office program.

2 If a dialog box appears, click the Save button to save any changes made to the document since the last save.

Excel

Excel is a powerful spreadsheet program that allows users to organize data, complete calculations, make decisions, graph data, develop professional-looking reports (Figure 63), publish organized data to the Web, and access real-time data from Web sites. The four major parts of Excel are:

- **Workbooks and Worksheets** - A **workbook** is like a notebook. Inside the workbook are sheets, each of which is called a **worksheet**. In other words, a workbook is a collection of worksheets. Worksheets allow users to enter, calculate, manipulate, and analyze data such as numbers and text. The terms worksheet and spreadsheet are interchangeable.

- **Charts** - Excel can draw a variety of charts.

- **Tables** - Tables organize and store data within worksheets. For example, once a user enters data into a worksheet, an Excel table can sort the data, search for specific data, and select data that satisfies defined criteria.

- **Web Support** - Web support allows users to save Excel worksheets or parts of a worksheet in HTML format, so that a user can view and manipulate the worksheet using a browser. Excel Web support also provides access to real-time data, such as stock quotes, using Web queries.

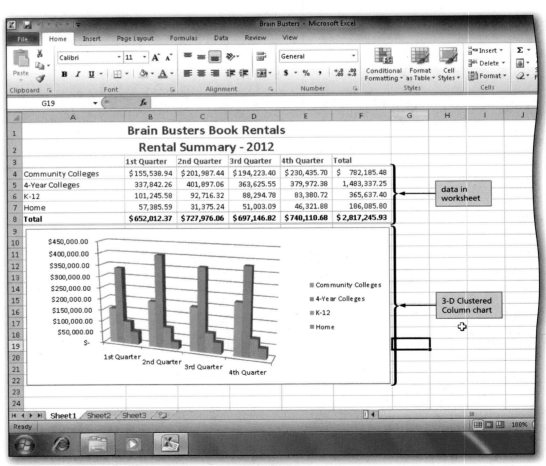

Figure 63

To Create a New Blank Office Document from Windows Explorer

Windows Explorer provides a means to create a blank Office document without ever starting an Office program. The following steps use Windows Explorer to create a blank Excel document.

1

- If necessary, click the Windows Explorer program button on the taskbar to make the folder window the active window in Windows Explorer.

- Double-click your class folder (CIS 101, in this case) in the navigation pane to display the contents of the selected folder.

- Double-click the Excel folder to display its contents in the right pane.

- With the Excel folder selected, right-click an open area in the right pane to display a shortcut menu.

- Point to New on the shortcut menu to display the New submenu (Figure 64).

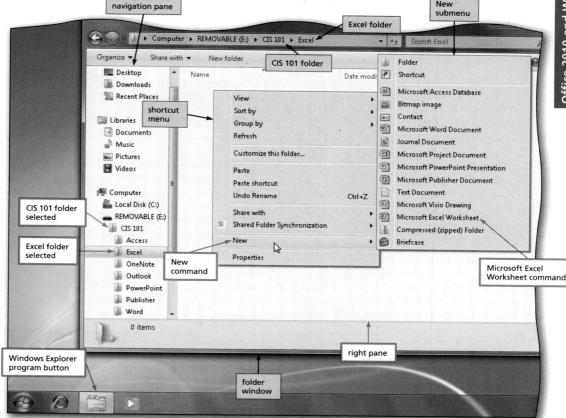

Figure 64

2

- Click Microsoft Excel Worksheet on the New submenu to display an icon and text box for a new file in the current folder window (Figure 65).

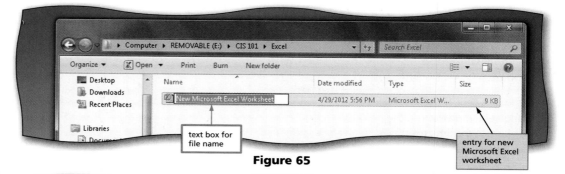

Figure 65

3

- Type **Brain Busters** in the text box and then press the ENTER key to assign a name to the new file in the current folder (Figure 66).

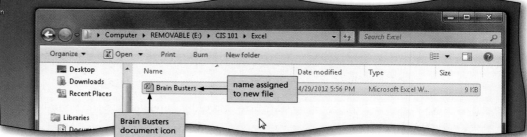

Figure 66

To Start a Program from Windows Explorer and Open a File

Previously, you learned how to start an Office program using the Start menu and the search box. Another way start an Office program is to open an existing file from Windows Explorer, which causes the program in which the file was created to start and then open the selected file. The following steps, which assume Windows 7 is running, use Windows Explorer to start the Excel Office program based on a typical installation. You may need to ask your instructor how to start Office programs for your computer.

- If necessary, display the file to open in the folder window in Windows Explorer (shown in Figure 66 on the previous page).

- Right-click the file icon or file name (Brain Busters, in this case) to display a shortcut menu (Figure 67).

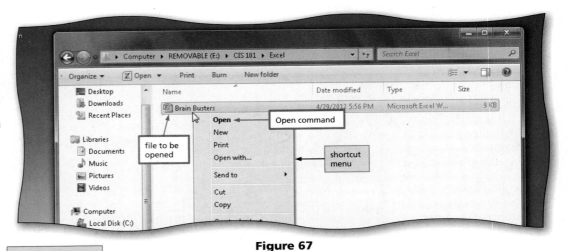

Figure 67

- Click Open on the shortcut menu to open the selected file in the program used to create the file, Microsoft Excel in this case (Figure 68).

- If the program window is not maximized, click the Maximize button on the title bar to maximize the window.

- For Excel users, if the worksheet window in Excel is not maximized, click the worksheet window Maximize button to maximize the worksheet window within Excel.

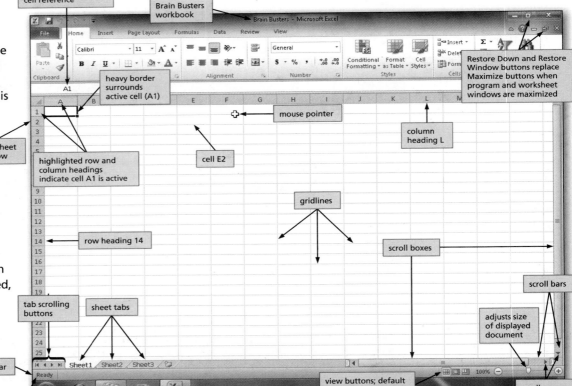

Figure 68

Q&A

Instead of using Windows Explorer, can I start Excel using the same method shown previously for Word and PowerPoint?

Yes, you can use any method of starting an Office program to start Excel.

Unique Features of Excel

The Excel window consists of a variety of components to make your work more efficient and worksheets more professional. These include the document window, Ribbon, Mini toolbar and shortcut menus, Quick Access Toolbar, and the Backstage view. Some of these components are common to other Microsoft Office 2010 programs; others are unique to Excel.

Excel opens a new workbook with three worksheets. If necessary, you can add additional worksheets as long as your computer has enough memory to accommodate them.

Each worksheet has a sheet name that appears on a **sheet tab** at the bottom of the workbook. For example, Sheet1 is the name of the active worksheet displayed in the Brain Busters workbook. If you click the sheet tab labeled Sheet2, Excel displays the Sheet2 worksheet.

The Worksheet The worksheet is organized into a rectangular grid containing vertical columns and horizontal rows. A column letter above the grid, also called the **column heading**, identifies each column. A row number on the left side of the grid, also called the **row heading**, identifies each row. With the screen resolution set to 1024 × 768 and the Excel window maximized, Excel displays 15 columns (A through O) and 25 rows (1 through 25) of the worksheet on the screen, as shown in Figure 68.

The intersection of each column and row is a cell. A **cell** is the basic unit of a worksheet into which you enter data. Each worksheet in a workbook has 16,384 columns and 1,048,576 rows for a total of 17,179,869,180 cells. Only a small fraction of the active worksheet appears on the screen at one time.

A cell is referred to by its unique address, or **cell reference**, which is the coordinates of the intersection of a column and a row. To identify a cell, specify the column letter first, followed by the row number. For example, cell reference E2 refers to the cell located at the intersection of column E and row 2 (Figure 68).

One cell on the worksheet, designated the **active cell**, is the one into which you can enter data. The active cell in Figure 68 is A1. The active cell is identified in three ways. First, a heavy border surrounds the cell; second, the active cell reference shows immediately above column A in the Name box; and third, the column heading A and row heading 1 are highlighted so it is easy to see which cell is active (Figure 68).

The horizontal and vertical lines on the worksheet itself are called **gridlines**. Gridlines make it easier to see and identify each cell in the worksheet. If desired, you can turn the gridlines off so that they do not show on the worksheet, but it is recommended that you leave them on for now.

The mouse pointer in Figure 68 has the shape of a block plus sign. The mouse pointer appears as a block plus sign whenever it is located in a cell on the worksheet. Another common shape of the mouse pointer is the block arrow. The mouse pointer turns into the block arrow when you move it outside the worksheet or when you drag cell contents between rows or columns. The other mouse pointer shapes are described when they appear on the screen.

Ribbon When you start Excel, the Ribbon displays eight main tabs: File, Home, Insert, Page Layout, Formulas, Data, Review, and View. The Formulas and Data tabs are specific to Excel. The Formulas tab allows you to work with Excel formulas, and the Data tab allows you to work with data processing features such as importing and sorting data.

BTW

The Worksheet Size and Window
The 16,384 columns and 1,048,576 rows in Excel make for a huge worksheet that – if you could imagine – takes up the entire side of a building to display in its entirety. Your computer screen, by comparison, is a small window that allows you to view only a minute area of the worksheet at one time. While you cannot see the entire worksheet, you can move the window over the worksheet to view any part of it.

BTW

Customizing the Ribbon
In addition to customizing the Quick Access Toolbar, you can add items to and remove items from the Ribbon. To customize the Ribbon, click File on the Ribbon to open the Backstage view, click Options in the Backstage view, and then click Customize Ribbon in the left pane of the Options dialog box. More information about customizing the Ribbon is presented in a later chapter.

Formula Bar   The formula bar appears below the Ribbon (Figure 69). As you type, Excel displays the entry in the **formula bar**. You can make the formula bar larger by dragging the sizing handle at the bottom of the formula bar or clicking the expand button to the right of the formula bar. Excel also displays the active cell reference in the **Name box** on the left side of the formula bar.

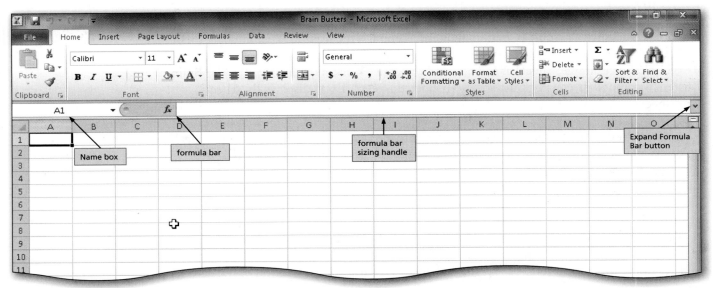

Figure 69

To Enter a Worksheet Title

To enter data into a cell, you first must select it. The easiest way to select a cell (make it active) is to use the mouse to move the block plus sign mouse pointer to the cell and then click. An alternative method is to use the arrow keys that are located just to the right of the typewriter keys on the keyboard. An arrow key selects the cell adjacent to the active cell in the direction of the arrow on the key.

In Excel, any set of characters containing a letter, hyphen (as in a telephone number), or space is considered text. **Text** is used to place titles, such as worksheet titles, column titles, and row titles, on the worksheet. The following steps enter the worksheet title in cell A1.

- If it is not already the active cell, click cell A1 to make it the active cell (Figure 70).

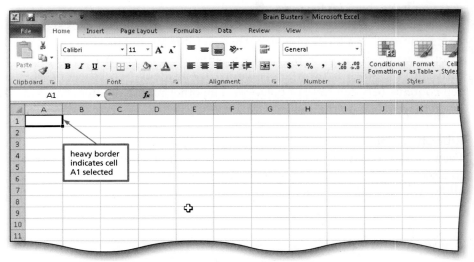

Figure 70

2

- Type **Brain Buster Book Rentals** in cell A1 (Figure 71).

Q&A

Why did the appearance of the formula bar change?

Excel displays the title in the formula bar and in cell A1. When you begin typing a cell entry, Excel displays two additional boxes in the formula bar: the Cancel box and the Enter box. Clicking the Enter box completes an entry. Clicking the Cancel box cancels an entry.

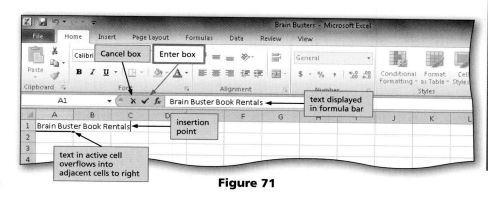

Figure 71

3

- Click the Enter box to complete the entry and enter the worksheet title in cell A1 (Figure 72).

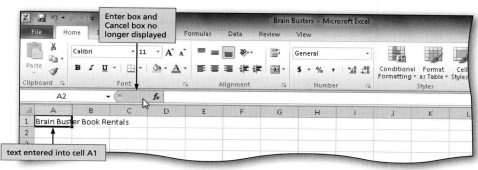

Figure 72

Other Ways		
1. To complete entry, click any cell other than active cell	2. To complete entry, press ENTER, HOME, PAGE UP, PAGE DOWN, END,	UP, DOWN, LEFT ARROW, or RIGHT ARROW

To Save an Existing Office Document with the Same File Name

Saving frequently cannot be overemphasized. You have made modifications to the file (spreadsheet) since you created it. Thus, you should save again. Similarly, you should continue saving files frequently so that you do not lose your changes since the time you last saved the file. You can use the same file name, such as Brain Busters, to save the changes made to the document. The following step saves a file again.

1

- Click the Save button on the Quick Access Toolbar to overwrite the previously saved file (Brain Busters, in this case) on the USB flash drive (Figure 73).

Q&A

Why did the Save As dialog box not appear?

Office programs, including Excel, overwrite the document using the setting specified the first time you saved the document.

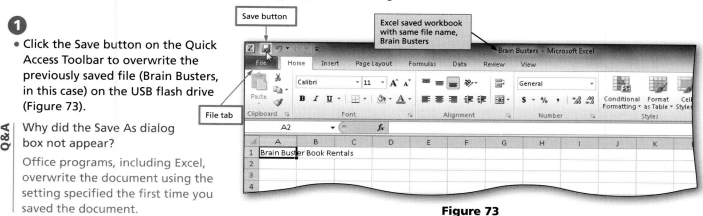

Figure 73

Other Ways
1. Press CTRL+S or press SHIFT+F12

To Use Save As to Change the Name of a File

You might want to save a file with a different name and even to a different location. For example, you might start a homework assignment with a data file and then save it with a final file name for submitting to your instructor, saving it to a location designated by your instructor. The following steps save a file with a different file name.

1 With your USB flash drive connected to one of the computer's USB ports, click File on the Ribbon to open the Backstage view.

2 Click Save As in the Backstage view to display the Save As dialog box.

3 Type **Brain Busters Rental Summary** in the File name text box (Save As dialog box) to change the file name. Do not press the ENTER key after typing the file name because you do not want to close the dialog box at this time.

4 Navigate to the desired save location (the Excel folder in the CIS 101 folder [or your class folder] on the USB flash drive, in this case). For specific instructions, perform the tasks in steps 4a through 4g.

4a If a navigation pane is not displayed in the Save As dialog box, click the Browse Folders button to expand the dialog box.

4b If Computer is not displayed in the navigation pane, drag the navigation pane scroll bar (Save As dialog box) until Computer appears.

4c If Computer is not expanded in the navigation pane, double-click Computer to display a list of available storage devices in the navigation pane.

4d If necessary, scroll through the Save As dialog box until your USB flash drive appears in the list of available storage devices in the navigation pane.

4e If your USB flash drive is not expanded, double-click the USB flash drive in the list of available storage devices in the navigation pane to select that drive as the new save location and display its contents in the right pane.

4f If your class folder (CIS 101, in this case) is not expanded, double-click the CIS 101 folder to select the folder and display its contents.

4g Double-click the Excel folder to select it and display its contents in the right pane.

5 Click the Save button (Save As dialog box) to save the file in the selected folder on the selected drive with the new file name.

To Quit an Office Program

You are finished using Excel. The following steps quit Excel.

1 If you have one Office document open, click the Close button on the right side of the title bar to close the document and quit the Office program; or if you have multiple Office documents open, click File on the Ribbon to open the Backstage view and then click Exit in the Backstage view to close all open documents and quit the Office program.

2 If a dialog box appears, click the Save button to save any changes made to the file since the last save.

Access

The term **database** describes a collection of data organized in a manner that allows access, retrieval, and use of that data. **Microsoft Access 2010**, usually referred to as simply **Access,** is a database management system. A **database management system** is software that allows you to use a computer to create a database; add, change, and delete data in the database; create queries that allow you to ask questions concerning the data in the database; and create forms and reports using the data in the database.

To Start a Program

The following steps, which assume Windows 7 is running, start the Access program based on a typical installation. You may need to ask your instructor how to start programs for your computer.

1 Click the Start button on the Windows 7 taskbar to display the Start menu.

2 Type the name of the program, **Microsoft Access** in this case, as the search text in the 'Search programs and files' text box and watch the search results appear on the Start menu.

3 Click the name of the program, Microsoft Access 2010 in this case, in the search results on the Start menu to start Access.

4 If the program window is not maximized, click the Maximize button on its title bar to maximize the window (Figure 74).

Q&A Do I have to start Access using these steps?

No. You can use any previously discussed method of starting an Office program to start Access.

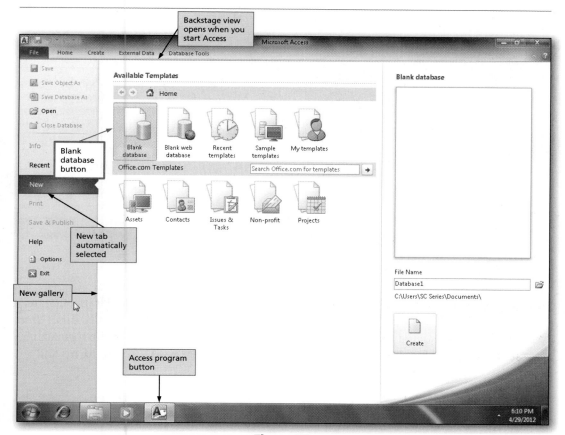

Figure 74

Unique Elements in Access

You work on objects such as tables, forms, and reports in the **Access work area**. In Figure 74, the Access window contains no open objects. Figure 75 shows a work area with multiple objects open. **Object tabs** for the open objects appear at the top of the work area. You select an open object by clicking its tab. In the figure, the Suppliers Split Form is the selected object. To the left of the work area is the Navigation Pane, which contains a list of all the objects in the database. You use this pane to open an object. You also can customize the way objects are displayed in the Navigation Pane.

Because the Navigation Pane can take up space in the window, you may not have as much open space for working as you would with Word or Excel. You can use the Shutter Bar Open/Close button to minimize the Navigation Pane when you are not using it, which allows more space to work with tables, forms, reports, and other database elements.

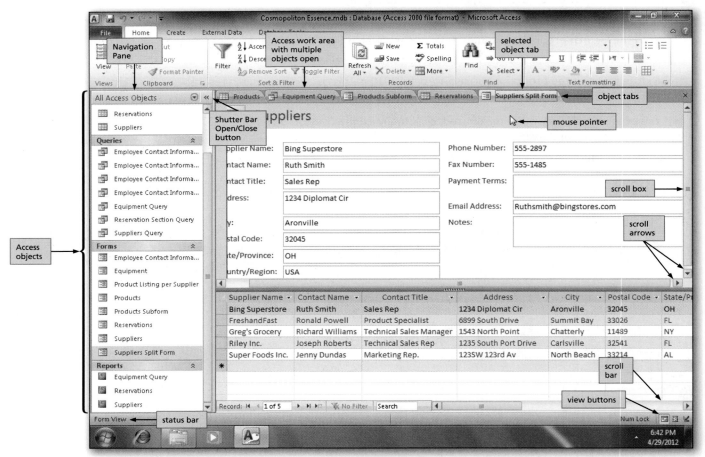

Figure 75

Ribbon When you start Access, the Ribbon displays five main tabs: File, Home, Create, External Data, and Database Tools. Access has unique groupings such as Sort & Filter and Records that are designed specifically for working with databases. Many of the formatting options are reserved for the tool tabs that appear when you are working with forms and reports.

To Create an Access Database

Unlike the other Office programs, Access saves a database when you first create it. When working in Access, you will add data to an Access database. As you add data to a database, Access automatically saves your changes rather than waiting until you manually save the database or quit Access. Recall that in Word and Excel, you entered the data first and then saved it.

Because Access automatically saves the database as you add and change data, you do not have to always click the Save button. In fact, the Save button in Access is used for saving the objects (including tables, queries, forms, reports, and other database objects) a database contains. You can use either the Blank Database option or a template to create a new database. If you already know the organization of your database, you would use the Blank Database option. If not, you can use a template. Templates can guide you by suggesting some commonly used database organizations.

The following steps use the Blank Database option to create a database named Charmed Excursions in the Access folder in the class folder (CIS 101, in this case) on a USB flash drive.

1

- If necessary, click the Blank database button in the New gallery (shown in Figure 74 on page OFF 53) in the Backstage view to select the template type.

- Click the File Name text box to select the default database name.

- Type **Charmed Excursions** in the File Name text box to enter the new file name. Do not press the ENTER key after typing the file name because you do not want to create the database at this time (Figure 76).

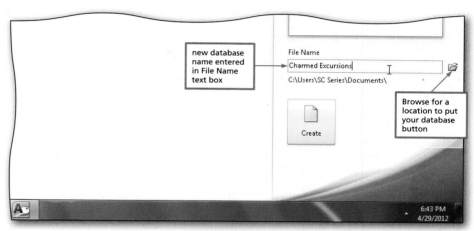

Figure 76

Q&A Why is the Backstage view automatically open when you start Access?

Unlike other Office programs, you first must save a database before adding any data. For this reason, the Backstage view opens automatically when you start Access.

2

- Click the 'Browse for a location to put your database' button to display the File New Database dialog box.

- Navigate to the location for the database, that is, the USB flash drive, then to the folder identifying your class (CIS 101, in this case), and then to the Access folder (Figure 77). For detailed steps about navigating, see Steps 3a – 3c on pages OFF 28 and OFF 29.

Q&A Why does the 'Save as type' box say Microsoft Access 2007 Databases?

Microsoft Access database formats change with some new versions of Microsoft Access. The most recent format is the Microsoft Access 2007 Databases format, which was released with Access 2007.

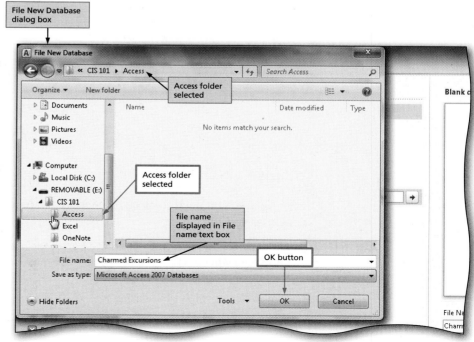

Figure 77

3

- Click the OK button (File New Database dialog box) to select the Access folder as the location for the database and close the dialog box (Figure 78).

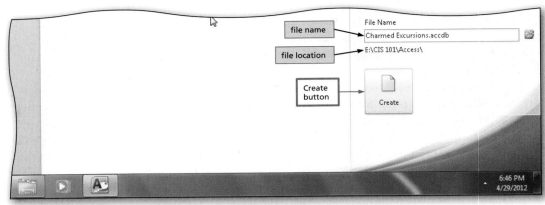

file name	File Name
	Charmed Excursions.accdb
file location	E:\CIS 101\Access\
Create button	Create

6:46 PM
4/29/2012

Figure 78

4

- Click the Create button in the Backstage view to create the database on the selected drive in the selected folder with the file name, Charmed Excursions. If necessary, click the Enable Content button (Figure 79).

Q&A How do I know that the Charmed Excursions database is created?

The name of the database appears on the title bar.

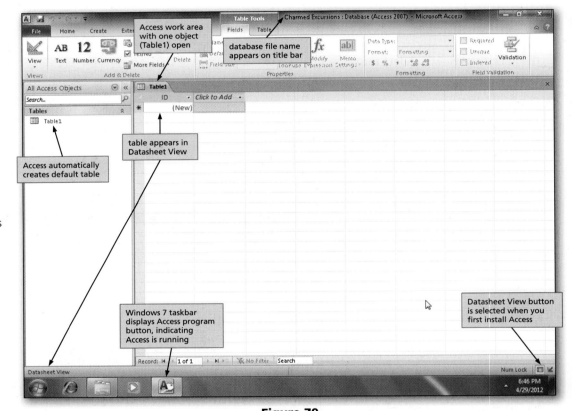

Access work area with one object (Table1) open

database file name appears on title bar

table appears in Datasheet View

Access automatically creates default table

Windows 7 taskbar displays Access program button, indicating Access is running

Datasheet View button is selected when you first install Access

Figure 79

To Close an Office File

Assume you need to close the Access database and return to it later. The following step closes an Office file.

1 Click File on the Ribbon to open the Backstage view and then click Close Database in the Backstage view to close the open file (Charmed Excursions, in this case) without quitting the active program.

Q&A Why is Access still on the screen?

When you close a database, the program remains open.

To Open an Existing Office File

Assume you wish to continue working on an existing file, that is, a file you previously saved. Earlier in this chapter, you learned how to open a recently used file through the Backstage view. The following steps open a database, specifically the Charmed Excursions database, from the USB flash drive.

1

- With your USB flash drive connected to one of the computer's USB ports, if necessary, click File on the Ribbon to open the Backstage view.

- Click Open in the Backstage view to display the Open dialog box (Figure 80).

2

- Navigate to the location of the file to be opened (in this case, the USB flash drive, then to the CIS 101 folder [or your class folder], and then to the Access folder). For detailed steps about navigating, see Steps 3a – 3c on pages OFF 28 and OFF 29.

What if I did not save my file in a folder?

If you did not save your file in a folder, the file you wish to open should be displayed in the Open dialog box before navigating to any folders.

Figure 80

3

- Click the file to be opened, Charmed Excursions in this case, to select the file (Figure 81).

4

- Click the Open button (Open dialog box) to open the selected file and display the opened file in the current program window (shown in Figure 79).

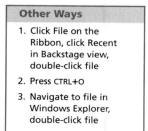

Other Ways

1. Click File on the Ribbon, click Recent in Backstage view, double-click file
2. Press CTRL+O
3. Navigate to file in Windows Explorer, double-click file

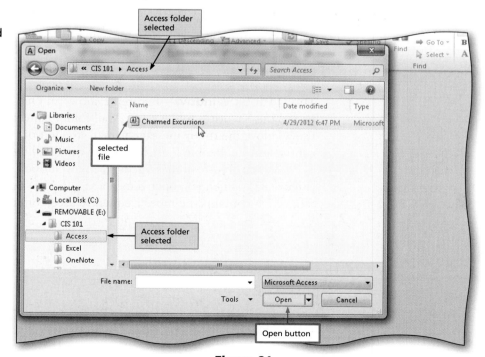

Figure 81

To Quit an Office Program

You are finished using Access. The following step quits Access.

1 Click the Close button on the right side of the title bar to close the file and quit the Office program.

Other Office Programs

In addition to the Office programs discussed thus far, three other programs are useful when collaborating and communicating with others: Outlook, Publisher, and OneNote.

Outlook

Outlook is a powerful communications and scheduling program that helps you communicate with others, keep track of contacts, and organize your calendar. Personal information manager (PIM) programs such as Outlook provide a way for individuals and workgroups to organize, find, view, and share information easily. Outlook allows you to send and receive electronic mail (e-mail) and permits you to engage in real-time messaging with family, friends, or coworkers using instant messaging. Outlook also provides a means to organize contacts. Users can track e-mail messages, meetings, and notes related to a particular contact. Outlook's Calendar, Contacts, Tasks, and Notes components aid in this organization. Contact information readily is available from the Outlook Calendar, Mail, Contacts, and Task components by accessing the Find a Contact feature.

Electronic mail (e-mail) is the transmission of messages and files over a computer network. E-mail has become an important means of exchanging information and files between business associates, classmates and instructors, friends, and family. Businesses find that using e-mail to send documents electronically saves both time and money. Parents with students away at college or relatives who live across the country find that communicating by e-mail is an inexpensive and easy way to stay in touch with their family members. Exchanging e-mail messages is one of the more widely used features of the Internet.

The Outlook Window   Figure 82 shows an Outlook window, which is divided into six panes: the Favorites folder pane, Mail folder pane, and Navigation Pane on the left side of the window, the Inbox message pane to the left of center, the Reading Pane to the right of center, and the People Pane just below the Reading Pane.

When an e-mail message is open in Outlook, it is displayed in a Message window (Figure 83). When you open a message, the Message window Ribbon displays the Message tab, which contains the more frequently used commands.

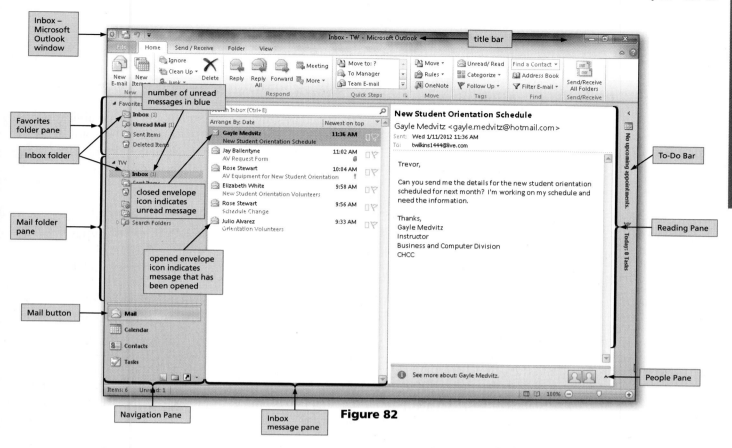

Figure 82

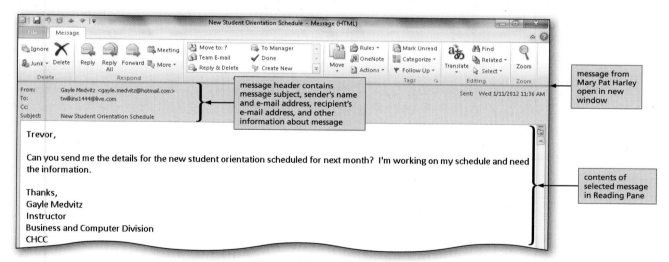

Figure 83

Publisher

Publisher is a powerful desktop publishing (DTP) program that assists you in designing and producing professional-quality documents that combine text, graphics, illustrations, and photos. DTP software provides additional tools beyond those typically found in word processing programs, including design templates, graphic manipulation tools, color schemes or libraries, advanced layout and printing tools, and Web components. For large jobs, businesses use DTP software to design publications that are camera ready, which means the files are suitable for outside commercial printing. In addition, DTP software can be used to create Web pages and interactive Web forms.

Publisher is used by people who regularly produce high-quality color publications, such as newsletters, brochures, flyers, logos, signs, catalogs, cards, and business forms. Saving publications as Web pages or complete Web sites is a powerful component of Publisher. All publications can be saved in a format that easily is viewed and manipulated using a browser.

Publisher has many features designed to simplify production and make publications visually appealing. Using Publisher, you easily can change the shape, size, and color of text and graphics. You can include many kinds of graphical objects, including mastheads, borders, tables, images, pictures, charts, and Web objects in publications, as well as integrate spreadsheets and databases.

BTW

Starting Publisher
When you first start Publisher, the New templates gallery usually is displayed in the Backstage view. If it is not displayed, click File on the Ribbon, click Options in the Backstage view, click General (Options dialog box), and then click Show the New template gallery when starting Publisher to select the check box in the General panel.

The Publisher Window On the right side of the Backstage view, Publisher displays the New template gallery, which includes a list of publication types. **Publication types** are typical publications used by desktop publishers. The more popular types are displayed in the center of the window. Each publication type is a link to display various templates and blank publications from which you may choose.

Once you select a publication type, the window changes to allow you to select a specific template (Figure 84). Some templates are installed with Publisher, and others are available online. Clicking a publication type causes template previews to be displayed in the center of the window. The templates are organized by purpose (for example, Sales) and then alphabetically by design type. On the right, Publisher will display a larger preview of the selected template, along with some customization options if the template is installed or a download option if the template is online. In Figure 84, the installed Arrows template is selected so that the customize options appear.

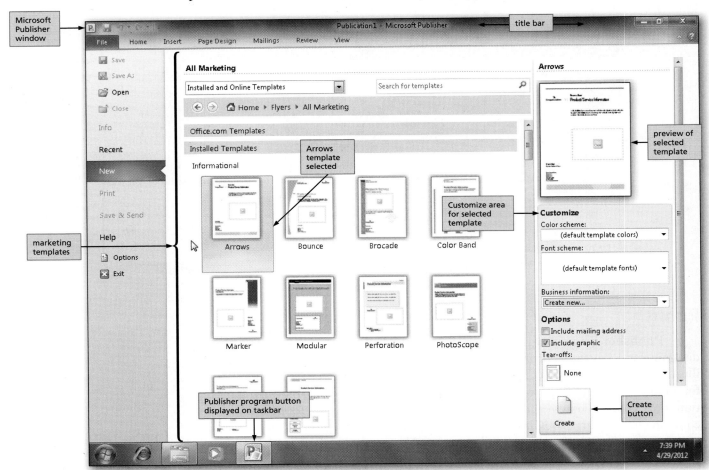

Figure 84

When you click the Create button, Publisher creates the document and sets it up for you to edit. Figure 85 shows the Arrows document that Publisher creates when default options are selected.

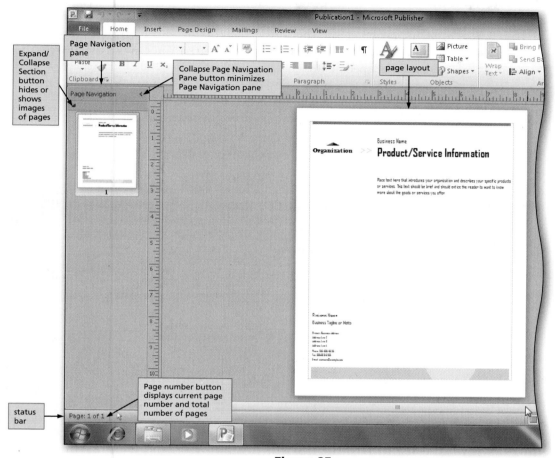

Figure 85

OneNote

OneNote is a note taking program that assists you in entering, saving, organizing, searching, and using notes. It enables you to create pages, which are organized in sections, just as in a physical notebook. In OneNote, you can type notes anywhere on a page and then easily move the notes around on the page. You can create lists and outlines, use handwriting to enter notes, and create drawings. If you use a Tablet PC to add handwritten notes to a document, OneNote can convert the handwriting to text. It also can perform searches on the handwritten entries. Pictures and data from other programs easily are incorporated in your notes.

In addition to typing and handwriting, you can take audio notes. For example, you could record conversations during a meeting or lecture. As you record, you can take additional notes. When you play back the audio notes, you can synchronize the additional notes you took; that is, OneNote will show you during playback the exact points at which you added the notes. A variety of note flags, which are symbols that call your attention to notes on a page, enable you to flag notes as being important. You then can use the Note Flags summary to view the flagged notes, which can be sorted in a variety of ways.

OneNote includes tools to assist you with organizing a notebook and navigating its contents. It also includes a search facility, making it easy to find the specific notes in which you are interested. For short notes that you always want to have available readily, you can use Side Notes, which are used much like the sticky notes that you might use in a physical notebook.

OneNote Window   All activity in OneNote takes place in the **notebook** (Figure 86). Like a physical notebook, the OneNote notebook consists of notes that are placed on **pages**. The pages are grouped into **sections**, which can be further grouped into **folders**. (No folders are shown in the notebook in the figure.) You can use the Search All Notebooks box to search for specific text in your notes.

You can add pages to the notebook using the New Page button in the Page Tabs pane. If Page Tabs are displayed, then you can switch to a page by clicking its tab. Figure 86 shows the Top Uses page being displayed for the General notebook.

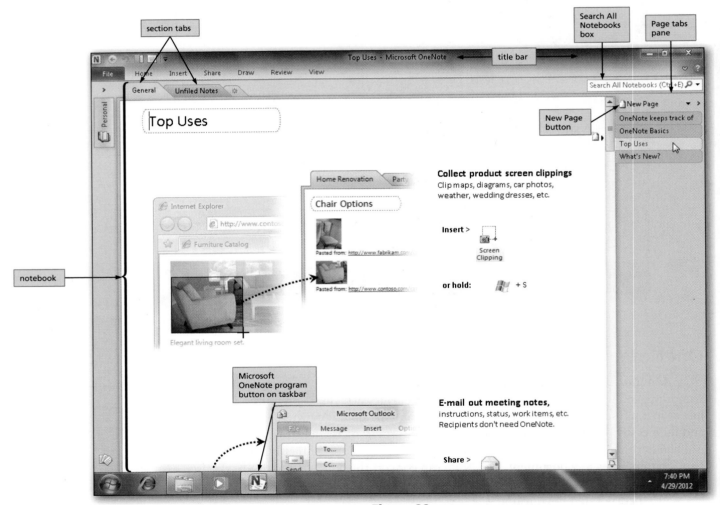

Figure 86

Break Point: If you wish to take a break, this is a good place to do so. To resume at a later time, continue to follow the steps from this location forward.

Moving, Renaming, and Deleting Files

Earlier in this chapter, you learned how to organize files in folders, which is part of a process known as **file management**. The following sections cover additional file management topics including renaming, moving, and deleting files.

To Rename a File

In some circumstances, you may want to change the name of, or rename, a file or a folder. For example, you may want to distinguish a file in one folder or drive from a copy of a similar file, or you may decide to rename a file to better identify its contents. The Word folder shown in Figure 87 contains the Word document, Koala Exhibit. The following steps change the name of the Koala Exhibit file in the Word folder to Koala Exhibit Flyer.

1

- If necessary, click the Windows Explorer program button on the taskbar to display the folder window in Windows Explorer.

- Navigate to the location of the file to be renamed (in this case, the Word folder in the CIS 101 [or your class folder] folder on the USB flash drive) to display the file(s) it contains in the right pane.

- Right-click the Koala Exhibit icon or file name in the right pane to select the Koala Exhibit file and display a shortcut menu that presents a list of commands related to files (Figure 87).

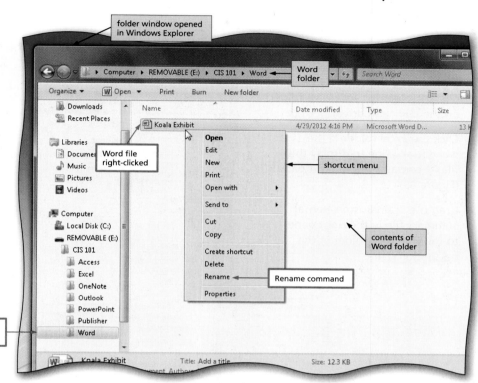

Figure 87

2

- Click Rename on the shortcut menu to place the current file name in a text box.

- Type **Koala Exhibit Flyer** in the text box and then press the ENTER key (Figure 88).

Q&A Are any risks involved in renaming files that are located on a hard disk?

If you inadvertently rename a file that is associated with certain programs, the programs may not be able to find the file and, therefore, may not execute properly. Always use caution when renaming files.

Q&A Can I rename a file when it is open?

No, a file must be closed to change the file name.

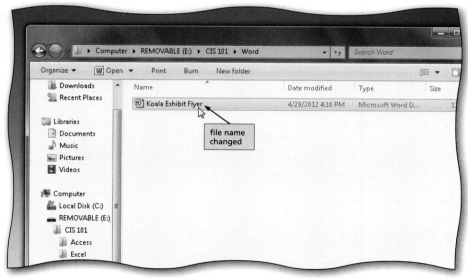

Figure 88

Other Ways
1. Select file, press F2, type new file name, press ENTER

To Move a File

At some time, you may want to move a file from one folder, called the source folder, to another, called the destination. When you move a file, it no longer appears in the original folder. If the destination and the source folders are on the same disk drive, you can move a file by dragging it. If the folders are on different disk drives, then you will need to right-drag the file. The following step moves the Brain Busters Rental Summary file from the Excel folder to the OneNote folder.

- In Windows Explorer, navigate to the location of the file to be moved (in this case, the Excel folder in the CIS 101 folder [or your class folder] on the USB flash drive).

- Click the Excel folder in the navigation pane to display the files it contains in the right pane (Figure 89).

- Drag the Brain Busters Rental Summary file in the right pane to the OneNote folder in the navigation pane.

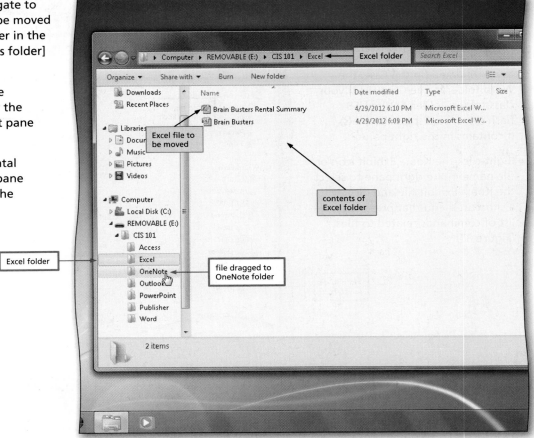

Figure 89

Other Ways
1. Right-click file, drag file to destination folder, click Move here
2. Right-click file to copy, click Cut on shortcut menu, right-click destination folder, click Paste on shortcut menu
3. Select file to copy, press CTRL+X, select destination folder, press CTRL+V

To Delete a File

A final task you may want to perform is to delete a file. Exercise extreme caution when deleting a file or files. When you delete a file from a hard disk, the deleted file is stored in the Recycle Bin where you can recover it until you empty the Recycle Bin. If you delete a file from removable media, such as a USB flash drive, the file is deleted permanently. The next steps delete the Koala Exhibit Gala file from the PowerPoint folder.

1

- In Windows Explorer, navigate to the location of the file to be deleted (in this case, the PowerPoint folder in the CIS 101 folder [or your class folder] on the USB flash drive).

- Click the PowerPoint folder in the navigation pane to display the files it contains in the right pane.

- Right-click the Koala Exhibit Gala icon or file name in the right pane to select the file and display a shortcut menu (Figure 90).

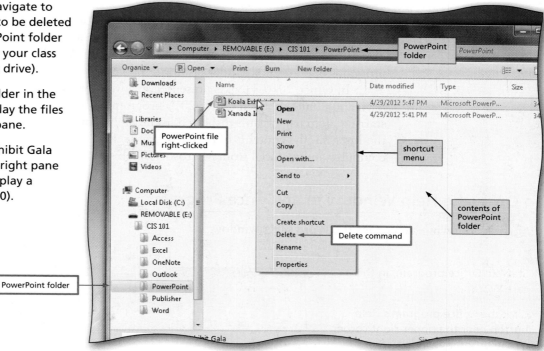

Figure 90

2

- Click Delete on the shortcut menu to display the Delete File dialog box (Figure 91).

- Click the Yes button (Delete File dialog box) to delete the selected file.

Q&A

Can I use this same technique to delete a folder?

Yes. Right-click the folder and then click Delete on the shortcut menu. When you delete a folder, all of the files and folders contained in the folder you are deleting, together with any files and folders on lower hierarchical levels, are deleted as well.

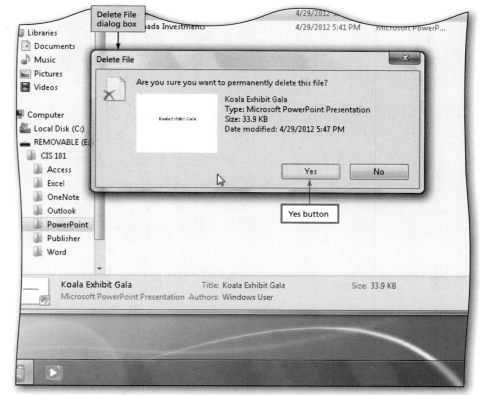

Figure 91

Other Ways
1. Select icon, press DELETE

Microsoft Office and Windows Help

At any time while you are using one of the Microsoft Office 2010 programs, you can use Office Help to display information about all topics associated with the program. To illustrate the use of Office Help, this section uses Word. Help in other Office 2010 programs operates in a similar fashion.

In Office 2010, Help is presented in a window that has Web-browser-style navigation buttons. Each Office 2010 program has its own Help home page, which is the starting Help page that is displayed in the Help window. If your computer is connected to the Internet, the contents of the Help page reflect both the local help files installed on the computer and material from Microsoft's Web site.

To Open the Help Window in an Office Program

The following step opens the Word Help window.

- Start an Office program, in this case Word.

- Click the Office program's Help button near the upper-right corner of the program window (the Microsoft Word Help button, in this case) to open the program's Help window (Figure 92).

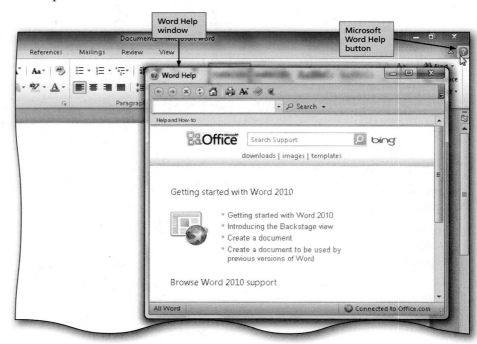

Figure 92

Other Ways
1. Press F1

Moving and Resizing Windows

Up to this point, this chapter has used minimized and maximized windows. At times, however, it is useful, or even necessary, to have more than one window open and visible on the screen at the same time. You can resize and move these open windows so that you can view different areas of and elements in the window. In the case of the Help window, for example, it could be covering document text in the Word window that you need to see.

To Move a Window by Dragging

You can move any open window that is not maximized to another location on the desktop by dragging the title bar of the window. The following step drags the Word Help window to the top left of the desktop.

1

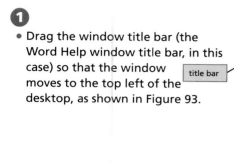

- Drag the window title bar (the Word Help window title bar, in this case) so that the window moves to the top left of the desktop, as shown in Figure 93.

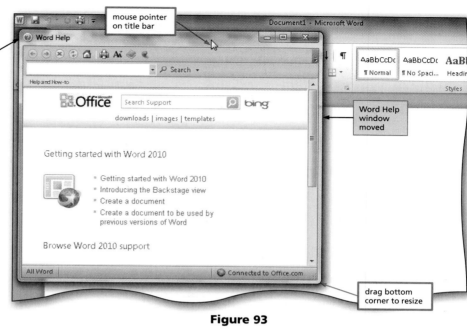

Figure 93

Other Ways

1. Right-click title bar, click Move on shortcut menu, drag window

To Resize a Window by Dragging

Sometimes, information is not visible completely in a window. A method used to change the size of the window is to drag the window borders. The following step changes the size of the Word Help window by dragging its borders.

1

- Point to the lower-right corner of the window (the Word Help window, in this case) until the mouse pointer changes to a two-headed arrow.

- Drag the bottom border downward to display more of the active window (Figure 94).

Q&A Can I drag other borders on the window to enlarge or shrink the window?

Yes, you can drag the left, right, and top borders and any window corner to resize a window.

Q&A Will Windows 7 remember the new size of the window after I close it?

Yes. When you reopen the window, Windows 7 will display it at the same size it was when you closed it.

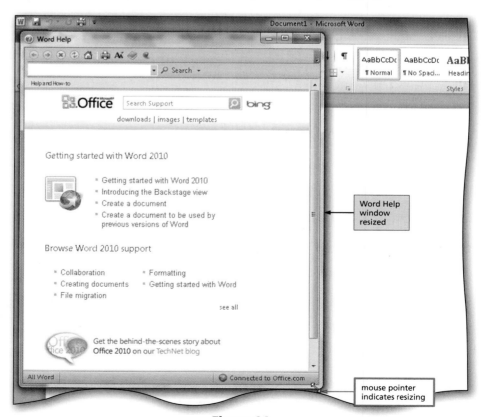

Figure 94

Using Office Help

Once an Office program's Help window is open, several methods exist for navigating Help. You can search for help by using any of the three following methods from the Help window:

1. Enter search text in the 'Type words to search for' text box
2. Click the links in the Help window
3. Use the Table of Contents

To Obtain Help Using the 'Type words to search for' Text Box

Assume for the following example that you want to know more about the Backstage view. The following steps use the 'Type words to search for' text box to obtain useful information about the Backstage view by entering the word, Backstage, as search text.

1

- Type **Backstage** in the 'Type words to search for' text box at the top of the Word Help window to enter the search text.

- Click the Search button arrow to display the Search menu (Figure 95).

- If it is not selected already, click All Word on the Search menu, so that Help performs the most complete search of the current program (Word, in this case). If All Word already is selected, click the Search button arrow again to close the Search menu.

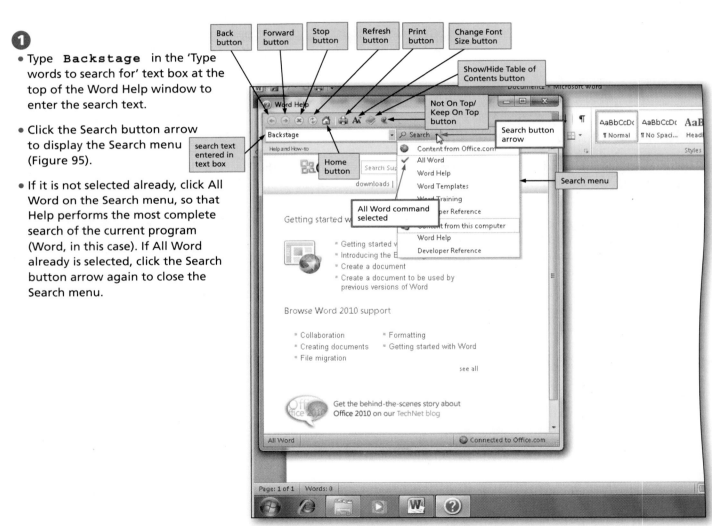

Figure 95

Q&A

Why select All Word on the Search menu?

Selecting All Word on the Search menu ensures that Word Help will search all possible sources for information about your search term. It will produce the most complete search results.

2

• Click the Search button to display the search results (Figure 96).

Q&A

Why do my search results differ?

If you do not have an Internet connection, your results will reflect only the content of the Help files on your computer. When searching for help online, results also can change as material is added, deleted, and updated on the online Help Web pages maintained by Microsoft.

Q&A

Why were my search results not very helpful?

When initiating a search, be sure to check the spelling of the search text; also, keep your search specific, with fewer than seven words, to return the most accurate results.

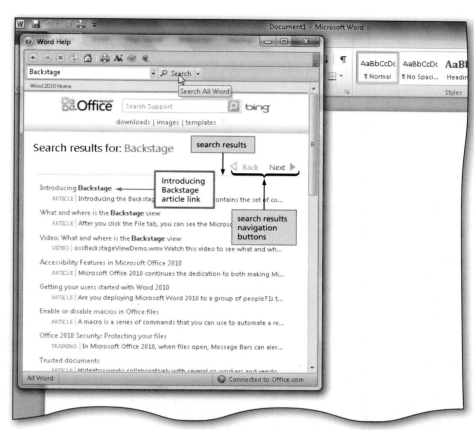

Figure 96

3

• Click the Introducing Backstage link to open the Help document associated with the selected topic (Figure 97).

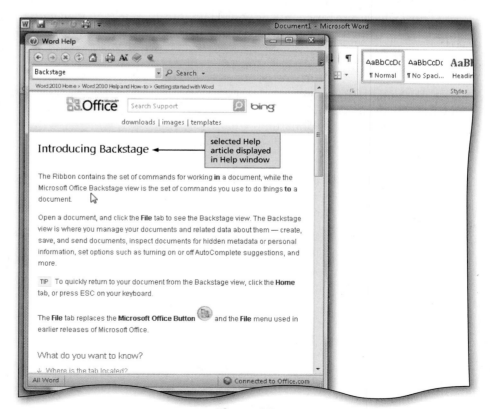

Figure 97

4

- Click the Home button on the toolbar to clear the search results and redisplay the Help home page (Figure 98).

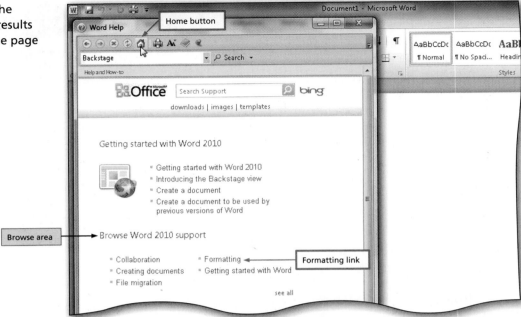

Figure 98

To Obtain Help Using the Help Links

If your topic of interest is listed in the Browse area of the Help window, you can click the link to begin browsing the Help categories instead of entering search text. You browse Help just as you would browse a Web site. If you know which category contains your Help information, you may wish to use these links. The following step finds the Formatting Help information using the category links from the Word Help home page.

1

- Click the Formatting link on the Help home page (shown in Figure 98) to display the Formatting page (Figure 99).

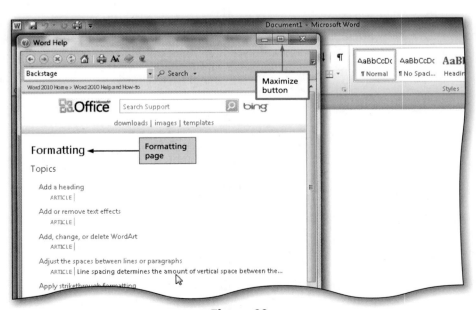

Figure 99

To Obtain Help Using the Help Table of Contents

A third way to find Help in Office programs is through the Help Table of Contents. You can browse through the Table of Contents to display information about a particular topic or to familiarize yourself with an Office program. The following steps access the Help information about themes by browsing through the Table of Contents.

1

- Click the Home button on the toolbar to display the Help home page.

- Click the Show Table of Contents button on the toolbar to display the Table of Contents pane on the left side of the Help window. If necessary, click the Maximize button on the Help title bar to maximize the window (Figure 100).

Q&A

Why does the appearance of the Show Table of Contents button change?

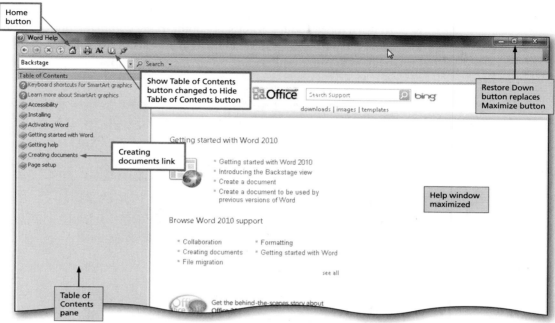

Figure 100

When the Table of Contents is displayed in the Help window, the Hide Table of Contents button replaces the Show Table of Contents button.

2

- Click the Creating documents link in the Table of Contents pane to view a list of Help subtopics.

- Click the Apply themes to Word documents link in the Table of Contents pane to view the selected Help document in the right pane (Figure 101).

- After reviewing the page, click the Close button to quit Help.

- Click the Office program's Close button (Word, in this case) to quit the Office program.

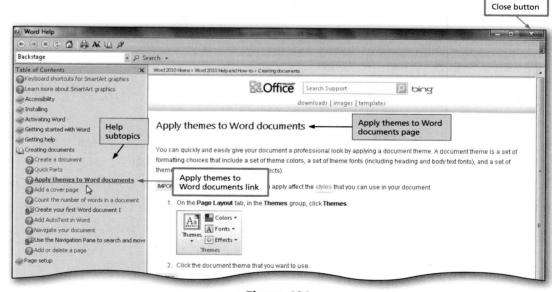

Figure 101

Q&A

How do I remove the Table of Contents pane when I am finished with it?

The Show Table of Contents button acts as a toggle. When the Table of Contents pane is visible, the button changes to Hide Table of Contents. Clicking it hides the Table of Contents pane and changes the button to Show Table of Contents.

Obtaining Help while Working in an Office Program

Help in the Office programs provides you with the ability to obtain help directly, without the need to open the Help window and initiate a search. For example, you may be unsure about how a particular command works, or you may be presented with a dialog box that you are not sure how to use.

Figure 102 shows one option for obtaining help while working in Word. If you want to learn more about a command, point to the command button and wait for the Enhanced ScreenTip to appear. If the Help icon appears in the Enhanced ScreenTip, press the F1 key while pointing to the command to open the Help window associated with that command.

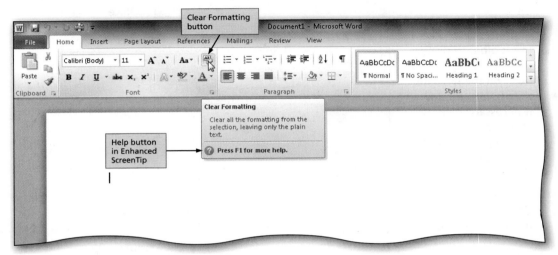

Figure 102

Figure 103 shows a dialog box that contains a Help button. Pressing the F1 key while the dialog box is displayed opens a Help window. The Help window contains help about that dialog box, if available. If no help file is available for that particular dialog box, then the main Help window opens.

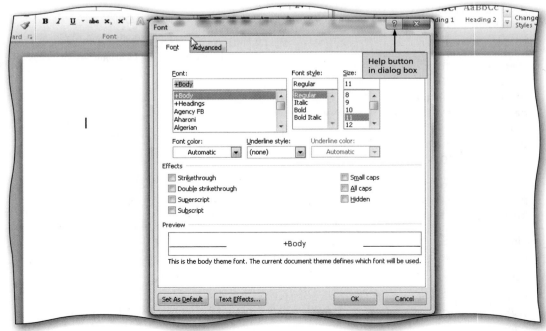

Figure 103

Using Windows Help and Support

One of the more powerful Windows 7 features is Windows Help and Support. **Windows Help and Support** is available when using Windows 7 or when using any Microsoft program running under Windows 7. This feature is designed to assist you in using Windows 7 or the various programs. Table 4 describes the content found in the Help and Support Center. The same methods used for searching Microsoft Office Help can be used in Windows Help and Support. The difference is that Windows Help and Support displays help for Windows 7, instead of for Microsoft Office.

Table 4 Windows Help and Support Center Content Areas	
Area	**Function**
Find an answer quickly	This area contains instructions about how to do a quick search using the search box.
Not sure where to start?	This area displays three topics to help guide a user: How to get started with your computer, Learn about Windows Basics, and Browse Help topics. Clicking one of the options navigates to corresponding Help and Support pages.
More on the Windows Website	This area contains links to online content from the Windows Web site. Clicking the links navigates to the corresponding Web pages on the Web site.

To Start Windows Help and Support

The following steps start Windows Help and Support and display the Windows Help and Support window, containing links to more information about Windows 7.

- Click the Start button on the taskbar to display the Start menu (Figure 104).

Why are the programs that are displayed on the Start menu different?

Windows adds the programs you have used recently to the left pane on the Start menu. You have started several programs while performing the steps in this chapter, so those programs now are displayed on the Start menu.

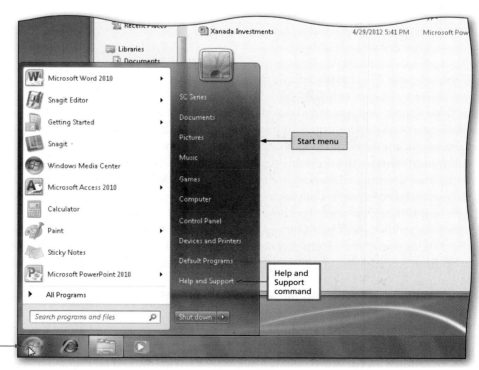

Figure 104

2

- Click Help and Support on the Start menu to open the Windows Help and Support window (Figure 105).

- After reviewing the Windows Help and Support window, click the Close button to quit Windows Help and Support.

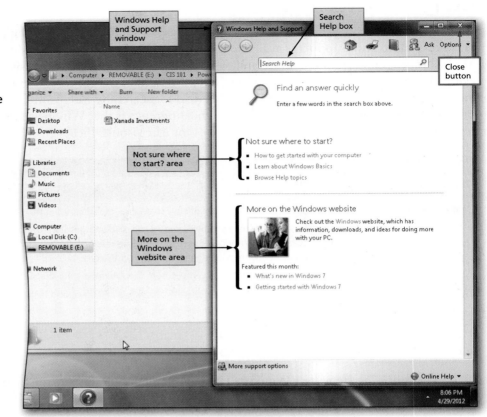

Figure 105

Other Ways

1. Press CTRL+ESC, press RIGHT ARROW, press UP ARROW, press ENTER
2. Press WINDOWS + F1

Chapter Summary

In this chapter, you learned about the Windows 7 interface. You started Windows 7, were introduced to the components of the desktop, and learned several mouse operations. You opened, closed, moved, resized, minimized, maximized, and scrolled a window. You used folder windows to expand and collapse drives and folders, display drive and folder contents, create folders, and rename and then delete a file.

You also learned some basic features of some Microsoft Office 2010 programs, including Word, PowerPoint, Excel, and Access. As part of this learning process, you discovered the common elements that exist among these different Office programs. You now can save basic document, presentation, spreadsheet, and database files. Additional Office programs, including Outlook, Publisher, and OneNote also were discussed.

Microsoft Office Help was demonstrated, and you learned how to use the Office Help window. You were introduced to the Windows 7 Help and Support Center and learned how to use it to obtain more information about Windows 7.

The items listed below include all of the new Windows 7 and Office 2010 skills you have learned in this chapter.

1. Log On to the Computer (OFF 6)
2. Start a Program Using the Start Menu (OFF 10)
3. Maximize a Window (OFF 12)
4. Display a Different Tab on the Ribbon (OFF 16)
5. Minimize, Display, and Restore the Ribbon (OFF 17)
6. Display and Use a Shortcut Menu (OFF 18)
7. Customize the Quick Access Toolbar (OFF 19)
8. Enter Text in a Document (OFF 20)
9. Create a Folder (OFF 22)
10. Create a Folder within a Folder (OFF 24)
11. Expand a Folder, Scroll through Folder Contents, and Collapse a Folder (OFF 26)
12. Switch from One Program to Another (OFF 27)
13. Save a File in a Folder (OFF 27)
14. Minimize and Restore a Window (OFF 30)
15. Change the Screen Resolution (OFF 33)

If you have a SAM 2010 user profile, your instructor may have assigned an autogradable version of this assignment. If so, log into the SAM 2010 Web site at www.cengage.com/sam2010 to download the instruction and start files.

Learn It Online

Test your knowledge of chapter content and key terms.

Instructions: To complete the Learn It Online exercises, start your browser, click the Address bar, and then enter the Web address **scsite.com/office2010/learn**. When the Office 2010 Learn It Online page is displayed, click the link for the exercise you want to complete and then read the instructions.

Chapter Reinforcement TF, MC, and SA
A series of true/false, multiple choice, and short answer questions that test your knowledge of the chapter content.

Flash Cards
An interactive learning environment where you identify chapter key terms associated with displayed definitions.

Practice Test
A series of multiple choice questions that test your knowledge of chapter content and key terms.

Who Wants To Be a Computer Genius?
An interactive game that challenges your knowledge of chapter content in the style of a television quiz show.

Wheel of Terms
An interactive game that challenges your knowledge of chapter key terms in the style of the television show *Wheel of Fortune*.

Crossword Puzzle Challenge
A crossword puzzle that challenges your knowledge of key terms presented in the chapter.

Apply Your Knowledge

Reinforce the skills and apply the concepts you learned in this chapter.

Creating a Folder and a Document

Instructions: You will create a Word folder and then create a Word document and save it in the folder.

Perform the following tasks:

1. Connect a USB flash drive to an available USB port and then open the USB flash drive window.

2. Click the New folder button on the toolbar to display a new folder icon and text box for the folder name.

3. Type **Word** in the text box to name the folder. Press the ENTER key to create the folder on the USB flash drive.

4. Start Word.

5. Enter the text shown in Figure 106.

6. Click the Save button on the Quick Access Toolbar. Navigate to the Word folder on the USB flash drive and then save the document using the file name, Apply 1 Class List.

7. If your Quick Access Toolbar does not show the Quick Print button, add the Quick Print button to the Quick Access Toolbar. Print the document using the Quick Print button on the Quick Access Toolbar. When you are finished printing, remove the Quick Print button from the Quick Access Toolbar.

8. Submit the printout to your instructor.

9. Quit Word.

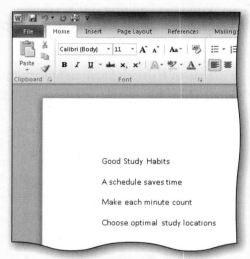

Figure 106

Extend Your Knowledge

Extend the skills you learned in this chapter and experiment with new skills. You will use Help to complete the assignment.

Using Help

Instructions: Use Office Help to perform the following tasks.

Perform the following tasks:

1. Start Word.

2. Click the Microsoft Word Help button to open the Word Help window (Figure 107).

3. Search Word Help to answer the following questions.

    a. What are the steps to add a new group to the Ribbon?

    b. What are Quick Parts?

4. With the Word program still running, start PowerPoint.

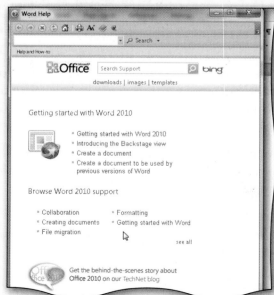

Figure 107

5. Click the Microsoft PowerPoint Help button on the title bar to open the PowerPoint Help window.

6. Search PowerPoint Help to answer the following questions.

   a. What is a slide master?

   b. How do you copy slides from another presentation into the existing presentation?

7. Quit PowerPoint.

8. Start Excel.

9. Click the Microsoft Excel Help button to open the Excel Help window.

10. Search Excel Help to answer the following questions.

    a. What are three different functions available in Excel?

    b. What are sparklines?

11. Quit Excel.

12. Start Access.

13. Click the Microsoft Access Help button to open the Access Help window.

14. Search Access Help to answer the following questions.

    a. What is SQL?

    b. What is a data macro?

15. Quit Access.

16. Type the answers from your searches in the Word document. Save the document with a new file name and then submit it in the format specified by your instructor.

17. Quit Word.

Make It Right

Analyze a file structure and correct all errors and/or improve the design.

Organizing Vacation Photos

Instructions: See the inside back cover of this book for instructions on downloading the Data Files for Students, or contact your instructor for information on accessing the required files.

Traditionally, you have stored photos from past vacations together in one folder. The photos are becoming difficult to manage, and you now want to store them in appropriate folders. You will create the folder structure shown in Figure 108. You then will move the photos to the folders so that they will be organized properly.

1. Connect a USB flash drive to an available USB port to open the USB flash drive window.

2. Using the techniques presented in the chapter, create the hierarchical folder structure shown in Figure 108.

3. Using the techniques presented in the chapter, move the vacation photos to their appropriate folders.

4. Submit your work in the format specified by your instructor.

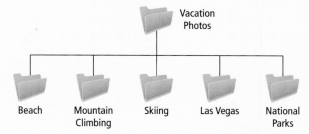

Figure 108

In the Lab

Use the guidelines, concepts, and skills presented in this chapter to increase your knowledge of Windows 7 and Office 2010. Labs are listed in order of increasing difficulty.

Lab 1: Using Windows Help and Support

Problem: You have a few questions about using Windows 7 and would like to answer these questions using Windows Help and Support.

Instructions: Use Windows Help and Support to perform the following tasks:

1. Display the Start menu and then click Help and Support to start Windows Help and Support.
2. Use the Help and Support Content page to answer the following questions.
   a. How do you reduce computer screen flicker?
   b. Which dialog box do you use to change the appearance of the mouse pointer?
   c. How do you minimize all windows?
   d. What is a VPN?
3. Use the Search Help text box in Windows Help and Support to answer the following questions.
   a. How can you minimize all open windows on the desktop?
   b. How do you start a program using the Run command?
   c. What are the steps to add a toolbar to the taskbar?
   d. What wizard do you use to remove unwanted desktop icons?
4. The tools to solve a problem while using Windows 7 are called **troubleshooters**. Use Windows Help and Support to find the list of troubleshooters (Figure 109), and answer the following questions.
   a. What problems does the HomeGroup troubleshooter allow you to resolve?
   b. List five Windows 7 troubleshooters that are not listed in Figure 109.
5. Use Windows Help and Support to obtain information about software licensing and product activation, and answer the following questions.
   a. What is genuine Windows?
   b. What is activation?
   c. What steps are required to activate Windows?
   d. What steps are required to read the Microsoft Software License Terms?
   e. Can you legally make a second copy of Windows 7 for use at home, work, or on a mobile computer or device?
   f. What is registration?
6. Close the Windows Help and Support window.

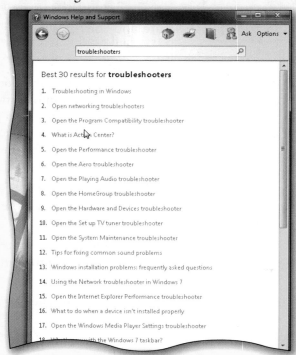

Figure 109

In the Lab

Lab 2: Creating Folders for a Pet Supply Store

Problem: Your friend works for Pete's Pet Supplies. He would like to organize his files in relation to the types of pets available in the store. He has five main categories: dogs, cats, fish, birds, and exotic. You are to create a folder structure similar to Figure 110.

Instructions: Perform the following tasks:

1. Connect a USB flash drive to an available USB port and then open the USB flash drive window.

2. Create the main folder for Pete's Pet Supplies.

3. Navigate to the Pete's Pet Supplies folder.

4. Within the Pete's Pet Supplies folder, create a folder for each of the following: Dogs, Cats, Fish, Birds, and Exotic.

5. Within the Exotic folder, create two additional folders, one for Primates and the second for Reptiles.

6. Submit the assignment in the format specified by your instructor.

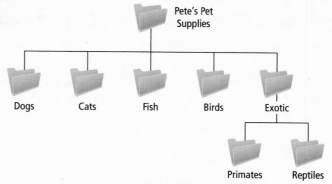

Figure 110

In the Lab

Lab 3: Creating Office Documents

Problem: You are taking a class that requires you to create a Word, PowerPoint, Excel, and Access file. You will save these files to folders named for four different Office programs (Figure 111).

Instructions: Create the folders shown in Figure 111. Then, using the respective Office program, create a small file to save in each folder (i.e., create a Word document to save in the Word folder, a PowerPoint presentation to save in the PowerPoint folder, and so on).

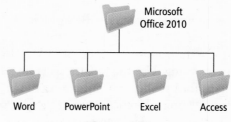

Figure 111

1. Connect a USB flash drive to an available USB port and then open the USB flash drive window.

2. Create the folder structure shown in Figure 111.

3. Navigate to the Word folder.

4. Create a Word document containing the text, My First Word Document, and then save it in the Word folder.

5. Navigate to the PowerPoint folder.

6. Create a PowerPoint presentation containing the title text, My First PowerPoint Presentation, and then save it in the PowerPoint folder.

7. Navigate to the Excel folder.

Continued >

In the Lab *continued*

8. Create an Excel spreadsheet containing the text, My First Excel Spreadsheet, in cell A1 and then save it in the Excel folder.

9. Navigate to the Access folder.

10. Save an Access database named, My First Database, in the Access folder.

11. Close all open Office programs.

12. Submit the assignment in the format specified by your instructor.

Cases and Places

Apply your creative thinking and problem solving skills to design and implement a solution.

Note: To complete these assignments, you may be required to use the Data Files for Students. See the inside back cover of this book for instructions on downloading the Data Files for Students, or contact your instructor for information about accessing the required files.

1: Creating Beginning Files for Classes

Academic

You are taking the following classes: Introduction to Engineering, Beginning Psychology, Introduction to Biology, and Accounting. Create folders for each of the classes. Use the following folder names: Engineering, Psychology, Biology, and Accounting, when creating the folder structure. In the Engineering folder, use Word to create a Word document with the name of the class and the class meeting location and time (MW 10:30 – 11:45, Room 317). In the Psychology folder, use PowerPoint to create your first lab presentation. It should begin with a title slide containing the text, Behavioral Observations. In the Biology folder, save a database named Research in the Biology folder. In the Accounting folder, create an Excel spreadsheet with the text, Tax Information, in cell A1. Use the concepts and techniques presented in this chapter to create the folders and files.

2: Using Help

Personal

Your parents enjoy working and playing games on their home computers. Your mother uses a notebook computer downstairs, and your father uses a desktop computer upstairs. They expressed interest in sharing files between their computers and sharing a single printer, so you offered to research various home networking options. Start Windows Help and Support, and search Help using the keywords, home networking. Use the link for installing a printer on a home network. Start Word and then type the main steps for installing a printer. Use the link for setting up a HomeGroup and then type the main steps for creating a HomeGroup in the Word document. Use the concepts and techniques presented in this chapter to use Help and create the Word document.

3: Creating Folders

Professional

Your boss at the bookstore where you work part-time has asked for help with organizing her files. After looking through the files, you decided upon a file structure for her to use, including the following folders: books, magazines, tapes, DVDs, and general merchandise. Within the books folder, create folders for hardback and paperback books. Within magazines, create folders for special issues and periodicals. In the tapes folder, create folders for celebrity and major release. In the DVDs folder, create a folder for book to DVD. In the general merchandise folder, create folders for novelties, posters, and games. Use the concepts and techniques presented in this chapter to create the folders.

1 Creating, Formatting, and Editing a Word Document with Pictures

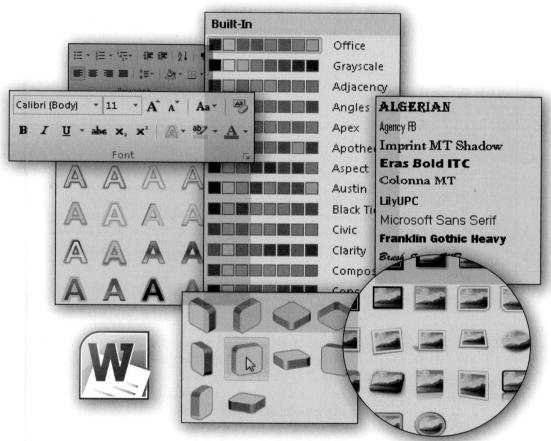

Objectives

You will have mastered the material in this chapter when you can:

- Enter text in a Word document
- Check spelling as you type
- Format paragraphs
- Format text
- Undo and redo commands or actions
- Change theme colors

- Insert digital pictures in a Word document
- Format pictures
- Add a page border
- Correct errors and revise a document
- Change document properties
- Print a document

1 | Creating, Formatting, and Editing a Word Document with Pictures

Introduction

To advertise a sale, promote a business, publicize an event, or convey a message to the community, you may want to create a flyer and hand it out in person or post it in a public location. Libraries, schools, religious organizations, grocery stores, coffee shops, and other places often provide bulletin boards or windows for flyers. These flyers announce personal items for sale or rent (car, boat, apartment); garage or block sales; services being offered (animal care, housecleaning, lessons); membership, sponsorship, or donation requests (club, religious organization, charity); and other messages such as a lost or found pet.

Project Planning Guidelines

> The process of developing a document that communicates specific information requires careful analysis and planning. As a starting point, establish why the document is needed. Once the purpose is determined, analyze the intended readers of the document and their unique needs. Then, gather information about the topic and decide what to include in the document. Finally, determine the document design and style that will be most successful at delivering the message. Details of these guidelines are provided in Appendix A. In addition, each project in this book provides practical applications of these planning considerations.

Project — Flyer with Pictures

Individuals and businesses create flyers to gain public attention. Flyers, which usually are a single page in length, are an inexpensive means of reaching the community. Many flyers, however, go unnoticed because they are designed poorly.

The project in this chapter follows general guidelines and uses Word to create the flyer shown in Figure 1–1. This colorful, eye-catching flyer announces that a dog has been found. The pictures of the dog, taken with a camera phone, entice passersby to stop and look at the flyer. The headline on the flyer is large and colorful to draw attention into the text. The body copy below the pictures briefly describes where and when the dog was found, along with a bulleted list that concisely highlights important identifying information. The signature line of the flyer calls attention to the contact phone number. The dog's name, Bailey, and signature line are in a different color so that they stand apart from the rest of the text on the flyer. Finally, the graphical page border nicely frames and complements the contents of the flyer.

FOUND DOG

page border

headline

digital photos of dog

Adorable, loving, friendly, well-behaved dog found early Friday morning, June 1, wandering on the bike trail at Filcher Park in Hampton Township.

- Male, adult cocker spaniel
- Tan color with patches of white on his chest
- Green and silver collar with the name, *Bailey*, on the tag

bulleted list

body copy

If this is your lost dog, <u>call 555-1029</u>.

signature line

Figure 1–1

Overview

As you read this chapter, you will learn how to create the flyer shown in Figure 1–1 on the previous page by performing these general tasks:

- Enter text in the document.
- Format the text in the document.
- Insert the pictures in the document.
- Format the pictures in the document.
- Enhance the page with a border and additional spacing.
- Correct errors and revise the document.
- Print the document.

Plan Ahead

General Project Guidelines

When creating a Word document, the actions you perform and decisions you make will affect the appearance and characteristics of the finished document. As you create a flyer, such as the project shown in Figure 1–1, you should follow these general guidelines:

1. **Choose the words for the text.** Follow the *less is more* principle. The less text, the more likely the flyer will be read. Use as few words as possible to make a point.

2. **Identify how to format various elements of the text.** The overall appearance of a document significantly affects its ability to communicate clearly. Examples of how you can modify the appearance, or **format**, of text include changing its shape, size, color, and position on the page.

3. **Find the appropriate graphical image(s).** An eye-catching graphical image should convey the flyer's overall message. It could show a product, service, result, or benefit, or visually convey a message that is not expressed easily with words.

4. **Establish where to position and how to format the graphical image(s).** The position and format of the graphical image(s) should grab the attention of passersby and draw them into reading the flyer.

5. **Determine whether the page needs enhancements such as a border or spacing adjustments.** A graphical, color-coordinated page border can further draw attention to a flyer and nicely frame its contents. Increasing or decreasing spacing between elements on a flyer can improve its readability and overall appearance.

6. **Correct errors and revise the document as necessary.** Post the flyer on a wall and make sure all text and images are legible from a distance. Ask someone else to read the flyer and give you suggestions for improvements.

7. **Determine the best method for distributing the document.** Documents can be distributed on paper or electronically. A flyer should be printed on paper so that it can be posted.

When necessary, more specific details concerning the above guidelines are presented at appropriate points in the chapter. The chapter also will identify the actions performed and decisions made regarding these guidelines during the creation of the flyer shown in Figure 1–1.

For an introduction to Windows 7 and instruction about how to perform basic Windows 7 tasks, read the Office 2010 and Windows 7 chapter at the beginning of this book, where you can learn how to resize windows, change screen resolution, create folders, move and rename files, use Windows Help, and much more.

To Start Word

If you are using a computer to step through the project in this chapter and you want your screens to match the figures in this book, you should change your screen's resolution to 1024 × 768. For information about how to change a computer's resolution, refer to the Office 2010 and Windows 7 chapter at the beginning of this book.

The following steps, which assume Windows 7 is running, start Word based on a typical installation. You may need to ask your instructor how to start Word for your computer. For a detailed example of the procedure summarized below, refer to the Office 2010 and Windows 7 chapter.

1 Click the Start button on the Windows 7 taskbar to display the Start menu.

2 Type **Microsoft Word** as the search text in the 'Search programs and files' text box and watch the search results appear on the Start menu.

3 Click Microsoft Word 2010 in the search results on the Start menu to start Word and display a new blank document in the Word window.

4 If the Word window is not maximized, click the Maximize button next to the Close button on its title bar to maximize the window.

5 If the Print Layout button on the status bar is not selected (shown in Figure 1–2 on the next page), click it so that your screen is in Print Layout view.

Q&A What is Print Layout view?

The default (preset) view in Word is **Print Layout view**, which shows the document on a mock sheet of paper in the document window.

6 If Normal (Home tab | Styles group) is not selected in the Quick Style gallery (shown in Figure 1–2), click it so that your document uses the Normal style.

Q&A What is the Normal style?

When you create a document, Word formats the text using a particular style. The default style in Word is called the **Normal style**, which is discussed later in this book.

Q&A What if rulers appear on my screen?

Click the View Ruler button above the vertical scroll bar to hide the rulers, or click View on the Ribbon to display the View tab and then place a check mark in the Ruler check box.

For an introduction to Office 2010 and instruction about how to perform basic tasks in Office 2010 programs, read the Office 2010 and Windows 7 chapter at the beginning of this book, where you can learn how to start a program, use the Ribbon, save a file, open a file, quit a program, use Help, and much more.

BTW The Word Window The chapters in this book begin with the Word window appearing as it did at the initial installation of the software. Your Word window may look different depending on your screen resolution and other Word settings.

Entering Text

The first step in creating a document is to enter its text. With the projects in this book, you enter text by typing on the keyboard. By default, Word positions text you type at the left margin. In a later section of this chapter, you will learn how to format, or change the appearance of, the entered text.

Choose the words for the text.
The text in a flyer is organized into three areas: headline, body copy, and signature line.

- The **headline** is the first line of text on the flyer. It conveys the product or service being offered, such as a car for sale or personal lessons, or the benefit that will be gained, such as a convenience, better performance, greater security, higher earnings, or more comfort; or it can contain a message such as a lost or found pet.

- The **body copy** consists of all text between the headline and the signature line. This text highlights the key points of the message in as few words as possible. It should be easy to read and follow. While emphasizing the positive, the body copy must be realistic, truthful, and believable.

- The **signature line**, which is the last line of text on the flyer, contains contact information or identifies a call to action.

Plan Ahead

BTW Zooming If text is too small for you to read on the screen, you can zoom the document by dragging the Zoom slider on the status bar or clicking the Zoom Out or Zoom In buttons on the status bar. Changing the zoom has no effect on the printed document.

To Type Text

To begin creating the flyer in this chapter, type the headline in the document window. The following steps type this first line of text in the document.

1

- Type **Found Dog** as the headline (Figure 1–2).

Q&A What if I make an error while typing?

You can press the BACKSPACE key until you have deleted the text in error and then retype the text correctly.

Q&A Why did the Spelling and Grammar Check icon appear on the status bar?

When you begin typing text, the **Spelling and Grammar Check icon** appears on the status bar with an animated pencil writing on paper to indicate that Word is checking for spelling and grammar errors. When you stop typing, the pencil changes to a blue check mark (no errors) or a red X (potential errors found). Word flags potential errors in the document with a red, green, or blue wavy underline. Later in this chapter, you will learn how to fix flagged errors.

Home tab

document window

Normal style automatically selected when you first install Word

Styles group

View Ruler button shows or hides rulers

insertion point moves to the right as you type

Found Dog

text typed

mouse pointer's shape changes depending on task you are performing in Word and pointer's location on screen

Note: To help you locate screen elements that are referenced in the step instructions, such as buttons and commands, this book uses red boxes to point to these screen elements.

number of words in document

Spelling and Grammar Check icon contains a blue check mark, indicating the entered text contains no spelling or grammar errors

Print Layout button automatically selected when you first install Word

Zoom slider

Page: 1 of 1   Words: 2

Figure 1–2

2

- Press the ENTER key to move the insertion point to the beginning of the next line (Figure 1–3).

Q&A Why did blank space appear between the headline and the insertion point?

Each time you press the ENTER key, Word creates a new paragraph and inserts blank space between the two paragraphs. Later in this chapter, you will learn how to adjust the spacing between paragraphs.

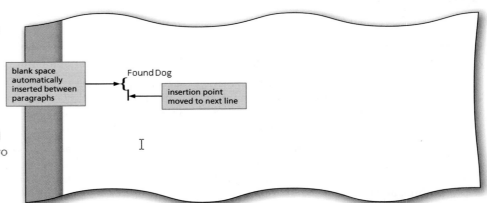

blank space automatically inserted between paragraphs

Found Dog

insertion point moved to next line

Figure 1–3

To Display Formatting Marks

To indicate where in a document you press the ENTER key or SPACEBAR, you may find it helpful to display formatting marks. A **formatting mark**, sometimes called a **nonprinting character**, is a character that Word displays on the screen but is not visible on a printed document. For example, the paragraph mark (¶) is a formatting mark that indicates where you press the ENTER key. A raised dot (·) shows where you press the SPACEBAR. Other formatting marks are discussed as they appear on the screen.

Depending on settings made during previous Word sessions, your Word screen already may display formatting marks (Figure 1–4). The following step displays formatting marks, if they do not show already on the screen.

1

• If the Home tab is not the active tab, click Home on the Ribbon to display the Home tab.

• If it is not selected already, click the Show/Hide ¶ button (Home tab | Paragraph group) to display formatting marks on the screen (Figure 1–4).

Q&A

What if I do not want formatting marks to show on the screen?

You can hide them by clicking the Show/Hide ¶ button (Home tab | Paragraph group) again. It is recommended that you display formatting marks so that you visually can identify when you press the ENTER key, SPACEBAR, and other keys associated with nonprinting characters; therefore, most of the document windows presented in this book show formatting marks.

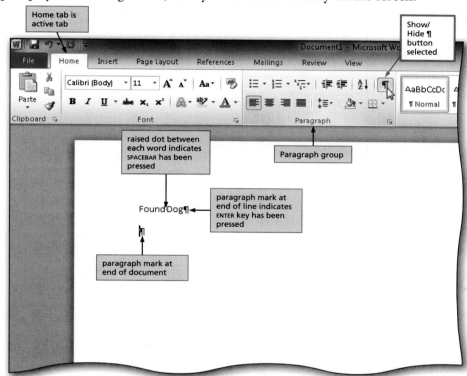

Figure 1–4

Other Ways
1. Press CTRL+SHIFT+*

To Insert a Blank Line

In the flyer, the digital pictures of the dog appear between the headline and body copy. You will not insert these pictures, however, until after you enter and format all text. Thus, you leave a blank line in the document as a placeholder for the pictures. To enter a blank line in a document, press the ENTER key without typing any text on the line. The following step inserts one blank line below the headline.

1

• Press the ENTER key to insert a blank line in the document (Figure 1–5).

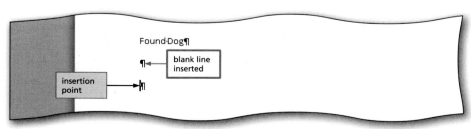

Figure 1–5

Wordwrap

Wordwrap allows you to type words in a paragraph continually without pressing the ENTER key at the end of each line. As you type, if a word extends beyond the right margin, Word also automatically positions that word on the next line along with the insertion point.

Word creates a new paragraph each time you press the ENTER key. Thus, as you type text in the document window, do not press the ENTER key when the insertion point reaches the right margin. Instead, press the ENTER key only in these circumstances:

1. To insert a blank line(s) in a document (as shown in the steps on the previous page)
2. To begin a new paragraph
3. To terminate a short line of text and advance to the next line
4. To respond to questions or prompts in Word dialog boxes, task panes, and other on-screen objects

BTW

The Ribbon and Screen Resolution
Word may change how the groups and buttons within the groups appear on the Ribbon, depending on the computer's screen resolution. Thus, your Ribbon may look different from the ones in this book if you are using a screen resolution other than 1024 × 768.

To Wordwrap Text as You Type

The next step in creating the flyer is to type the body copy. The following step illustrates how the body copy text wordwraps as you enter it in the document.

1

• Type the first sentence of the body copy: `Adorable, loving, friendly, well-behaved dog found early Friday morning, June 1, wandering on the bike trail at Filcher Park in Hampton Township.`

Q&A

Why does my document wrap on different words?

The printer connected to a computer is one factor that can control where wordwrap occurs for each line in a document. Thus, it is possible that the same document could wordwrap differently if printed on different printers.

• Press the ENTER key to position the insertion point on the next line in the document (Figure 1–6).

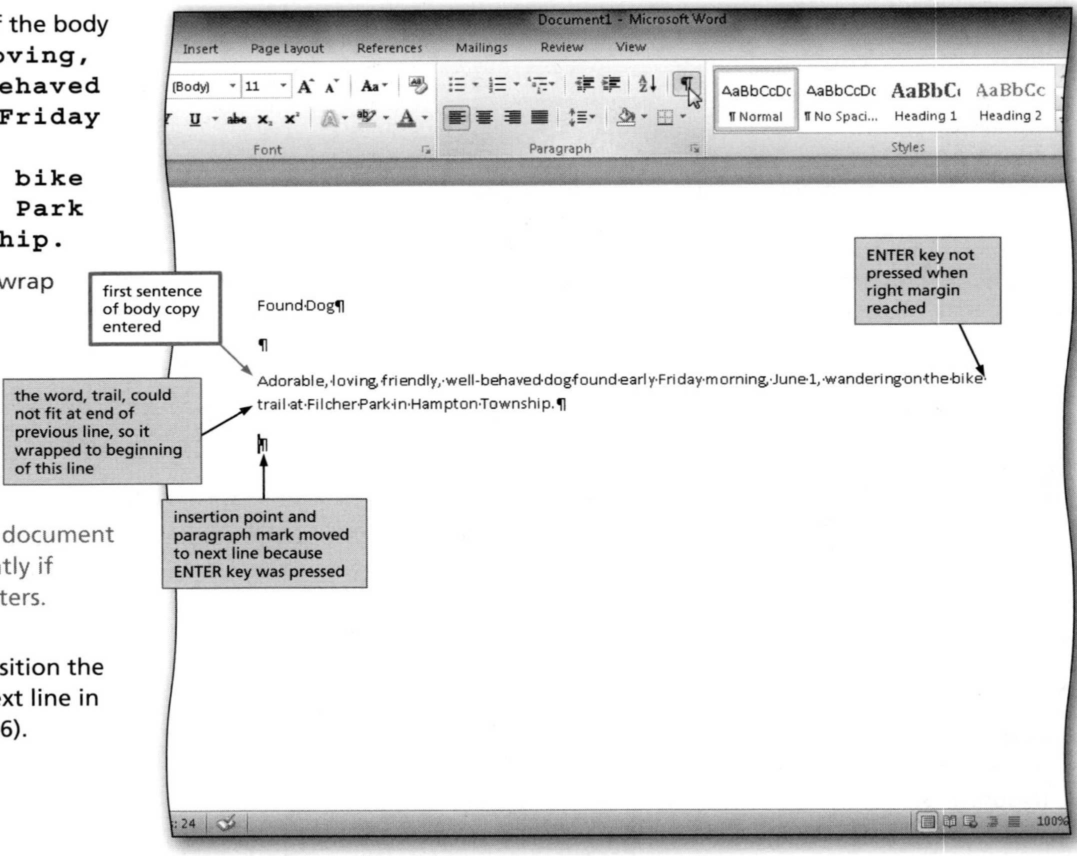

Figure 1–6

Spelling and Grammar Check

As you type text in a document, Word checks your typing for possible spelling and grammar errors. If all of the words you have typed are in Word's dictionary and your grammar is correct, as mentioned earlier, the Spelling and Grammar Check icon on the status bar displays a blue check mark. Otherwise, the icon shows a red X. In this case, Word flags the potential error in the document window with a red, green, or blue wavy underline. A red wavy underline means the flagged text is not in Word's dictionary (because it is a proper name or misspelled). A green wavy underline indicates the text may be incorrect grammatically. A blue wavy underline indicates the text may contain a contextual spelling error such as the misuse of homophones (words that are pronounced the same but that have different spellings or meanings, such as one and won). Although you can check the entire document for spelling and grammar errors at once, you also can check flagged errors as they appear on the screen.

A flagged word is not necessarily misspelled. For example, many names, abbreviations, and specialized terms are not in Word's main dictionary. In these cases, you can instruct Word to ignore the flagged word. As you type, Word also detects duplicate words while checking for spelling errors. For example, if your document contains the phrase, to the the store, Word places a red wavy underline below the second occurrence of the word, the.

BTW

Automatic Spelling Correction

As you type, Word automatically corrects some misspelled words. For example, if you type recieve, Word automatically corrects the misspelling and displays the word, receive, when you press the SPACEBAR or type a punctuation mark. To see a complete list of automatically corrected words, click File on the Ribbon to open the Backstage view, click Options in the Backstage view, click Proofing in the left pane (Word Options dialog box), click the AutoCorrect Options button, and then scroll through the list near the bottom of the dialog box.

To Check Spelling and Grammar as You Type

In the following steps, the word, patches, has been misspelled intentionally as paches to illustrate Word's check spelling as you type feature. If you are doing this project on a computer, your flyer may contain different misspelled words, depending on the accuracy of your typing.

1

• Type **Tan color with paches** and then press the SPACEBAR so that a red wavy line appears below the misspelled word (Figure 1–7).

Q&A

What if Word does not flag my spelling and grammar errors with wavy underlines?

To verify that the check spelling and grammar as you type features are enabled, click File on the Ribbon to open the Backstage view and then click Options in the Backstage view. When the Word Options dialog box is displayed, click Proofing in the left pane, and then ensure the 'Check spelling as you type' and 'Mark grammar errors as you type' check boxes contain check marks. Also ensure the 'Hide spelling errors in this document only' and 'Hide grammar errors in this document only' check boxes do not have check marks. Click the OK button.

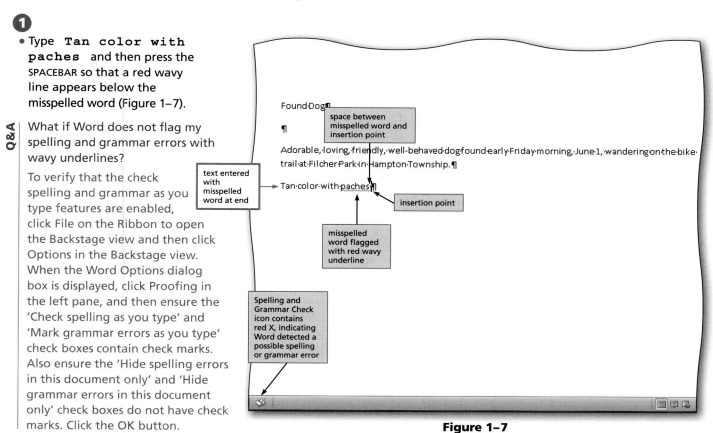

Figure 1–7

2

- Right-click the flagged word (paches, in this case) to display a shortcut menu that presents a list of suggested spelling corrections for the flagged word (Figure 1–8).

Q&A What if, when I right-click the misspelled word, my desired correction is not in the list on the shortcut menu?

You can click outside the shortcut menu to close the shortcut menu and then retype the correct word, or you can click Spelling on the shortcut menu to display the Spelling dialog box. Chapter 2 discusses the Spelling dialog box.

Q&A What if a flagged word actually is, for example, a proper name and spelled correctly?

Right-click it and then click Ignore All on the shortcut menu to instruct Word not to flag future occurrences of the same word in this document.

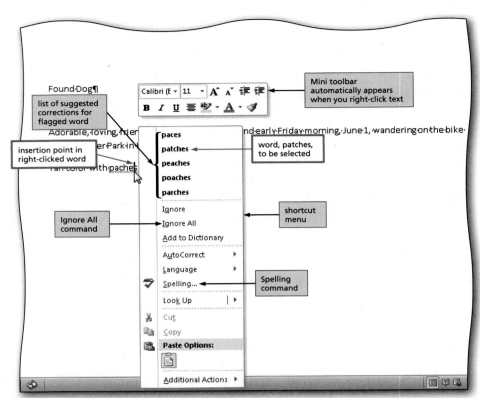

Figure 1–8

3

- Click patches on the shortcut menu to replace the misspelled word in the document with a correctly spelled word (Figure 1–9).

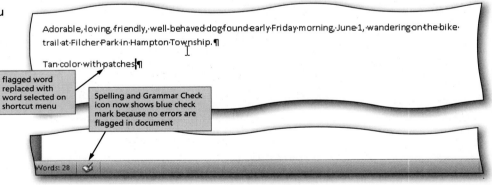

Figure 1–9

Other Ways
1. Click Spelling and Grammar Check icon on status bar, click desired word on shortcut menu

BTW

Character Widths
Many word processing documents use variable character fonts, where some characters are wider than others; for example, the letter w is wider than the letter i.

To Enter More Text

In the flyer, the text yet to be entered includes the remainder of the body copy, which will be formatted as a bulleted list, and the signature line. The next steps enter the remainder of text in the flyer.

① Press the END key to move the insertion point to the end of the current line.

② Type `of white on his chest` and then press the ENTER key.

③ Type `Male, adult cocker spaniel` and then press the ENTER key.

④ Type `Green and silver collar with the name, Bailey, on the tag` and then press the ENTER key.

⑤ Type the signature line in the flyer (Figure 1–10):
`If this is your lost dog, call 555-1029.`

Figure 1–10

Navigating a Document

You view only a portion of a document on the screen through the document window. At some point when you type text or insert graphics, Word probably will **scroll** the top or bottom portion of the document off the screen. Although you cannot see the text and graphics once they scroll off the screen, they remain in the document.

You can use either the keyboard or the mouse to scroll to a different location in a document and/or move the insertion point around a document. When you use the keyboard, the insertion point automatically moves when you press the desired keys. For example, the previous steps used the END key to move the insertion point to the end of the current line. Table 1–1 outlines various techniques to navigate a document using the keyboard.

With the mouse, you can use the scroll arrows or the scroll box on the scroll bar to display a different portion of the document in the document window and then click the mouse to move the insertion point to that location. Table 1–2 explains various techniques for using the scroll bar to scroll vertically with the mouse.

BTW

Minimize Wrist Injury
Computer users frequently switch between the keyboard and the mouse during a word processing session; such switching strains the wrist. To help prevent wrist injury, minimize switching. For instance, if your fingers already are on the keyboard, use keyboard keys to scroll. If your hand already is on the mouse, use the mouse to scroll.

Table 1–1 Moving the Insertion Point with the Keyboard

Insertion Point Direction	Key(s) to Press	Insertion Point Direction	Key(s) to Press
Left one character	LEFT ARROW	Up one paragraph	CTRL+UP ARROW
Right one character	RIGHT ARROW	Down one paragraph	CTRL+DOWN ARROW
Left one word	CTRL+LEFT ARROW	Up one screen	PAGE UP
Right one word	CTRL+RIGHT ARROW	Down one screen	PAGE DOWN
Up one line	UP ARROW	To top of document window	ALT+CTRL+PAGE UP
Down one line	DOWN ARROW	To bottom of document window	ALT+CTRL+PAGE DOWN
To end of line	END	To beginning of document	CTRL+HOME
To beginning of line	HOME	To end of document	CTRL+END

Table 1–2 Using the Scroll Bar to Scroll Vertically with the Mouse

Scroll Direction	Mouse Action	Scroll Direction	Mouse Action
Up	Drag the scroll box upward.	Down one screen	Click anywhere below the scroll box on the vertical scroll bar.
Down	Drag the scroll box downward.	Up one line	Click the scroll arrow at the top of the vertical scroll bar.
Up one screen	Click anywhere above the scroll box on the vertical scroll bar.	Down one line	Click the scroll arrow at the bottom of the vertical scroll bar.

BTW

Organizing Files and Folders
You should organize and store files in folders so that you easily can find the files later. For example, if you are taking an introductory computer class called CIS 101, a good practice would be to save all Word files in a Word folder in a CIS 101 folder. For a discussion of folders and detailed examples of creating folders, refer to the Office 2010 and Windows 7 chapter at the beginning of this book.

To Save a Document

You have performed many tasks while creating this flyer and do not want to risk losing work completed thus far. Accordingly, you should save the document.

The following steps assume you already have created folders for storing your files, for example, a CIS 101 folder (for your class) that contains a Word folder (for your assignments). Thus, these steps save the document in the Word folder in the CIS 101 folder on a USB flash drive using the file name, Found Dog Flyer. For a detailed example of the procedure summarized below, refer to the Office 2010 and Windows 7 chapter at the beginning of this book.

1 With a USB flash drive connected to one of the computer's USB ports, click the Save button on the Quick Access Toolbar to display the Save As dialog box.

2 Type **Found Dog Flyer** in the File name text box to change the file name. Do not press the ENTER key after typing the file name because you do not want to close the dialog box at this time.

3 Navigate to the desired save location (in this case, the Word folder in the CIS 101 folder [or your class folder] on the USB flash drive).

4 Click the Save button (Save As dialog box) to save the document in the selected folder on the selected drive with the entered file name.

Formatting Paragraphs and Characters

With the text for the flyer entered, the next step is to **format**, or change the appearance of, its text. A paragraph encompasses the text from the first character in the paragraph up to and including its paragraph mark (¶). **Paragraph formatting** is the process of changing the appearance of a paragraph. For example, you can center or add bullets to a paragraph. Characters include letters, numbers, punctuation marks, and symbols. **Character formatting** is the process of changing the way characters appear on the screen and in print. You use character formatting to emphasize certain words and improve readability of a document. For example, you can color or underline characters. Often, you apply both paragraph and character formatting to the same text. For example, you may center a paragraph (paragraph formatting) and underline some of the characters in the same paragraph (character formatting).

Although you can format paragraphs and characters before you type, many Word users enter text first and then format the existing text. Figure 1–11a shows the flyer in this chapter before formatting its paragraphs and characters. Figure 1–11b shows the flyer after formatting. As you can see from the two figures, a document that is formatted is easier to read and looks more professional. The following pages discuss how to format the flyer so that it looks like Figure 1–11b.

Characters that appear on the screen are a specific shape and size. The **font**, or typeface, defines the appearance and shape of the letters, numbers, and special characters. In Word, the default font usually is Calibri (shown in Figure 1–12 on page WD 14). You can leave characters in the default font or change them to a different font. **Font size** specifies the size of the characters and is determined by a measurement system called points. A single **point** is about 1/72 of one inch in height. The default font size in Word typically is 11 (Figure 1–12). Thus, a character with a font size of 11 is about 11/72 or a little less than 1/6 of one inch in height. You can increase or decrease the font size of characters in a document.

A document **theme** is a set of unified formats for fonts, colors, and graphics. Word includes a variety of document themes to assist you with coordinating these visual elements in a document. The default theme fonts are Cambria for headings and Calibri for body text. By changing the document theme, you quickly can give your document a new look. You also can define your own document themes.

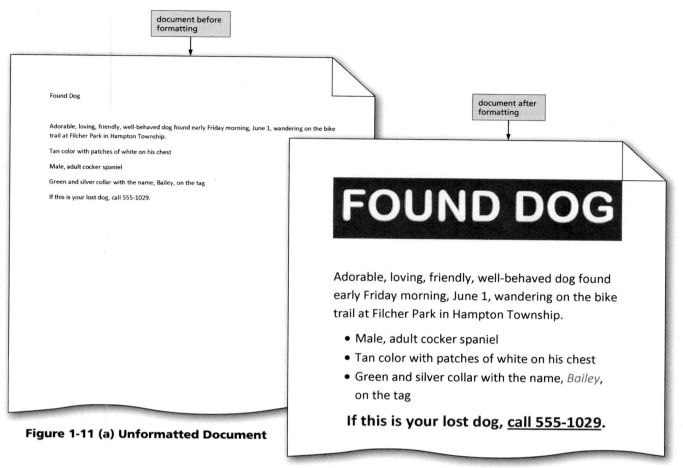

Figure 1-11 (a) Unformatted Document

Figure 1-11 (b) Formatted Document

Identify how to format various elements of the text.

By formatting the characters and paragraphs in a document, you can improve its overall appearance. In a flyer, consider the following formatting suggestions.

Plan Ahead

- **Increase the font size of characters.** Flyers usually are posted on a bulletin board or in a window. Thus, the font size should be as large as possible so that passersby easily can read the flyer. To give the headline more impact, its font size should be larger than the font size of the text in the body copy. If possible, make the font size of the signature line larger than the body copy but smaller than the headline.

- **Change the font of characters.** Use fonts that are easy to read. Try to use only two different fonts in a flyer, for example, one for the headline and the other for all other text. Too many fonts can make the flyer visually confusing.

- **Change paragraph alignment.** The default alignment for paragraphs in a document is **left-aligned,** that is, flush at the left margin of the document with uneven right edges. Consider changing the alignment of some of the paragraphs to add interest and variety to the flyer.

- **Highlight key paragraphs with bullets.** A bulleted paragraph is a paragraph that begins with a dot or other symbol. Use bulleted paragraphs to highlight important points in a flyer.

- **Emphasize important words.** To call attention to certain words or lines, you can underline them, italicize them, or bold them. Use these formats sparingly, however, because overuse will minimize their effect and make the flyer look too busy.

- **Use color.** Use colors that complement each other and convey the meaning of the flyer. Vary colors in terms of hue and brightness. Headline colors, for example, can be bold and bright. Signature lines should stand out more than body copy but less than headlines. Keep in mind that too many colors can detract from the flyer and make it difficult to read.

To Center a Paragraph

The headline in the flyer currently is left-aligned (Figure 1–12). You want the headline to be **centered**, that is, positioned horizontally between the left and right margins on the page. Recall that Word considers a single short line of text, such as the two-word headline, a paragraph. Thus, you will center the paragraph containing the headline. The following steps center a paragraph.

1

- Click somewhere in the paragraph to be centered (in this case, the headline) to position the insertion point in the paragraph to be formatted (Figure 1–12).

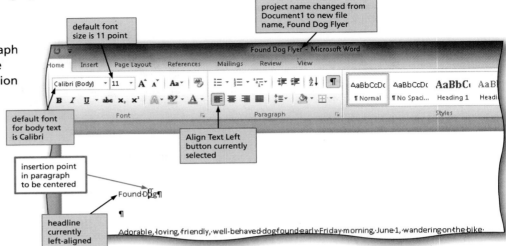

Figure 1–12

2

- Click the Center button (Home tab | Paragraph group) to center the paragraph containing the insertion point (Figure 1–13).

Q&A

What if I want to return the paragraph to left-aligned?

You would click the Center button again or click the Align Text Left button (Home tab | Paragraph group).

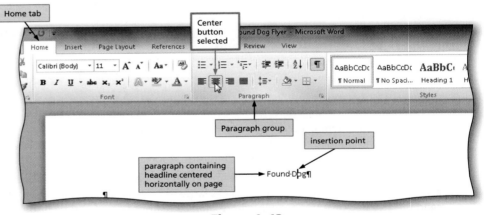

Figure 1–13

Other Ways

1. Right-click paragraph, click Center button on Mini toolbar
2. Right-click paragraph, click Paragraph on shortcut menu, click Indents and Spacing tab
3. Click Paragraph Dialog Box Launcher (Home tab or Page Layout tab | Paragraph group), click Indents and Spacing tab (Paragraph dialog box), click Alignment box arrow, click Centered, click OK button

(Paragraph dialog box), click Alignment box arrow, click Centered, click OK button

4. Press CTRL+E

BTW

File Type
Depending on your Windows settings, the file type .docx may be displayed on the title bar immediately to the right of the file name after you save the file. The file type .docx is a Word 2010 document.

To Center Another Paragraph

In the flyer, the signature line is to be centered to match the paragraph alignment of the headline. The following steps center the signature line.

1 Click somewhere in the paragraph to be centered (in this case, the signature line) to position the insertion point in the paragraph to be formatted.

2 Click the Center button (Home tab | Paragraph group) to center the paragraph containing the insertion point (shown in Figure 1–14).

Formatting Single versus Multiple Paragraphs and Characters

As shown on the previous pages, to format a single paragraph, simply move the insertion point in the paragraph, to make it the current paragraph, and then format the paragraph. Similarly, to format a single word, position the insertion point in the word, to make it the current word, and then format the word.

To format multiple paragraphs or words, however, you first must select the paragraphs or words you want to format and then format the selection. If your screen normally displays dark letters on a light background, which is the default setting in Word, then selected text displays light letters on a dark background.

To Select a Line

The default font size of 11 point is too small for a headline in a flyer. To increase the font size of the characters in the headline, you first must select the line of text containing the headline. The following steps select a line.

1

- Move the mouse pointer to the left of the line to be selected (in this case, the headline) until the mouse pointer changes to a right-pointing block arrow (Figure 1–14).

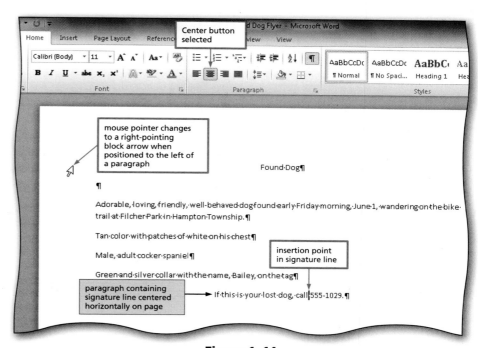

Figure 1–14

2

- While the mouse pointer is a right-pointing block arrow, click the mouse to select the entire line to the right of the mouse pointer (Figure 1–15).

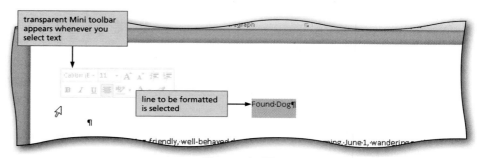

Figure 1–15

Other Ways	
1. Drag mouse through line	2. With insertion point at beginning of desired line, press SHIFT+DOWN ARROW

To Change the Font Size of Selected Text

The next step is to increase the font size of the characters in the selected headline. You would like the headline to be as large as possible and still fit on a single line, which in this case is 72 point. The following steps increase the font size of the headline from 11 to 72 point.

1

• With the text selected, click the Font Size box arrow (Home tab | Font group) to display the Font Size gallery (Figure 1–16).

Q&A Why are the font sizes in my Font Size gallery different from those in Figure 1–16?

Font sizes may vary depending on the current font and your printer driver.

Q&A What happened to the Mini toolbar?

The Mini toolbar disappears if you do not use it. These steps use the Font Size box arrow on the Home tab instead of the Font Size box arrow on the Mini toolbar.

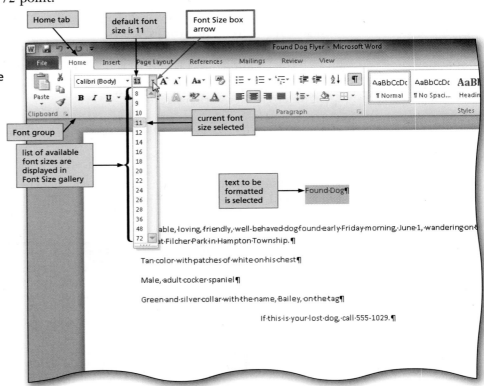

Figure 1–16

2

• Point to 72 in the Font Size gallery to display a live preview of the selected text at the selected point size (Figure 1–17).

Experiment

• Point to various font sizes in the Font Size gallery and watch the font size of the selected text change in the document window.

3

• Click 72 in the Font Size gallery to increase the font size of the selected text.

Figure 1–17

Other Ways

1. Click Font Size box arrow on Mini toolbar, click desired font size in Font Size gallery

2. Right-click selected text, click Font on shortcut menu, click Font tab (Font dialog box), select desired font size in Size list, click OK button

3. Click Font Dialog Box Launcher, click Font tab (Font dialog box), select desired font size in Size list, click OK button

4. Press CTRL+D, click Font tab (Font dialog box), select desired font size in Size list, click OK button

To Change the Font of Selected Text

The default theme font for headings is Cambria and for all other text, called body text in Word, is Calibri. Many other fonts are available, however, so that you can add variety to documents.

To draw more attention to the headline, you change its font so that it differs from the font of other text in the flyer. The following steps change the font of the headline from Calibri to Arial Rounded MT Bold.

1

- With the text selected, click the Font box arrow (Home tab | Font group) to display the Font gallery (Figure 1–18).

Q&A Will the fonts in my Font gallery be the same as those in Figure 1–18?

Your list of available fonts may differ, depending on the type of printer you are using and other settings.

Q&A What if the text is no longer selected?

Follow the steps on page WD 15 to select a line.

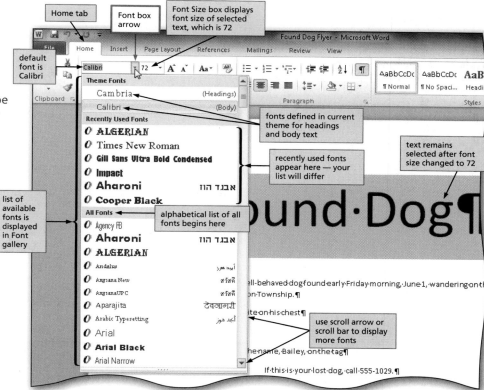

Figure 1–18

2

- Scroll through the Font gallery, if necessary, and then point to Arial Rounded MT Bold (or a similar font) to display a live preview of the selected text in the selected font (Figure 1–19).

 **Experiment**

- Point to various fonts in the Font gallery and watch the font of the selected text change in the document window.

3

- Click Arial Rounded MT Bold (or a similar font) to change the font of the selected text.

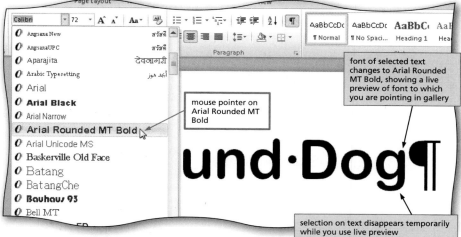

Figure 1–19

Other Ways

1. Click Font box arrow on Mini toolbar, click desired font in Font gallery

2. Right-click selected text, click Font on shortcut menu, click Font tab (Font dialog box), select desired font in Font list, click OK button

3. Click Font Dialog Box Launcher (Home tab | Font group), click Font tab (Font dialog box), select desired font in Font list, click OK button

4. Press CTRL+D, click Font tab (Font dialog box), select desired font in the Font list, click OK button

To Change the Case of Selected Text

The headline currently shows the first letter in each word capitalized, which sometimes is referred to as initial cap. To draw more attention to the headline, you would like the entire line of text to be capitalized, or in uppercase letters. The following steps change the headline to uppercase.

1
- With the text selected, click the Change Case button (Home tab | Font group) to display the Change Case gallery (Figure 1–20).

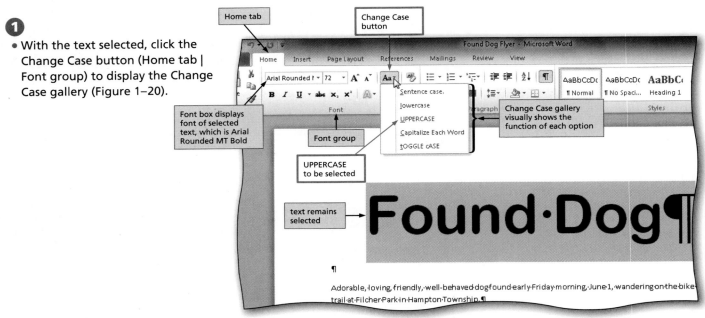

Figure 1–20

2
- Click UPPERCASE in the Change Case gallery to change the case of the selected text (Figure 1–21).

Q&A

What if a ruler appears on the screen or the mouse pointer shape changes?

Depending on the position of your mouse pointer and locations you click on the screen, a ruler may automatically appear or the mouse pointer shape may change. Simply move the mouse and the ruler should disappear and/or the mouse pointer shape will change.

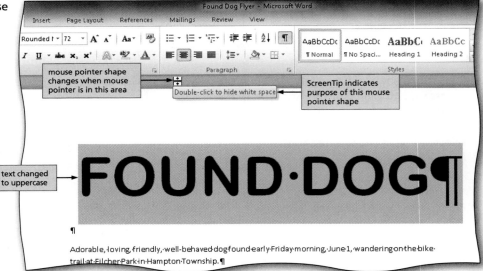

Figure 1–21

Other Ways		
1. Right-click selected text, click Font on shortcut menu, click Font tab (Font dialog box), select All caps in Effects area, click OK button	2. Click Font Dialog Box Launcher (Home tab | Font group), click Font tab (Font dialog box), select All caps in Effects area, click OK button	3. Press SHIFT+F3 repeatedly until text is desired case

To Apply a Text Effect to Selected Text

You would like the text in the headline to be even more noticeable. Word provides many text effects to add interest and variety to text. The following steps apply a text effect to the headline.

- With the text selected, click the Text Effects button (Home tab | Font group) to display the Text Effects gallery (Figure 1–22).

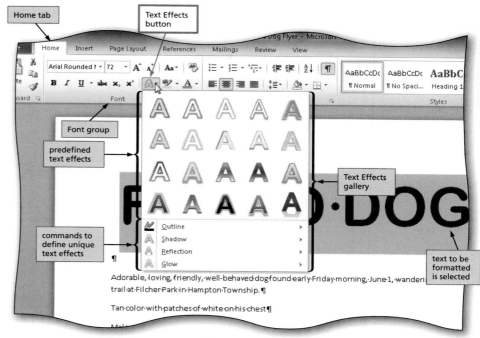

Figure 1–22

- Point to Fill – White, Gradient Outline – Accent 1 (first text effect in third row) to display a live preview of the selected text in the selected text effect (Figure 1–23).

Experiment

- Point to various text effects in the Text Effects gallery and watch the text effects of the selected text change in the document window.

- Click Fill – White, Gradient Outline – Accent 1 to change the text effect of the selected text.

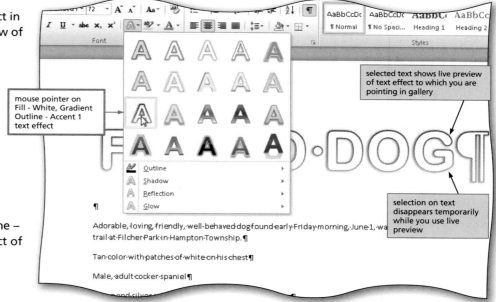

Figure 1–23

- Click anywhere in the document window to remove the selection from the selected text.

Other Ways

1. Right-click selected text, click Font on shortcut menu, click Font tab (Font dialog box), click Text Effects button, select desired text effects

   (Format Text Effects dialog box), click Close button, click OK button

2. Click Font Dialog Box Launcher (Home tab | Font group), click Font

   tab (Font dialog box), click Text Effects button, select desired text effects (Format Text Effects dialog box), click Close button, click OK button

To Shade a Paragraph

To make the headline of the flyer more eye-catching, you would like to shade it. When you **shade** text, Word colors the rectangular area behind any text or graphics. If the text to shade is a paragraph, Word shades the area from the left margin to the right margin of the current paragraph. To shade a paragraph, place the insertion point in the paragraph. To shade any other text, you must first select the text to be shaded. This flyer uses brown as the shading color for the headline. The following steps shade a paragraph.

- Click somewhere in the paragraph to be shaded (in this case, the headline) to position the insertion point in the paragraph to be formatted.

- Click the Shading button arrow (Home tab | Paragraph group) to display the Shading gallery (Figure 1–24).

 What if I click the Shading button by mistake?

Click the Shading button arrow and proceed with Step 2.

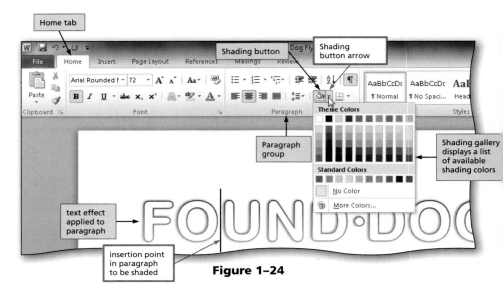

Figure 1–24

- Point to Orange, Accent 6, Darker 50% (rightmost color in the sixth row) to display a live preview of the selected shading color (Figure 1–25).

Experiment

- Point to various colors in the Shading gallery and watch the shading color of the current paragraph change.

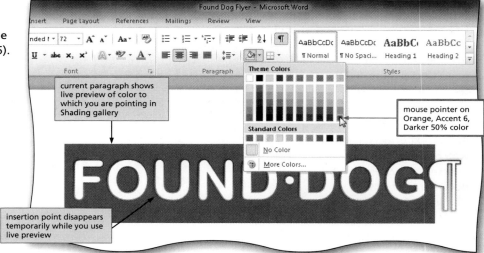

Figure 1–25

- Click Orange, Accent 6, Darker 50% to shade the current paragraph.

Q&A What if I apply a dark shading color to dark text?

When the font color of text is Automatic, it usually is black. If you select a dark shading color, Word automatically may change the text color to white so that the shaded text is easier to read.

Other Ways
1. Click Border button arrow (Home tab | Paragraph group), click Borders and Shading, click Shading tab (Borders and Shading dialog box), click Fill box arrow, select desired color, click OK button

To Select Multiple Lines

The next formatting step for the flyer is to increase the font size of the characters between the headline and the signature line so that they are easier to read from a distance. To change the font size of the characters in multiple lines, you first must select all the lines to be formatted. The following steps select multiple lines.

1

- Move the mouse pointer to the left of the first paragraph to be selected until the mouse pointer changes to a right-pointing block arrow (Figure 1–26).

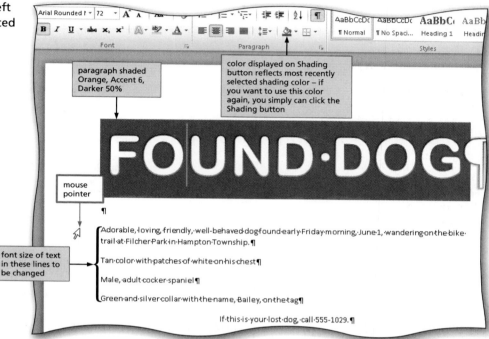

Figure 1–26

2

- Drag downward to select all lines that will be formatted (Figure 1–27).

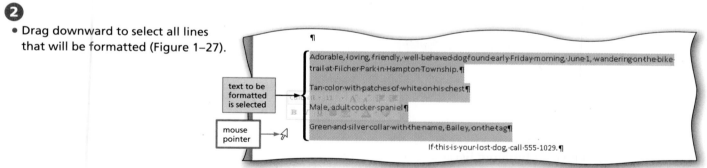

Figure 1–27

Other Ways

1. With insertion point at beginning of desired line, press SHIFT+DOWN ARROW repeatedly until all lines are selected

To Change the Font Size of Selected Text

The characters between the headline and the signature line in the flyer currently are 11 point. To make them easier to read from a distance, this flyer uses 22 point for these characters. The steps on the next page change the font size of the selected text.

1 With the text selected, click the Font Size box arrow (Home tab | Font group) to display the Font Size gallery.

2 Click 22 in the Font Size gallery to increase the font size of the selected text.

3 Click anywhere in the document window to remove the selection from the text.

4 If necessary, scroll so that you can see all the text on the screen (Figure 1–28).

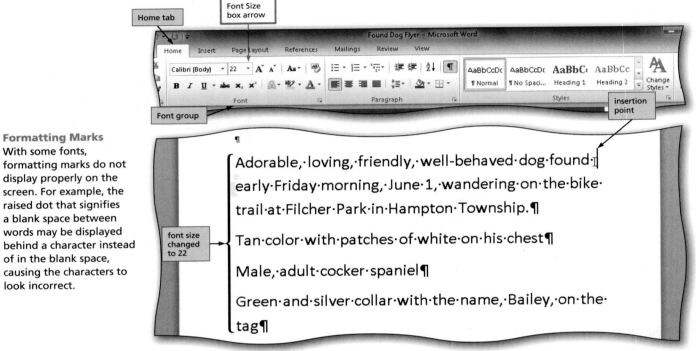

Formatting Marks
With some fonts, formatting marks do not display properly on the screen. For example, the raised dot that signifies a blank space between words may be displayed behind a character instead of in the blank space, causing the characters to look incorrect.

Figure 1–28

To Bullet a List of Paragraphs

The next step is to format as a bulleted list the three paragraphs of identifying information that are above the signature line in the flyer. A **bulleted list** is a series of paragraphs, each beginning with a bullet character.

To format a list of paragraphs with bullets, you first must select all the lines in the paragraphs. The following steps bullet a list of paragraphs.

1

• Move the mouse pointer to the left of the first paragraph to be selected until the mouse pointer changes to a right-pointing block arrow.

• Drag downward until all paragraphs that will be formatted with a bullet character are selected (Figure 1–29).

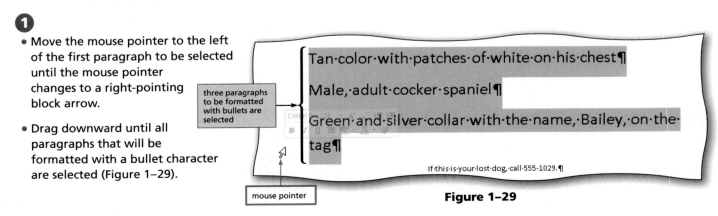

Figure 1–29

2

- Click the Bullets button (Home tab | Paragraph group) to place a bullet character at the beginning of each selected paragraph (Figure 1–30).

Q&A How do I remove bullets from a list or paragraph?

Select the list or paragraph and then click the Bullets button again.

Q&A What if I accidentally click the Bullets button arrow?

Press the ESCAPE key to remove the Bullets gallery from the screen and then repeat Step 2.

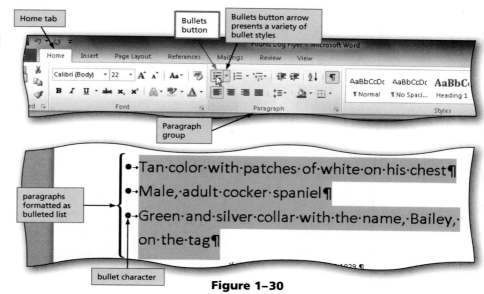

Figure 1–30

To Undo and Redo an Action

Word provides a means of canceling your recent command(s) or action(s). For example, if you format text incorrectly, you can undo the format and try it again. When you point to the Undo button, Word displays the action you can undo as part of a ScreenTip.

If, after you undo an action, you decide you did not want to perform the undo, you can redo the undone action. Word does not allow you to undo or redo some actions, such as saving or printing a document. The next steps undo the bullet format just applied and then redo the bullet format.

1

- Click the Undo button on the Quick Access Toolbar to reverse your most recent action (in this case, remove the bullets from the paragraphs) (Figure 1–31).

2

- Click the Redo button on the Quick Access Toolbar to reverse your most recent undo (in this case, place a bullet character on the paragraphs again) (shown in Figure 1–30).

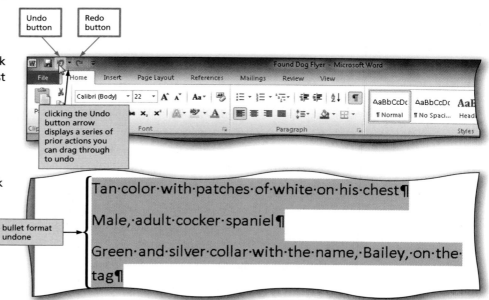

Figure 1–31

To Italicize Text

The next step is to italicize the dog's name, Bailey, in the flyer to further emphasize it. **Italicized** text has a slanted appearance. As with a single paragraph, if you want to format a single word, you do not need to select it. Simply position the insertion point somewhere in the word and apply the desired format. The following step formats a word in italics.

- Click somewhere in the word to be italicized (Bailey, in this case) to position the insertion point in the word to be formatted.

- Click the Italic button (Home tab | Font group) to italicize the word containing the insertion point (Figure 1–32).

Q&A
How would I remove an italic format?

You would click the Italic button a second time, or you immediately could click the Undo button on the Quick Access Toolbar or press CTRL+Z.

Q&A
How can I tell what formatting has been applied to text?

The selected buttons and boxes on the Home tab show formatting characteristics of the location of the insertion point. With the insertion point in the word, Bailey, the Home tab shows these formats: 22-point Calibri italic font, bulleted paragraph.

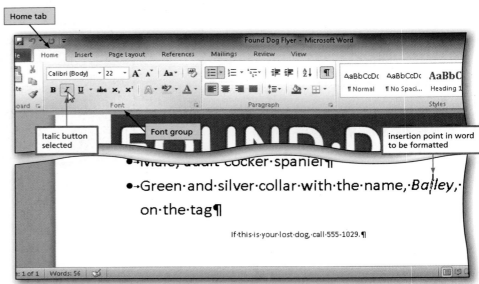

Figure 1–32

Other Ways
1. Click Italic button on Mini toolbar
2. Right-click selected text, click Font on shortcut menu, click Font tab
3. Click Font Dialog Box Launcher (Home tab	(Font dialog box), click Italic in Font style list, click OK button
Font group), click Font tab (Font dialog box), click Italic in Font style list, click OK button
4. Press CTRL+I

Plan Ahead

Use color.
When choosing color, associate the meaning of color to your message:

- Red expresses danger, power, or energy, and often is associated with sports or physical exertion.
- Brown represents simplicity, honesty, and dependability.
- Orange denotes success, victory, creativity, and enthusiasm.
- Yellow suggests sunshine, happiness, hope, liveliness, and intelligence.
- Green symbolizes growth, healthiness, harmony, blooming, and healing, and often is associated with safety or money.
- Blue indicates integrity, trust, importance, confidence, and stability.
- Purple represents wealth, power, comfort, extravagance, magic, mystery, and spirituality.
- White stands for purity, goodness, cleanliness, precision, and perfection.
- Black suggests authority, strength, elegance, power, and prestige.
- Gray conveys neutrality and thus often is found in backgrounds and other effects.

BTW
Q&As
For a complete list of the Q&As found in many of the step-by-step sequences in this book, visit the Word 2010 Q&A Web page (scsite.com/wd2010/qa).

To Color Text

To emphasize the dog's name even more, its color is changed to a shade of blue. The following steps change the color of the word, Bailey.

1

- With the insertion point in the word to format, click the Font Color button arrow (Home tab | Font group) to display the Font Color gallery (Figure 1–33).

Q&A What if I click the Font Color button by mistake?

Click the Font Color button arrow and then proceed with Step 2.

2

- Point to Blue, Accent 1, Darker 25% (fifth color in the fifth row) to display a live preview of the selected font color.

 **Experiment**

- Point to various colors in the Font Color gallery and watch the color of the current word change.

Figure 1–33

3

- Click Blue, Accent 1, Darker 25% to change the color of the text (Figure 1–34).

Q&A How would I change the text color back to black?

You would position the insertion point in the word or select the text, click the Font Color button arrow (Home tab | Font group) again, and then click Automatic in the Font Color gallery.

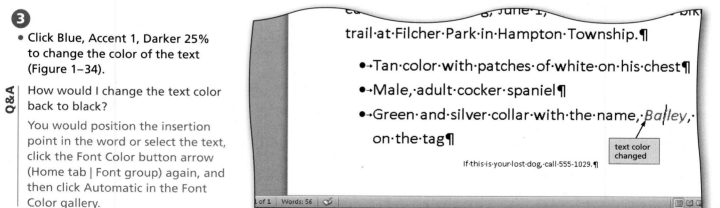

Figure 1–34

Other Ways		
1. Click Font Color button arrow on Mini toolbar, click desired color	(Font dialog box), click Font color box arrow, click desired color, click OK button	Font group), click Font tab (Font dialog box), click Font color box arrow, click desired color, click OK button
2. Right-click selected text, click Font on shortcut menu, click Font tab	3. Click Font Dialog Box Launcher (Home tab |	

To Use the Mini Toolbar to Format Text

Recall from the Office 2010 and Windows 7 chapter at the beginning of this book that the Mini toolbar, which automatically appears based on certain tasks you perform, contains commands related to changing the appearance of text in a document. All commands on the Mini toolbar also exist on the Ribbon.

When the Mini toolbar appears, it initially is transparent. If you do not use the transparent Mini toolbar, it disappears from the screen. The following steps use the Mini toolbar to change the color and font size of text in the signature line of the flyer.

1
- Move the mouse pointer to the left of the line to be selected (in this case, the signature line) until the mouse pointer changes to a right-pointing block arrow and then click the mouse to select the line (Figure 1–35).

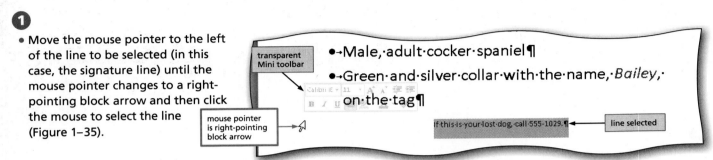

Figure 1–35

2
- Move the mouse pointer into the transparent Mini toolbar, so that it changes to a bright toolbar.

- Click the Font Size box arrow on the Mini toolbar to display the Font Size gallery and then point to 28 in the Font Size gallery to display a live preview of the selected font size (Figure 1–36).

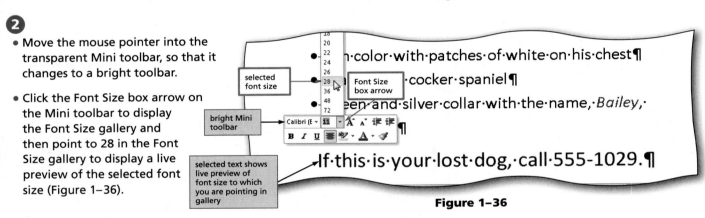

Figure 1–36

3
- Click 28 in the Font Size gallery to increase the font size of the selected text.

4
- With the text still selected and the Mini toolbar still displayed, click the Font Color button arrow on the Mini toolbar to display the Font Color gallery and then point to Purple, Accent 4, Darker 50% (eighth color in the sixth row) to display a live preview of the selected font color (Figure 1–37).

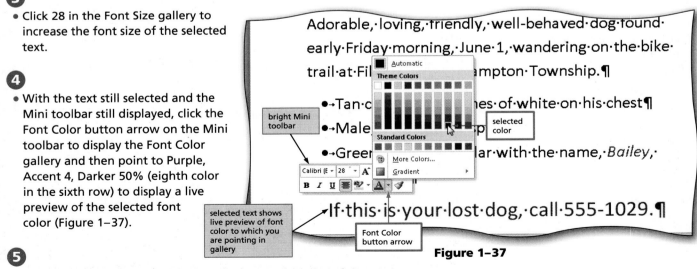

Figure 1–37

5
- Click Purple, Accent 4, Darker 50% to change the color of the text.

- Click anywhere in the document window to remove the selection from the text.

To Select a Group of Words

To emphasize the contact information (call 555-1029), these words are underlined in the flyer. To format a group of words, you first must select them. The following steps select a group of words.

- Position the mouse pointer immediately to the left of the first character of the text to be selected, in this case, the c in call (Figure 1–38).

Q&A Why did the shape of the mouse pointer change?

The mouse pointer's shape is an I-beam when positioned in unselected text in the document window.

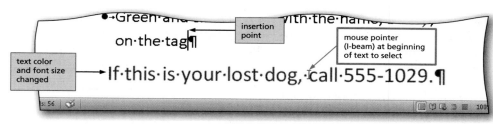

Figure 1–38

- Drag the mouse pointer through the last character of the text to be selected, in this case, the 9 in the phone number (Figure 1–39).

Q&A Why did the mouse pointer shape change again?

When the mouse pointer is positioned in selected text, its shape is a left-pointing block arrow.

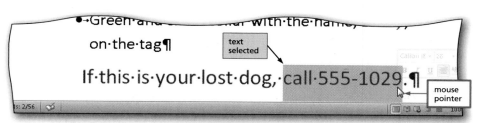

Figure 1–39

Other Ways	
1. With insertion point at beginning of first word in group, press	CTRL+SHIFT+RIGHT ARROW repeatedly until all words are selected

To Underline Text

Underlines are used to emphasize or draw attention to specific text. **Underlined** text prints with an underscore (_) below each character. In the flyer, the contact information, call 555-1029, in the signature line is emphasized with an underline. The following step formats selected text with an underline.

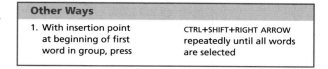

- With the text selected, click the Underline button (Home tab | Font group) to underline the selected text (Figure 1–40).

Q&A How would I remove an underline?

You would click the Underline button a second time, or you immediately could click the Undo button on the Quick Access Toolbar.

Figure 1–40

Other Ways		
1. Right-click text, click Font on shortcut menu, click Font tab (Font dialog box), click Underline style box arrow, click desired	underline style, click OK button 2. Click Font Dialog Box Launcher (Home tab | Font group), click Font tab	(Font dialog box), click Underline style box arrow, click desired underline style, click OK button 3. Press CTRL+U

To Bold Text

Bold characters appear somewhat thicker and darker than those that are not bold. To further emphasize the signature line, it is bold in the flyer. To format the line, as you have learned previously, you select the line first. The following steps format the signature line bold.

1

- Move the mouse pointer to the left of the line to be selected (in this case, the signature line) until the mouse pointer changes to a right-pointing block arrow and then click the mouse to select the text to be formatted.

- With the text selected, click the Bold button (Home tab | Font group) to bold the selected text (Figure 1–41).

Q&A

How would I remove a bold format?
You would click the Bold button a second time, or you immediately could click the Undo button on the Quick Access Toolbar.

2

- Click anywhere in the document window to remove the selection from the screen.

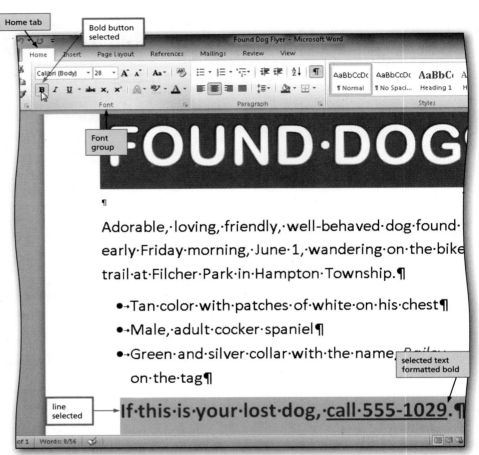

Figure 1–41

Other Ways
1. Click Bold button on Mini toolbar
2. Right-click selected text, click Font on shortcut menu, click Font tab (Font dialog box), click Bold in Font style list, click OK button
3. Click Font Dialog Box Launcher (Home tab | Font group), click Font tab (Font dialog box), click Bold in Font style list, click OK button
4. Press CTRL+B

To Change Theme Colors

A **color scheme** in Word is a document theme that identifies 12 complementary colors for text, background, accents, and links in a document. With more than 20 predefined color schemes, Word provides a simple way to select colors that work well together.

In the flyer, you want all the colors to convey honesty, dependability, and healing, that is, shades of browns and greens. In Word, the Aspect color scheme uses these colors. Thus, you will change the color scheme from the default, Office, to Aspect. The next steps change theme colors.

1

- Click the Change Styles button (Home tab | Styles group) to display the Change Styles menu.

- Point to Colors on the Change Styles menu to display the Colors gallery (Figure 1–42).

Experiment

- Point to various color schemes in the Colors gallery and watch the colors change in the document window.

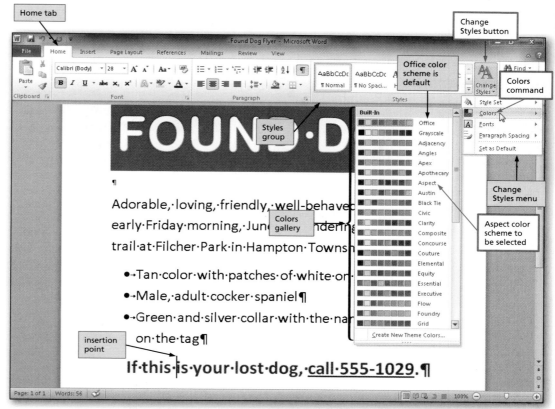

Figure 1–42

2

- Click Aspect in the Colors gallery to change the document theme colors (Figure 1–43).

Q&A

What if I want to return to the original color scheme?

You would click the Change Styles button again, click Colors on the Change Styles menu, and then click Office in the Colors gallery.

Figure 1–43

Other Ways

1. Click Theme Colors button (Page Layout tab | Themes group), select desired color scheme

Selecting Text

In many of the previous steps, you have selected text. Table 1–3 summarizes the techniques used to select various items.

Table 1–3 Techniques for Selecting Text		
Item to Select	**Mouse**	**Keyboard (where applicable)**
Block of text	Click at beginning of selection, scroll to end of selection, position mouse pointer at end of selection, hold down SHIFT key and then click; or drag through the text.	
Character(s)	Drag through character(s).	SHIFT+RIGHT ARROW or SHIFT+LEFT ARROW
Document	Move mouse to left of text until mouse pointer changes to a right-pointing block arrow and then triple-click.	CTRL+A
Graphic	Click the graphic.	
Line	Move mouse to left of line until mouse pointer changes to a right-pointing block arrow and then click.	HOME, then SHIFT+END or END, then SHIFT+HOME
Lines	Move mouse to left of first line until mouse pointer changes to a right-pointing block arrow and then drag up or down.	HOME, then SHIFT+DOWN ARROW or END, then SHIFT+UP ARROW
Paragraph	Triple-click paragraph; or move mouse to left of paragraph until mouse pointer changes to a right-pointing block arrow and then double-click.	CTRL+SHIFT+DOWN ARROW or CTRL+SHIFT+UP ARROW
Paragraphs	Move mouse to left of paragraph until mouse pointer changes to a right-pointing block arrow, double-click, and then drag up or down.	CTRL+SHIFT+DOWN ARROW or CTRL+SHIFT+UP ARROW repeatedly
Sentence	Press and hold down CTRL key and then click sentence.	
Word	Double-click the word.	CTRL+SHIFT+RIGHT ARROW or CTRL+SHIFT+LEFT ARROW
Words	Drag through words.	CTRL+SHIFT+RIGHT ARROW or CTRL+SHIFT+LEFT ARROW repeatedly

To Save an Existing Document with the Same File Name

You have made several modifications to the document since you last saved it. Thus, you should save it again. The following step saves the document again. For an example of the step listed below, refer to the Office 2010 and Windows 7 chapter at the beginning of this book.

 Click the Save button on the Quick Access Toolbar to overwrite the previously saved file.

Break Point: If you wish to take a break, this is a good place to do so. You can quit Word now (refer to page WD 44 for instructions). To resume at a later time, start Word (refer to pages WD 4 and WD 5 for instructions), open the file called Found Dog Flyer (refer to page WD 45 for instructions), and continue following the steps from this location forward.

Inserting and Formatting Pictures in a Word Document

With the text formatted in the flyer, the next step is to insert digital pictures in the flyer and format the pictures. Flyers usually contain graphical images, such as a picture, to attract the attention of passersby. In the following pages, you will perform these tasks:

1. Insert the first digital picture into the flyer and then reduce its size.
2. Insert the second digital picture into the flyer and then reduce its size.
3. Change the look of the first picture and then the second picture.

Find the appropriate graphical image.
To use a graphical image, also called a graphic, in a Word document, the image must be stored digitally in a file. Files containing graphical images are available from a variety of sources:

- Word includes a collection of predefined graphical images that you can insert in a document.
- Microsoft has free digital images on the Web for use in a document. Other Web sites also have images available, some of which are free, while others require a fee.
- You can take a picture with a digital camera or camera phone and **download** it, which is the process of copying the digital picture from the camera or phone to your computer.
- With a scanner, you can convert a printed picture, drawing, or diagram to a digital file.

If you receive a picture from a source other than yourself, do not use the file until you are certain it does not contain a virus. A **virus** is a computer program that can damage files and programs on your computer. Use an antivirus program to verify that any files you use are virus free.

Plan Ahead

Establish where to position and how to format the graphical image.
The content, size, shape, position, and format of a graphic should capture the interest of passersby, enticing them to stop and read the flyer. Often, the graphic is the center of attraction and visually the largest element on a flyer. If you use colors in the graphical image, be sure they are part of the document's color scheme.

Plan Ahead

To Insert a Picture

The next step in creating the flyer is to insert one of the digital pictures of the dog so that it is centered on the blank line below the headline. The picture, which was taken with a camera phone, is available on the Data Files for Students. See the inside back cover of this book for instructions on downloading the Data Files for Students, or contact your instructor for information about accessing the required files.

The following steps insert a centered picture, which, in this example, is located in the Chapter 01 folder in the Word folder in the Data Files for Students folder on a USB flash drive.

1
- Position the insertion point on the blank line below the headline, which is the location where you want to insert the picture.

- Click the Center button (Home tab | Paragraph group) to center the paragraph that will contain the picture.

- Click Insert on the Ribbon to display the Insert tab (Figure 1–44).

Figure 1–44

2
- With your USB flash drive connected to one of the computer's USB ports, click the Insert Picture from File button (Insert tab | Illustrations group) (shown in Figure 1-44) to display the Insert Picture dialog box (shown in Figure 1-45 on the next page).

3

- Navigate to the picture location (in this case, the Chapter 01 folder in the Word folder in the Data Files for Students folder on a USB flash drive). For a detailed example of this procedure, refer to Steps 3a – 3c in the To Save a File in a Folder section in the Office 2010 and Windows 7 chapter at the beginning of this book.

- Click Dog Picture 1 to select the file (Figure 1–45).

Q&A What if the picture is not on a USB flash drive?

Use the same process, but select the storage location containing the picture.

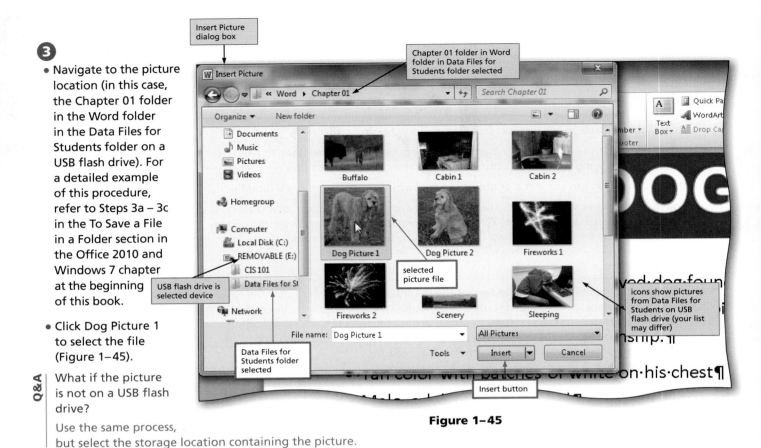

Figure 1–45

4

- Click the Insert button (Insert Picture dialog box) to insert the picture at the location of the insertion point in the document (Figure 1–46).

Q&A What are the symbols around the picture?

A selected graphic appears surrounded by a **selection rectangle**, which has small squares and circles, called **sizing handles**, at each corner and middle location.

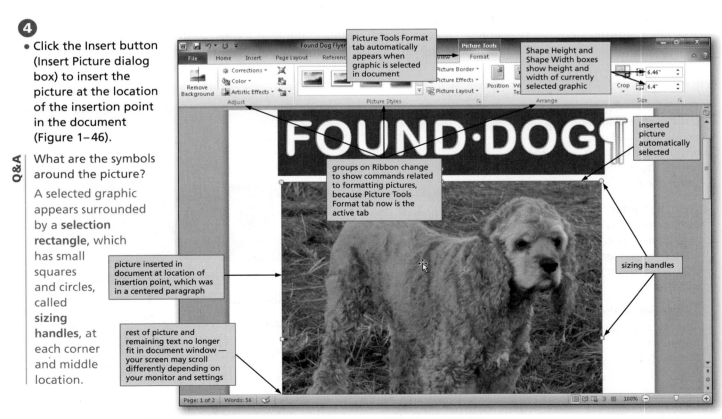

Figure 1–46

To Zoom the Document

The next step is to reduce the size of the picture so that both pictures will fit side-by-side on the same line. With the current picture size, the flyer now has expanded to two pages. The final flyer, however, should fit on a single page. In Word, you can change the zoom so that you can see the entire document (that is, both pages) on the screen at once. Seeing the entire document at once helps you determine the appropriate size for the picture. The following step zooms the document.

 1

Experiment

- Repeatedly click the Zoom Out and Zoom In buttons on the status bar and watch the size of the document change in the document window.

- Click the Zoom Out or Zoom In button as many times as necessary until the Zoom button on the status bar displays 50% on its face (Figure 1–47).

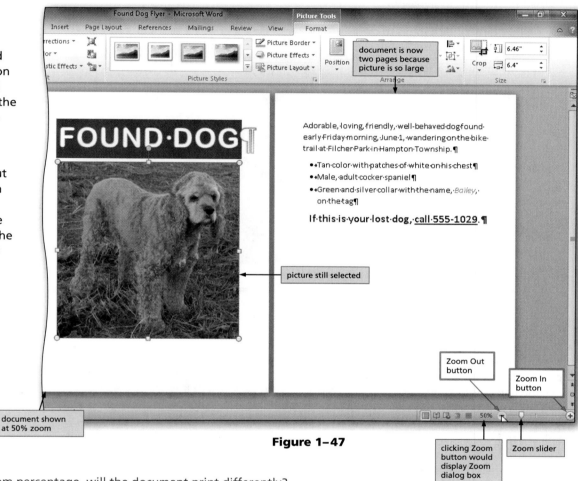

Figure 1–47

Q&A If I change the zoom percentage, will the document print differently?

Changing the zoom has no effect on the printed document.

Q&A Are there predefined zoom options?

Yes. Through the View tab | Zoom group or the Zoom dialog box, you can zoom to one page, two pages, many pages, page width, text width, and a variety of set percentages. Page width zoom places the edges of the page at the edges of the Word window, whereas Text width zoom places the contents of the page at the edges of the Word window.

Other Ways	
1. Drag Zoom slider on status bar	3. Click Zoom button (View tab | Zoom group), select desired zoom percent or type (Zoom dialog box), click OK button
2. Click Zoom button on status bar, select desired zoom percent or type (Zoom dialog box), click OK button	

To Resize a Graphic

The next step is to resize the picture so that both pictures will fit side-by-side on the same line below the headline. **Resizing** includes both enlarging and reducing the size of a graphic. In this flyer, you will reduce the size of the picture. With the entire document displayed in the document window, you will be able to see how the resized graphic will look on the entire page. The following steps resize a selected graphic.

- With the graphic still selected, point to the upper-right corner sizing handle on the picture so that the mouse pointer shape changes to a two-headed arrow (Figure 1–48).

Q&A What if my graphic (picture) is not selected?

To select a graphic, click it.

Figure 1–48

- Drag the sizing handle diagonally inward until the crosshair mouse pointer is positioned approximately as shown in Figure 1–49.

- Release the mouse button to resize the graphic, which in this case should have a height of about 2.74" and a width of about 2.73".

Q&A How can I see the height and width measurements?

Look in the Size group on the Picture Tools Format tab to see the height and width measurements of the currently selected graphic (shown in Figure 1–46 on page WD 32).

Q&A What if the graphic is the wrong size?

Repeat Steps 1, 2, and 3; or enter the desired height and width values in the Shape Height and Shape Width boxes (Picture Tools Format tab | Size group).

Figure 1–49

4

- Click to the right of the graphic to deselect it (Figure 1–50).

Q&A What happened to the Picture Tools Format tab?

When you click outside of a graphic or press a key to scroll through a document, Word deselects the graphic and removes the Picture Tools Format tab from the screen.

Q&A What if I want to return a graphic to its original size and start again?

With the graphic selected, click the Size Dialog Box Launcher (Picture Tools Format tab | Size group), click the Size tab (Layout dialog box), click the Reset button, and then click the OK button.

Figure 1–50

Other Ways
1. Enter height and width of graphic in Shape Height and Shape Width boxes (Picture Tools Format tab | Size group)   2. Click Size Dialog Box Launcher (Picture Tools Format tab | Size group), click Size tab (Layout dialog box), enter desired   height and width values in boxes, click OK button

To Insert Another Picture

The next step is to insert the other digital picture of the dog immediately to the right of the current picture. This second picture also is available on the Data Files for Students. See the inside back cover of this book for instructions on downloading the Data Files for Students, or contact your instructor for information about accessing the required files.

The following steps insert another picture immediately to the right of the current picture.

1 With the insertion point positioned as shown in Figure 1–50, click Insert on the Ribbon to display the Insert tab.

2 With your USB flash drive connected to one of the computer's USB ports, click the Insert Picture from File button (Insert tab | Illustrations group) to display the Insert Picture dialog box.

3 If necessary, navigate to the picture location (in this case, the Word folder in the CIS 101 folder [or your class folder] on the USB flash drive). For a detailed example of this procedure, refer to Steps 3a – 3c in the To Save a File in a Folder section in the Office 2010 and Windows 7 chapter at the beginning of this book.

4 Click Dog Picture 2 to select the file.

5 Click the Insert button (Insert Picture dialog box) to insert the picture at the location of the insertion point in the document.

BTW

Word Help
At any time while using Word, you can find answers to questions and display information about various topics through Word Help. Used properly, this form of assistance can increase your productivity and reduce your frustrations by minimizing the time you spend learning how to use Word. For instruction about Word Help and exercises that will help you gain confidence in using it, read the Office 2010 and Windows 7 chapter at the beginning of this book.

To Resize a Graphic by Entering Exact Measurements

The next step is to resize the second picture so that it is the exact same size as the first picture. The height and width measurements of the first graphic are approximately 2.74" and 2.73", respectively. When a graphic is selected, its height and width measurements show in the Size group of the Picture Tools Format tab. The following steps resize a selected graphic by entering its desired exact measurements.

- With the second graphic still selected, click the Shape Height box (Picture Tools Format tab | Size group) to select the contents in the box and then type **2.74** as the height.

Q&A What if the Picture Tools Format tab no longer is displayed on my Ribbon?

Double-click the picture to display the Picture Tools Format tab.

Q&A What if the contents of the Shape Height box are not selected?

Triple-click the Shape Height box.

Figure 1–51

- Click the Shape Width box to select the contents in the box, type **2.73** as the width, and then click the picture to apply the settings.

- If necessary, scroll up to display the entire document in the window (Figure 1–51).

Q&A Why did my measurements change slightly?

Depending on relative measurements, the height and width values entered may change slightly.

Other Ways

1. Right-click picture, enter shape height and width values in boxes on shortcut menu
2. Right-click picture, click Size and Position on shortcut menu, click Size tab (Layout dialog box), enter shape height and width values in boxes, click OK button

To Zoom the Document

You are finished resizing the graphics and no longer need to view the entire page in the document window. Thus, the following step changes the zoom back to 100 percent.

1. Click the Zoom In button on the status bar as many times as necessary until the Zoom button displays 100% on its face (shown in Figure 1–52).

To Apply a Picture Style

A **style** is a named group of formatting characteristics. Word provides more than 25 picture styles that enable you easily to change a picture's look to a more visually appealing style, including a variety of shapes, angles, borders, and reflections. The flyer in this chapter uses a style that applies soft edges to the picture. The following steps apply a picture style to a picture.

1
- Click the leftmost dog picture to select it (Figure 1–52).

Q&A What is the green circle attached to the selected graphic?

It is called a rotate handle. When you drag a graphic's rotate handle, the graphic moves in either a clockwise or counterclockwise direction.

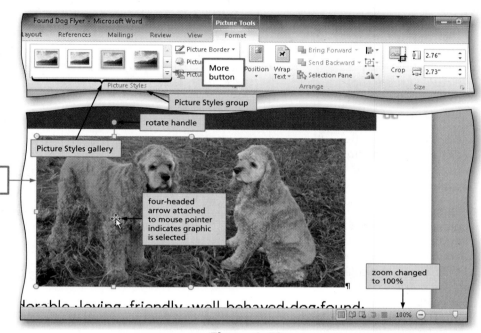

Figure 1–52

2
- Click the More button in the Picture Styles gallery (Picture Tools Format tab | Picture Styles group) (shown in Figure 1–52) to expand the gallery.

- Point to Soft Edge Rectangle in the Picture Styles gallery to display a live preview of that style applied to the picture in the document (Figure 1–53).

Experiment
- Point to various picture styles in the Picture Styles gallery and watch the style of the picture change in the document window.

3
- Click Soft Edge Rectangle in the Picture Styles gallery to apply the style to the selected picture.

Figure 1–53

To Apply Picture Effects

Word provides a variety of picture effects so that you can further customize a picture. Effects include shadows, reflections, glow, soft edges, bevel, and 3-D rotation. The difference between the effects and the styles is that each effect has several options, providing you with more control over the exact look of the image.

In this flyer, the leftmost dog picture has a slight tan glow effect and is turned inward toward the center of the page. The following steps apply picture effects to the selected picture.

1

- Click the Picture Effects button (Picture Tools Format tab | Picture Styles group) to display the Picture Effects menu.

- Point to Glow on the Picture Effects menu to display the Glow gallery.

- Point to Tan, 5 pt glow, Accent color 6 in the Glow Variations area (rightmost glow in first row) to display a live preview of the selected glow effect applied to the picture in the document window (Figure 1–54).

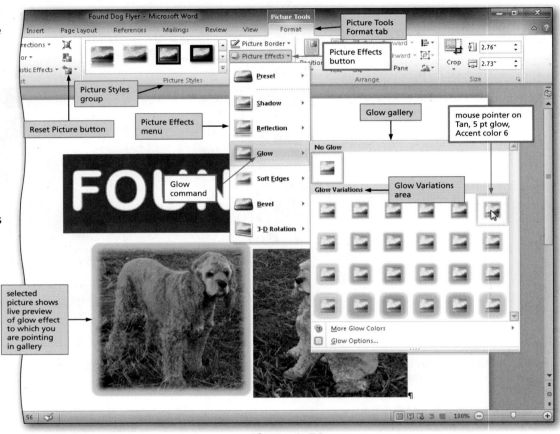

Figure 1–54

(P) **Experiment**

- Point to various glow effects in the Glow gallery and watch the picture change in the document window.

2

- Click Tan, 5 pt glow, Accent color 6 in the Glow gallery to apply the selected picture effect.

Q&A

What if I wanted to discard formatting applied to a picture?

You would click the Reset Picture button (Picture Tools Format tab | Adjust group). To reset formatting and size, you would click the Reset Picture button arrow (Picture Tools Format tab | Adjust group) and then click Reset Picture & Size on the Reset Picture menu.

- Click the Picture Effects button (Picture Tools Format tab | Picture Styles group) to display the Picture Effects menu again.

- Point to 3-D Rotation on the Picture Effects menu to display the 3-D Rotation gallery.

- Point to Off Axis 1 Right in the Parallel area (second rotation in second row) to display a live preview of the selected 3-D effect applied to the picture in the document window (Figure 1–55).

 Experiment

- Point to various 3-D rotation effects in the 3-D Rotation gallery and watch the picture change in the document window.

4

- Click Off Axis 1 Right in the 3-D Rotation gallery to apply the selected picture effect.

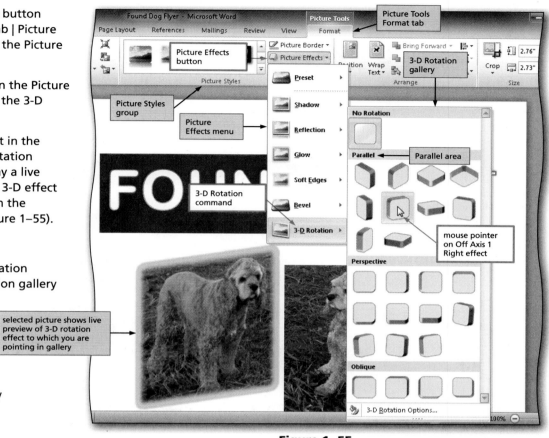

Figure 1–55

Other Ways
1. Right-click picture, click Format Picture on shortcut menu, select desired options (Format Picture | dialog box), click Close button 2. Click Format Shape Dialog Box Launcher (Picture | Tools Format tab | Picture Styles group), select desired options (Format Picture dialog box), click Close button

To Apply a Picture Style and Effects to Another Picture

In this flyer, the rightmost dog picture also uses the soft edge picture style, has a slight tan glow effect, and is turned inward toward the center of the page. The following steps apply the picture style and picture effects to the picture.

1 Click the rightmost dog picture to select it.

2 Click the More button in the Picture Styles gallery (Picture Tools Format tab | Picture Styles group) to expand the gallery and then click Soft Edge Rectangle in the Picture Styles gallery to apply the selected style to the picture.

3 Click the Picture Effects button (Picture Tools Format tab | Picture Styles group) to display the Picture Effects menu and then point to Glow on the Picture Effects menu to display the Glow gallery.

4 Click Tan, 5 pt glow, Accent color 6 (rightmost glow in first row) in the Glow gallery to apply the picture effect to the picture.

5 Click the Picture Effects button (Picture Tools Format tab | Picture Styles group) to display the Picture Effects menu again and then point to 3-D Rotation on the Picture Effects menu to display the 3-D Rotation gallery.

6 Click Off Axis 2 Left (rightmost rotation in second row) in the Parallel area in the 3-D Rotation gallery to apply the picture effect to the selected picture.

7 Click to the right of the picture to deselect it (Figure 1–56).

picture style and picture effects applied to picture

Figure 1–56

Enhancing the Page

With the text and graphics entered and formatted, the next step is to look at the page as a whole and determine if it looks finished in its current state. As you review the page, answer these questions:

- Does it need a page border to frame its contents, or would a page border make it look too busy?
- Is the spacing between paragraphs and graphics on the page adequate? Do any sections of text or graphics look as if they are positioned too closely to the items above or below them?

You determine that a graphical, color-coordinated border would enhance the flyer. You also notice that the flyer would look more proportionate if it had a little more space above and below the pictures. The following pages make these enhancements to the flyer.

To View One Page

Earlier in this chapter, you changed the zoom using the Zoom Out and Zoom In buttons on the status bar. If you want to display an entire page as large as possible in the document window, Word can compute the correct zoom percentage for you. The next steps display a single page in its entirety in the document window as large as possible.

1

- Click View on the Ribbon to display the View tab.

2

- Click the One Page button (View tab | Zoom group) to display the entire page in the document window as large as possible (Figure 1–57).

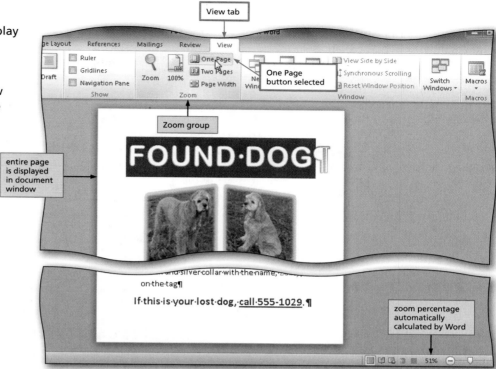

Figure 1–57

To Add a Page Border

In Word, you can add a border around the perimeter of an entire page. The flyer in this chapter has a light green dashed border. The following steps add a page border.

1

- Click Page Layout on the Ribbon to display the Page Layout tab.

- Click the Page Borders button (Page Layout tab | Page Background group) to display the Borders and Shading dialog box (Figure 1–58).

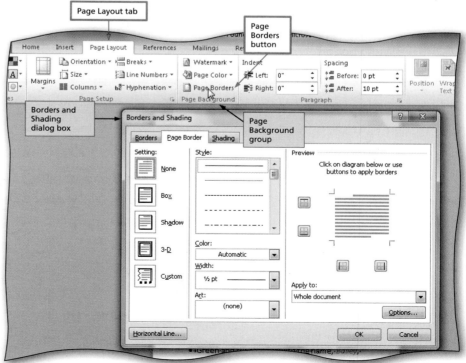

Figure 1–58

2

- Scroll through the Style list (Borders and Shading dialog box) and select the style shown in Figure 1–59.

- Click the Color box arrow to display a Color palette (Figure 1–59).

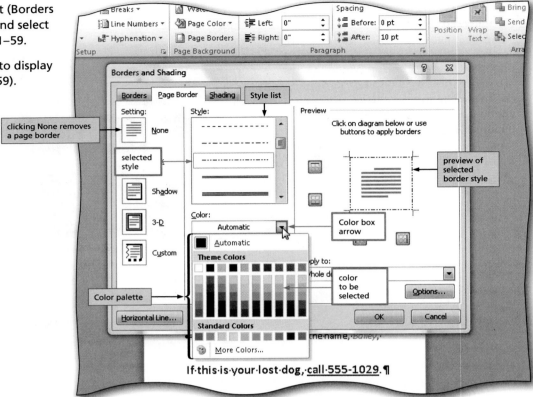

Figure 1–59

3

- Click Dark Green, Accent 4, Lighter 60% (eighth color in third row) in the Color palette to select the color for the page border.

- Click the Width box arrow and then click 3 pt to select the thickness of the page border (Figure 1–60).

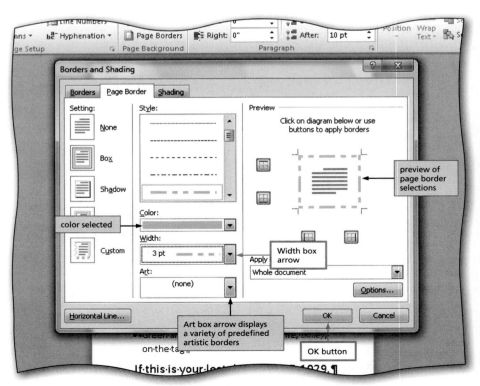

Figure 1–60

4

- Click the OK button to add the border to the page (Figure 1–61).

Q&A

What if I wanted to remove the border?

You would click None in the Setting list in the Borders and Shading dialog box.

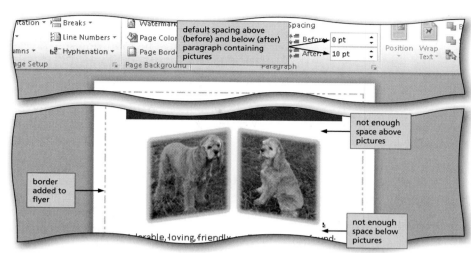

Figure 1–61

To Change Spacing before and after a Paragraph

The default spacing above (before) a paragraph in Word is 0 points and below (after) is 10 points. In the flyer, you want to increase the spacing above and below the paragraph containing the pictures. The following steps change the spacing above and below a paragraph.

1

- Position the insertion point in the paragraph to be adjusted, in this case, the paragraph containing the pictures.

- Click the Spacing Before box up arrow (Page Layout tab | Paragraph group) as many times as necessary until 24 pt is displayed in the Spacing Before box to increase the space above the current paragraph.

2

- Click the Spacing After box up arrow (Page Layout tab | Paragraph group) so that 12 pt is displayed in the Spacing After box to increase the space below the current paragraph (Figure 1–62).

- If the text flows to two pages, reduce the spacing above and below paragraphs as necessary.

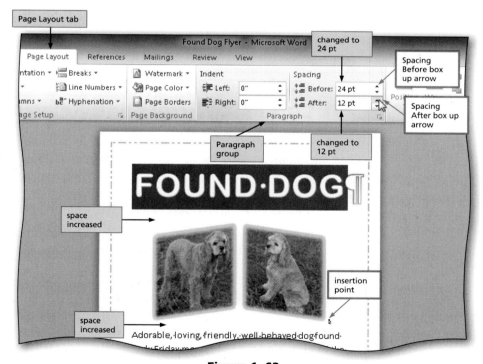

Figure 1–62

Other Ways

1. Right-click paragraph, click Paragraph on shortcut menu, click Indents and Spacing tab (Paragraph dialog box), enter spacing before and after values, click OK button

2. Click Paragraph Dialog Box Launcher (Home tab or Page Layout tab | Paragraph group), click Indents and Spacing tab (Paragraph dialog box), enter spacing before and after values, click OK button

To Save an Existing Document with the Same File Name

You have made several modifications to the document since you last saved it. Thus, you should save it again. The following step saves the document again. For an example of the step listed below, refer to the Office 2010 and Windows 7 chapter at the beginning of this book.

1 Click the Save button on the Quick Access Toolbar to overwrite the previously saved file.

To Quit Word

Although you still need to make some edits to this document, you want to quit Word and resume working on the project at a later time. Thus, the following steps quit Word. For a detailed example of the procedure summarized below, refer to the Office 2010 and Windows 7 chapter at the beginning of this book.

1 If you have one Word document open, click the Close button on the right side of the title bar to close the document and quit Word; or if you have multiple Word documents open, click File on the Ribbon to open the Backstage view and then click Exit in the Backstage view to close all open documents and quit Word.

2 If a Microsoft Word dialog box appears, click the Save button to save any changes made to the document since the last save.

BTW

Certification
The Microsoft Office Specialist (MOS) program provides an opportunity for you to obtain a valuable industry credential — proof that you have the Word 2010 skills required by employers. For more information, visit the Word 2010 Certification Web page (scsite.com/wd2010/cert).

> **Break Point:** If you wish to take a break, this is a good place to do so. To resume at a later time, continue following the steps from this location forward.

Correcting Errors and Revising a Document

After creating a document, you may need to change it. For example, the document may contain an error, or new circumstances may require you to add text to the document.

Types of Changes Made to Documents

The types of changes made to documents normally fall into one of the three following categories: additions, deletions, or modifications.

Additions   Additional words, sentences, or paragraphs may be required in a document. Additions occur when you omit text from a document and want to insert it later. For example, you may want to add your e-mail address to the flyer.

Deletions   Sometimes, text in a document is incorrect or is no longer needed. For example, you may discover the dog's collar is just green. In this case, you would delete the words, and silver, from the flyer.

Modifications   If an error is made in a document or changes take place that affect the document, you might have to revise a word(s) in the text. For example, the dog may have been found in Hampton Village instead of Hampton Township.

To Start Word

Once you have created and saved a document, you may need to retrieve it from your storage medium. For example, you might want to revise the document or print it. The following steps, which assume Windows 7 is running, start Word so that you can open and modify the flyer. You may need to ask your instructor how to start Word for your computer. For a detailed example of the procedure summarized below, refer to the Office 2010 and Windows 7 chapter at the beginning of this book.

1 Click the Start button on the Windows 7 taskbar to display the Start menu.

2 Type `Microsoft Word` as the search text in the 'Search programs and files' text box and watch the search results appear on the Start menu.

3 Click Microsoft Word 2010 in the search results on the Start menu to start Word and display a new blank document in the Word window.

4 If the Word window is not maximized, click the Maximize button next to the Close button on its title bar to maximize the window.

To Open a Document from Word

Earlier in this chapter, you saved your project on a USB flash drive using the file name, Found Dog Flyer. The following steps open the Found Dog Flyer file from the Word folder in the CIS 101 folder on the USB flash drive. For a detailed example of the procedure summarized below, refer to the Office 2010 and Windows 7 chapter at the beginning of this book.

1 With your USB flash drive connected to one of the computer's USB ports, click File on the Ribbon to open the Backstage view.

2 Click Open in the Backstage view to display the Open dialog box.

3 Navigate to the location of the file to be opened (in this case, the Word folder in the CIS 101 folder [or your class folder] on the USB flash drive). For a detailed example of this procedure, refer to Steps 3a – 3c in the To Save a File in a Folder section in the Office 2010 and Windows 7 chapter at the beginning of this book.

4 Click Found Dog Flyer to select the file to be opened.

5 Click the Open button (Open dialog box) to open the selected file and display the opened document in the Word window.

Q&A Could I have clicked the Recent tab to open the file?

Yes. Because the file was recently closed, it should appear in the Recent Documents list.

To Zoom the Document

While modifying the document, you prefer the document at 100 percent so that it is easier to read. Thus, the following step changes the zoom back to 100 percent.

1 If necessary, click the Zoom In button on the status bar as many times as necessary until the Zoom button displays 100% on its face (shown in Figure 1–63 on the next page).

To Insert Text in an Existing Document

Word inserts text to the left of the insertion point. The text to the right of the insertion point moves to the right and downward to fit the new text. The following steps insert the word, very, to the left of the word, early, in the flyer.

1

- Scroll through the document and then click to the left of the location of text to be inserted (in this case, the e in early) to position the insertion point where text should be inserted (Figure 1–63).

Figure 1–63

2

- Type **very** and then press the SPACEBAR to insert the word to the left of the insertion point (Figure 1–64).

Q&A

Why did the text move to the right as I typed?

In Word, the default typing mode is **insert mode**, which means as you type a character, Word moves all the characters to the right of the typed character one position to the right.

Figure 1–64

Deleting Text from a Document

It is not unusual to type incorrect characters or words in a document. As discussed earlier in this chapter, you can click the Undo button on the Quick Access Toolbar to undo a command or action immediately — this includes typing. Word also provides other methods of correcting typing errors.

To delete an incorrect character in a document, simply click next to the incorrect character and then press the BACKSPACE key to erase to the left of the insertion point, or press the DELETE key to erase to the right of the insertion point.

To Delete Text

To delete a word or phrase, you first must select the word or phrase. The following steps select the word, very, that was just added in the previous steps and then delete the selection.

1
- Position the mouse pointer somewhere in the word to be selected (in this case, very) and then double-click to select the word (Figure 1–65).

Adorable, loving, friendly, well-behaved dog found very early Friday morning, June 1, wandering on the bike trail at Filcher Park in Hampton Township.¶

text to be deleted is selected

mouse pointer

Figure 1–65

2
- With the text selected, press the DELETE key to delete the selected text (shown in Figure 1–63).

To Move Text

While proofreading the flyer, you realize that the body copy would read better if the first two bulleted paragraphs were reversed. An efficient way to move text a short distance, such as reversing two paragraphs, is drag-and-drop editing. With **drag-and-drop editing**, you select the text to be moved and then drag the selected item to the new location and then *drop*, or insert, it there. Another technique for moving text is the cut-and-paste technique, which is discussed in the next chapter. The following steps use drag-and-drop editing to move text.

1
- Position the mouse pointer in the paragraph to be moved (in this case, the second bulleted item) and then triple-click to select the paragraph.

- With the mouse pointer in the selected text, press and hold down the mouse button, which displays a dotted insertion point and a small dotted box with the mouse pointer (Figure 1–66).

- Tan color with patches of white on his chest¶
- Male, adult cocker spaniel¶

text to be moved is selected

- Green and silver collar with the name, *Bailey*,

mouse pointer has small box below it when you begin to drag selected text

If ... ur lost dog, call 555-1029.¶

100%

Figure 1–66

2

- Drag the dotted insertion point to the location where the selected text is to be moved, as shown in Figure 1–67.

selected text to be dropped at location of dotted insertion point

Adorable, loving, friendly, well-behaved dog found early Friday morning, June 1, wandering on the bike trail at Filcher Park in Hampton Township.¶

- → Tan color with patches of white on his chest¶
- → Male, adult cocker spaniel¶
- → Green and silver collar with the name, *Bailey*, on the tag¶

If this is your lost dog, call 555-1029.¶

Figure 1–67

3

- Release the mouse button to move the selected text to the location of the dotted insertion point (Figure 1–68).

Q&A What if I accidentally drag text to the wrong location?

Click the Undo button on the Quick Access Toolbar and try again.

Q&A Can I use drag-and-drop editing to move any selected item?

Yes, you can select words, sentences, phrases, and graphics and then use drag-and-drop editing to move them.

Q&A What is the purpose of the Paste Options button?

If you click the Paste Options button, a menu appears that allows you to change the format of the item that was moved. The next chapter discusses the Paste Options menu.

- Click anywhere in the document window to remove the selection from the bulleted item.

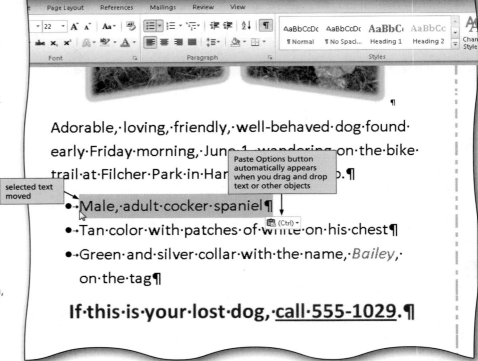

Figure 1–68

Other Ways

1. Click Cut button (Home tab | Clipboard group), click where text or object is to be pasted, click Paste button (Home tab | Clipboard group)

2. Right-click selected text, click Cut on shortcut menu, right-click where text or object is to be pasted, click Keep Source Formatting on shortcut menu

3. Press CTRL+X, position insertion point where text or object is to be pasted, press CTRL+V

Changing Document Properties

Word helps you organize and identify your files by using **document properties**, which are the details about a file. Document properties, also known as **metadata**, can include information such as the project author, title, subject, and keywords. A **keyword** is a word or phrase that further describes the document. For example, a class name or document topic can describe the file's purpose or content.

Document properties are valuable for a variety of reasons:

- Users can save time locating a particular file because they can view a document's properties without opening the document.

- By creating consistent properties for files having similar content, users can better organize their documents.

- Some organizations require Word users to add document properties so that other employees can view details about these files.

Five different types of document properties exist, but the more common ones used in this book are standard and automatically updated properties. **Standard properties** are associated with all Microsoft Office documents and include author, title, and subject. **Automatically updated properties** include file system properties, such as the date you create or change a file, and statistics, such as the file size.

BTW

Printing Document Properties
To print document properties, click File on the Ribbon to open the Backstage view, click the Print tab in the Backstage view to display the Print gallery, click the first button in the Settings area to display a list of options specifying what you can print, click Document Properties in the list to specify you want to print the document properties instead of the actual document, and then click the Print button in the Print gallery to print the document properties on the currently selected printer.

To Change Document Properties

The **Document Information Panel** contains areas where you can view and enter document properties. You can view and change information in this panel at any time while you are creating a document. Before saving the flyer again, you want to add your name and course information as document properties. The following steps use the Document Information Panel to change document properties.

1

- Click File on the Ribbon to open the Backstage view.

- If necessary, click the Info tab to display the Info gallery (Figure 1–69).

Q&A

How do I close the Backstage view?

Click File on the Ribbon or click the preview of the document in the Info gallery to return to the Word document window.

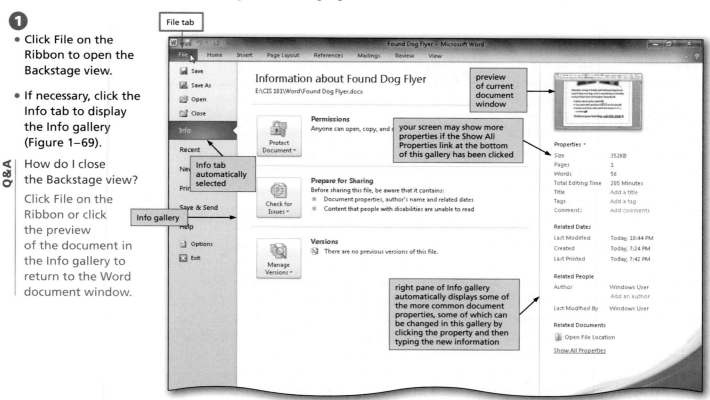

Figure 1–69

2

- Click the Properties button in the right pane of the Info gallery to display the Properties menu (Figure 1–70).

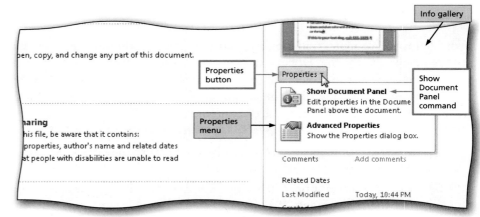

Figure 1–70

3

- Click Show Document Panel on the Properties menu to close the Backstage view and display the Document Information Panel in the Word document window (Figure 1–71).

Q&A Why are some of the document properties in my Document Information Panel already filled in?

The person who installed Microsoft Office 2010 on your computer or network may have set or customized the properties.

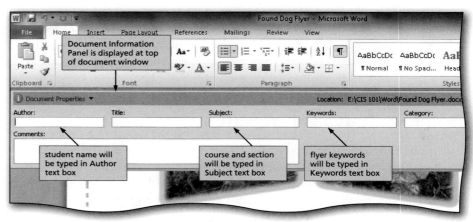

Figure 1–71

4

- Click the Author text box, if necessary, and then type your name as the Author property. If a name already is displayed in the Author text box, delete it before typing your name.

- Click the Subject text box, if necessary delete any existing text, and then type your course and section as the Subject property.

- If an AutoComplete dialog box appears, click its Yes button.

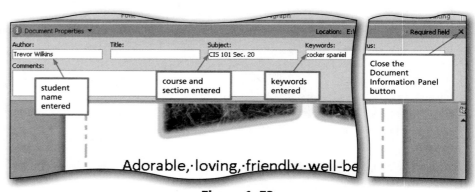

Figure 1–72

- Click the Keywords text box, if necessary delete any existing text, and then type **cocker spaniel** as the Keywords property (Figure 1–72).

Q&A What types of document properties does Word collect automatically?

Word records details such as time spent editing a document, the number of times a document has been revised, and the fonts and themes used in a document.

5

- Click the Close the Document Information Panel button so that the Document Information Panel no longer is displayed.

Other Ways

1. Click File on Ribbon, click Info in Backstage view, if necessary click Show All Properties link in Info gallery, click property to change and then type new information, close Backstage view

To Save an Existing Document with the Same File Name

You are finished editing the flyer. Thus, you should save it again. The following step saves the document again. For an example of the step listed below, refer to the Office 2010 and Windows 7 chapter at the beginning of this book.

 Click the Save button on the Quick Access Toolbar to overwrite the previously saved file.

Printing a Document

After creating a document, you may want to print it. Printing a document enables you to distribute the document to others in a form that can be read or viewed but typically not edited. It is a good practice to save a document before printing it, in the event you experience difficulties printing.

Determine the best method for distributing the document.
The traditional method of distributing a document uses a printer to produce a hard copy. A **hardcopy** or **printout** is information that exists on a physical medium such as paper. For users that can receive fax documents, you can elect to print a hard copy on a remote fax machine. Hard copies can be useful for the following reasons:

- Many people prefer proofreading a hard copy of a document rather than viewing it on the screen to check for errors and readability.

- Hard copies can serve as reference material if your storage medium is lost or becomes corrupted and you need to recreate the document.

Instead of distributing a hard copy of a document, users can choose to distribute the document as an electronic image that mirrors the original document's appearance. The electronic image of the document can be e-mailed, posted on a Web site, or copied to a portable storage medium such as a USB flash drive. Two popular electronic image formats, sometimes called fixed formats, are PDF by Adobe Systems and XPS by Microsoft. In Word, you can create electronic image files through the Print tab in the Backstage view, the Send & Save tab in the Backstage view, and the Save As dialog box. Electronic images of documents, such as PDF and XPS, can be useful for the following reasons:

- Users can view electronic images of documents without the software that created the original document (e.g., Word). Specifically, to view a PDF file, you use a program called Acrobat Reader, which can be downloaded free from Adobe's Web site. Similarly, to view an XPS file, you use a program called an XPS Viewer, which is included in the latest versions of Windows and Internet Explorer.

- Sending electronic documents saves paper and printer supplies. Society encourages users to contribute to **green computing**, which involves reducing the environmental waste generated when using a computer.

Plan Ahead

BTW

Conserving Ink and Toner
If you want to conserve ink or toner, you can instruct Word to print draft quality documents by clicking File on the Ribbon to open the Backstage view, clicking Options in the Backstage view to display the Word Options dialog box, clicking Advanced in the left pane (Word Options dialog box), scrolling to the Print area in the right pane, placing a check mark in the 'Use draft quality' check box, and then clicking the OK button. Then, use the Backstage view to print the document as usual.

To Print a Document

With the completed document saved, you may want to print it. Because this flyer is being posted, you will print a hard copy on a printer. The steps on the next page print a hard copy of the contents of the saved Found Dog Flyer document.

1

- Click File on the Ribbon to open the Backstage view.

- Click the Print tab in the Backstage view to display the Print gallery (Figure 1–73).

Q&A How can I print multiple copies of my document?

Increase the number in the Copies box in the Print gallery.

Q&A What if I decide not to print the document at this time?

Click File on the Ribbon to close the Backstage view and return to the Word document window.

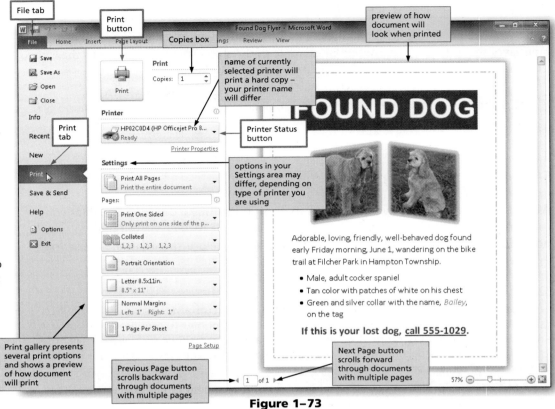

Figure 1–73

2

- Verify the printer name that appears on the Printer Status button will print a hard copy of the document. If necessary, click the Printer Status button to display a list of available printer options and then click the desired printer to change the currently selected printer.

3

- Click the Print button in the Print gallery to print the document on the currently selected printer.

- When the printer stops, retrieve the hard copy (Figure 1–74).

Q&A Do I have to wait until my document is complete to print it?

No, you can follow these steps to print a document at any time while you are creating it.

Q&A What if I want to print an electronic image of a document instead of a hard copy?

You would click the Printer Status button in the Print gallery and then select the desired electronic image option such as a Microsoft XPS Document Writer, which would create an XPS file.

Figure 1–74

Other Ways

1. Press CTRL+P, press ENTER

To Quit Word

The project now is complete. Thus, the following steps quit Word. For an example of the step listed below, refer to the Office 2010 and Windows 7 chapter at the beginning of this book.

1 If you have one Word document open, click the Close button on the right side of the title bar to close the document and quit Word; or if you have multiple Word documents open, click File on the Ribbon to open the Backstage view and then click Exit in the Backstage view to close all open documents and quit Word.

2 If a Microsoft Word dialog box appears, click the Save button to save any changes made to the document since the last save.

Chapter Summary

In this chapter, you have learned how to enter text in a document, format text, insert a picture, format a picture, add a page border, and print a document. The items listed below include all the new Word skills you have learned in this chapter.

1. Start Word (WD 4)
2. Type Text (WD 6)
3. Display Formatting Marks (WD 7)
4. Insert a Blank Line (WD 7)
5. Wordwrap Text as You Type (WD 8)
6. Check Spelling and Grammar as You Type (WD 9)
7. Save a Document (WD 12)
8. Center a Paragraph (WD 14)
9. Select a Line (WD 15)
10. Change the Font Size of Selected Text (WD 16)
11. Change the Font of Selected Text (WD 17)
12. Change the Case of Selected Text (WD 18)
13. Apply a Text Effect to Selected Text (WD 19)
14. Shade a Paragraph (WD 20)
15. Select Multiple Lines (WD 21)
16. Bullet a List of Paragraphs (WD 22)
17. Undo and Redo an Action (WD 23)
18. Italicize Text (WD 24)
19. Color Text (WD 25)
20. Use the Mini Toolbar to Format Text (WD 26)
21. Select a Group of Words (WD 27)
22. Underline Text (WD 27)
23. Bold Text (WD 28)
24. Change Theme Colors (WD 28)
25. Save an Existing Document with the Same File Name (WD 30)
26. Insert a Picture (WD 31)
27. Zoom the Document (WD 33)
28. Resize a Graphic (WD 34)
29. Resize a Graphic by Entering Exact Measurements (WD 36)
30. Apply a Picture Style (WD 37)
31. Apply Picture Effects (WD 38)
32. View One Page (WD 40)
33. Add a Page Border (WD 41)
34. Change Spacing before and after a Paragraph (WD 44)
35. Quit Word (WD 44)
36. Open a Document from Word (WD 45)
37. Insert Text in an Existing Document (WD 46)
38. Delete Text (WD 47)
39. Move Text (WD 47)
40. Change Document Properties (WD 49)
41. Print a Document (WD 51)

If you have a SAM 2010 user profile, your instructor may have assigned an autogradable version of this assignment. If so, log into the SAM 2010 Web site at www.cengage.com/sam2010 to download the instruction and start files.

Learn It Online

Test your knowledge of chapter content and key terms.

Instructions: To complete the Learn It Online exercises, start your browser, click the Address bar, and then enter the Web address **scsite.com/wd2010/learn**. When the Word 2010 Learn It Online page is displayed, click the link for the exercise you want to complete and then read the instructions.

Chapter Reinforcement TF, MC, and SA
A series of true/false, multiple choice, and short answer questions that test your knowledge of the chapter content.

Flash Cards
An interactive learning environment where you identify chapter key terms associated with displayed definitions.

Practice Test
A series of multiple choice questions that test your knowledge of chapter content and key terms.

Who Wants To Be a Computer Genius?
An interactive game that challenges your knowledge of chapter content in the style of a television quiz show.

Wheel of Terms
An interactive game that challenges your knowledge of chapter key terms in the style of the television show *Wheel of Fortune*.

Crossword Puzzle Challenge
A crossword puzzle that challenges your knowledge of key terms presented in the chapter.

Apply Your Knowledge

Reinforce the skills and apply the concepts you learned in this chapter.

Modifying Text and Formatting a Document
Note: To complete this assignment, you will be required to use the Data Files for Students. See the inside back cover of this book for instructions on downloading the Data Files for Students, or contact your instructor for information about accessing the required files.

Instructions: Start Word. Open the document, Apply 1-1 Buffalo Photo Shoot Flyer Unformatted, from the Data Files for Students. The document you open is an unformatted flyer. You are to modify text, format paragraphs and characters, and insert a picture in the flyer.

Perform the following tasks:
1. Delete the word, single, in the sentence of body copy below the headline.
2. Insert the word, Creeks, between the words, Twin Buffalo, in the sentence of body copy below the headline.
3. At the end of the signature line, change the period to an exclamation point.
4. Center the headline and the signature line.
5. Change the theme colors to the Aspect color scheme.
6. Change the font and font size of the headline to 48-point Impact, or a similar font. Change the case of the headline text to all capital letters. Apply the text effect called Gradient Fill – Orange, Accent 1, Outline – White to the headline.
7. Change the font size of body copy between the headline and the signature line to 20 point.
8. Use the Mini toolbar to change the font size of the signature line to 26 point.
9. Select the words, hundreds of buffalo, in the paragraph below the headline and underline them.

10. Italicize the word, every, in the paragraph below the headline. Undo this change and then redo the change.

11. Select the three lines (paragraphs) of text above the signature line and add bullets to the selected paragraphs.

12. Switch the last two bulleted paragraphs. That is, select the Questions bullet and move it so that it is the last bulleted paragraph.

13. Bold the first word of each bulleted paragraph. Change the font color of these same three words to Dark Green, Accent 4, Darker 50%.

14. Bold the text in the signature line. Shade the signature line Dark Green, Accent 4, Darker 50%. If the font color does not automatically change to a lighter color, change it to a shade of white.

15. Change the zoom so that the entire page is visible in the document window.

16. Insert the picture of the buffalo centered on the blank line below the headline. The picture is called Buffalo and is available on the Data Files for Students. Apply the Snip Diagonal Corner, White picture style to the inserted picture. Apply the glow called Dark Green, 5 pt glow, Accent color 4 to the picture.

17. Change the spacing after the headline paragraph to 6 point.

18. The entire flyer now should fit on a single page. If it flows to two pages, resize the picture or decrease spacing before and after paragraphs until the entire flyer text fits on a single page.

19. Change the zoom to text width, then page width, then 100% and notice the differences.

20. Enter the text, Twin Creeks, as the keywords in the document properties. Change the other document properties, as specified by your instructor.

21. Click File on the Ribbon and then click Save As. Save the document using the file name, Apply 1-1 Buffalo Photo Shoot Flyer Formatted.

22. Print the document. Submit the revised document, shown in Figure 1–75, in the format specified by your instructor.

23. Quit Word.

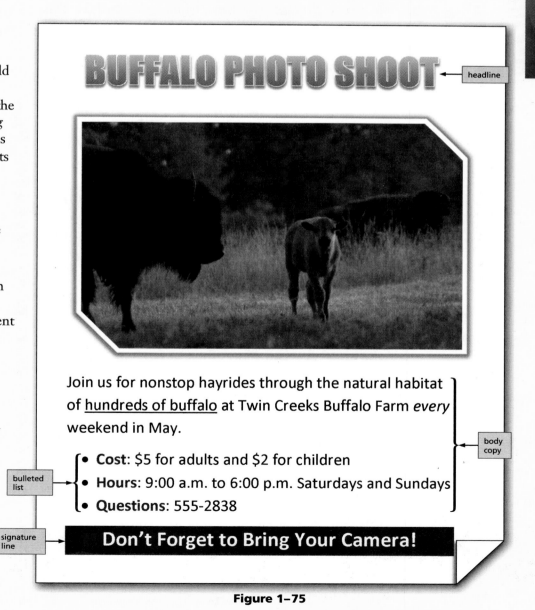

Figure 1–75

Extend Your Knowledge

Extend the skills you learned in this chapter and experiment with new skills. You may need to use Help to complete the assignment.

Modifying Text and Picture Formats and Adding Page Borders

Note: To complete this assignment, you will be required to use the Data Files for Students. See the inside back cover of this book for instructions on downloading the Data Files for Students, or contact your instructor for information about accessing the required files.

Instructions: Start Word. Open the document, Extend 1-1 TVC Cruises Flyer, from the Data Files for Students. You will enhance the look of the flyer shown in Figure 1–76. *Hint:* Remember, if you make a mistake while formatting the picture, you can reset it by clicking the Reset Picture button or Reset Picture button arrow (Picture Tools Format tab | Adjust group).

Perform the following tasks:

1. Use Help to learn about the following formats: remove bullets, grow font, shrink font, art page borders, decorative underline(s), picture bullets, picture border shading, shadow picture effects, and color saturation and tone.
2. Remove the bullet from the paragraph below the picture.

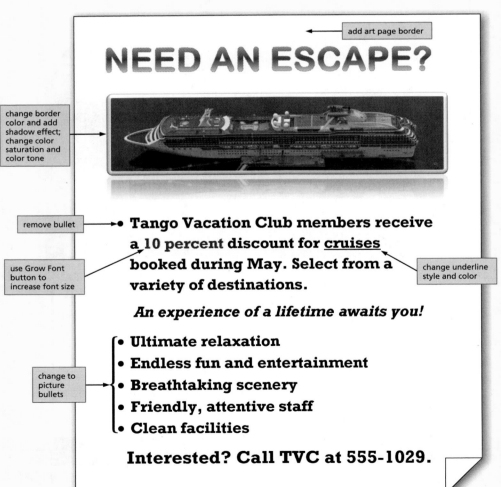

3. Select the text, 10 percent, and use the Grow Font button to increase its font size.
4. Add an art page border to the flyer. If the border is not in color, add color to it.
5. Change the solid underline below the word, cruises, to a decorative underline. Change the color of the underline.
6. Change the style of the bullets to picture bullet(s).
7. Change the color of the picture border. Add a shadow picture effect to the picture.
8. Change the color saturation and color tone of the picture.
9. Change the document properties, including keywords, as specified by your instructor. Save the revised document with a new file name and then submit it in the format specified by your instructor.

Figure 1–76

Make It Right

Analyze a document and correct all errors and/or improve the design.

Correcting Spelling and Grammar Errors

Note: To complete this assignment, you will be required to use the Data Files for Students. See the inside back cover of this book for instructions on downloading the Data Files for Students, or contact your instructor for information about accessing the required files.

Instructions: Start Word. Open the document, Make It Right 1-1 Karate Academy Flyer Unchecked, from the Data Files for Students. The document is a flyer that contains spelling and grammar errors, as shown in Figure 1–77. You are to correct each spelling (red wavy underline) and grammar error (green and blue wavy underlines) by right-clicking the flagged text and then clicking the appropriate correction on the shortcut menu.

If your screen does not display the wavy underlines, click File on the Ribbon and then click Options in the Backstage view. When the Word Options dialog box is displayed, click Proofing in the left pane, be sure the 'Hide spelling errors in this document only' and 'Hide grammar errors in this document only' check boxes do not contain check marks, and then click the OK button. If your screen still does not display the wavy underlines, redisplay the Word Options dialog box, click Proofing, and then click the Recheck Document button.

Change the document properties, including keywords, as specified by your instructor. Save the revised document with the name, Make It Right 1-1 Karate Academy Flyer, and then submit it in the format specified by your instructor.

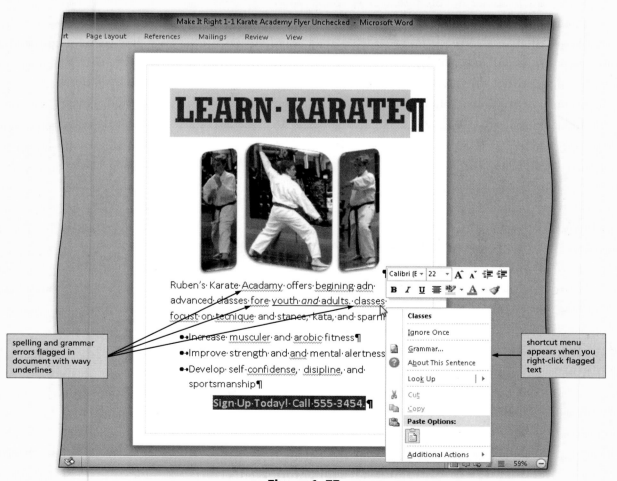

Figure 1–77

In the Lab

Design and/or create a document using the guidelines, concepts, and skills presented in this chapter. Labs are listed in order of increasing difficulty.

Lab 1: Creating a Flyer with a Picture

Problem: As a part-time employee in the Student Services Center at school, you have been asked to prepare a flyer that advertises study habits classes. First, you prepare the unformatted flyer shown in Figure 1–78a, and then you format it so that it looks like Figure 1–78b. *Hint:* Remember, if you make a mistake while formatting the flyer, you can click the Undo button on the Quick Access Toolbar to undo your last action.

Note: To complete this assignment, you will be required to use the Data Files for Students. See the inside back cover of this book for instructions on downloading the Data Files for Students, or contact your instructor for information about accessing the required files.

Instructions: Perform the following tasks:
1. Start Word. Display formatting marks on the screen.
2. Type the flyer text, unformatted, as shown in Figure 1–78a, inserting a blank line between the headline and the body copy. If Word flags any misspelled words as you type, check their spelling and correct them.
3. Save the document using the file name, Lab 1-1 Study Habits Flyer.
4. Center the headline and the signature line.
5. Change the theme colors to Concourse.
6. Change the font size of the headline to 36 point and the font to Ravie, or a similar font. Apply the text effect called Gradient Fill – Dark Red, Accent 6, Inner Shadow.
7. Change the font size of body copy between the headline and the signature line to 20 point.
8. Change the font size of the signature line to 22 point. Bold the text in the signature line.

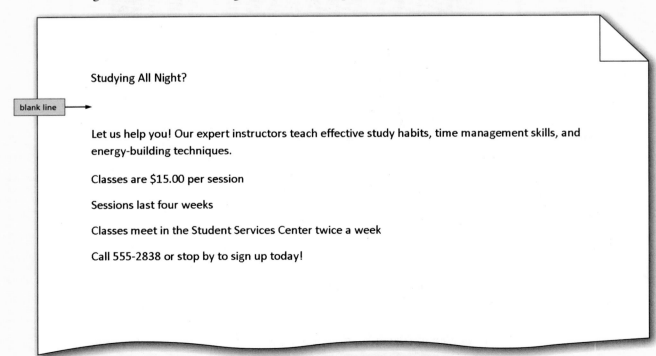

Figure 1–78 (a) Unformatted Flyer

9. Change the font of the body copy and signature line to Rockwell, and change the color of the signature line to Dark Red, Accent 6.

10. Bullet the three lines (paragraphs) of text above the signature line.

11. Bold and capitalize the text, Let us help you!, and change its color to Dark Red, Accent 6.

12. Italicize the word, or, in the signature line.

13. Underline the text, Student Services Center, in the third bulleted paragraph.

14. Change the zoom so that the entire page is visible in the document window.

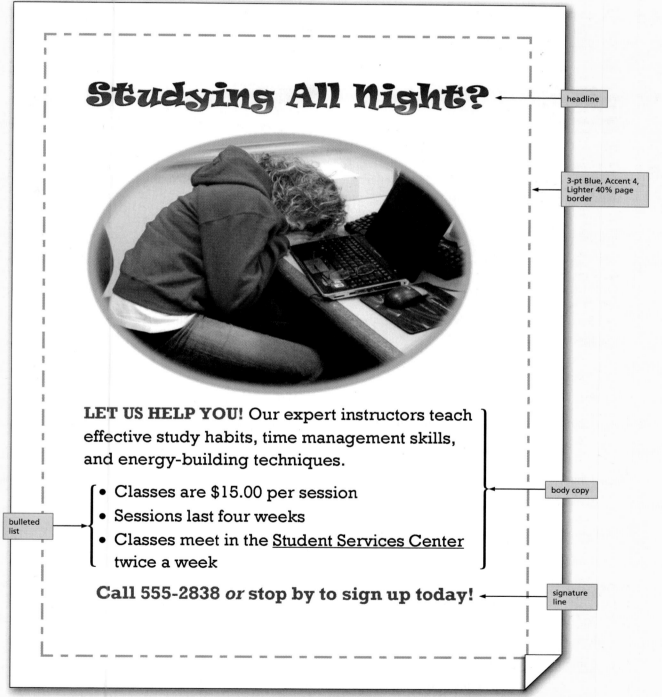

Figure 1–78 (b) Formatted Flyer

Continued >

In the Lab *continued*

15. Insert the picture centered on a blank line below the headline. The picture is called Sleeping and is available on the Data Files for Students.

16. Apply the Soft Edge Oval picture style to the inserted picture. Apply the glow effect called Blue, 5 pt glow, Accent color 4 to the picture.

17. The entire flyer should fit on a single page. If it flows to two pages, resize the picture or decrease spacing before and after paragraphs until the entire flyer text fits on a single page.

18. Add the page border shown in Figure 1–78b on the previous page.

19. Change the document properties, including keywords, as specified by your instructor. Save the flyer again with the same file name. Submit the document, shown in Figure 1–78b, in the format specified by your instructor.

In the Lab

Lab 2: Creating a Flyer with a Resized Picture

Problem: Your boss at Granger Camera House has asked you to prepare a flyer that announces the upcoming photography contest. You prepare the flyer shown in Figure 1–79. *Hint:* Remember, if you make a mistake while formatting the flyer, you can click the Undo button on the Quick Access Toolbar to undo your last action.

Note: To complete this assignment, you will be required to use the Data Files for Students. See the inside back cover of this book for instructions on downloading the Data Files for Students, or contact your instructor for information about accessing the required files.

Instructions: Perform the following tasks:

1. Start Word. Type the flyer text, unformatted. If Word flags any misspelled words as you type, check their spelling and correct them.

2. Save the document using the file name, Lab 1-2 Photography Contest Flyer.

3. Change the theme colors to the Apex color scheme.

4. Center the headline, the line that says RULES, and the signature line.

5. Change the font size of the headline to 36 point and the font to Stencil, or a similar font. Shade the headline paragraph Lavender, Background 2, Darker 50%. Apply the text effect called Fill – Lavender, Accent 6, Outline – Accent 6, Glow – Accent 6.

6. Change the font size of body copy between the headline and the signature line to 18 point.

7. Change the font size of the signature line to 24 point and the font to Stencil. Bold the text in the signature line. Change the font color of the text in the signature line to Gray-50%, Text 2.

8. Bullet the three paragraphs of text above the signature line.

9. Italicize the word, not.

10. Bold the word, landscape.

11. Underline the text, August 31.

12. Shade the line that says RULES to the Gray-50%, Text 2 color. If the font color does not automatically change to a lighter color, change it to White, Background 1.

13. Change the zoom so that the entire page is visible in the document window.

14. Insert the picture on a blank line below the headline. The picture is called Wind Power and is available on the Data Files for Students.

15. Resize the picture so that it is approximately 3.5" × 5.25". Apply the Rotated, White picture style to the inserted picture. Apply the glow effect called Lavender, 5 pt glow, Accent color 6 to the picture.

16. The entire flyer should fit on a single page. If it flows to two pages, resize the picture or decrease spacing before and after paragraphs until the entire flyer text fits on a single page.

17. Add the page border shown in Figure 1–79.

18. Change the document properties, including keywords, as specified by your instructor. Save the flyer again with the same file name. Submit the document, shown in Figure 1–79, in the format specified by your instructor.

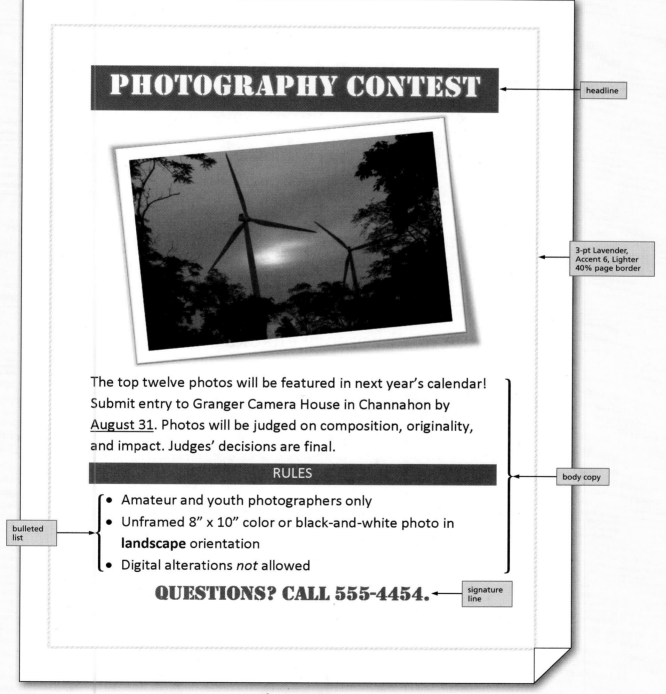

Figure 1–79

In the Lab

Lab 3: Creating a Flyer with Pictures

Problem: Your boss at Warner Depot has asked you to prepare a flyer that advertises its scenic train ride. You prepare the flyer shown in Figure 1–80.

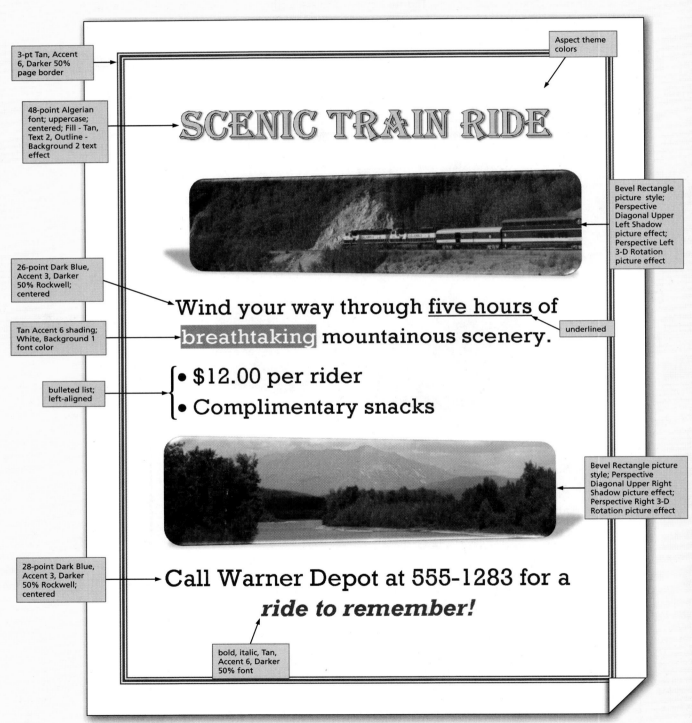

Figure 1–80

Note: To complete this assignment, you will be required to use the Data Files for Students. See the inside back cover of this book for instructions on downloading the Data Files for Students, or contact your instructor for information about accessing the required files.

Instructions: Start Word. Enter the text in the flyer, checking spelling as you type, and then format it as shown in Figure 1–80. The pictures to be inserted are called Train and Scenery and are available on the Data Files for Students. Adjust spacing before and after paragraphs and resize pictures as necessary so that the flyer fits on a single page.

Change the document properties, including keywords, as specified by your instructor. Save the document using the file name, Lab 1-3 Train Ride Flyer. Submit the document, shown in Figure 1–80, in the format specified by your instructor.

Cases and Places

Apply your creative thinking and problem solving skills to design and implement a solution.

Note: To complete these assignments, you may be required to use the Data Files for Students. See the inside back cover of this book for instructions on downloading the Data Files for Students, or contact your instructor for information about accessing the required files.

1: Design and Create a Spring Break Flyer

Academic

As secretary of your school's Student Government Association, you are responsible for creating and distributing flyers for spring break group outings. This year, you have planned a trip to Settlers Resort. The flyer should contain two digital pictures appropriately resized; the Data Files for Students contains two pictures called Cabin 1 and Cabin 2, or you can use your own digital pictures if they are appropriate for the topic of the flyer. The flyer should contain the headline, Feeling Adventurous?, and this signature line: Call Lyn at 555-9901 to sign up. The body copy consists of the following, in any order: Spring Break – Blast to the Past. Settlers Resort is like a page right out of a history textbook! Spend five days living in the 1800s. The bulleted list in the body copy is as follows: One-room cabins with potbelly stoves, Campfire dining with authentic meals, and Horseback riding and much more.

Use the concepts and techniques presented in this chapter to create and format this flyer. Be sure to check spelling and grammar. Submit your assignment in the format specified by your instructor.

2: Design and Create a Yard Sale Flyer

Personal

You are planning a yard sale and would like to create and post flyers around town advertising the upcoming sale. The flyer should contain two digital pictures appropriately resized; the Data Files for Students contains two pictures called Yard Sale 1 and Yard Sale 2, or you can use your own digital pictures if they are appropriate for the topic of the flyer. The flyer should contain the headline, Yard Sale!, and this signature line: Questions? Call 555-9820. The body copy consists of the following, in any order: Hundreds of items for sale. After 20 years, we are moving to a smaller house and are selling anything that won't fit. Everything for sale must go! The bulleted list in the body copy is as follows: When: August 7, 8, 9 from 9:00 a.m. to 7:00 p.m.; Where: 139 Ravel Boulevard; and What: something for everyone – from clothing to collectibles.

Use the concepts and techniques presented in this chapter to create and format this flyer. Be sure to check spelling and grammar. Submit your assignment in the format specified by your instructor.

Continued >

Cases and Places *continued*

3: Design and Create a Village Fireworks Flyer

Professional

As a part-time employee at the Village of Crestwood, your boss has asked you to create and distribute flyers for the upcoming fireworks extravaganza. The flyer should contain two digital pictures appropriately resized; the Data Files for Students contains two pictures called Fireworks 1 and Fireworks 2, or you can use your own digital pictures if they are appropriate for the topic of the flyer. The flyer should contain the headline, Light Up The Sky, and this signature line: Call 555-2983 with questions. The body copy consists of the following, in any order: Join Us! The Village of Crestwood will present its tenth annual Light Up The Sky fireworks extravaganza on August 8 at 9:00 p.m. during the end of summer celebration in Douglas Park. The bulleted list in the body copy is as follows: Pork chop dinners will be sold for $3.00 beginning at 6:00 p.m., Bring chairs and blankets, and Admission is free.

Use the concepts and techniques presented in this chapter to create and format this flyer. Be sure to check spelling and grammar. Submit your assignment in the format specified by your instructor.

2 | Creating a Research Paper with Citations and References

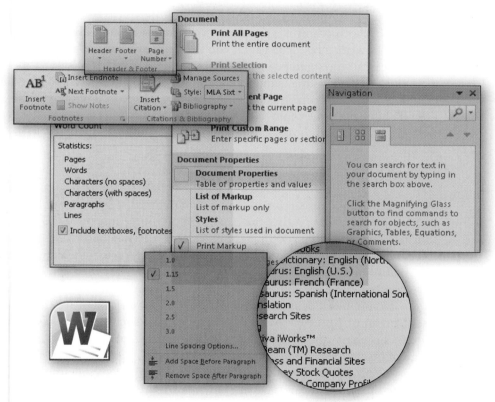

Objectives

You will have mastered the material in this chapter when you can:

- Describe the MLA documentation style for research papers
- Change line and paragraph spacing in a document
- Modify a style
- Use a header to number pages of a document
- Apply formatting using shortcut keys
- Modify paragraph indentation

- Insert and edit citations and their sources
- Add a footnote to a document
- Insert a manual page break
- Create a bibliographical list of sources
- Cut, copy, and paste text
- Find text and replace text
- Find a synonym
- Use the Research task pane to look up information

2 Creating a Research Paper with Citations and References

Introduction

In both academic and business environments, you will be asked to write reports. Business reports range from proposals to cost justifications to five-year plans to research findings. Academic reports focus mostly on research findings.

A **research paper** is a document you can use to communicate the results of research findings. To write a research paper, you learn about a particular topic from a variety of sources (research), organize your ideas from the research results, and then present relevant facts and/or opinions that support the topic. Your final research paper combines properly credited outside information along with personal insights. Thus, no two research papers — even if about the same topic — will or should be the same.

Project — Research Paper

When preparing a research paper, you should follow a standard documentation style that defines the rules for creating the paper and crediting sources. A variety of documentation styles exists, depending on the nature of the research paper. Each style requires the same basic information; the differences in styles relate to requirements for presenting the information. For example, one documentation style uses the term bibliography for the list of sources, whereas another uses references, and yet a third prefers the title works cited. Two popular documentation styles for research papers are the **Modern Language Association of America** (**MLA**) and **American Psychological Association** (**APA**) styles. This chapter uses the MLA documentation style because it is used in a wide range of disciplines.

The project in this chapter follows research paper guidelines and uses Word to create the short research paper shown in Figure 2–1. This paper, which discusses triangulation, follows the MLA documentation style. Each page contains a page number. The first two pages present the name and course information (student name, instructor name, course name, and paper due date), paper title, an introduction with a thesis statement, details that support the thesis, and a conclusion. This section of the paper also includes references to research sources and a footnote. The third page contains a detailed, alphabetical list of the sources referenced in the research paper. All pages include a header at the upper-right edge of the page.

BTW

APA Appendix
If your version of this book includes the Word APA Appendix and you are required to create a research paper using the APA documentation style instead of the MLA documentation style, the appendix shows the steps required to create the research paper in this chapter using the APA guidelines. If your version of this book does not include the Word APA Appendix, see print publications or search the Web for the APA guidelines.

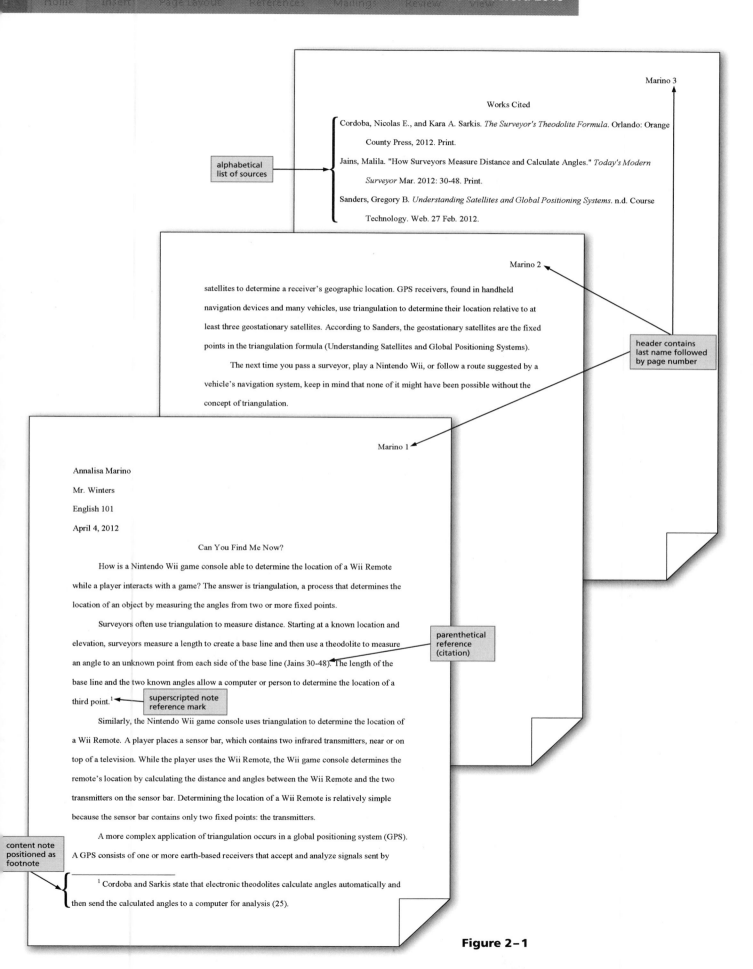

alphabetical list of sources

Marino 3

Works Cited

Cordoba, Nicolas E., and Kara A. Sarkis. *The Surveyor's Theodolite Formula*. Orlando: Orange County Press, 2012. Print.

Jains, Malila. "How Surveyors Measure Distance and Calculate Angles." *Today's Modern Surveyor* Mar. 2012: 30-48. Print.

Sanders, Gregory B. *Understanding Satellites and Global Positioning Systems*. n.d. Course Technology. Web. 27 Feb. 2012.

Marino 2

satellites to determine a receiver's geographic location. GPS receivers, found in handheld navigation devices and many vehicles, use triangulation to determine their location relative to at least three geostationary satellites. According to Sanders, the geostationary satellites are the fixed points in the triangulation formula (Understanding Satellites and Global Positioning Systems).

The next time you pass a surveyor, play a Nintendo Wii, or follow a route suggested by a vehicle's navigation system, keep in mind that none of it might have been possible without the concept of triangulation.

header contains last name followed by page number

Marino 1

Annalisa Marino

Mr. Winters

English 101

April 4, 2012

Can You Find Me Now?

How is a Nintendo Wii game console able to determine the location of a Wii Remote while a player interacts with a game? The answer is triangulation, a process that determines the location of an object by measuring the angles from two or more fixed points.

Surveyors often use triangulation to measure distance. Starting at a known location and elevation, surveyors measure a length to create a base line and then use a theodolite to measure an angle to an unknown point from each side of the base line (Jains 30-48). The length of the base line and the two known angles allow a computer or person to determine the location of a third point.[1]

parenthetical reference (citation)

superscripted note reference mark

Similarly, the Nintendo Wii game console uses triangulation to determine the location of a Wii Remote. A player places a sensor bar, which contains two infrared transmitters, near or on top of a television. While the player uses the Wii Remote, the Wii game console determines the remote's location by calculating the distance and angles between the Wii Remote and the two transmitters on the sensor bar. Determining the location of a Wii Remote is relatively simple because the sensor bar contains only two fixed points: the transmitters.

A more complex application of triangulation occurs in a global positioning system (GPS). A GPS consists of one or more earth-based receivers that accept and analyze signals sent by

content note positioned as footnote

[1] Cordoba and Sarkis state that electronic theodolites calculate angles automatically and then send the calculated angles to a computer for analysis (25).

Figure 2–1

Overview

As you read through this chapter, you will learn how to create the research paper shown in Figure 2–1 on the previous page by performing these general tasks:

- Change the document settings.
- Type the research paper.
- Save the research paper.
- Create an alphabetical list of sources.
- Proof and revise the research paper.
- Print the research paper.

Plan Ahead

General Project Guidelines

When creating a Word document, the actions you perform and decisions you make will affect the appearance and characteristics of the finished document. As you create a research paper, such as the project shown in Figure 2–1, you should follow these general guidelines:

1. **Select a topic.** Spend time brainstorming ideas for a topic. Choose one you find interesting. For shorter papers, narrow the scope of the topic; for longer papers, broaden the scope. Identify a tentative thesis statement, which is a sentence describing the paper's subject matter.

2. **Research the topic and take notes.** Gather credible, relevant information about the topic that supports the thesis statement. Sources of research include books, magazines, newspapers, and the Internet. As you record facts and ideas, list details about the source: title, author, place of publication, publisher, date of publication, etc. When taking notes, be careful not to **plagiarize**. That is, do not use someone else's work and claim it to be your own. If you copy information directly, place it in quotation marks and identify its source.

3. **Organize your ideas.** Classify your notes into related concepts. Make an outline from the categories of notes. In the outline, identify all main ideas and supporting details.

4. **Write the first draft, referencing sources.** From the outline, compose the paper. Every research paper should include an introduction containing the thesis statement, supporting details, and a conclusion. Follow the guidelines identified in the required documentation style. Reference all sources of information.

5. **Create the list of sources.** Using the formats specified in the required documentation style, completely list all sources referenced in the body of the research paper in alphabetical order.

6. **Proofread and revise the paper.** If possible, proofread the paper with a fresh set of eyes, that is, at least one to two days after completing the first draft. Proofreading involves reading the paper with the intent of identifying errors (spelling, grammar, etc.) and looking for ways to improve the paper (wording, transitions, flow, etc.). Try reading the paper out loud, which helps to identify unclear or awkward wording. Ask someone else to proofread the paper and give you suggestions for improvements.

When necessary, more specific details concerning the above guidelines are presented at appropriate points in the chapter. The chapter also will identify the actions performed and decisions made regarding these guidelines during the creation of the research paper shown in Figure 2–1.

MLA Documentation Style

The research paper in this project follows the guidelines presented by the MLA. To follow the MLA documentation style, use 12-point Times New Roman, or a similar, font. Double-space text on all pages of the paper using one-inch top, bottom, left, and right margins. Indent the first word of each paragraph one-half inch from the left margin. At the right margin of each page, place a page number one-half inch from the top margin. On each page, precede the page number by your last name.

The MLA documentation style does not require a title page. Instead, place your name and course information in a block at the left margin beginning one inch from the top of the page. Center the title one double-spaced line below your name and course information.

In the text of the paper, place author references in parentheses with the page number(s) of the referenced information. The MLA documentation style uses in-text **parenthetical references** instead of noting each source at the bottom of the page or at the end of the paper. In the MLA documentation style, notes are used only for optional content or bibliographic notes.

If used, content notes elaborate on points discussed in the paper, and bibliographic notes direct the reader to evaluations of statements in a source or provide a means for identifying multiple sources. Use a superscript (raised number) both to signal that a note exists and to sequence the notes (shown in Figure 2-1 on page WD 67). Position notes at the bottom of the page as footnotes or at the end of the paper as endnotes. Indent the first line of each note one-half inch from the left margin. Place one space following the superscripted number before beginning the note text. Double-space the note text (shown in Figure 2–1).

The MLA documentation style uses the term **works cited** to refer to the bibliographic list of sources at the end of the paper. The works cited page alphabetically lists sources that are referenced directly in the paper. Place the list of sources on a separate numbered page. Center the title, Works Cited, one inch from the top margin. Double-space all lines. Begin the first line of each source at the left margin, indenting subsequent lines of the same source one-half inch from the left margin. List each source by the author's last name, or, if the author's name is not available, by the title of the source.

BTW

APA Documentation Style
In the APA documentation style, a separate title page is required instead of placing name and course information on the paper's first page. Double-space all pages of the paper with one-inch top, bottom, left, and right margins. Indent the first word of each paragraph one-half inch from the left margin. In the upper-right margin of each page, including the title page, place a running head that consists of the page number preceded by a brief summary of the paper title.

Changing Document Settings

The MLA documentation style defines some global formats that apply to the entire research paper. Some of these formats are the default in Word. For example, the default left, right, top, and bottom margin settings in Word are one inch, which meets the MLA documentation style. You will modify, however, the font, font size, line and paragraph spacing, and header formats as required by the MLA documentation style.

To Start Word

If you are using a computer to step through the project in this chapter and you want your screens to match the figures in this book, you should change your screen's resolution to 1024 × 768. For information about how to change a computer's resolution, refer to the Office 2010 and Windows 7 chapter at the beginning of this book.

For an introduction to Windows 7 and instruction about how to perform basic Windows 7 tasks, read the Office 2010 and Windows 7 chapter at the beginning of this book, where you can learn how to resize windows, change screen resolution, create folders, move and rename files, use Windows Help, and much more.

BTW

New Document Window
If you wanted to open a new blank document window, you could press CTRL+N or click File on the Ribbon to open the Backstage view, click the New tab to display the New gallery, click the Blank document button, and then click the Create button.

The following steps, which assume Windows 7 is running, start Word based on a typical installation. You may need to ask your instructor how to start Word for your computer. For a detailed example of the procedure summarized below, refer to the Office 2010 and Windows 7 chapter.

1 Click the Start button on the Windows 7 taskbar to display the Start menu.

2 Type **Microsoft Word** as the search text in the 'Search programs and files' text box and watch the search results appear on the Start menu.

3 Click Microsoft Word 2010 in the search results on the Start menu to start Word and display a new blank document in the Word window.

4 If the Word window is not maximized, click the Maximize button next to the Close button on its title bar to maximize the window.

5 If the Print Layout button on the status bar is not selected (shown in Figure 2–2), click it so that your screen is in Print Layout view.

6 If Normal (Home tab | Styles group) is not selected in the Quick Style gallery (shown in Figure 2–2), click it so that your document uses the Normal style.

7 If your zoom percent is not 100, click the Zoom Out or Zoom In button as many times as necessary until the Zoom button displays 100% on its face (shown in Figure 2–2).

BTW

Style Formats
To see the formats assigned to a particular style in a document, click the Styles Dialog Box Launcher (Home tab | Styles group) and then click the Style Inspector button in the Styles task pane. Position the insertion point in the style in the document and then point to the Paragraph formatting or Text level formatting areas in the Style Inspector task pane to display an Enhanced ScreenTip describing formats assigned to the location of the insertion point. You also can click the Reveal Formatting button in the Style Inspector task pane to display the Reveal Formatting task pane.

To Display Formatting Marks

As discussed in Chapter 1, it is helpful to display formatting marks that indicate where in the document you press the ENTER key, SPACEBAR, and other keys. The following steps display formatting marks.

1 If the Home tab is not the active tab, click Home on the Ribbon to display the Home tab.

2 If the Show/Hide ¶ button (Home tab | Paragraph group) is not selected already, click it to display formatting marks on the screen.

Styles

When you create a document, Word formats the text using a particular style. A **style** is a named group of formatting characteristics, including font and font size. The default style in Word is called the **Normal style**, which most likely uses 11-point Calibri font. If you do not specify a style for text you type, Word applies the Normal style to the text. In addition to the Normal style, Word has many other built-in, or predefined, styles that you can use to format text. Styles make it easy to apply many formats at once to text. You can modify existing styles and create your own styles. Styles are discussed as they are used in this book.

To Modify a Style

The MLA documentation style requires that all text in the research paper use 12-point Times New Roman, or a similar, font. If you change the font and font size using buttons on the Ribbon, you will need to make the change many times during the course of creating the paper because Word formats different areas of a document using the Normal style, which uses 11-point Calibri font. For example, body text, headers, and bibliographies all display text based on the Normal style. Thus, instead of changing the font and font size for each of these document elements, a more efficient technique would be to change the Normal style for this document to 12-point Times New Roman. By changing the Normal style, you ensure that all text in the document will use the format required by the MLA. The next steps change the Normal style.

1

- Right-click Normal in the Quick Style gallery (Home tab | Styles group) to display a shortcut menu related to styles (Figure 2–2).

Note: To help you locate screen elements that are referenced in the step instructions, such as buttons and commands, this book uses red boxes to point to these screen elements.

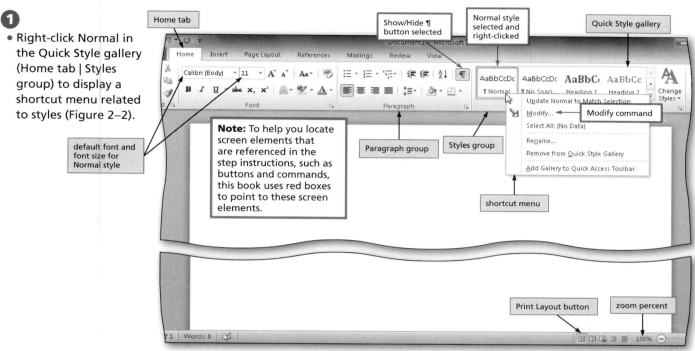

Home tab

Show/Hide ¶ button selected

Normal style selected and right-clicked

Quick Style gallery

default font and font size for Normal style

Paragraph group

Styles group

Modify command

shortcut menu

Print Layout button

zoom percent

Figure 2–2

2

- Click Modify on the shortcut menu to display the Modify Style dialog box (Figure 2–3).

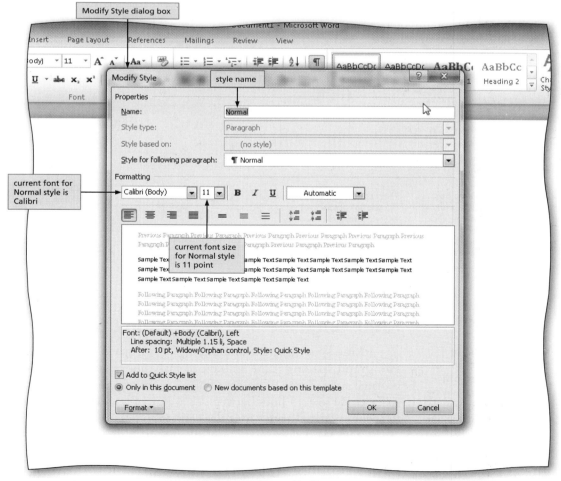

Modify Style dialog box

style name

current font for Normal style is Calibri

current font size for Normal style is 11 point

Figure 2–3

3

- Click the Font box arrow (Modify Style dialog box) to display the Font list. Scroll to and then click Times New Roman in the list to change the font for the style being modified.

- Click the Font Size box arrow (Modify Style dialog box) and then click 12 in the Font Size list to change the font size for the style being modified.

- Ensure that the 'Only in this document' option button is selected (Figure 2–4).

Q&A

Will all future documents use the new font and font size?

No, because the 'Only in this document' option button is selected. If you want all future documents to use a new setting, you would select the 'New documents based on this template' option button.

4

- Click the OK button (Modify Style dialog box) to update the Normal style to the specified settings.

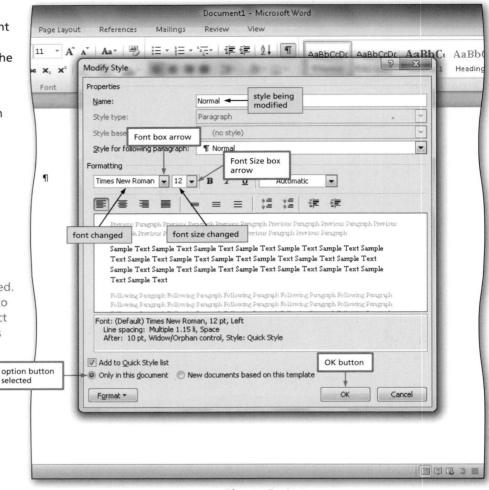

Figure 2–4

Other Ways

1. Click Styles Dialog Box Launcher, click box arrow next to style name, click Modify on menu, change settings (Modify Style dialog box), click OK button

2. Press ALT+CTRL+SHIFT+S, click box arrow next to style name, click Modify on menu, change settings (Modify Style dialog box), click OK button

---

Adjusting Line and Paragraph Spacing

Line spacing is the amount of vertical space between lines of text in a paragraph. **Paragraph spacing** is the amount of space above and below a paragraph. By default, the Normal style places 10 points of blank space after each paragraph and inserts a vertical space equal to 1.15 lines between each line of text. It also automatically adjusts line height to accommodate various font sizes and graphics.

The MLA documentation style requires that you **double-space** the entire research paper. That is, the amount of vertical space between each line of text and above and below paragraphs should be equal to one blank line. The next sets of steps adjust line spacing and paragraph spacing according to the MLA documentation style.

To Change Line Spacing

The lines of the research paper should be double-spaced, according to the MLA documentation style. In Word, you change the line spacing to 2.0 to double-space lines in a paragraph. The following steps change the line spacing to double.

1

- Click the Line and Paragraph Spacing button (Home tab | Paragraph group) to display the Line and Paragraph Spacing gallery (Figure 2–5).

Q&A

What do the numbers in the Line and Paragraph Spacing gallery represent?

The default line spacing is 1.15 lines. The options 1.0, 2.0, and 3.0 set line spacing to single, double, and triple, respectively. Similarly, the 1.5 and 2.5 options set line spacing to 1.5 and 2.5 lines. All these options adjust line spacing automatically to accommodate the largest font or graphic on a line.

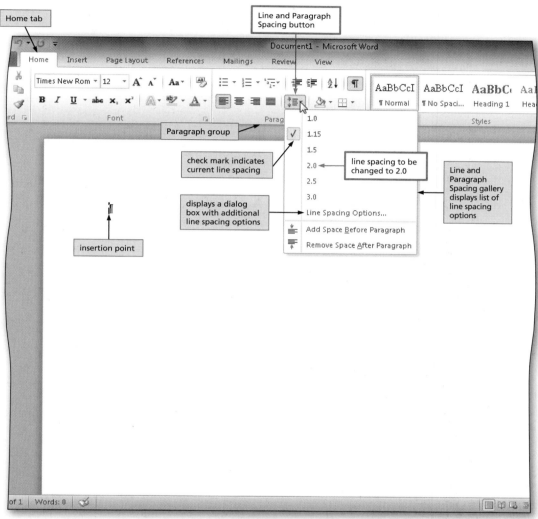

Figure 2–5

2

- Click 2.0 in the Line and Paragraph Spacing gallery to change the line spacing at the location of the insertion point.

Q&A

Can I change the line spacing of existing text?

Yes. Select the text first and then change the line spacing as described in these steps.

Other Ways

1. Right-click paragraph, click Paragraph on shortcut menu, click Indents and Spacing tab (Paragraph dialog box), click Line spacing box arrow, click desired spacing, click OK button

2. Click Paragraph Dialog Box Launcher (Home

tab or Page Layout tab | Paragraph group), click Indents and Spacing tab (Paragraph dialog box), click Line spacing box arrow, click desired spacing, click OK button

3. Press CTRL+2 for double-spacing

To Remove Space after a Paragraph

The research paper should not have additional blank space after each paragraph. The following steps remove space after a paragraph.

1
- Click the Line and Paragraph Spacing button (Home tab | Paragraph group) to display the Line and Paragraph Spacing gallery (Figure 2–6).

2
- Click Remove Space After Paragraph in the Line and Paragraph Spacing gallery so that no blank space appears after paragraphs.

Q&A

Can I remove space after existing paragraphs?

Yes. Select the paragraphs first and then remove the space as described in these steps.

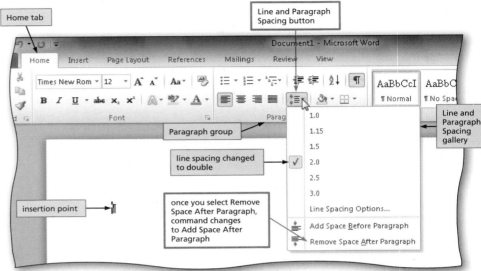

Figure 2–6

Other Ways

1. Click Spacing After box arrows (Page Layout tab | Paragraph group) until 0 pt is displayed

2. Right-click paragraph, click Paragraph on shortcut menu, click

Indents and Spacing tab (Paragraph dialog box), click After box arrows until 0 pt is displayed, click OK button

3. Click Paragraph Dialog Box Launcher (Home

tab or Page Layout tab | Paragraph group), click Indents and Spacing tab (Paragraph dialog box), click After box arrows until 0 pt is displayed, click OK button

To Update a Style to Match a Selection

To ensure that all paragraphs in the paper will be double-spaced and do not have space after the paragraphs, you want the Normal style to include the line and paragraph spacing changes made in the previous two sets of steps. You can update a style to reflect the settings of the location of the insertion point or selected text. Because no text has yet been typed in the research paper, you do not need to select text prior to updating the Normal style. The following steps update the Normal style.

1
- Right-click Normal in the Quick Style gallery (Home tab | Styles group) to display a shortcut menu (Figure 2–7).

2
- Click Update Normal to Match Selection on the shortcut menu to update the selected (or current) style to reflect the settings at the location of the insertion point.

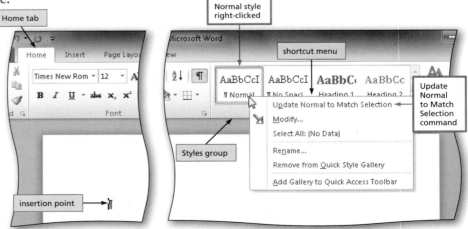

Figure 2–7

Other Ways

1. Right-click text, point to Styles on shortcut menu, click Update [style name] to Match Selection on submenu

Headers and Footers

A **header** is text and graphics that print at the top of each page in a document. Similarly, a **footer** is text and graphics that print at the bottom of every page. In Word, headers print in the top margin one-half inch from the top of every page, and footers print in the bottom margin one-half inch from the bottom of each page, which meets the MLA documentation style. In addition to text and graphics, headers and footers can include document information such as the page number, current date, current time, and author's name.

In this research paper, you are to precede the page number with your last name placed one-half inch from the upper-right edge of each page. The procedures on the following pages enter your name and the page number in the header, as specified by the MLA documentation style.

BTW

The Ribbon and Screen Resolution
Word may change how the groups and buttons within the groups appear on the Ribbon, depending on the computer's screen resolution. Thus, your Ribbon may look different from the ones in this book if you are using a screen resolution other than 1024 x 768.

To Switch to the Header

To enter text in the header, you instruct Word to edit the header. The following steps switch from editing the document text to editing the header.

1

- Click Insert on the Ribbon to display the Insert tab.

- Click the Header button (Insert tab | Header & Footer group) to display the Header gallery (Figure 2–8).

Q&A

Can I use a built-in header for this research paper?

None of the built-in headers adheres to the MLA documentation style. Thus, you enter your own header content, instead of using a built-in header, for this research paper.

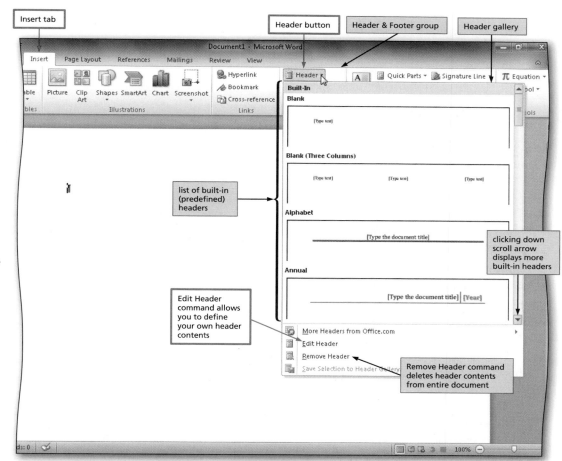

Figure 2–8

Q&A

How would I remove a header from a document?

You would click Remove Header in the Header gallery (shown in Figure 2–8). Similarly, to remove a footer, you would click Remove Footer in the Footer gallery.

 **Experiment**

- Click the down scroll arrow in the Header gallery to see the available built-in headers.

2

- Click Edit Header in the Header gallery to switch from the document text to the header, which allows you to edit the contents of the header (Figure 2–9).

Q&A

How do I remove the Header & Footer Tools Design tab from the Ribbon?

When you are finished editing the header, you will close it, which removes the Header & Footer Tools Design tab.

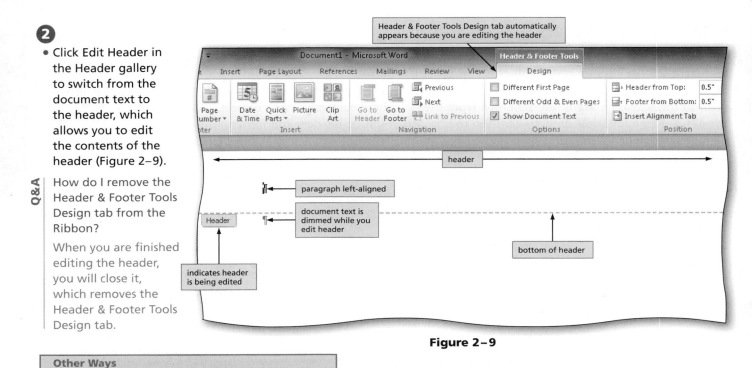

Figure 2–9

Other Ways	
1. Double-click dimmed header	2. Right-click header in document, click Edit Header button that appears

To Right-Align a Paragraph

The paragraph in the header currently is left-aligned (Figure 2–9). Your last name and the page number should print **right-aligned**, that is, at the right margin. The following step right-aligns a paragraph.

1

- Click Home on the Ribbon to display the Home tab.

- Click the Align Text Right button (Home tab | Paragraph group) to right-align the current paragraph (Figure 2–10).

Q&A

What if I wanted to return the paragraph to left-aligned?

Click the Align Text Right button again, or click the Align Text Left button.

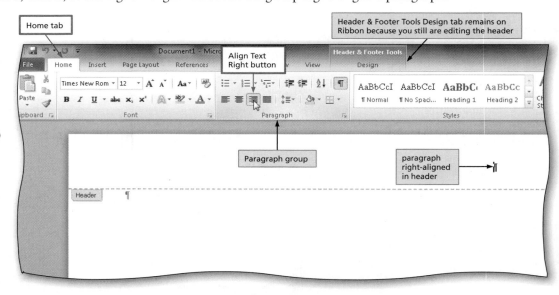

Figure 2–10

Other Ways		
1. Right-click paragraph, click Paragraph on shortcut menu, click Indents and Spacing tab (Paragraph dialog box), click Alignment box arrow, click Right, click OK button	2. Click Paragraph Dialog Box Launcher (Home tab or Page Layout tab | Paragraph group), click Indents and Spacing tab (Paragraph dialog box),	click Alignment box arrow, click Right, click OK button 3. Press CTRL+R

To Enter Text

The following steps enter your last name right-aligned in the header area.

1 Click Design on the Ribbon to display the Header & Footer Tools Design tab.

2 Type **Marino** and then press the SPACEBAR to enter the last name in the header.

BTW

Footers
If you wanted to create a footer, you would click the Footer button (Insert tab | Header & Footer group) and then select the desired built-in footer or click Edit Footer to create a customized footer; you also could double-click the dimmed footer, or right-click the footer and then click the Edit Footer button that appears.

To Insert a Page Number

The next task is to insert the current page number in the header. The following steps insert a page number at the location of the insertion point.

1

• Click the Insert Page Number button (Header & Footer Tools Design tab | Header & Footer group) to display the Insert Page Number menu.

• Point to Current Position on the Insert Page Number menu to display the Current Position gallery (Figure 2–11).

Experiment

• Click the down scroll arrow in the Current Position gallery to see the available page number formats.

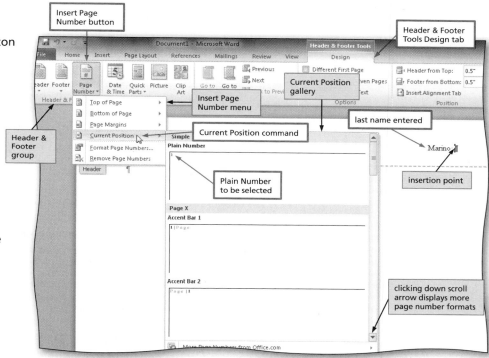

Figure 2–11

2

• If necessary, scroll to the top of the Current Position gallery. Click Plain Number in the Current Position gallery to insert an unformatted page number at the location of the insertion point (Figure 2–12).

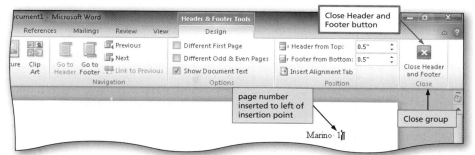

Figure 2–12

Other Ways		
1. Click Insert Page Number button (Insert tab | Header & Footer group)	2. Click Quick Parts button (Insert tab | Text group or Header & Footer Tools Design tab | Insert group),	click Field on Quick Parts menu, select Page in Field names list (Field dialog box), click OK button

To Close the Header

You are finished entering text in the header. Thus, the next task is to switch back to the document text. The following step closes the header.

- Click the Close Header and Footer button (Header & Footer Tools Design tab | Close group) (shown in Figure 2–12 on the previous page) to close the header and switch back to the document text (Figure 2–13).

Q&A

How do I make changes to existing header text?

Switch to the header using the steps described on pages WD 75 and WD 76, edit the header as you would edit text in the document window, and then switch back to the document text.

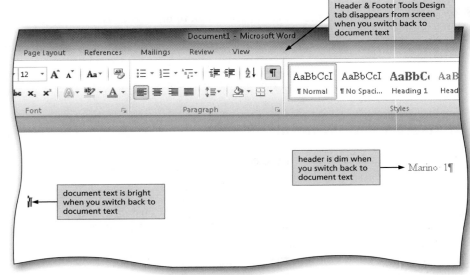

Figure 2–13

Other Ways

1. Double-click dimmed document text

Typing the Research Paper Text

The text of the research paper in this chapter encompasses the first two pages of the paper. You will type the text of the research paper and then modify it later in the chapter, so that it matches Figure 2–1 on page WD 67.

Plan Ahead

Write the first draft, referencing sources.
As you write the first draft of a research paper, be sure it includes the proper components, uses credible sources, and does not contain any plagiarized material.

- **Include an introduction, body, and conclusion.** The first paragraph of the paper introduces the topic and captures the reader's attention. The body, which follows the introduction, consists of several paragraphs that support the topic. The conclusion summarizes the main points in the body and restates the topic.

- **Evaluate sources for authority, currency, and accuracy.** Be especially wary of information obtained from the Web. Any person, company, or organization can publish a Web page on the Internet. Ask yourself these questions about the source:

  - Authority: Does a reputable institution or group support the source? Is the information presented without bias? Are the author's credentials listed and verifiable?

  - Currency: Is the information up to date? Are dates of sources listed? What is the last date revised or updated?

  - Accuracy: Is the information free of errors? Is it verifiable? Are the sources clearly identified?

(continued)

(continued)

Plan Ahead

- **Acknowledge all sources of information; do not plagiarize.** Not only is plagiarism unethical, but it is considered an academic crime that can have severe punishments such as failing a course or being expelled from school.

  When you summarize, paraphrase (rewrite information in your own words), present facts, give statistics, quote exact words, or show a map, chart, or other graphical image, you must acknowledge the source. Information that commonly is known or accessible to the audience constitutes common knowledge and does not need to be acknowledged. If, however, you question whether certain information is common knowledge, you should document it — just to be safe.

To Enter Name and Course Information

As discussed earlier in this chapter, the MLA documentation style does not require a separate title page for research papers. Instead, place your name and course information in a block at the top of the page, below the header, at the left margin. The following steps enter the name and course information in the research paper.

1 Type **Annalisa Marino** as the student name and then press the ENTER key.

2 Type **Mr. Winters** as the instructor name and then press the ENTER key.

3 Type **English 101** as the course name and then press the ENTER key.

4 Type **April 4, 2012** as the paper due date and then press the ENTER key (Figure 2–14).

BTW

Date Formats
The MLA documentation style prefers the day-month-year (4 April 2012) or month-day-year (April 4, 2012) format.

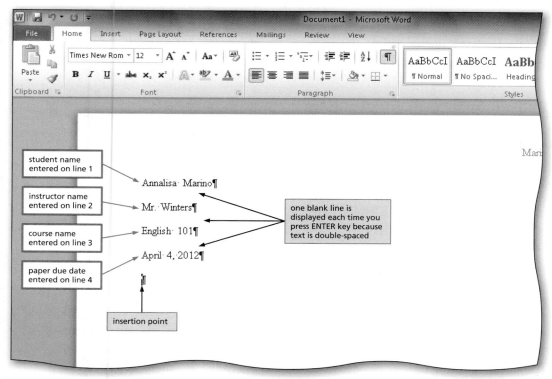

student name entered on line 1

instructor name entered on line 2

course name entered on line 3

paper due date entered on line 4

insertion point

one blank line is displayed each time you press ENTER key because text is double-spaced

Figure 2–14

To Click and Type

   The next step is to enter the title of the research paper centered between the page margins. In Chapter 1, you used the Center button (Home tab | Paragraph group) to center text and graphics. As an alternative, you can use Word's **Click and Type** feature to format and enter text, graphics, and other items. To use Click and Type, you double-click a blank area of the document window. Word automatically formats the item you type or insert according to the location where you double-clicked. The following steps use Click and Type to center and then type the title of the research paper.

Experiment

- Move the mouse pointer around the document below the entered name and course information and observe the various icons that appear with the I-beam.

- Position the mouse pointer in the center of the document at the approximate location for the research paper title until a center icon appears below the I-beam (Figure 2–15).

Q&A

What are the other icons that appear in the Click and Type pointer?

A left-align icon appears to the right of the I-beam when the Click and Type pointer is in certain locations on the left side of the document window. A right-align icon appears to the left of the I-beam when the Click and Type pointer is in certain locations on the right side of the document window.

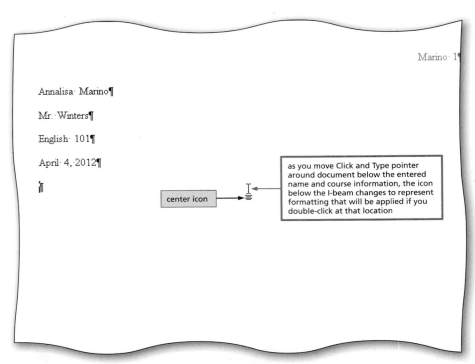

Figure 2–15

- Double-click to center the paragraph mark and insertion point between the left and right margins.

- Type `Can You Find Me Now?` as the paper title and then press the ENTER key to position the insertion point on the next line (Figure 2–16).

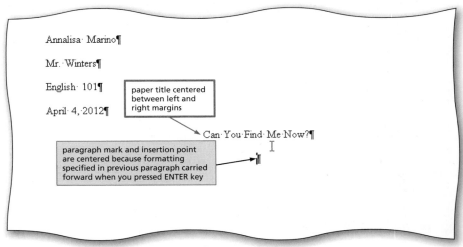

Figure 2–16

Shortcut Keys

Word has many **shortcut keys**, or keyboard key combinations, for your convenience while typing. Table 2–1 lists the common shortcut keys for formatting characters. Table 2–2 lists common shortcut keys for formatting paragraphs.

Table 2–1 Shortcut Keys for Formatting Characters

Character Formatting Task	Shortcut Keys	Character Formatting Task	Shortcut Keys
All capital letters	CTRL+SHIFT+A	Italic	CTRL+I
Bold	CTRL+B	Remove character formatting (plain text)	CTRL+SPACEBAR
Case of letters	SHIFT+F3	Small uppercase letters	CTRL+SHIFT+K
Decrease font size	CTRL+SHIFT+<	Subscript	CTRL+EQUAL SIGN
Decrease font size 1 point	CTRL+[	Superscript	CTRL+SHIFT+PLUS SIGN
Double-underline	CTRL+SHIFT+D	Underline	CTRL+U
Increase font size	CTRL+SHIFT+>	Underline words, not spaces	CTRL+SHIFT+W
Increase font size 1 point	CTRL+]		

Table 2–2 Shortcut Keys for Formatting Paragraphs

Paragraph Formatting	Shortcut Keys	Paragraph Formatting	Shortcut Keys
1.5 line spacing	CTRL+5	Justify paragraph	CTRL+J
Add/remove one line above paragraph	CTRL+0 (zero)	Left-align paragraph	CTRL+L
Center paragraph	CTRL+E	Remove hanging indent	CTRL+SHIFT+T
Decrease paragraph indent	CTRL+SHIFT+M	Remove paragraph formatting	CTRL+Q
Double-space lines	CTRL+2	Right-align paragraph	CTRL+R
Hanging indent	CTRL+T	Single-space lines	CTRL+1
Increase paragraph indent	CTRL+M		

To Format Text Using Shortcut Keys

The paragraphs below the paper title should be left-aligned, instead of centered. Thus, the next step is to left-align the paragraph below the paper title. When your fingers are already on the keyboard, you may prefer using shortcut keys to format text as you type it. The following step left-aligns a paragraph using the shortcut keys CTRL+L. (Recall from Chapter 1 that a notation such as CTRL+L means to press the letter L on the keyboard while holding down the CTRL key.)

1 Press CTRL+L to left-align the current paragraph, that is, the paragraph containing the insertion point (shown in Figure 2–17 on the next page).

Q&A Why would I use a keyboard shortcut instead of the Ribbon to format text?

Switching between the mouse and the keyboard takes time. If your hands are already on the keyboard, use a shortcut key. If your hand is on the mouse, use the Ribbon.

BTW

Shortcut Keys
To print a complete list of shortcut keys in Word, click the Microsoft Word Help button near the upper-right corner of the Word window, type **shortcut keys** in the 'Type words to search for' text box at the top of the Word Help window, press the ENTER key, click the Keyboard shortcuts for Microsoft Word link, click the Show All link in the upper-right corner of the Help window, click the Print button in the Help window, and then click the Print button in the Print dialog box.

an introduction
to Office 2010 and
instruction about
how to perform
basic tasks in Office
2010 programs, read
the Office 2010 and
Windows 7 chapter
at the beginning of
this book, where you
can learn how to start
a program, use the
Ribbon, save a file,
open a file, quit a
program, use Help,
and much more.

To Save a Document

You have performed many tasks while creating this research paper and do not want to risk losing work completed thus far. Accordingly, you should save the document. The following steps assume you already have created folders for storing your files, for example, a CIS 101 folder (for your class) that contains a Word folder (for your assignments). Thus, these steps save the document in the Word folder in the CIS 101 folder on a USB flash drive using the file name, Triangulation Paper.

1 With a USB flash drive connected to one of the computer's USB ports, click the Save button on the Quick Access Toolbar to display the Save As dialog box.

2 Type **Triangulation Paper** in the File name text box to change the file name. Do not press the ENTER key after typing the file name because you do not want to close the dialog box at this time.

3 Navigate to the desired save location (in this case, the Word folder in the CIS 101 folder [or your class folder] on the USB flash drive).

4 Click the Save button (Save As dialog box) to save the document in the selected folder on the selected drive with the entered file name.

To Display the Rulers

According to the MLA documentation style, the first line of each paragraph in the research paper is to be indented one-half inch from the left margin. Although you can use a dialog box to indent paragraphs, Word provides a quicker way through the **horizontal ruler**. This ruler is displayed at the top edge of the document window just below the Ribbon. Word also provides a **vertical ruler** that is displayed along the left edge of the Word window. The following step displays the rulers because you want to use the ruler to indent paragraphs.

Experiment

• Repeatedly click the View Ruler button on the vertical scroll bar to see the how this button is used to both show and hide the rulers.

• If the rulers are not displayed, click the View Ruler button on the vertical scroll bar to display the horizontal and vertical rulers on the screen (Figure 2–17).

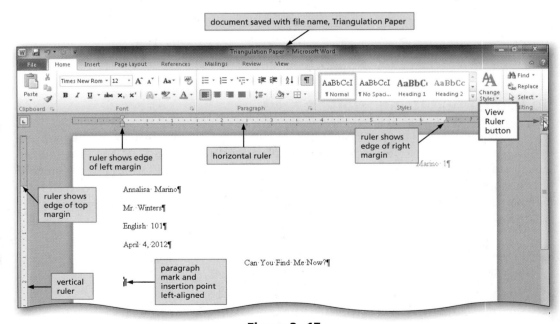

Figure 2–17

Q&A For what tasks would I use the rulers?

You can use the rulers to indent paragraphs, set tab stops, change page margins, and adjust column widths.

To First-Line Indent Paragraphs

The first line of each paragraph in the research paper is to be indented one-half inch from the left margin. You can use the horizontal ruler, usually simply called the **ruler**, to indent just the first line of a paragraph, which is called a **first-line indent**.

The left margin on the ruler contains two triangles above a square. The **First Line Indent marker** is the top triangle at the 0" mark on the ruler (Figure 2–18). The bottom triangle is discussed later in this chapter. The small square at the 0" mark is the Left Indent marker. The **Left Indent marker** allows you to change the entire left margin, whereas the First Line Indent marker indents only the first line of the paragraph. The following steps first-line indent paragraphs in the research paper.

1

• With the insertion point on the paragraph mark below the research paper title, point to the First Line Indent marker on the ruler (Figure 2–18).

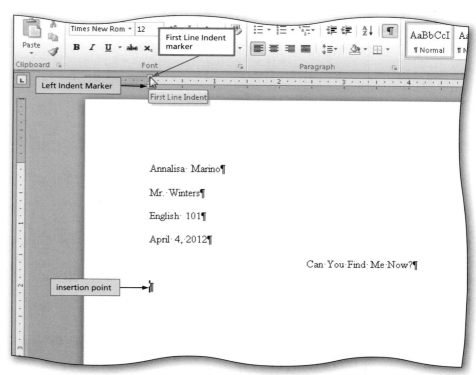

Figure 2–18

2

• Drag the First Line Indent marker to the .5" mark on the ruler to display a vertical dotted line in the document window, which indicates the proposed location of the first line of the paragraph (Figure 2–19).

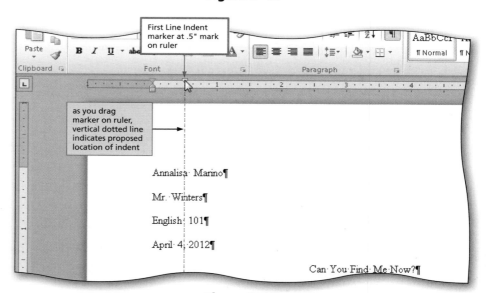

Figure 2–19

- Release the mouse button to place the First Line Indent marker at the .5" mark on the ruler, or one-half inch from the left margin (Figure 2–20).

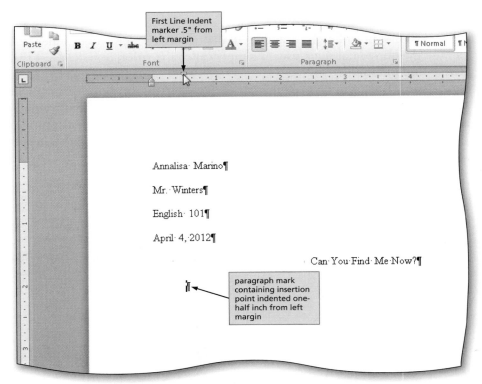

Figure 2–20

- Type **How is a Nintendo Wii console able to determine the location of a Wii Remote while a player interacts with a game?** and notice that Word automatically indented the first line of the paragraph by one-half inch (Figure 2–21).

Q&A

Will I have to set a first-line indent for each paragraph in the paper?

No. Each time you press the ENTER key, paragraph formatting in the previous paragraph carries forward to the next paragraph. Thus, once you set the first-line indent, its format carries forward automatically to each subsequent paragraph you type.

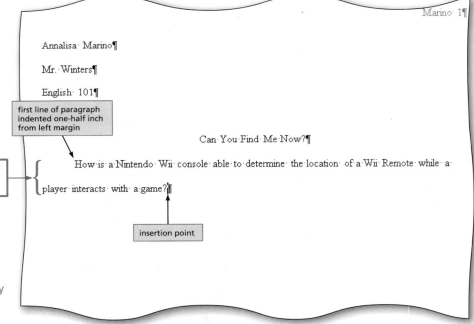

Figure 2–21

Other Ways

1. Right-click paragraph, click Paragraph on shortcut menu, click Indents and Spacing tab (Paragraph dialog box), click Special box arrow, click First line, click OK button

2. Click Paragraph Dialog Box Launcher (Home tab or Page Layout tab | Paragraph group), click Indents and Spacing tab (Paragraph dialog box), click Special box arrow, click First line, click OK button

3. Press TAB key at beginning of paragraph

To AutoCorrect as You Type

As you type, you may make typing, spelling, capitalization, or grammar errors. For this reason, Word provides an **AutoCorrect** feature that automatically corrects these kinds of errors as you type them in the document. For example, if you type ahve, Word automatically changes it to the correct spelling, have, when you press the SPACEBAR or a punctuation mark key such as a period or comma.

Word has predefined many commonly misspelled words, which it automatically corrects for you. The following steps intentionally misspell the word, the, as teh to illustrate the AutoCorrect feature.

1

- Press the SPACEBAR.

- Type the beginning of the next sentence, misspelling the word, the, as follows:
  The answer is triangulation, a process that determines teh
  (Figure 2–22).

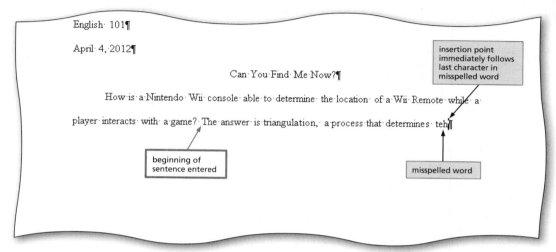

Figure 2–22

2

- Press the SPACEBAR and watch Word automatically correct the misspelled word.

- Type the rest of the sentence (Figure 2–23):
  location of an object by measuring the angles from two or more fixed points.

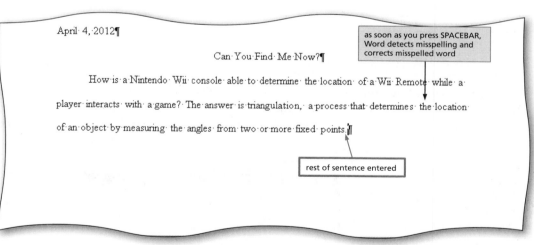

Figure 2–23

To Use the AutoCorrect Options Button

When you position the mouse pointer on text that Word automatically corrected, a small blue box appears below the text. If you point to the small blue box, Word displays the AutoCorrect Options button. When you click the **AutoCorrect Options button**, Word displays a menu that allows you to undo a correction or change how Word handles future automatic corrections of this type. The steps on the next page illustrate the AutoCorrect Options button and menu.

● Position the mouse pointer in the text automatically corrected by Word (the word, the, in this case) to display a small blue box below the automatically corrected word (Figure 2–24).

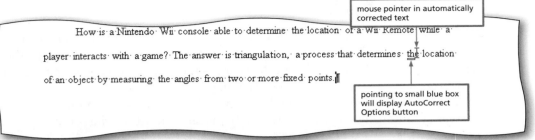

Figure 2–24

● Point to the small blue box to display the AutoCorrect Options button.

● Click the AutoCorrect Options button to display the AutoCorrect Options menu (Figure 2–25).

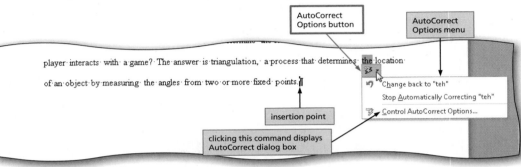

Figure 2–25

● Press the ESCAPE key to remove the AutoCorrect Options menu from the screen.

Q&A

Do I need to remove the AutoCorrect Options button from the screen?

No. When you move the mouse pointer, the AutoCorrect Options button will disappear from the screen. If, for some reason, you wanted to remove the AutoCorrect Options button from the screen, you could press the ESCAPE key a second time.

To Create an AutoCorrect Entry

In addition to the predefined list of AutoCorrect spelling, capitalization, and grammar errors, you can create your own AutoCorrect entries to add to the list. For example, if you tend to mistype the word sensor as senser, you should create an AutoCorrect entry for it. The following steps create an AutoCorrect entry.

● Click File on the Ribbon to open the Backstage view (Figure 2–26).

Figure 2–26

2

- Click Options in the Backstage view to display the Word Options dialog box.

- Click Proofing in the left pane (Word Options dialog box) to display proofing options in the right pane.

- Click the AutoCorrect Options button in the right pane to display the AutoCorrect dialog box.

- When Word displays the AutoCorrect dialog box, type **senser** in the Replace text box.

- Press the TAB key and then type **sensor** in the With text box (Figure 2–27).

Figure 2–27

How would I delete an existing AutoCorrect entry?

You would select the entry to be deleted in the list of defined entries in the AutoCorrect dialog box and then click the Delete button.

3

- Click the Add button (AutoCorrect dialog box) to add the entry alphabetically to the list of words to correct automatically as you type. (If your dialog box displays a Replace button instead, click it and then click the Yes button in the Microsoft Word dialog box to replace the previously defined entry.)

- Click the OK button (AutoCorrect dialog box) to close the dialog box.

- Click the OK button (Word Options dialog box) to close the dialog box.

The AutoCorrect Dialog Box

In addition to creating AutoCorrect entries for words you commonly misspell or mistype, you can create entries for abbreviations, codes, and so on. For example, you could create an AutoCorrect entry for asap, indicating that Word should replace this text with the phrase, as soon as possible.

If, for some reason, you do not want Word to correct automatically as you type, you can turn off the 'Replace text as you type' feature by clicking Options in the Backstage view, clicking Proofing in the left pane (Word Options dialog box), clicking the AutoCorrect Options button in the right pane (Figure 2–27), removing the check mark from the 'Replace text as you type' check box, and then clicking the OK button in each open dialog box.

The AutoCorrect sheet in the AutoCorrect dialog box (Figure 2–27) contains other check boxes that correct capitalization errors if the check boxes are selected. If you

BTW

Automatic Corrections
If you do not want to keep a change automatically made by Word and you immediately notice the automatic correction, you can undo the change by clicking the Undo button on the Quick Access Toolbar or pressing CTRL+Z. You also can undo a correction through the AutoCorrect Options button, which was shown above.

type two capital letters in a row, such as TH, Word makes the second letter lowercase, Th. If you begin a sentence with a lowercase letter, Word capitalizes the first letter of the sentence. If you type the name of a day in lowercase letters, such as tuesday, Word capitalizes the first letter in the name of the day, Tuesday. If you leave the CAPS LOCK key on and begin a new sentence, such as aFTER, Word corrects the typing, After, and turns off the CAPS LOCK key. If you do not want Word to automatically perform any of these corrections, simply remove the check mark from the appropriate check box in the AutoCorrect dialog box.

Sometimes you do not want Word to AutoCorrect a particular word or phrase. For example, you may use the code WD. in your documents. Because Word automatically capitalizes the first letter of a sentence, the character you enter following the period will be capitalized (in the previous sentence, it would capitalize the letter i in the word, in). To allow the code WD. to be entered into a document and still leave the AutoCorrect feature turned on, you would set an exception. To set an exception to an AutoCorrect rule, click Options in the Backstage view, click Proofing in the left pane (Word Options dialog box), click the AutoCorrect Options button in the right pane, click the Exceptions button (Figure 2–27 on the previous page), click the appropriate tab in the AutoCorrect Exceptions dialog box, type the exception entry in the text box, click the Add button, click the Close button (AutoCorrect Exceptions dialog box), and then click the OK button in each of the remaining dialog boxes.

To Enter More Text

The next step is to continue typing text in the research paper up to the location of the in-text parenthetical reference. The following steps enter this text.

1 With the insertion point positioned at the end of the first paragraph in the paper, as shown in Figure 2–25 on page WD 86, press the ENTER key, so that you can begin typing the text in the second paragraph.

2 Type `Surveyors often use triangulation to measure distance. Starting at a known location and elevation, surveyors measure a length to create a base line and then use a theodolite to measure an angle to an unknown point from each side of the base line` and then press the SPACEBAR.

Citations

Both the MLA and APA guidelines suggest the use of in-text parenthetical references (placed at the end of a sentence), instead of footnoting each source of material in a paper. These parenthetical references, called citations in Word, guide the reader to the end of the paper for complete information about the source.

BTW

Spacing after Punctuation
Because word processing documents use variable character fonts, it often is difficult to determine in a printed document how many times someone has pressed the SPACEBAR between sentences. Thus, the rule is to press the SPACEBAR only once after periods, colons, and other punctuation marks.

Plan Ahead

Reference all sources.
During your research, be sure to record essential publication information about each of your sources. Following is a sample list of types of required information for the MLA documentation style.

- Book: full name of author(s), complete title of book, edition (if available), volume (if available), publication city, publisher name, publication year, publication medium

- Magazine: full name of author(s), complete title of article, magazine title, issue number (if available), date of magazine, page numbers of article, publication medium

- Web site: full name of author(s), title of Web site, Web site publisher or sponsor (if none, write N.p.), publication date (if none, write n.d.), publication medium, date viewed

Word provides tools to assist you with inserting citations in a paper and later generating a list of sources from the citations. With a documentation style selected, Word automatically formats the citations and list of sources according to that style. The process for adding citations in Word is as follows:

1. Modify the documentation style, if necessary.
2. Insert a citation placeholder.
3. Enter the source information for the citation.

You can combine Steps 2 and 3, where you insert the citation placeholder and enter the source information at once. Or, you can insert the citation placeholder as you write and then enter the source information for the citation at a later time. While creating the research paper in this chapter, you will use both methods.

To Change the Bibliography Style

The first step in inserting a citation is to be sure the citations and sources will be formatted using the correct documentation style, called the bibliography style in Word. The following steps change the specified documentation style.

1

- Click References on the Ribbon to display the References tab.

- Click the Bibliography Style box arrow (References tab | Citations & Bibliography group) to display a gallery of predefined documentation styles (Figure 2–28).

2

- Click MLA Sixth Edition in the Bibliography Style gallery to change the documentation style to MLA.

Q&A What if I am using a different edition of a documentation style shown in the Bibliography Style gallery?

Select the closest one and then, if necessary, perform necessary edits before submitting the paper.

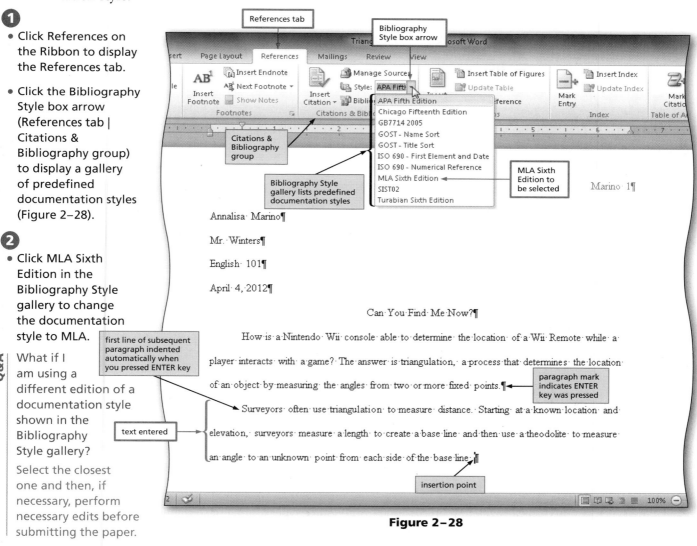

Figure 2–28

To Insert a Citation and Create Its Source

With the documentation style selected, the next task is to insert a citation placeholder and enter the source information for the citation. You can accomplish these steps at once by instructing Word to add a new source. The following steps add a new source for a magazine (periodical) article.

- Click the Insert Citation button (References tab | Citations & Bibliography group) to display the Insert Citation menu (Figure 2–29).

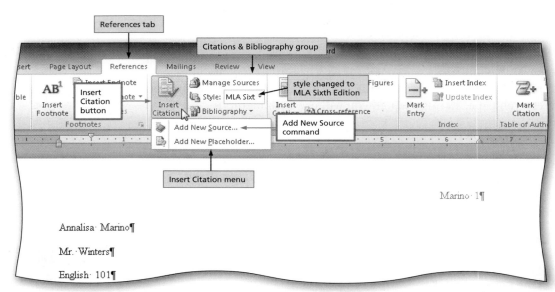

Figure 2–29

- Click Add New Source on the Insert Citation menu to display the Create Source dialog box (Figure 2–30).

 What are the Bibliography Fields in the Create Source dialog box?

A **field** is a placeholder for data whose contents can change. You enter data in some fields; Word supplies data for others. In this case, you enter the contents of the fields for a particular source, for example, the author name in the Author field.

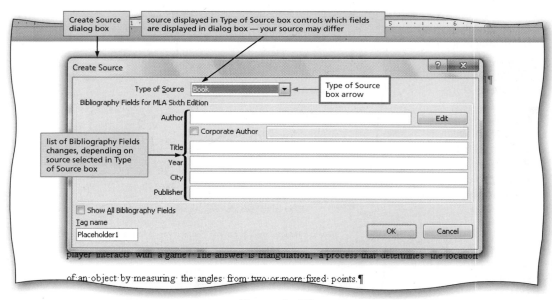

Figure 2–30

 **Experiment**

- Click the Type of Source box arrow and then click one of the source types in the list, so that you can see how the list of fields changes to reflect the type of source you selected.

- If necessary, click the Type of Source box arrow (Create Source dialog box) and then click Article in a Periodical, so that the list shows fields required for a magazine (periodical).

- Click the Author text box. Type **Jains, Malila** as the author.

- Click the Title text box. Type **How Surveyors Measure and Calculate Angles** as the article title.

- Press the TAB key and then type **Today's Modern Surveyor** as the periodical title.

- Press the TAB key and then type **2012** as the year.

- Press the TAB key and then type **Mar.** as the month.

- Press the TAB key twice and then type **30-48** as the pages (Figure 2–31).

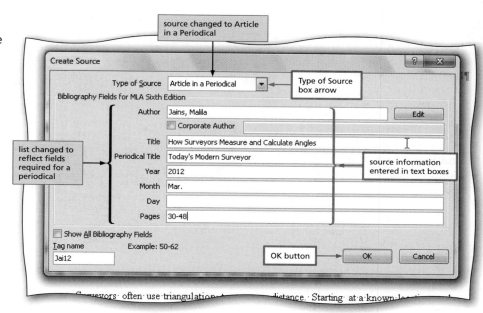

Figure 2–31

- Click the OK button to close the dialog box, create the source, and insert the citation in the document at the location of the insertion point (Figure 2–32).

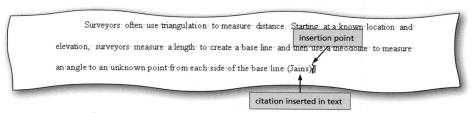

Figure 2–32

To Edit a Citation

In the MLA documentation style, if a source has page numbers, you should include them in the citation. Thus, Word provides a means to enter the page numbers to be displayed in the citation. The following steps edit a citation, so that the page numbers appear in it.

1

- Click somewhere in the citation to be edited, in this case somewhere in (Jains), which selects the citation and displays the Citation Options box arrow.

- Click the Citation Options box arrow to display the Citation Options menu (Figure 2–33).

Q&A What is the purpose of the tab to the left of the selected citation?

If, for some reason, you wanted to move a citation to a different location in the document, you would select the citation and then drag the citation tab to the desired location.

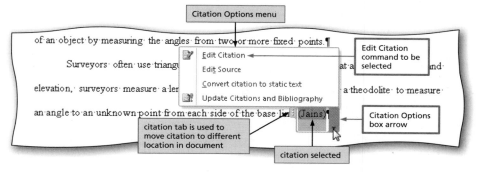

Figure 2–33

- Click Edit Citation on the Citation Options menu to display the Edit Citation dialog box.

- Type 30-48 in the Pages text box (Edit Citations dialog box) (Figure 2–34).

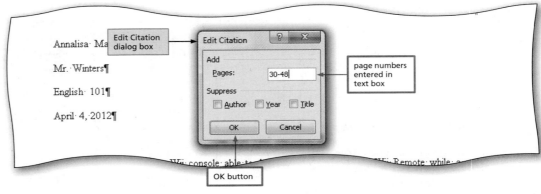

Figure 2–34

- Click the OK button to close the dialog box and add the page numbers to the citation in the document (Figure 2–35).

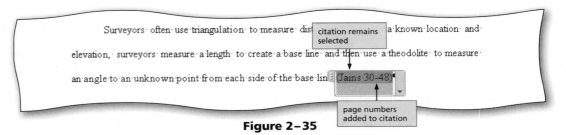

Figure 2–35

4

- Press the END key to move the insertion point to the end of the line, which also deselects the citation.

- Press the PERIOD key to end the sentence.

BTW

Edit a Source
To edit a source, click somewhere in the citation, click the Citation Options box arrow, and then click Edit Source on the Citation Options menu to display the Edit Source dialog box (which resembles the Create Source dialog box). Make necessary changes and then click the OK button.

To Enter More Text

The next step is to continue typing text in the research paper up to the location of the footnote. The following steps enter this text.

1. Press the SPACEBAR.

2. Type the next sentence (Figure 2–36): **The length of the base line and the two known angles allow a computer or person to determine the location of a third point.**

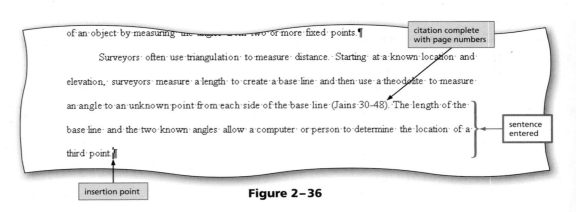

Figure 2–36

To Save an Existing Document with the Same File Name

You have made several modifications to the document since you last saved it. Thus, you should save it again. The following step saves the document again.

1 Click the Save button on the Quick Access Toolbar to overwrite the previously saved file.

Footnotes

As discussed earlier in this chapter, notes are optional in the MLA documentation style. If used, content notes elaborate on points discussed in the paper, and bibliographic notes direct the reader to evaluations of statements in a source or provide a means for identifying multiple sources. The MLA documentation style specifies that a superscript (raised number) be used for a **note reference mark** to signal that a note exists either at the bottom of the page as a **footnote** or at the end of the document as an **endnote**.

In Word, **note text** can be any length and format. Word automatically numbers notes sequentially by placing a note reference mark both in the body of the document and to the left of the note text. If you insert, rearrange, or remove notes, Word renumbers any subsequent note reference marks according to their new sequence in the document.

To Insert a Footnote Reference Mark

The following step inserts a footnote reference mark in the document at the location of the insertion point and at the location where the footnote text will be typed.

1

• With the insertion point positioned as shown in Figure 2–36, click the Insert Footnote button (References tab | Footnotes group) to display a note reference mark (a superscripted 1) in two places: (1) in the document window at the location of the insertion point and (2) at the bottom of the page where the footnote will be positioned, just below a separator line (Figure 2–37).

Q&A

What if I wanted notes to be positioned as endnotes instead of as footnotes?

You would click the Insert Endnote button (References tab | Footnotes group), which places the separator line and the endnote text at the end of the document, instead of the bottom of the page containing the reference.

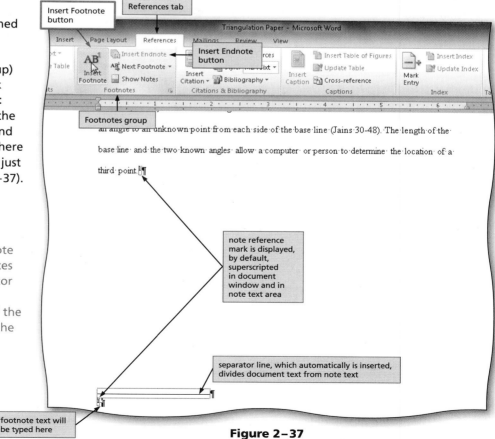

Figure 2–37

Other Ways
1. Press CTRL+ALT+F

To Enter Footnote Text

The following step types the footnote text to the right of the note reference mark below the separator line.

1 Type the footnote text up to the citation: `Cordoba and Sarkis state that electronic theodolites calculate angles automatically and then send the calculated angles to a computer for analysis` and then press the SPACEBAR.

To Insert a Citation Placeholder

Earlier in this chapter, you inserted a citation and its source at once. Sometimes, you may not have the source information readily available and would prefer entering it at a later time.

In the footnote, you will insert a placeholder for the citation and enter the source information later. The following steps insert a citation placeholder.

1
- With the insertion point positioned as shown in Figure 2–38, click the Insert Citation button (References tab | Citations & Bibliography group) to display the Insert Citation menu (Figure 2–38).

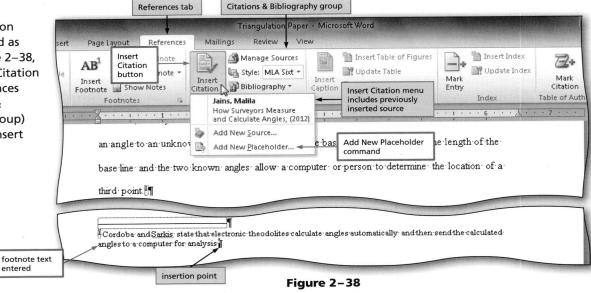

Figure 2–38

2
- Click Add New Placeholder on the Insert Citation menu to display the Placeholder Name dialog box.

- Type `Cordoba` as the tag name for the source (Figure 2–39).

Q&A What is a tag name?

A tag name is an identifier that links a citation to a source. Word automatically creates a tag name when you enter a source. When you create a citation placeholder, enter a meaningful tag name, which will appear in the citation placeholder until you edit the source.

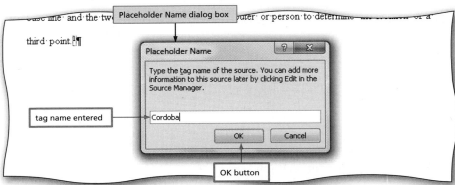

Figure 2–39

3
- Click the OK button (Placeholder Name dialog box) to close the dialog box and insert the entered tag name in the citation placeholder in the document.

- Press the PERIOD key to end the sentence.

Footnote Text Style

When you insert a footnote, Word formats it using the Footnote Text style, which does not adhere to the MLA documentation style. For example, notice in Figure 2–38 that the footnote text is single-spaced, left-aligned, and a smaller font size than the text in the research paper. According to the MLA documentation style, notes should be formatted like all other paragraphs in the paper.

You could change the paragraph formatting of the footnote text to first-line indent and double-spacing and then change the font size from 10 to 12 point. If you use this technique, however, you will need to change the format of the footnote text for each footnote you enter into the document.

A more efficient technique is to modify the format of the Footnote Text style so that every footnote you enter in the document will use the formats defined in this style.

To Modify a Style Using a Shortcut Menu

The Footnote Text style specifies left-aligned single-spaced paragraphs with a 10-point font size for text. To meet MLA documentation style, the footnotes should be double-spaced with a first line indent and a 12-point font size for text. The following steps modify the Footnote Text style.

1

• Right-click the note text in the footnote to display a shortcut menu related to footnotes (Figure 2–40).

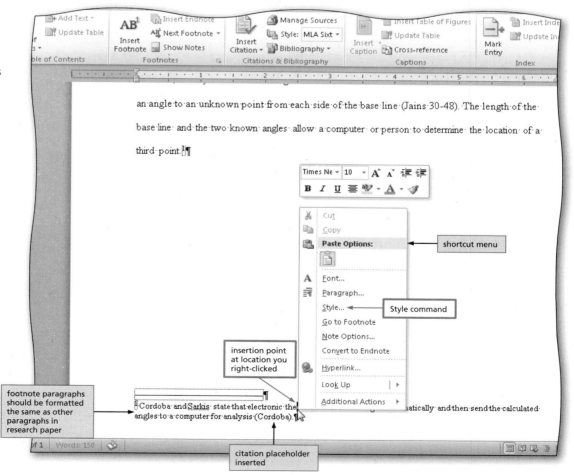

Figure 2–40

2

- Click Style on the shortcut menu to display the Style dialog box. If necessary, click the Category box arrow, click All styles in the Cagetory list, and then click Footnote Text in the Styles list.

- Click the Modify button (Style dialog box) to display the Modify Style dialog box.

- Click the Font Size box arrow (Modify Style dialog box) to display the Font Size list and then click 12 in the Font Size list to change the font size.

- Click the Double Space button to change the line spacing.

- Click the Format button to display the Format menu (Figure 2–41).

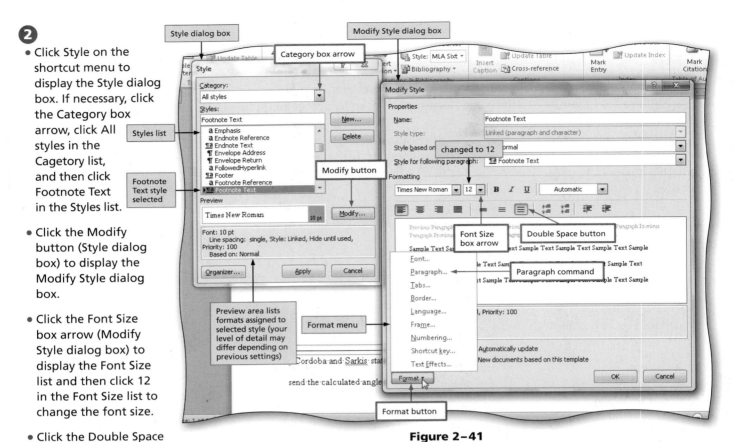

Figure 2–41

3

- Click Paragraph on the Format menu (Modify Style dialog box) to display the Paragraph dialog box.

- Click the Special box arrow (Paragraph dialog box) and then click First line (Figure 2–42).

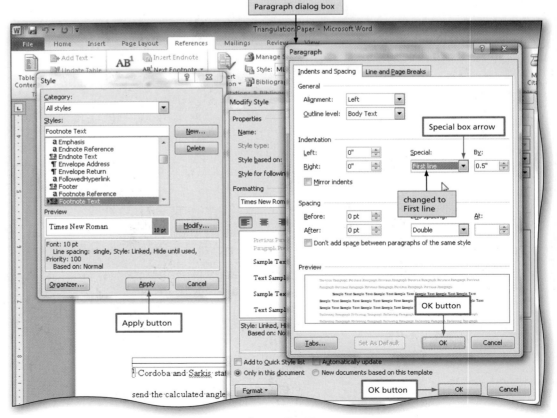

Figure 2–42

4

- Click the OK button (Paragraph dialog box) to close the dialog box.

- Click the OK button (Modify Style dialog box) to close the dialog box.

- Click the Apply button (Style dialog box) to apply the style changes to the footnote text (Figure 2–43).

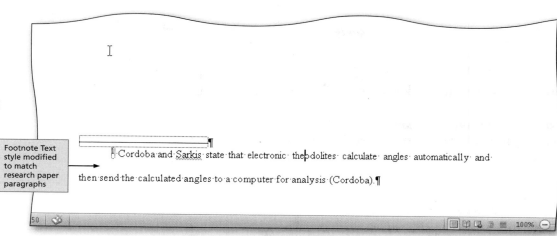

Footnote Text style modified to match research paper paragraphs

Figure 2–43

Q&A

Will all footnotes use this modified style?

Yes. Any future footnotes entered in the document will use a 12-point font with the paragraphs first-line indented and double-spaced.

Other Ways		
1. Click Styles Dialog Box Launcher (Home tab | Styles group), point to style name in list, click style name box arrow, click Modify, change settings	(Modify Style dialog box), click OK button 2. Click Styles Dialog Box Launcher (Home tab | Styles group), click Manage Styles button	in task pane, select style name in list, click Modify button, change settings (Modify Style dialog box), click OK button in each dialog box

To Edit a Source

When you typed the footnote text for this research paper, you inserted a citation placeholder for the source. Assume you now have the source information and are ready to enter it. The following steps edit a source.

1

- Click somewhere in the citation placeholder to be edited, in this case (Cordoba), to select the citation placeholder.

- Click the Citation Options box arrow to display the Citation Options menu (Figure 2–44).

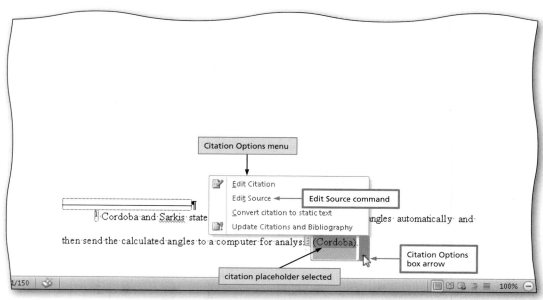

Citation Options menu

Edit Source command

Citation Options box arrow

citation placeholder selected

Figure 2–44

2

- Click Edit Source on the Citation Options menu to display the Edit Source dialog box.

- If necessary, click the Type of Source box arrow (Edit Source dialog box) and then click Book, so that the list shows fields required for a book.

- Click the Author text box. Type **Cordoba, Nicolas E.,; Sarkis, Kara A.** as the author.

What if I do not know how to punctuate the author entry so that Word formats it properly?

Click the Edit button (Edit Source dialog box) to the right of the Author entry for assistance. For example, you should separate multiple author names with a semicolon as shown in this figure.

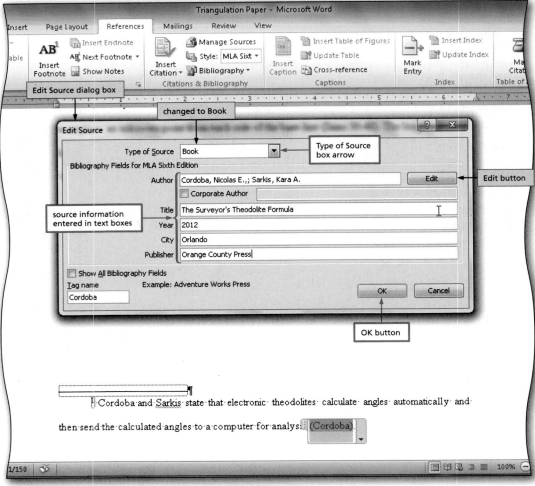

Figure 2–45

- Click the Title text box. Type **The Surveyor's Theodolite Formula** as the book title.

- Press the TAB key and then type **2012** as the year.

- Press the TAB key and then type **Orlando** as the city.

- Press the TAB key and then type **Orange County Press** as the publisher (Figure 2–45).

3

- Click the OK button to close the dialog box and create the source.

Other Ways
1. Click Manage Sources button (References tab | Citations & Bibliography group), click placeholder source in Current List, click Edit button (Source Manager dialog box)

Q&As
For a complete list of the Q&As found in many of the step-by-step sequences in this book, visit the Word 2010 Q&A Web page (scsite.com/wd2010/qa).

To Edit a Citation

In the MLA documentation style, if you reference the author's name in the text, you should not list it again in the parenthetical citation. Instead, just list the page number in the citation. To do this, you instruct Word to suppress author and title. The following steps edit the citation, suppressing the author and title but displaying the page numbers.

1 If necessary, click somewhere in the citation to be edited, in this case (Cordoba), to select the citation and display the Citation Options box arrow.

2 Click the Citation Options box arrow to display the Citation Options menu.

3 Click Edit Citation on the Citation Options menu to display the Edit Citation dialog box.

4 Type **25** in the Pages text box (Edit Citation dialog box).

5 Click the Author check box to place a check mark in it.

6 Click the Title check box to place a check mark in it (Figure 2–46).

7 Click the OK button to close the dialog box, remove the author name from the citation in the footnote, suppress the title from showing, and add a page number to the citation (shown in Figure 2-47 on page WD 101).

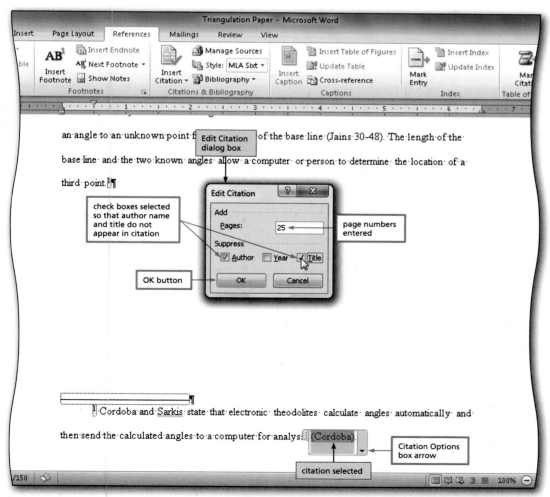

Figure 2–46

Working with Footnotes and Endnotes

You edit footnote text just as you edit any other text in the document. To delete or move a note reference mark, however, the insertion point must be in the document text (not in the footnote text).

To delete a note, select the note reference mark in the document text (not in the footnote text) by dragging through the note reference mark and then click the Cut button (Home tab | Clipboard group). Or, click immediately to the right of the note reference mark in the document text and then press the BACKSPACE key twice, or click immediately to the left of the note reference mark in the document text and then press the DELETE key twice.

To move a note to a different location in a document, select the note reference mark in the document text (not in the footnote text), click the Cut button (Home tab | Clipboard group), click the location where you want to move the note, and then click the Paste button (Home tab | Clipboard group). When you move or delete notes, Word automatically renumbers any remaining notes in the correct sequence.

If you position the mouse pointer on the note reference mark in the document text, the note text is displayed above the note reference mark as a ScreenTip. To remove the ScreenTip, move the mouse pointer.

If, for some reason, you wanted to change the format of note reference marks in footnotes or endnotes (i.e., from 1, 2, 3, to A, B, C), you would click the Footnote & Endnote Dialog Box Launcher (References tab | Footnotes group) to display the Footnote and Endnote dialog box, click the Number format box arrow (Footnote and Endnote dialog box), click the desired number format in the list, and then click the Apply button.

If, for some reason, you wanted to convert footnotes to endnotes, you would click the Footnote & Endnote Dialog Box Launcher (References tab | Footnotes group) to display the Footnote and Endnote dialog box, click the Convert button (Footnote and Endnote dialog box), select the 'Convert all footnotes to endnotes' option button, click the OK button, and then click the Close button (Footnote and Endnote dialog box).

BTW

Footnote and Endnote Location
You can change the location of footnotes from the bottom of the page to the end of the text by clicking the Footnotes and Endnote Dialog Box Launcher (References tab | Footnotes group), clicking the Footnotes box arrow (Footnote and Endnote dialog box), and then clicking Below text. Similarly, clicking the Endnotes box arrow (Footnote and Endnote dialog box) enables you to change the location of endnotes from the end of the document to the end of a section.

To Enter More Text

The next step is to continue typing text in the body of the research paper. The following steps enter this text.

1 Position the insertion point after the note reference mark in the document and then press the ENTER key.

2 Type the third paragraph of the research paper (Figure 2–47): `Similarly, the Nintendo Wii console uses triangulation to determine the location of a Wii Remote. A player places a sensor bar, which contains two infrared transmitters, near or on top of a television. While the player uses the Wii Remote, the Wii console determines the remote's location by calculating the distance and angles between the Wii Remote and the two transmitters on the sensor bar. Determining the location of a Wii Remote is relatively simple because the sensor bar contains only two fixed points: the transmitters.`

To Count Words

Often when you write papers, you are required to compose the papers with a minimum number of words. The minimum requirement for the research paper in this chapter is 325 words. You can look on the status bar and see the total number of words thus far in a document. For example, Figure 2–47 shows the research paper has 236 words, but you are not sure if that count includes the words in your footnote. The following steps display the Word Count dialog box, so that you can verify the footnote text is included in the count.

1
- Click the Word Count indicator on the status bar to display the Word Count dialog box.

- If necessary, place a check mark in the 'Include textboxes, footnotes and endnotes' check box (Word Count dialog box) (Figure 2–47).

Q&A Why do the statistics in my Word Count dialog box differ from Figure 2–47?

Depending on the accuracy of your typing, your statistics may differ.

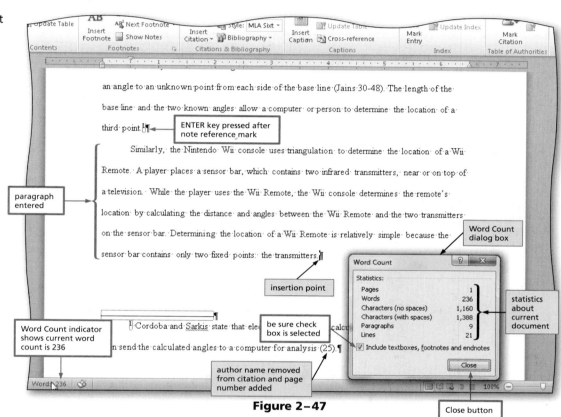

Figure 2–47

2
- Click the Close button to close the dialog box.

Q&A Can I display statistics for just a section of the document?

Yes. Select the section and then click the Word Count indicator on the status bar to display statistics about the selected text.

Automatic Page Breaks

As you type documents that exceed one page, Word automatically inserts page breaks, called **automatic page breaks** or **soft page breaks**, when it determines the text has filled one page according to paper size, margin settings, line spacing, and other settings. If you add text, delete text, or modify text on a page, Word recomputes the location of automatic page breaks and adjusts them accordingly.

Word performs page recomputation between the keystrokes, that is, in between the pauses in your typing. Thus, Word refers to the automatic page break task as **background repagination**. The steps on the next page illustrate Word's automatic page break feature.

To Enter More Text and Insert a Citation Placeholder

The next task is to type the fourth paragraph in the body of the research paper. The following steps enter this text and a placeholder.

1 With the insertion point positioned at the end of the third paragraph as shown in Figure 2–47 on the previous page, press the ENTER key.

2 Type the fourth paragraph of the research paper (Figure 2–48): **A more complex application of triangulation occurs in a global positioning system (GPS). A GPS consists of one or more earth-based receivers that accept and analyze signals sent by satellites to determine a receiver's geographic location. GPS receivers, found in handheld navigation devices and many vehicles, use triangulation to determine their location relative to at least three geostationary satellites. According to Sanders, the satellites are the fixed points in the triangulation formula** and then press the SPACEBAR.

Page Break Locations
As you type, your page break may occur at different locations depending on Word settings and the type of printer connected to the computer.

Q&A

Why does the text move from the second page to the first page as I am typing?

Word, by default, will not allow the first line of a paragraph to be by itself at the bottom of a page (an orphan) or the last line of a paragraph to be by itself at the top of a page (a widow). As you type, Word adjusts the placement of the paragraph to avoid orphans and widows.

3 Click the Insert Citation button (References tab | Citations & Bibliography group) to display the Insert Citation menu. Click Add New Placeholder on the Insert Citation menu to display the Placeholder Name dialog box.

4 Type **Sanders** as the tag name for the source.

5 Click the OK button to close the dialog box and insert the tag name in the citation placeholder.

6 Press the PERIOD key to end the sentence.

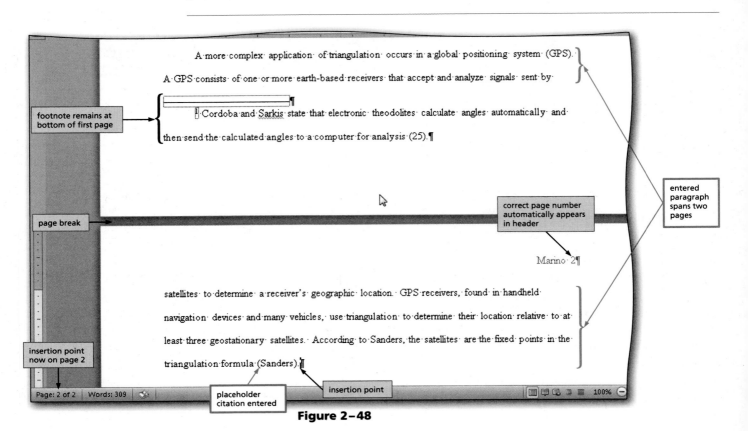

Figure 2–48

To Edit a Source

When you typed the fourth paragraph of the research paper, you inserted a citation placeholder, Sanders, for the source. You now have the source information, which is for a Web site, and are ready to enter it. The following steps edit the source for the Sanders citation placeholder.

1 Click somewhere in the citation placeholder to be edited, in this case (Sanders), to select the citation placeholder.

2 Click the Citation Options box arrow to display the Citation Options menu.

3 Click Edit Source on the Citation Options menu to display the Edit Source dialog box.

4 If necessary, click the Type of Source box arrow (Edit Source dialog box); scroll to and then click Web site, so that the list shows fields required for a Web site.

5 Place a check mark in the Show All Bibliography Fields check box to display more fields related to Web sites.

6 Click the Author text box. Type **Sanders, Gregory B.** as the author.

7 Click the Name of Web Page text box. Type **Understanding Satellites and Global Positioning Systems** as the Web page name.

8 Click the Production Company text box. Type **Course Technology** as the production company.

9 Click the Year Accessed text box. Type **2012** as the year accessed.

10 Press the TAB key and then type **Feb.** as the month accessed.

Q&A What if some of the text boxes disappear as I enter the Web site fields?

With the Show All Bibliography Fields check box selected, the dialog box may not be able to display all Web site fields at the same time. In this case, some may scroll up.

11 Press the TAB key and then type **27** as the day accessed (Figure 2–49).

Q&A Do I need to enter a Web address (URL)?

The latest MLA documentation style update does not require the Web address in the source.

12 Click the OK button to close the dialog box and create the source.

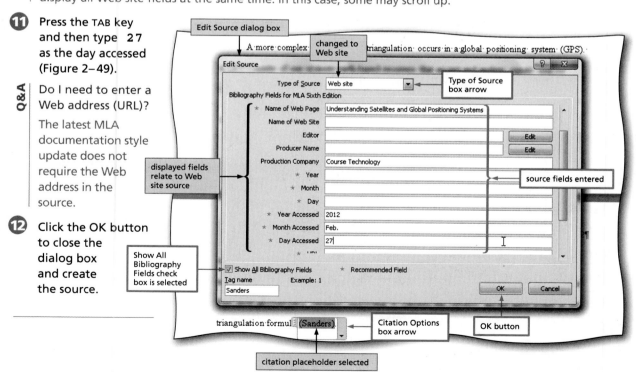

Figure 2–49

To Edit a Citation

As mentioned earlier, if you reference the author's name in the text, you should not list it again in the parenthetical citation. For Web site citations, when you suppress the author's name, the citation shows the Web site name because page numbers do not apply. The following steps edit the citation, suppressing the author and displaying the name of the Web site instead.

1 If necessary, click somewhere in the citation to be edited, in this case (Sanders), to select the citation and display the Citation Options box arrow.

2 Click the Citation Options box arrow and then click Edit Citation on the Citation Options menu to display the Edit Citation dialog box.

3 Click the Author check box (Edit Citation dialog box) to place a check mark in it (Figure 2–50).

4 Click the OK button to close the dialog box, remove the author name from the citation, and show the name of the Web site in the citation (shown in Figure 2–51).

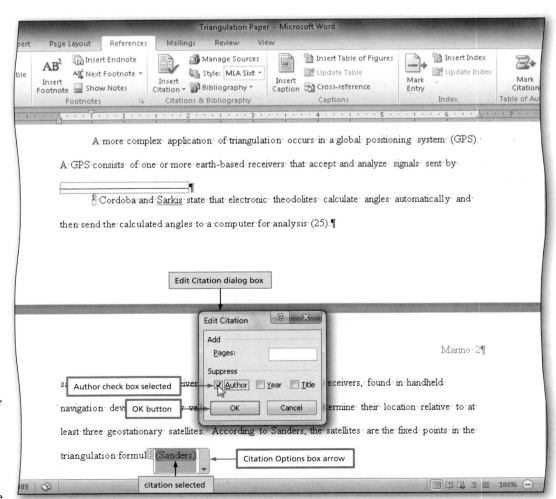

Figure 2–50

To Enter More Text

The next step is to type the last paragraph of text in the research paper. The following steps enter this text.

1 Press the END key to position the insertion point at the end of the fourth paragraph and then press the ENTER key.

2 Type the last paragraph of the research paper (Figure 2–51): **The next time you pass a surveyor, play a Nintendo Wii, or follow a route prescribed by a vehicle's navigation system, keep in mind that none of it might have been possible without the concept of triangulation.**

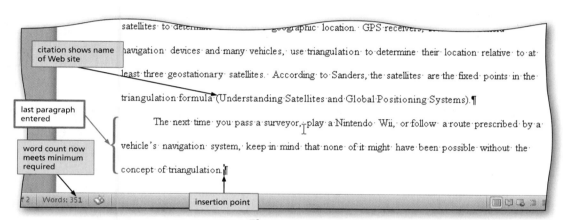

satellites to determine .... geographic location. GPS receivers, ...

citation shows name of Web site navigation devices and many vehicles, use triangulation to determine their location relative to at least three geostationary satellites. According to Sanders, the satellites are the fixed points in the triangulation formula (Understanding Satellites and Global Positioning Systems).¶

last paragraph entered The next time you pass a surveyor, play a Nintendo Wii, or follow a route prescribed by a vehicle's navigation system, keep in mind that none of it might have been possible without the concept of triangulation.¶

word count now meets minimum required

f 2 | Words: 351 | **insertion point**

Figure 2–51

To Save an Existing Document with the Same File Name

You have made several modifications to the document since you last saved it. Thus, you should save it again. The following step saves the document again.

1 Click the Save button on the Quick Access Toolbar to overwrite the previously saved file.

> **Break Point:** If you wish to take a break, this is a good place to do so. You can quit Word now (refer to page WD 125 for instructions). To resume at a later time, start Word (refer to page WD 70 for instructions), open the file called Triangulation Paper (refer to page WD 45 for instructions), and continue following the steps from this location forward.

Creating an Alphabetical Works Cited Page

According to the MLA documentation style, the **works cited page** is a list of sources that are referenced directly in a research paper. You place the list on a separate numbered page with the title, Works Cited, centered one inch from the top margin. The works are to be alphabetized by the author's last name or, if the work has no author, by the work's title. The first line of each entry begins at the left margin. Indent subsequent lines of the same entry one-half inch from the left margin.

Plan
Ahead

> **Create the list of sources.**
> A **bibliography** is an alphabetical list of sources referenced in a paper. Whereas the text of the research paper contains brief references to the source (the citations), the bibliography lists all publication information about the source. Documentation styles differ significantly in their guidelines for preparing a bibliography. Each style identifies formats for various sources, including books, magazines, pamphlets, newspapers, Web sites, television programs, paintings, maps, advertisements, letters, memos, and much more. You can find information about various styles and their guidelines in printed style guides and on the Web.

To Page Break Manually

The works cited are to be displayed on a separate numbered page. Thus, you must insert a manual page break following the body of the research paper so that the list of sources is displayed on a separate page. A **manual page break**, or **hard page break**, is one that you force into the document at a specific location.

Word never moves or adjusts manual page breaks. Word, however, does adjust any automatic page breaks that follow a manual page break. Word inserts manual page breaks immediately above or to the left of the location of the insertion point. The following step inserts a manual page break after the text of the research paper.

- Verify that the insertion point is positioned at the end of the text of the research paper, as shown in Figure 2–51 on the previous page.

- Click Insert on the Ribbon to display the Insert tab.

- Click the Page Break button (Insert tab | Pages group) to insert a manual page break immediately to the left of the insertion point and position the insertion point immediately below the manual page break (Figure 2–52).

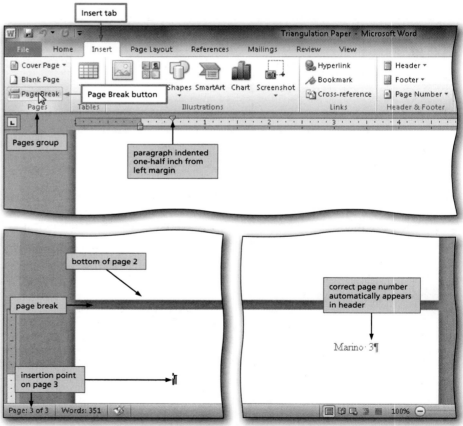

Figure 2–52

Other Ways
1. Press CTRL+ENTER

To Apply a Style

The works cited title is to be centered between the margins of the paper. If you simply issue the Center command, the title will not be centered properly. Instead, it will be one-half inch to the right of the center point because earlier you set the first-line indent for paragraphs to one-half inch.

To properly center the title of the works cited page, you could drag the First Line Indent marker back to the left margin before centering the paragraph, or you could apply the Normal style to the location of the insertion point. Recall that you modified the Normal style for this document to 12-point Times New Roman with double-spaced, left-aligned paragraphs that have no space after the paragraphs.

To apply a style to a paragraph, first position the insertion point in the paragraph and then apply the style. The following step applies the modified Normal style to the location of the insertion point.

1

- Click Home on the Ribbon to display the Home tab.

- With the insertion point on the paragraph mark at the top of page 3 (as shown in Figure 2–52) even if Normal is selected, click Normal in the Quick Style gallery (Home tab | Styles group) to apply the Normal style to the paragraph containing the insertion point (Figure 2–53).

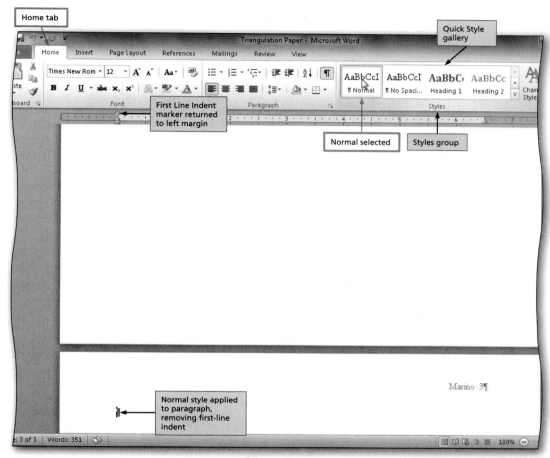

Figure 2–53

Other Ways
1. Click Styles Dialog Box Launcher (Home tab | Styles group), click desired style in Styles task pane	2. Press CTRL+SHIFT+S, click Style Name box arrow in Apply Styles task pane, click desired style in list

To Center Text

The next step is to enter the title, Works Cited, centered between the margins of the paper. The following steps use shortcut keys to format the title.

1 Press CTRL+E to center the paragraph mark.

2 Type **Works Cited** as the title.

3 Press the ENTER key.

4 Press CTRL+L to left-align the paragraph mark (shown in Figure 2–54 on the next page).

BTW

BTWs
For a complete list of the BTWs found in the margins of this book, visit the Word 2010 BTW Web page (scsite.com/wd2010/btw).

To Create the Bibliographical List

While typing the research paper, you created several citations and their sources. Word can format the list of sources and alphabetize them in a **bibliographical list**, saving you time looking up style guidelines. That is, Word will create a bibliographical list with each element of the source placed in its correct position with proper punctuation, according to the specified style. For example, in this research paper, the book source will list, in this order, the author name(s), book title, publisher city, publishing company name, and publication year with the correct punctuation between each element according to the MLA documentation style. The following steps create an MLA-styled bibliographical list from the sources previously entered.

1

- Click References on the Ribbon to display the References tab.

- With the insertion point positioned as shown in Figure 2–54, click the Bibliography button (References tab | Citations & Bibliography group) to display the Bibliography gallery (Figure 2–54).

Q&A

Will I select the Works Cited option from the Bibliography gallery?

No. The title it inserts is not formatted according to the MLA documentation style. Thus, you will use the Insert Bibliography command instead.

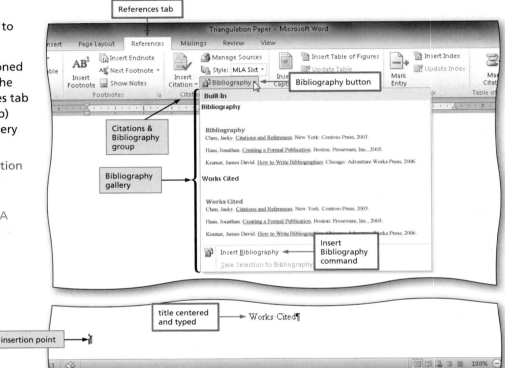

Figure 2–54

2

- Click Insert Bibliography in the Bibliography gallery to insert a list of sources at the location of the insertion point.

- If necessary, scroll to display the entire list of sources in the document window (Figure 2–55).

Q&A

What is the n.d. in the last work?

The MLA documentation style uses the abbreviation n.d. for no date, for example, no date on the Web page.

Figure 2–55

To Format Paragraphs with a Hanging Indent

Notice in Figure 2–55 that the first line of each source entry begins at the left margin, and subsequent lines in the same paragraph are indented one-half inch from the left margin. In essence, the first line hangs to the left of the rest of the paragraph; thus, this type of paragraph formatting is called a **hanging indent**. The Bibliography style in Word automatically formats the works cited paragraphs with a hanging indent.

If you wanted to format paragraphs with a hanging indent, you would use one of the following techniques.

- With the insertion point in the paragraph to format, drag the **Hanging Indent marker** (the bottom triangle) on the ruler to the desired mark on the ruler (i.e., .5") to set the hanging indent at that location from the left margin.

or

- Right-click the paragraph to format, click Paragraph on shortcut menu, click Indents and Spacing tab (Paragraph dialog box), click Special box arrow, click Hanging, and then click the OK button.

or

- Click the Paragraph Dialog Box Launcher (Home tab or Page Layout tab | Paragraph group), click Indents and Spacing tab (Paragraph dialog box), click Special box arrow, click Hanging, and then click the OK button.

or

- With the insertion point in the paragraph to format, press CTRL+T.

To Modify a Source and Update the Bibliographical List

If you modify the contents of any source, the list of sources automatically updates because the list is a field. The following steps modify the title of the magazine article.

1

- Click the Manage Sources button (References tab | Citations & Bibliography group) to display the Source Manager dialog box.

- Click the source you wish to edit in the Current List, in this case the article by Jains, to select the source.

- Click the Edit button (Source Manager dialog box) to display the Edit Source dialog box.

- In the Title text box, insert the word, Distance, between the words, Measure and, in the title (Figure 2–56).

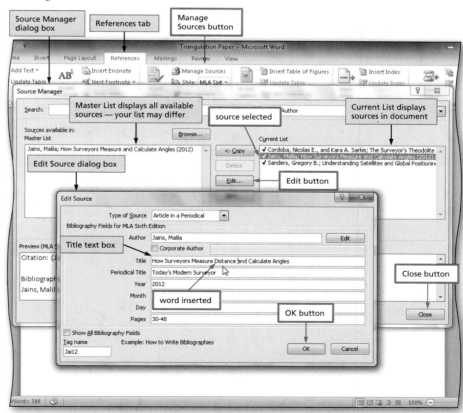

Figure 2–56

- Click the OK button (Edit Source dialog box) to close the dialog box.

- If a Microsoft Word dialog box appears, click its Yes button to update all occurrences of the source.

- Click the Close button (Source Manager dialog box) to update the list of sources in the document and close the dialog box (Figure 2–57).

Q&A What if the list of sources in the document is not updated automatically?

Click in the list of sources and then press the F9 key, which is the shortcut key to update a field.

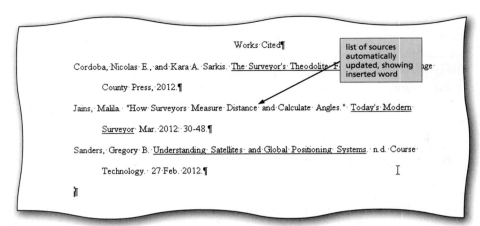

Figure 2–57

To Convert a Field to Regular Text

Word may use an earlier version of the MLA documentation style to format the bibliography. The latest guidelines for the MLA documentation style, for example, state that titles should be italicized instead of underlined, and each work should identify the source's publication medium (e.g., Print for printed media, Web for online media, etc.). If you format or add text to the bibliography, Word automatically will change it back to the Bibliography style's predetermined formats when the bibliography field is updated. To preserve modifications you make to the format of the bibliography, you can convert the bibliography field to regular text. Keep in mind, though, once you convert the field to regular text, it no longer is a field that can be updated. The following step converts a field to regular text.

1

- Click somewhere in the field to select it, in this case, somewhere in the bibliography (Figure 2–58).

Q&A What if the bibliography field is not shaded gray?

Click File on the Ribbon to open the Backstage view, click Options in the Backstage view, click Advanced in the left pane (Word Options dialog box), scroll to the 'Show document content' area, click the Field shading box arrow, click When selected, and then click the OK button.

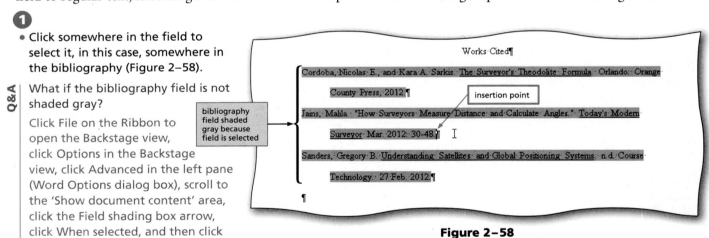

Figure 2–58

Q&A Why are all the words in the bibliography shaded?

The bibliography field consists of all text in the bibliography.

2

- Press CTRL+SHIFT+F9 to convert the selected field to regular text.

Q&A Why did the gray shading disappear?

The bibliography no longer is a field, so it is not shaded gray.

- Click anywhere in the document to remove the selection from the text.

To Format the Works Cited to the Latest MLA Documentation Style

As mentioned earlier, the latest the MLA documentation style guidelines state that titles should be italicized instead of underlined, and each work should identify the source's publication medium (e.g., Print, Web, Radio, Television, CD, DVD, Film, etc.). The following steps format and modify the Works Cited as specified by the latest MLA guidelines, if yours are not already formatted this way.

1 Drag through the book title, The Surveyor's Theodolite Formula, to select it.

2 Click Home on the Ribbon to display the Home tab. Click the Underline button (Home tab | Font group) to remove the underline from the selected text and then click the Italic button (Home tab | Font group) to italicize the selected text.

3 Select the magazine title, Today's Modern Surveyor. Remove the underline from the selected title and then italicize the selected title.

4 Select the Web page title, Understanding Satellites and Global Positioning Systems. Remove the underline from the selected title and then italicize the selected title.

5 After the period following the year in the first work, press the SPACEBAR and then type **Print.**

6 After the period following the page range in the second work, press the SPACEBAR and then type **Print.**

7 Before the date in the third work, type **Web.** and then press the SPACEBAR (Figure 2–59).

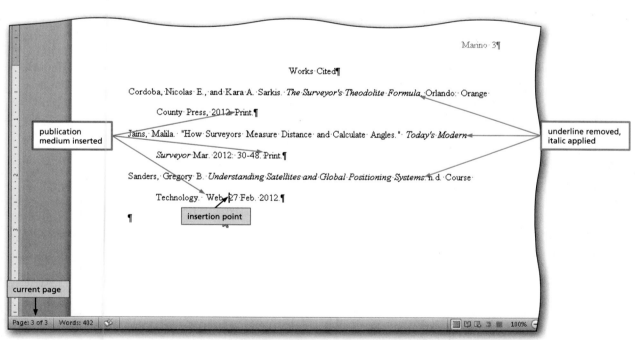

Figure 2–59

To Save an Existing Document with the Same File Name

You have made several modifications to the document since you last saved it. Thus, you should save it again. The following step saves the document again.

1 Click the Save button on the Quick Access Toolbar to overwrite the previously saved file.

Proofing and Revising the Research Paper

As discussed in Chapter 1, once you complete a document, you might find it necessary to make changes to it. Before submitting a paper to be graded, you should proofread it. While **proofreading**, look for grammatical errors and spelling errors. You also should ensure the transitions between sentences flow smoothly and the sentences themselves make sense.

Plan Ahead

Proofread and revise the paper.
As you proofread the paper, look for ways to improve it. Check all grammar, spelling, and punctuation. Be sure the text is logical and transitions are smooth. Where necessary, add text, delete text, reword text, and move text to different locations. Ask yourself these questions:

- Does the title suggest the topic?
- Is the thesis clear?
- Is the purpose of the paper clear?
- Does the paper have an introduction, body, and conclusion?
- Does each paragraph in the body relate to the thesis?
- Is the conclusion effective?
- Are all sources acknowledged?

To assist you with the proofreading effort, Word provides several tools. You can browse through pages, copy text, find text, replace text, insert a synonym, check spelling and grammar, and look up information. The following pages discuss these tools.

To Scroll Page by Page through a Document

The next step is to modify text on the second page of the paper. Currently, the third page is the active page (Figure 2–59 on the previous page). The following step scrolls up one page in the document.

1

- With the insertion point on the third page of the paper, click the Previous Page button on the vertical scroll bar to position the insertion point at the top of the previous page (Figure 2–60).

Q&A The button on my screen shows a ScreenTip different from Previous Page. Why?

By default, the functions of the buttons above and below the Select Browse Object button are Previous Page and Next Page, respectively. You can change the commands associated with these buttons by clicking the Select Browse Object button and then clicking the desired browse object. The Browse by Page command on the Select Browse Object menu, for example, changes the buttons back to Previous Page and Next Page.

Q&A How do I display the next page?
Click the Next Page button on the vertical scroll bar.

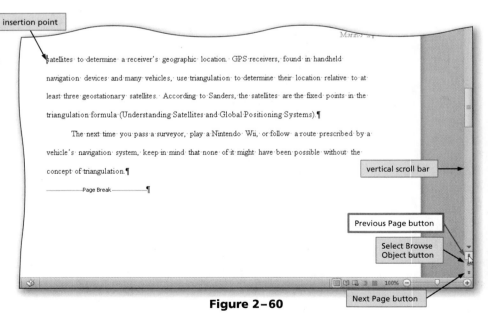

Figure 2–60

Other Ways

1. Click Page Number indicator on status bar, click Page in 'Go to what' list (Find and Replace dialog box), type desired page number in 'Enter page number' text box, click Go To button

2. Press CTRL+PAGE UP or CTRL+PAGE DOWN

Copying, Cutting, and Pasting

While proofreading the research paper, you decide it would read better if the word, geostationary, appeared in front of the word, satellites, in the last sentence of the fourth paragraph. You could type the word at the desired location, but because this is a difficult word to spell, you decide to use the Office Clipboard. The **Office Clipboard** is a temporary storage area that holds up to 24 items (text or graphics) copied from any Office program.

Copying is the process of placing items on the Office Clipboard, leaving the item in the document. **Cutting**, by contrast, removes the item from the document before placing it on the Office Clipboard. **Pasting** is the process of copying an item from the Office Clipboard into the document at the location of the insertion point.

To Copy and Paste

In the research paper, you copy a word from one sentence to another. The following steps copy and paste a word.

1
- Select the item to be copied (the word, geostationary, in this case).

- Click the Copy button (Home tab | Clipboard group) to copy the selected item in the document to the Office Clipboard (Figure 2–61).

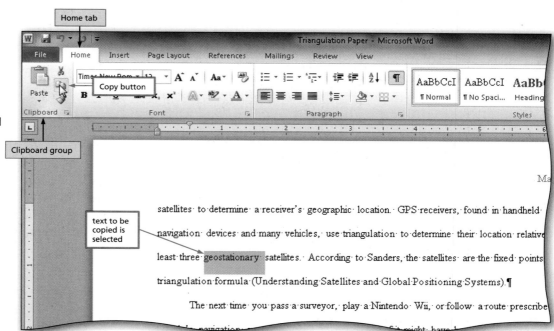

Figure 2–61

2
- Position the insertion point at the location where the item should be pasted (immediately to the left of the word, satellites, in this case) (Figure 2–62).

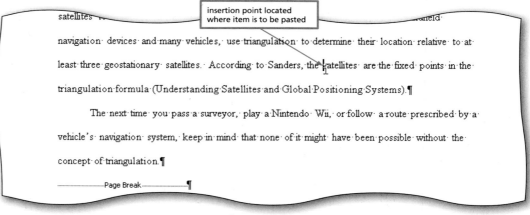

Figure 2–62

3

- Click the Paste button (Home tab | Clipboard group) to paste the copied item in the document at the location of the insertion point (Figure 2–63).

Q&A

What if I click the Paste button arrow by mistake?

Click the Paste button arrow again to remove the Paste menu.

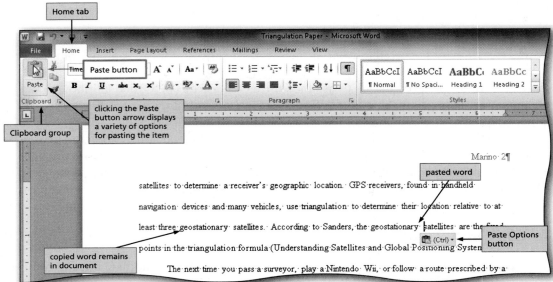

Figure 2–63

Other Ways

1. Right-click selected item, click Copy on shortcut menu, right-click where item is to be pasted, click Keep Source Formatting in Paste Options area on shortcut menu

2. Select item, press CTRL+C, position insertion point at paste location, press CTRL+V

To Display the Paste Options Menu

When you paste an item or move an item using drag-and-drop editing, which was discussed in the previous chapter, Word automatically displays a Paste Options button near the pasted or moved text (Figure 2–63). The Paste Options button allows you to change the format of a pasted item. For example, you can instruct Word to format the pasted item the same way as where it was copied, or format it the same way as where it is being pasted. The following steps display the Paste Options menu.

1

- Click the Paste Options button to display the Paste Options menu (Figure 2–64).

Q&A

What are the functions of the buttons on the Paste Options menu?

In general, the left button indicates the pasted item should look the same as it did in its original location. The second button formats the pasted text to match the rest of the item where it was pasted. The third button removes all formatting from the pasted item. The Set Default Paste command displays the Word Options dialog box. Keep in mind that the buttons shown on a Paste Options menu will vary, depending on the item being pasted.

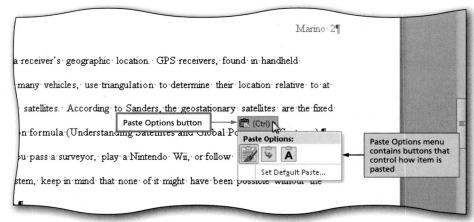

Figure 2–64

2

- Press the ESCAPE key to remove the Paste Options menu from the window.

To Find Text

While proofreading the paper, you would like to locate all occurrences of Wii console because you are contemplating changing this text to Wii game console. The following steps find all occurrences of specific text in a document.

1

- Click the Find button (Home tab | Editing group) to display the Navigation Pane (Figure 2–65).

Q&A

What is the Navigation Pane?

The **Navigation Pane** is a window that enables you to search for text in a document, browse through pages in a document, or browse through headings in a document.

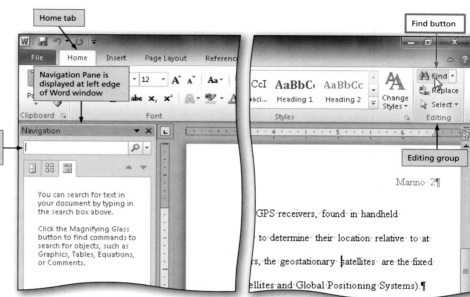

Figure 2–65

2

- Type **Wii console** in the Navigation Pane text box to display all occurrences of the typed text, called the search text, in the Navigation Pane and to highlight the occurrences of the search text in the document window (Figure 2–66).

3

 Experiment

- Type various search text in the Navigation Pane text box, and watch Word both list matches in the Navigation Pane and highlight matches in the document window. When you are finished experimenting, repeat Step 2.

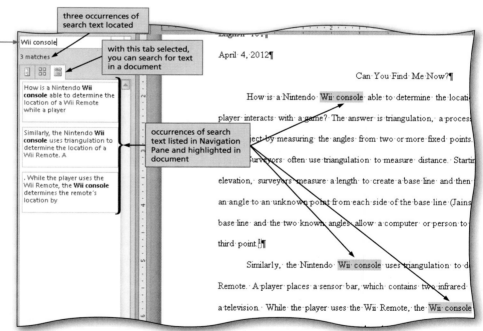

Figure 2–66

Other Ways

1. Click Find button arrow (Home tab | Editing group), click Find on Find menu, enter search text in Navigation Pane
2. Click Select Browse Object button on vertical scroll bar, click Find icon on Select Browse Object menu, enter search text (Find and Replace dialog box), click Find Next button
3. Click Page Number indicator on status bar, click Find tab (Find and Replace dialog box), enter search text, click Find Next button
4. Press CTRL+F

To Replace Text

You decide to change all occurrences of Wii console to Wii game console. To do this, you can use Word's find and replace feature, which automatically locates each occurrence of a word or phrase and then replaces it with specified text. The following steps replace all occurrences of Wii console with Wii game console.

- Click the Replace button (Home tab | Editing group) to display the Replace sheet in the Find and Replace dialog box.

- If necessary, type **Wii console** in the Find what text box (Find and Replace dialog box).

- Press the TAB key. Type **Wii game console** in the Replace with text box (Figure 2–67).

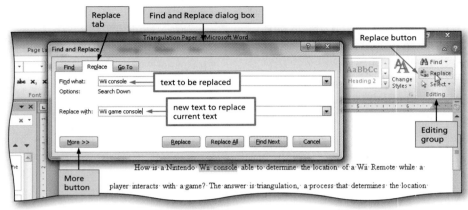

Figure 2–67

- Click the Replace All button to instruct Word to replace all occurrences of the Find what text with the Replace with text (Figure 2–68). If Word displays a dialog box asking if you want to continue searching from the beginning of the document, click the Yes button.

Q&A

Does Word search the entire document?

If the insertion point is at the beginning of the document, Word searches the entire document; otherwise, Word searches from the location of the insertion point to the end of the document and then displays a dialog box asking if you want to continue searching from the beginning. You also can search a section of text by selecting the text before clicking the Replace button.

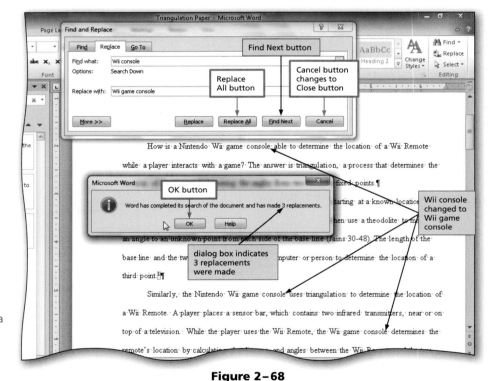

Figure 2–68

- Click the OK button (Microsoft Word dialog box) to close the dialog box.

- Click the Close button (Find and Replace dialog box) to close the dialog box.

Other Ways

1. Click Select Browse Object button on vertical scroll bar, click Find icon on Select Browse Object menu, click Replace tab

2. Click Page Number indicator on status bar, click Replace tab (Find and Replace dialog box)

3. Press CTRL+H

Find and Replace Dialog Box

The Replace All button (Find and Replace dialog box) replaces all occurrences of the Find what text with the Replace with text. In some cases, you may want to replace only certain occurrences of a word or phrase, not all of them. To instruct Word to confirm each change, click the Find Next button (Find and Replace dialog box) (Figure 2–68), instead of the Replace All button. When Word locates an occurrence of the text, it pauses and waits for you to click either the Replace button or the Find Next button. Clicking the Replace button changes the text; clicking the Find Next button instructs Word to disregard the replacement and look for the next occurrence of the Find what text.

If you accidentally replace the wrong text, you can undo a replacement by clicking the Undo button on the Quick Access Toolbar. If you used the Replace All button, Word undoes all replacements. If you used the Replace button, Word undoes only the most recent replacement.

BTW

Finding Formatting
To search for formatting or a special character, click the More button (shown in Figure 2–67) to expand the Find dialog box. To find formatting, use the Format button in the expanded Find dialog box. To find a special character, use the Special button.

To Go to a Page

The next step in revising the paper is to change a word on the second page of the document. You could scroll to the location in the document, or as mentioned earlier, you can use the Navigation Pane to browse through pages in a document. The following steps display the top of the second page in the document window and position the insertion point at the beginning of that page.

1
- Click the 'Browse the pages in your document' tab in the Navigation Pane to display thumbnail images of the pages in the document (Figure 2–69).

Q&A What if the Navigation Pane is not on the screen anymore?

Click View on the Ribbon to display the View tab and then click Navigation Pane (View tab | Show group) to select the check box.

2
- Click the thumbnail of the second page, even if the second page already is selected, to display the top of the selected page in the top of the document window (shown in Figure 2–70 on the next page).

3
- Click the Close button in the Navigation Pane to close the pane.

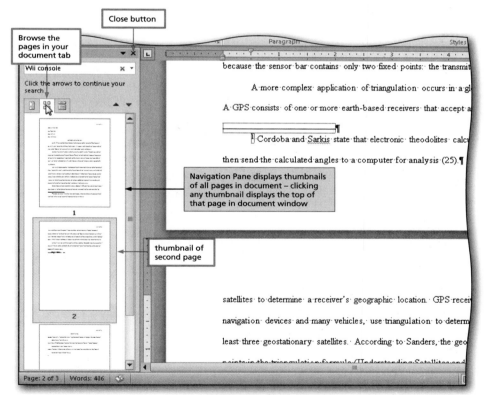

Figure 2–69

Other Ways		
1. Click Find button arrow (Home tab | Editing group), click Go To on Find menu, click Go To tab (Find and Replace dialog box), enter page number, click Go To button	2. Click Select Browse Object button on vertical scroll bar, click Go To icon on Select Browse Object menu, enter page number (Find and Replace dialog box), click Go To button	3. Click Page Number indicator on status bar, click Go To tab (Find and Replace dialog box), enter page number, click Go To button 4. Press CTRL+G

To Find and Insert a Synonym

When writing, you may discover that you used the same word in multiple locations or that a word you used was not quite appropriate. In these instances, you will want to look up a **synonym,** or a word similar in meaning, to the duplicate or inappropriate word. A **thesaurus** is a book of synonyms. Word provides synonyms and a thesaurus for your convenience.

In this project, you would like a synonym for the word, prescribed, in the fourth paragraph of the research paper. The following steps find a suitable synonym.

1

- Locate and then right-click the word for which you want to find a synonym (in this case, prescribed) to display a shortcut menu related to the word you right-clicked.

- Point to Synonyms on the shortcut menu to display a list of synonyms for the word you right-clicked (Figure 2–70).

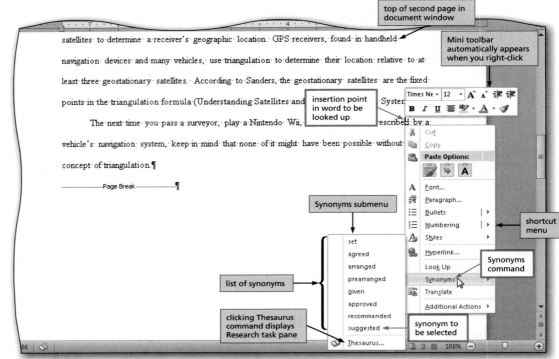

Figure 2–70

2

- Click the synonym you want (in this case, suggested) on the Synonyms submenu to replace the selected word in the document with the selected synonym (Figure 2–71).

Figure 2–71

Q&A

What if the synonyms list on the shortcut menu does not display a suitable word?

You can display the thesaurus in the Research task pane by clicking Thesaurus on the Synonyms submenu. The Research task pane displays a complete thesaurus, in which you can look up synonyms for various meanings of a word. You also can look up an **antonym,** or word with an opposite meaning. The Research task pane is discussed later in this chapter.

Other Ways

1. Click Thesaurus (Review tab | Proofing group)
2. Press SHIFT+F7

To Check Spelling and Grammar at Once

As discussed in Chapter 1, Word checks spelling and grammar as you type and places a wavy underline below possible spelling or grammar errors. Chapter 1 illustrated how to check these flagged words immediately. As an alternative, you can wait and check the entire document for spelling and grammar errors at once. The next steps check spelling and grammar at once.

Note: In the following steps, the word, theodolite, has been misspelled intentionally as theadalight to illustrate the use of Word's check spelling and grammar at once feature. If you are completing this project on a personal computer, your research paper may contain different misspelled words, depending on the accuracy of your typing.

1

• Press CTRL+HOME because you want the spelling and grammar check to begin from the top of the document.

• Click Review on the Ribbon to display the Review tab.

• Click the Spelling & Grammar button (Review tab | Proofing group) to begin the spelling and grammar check at the location of the insertion point, which in this case, is at the beginning of the document.

• Click the desired spelling in the Suggestions list (theodolite, in this case) (Figure 2–72).

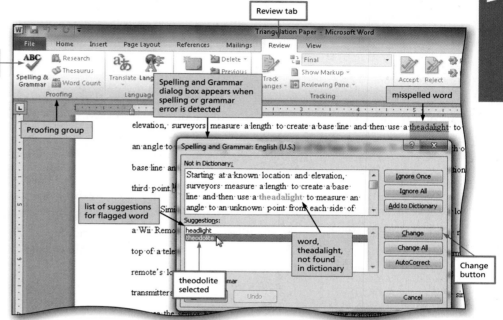

Figure 2–72

2

• With the word, theodolite, selected in the Suggestions list, click the Change button (Spelling and Grammar dialog box) to change the flagged word to the selected suggestion and then continue the spelling and grammar check until the next error is identified or the end of the document is reached (Figure 2–73).

3

• Click the Ignore All button (Spelling and Grammar dialog box) to ignore this and future occurrences of the flagged proper noun and then continue the spelling and grammar check until the next error is identified or the end of the document is reached.

4

• When the spelling and grammar check is finished and Word displays a dialog box, click its OK button.

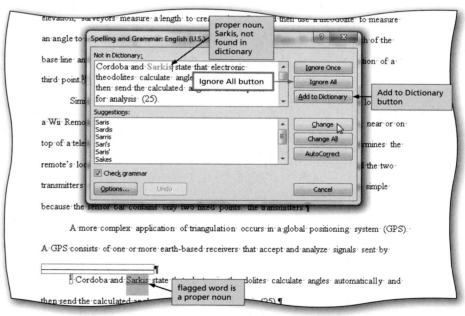

Figure 2–73

 Can I check spelling of just a section of a document?

Yes, select the text before starting the spelling and grammar check.

Other Ways
1. Click Spelling and Grammar Check icon on status bar, click Spelling on shortcut menu   2. Right-click flagged word, click Spelling on shortcut menu   3. Press F7

BTW

Readability Statistics
You can instruct Word to display readability statistics when it has finished a spelling and grammar check on a document. Three readability statistics presented are the percent of passive sentences, the Flesch Reading Ease score, and the Flesch-Kincaid Grade Level score. The Flesch Reading Ease score uses a 100-point scale to rate the ease with which a reader can understand the text in a document. A higher score means the document is easier to understand. The Flesch-Kincaid Grade Level score rates the text in a document on a U.S. school grade level. For example, a score of 10.0 indicates a student in the tenth grade can understand the material. To show readability statistics when the spelling and grammar check is complete, open the Backstage view, click Options in the Backstage view, click Proofing in the left pane (Word Options dialog box), place a check mark in the 'Show readability statistics' check box, and then click the OK button. Readability statistics will be displayed the next time you check spelling and grammar at once in the document.

The Main and Custom Dictionaries

As shown in the steps on the previous page, Word may flag a proper noun as an error because the proper noun is not in its main dictionary. To prevent Word from flagging proper nouns as errors, you can add the proper nouns to the custom dictionary. To add a correctly spelled word to the custom dictionary, click the Add to Dictionary button (Spelling and Grammar dialog box) or right-click the flagged word and then click Add to Dictionary on the shortcut menu. Once you have added a word to the custom dictionary, Word no longer will flag it as an error.

TO VIEW OR MODIFY ENTRIES IN A CUSTOM DICTIONARY

To view or modify the list of words in a custom dictionary, you would follow these steps.

1. Click File on the Ribbon and then click Options in the Backstage view.
2. Click Proofing in the left pane (Word Options dialog box).
3. Click the Custom Dictionaries button.
4. When Word displays the Custom Dictionaries dialog box, place a check mark next to the dictionary name to view or modify. Click the Edit Word List button (Custom Dictionaries dialog box). (In this dialog box, you can add or delete entries to and from the selected custom dictionary.)
5. When finished viewing and/or modifying the list, click the OK button in the dialog box.
6. Click the OK button (Custom Dictionaries dialog box).
7. If the 'Suggest from main dictionary only' check box is selected in the Word Options dialog box, remove the check mark. Click the OK button (Word Options dialog box).

TO SET THE DEFAULT CUSTOM DICTIONARY

If you have multiple custom dictionaries, you can specify which one Word should use when checking spelling. To set the default custom dictionary, you would follow these steps.

1. Click File on the Ribbon and then click Options in the Backstage view.
2. Click Proofing in the left pane (Word Options dialog box).
3. Click the Custom Dictionaries button.
4. When the Custom Dictionaries dialog box is displayed, place a check mark next to the desired dictionary name. Click the Change Default button (Custom Dictionaries dialog box).
5. Click the OK button (Custom Dictionaries dialog box).
6. If the 'Suggest from main dictionary only' check box is selected in the Word Options dialog box, remove the check mark. Click the OK button (Word Options dialog box).

To Use the Research Task Pane to Look Up Information

From within Word, you can search through various forms of reference information. Earlier, this chapter discussed the Research task pane with respect to looking up a synonym in a thesaurus. Other services available in the Research task pane include a dictionary and, if you are connected to the Web, a search engine and other Web sites that provide information such as stock quotes, news articles, and company profiles.

Assume you want to know more about the word, geostationary. The following steps use the Research task pane to look up a definition of a word.

1

- Locate the word you want to look up.

- While holding down the ALT key, click the word you want to look up (in this case, geostationary) to open the Research task pane and display a dictionary entry for the ALT+clicked word. Release the ALT key.

2

- Click the Search for box arrow in the Research task pane to display a list of search locations (Figure 2–74).

Why does my Research task pane look different?

Depending on your settings and Microsoft's Web site search settings, your Research task pane may appear different from the figures shown here.

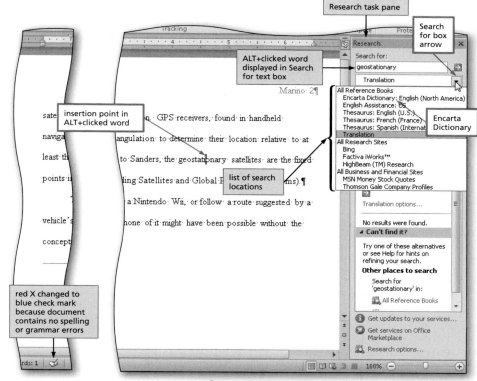

Figure 2–74

- Click Encarta Dictionary in the list to display a definition for the ALT+clicked word (Figure 2–75).

Can I copy information from the Research task pane into my document?

Yes, you can use the Copy and Paste commands. When using Word to insert material from the Research task pane or any other online reference, however, be careful not to plagiarize.

3

- Click the Close button in the Research task pane.

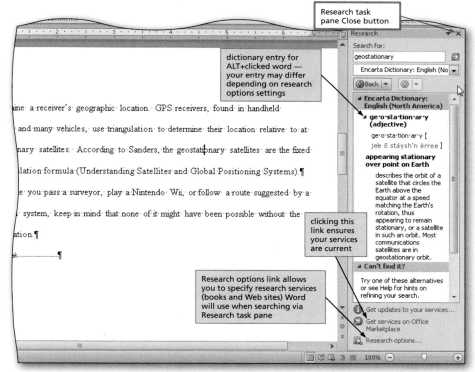

Figure 2–75

Other Ways

1. Click Research button (Review tab | Proofing group)

Research Task Pane Options

When you install Word, it selects a series of services (reference books and Web sites) that it searches through when you use the Research task pane. You can view, modify, and update the list of services at any time.

Clicking the Research options link at the bottom of the Research task pane (shown in Figure 2–75 on the previous page) displays the Research Options dialog box, where you can view or modify the list of installed services. You can view information about any installed service by clicking the service in the list and then clicking the Properties button. To activate an installed service, click the check box to its left; likewise, to deactivate a service, remove the check mark. To add a particular Web site to the list, click the Add Services button, enter the Web address in the Address text box, and then click the Add button (Add Services dialog box). To update or remove services, click the Update/Remove button, select the service in the list, click the Update (or Remove) button (Update or Remove Services dialog box), and then click the Close button. You also can install parental controls through the Parental Control button (Research Options dialog box), for example, if you want to prevent minor children who use Word from accessing the Web.

To Change Document Properties

Before saving the research paper again, you want to add your name, course information, and some keywords as document properties. The following steps use the Document Information Panel to change document properties.

1 Click File on the Ribbon to open the Backstage view and, if necessary, select the Info tab.

2 Click the Properties button in the right pane of the Info gallery to display the Properties menu and then click Show Document Panel on the Properties menu to close the Backstage view and display the Document Information Panel in the Word document window.

3 Click the Author text box, if necessary, and then type your name as the Author property. If a name already is displayed in the Author text box, delete it before typing your name.

4 Click the Subject text box, if necessary delete any existing text, and then type your course and section as the Subject property.

5 Click the Keywords text box, if necessary delete any existing text, and then type **surveyor, Wii, GPS** as the Keywords property.

6 Click the Close the Document Information Panel button so that the Document Information Panel no longer is displayed.

To Save an Existing Document with the Same File Name

You have made several modifications to the document since you last saved it. Thus, you should save it again. The following step saves the document again.

1 Click the Save button on the Quick Access Toolbar to overwrite the previously saved file.

BTW

Conserving Ink and Toner
If you want to conserve ink or toner, you can instruct Word to print draft quality documents by clicking File on the Ribbon to open the Backstage view, clicking Options in the Backstage view to display the Word Options dialog box, clicking Advanced in the left pane (Word Options dialog box), scrolling to the Print area in the right pane, placing a check mark in the 'Use draft quality' check box, and then clicking the OK button. Then, use the Backstage view to print the document as usual.

To Print Document Properties

With the document properties entered and the completed document saved, you may want to print the document properties along with the document. The following steps print the document properties for the Triangulation Paper.

1
- Click File on the Ribbon to open the Backstage view and then click the Print tab in the Backstage view to display the Print gallery.

- Verify the printer name that appears on the Printer Status button will print a hard copy of the document. If necessary, click the Printer Status button to display a list of available printer options and then click the desired printer to change the currently selected printer.

- Click the first button in the Settings area to display a list of options specifying what you can print (Figure 2–76).

2
- Click Document Properties in the list to specify you want to print the document properties instead of the actual document.

- Click the Print button in the Print gallery to print the document properties on the currently selected printer (Figure 2–77).

 Q&A

What if the currently updated document properties do not print on the hard copy?

Try closing the document, reopening the document, and then repeating these steps.

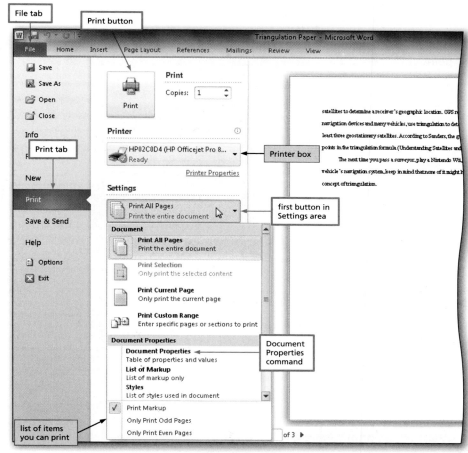

Figure 2–76

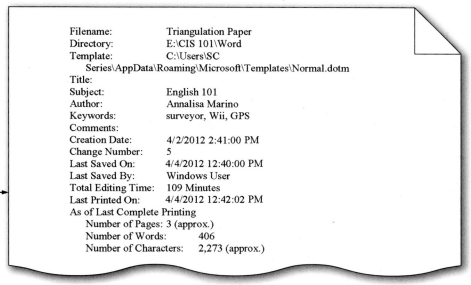

Filename:	Triangulation Paper
Directory:	E:\CIS 101\Word
Template:	C:\Users\SC Series\AppData\Roaming\Microsoft\Templates\Normal.dotm
Title:	
Subject:	English 101
Author:	Annalisa Marino
Keywords:	surveyor, Wii, GPS
Comments:	
Creation Date:	4/2/2012 2:41:00 PM
Change Number:	5
Last Saved On:	4/4/2012 12:40:00 PM
Last Saved By:	Windows User
Total Editing Time:	109 Minutes
Last Printed On:	4/4/2012 12:42:02 PM

As of Last Complete Printing
Number of Pages: 3 (approx.)
Number of Words: 406
Number of Characters: 2,273 (approx.)

printed document properties — your properties may differ, depending on settings

Figure 2–77

Other Ways

1. Press CTRL+P, press ENTER

To Preview the Document and Then Print It

Before printing the research paper, you want to verify the page layouts. The following steps change the print option to print the document (instead of the document properties), preview the printed pages in the research paper, and then print the document.

- Position the insertion point at the top of the document because you want initially to view the first page in the document.

- Click File on the Ribbon to open the Backstage view and then click the Print tab in the Backstage view to display the Print gallery.

- Verify the printer name that appears on the Printer Status button will print a hard copy of the document. If necessary, select a different printer.

- Click the first button in the Settings area to display a list of options specifying what you can print (Figure 2–78).

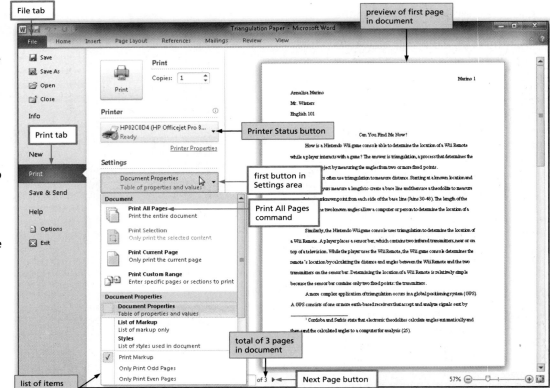

Figure 2–78

- Click Print All Pages in the list to specify you want to print all pages in the actual document.

- Click the Next Page button in the Print gallery to preview the second page of the research paper in the Print gallery.

- Click the Next Page button again to preview the third page of the research paper in the Print gallery (Figure 2–79).

- Click the Print button in the Print gallery to print the research paper on the currently selected printer (shown in Figure 2–1 on page WD 67).

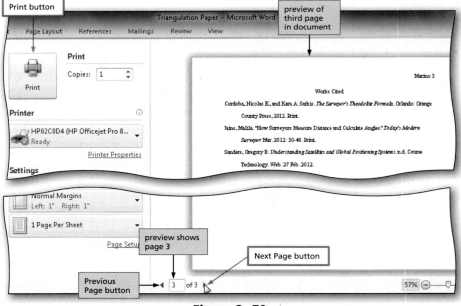

Figure 2–79

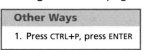

Other Ways

1. Press CTRL+P, press ENTER

To Quit Word

This project now is complete. The following steps quit Word. For a detailed example of the procedure summarized below, refer to the Office 2010 and Windows 7 chapter at the beginning of this book.

1 If you have one Word document open, click the Close button on the right side of the title bar to close the document and quit Word; or if you have multiple Word documents open, click File on the Ribbon to open the Backstage view and then click Exit in the Backstage view to close all open documents and quit Word.

2 If a Microsoft Word dialog box appears, click the Save button to save any changes made to the document since the last save.

BTW

Quick Reference
For a table that lists how to complete the tasks covered in this book using the mouse, Ribbon, shortcut menu, and keyboard, see the Quick Reference Summary at the back of this book, or visit the Word 2010 Quick Reference Web page (scsite.com/wd2010/qr).

Chapter Summary

In this chapter, you have learned how to change document settings, use headers to number pages, modify a style, insert and edit citations and their sources, add footnotes, create a bibliographical list of sources, and use the Research task pane. The items listed below include all the new Word skills you have learned in this chapter.

1. Modify a Style (WD 70)
2. Change Line Spacing (WD 73)
3. Remove Space after a Paragraph (WD 74)
4. Update a Style to Match a Selection (WD 74)
5. Switch to the Header (WD 75)
6. Right-Align a Paragraph (WD 76)
7. Insert a Page Number (WD 77)
8. Close the Header (WD 78)
9. Click and Type (WD 80)
10. Display the Rulers (WD 82)
11. First-Line Indent Paragraphs (WD 83)
12. AutoCorrect as You Type (WD 85)
13. Use the AutoCorrect Options Button (WD 85)
14. Create an AutoCorrect Entry (WD 86)
15. Change the Bibliography Style (WD 89)
16. Insert a Citation and Create Its Source (WD 90)
17. Edit a Citation (WD 91)
18. Insert a Footnote Reference Mark (WD 93)
19. Insert a Citation Placeholder (WD 94)
20. Modify a Style Using a Shortcut Menu (WD 95)
21. Edit a Source (WD 97)
22. Count Words (WD 101)
23. Page Break Manually (WD 106)
24. Apply a Style (WD 106)
25. Create the Bibliographical List (WD 108)
26. Format Paragraphs with a Hanging Indent (WD 109)
27. Modify a Source and Update the Bibliographical List (WD 109)
28. Convert a Field to Regular Text (WD 110)
29. Scroll Page by Page through a Document (WD 112)
30. Copy and Paste (WD 113)
31. Display the Paste Options Menu (WD 114)
32. Find Text (WD 115)
33. Replace Text (WD 116)
34. Go to a Page (WD 117)
35. Find and Insert a Synonym (WD 118)
36. Check Spelling and Grammar at Once (WD 118)
37. View or Modify Entries in a Custom Dictionary (WD 120)
38. Set the Default Custom Dictionary (WD 120)
39. Use the Research Task Pane to Look Up Information (WD 120)
40. Print Document Properties (WD 123)
41. Preview the Document and Then Print It (WD 124)

If you have a SAM 2010 user profile, your instructor may have assigned an autogradable version of this assignment. If so, log into the SAM 2010 Web site at www.cengage.com/sam2010 to download the instruction and start files.

Learn It Online

Test your knowledge of chapter content and key terms.

Instructions: To complete the Learn It Online exercises, start your browser, click the Address bar, and then enter the Web address **scsite.com/wd2010/learn**. When the Word 2010 Learn It Online page is displayed, click the link for the exercise you want to complete and then read the instructions.

Chapter Reinforcement TF, MC, and SA
A series of true/false, multiple choice, and short answer questions that test your knowledge of the chapter content.

Flash Cards
An interactive learning environment where you identify chapter key terms associated with displayed definitions.

Practice Test
A series of multiple choice questions that test your knowledge of chapter content and key terms.

Who Wants To Be a Computer Genius?
An interactive game that challenges your knowledge of chapter content in the style of a television quiz show.

Wheel of Terms
An interactive game that challenges your knowledge of chapter key terms in the style of the television show *Wheel of Fortune*.

Crossword Puzzle Challenge
A crossword puzzle that challenges your knowledge of key terms presented in the chapter.

Apply Your Knowledge

Reinforce the skills and apply the concepts you learned in this chapter.

Revising Text and Paragraphs in a Document
Note: To complete this assignment, you will be required to use the Data Files for Students. See the inside back cover of this book for instructions on downloading the Data Files for Students, or contact your instructor for information about accessing the required files.

Instructions: Start Word. Open the document, Apply 2-1 Space Paragraph Draft, from the Data Files for Students. The document you open contains a paragraph of text. You are to revise the document as follows: move a word, move another word and change the format of the moved word, change paragraph indentation, change line spacing, find all occurrences of a word, replace all occurrences of a word with another word, locate a synonym, and edit the header.

Perform the following tasks:
1. Copy the word, exploration, from the first sentence and paste it in the last sentence after the word, space, so that it is the eighth word in the sentence.
2. Select the underlined word, safe, in the paragraph. Use drag-and-drop editing to move the selected word, safe, so that it is before the word, mission, in the same sentence. Click the Paste Options button that displays to the right of the moved word, safe. Remove the underline format from the moved sentence by clicking Keep Text Only on the Paste Options menu.
3. Display the ruler, if necessary. Use the ruler to indent the first line of the paragraph one-half inch.
4. Change the line spacing of the paragraph to double.
5. Use the Navigation Pane to find all occurrences of the word, sensors. How many are there?
6. Use the Find and Replace dialog box to replace all occurrences of the word, issues, with the word, problems. How many replacements were made?

7. Use Word to find the word, height. Use Word's thesaurus to change the word, height, to the word, altitude.

8. Switch to the header so that you can edit it. In the first line of the header, change the word, Draft, to the word, Modified, so that it reads: Space Paragraph Modified.

9. In the second line of the header, insert the page number (with no formatting) one space after the word, Page.

10. Change the alignment of both lines of text in the header from left-aligned to right-aligned. Switch back to the document text.

11. Change the document properties, as specified by your instructor.

12. Click File on the Ribbon and then click Save As. Save the document using the file name, Apply 2-1 Space Paragraph Modified.

13. Print the document properties and then print the revised document, shown in Figure 2–80.

14. Use the Research task pane to look up the definition of the word, NASA, in the paragraph. Handwrite the definition of the word on your printout, as well as your response to the question in #6.

15. Change the Search for box to All Research Sites. Print an article from one of the sites.

16. Display the Research Options dialog box and, on your printout, handwrite the currently active Reference Books, Research Sites, and Business and Financial Sites. If your instructor approves, activate one of the services.

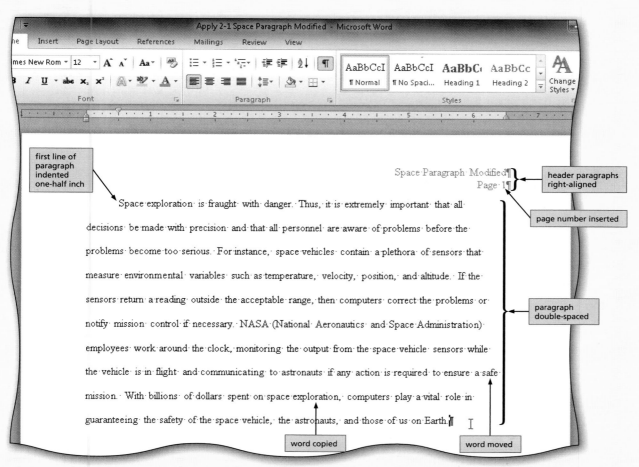

Figure 2–80

Extend Your Knowledge

Extend the skills you learned in this chapter and experiment with new skills. You may need to use Help to complete the assignment.

Working with References and Proofing Tools

Note: To complete this assignment, you will be required to use the Data Files for Students. See the inside back cover of this book for instructions on downloading the Data Files for Students, or contact your instructor for information about accessing the required files.

Instructions: Start Word. Open the document, Extend 2-1 Digital Camera Paper Draft, from the Data Files for Students. You will add another footnote to the paper, use the thesaurus, convert the document from MLA to APA documentation style, convert the footnotes to endnotes, modify the Endnote Text style, change the format of the note reference marks, and translate the document to another language (Figure 2–81).

research paper translated from English to German

Figure 2–81

Perform the following tasks:

1. Use Help to learn more about footers, footnotes and endnotes, bibliography styles, AutoCorrect, and the Mini Translator.

2. Delete the footer from the document.

3. Insert a second footnote at an appropriate place in the research paper. Use the following footnote text: For instance, Adams states that you may be able to crop photos, change the brightness, or remove red eye effects.

4. Change the location of the footnotes from bottom of page to below text.

5. Use the Find and Replace dialog box to find the word, small, in the document and then replace it with a word of your choice.

6. Save the document with a new file name and then print it. On the printout, write the number of words, characters without spaces, characters with spaces, paragraphs, and lines in the document. Be sure to include footnote text in the statistics.

7. Select the entire document and then change the documentation style of the citations and bibliography from MLA to APA. Save the APA version of the document with a new file name and then print it. Compare the two versions. Circle the differences between the two documents.

8. Convert the footnotes to endnotes.

9. Modify the Endnote Text style to 12-point Times New Roman font, double-spaced text with a hanging-line indent.

10. Change the format of the note reference marks to capital letters (A, B, etc.).

11. Add an AutoCorrect entry that replaces the word, camora, with the word, camera. Add this sentence, A field camora usually is more than sufficient for most users., to the end of the second paragraph, misspelling the word camera to test the AutoCorrect entry. Delete the AutoCorrect entry that replaces camora with the word, camera.

12. Display readability statistics. What are the Flesch-Kincaid Grade Level, the Flesch Reading Ease score, and the percent of passive sentences?

13. Save the revised document with endnotes with a new file name and then print it. On the printout, write your response to the question in #12.

14. If you have an Internet connection, translate the research paper into a language of your choice using the Translate button (Review tab | Language group). Submit the translated document in the format specified by your instructor. Use the Mini Translator to hear how to pronounce three words in your paper.

Make It Right

Analyze a document and correct all errors and/or improve the design.

Inserting Missing Elements in an MLA-Styled Research Paper

Note: To complete this assignment, you will be required to use the Data Files for Students. See the inside back cover of this book for instructions on downloading the Data Files for Students, or contact your instructor for information about accessing the required files.

Instructions: Start Word. Open the document, Make It Right 2-1 Biometrics Paper Draft, from the Data Files for Students. The document is a research paper that is missing several elements. You are to insert these missing elements, all formatted according to the MLA documentation style: header with a page number, name and course information, paper title, footnote, and source information for a citation.

Perform the following tasks:

1. Insert a header with a page number (use your own last name), name and course information (your name, your instructor name, your course name, and today's date), and an appropriate paper title, all formatted according to the MLA documentation style.

2. The Jenkins citation placeholder is missing its source information (Figure 2–82). Use the following source information to edit the source: magazine article titled "Fingerprint Readers" written by Arthur D. Jenkins and Marissa K. Weavers, magazine name is *Security Today*, publication date is February 2012, article is on pages 55–60. Edit the citation so that it displays the author name and the page numbers of 55–56 for this reference.

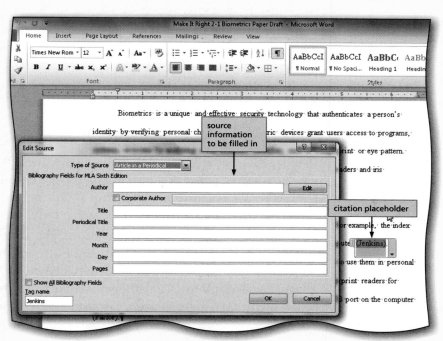

Figure 2–82

Continued >

Make It Right *continued*

3. Modify the source of the book authored by Carolina Doe, so that the publisher city is Chicago instead of Dallas.

4. Change the Footnote Text style to 12-point Times New Roman, double-spaced paragraphs with a first-line indent.

5. Insert the following footnote with the note reference at an appropriate place in the paper, formatted according to the MLA documentation style: Parlor states that one use of fingerprint readers is for users to log on to programs and Web sites via their fingerprint instead of entering a user name and password.

6. Use the Navigation Pane to display page 3. Use Word to insert the bibliographical list (bibliography). Convert the works cited to regular text. Change the underline format on the titles of the works to the italic format, and insert the correct publication medium for each work.

7. Change the document properties, as specified by your instructor. Save the revised document with the file name, Make It Right 2-1 Biometrics Paper Modified, and then submit it in the format specified by your instructor.

In the Lab

Design and/or create a document using the guidelines, concepts, and skills presented in this chapter. Labs are listed in order of increasing difficulty.

Lab 1: Preparing a Short Research Paper

Problem: You are a college student currently enrolled in an introductory business class. Your assignment is to prepare a short research paper (275–300 words) about video or computer games. The requirements are that the paper be presented according to the MLA documentation style and have three references. One of the three references must be from the Web. You prepare the paper shown in Figure 2–83 on pages WD 131 and WD 132, which discusses game controllers.

Instructions: Perform the following tasks:

1. Start Word. If necessary, display formatting marks on the screen.

2. Modify the Normal style to 12-point Times New Roman font.

3. Adjust line spacing to double.

4. Remove space below (after) paragraphs.

5. Update the Normal style to reflect the adjusted line and paragraph spacing.

6. Create a header to number pages.

7. Type the name and course information at the left margin. Center and type the title.

8. Set a first-line indent to one-half inch for paragraphs in the body of the research paper.

9. Type the research paper as shown in Figures 2–83a and 2–83b. Change the bibliography style to MLA. As you insert citations, enter their source information (shown in Figure 2–83c). Edit the citations so that they are displayed according to Figures 2–83a and 2–83b.

10. At the end of the research paper text, press the ENTER key and then insert a manual page break so that the Works Cited page begins on a new page. Enter and format the works cited title (Figure 2–83c). Use Word to insert the bibliographical list (bibliography). Convert the bibliography field to text. Change the underline format on the titles of the works to the italic format and insert the correct publication medium for each work (shown in Figure 2–83c).

(b) Page 2

Kimble 2

Game controllers are used primarily to direct movement and actions of on-screen objects. Two popular types are gamepads and motion-sensing game controllers. Games become more enjoyable every day with the use of new and exciting game controllers. What will be next?

(a) Page 1

Kimble 1

Harley Kimble

Ms. Longherst

English 101

April 30, 2012

From One Controller to Another

Video games and computer games use a game controller as the input device that directs movements and actions of on-screen objects. Two commonly used game controllers are gamepads and motion-sensing game controllers (Joyce). Game controllers not only enrich the gaming experience but also aid in the movements and actions of players.

A gamepad is held by the player with both hands, allowing the player to control the movement or actions of the objects in the video or computer games. Players press buttons on the gamepad, often with their thumbs, to carry out actions. Some gamepads have swiveling sticks that also can trigger events during game play (Cortez 20-24). Some gamepads include wireless capabilities; others connect via a cable directly to the game console or a personal computer.

Motion-sensing game controllers allow the user to guide on-screen elements or trigger events by moving a handheld input device in predetermined directions through the air. These controllers communicate with a game console or personal computer via wired or wireless technology. A variety of games, from sports to simulations, use motion-sensing game controllers. Some of these controllers, such as baseball bats and golf clubs, are designed for only one specific kind of game; others are general purpose. A popular, general-purpose, motion-sensing game controller is Nintendo's Wii Remote. Shaped like a television remote control and operated with one hand, the Wii Remote uses Bluetooth wireless technology to communicate with the Wii game console (Bloom 56-59).

Figure 2–83

Continued >

In the Lab *continued*

(c) Page 3

Kimble 3

Works Cited

Bloom, June. *The Gaming Experience*. New York: Buffalo Works Press, 2012. Print.

Cortez, Domiciano Isachar. "Today's Game Controllers." *Gaming, Gaming, Gaming* Jan. 2012:

12-34. Print.

Joyce, Andrea D. *What Gamers Want*. 15 Feb. 2012. Web. 28 Mar. 2012.

11. Check the spelling and grammar of the paper at once.

12. Change the document properties, as specified by your instructor. Save the document using Lab 2-1 Game Controllers Paper as the file name.

13. Print the research paper. Handwrite the number of words, paragraphs, and characters in the research paper above the title of your printed research paper.

In the Lab

Lab 2: Preparing a Research Report with a Footnote

Problem: You are a college student enrolled in an introductory English class. Your assignment is to prepare a short research paper in any area of interest to you. The requirements are that the paper be presented according to the MLA documentation style, contain at least one note positioned as a footnote, and have three references. One of the three references must be from the Internet. You prepare a paper about trends in agriculture (Figure 2–84).

Instructions: Perform the following tasks:
1. Start Word. Modify the Normal style to 12-point Times New Roman font. Adjust line spacing to double and remove space below (after) paragraphs. Update the Normal style to include the adjusted line and paragraph spacing. Create a header to number pages. Type the name and course information at the left margin. Center and type the title. Set a first-line indent for paragraphs in the body of the research paper.

2. Type the research paper as shown in Figures 2–84a and 2–84b. Insert the footnote as shown in Figure 2–84a. Change the Footnote Text style to the format specified in the MLA documentation style. Change the bibliography style to MLA. As you insert citations, use the source information listed below and on page WD 134:
   a. Type of Source: Article in a Periodical
      Author: Barton, Blake
      Title: Computers in Agriculture
      Periodical Title: Agriculture Today and Tomorrow
      Year: 2012
      Month: Feb.
      Pages 53–86
      Publication Medium: Print

(b) Page 2

Gander 2

Brewster, the discovery of pests might trigger a pesticide to discharge in the affected area

automatically (Agriculture: Expanding and Growing).

Many farmers use technology on a daily basis to regulate soil moisture and to keep their

crops pest free. With technology, farming can be much more convenient and efficient.

(a) Page 1

Gander 1

Samuel Gander

Mr. Dunham

English 102

April 25, 2012

Farming on a Whole New Level

Although people have worked in agriculture for more than 10,000 years, advances in

technology assist with maintaining and protecting land, crops, and animals. The demand to keep

food prices affordable encourages those working in the agriculture industry to operate as

efficiently as possible (Newman and Ruiz 33-47).

Almost all people and companies in this industry have many acres of land they must

maintain, and it is not always feasible for farmers to take frequent trips around the property to

perform basic tasks such as watering soil in the absence of rain. The number of people-hours

required to water soil manually on several thousand acres of land might result in businesses

spending thousands of dollars in labor and utility costs. If the irrigation process is automated,

sensors detect how much rain has fallen recently, as well as whether the soil is in need of

watering. The sensors then send this data to a computer that processes it and decides when and

how much to water.[1]

In addition to keeping the soil moist and reducing maintenance costs, computers also can

utilize sensors to analyze the condition of crops in the field and determine whether pests or

diseases are affecting the crops. If sensors detect pests and/or diseases, computers send a

notification to the appropriate individual to take corrective action. In some cases, according to

---

[1] Barton states that many automated home irrigation systems also are programmable and

use rain sensors (67-73).

Figure 2–84

Continued >

In the Lab *continued*

  b. Type of Source: Book
   Author: Newman, Albert D., and Carmen W. Ruiz
   Title: The Agricultural Industry Today
   Year: 2012
   City: New York
   Publisher: Alabama Press
   Publication Medium: Print
  c. Type of Source: Web site
   Author: Brewster, Letty
   Name of Web page: Agriculture: Expanding and Growing
   Year: 2012
   Month: Jan.
   Day: 3
   Publication Medium: Web
   Year Accessed: 2012
   Month Accessed: Feb.
   Day Accessed: 9

3. At the end of the research paper text, press the ENTER key once and insert a manual page break so that the Works Cited page begins on a new page. Enter and format the works cited title. Use Word to insert the bibliographical list. Convert the bibliography field to text. Change the underline format on the titles of the works to the italic format, and insert the correct publication medium for each work.

4. Check the spelling and grammar of the paper.

5. Save the document using Lab 2-2 Agriculture Paper as the file name.

6. Print the research paper. Handwrite the number of words, including the footnotes, in the research paper above the title of your printed research paper.

In the Lab

Lab 3: Composing a Research Paper from Notes

Problem: You have drafted the notes shown in Figure 2–85. Your assignment is to prepare a short research paper from these notes.

Instructions: Perform the following tasks:

1. Start Word. Review the notes in Figure 2–85 and then rearrange and reword them. Embellish the paper as you deem necessary. Present the paper according to the MLA documentation style.

  Create an AutoCorrect entry that automatically corrects the spelling of the misspelled word, digtal, to the correct spelling, digital. Set an AutoCorrect exception for CD., so that Word does not lowercase the next typed letter.

  Insert a footnote that refers the reader to the Web for more information. Enter citations and their sources as shown.

  Create the works cited page (bibliography) from the listed sources. Convert the bibliography field to text. Change the underline format on the titles of the works to the italic format, and insert the correct publication medium for each work.

2. If necessary, set the default dictionary. Add the word, Flickr, to the dictionary. Check the spelling and grammar of the paper.

3. Use the Research task pane to look up a definition of a word in the paper. Copy and insert the definition into the document as a footnote. Be sure to quote the definition and cite the source. *Hint:* Use a Web site as the type of source.

4. Save the document using Lab 2-3 Cloud Storage Paper as the file name. Print the research paper. Handwrite the number of words, including the footnotes, in the research paper above the title of the printed research paper.

Cloud Storage:
- When storing data using cloud storage, the user must locate the appropriate Web site. Some sites support only certain file types. Other sites provide more than just storage.
- Cloud storage is one of the many different features available on the Internet.
- Cloud storage allows users to store files on Web sites.
- Computer users may use this type of storage if they do not want to store their data locally on a hard disk or other type of media.

Different Web sites provide different types of cloud storage. Three are Google's Gmail, YouTube, and Windows Live SkyDrive (source: "Cloud Storage and the Internet," an article on pages 23-37 in March 2012 issue of *Internet Usage and Trends* by Leona Carter).
- Google's e-mail program, Gmail, is cloud storage that stores e-mail messages.
- YouTube is different from Gmail, however, because it stores only digital videos (source: pages 22-24 in a book called *Working with the Internet: Cloud Storage* by Robert M. Gaff, published at Jane Lewis Press in New York in 2012).
- Windows Live SkyDrive is a cloud storage provider that accepts any type of file. This type of Web site is used mainly for backup or additional storage space.

Some cloud storage Web sites also provide other services (source: a Web site titled *The Internet: Cloud Storage* by Rebecca A. Ford and Harry I. Garland of Course Technology dated January 2, 2012, viewed on March 7, 2012).
- Flickr provides cloud storage for digital photos and also enables users to manage their photos and share them with others.
- Facebook provides cloud storage for a number of different file types including digital photos, digital videos, messages, and personal information. Facebook also provides a means of social networking.
- Google Docs not only stores documents, spreadsheets, and presentations in its cloud, it also enables its users to create these documents.

Figure 2–85

Cases and Places

Apply your creative thinking and problem solving skills to design and implement a solution.

Note: To complete these assignments, you may be required to use the Data Files for Students. See the inside back cover of this book for instructions on downloading the Data Files for Students, or contact your instructor for information about accessing the required files.

1: Create a Research Paper about Preparing for a Career in the Computer Industry

Academic

As a student in an introductory computer class, your instructor has assigned a research paper that discusses educational options available for students pursuing a career in the computer industry. The source for the text in your research paper is in a file called Preparing for a Career in the Computer Industry, which is located on the Data Files for Students. In addition to this source, if your instructor requests, use the Research task pane to obtain information from another source. Include a note positioned as a footnote. Add an AutoCorrect entry to correct a word you commonly mistype.

Using the concepts and techniques presented in this chapter, along with the text in the file on the Data Files for Students, create and format this research paper according to the MLA documentation style. Be sure to check spelling and grammar of the finished paper. Submit your assignment in the format specified by your instructor.

2: Create a Research Paper about Computer Viruses

Personal

The computer you recently purchased included an antivirus program. Because you need practice writing research papers and you want to learn more about computer viruses, you decide to write a paper about computer viruses. The source for the text in your research paper is in a file called Computer Viruses, which is located on the Data Files for Students. In addition to this source, if your instructor requests, use the Research task pane to obtain information from another source. Include a note positioned as a footnote. Add an AutoCorrect entry to correct a word you commonly mistype.

Using the concepts and techniques presented in this chapter, along with the text in the file on the Data Files for Students, create and format this research paper according to the MLA documentation style. Be sure to check spelling and grammar of the finished paper. Submit your assignment in the format specified by your instructor.

3: Create a Research Paper about a Disaster Recovery Plan

Professional

Your boss has asked you to research the components of a disaster recovery plan. Because you learned in college how to write research papers, you decide to present your findings in a research paper. The source for the text in your research paper is in a file called Disaster Recovery Plan, which is located on the Data Files for Students. In addition to this source, if your instructor requests, use the Research task pane to obtain information from another source. Include a note positioned as a footnote. Add an AutoCorrect entry to correct a word you commonly mistype.

Using the concepts and techniques presented in this chapter, along with the text in the file on the Data Files for Students, create and format this research paper according to the MLA documentation style. Be sure to check spelling and grammar of the finished paper. Submit your assignment in the format specified by your instructor.

1 Creating and Editing a Presentation with Clip Art

Objectives

You will have mastered the material in this chapter when you can:

- Select a document theme
- Create a title slide and a text slide with a multi-level bulleted list
- Add new slides and change slide layouts
- Insert clips and pictures into a slide with and without a content placeholder
- Move and size clip art

- Change font size and color
- Bold and italicize text
- Duplicate a slide
- Arrange slides
- Select slide transitions
- View a presentation in Slide Show view
- Print a presentation

1 | Creating and Editing a Presentation with Clip Art

Introduction

A PowerPoint **presentation,** also called a **slide show,** can help you deliver a dynamic, professional-looking message to an audience. PowerPoint allows you to produce slides to use in an academic, business, or other environment. One of the more common uses of these slides is to enhance an oral presentation. A speaker may desire to convey information, such as urging students to volunteer at a fund-raising event, explaining changes in employee compensation packages, or describing a new laboratory procedure. The PowerPoint slides should reinforce the speaker's message and help the audience retain the information presented. Custom slides can fit your specific needs and contain diagrams, charts, tables, pictures, shapes, video, sound, and animation effects to make your presentation more effective. An accompanying handout gives audience members reference notes and review material for your presentation.

Project Planning Guidelines

The process of developing a presentation that communicates specific information requires careful analysis and planning. As a starting point, establish why the presentation is needed. Next, analyze the intended audience for the presentation and its unique needs. Then, gather information about the topic and decide what to include in the presentation. Finally, determine the presentation design and style that will be most successful at delivering the message. Details of these guidelines are provided in Appendix A. In addition, each project in this book provides practical applications of these planning considerations.

BTW

Energy-Saving Information
The U.S. Department of Energy's Web site has myriad information available on the topics of energy efficiency and renewable energy. These features can provide news and product research that you can share with audiences with the help of a PowerPoint presentation.

Project — Presentation with Bulleted Lists and Clip Art

In this chapter's project, you will follow proper design guidelines and learn to use PowerPoint to create, save, and print the slides shown in Figures 1–1a through 1–1e. The objective is to produce a presentation, called It Is Easy Being Green, to help consumers understand basic steps they can take to save energy in their homes. This slide show has a variety of clip art and visual elements to add interest and illustrate energy-cutting measures. Some of the text has formatting and color enhancements. Transitions help one slide flow gracefully into the next during a slide show. In addition, you will print a handout of your slides to distribute to audience members.

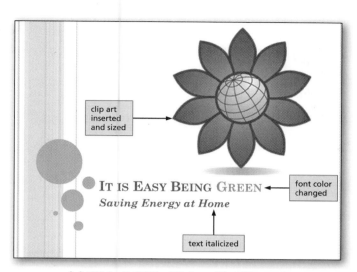

(a) Slide 1 (Title Slide with Clip Art)

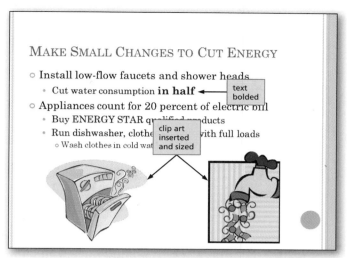

(b) Slide 2 (Multi-Level Bulleted List with Clip Art)

(c) Slide 3 (Title and Photograph)

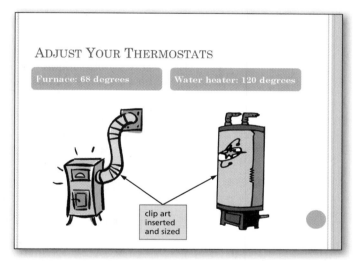

(d) Slide 4 (Comparison Layout and Clip Art)

(e) Slide 5 (Closing Slide)

Figure 1–1

Overview

As you read this chapter, you will learn how to create the presentation shown in Figure 1–1 on the previous page by performing these general tasks:

- Select an appropriate document theme.
- Enter titles and text on slides.
- Change the size, color, and style of text.
- Insert clips and a photograph.
- Add a transition to each slide.
- View the presentation on your computer.
- Print your slides.

Plan Ahead

General Project Guidelines

When creating a PowerPoint document, the actions you perform and decisions you make will affect the appearance and characteristics of the finished document. As you create a presentation such as the project shown in Figure 1–1, you should follow these general guidelines:

1. **Find the appropriate theme.** The overall appearance of a presentation significantly affects its capability to communicate information clearly. The slides' graphical appearance should support the presentation's overall message. Colors, fonts, and layouts affect how audience members perceive and react to the slide content.

2. **Choose words for each slide.** Use the less is more principle. The less text, the more likely the slides will enhance your speech. Use the fewest words possible to make a point.

3. **Format specific elements of the text.** Examples of how you can modify the appearance, or **format**, of text include changing its shape, size, color, and position on the slide.

4. **Determine where to save the presentation.** You can store a document permanently, or **save** it, on a variety of storage media, including a hard disk, USB flash drive, or CD. You also can indicate a specific location on the storage media for saving the document.

5. **Determine the best method for distributing the presentation.** Presentations can be distributed on paper or electronically. You can print a hard copy of the presentation slides for proofing or reference, or you can distribute an electronic image in various formats.

When necessary, more specific details concerning the above guidelines are presented at appropriate points in the chapter. The chapter also will identify the actions performed and decisions made regarding these guidelines during the creation of the slides shown in Figure 1–1.

To Start PowerPoint

If you are using a computer to step through the project in this chapter and you want your screens to match the figures in this book, you should change your screen's resolution to 1024 × 768. For information about how to change a computer's resolution, refer to the Office 2010 and Windows 7 chapter at the beginning of this book.

The following steps, which assume Windows 7 is running, start PowerPoint based on a typical installation. You may need to ask your instructor how to start PowerPoint for your computer. For a detailed example of the procedure summarized below, refer to the Office 2010 and Windows 7 chapter.

1 Click the Start button on the Windows 7 taskbar to display the Start menu.

2 Type **Microsoft PowerPoint** as the search text in the 'Search programs and files' text box and watch the search results appear on the Start menu.

3 Click Microsoft PowerPoint 2010 in the search results on the Start menu to start PowerPoint and display a new blank document in the PowerPoint window.

4 If the PowerPoint window is not maximized, click the Maximize button next to the Close button on its title bar to maximize the window.

Choosing a Document Theme

You can give a presentation a professional and integrated appearance easily by using a document theme. A **document theme** provides consistency in design and color throughout the entire presentation by setting the color scheme, font set, and layout of a presentation. This collection of formatting choices includes a set of colors (the Theme Colors group), a set of heading and content text fonts (the Theme Fonts group), and a set of lines and fill effects (the Theme Effects group). These groups allow you to choose and change the appearance of all the slides or individual slides in your presentation. The left edge of the status bar in Figure 1–2 shows the current slide number followed by the total number of slides in the document and a document theme identifier.

Find the appropriate theme.
In the initial steps of this project, you will select a document theme by locating a particular built-in theme in the Themes group. You could, however, apply a theme at any time while creating the presentation. Some PowerPoint slide show designers create presentations using the default Office Theme. This blank design allows them to concentrate on the words being used to convey the message and does not distract them with colors and various text attributes. Once the text is entered, the designers then select an appropriate document theme.

Plan Ahead

To Choose a Document Theme

The document theme identifier shows the theme currently used in the slide show. PowerPoint initially uses the **Office Theme** until you select a different theme. The following steps change the theme for this presentation from the Office Theme to the Oriel document theme.

1

- Click Design on the Ribbon to display the Design tab (Figure 1–2).

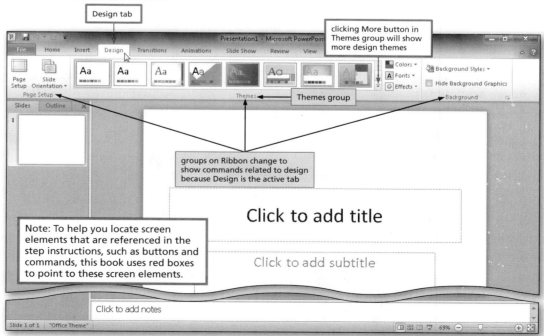

Figure 1–2

2

● Click the More button (Design tab | Themes group) to expand the gallery, which shows more Built-In theme gallery options (Figure 1–3).

Experiment

● Point to various document themes in the Themes gallery and watch the colors and fonts change on the title slide.

Q&A Are the themes displayed in a specific order?

Yes. They are arranged in alphabetical order running from left to right. If you point to a theme, a ScreenTip with the theme's name appears on the screen.

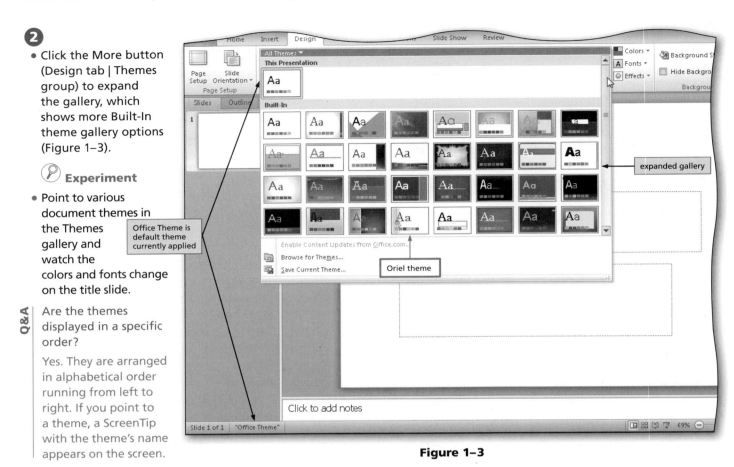

Figure 1–3

Q&A What if I change my mind and do not want to select a new theme?
Click anywhere outside the All Themes gallery to close the gallery.

3

● Click the Oriel theme to apply this theme to Slide 1 (Figure 1–4).

Q&A If I decide at some future time that this design does not fit the theme of my presentation, can I apply a different design?

Yes. You can repeat these steps at any time while creating your presentation.

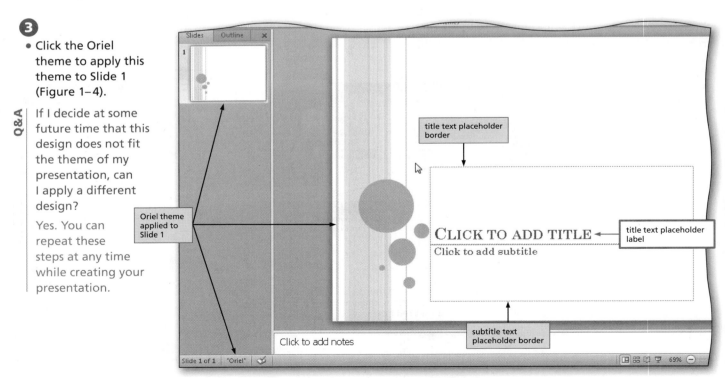

Figure 1–4

Creating a Title Slide

When you open a new presentation, the default **Title Slide** layout appears. The purpose of this layout is to introduce the presentation to the audience. PowerPoint includes eight other built-in standard layouts. The default (preset) slide layouts are set up in **landscape orientation**, where the slide width is greater than its height. In landscape orientation, the slide size is preset to 10 inches wide and 7.5 inches high when printed on a standard sheet of paper measuring 11 inches wide and 8.5 inches high.

Placeholders are boxes with dotted or hatch-marked borders that are displayed when you create a new slide. Most layouts have both a title text placeholder and at least one content placeholder. Depending on the particular slide layout selected, title and sub-title placeholders are displayed for the slide title and subtitle; a content text placeholder is displayed for text, art, or a table, chart, picture, graphic, or movie. The title slide has two text placeholders where you can type the main heading, or title, of a new slide and the subtitle.

With the exception of a blank slide, PowerPoint assumes every new slide has a title. To make creating a presentation easier, any text you type after a new slide appears becomes title text in the title text placeholder. The following steps create the title slide for this presentation.

Choose the words for the slide.
No doubt you have heard the phrase, "You get only one chance to make a first impression." The same philosophy holds true for a PowerPoint presentation. The title slide gives your audience an initial sense of what they are about to see and hear. It is, therefore, extremely important to choose the text for this slide carefully. Avoid stating the obvious in the title. Instead, create interest and curiosity using key ideas from the presentation.

Some PowerPoint users create the title slide as their last step in the design process so that it reflects the tone of the presentation. They begin by planning the final slide in the presentation so that they know where and how they want to end the slide show. All the slides in the presentation should work toward meeting this final slide.

Plan Ahead

To Enter the Presentation Title

The presentation title for Project 1 is It Is Easy Being Green. This title creates interest by introducing the concept of simple energy conservation tasks. The following step creates the slide show's title.

● Click the label, Click to add title, located inside the title text placeholder to select the placeholder (Figure 1–5).

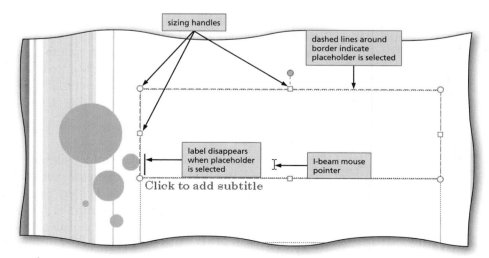

Figure 1–5

2

- Type It Is Easy Being Green in the title text placeholder. Do not press the ENTER key (Figure 1–6).

Q&A

Why does the text display with capital letters despite the fact I am typing uppercase and lowercase letters?

The Oriel theme uses the Small Caps effect for the title text. This effect converts lowercase letters to uppercase and reduces their size.

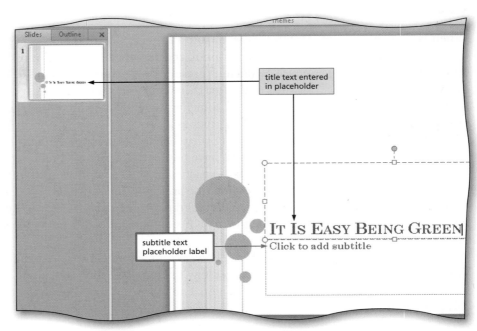

Figure 1–6

Correcting a Mistake When Typing

If you type the wrong letter, press the BACKSPACE key to erase all the characters back to and including the one that is incorrect. If you mistakenly press the ENTER key after typing the title and the insertion point is on the new line, simply press the BACKSPACE key to return the insertion point to the right of the letter n in the word, Green.

When you install PowerPoint, the default setting allows you to reverse up to the last 20 changes by clicking the Undo button on the Quick Access Toolbar. The ScreenTip that appears when you point to the Undo button changes to indicate the type of change just made. For example, if you type text in the title text placeholder and then point to the Undo button, the ScreenTip that appears is Undo Typing. For clarity, when referencing the Undo button in this project, the name displaying in the ScreenTip is referenced. You can reapply a change that you reversed with the Undo button by clicking the Redo button on the Quick Access Toolbar. Clicking the Redo button reverses the last undo action. The ScreenTip name reflects the type of reversal last performed.

For an introduction to Office 2010 and instruction about how to perform basic tasks in Office 2010 programs, read the Office 2010 and Windows 7 chapter at the beginning of this book, where you can learn how to start a program, use the Ribbon, save a file, open a file, quit a program, use Help, and much more.

Paragraphs

Text in the subtitle text placeholder supports the title text. It can appear on one or more lines in the placeholder. To create more than one subtitle line, you press the ENTER key after typing some words. PowerPoint creates a new line, which is the second paragraph in the placeholder. A **paragraph** is a segment of text with the same format that begins when you press the ENTER key and ends when you press the ENTER key again. This new paragraph is the same level as the previous paragraph. A **level** is a position within a structure, such as an outline, that indicates the magnitude of importance. PowerPoint allows for five paragraph levels.

To Enter the Presentation Subtitle Paragraph

The first subtitle paragraph links to the title by giving further detail that the presentation will focus on energy-saving measures at home. The following steps enter the presentation subtitle.

1
- Click the label, Click to add subtitle, located inside the subtitle text placeholder to select the placeholder (Figure 1–7).

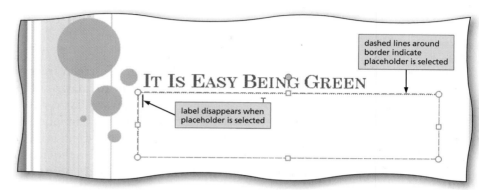

Figure 1–7

2
- Type **Saving Energy at Home** but do not press the ENTER key (Figure 1–8).

Figure 1–8

Identify how to format specific elements of the text.

Plan Ahead

Most of the time, you use the document theme's text attributes, color scheme, and layout. Occasionally, you may want to change the way a presentation looks, however, and still keep a particular document theme. PowerPoint gives you that flexibility.

Graphic designers use several rules when formatting text.

- Avoid all capital letters, if possible. Audiences have difficulty comprehending sentences typed in all capital letters, especially when the lines exceed seven words. All capital letters leaves no room for emphasis or inflection, so readers get confused about what material deserves particular attention. Some document themes, however, have a default title text style of all capital letters.

- Avoid text with a font size less than 30 point. Audience members generally will sit a maximum of 50 feet from a screen, and at this distance 30-point type is the smallest size text they can read comfortably without straining.

- Make careful color choices. Color evokes emotions, and a careless color choice may elicit the incorrect psychological response. PowerPoint provides a color gallery with hundreds of colors. The built-in document themes use complementary colors that work well together. If you stray from these themes and add your own color choices, without a good reason to make the changes, your presentation is apt to become ineffective.

Formatting Characters in a Presentation

Recall that each document theme determines the color scheme, font set, and layout of a presentation. You can use a specific document theme and then change the characters' formats any time before, during, or after you type the text.

BTW

Q&As
For a complete list of the Q&As found in many of the step-by-step sequences in this book, visit the PowerPoint 2010 Q&A Web page (scsite.com/ppt2010/qa).

Fonts and Font Styles

Characters that appear on the screen are a specific shape and size. Examples of how you can modify the appearance, or **format**, of these typed characters on the screen and in print include changing the font, style, size, and color. The **font**, or typeface, defines the appearance and shape of the letters, numbers, punctuation marks, and symbols. **Style** indicates how the characters are formatted. PowerPoint's text font styles include regular, italic, bold, and bold italic. **Size** specifies the height of the characters and is gauged by a measurement system that uses points. A **point** is 1/72 of an inch in height. Thus, a character with a font size of 36 is 36/72 (or 1/2) of an inch in height. **Color** defines the hue of the characters.

This presentation uses the Oriel document theme, which uses particular font styles and font sizes. The Oriel document theme default title text font is named Century Schoolbook. It has a bold style with no special effects, and its size is 30 point. The Oriel document theme default subtitle text font also is Century Schoolbook with a font size of 18 point.

To Select a Paragraph

You can use many techniques to format characters. When you want to apply the same formats to multiple words or paragraphs, it is efficient to select the desired text and then make the desired changes to all the characters simultaneously. The first formatting change you will make will apply to the title slide subtitle. The following step selects this paragraph.

1

- Triple-click the paragraph, Saving Energy at Home, in the subtitle text placeholder to select the paragraph (Figure 1–9).

Q&A

Can I select the paragraph using a technique other than triple-clicking?

Yes. You can move your mouse pointer to the left of the first paragraph and then drag to the end of the line.

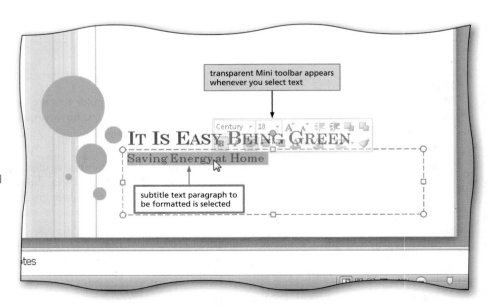

Figure 1–9

To Italicize Text

Different font styles often are used on slides to make them more appealing to the reader and to emphasize particular text. **Italicized** text has a slanted appearance. Used sparingly, it draws the readers' eyes to these characters. The following step adds emphasis to the second line of the subtitle text by changing regular text to italic text.

1

- With the subtitle text still selected, click the Italic button on the Mini toolbar to italicize that text on the slide (Figure 1–10).

If I change my mind and decide not to italicize the text, how can I remove this style?

Click the Italic button a second time or immediately click the Undo button on the Quick Access Toolbar or press CTRL+Z.

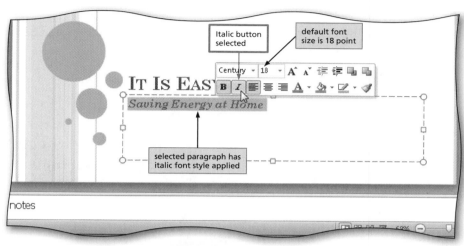

Figure 1–10

Other Ways		
1. Right-click selected text, click Font on shortcut menu, click Font tab (Font dialog box), click Italic in Font style list, click OK button	2. Select text, click Italic button (Home tab | Font group) 3. Click Font Dialog Box Launcher (Home tab | Font	group), click Font tab (Font dialog box), click Italic in Font style list, click OK button 4. Select text, press CTRL+I

To Increase Font Size

To add emphasis, you increase the font size for the subtitle text. The Increase Font Size button on the Mini toolbar increases the font size in preset increments. The following step uses this button to increase the font size.

1

- Click the Increase Font Size button on the Mini toolbar twice to increase the font size of the selected text from 18 to 24 point (Figure 1–11).

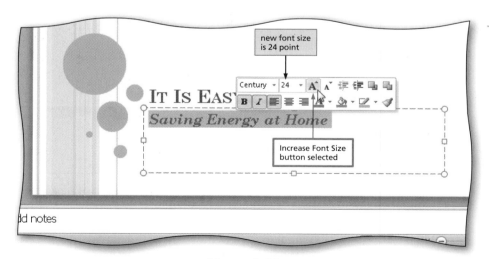

Figure 1–11

Other Ways		
1. Click Font Size box arrow on Mini toolbar, click desired font size in Font Size gallery	2. Click Increase Font Size button (Home tab | Font group) 3. Click Font Size box arrow (Home tab | Font group),	click desired font size in Font size gallery 4. Press CTRL+SHIFT+>

To Select a Word

PowerPoint designers use many techniques to emphasize words and characters on a slide. To add emphasis to the energy-saving concept of your slide show, you want to increase the font size and change the font color to green for the word, Green, in the title text. You could perform these actions separately, but it is more efficient to select the word and then change the font attributes. The following steps select a word.

- Position the mouse pointer somewhere in the word to be selected (in this case, in the word, Green) (Figure 1–12).

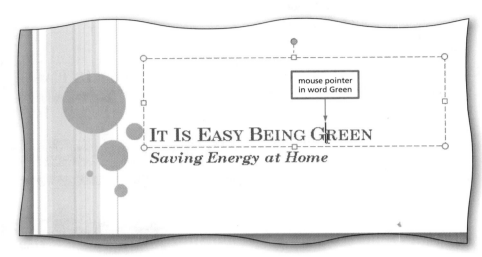

Figure 1–12

- Double-click the word to select it (Figure 1–13).

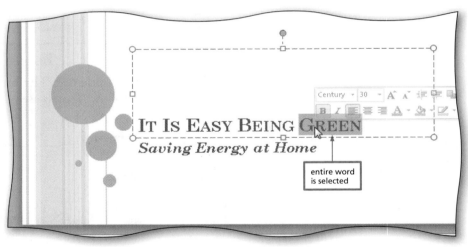

Figure 1–13

Other Ways

1. Position mouse pointer before first character, press CTRL+SHIFT+RIGHT ARROW

Plan Ahead

Format text colors.
When selecting text colors, try to limit using red. This color often is associated with dangerous or alarming situations. In addition, at least 15 percent of men have difficulty distinguishing varying shades of green or red. They also often see the color purple as blue and the color brown as green. This problem is more pronounced when the colors appear in small areas, such as slide paragraphs or line chart bars.

To Change the Text Color

PowerPoint allows you to use one or more text colors in a presentation. To add more emphasis to the word, Green, in the title slide text, you decide to change the color. The following steps add emphasis to this word by changing the font color from black to green.

1
- With the word, Green, selected, click the Font Color arrow on the Mini toolbar to display the gallery of Theme Colors and Standard Colors (Figure 1–14).

If the Mini toolbar disappears from the screen, how can I display it once again?

Right-click the text, and the Mini toolbar should appear.

Experiment
- Point to various colors in the gallery and watch the word's font color change.

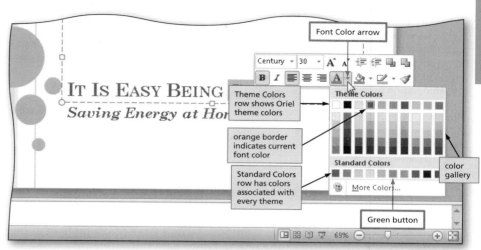

Figure 1–14

2
- Click the Green button in the Standard Colors row on the Mini toolbar (sixth color) to change the font color to green (Figure 1–15).

Why did I select the color Green?

Green is one of the 10 standard colors associated with every document theme, and it is a universal color to represent respecting natural resources. The color will emphasize the fact that the presentation focuses on green conservation measures.

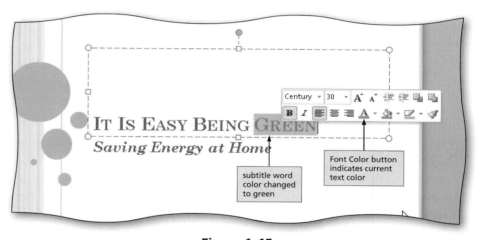

Figure 1–15

What is the difference between the colors shown in the Theme Colors area and the Standard Colors?

The 10 colors in the top row of the Theme Colors area are two text, two background, and six accent colors in the Oriel theme; the five colors in each column under the top row display different transparencies. These colors are available in every document theme.

3
- Click outside the selected area to deselect the word.

Other Ways
1. Right-click selected text, click Font on shortcut menu, click Font Color button, click Green in Standard Colors row   2. Click Font Color arrow (Home tab | Font group), click Green in Standard Colors row

Organizing Files and Folders
You should organize and store files in folders so that you easily can find the files later. For example, if you are taking an introductory computer class called CIS 101, a good practice would be to save all PowerPoint files in a PowerPoint folder in a CIS 101 folder. For a discussion of folders and detailed examples of creating folders, refer to the Office 2010 and Windows 7 chapter at the beginning of this book.

To Save a Presentation

You have performed many tasks while creating this slide and do not want to risk losing work completed thus far. Accordingly, you should save the document.

The following steps assume you already have created folders for storing your files, for example, a CIS 101 folder (for your class) that contains a PowerPoint folder (for your assignments). Thus, these steps save the document in the PowerPoint folder in the CIS 101 folder on a USB flash drive using the file name, Saving Energy. For a detailed example of the procedure summarized below, refer to the Office 2010 and Windows 7 chapter at the beginning of this book.

1 With a USB flash drive connected to one of the computer's USB ports, click the Save button on the Quick Access Toolbar to display the Save As dialog box.

2 Type `Saving Energy` in the File name text box to change the file name. Do not press the ENTER key after typing the file name because you do not want to close the dialog box at this time.

3 Navigate to the desired save location (in this case, the PowerPoint folder in the CIS 101 folder [or your class folder] on the USB flash drive).

4 Click the Save button (Save As dialog box) to save the document in the selected folder on the selected drive with the entered file name.

Adding a New Slide to a Presentation

With the text for the title slide for the presentation created, the next step is to add the first text slide immediately after the title slide. Usually, when you create a presentation, you add slides with text, clip art, graphics, or charts. Some placeholders allow you to double-click the placeholder and then access other objects, such as media clips, charts, diagrams, and organization charts. You can change the layout for a slide at any time during the creation of a presentation.

To Add a New Text Slide with a Bulleted List

When you add a new slide, PowerPoint uses the Title and Content slide layout. This layout provides a title placeholder and a content area for text, art, charts, and other graphics. A vertical scroll bar appears in the Slide pane when you add the second slide so that you can move from slide to slide easily. A thumbnail of this slide also appears in the Slides tab. The following steps add a new slide with the Title and Content slide layout.

1
- Click Home on the Ribbon to display the Home tab (Figure 1–16).

Figure 1–16

2

- Click the New Slide button (Home tab | Slides group) to insert a new slide with the Title and Content layout (Figure 1–17).

Q&A Why does the bullet character display an orange circle?

The Oriel document theme determines the bullet characters. Each paragraph level has an associated bullet character.

Q&A I clicked the New Slide arrow instead of the New Slide button. What should I do?

Click the Title and Content slide thumbnail in the layout gallery.

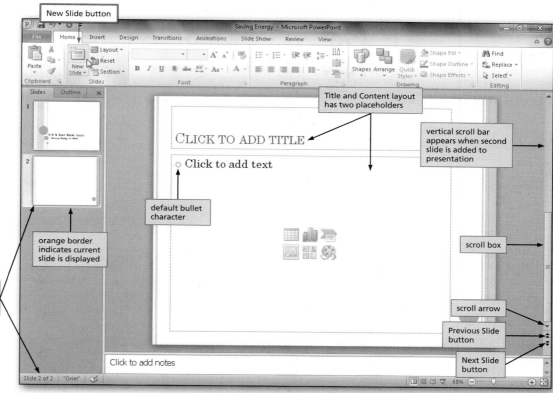

Figure 1–17

Other Ways

1. Press CTRL+M

Choose the words for the slide.

All presentations should follow the 7 × 7 rule, which states that each slide should have a maximum of seven lines, and each line should have a maximum of seven words. PowerPoint designers must choose their words carefully and, in turn, help viewers read the slides easily.

Avoid line wraps. Your audience's eyes want to stop at the end of a line. Thus, you must plan your words carefully or adjust the font size so that each point displays on only one line.

Plan Ahead

Creating a Text Slide with a Multi-Level Bulleted List

The information in the Slide 2 text placeholder is presented in a bulleted list with three levels. A **bulleted list** is a list of paragraphs, each of which is preceded by a bullet. A slide that consists of more than one level of bulleted text is called a **multi-level bulleted list slide**. In a multi-level bulleted list, a lower-level paragraph is a subset of a higher-level paragraph. It usually contains information that supports the topic in the paragraph immediately above it.

Two of the Slide 2 bullets appear at the same paragraph level, called the first level: Install low-flow faucets and shower heads, and Appliances count for 20 percent of electric bill. Beginning with the second level, each paragraph indents to the right of the preceding level and is pushed down to a lower level. For example, if you increase the indent of a first-level paragraph, it becomes a second-level paragraph. The second, fourth, and fifth paragraphs on Slide 2 are second-level paragraphs. The last paragraph, Wash clothes in cold water, is a third-level paragraph.

BTW

The Ribbon and Screen Resolution
PowerPoint may change how the groups and buttons within the groups appear on the Ribbon, depending on the computer's screen resolution. Thus, your Ribbon may look different from the ones in this book if you are using a screen resolution other than 1024 x 768.

Creating a text slide with a multi-level bulleted list requires several steps. Initially, you enter a slide title in the title text placeholder. Next, you select the content text placeholder. Then, you type the text for the multi-level bulleted list, increasing and decreasing the indents as needed. The next several sections add a slide with a multi-level bulleted list.

To Enter a Slide Title

PowerPoint assumes every new slide has a title. The title for Slide 2 is Make Small Changes to Cut Energy. The following step enters this title.

- Click the label, Click to add title, to select it and then type **Make Small Changes to Cut Energy** in the placeholder. Do not press the ENTER key (Figure 1–18).

Q&A

What are those six icons grouped in the middle of the slide?

You can click one of the icons to insert a specific type of content: table, chart, SmartArt graphic, picture, clip art, or media clip.

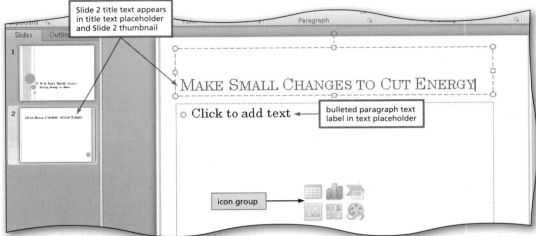

Figure 1–18

To Select a Text Placeholder

Before you can type text into the text placeholder, you first must select it. The following step selects the text placeholder on Slide 2.

- Click the label, Click to add text, to select the text placeholder (Figure 1–19).

Q&A

Why does my mouse pointer have a different shape?

If you move the mouse pointer away from the bullet, it will change shape.

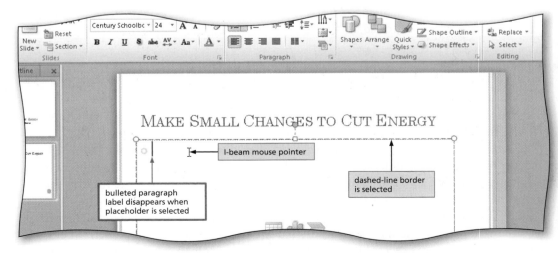

Figure 1–19

Other Ways

1. Press CTRL+ENTER

To Type a Multi-Level Bulleted List

The content placeholder provides an area for the text characters. When you click inside a placeholder, you then can type or paste text. As discussed previously, a bulleted list is a list of paragraphs, each of which is preceded by a bullet. A paragraph is a segment of text ended by pressing the ENTER key.

The content text placeholder is selected, so the next step is to type the multi-level bulleted list that consists of six paragraphs, as shown in Figure 1–1b on page PPT 3. Creating a lower-level paragraph is called **demoting** text; creating a higher-level paragraph is called **promoting** text. The following steps create a multi-level bulleted list consisting of three levels.

1

- Type `Install low-flow faucets and shower heads` and then press the ENTER key (Figure 1–20).

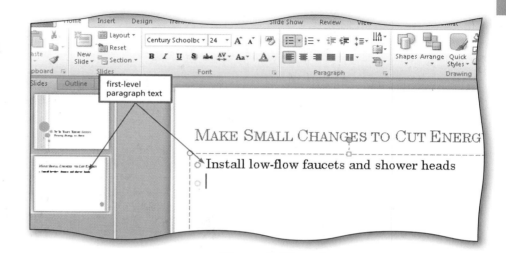

Figure 1–20

2

- Click the Increase List Level button (Home tab | Paragraph group) to indent the second paragraph below the first and create a second-level paragraph (Figure 1–21).

Q&A Why does the bullet for this paragraph have a different size and color?

A different bullet is assigned to each paragraph level.

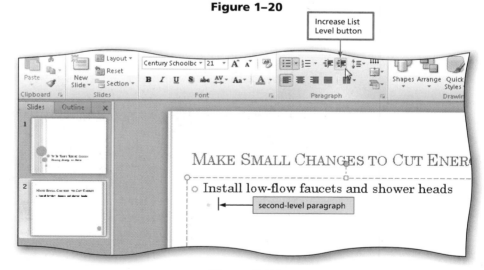

Figure 1–21

3

- Type `Cut water consumption in half` and then press the ENTER key (Figure 1–22).

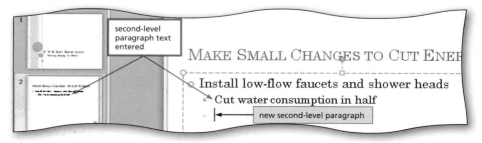

Figure 1–22

4

- Click the Decrease List Level button (Home tab | Paragraph group) so that the second-level paragraph becomes a first-level paragraph (Figure 1–23).

Q&A Can I delete bullets on a slide?

Yes. If you do not want bullets to display in a particular paragraph, click the Bullets button (Home tab | Paragraph group) or right-click the paragraph and then click the Bullets button on the shortcut menu.

Other Ways

1. Press TAB to promote paragraph; press SHIFT+TAB to demote paragraph

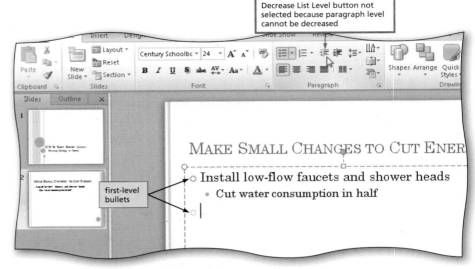

Figure 1–23

To Type the Remaining Text for Slide 2

The following steps complete the text for Slide 2.

1 Type `Appliances count for 20 percent of electric bill` and then press the ENTER key.

2 Click the Increase List Level button (Home tab | Paragraph group) to demote the paragraph to the second level.

3 Type `Buy ENERGY STAR qualified products` and then press the ENTER key to add a new paragraph at the same level as the previous paragraph.

4 Type `Run dishwasher, clothes washer with full loads` and then press the ENTER key.

5 Click the Increase List Level button (Home tab | Paragraph group) to demote the paragraph to the third level.

6 Type `Wash clothes in cold water` but do not press the ENTER key (Figure 1–24).

Q&A I pressed the ENTER key in error, and now a new bullet appears after the last entry on this slide. How can I remove this extra bullet?

Press the BACKSPACE key twice.

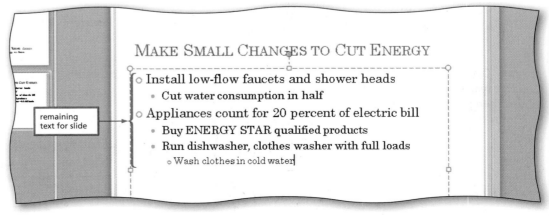

Figure 1–24

To Select a Group of Words

PowerPoint designers use many techniques to emphasize words and characters on a slide. To add emphasis to your slide show's concept of saving natural resources, you want to bold and increase the font size of the words, in half, in the body text. You could perform these actions separately, but it is more efficient to select the words and then change the font attributes. The following steps select two words.

1
- Position the mouse pointer immediately to the left of the first character of the text to be selected (in this case, the i in the word, in) (Figure 1–25).

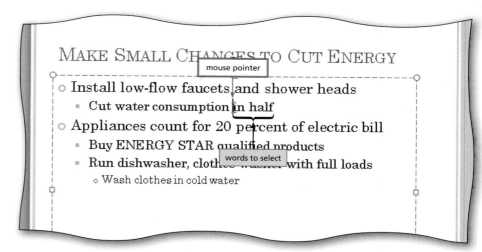

Figure 1–25

2
- Drag the mouse pointer through the last character of the text to be selected (in this case, the f in half) (Figure 1–26).

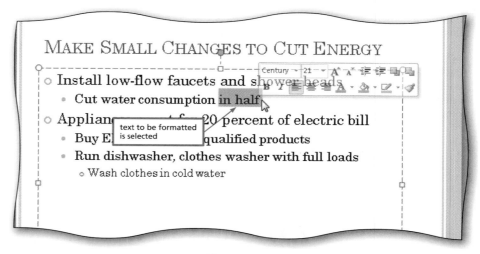

Figure 1–26

Other Ways
1. Press CTRL+SHIFT+RIGHT ARROW

To Bold Text

Bold characters display somewhat thicker and darker than those that display in a regular font style. Clicking the Bold button on the Mini toolbar is an efficient method of bolding text. To add more emphasis to the amount of water savings that can occur by installing low-flow faucets and shower heads, you want to bold the words, in half. The following step bolds this text.

1
● With the words, in half, selected, click the Bold button on the Mini toolbar to bold the two words (Figure 1–27).

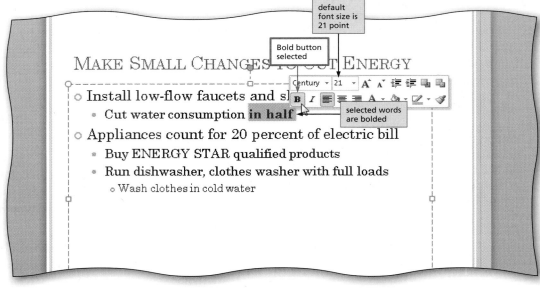

Figure 1–27

Other Ways

1. Click Bold button (Home tab | Font group)
2. Press CTRL+B

Formatting Words
To format one word, position the insertion point anywhere in the word. Then make the formatting changes you desire. The entire word does not need to be selected for the change to occur.

To Increase Font Size

To add emphasis, you increase the font size for the words, in half. The following step increases the font size from 21 to 24 point.

1 With the words, in half, still selected, click the Increase Font Size button on the Mini toolbar once (Figure 1–28).

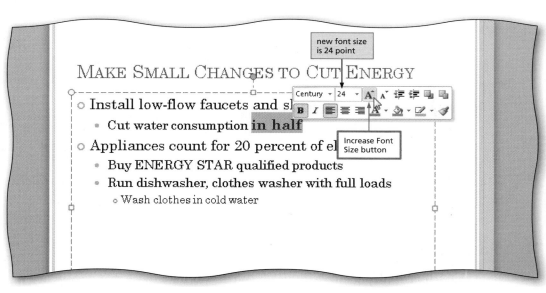

Figure 1–28

Adding New Slides and Changing the Slide Layouts

Slide 3 in Figure 1–1c on page PPT 3 contains a photograph and does not contain a bulleted list. When you add a new slide, PowerPoint applies the Title and Content layout. This layout along with the Title Slide layout for Slide 1 are the default styles. A **layout** specifies the arrangement of placeholders on a slide. These placeholders are arranged in various configurations and can contain text, such as the slide title or a bulleted list, or they can contain content, such as SmartArt graphics, pictures, charts, tables, shapes, and clip art. The placement of the text, in relationship to content, depends on the slide layout. You can specify a particular slide layout when you add a new slide to a presentation or after you have created the slide.

Using the **Layout gallery**, you can choose a slide layout. The nine layouts in this gallery have a variety of placeholders to define text and content positioning and formatting. Three layouts are for text: Title Slide, Section Header, and Title Only. Five are for text and content: Title and Content, Two Content, Comparison, Content with Caption, and Picture with Caption. The Blank layout has no placeholders. If none of these standard layouts meets your design needs, you can create a **custom layout**. A custom layout specifies the number, size, and location of placeholders, background content, and optional slide and placeholder-level properties.

When you change the layout of a slide, PowerPoint retains the text and objects and repositions them into the appropriate placeholders. Using slide layouts eliminates the need to resize objects and the font size because PowerPoint automatically sizes the objects and text to fit the placeholders.

BTW

Experimenting with Normal View
As you learn to use PowerPoint's features, experiment with using the Outline tab and with closing the Tabs pane to maximize the slide area. To close the Tabs pane, click the x to the right of the Outline tab. To redisplay the Tabs pane, click the View tab on the Ribbon and then click Normal in the Presentation Views group.

To Add a Slide with the Title Only Layout

The following steps add Slide 3 to the presentation with the Title Only slide layout style.

1
- If necessary, click Home on the Ribbon to display the Home tab.
- Click the New Slide arrow (Home tab | Slides group) to display the Layout gallery (Figure 1–29).

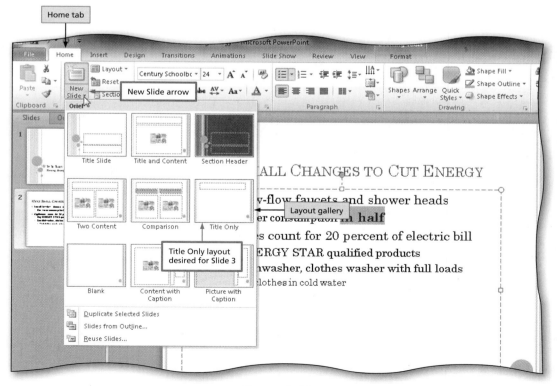

Figure 1–29

2
- Click Title Only to add a new slide and apply that layout to Slide 3 (Figure 1–30).

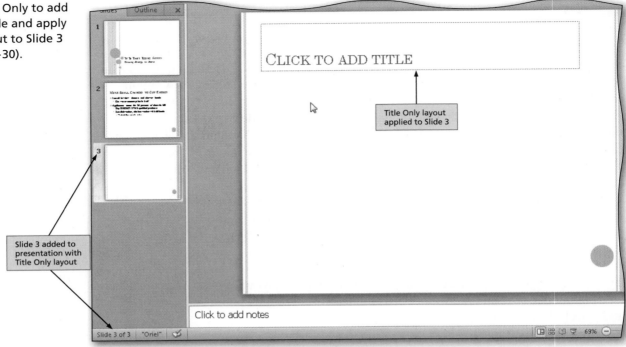

Figure 1–30

Other Ways

1. Press CTRL+M

To Enter a Slide Title

The only text on Slide 3 is the title. The following step enters the title text for this slide.

1 Type **`Use Energy Efficient Lighting`** as the title text but do not press the ENTER key (Figure 1–31).

BTW

Portrait Page Orientation
If your slide content is dominantly vertical, such as a skyscraper or a person, consider changing the slide layout to a portrait page orientation. To change the orientation, click the Slide Orientation button (Design tab | Page Setup group) and then click the desired orientation.

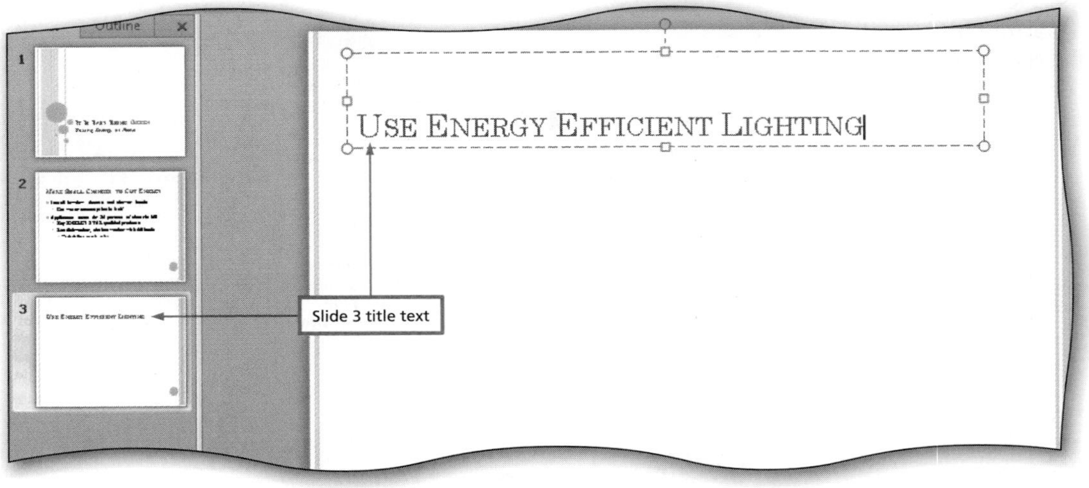

Figure 1–31

To Add a New Slide and Enter a Slide Title and Headings

The text on Slide 4 in Figure 1–1d on page PPT 3 consists of a title and two headings. The appropriate layout for this slide is named Comparison. The following steps add Slide 4 to the presentation with the Comparison layout and then enter the title and heading text for this slide.

1

- Click the New Slide arrow in the Slides group to display the Layout gallery (Figure 1–32).

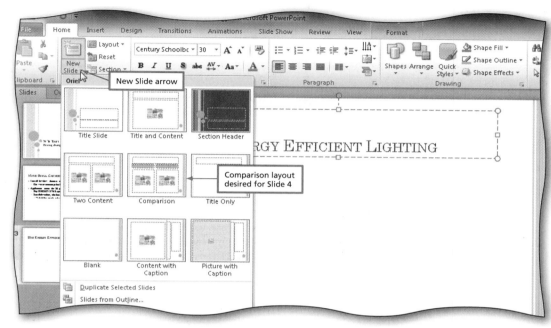

Figure 1–32

2

- Click Comparison to add Slide 4 and apply that layout.

- Type **Adjust Your Thermostats** in the title text placeholder but do not press the ENTER key.

- Click the left orange heading placeholder with the label, Click to add text, to select this placeholder (Figure 1–33).

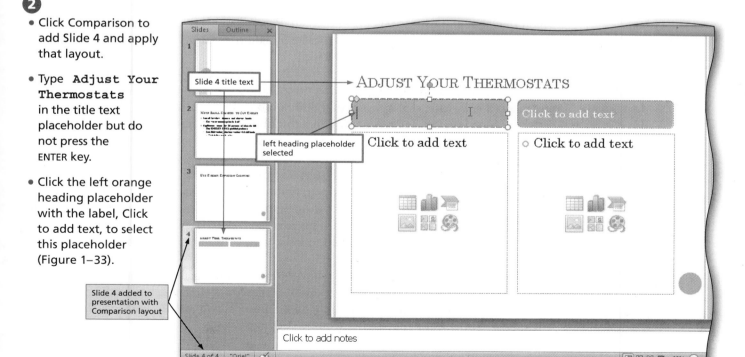

Figure 1–33

3

- Type **Furnace: 68 degrees** but do not press the ENTER key.

- Click the right orange heading placeholder and then type **Water heater: 120 degrees** but do not press the ENTER key (Figure 1–34).

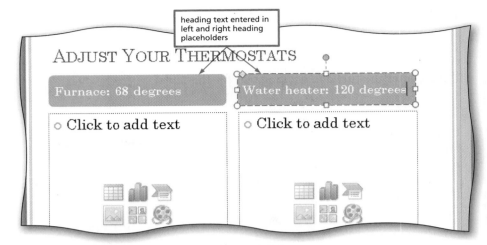

Figure 1–34

Break Point: If you wish to take a break, this is a good place to do so. You can quit PowerPoint now (refer to page PPT 50 for instructions). To resume at a later time, start PowerPoint (refer to pages PPT 4 and PPT 5 for instructions), open the file called Saving Energy (refer to pages PPT 50 and PPT 51 for instructions), and continue following the steps from this location forward.

PowerPoint Views

The PowerPoint window display varies depending on the view. A **view** is the mode in which the presentation appears on the screen. PowerPoint has four main views: Normal, Slide Sorter, Reading, and Slide Show. It also has another view, called Notes Page view, used for entering information about a slide.

The default view is **Normal view**, which is composed of three working areas that allow you to work on various aspects of a presentation simultaneously. The left side of the screen has a Tabs pane that consists of a **Slides tab** and an **Outline tab**. These tabs alternate between views of the presentation in a thumbnail, or miniature, view of the slides and an outline of the slide text. You can type the text of the presentation on the Outline tab and easily rearrange bulleted lists, paragraphs, and individual slides. As you type, you can view this text in the **Slide pane**, which shows a large view of the current slide on the right side of the window. You also can enter text, graphics, animations, and hyperlinks directly in the Slide pane. The **Notes pane** at the bottom of the window is an area where you can type notes and additional information. This text can consist of notes to yourself or remarks to share with your audience. If you want to work with your notes in full page format, you can display them in **Notes Page view**.

In Normal view, you can adjust the width of the Slide pane by dragging the **splitter bar** and the height of the Notes pane by dragging the pane borders. After you have created at least two slides, a scroll bar containing **scroll arrows** and **scroll boxes** will appear on the right edge of the window.

To Move to Another Slide in Normal View

When creating or editing a presentation in Normal view (the view you are currently using), you often want to display a slide other than the current one. Before continuing with developing this project, you want to display the title slide by dragging the scroll box on the vertical scroll bar. When you drag the scroll box, the **slide indicator** shows the number and title of the slide you are about to display. Releasing the mouse button shows the slide. The following steps move from Slide 4 to Slide 1 using the scroll box on the Slide pane.

- Position the mouse pointer on the scroll box.

- Press and hold down the mouse button so that Slide: 4 of 4 Adjust Your Thermostats appears in the slide indicator (Figure 1–35).

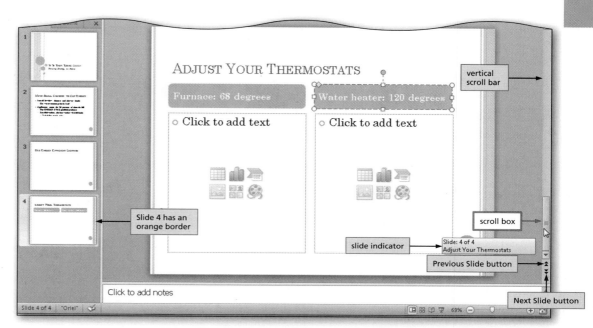

Figure 1–35

2

- Drag the scroll box up the vertical scroll bar until Slide: 1 of 4 It Is Easy Being Green appears in the slide indicator (Figure 1–36).

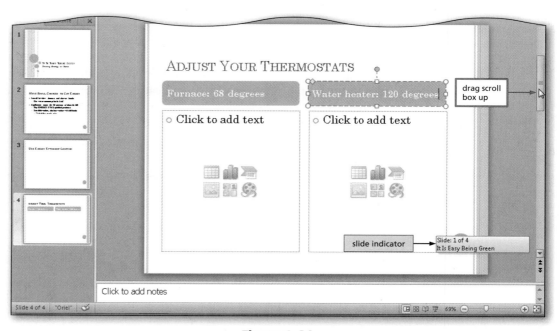

Figure 1–36

3

- Release the mouse button so that Slide 1 appears in the Slide pane and the Slide 1 thumbnail has an orange border in the Slides tab (Figure 1–37).

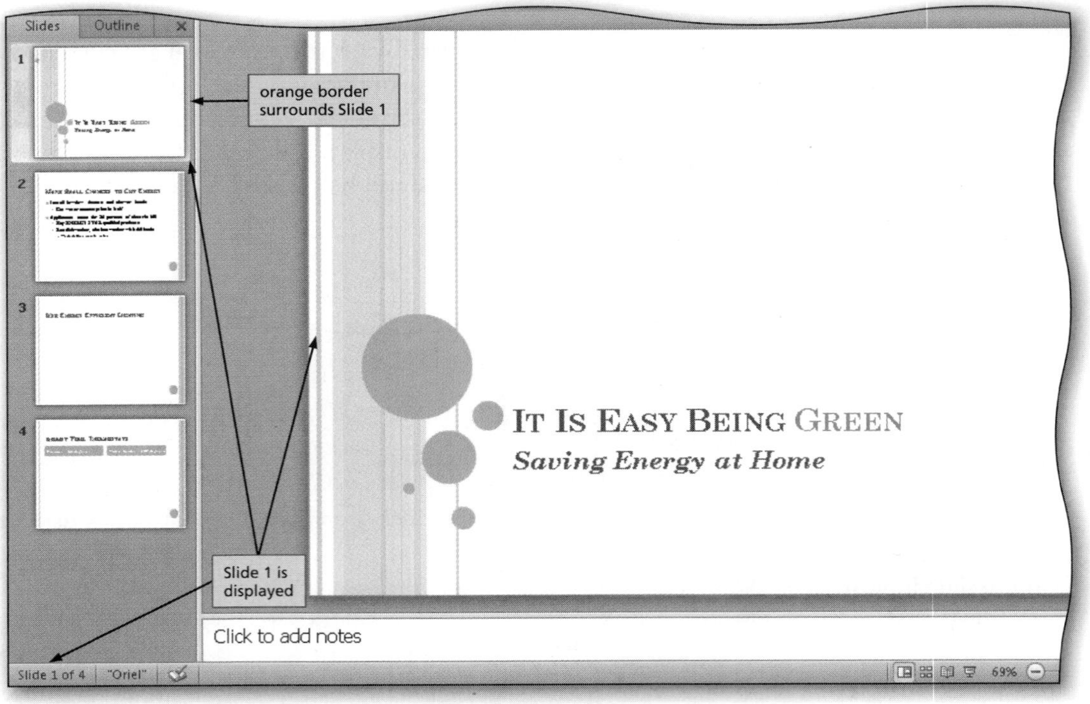

orange border surrounds Slide 1

Slide 1 is displayed

IT IS EASY BEING GREEN

Saving Energy at Home

Click to add notes

Slide 1 of 4   "Oriel"

Figure 1–37

Other Ways

1. Click Next Slide button or Previous Slide button to move forward or back one slide
2. Click slide thumbnail on Slides tab
3. Press PAGE DOWN or PAGE UP to move forward or back one slide

BTW

Today's Clip
Each day, Microsoft features "today's clip," which reflects events or themes specific to this time. For example, the pictures, illustrations, and clip art have back-to-school images, winter scenes, and holiday characters.

Inserting Clip Art and Photographs into Slides

A **clip** is a single media file that can include art, sound, animation, or movies. Adding a clip can help increase the visual appeal of many slides and can offer a quick way to add professional-looking graphic images and sounds to a presentation without creating these files yourself. This art is contained in the **Microsoft Clip Organizer**, a collection of drawings, photographs, sounds, videos, and other media files shared among Microsoft Office applications. The **Office Collections** contains all these media files included with Microsoft Office.

You also can add your own clips to slides. You can insert these files directly from a storage medium, such as a USB flash drive. In addition, you can add them to the other files in the Clip Organizer so that you can search for and reuse these images, sounds, animations, and movies. When you create these media files, they are stored on your hard disk in **My Collections**. The Clip Organizer will find these files and create a new collection with these files. Two other locations for clips are Shared Collections and Web Collections. Files in the **Shared Collections** typically reside on a shared network file server and are accessible to multiple users. The **Web Collections** clips reside on the Microsoft Clip Art and Media Home page on the Microsoft Office Online Web site. They are available only if you have an active Internet connection.

The Clip Art Task Pane

You can add clips to your presentation in two ways. One way is by selecting one of the slide layouts that includes a content placeholder with a Clip Art button. A second method is by clicking the Clip Art button in the Images area on the Insert tab. Clicking the Clip Art button opens the Clip Art task pane. The **Clip Art task pane** allows you to search for clips by using descriptive keywords, file names, media file formats, and clip collections. Specific file formats could be for clip art, photographs, movies, and sounds.

Clips are organized in hierarchical **clip collections** that combine topic-related clips into categories, such as Academic, Business, and Technology.

Clips have one or more keywords associated with various entities, activities, labels, and emotions. In most instances, the keywords give the name of the clip and related categories. For example, an image of a cow in the Animals category has the keywords animals, cattle, cows, dairies, farms, and Holsteins. You can enter these keywords in the Search for text box to find clips when you know one of the words associated with the image. Otherwise, you might find it necessary to scroll through several categories to find an appropriate clip.

Depending on the installation of the Microsoft Clip Organizer on your computer, you might not have the clip art used in this chapter. Contact your instructor if you are missing clips used in the following steps. If you have an active connection to the Internet, clips from the Microsoft Office Online Web site will display automatically as the result of your search results.

Adhere to copyright regulations. You have permission to use the clips from the Microsoft Clip Organizer. If you want to use a clip from another source, be certain you have the legal right to insert this file in your presentation. Read the copyright notices that may accompany the clip and may be posted on the Web site where you obtained the clip. The owners of these images and files often ask you to give them credit for using their work, which may be satisfied by stating where you obtained the images.

Plan Ahead

To Insert a Clip from the Clip Organizer into the Title Slide

Slide 1 uses the Title Slide layout, which has two placeholders for text but none for graphical content. You desire to place a graphic on Slide 1, so you will locate a clip art image of a green globe and flower and then insert it in this slide. Later in this chapter, you will size and position it in an appropriate location. The following steps add a clip to Slide 1.

1
- Click Insert on the Ribbon to display the Insert tab.

- Click the Clip Art button (Insert tab | Images group) to display the Clip Art task pane.

- Click the Search for text box in the Clip Art task pane, if necessary delete any letters that are present, and then type **green globe** in the Search for text box.

- If necessary, click the 'Include Office.com content' check box to select it (Figure 1–38).

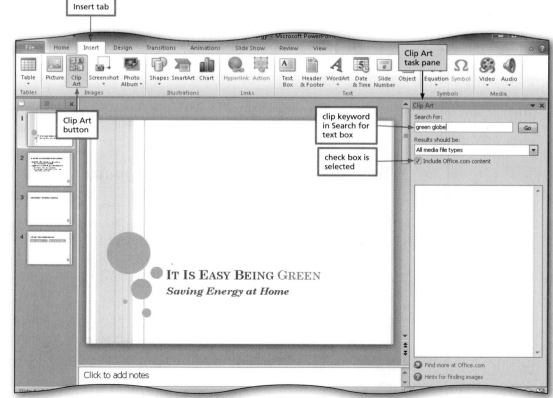

Figure 1–38

2

- Click the Go button so that the Microsoft Clip Organizer will search for and display all clips having the keywords, green globe.

- If necessary, click the Yes button if a Microsoft Clip Organizer dialog box appears asking if you want to include additional clip art images from Office.com.

- If necessary, scroll down the list to display the globe clip shown in Figure 1–39.

- Click the clip to insert it into the slide (Figure 1–39).

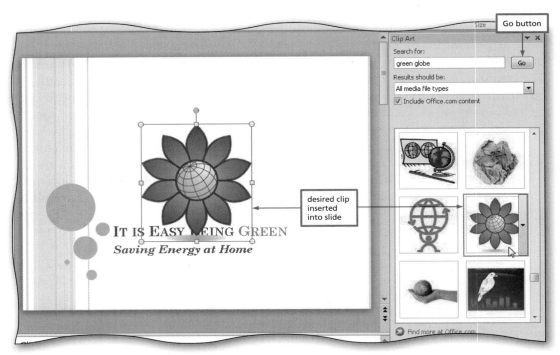

Figure 1–39

Q&A | What if the globe image displayed in Figure 1–39 is not shown in my Clip Art task pane?

Select a similar clip. Your clips may be different depending on the clips installed on your computer and if you have an active connection to the Internet.

Q&A | What is the yellow star image that displays in the lower-right corner of some clips in the Clip Art task pane?

The star indicates the image is animated and will move when the slide containing this clip is displayed during a slide show.

Q&A | Why is this globe clip displayed in this location on the slide?

The slide layout does not have a content placeholder, so PowerPoint inserts the clip in the center of the slide.

To Insert a Clip from the Clip Organizer into a Slide without a Content Placeholder

The next step is to add two clips to Slide 2. Slide 2 has a bulleted list in the text placeholder, so the icon group does not display in the center of the placeholder. Later in this chapter, you will resize the inserted clips. The Clip Art task pane is displayed and will remain open until you close it. The following steps add one clip to Slide 2.

1 Click the Next Slide button to display Slide 2.

2 Click the Search for text box in the Clip Art task pane and then delete the letters in the Search for text box.

3 Type `faucets` and then click the Go button.

4 If necessary, scroll down the list to display the faucet clip shown in Figure 1–40 and then click the clip to insert it into Slide 2 (Figure 1–40).

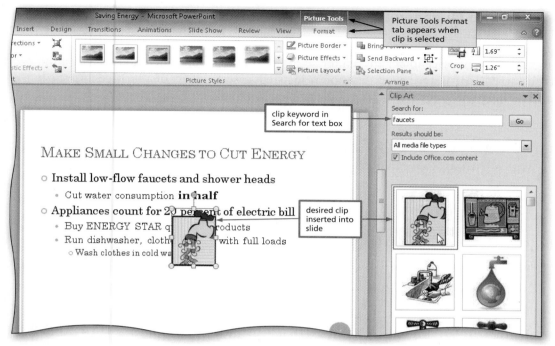

Figure 1–40

To Insert a Second Clip from the Clip Organizer into a Slide without a Content Placeholder

The following steps add a second clip to Slide 2. PowerPoint inserts this clip on top of the faucet clip in the center of the slide. Both clips will be moved and resized later in this project.

1 Click the Search for text box in the Clip Art task pane and then delete the letters in the text box.

2 Type **dishwasher,** click the Go button, locate the clip shown in Figure 1–41, and then click the clip to insert it into Slide 2 (Figure 1–41).

BTW

Clip Properties
Each clip has properties that identify its characteristics. When you right-click a clip in the Microsoft Clip Organizer, you will see details of the clip's name, file type, size, dimensions, keywords, and creation date. You also can preview the clip and edit its assigned keywords.

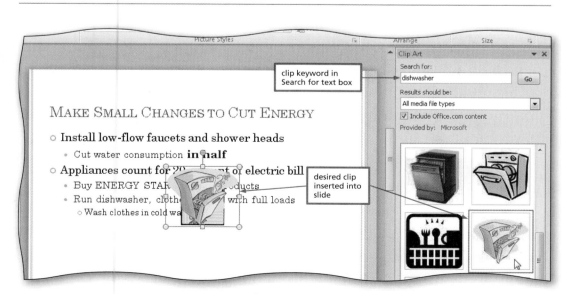

Figure 1–41

To Insert a Clip from the Clip Organizer into a Content Placeholder

Slide 4 uses the Comparison layout, which has a content placeholder below each of the two headings. You desire to insert clip art into both content placeholders to reinforce the concept that consumers should adjust the heating temperatures of their furnace and water heater. The following steps insert clip art of a furnace into the left content placeholder and a water heater into the right content placeholder on Slide 4.

1

- Click the Close button in the Clip Art task pane so that it no longer is displayed.

- Click the Next Slide button twice to display Slide 4.

- Click the Clip Art icon in the left content placeholder to select that placeholder and to open the Clip Art task pane (Figure 1–42).

Do I need to close the Clip Art task pane when I am finished inserting the two clips into Slide 2?

No. You can leave the Clip Art task pane open and then display Slide 4. It is often more convenient, however, to open this pane when you are working with a layout that has a content placeholder so that the clip is inserted in the desired location.

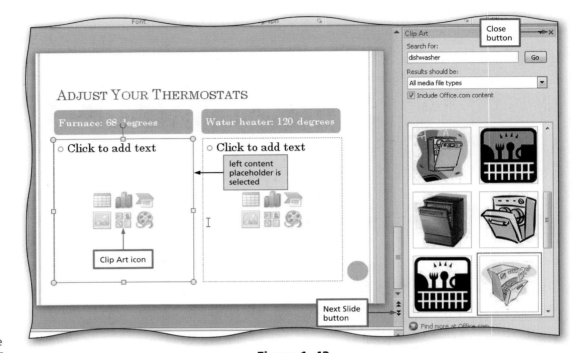

Figure 1–42

2

- Click the Search for text box in the Clip Art task pane, delete any letters that are present, type **furnace** in the Search for text box, and then click the Go button to search for and display all pictures having the keyword, furnace.

- If necessary, scroll down the list to display the furnace clip shown in Figure 1–43.

- Click the clip to insert it into the left content placeholder (Figure 1–43).

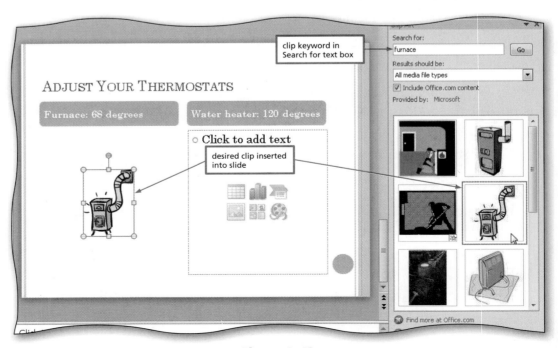

Figure 1–43

3
- Click anywhere in the right placeholder except one of the six icons to select the placeholder.

Q&A
I clicked the Clip Art icon by mistake, which closed the Clip Art task pane. How do I open it?

Click the Clip Art icon.

4
- Click the Search for text box in the Clip Art task pane, delete any letters that are present, type **water heater** in the Search for text box, and then click the Go button.

- If necessary, scroll down the list to display the water heater clip shown in Figure 1–44 and then click the clip to insert it into the right content placeholder (Figure 1–44).

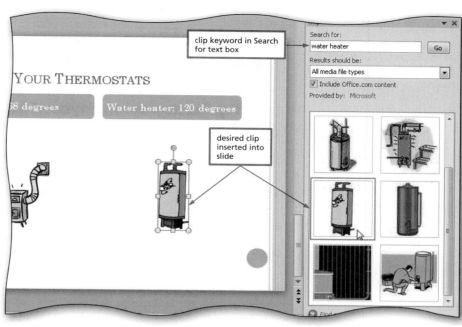

Figure 1–44

Photographs and the Clip Organizer

In addition to clip art, you can insert pictures into a presentation. These may include scanned photographs, line art, and artwork from storage media, such as USB flash drives, hard disks, optical discs, and memory cards. To insert a picture into a presentation, the picture must be saved in a format that PowerPoint can recognize. Table 1–1 identifies some of the formats PowerPoint recognizes.

Table 1–1 Primary File Formats PowerPoint Recognizes

Format	File Extension
Computer Graphics Metafile	.cgm
CorelDRAW	.cdr, .cdt, .cmx, and .pat
Encapsulated PostScript	.eps
Enhanced Metafile	.emf
FlashPix	.fpx
Graphics Interchange Format	.gif
Hanako	.jsh, .jah, and .jbh
Joint Photographic Experts Group (JPEG)	.jpg
Kodak PhotoCD	.pcd
Macintosh PICT	.pct
PC Paintbrush	.pcx
Portable Network Graphics	.png
Tagged Image File Format	.tif
Windows Bitmap	.bmp, .rle, .dib
Microsoft Windows Metafile	.wmf
WordPerfect Graphics	.wpg

BTW

Compressing File Size
When you add a picture to a presentation, PowerPoint automatically compresses this image. Even with this compression applied, a presentation that contains pictures usually has a large file size. To reduce this size, you can compress a picture further without affecting the quality of how it displays on the slide. To compress a picture, select the picture and then click the Compress Pictures button (Picture Tools Format tab | Adjust group). You can restore the picture's original settings by clicking the Reset Picture button (Picture Tools Format tab | Adjust group).

BTW

Wrapping Text around a Picture
PowerPoint 2010 does not allow you to wrap text around a picture or other graphics, such as tables, shapes, charts, or graphics. This feature, however, is available in Word 2010.

You can import files saved with the .emf, .gif, .jpg, .png, .bmp, .rle, .dib, and .wmf formats directly into PowerPoint presentations. All other file formats require separate filters that are shipped with the PowerPoint installation software and must be installed separately. You can download additional filters from the Microsoft Office Online Web site.

To Insert a Photograph from the Clip Organizer into a Slide without a Content Placeholder

Next, you will add a photograph to Slide 3. You will not insert this picture into a content placeholder, so it will display in the center of the slide. Later in this chapter, you will resize this picture. To start the process of locating this photograph, you do not need to click the Clip Art button icon in the content placeholder because the Clip Art task pane already is displayed. The following steps add a photograph to Slide 3.

1 Click the Previous Slide button to display Slide 3.

2 Click the Search for text box in the Clip Art task pane, delete the letters in the text box, type **CFL,** and then click the Go button.

3 If necessary, scroll down the list to display the picture of a light bulb shown in Figure 1–45, and then click the photograph to insert it into Slide 2 (Figure 1–45).

Q&A
Why is my photograph a different size from the one shown in Figure 1–1c on page PPT 3?

The photograph was inserted into the slide and not into a content placeholder. You will resize the picture later in this chapter.

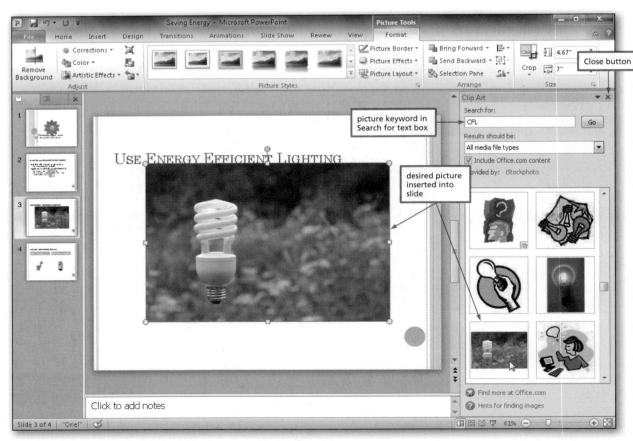

Figure 1–45

Break Point: If you wish to take a break, this is a good place to do so. You can quit PowerPoint now (refer to page PPT 50 for instructions). To resume at a later time, start PowerPoint (refer to pages PPT 4 and PPT 5 for instructions), open the file called Saving Energy (refer to pages PPT 50 and PPT 51 for instructions), and continue following the steps from this location forward.

Resizing Clip Art and Photographs

Sometimes it is necessary to change the size of clip art. **Resizing** includes enlarging or reducing the size of a clip art graphic. You can resize clip art using a variety of techniques. One method involves changing the size of a clip by specifying exact dimensions in a dialog box. Another method involves dragging one of the graphic's sizing handles to the desired location. A selected graphic appears surrounded by a **selection rectangle**, which has small squares and circles, called **sizing handles** or move handles, at each corner and middle location.

To Resize Clip Art

On Slides 1, 2, and 4, much space appears around the clips, so you can increase their sizes. Likewise, the photograph on Slide 3 can be enlarged to fill more of the space below the slide title. To change the size, drag the corner sizing handles to view how the clip will look on the slide. Using these corner handles maintains the graphic's original proportions. Dragging the square sizing handles alters the proportions so that the graphic's height and width become larger or smaller. The following steps increase the size of the Slide 1 clip using a corner sizing handle.

1
- Click the Close button in the Clip Art task pane so that it no longer is displayed.

- Click the Previous Slide button two times to display Slide 1.

- Click the globe clip to select it and display the selection rectangle.

- Point to the lower-left corner sizing handle on the clip so that the mouse pointer changes to a two-headed arrow (Figure 1–46).

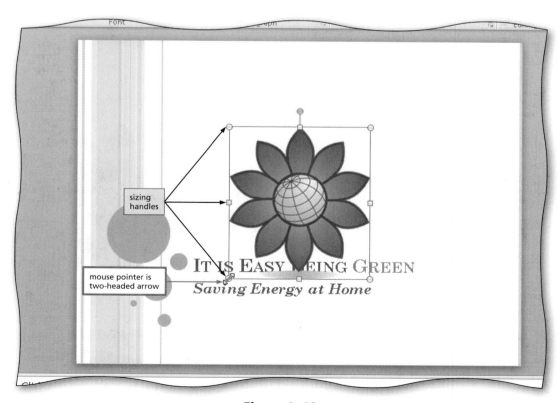

Figure 1–46

- Drag the sizing handle diagonally toward the lower-left corner of the slide until the mouse pointer is positioned approximately as shown in Figure 1–47.

Q&A What if the clip is not the same size as the one shown in Figure 1–47?

Repeat Steps 1 and 2.

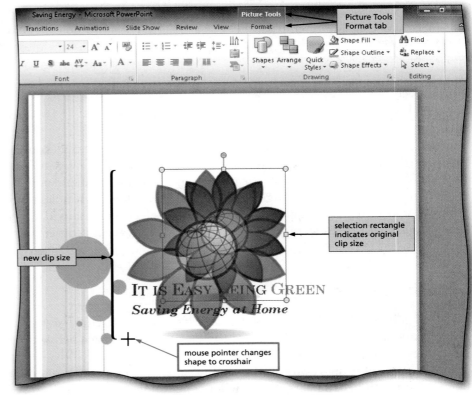

Figure 1–47

- Release the mouse button to resize the clip.
- Click outside the clip to deselect it (Figure 1–48).

Q&A What happened to the Picture Tools Format tab?

When you click outside the clip, PowerPoint deselects the clip and removes the Picture Tools Format tab from the screen.

Q&A What if I want to return the clip to its original size and start again?

With the graphic selected, click the Reset Picture button (Picture Tools Format tab | Adjust group).

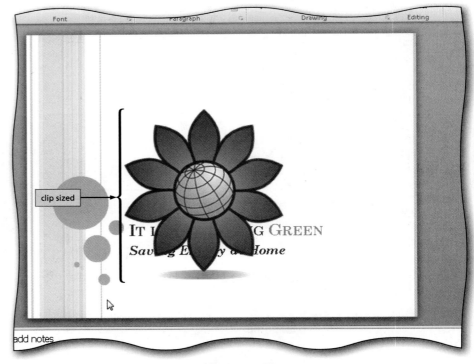

Figure 1–48

To Resize Clips on Slide 4

The two clip art images on Slide 4 also can be enlarged to fill much of the white space below the headings. You will reposition the clips in a later step. The following steps resize these clips using a sizing handle.

1 Click the Next Slide button three times to display Slide 4.

2 Click the furnace clip to select it.

3 Drag the lower-left corner sizing handle on the clip diagonally outward until the clip is resized approximately as shown in Figure 1–49.

4 Click the water heater clip to select it.

5 Drag the lower-right corner sizing handle on the clip diagonally outward until the clip is resized approximately as shown in Figure 1–49.

Figure 1–49

To Resize a Photograph

The light bulb picture in Slide 3 can be enlarged slightly to fill much of the space below the slide title. You resize a photograph in the same manner that you resize clip art. The following steps resize this photograph using a sizing handle.

1 Click the Previous Slide button to display Slide 3.

2 Click the light bulb photograph to select it.

BTW

Minimalist Design
Resist the urge to fill your slides with clips from the Microsoft Clip Organizer. Minimalist style reduces clutter and allows the slide content to display prominently. This simple, yet effective design helps audience members with short attention spans to focus on the message.

3 Drag the lower-left corner sizing handle on the photograph diagonally outward until the photograph is resized approximately as shown in Figure 1–50.

Figure 1–50

To Move Clips

After you insert clip art or a photograph on a slide, you might want to reposition it. The light bulb photograph on Slide 3 could be centered in the space between the slide title and the left and right edges of the slide. The clip on Slide 1 could be positioned in the upper-right corner of the slide. On Slide 4, the furnace and water heater clips could be centered under each heading. The following steps move these graphics.

1
- If necessary, click the light bulb photograph on Slide 3 to select it.

- Press and hold down the mouse button and then drag the photograph diagonally downward below the title text (Figure 1–51).

- If necessary, select the photograph and then use the ARROW keys to position it precisely as shown in Figure 1–51.

 Q&A The photograph still is not located exactly where I want it to display. What can I do to align the photograph?

Press the CTRL key while you press the ARROW keys. This key combination moves the clip in smaller increments than when you press only an ARROW key.

Figure 1–51

- Click the Next Slide button to display Slide 4.

- Click the furnace clip to select it, press and hold down the mouse button, and then drag the clip to center it under the furnace heading.

- Click the water heater clip and then drag the clip to center it under the water heater heading (Figure 1–52).

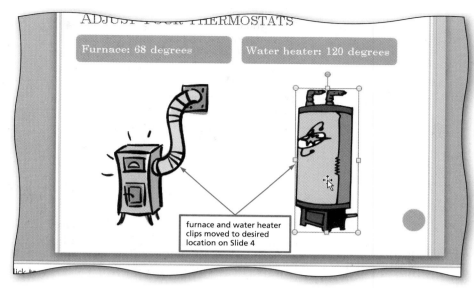

Figure 1–52

- Click the Previous Slide button twice to display Slide 2.

- Click the dishwasher clip, which is on top of the faucet clip, and then drag the clip to center it under the last bulleted paragraph, Wash clothes in cold water.

- Click the faucet clip and then drag the clip so that the faucet handle is centered under the words, full loads.

- Drag a corner sizing handle on the faucet clip diagonally outward until the clip is resized approximately as shown in Figure 1–53. You may need to drag the clip to position it in the desired location.

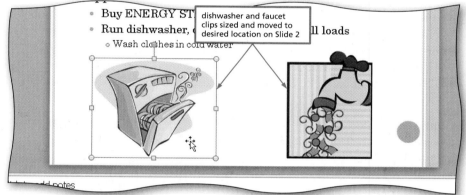

Figure 1–53

- Select the dishwasher clip and then resize and move it so that the clip displays approximately as shown in Figure 1–53.

- Click the Previous Slide button to display Slide 1.

- Click the globe clip and then drag it to the upper-right corner of the slide. You may want to adjust its size by selecting it and then dragging the corner sizing handles.

- Click outside the clip to deselect it (Figure 1–54).

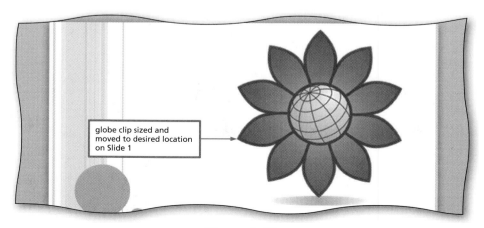

Figure 1–54

<table>
<tr>
<td>Plan
Ahead</td>
<td>

Choose a closing slide.

After the last slide appears during a slide show, the default PowerPoint setting is to end the presentation with a **black slide**. This black slide appears only when the slide show is running and concludes the slide show, so your audience never sees the PowerPoint window. It is a good idea, however, to end the presentation with a final closing slide to display at the end of the presentation. This slide ends the presentation gracefully and should be an exact copy, or a very similar copy, of your title slide. The audience will recognize that the presentation is drawing to a close when this slide appears. It can remain on the screen when the audience asks questions, approaches the speaker for further information, or exits the room.
</td>
</tr>
</table>

Ending a Slide Show with a Closing Slide

All the text for the slides in the Saving Energy slide show has been entered. This presentation thus far consists of a title slide, one text slide with a multi-level bulleted list, a third slide for a photograph, and a fourth slide with a Comparison layout. A closing slide that resembles the title slide is the final slide to create.

To Duplicate a Slide

When two slides contain similar information and have the same format, duplicating one slide and then making minor modifications to the new slide saves time and increases consistency.

Slide 5 will have the same layout and design as Slide 1. The most expedient method of creating this slide is to copy Slide 1 and then make minor modifications to the new slide. The following steps duplicate the title slide.

1

- With Slide 1 selected, click the New Slide arrow (Home tab | Slides group) to display the Oriel layout gallery (Figure 1–55).

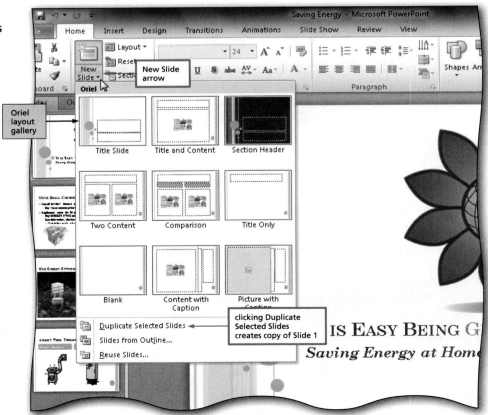

Figure 1–55

2

● Click Duplicate
Selected Slides in the
Oriel layout gallery
to create a new
Slide 2, which is a
duplicate of Slide 1
(Figure 1–56).

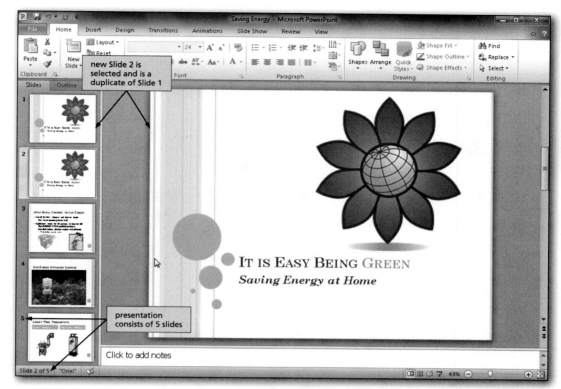

Figure 1–56

Break Point: If you wish to take a break, this is a good place to do so. You can quit PowerPoint now (refer to page
PPT 50 for instructions). To resume at a later time, start PowerPoint (refer to pages PPT 4 and PPT 5 for instructions),
open the file called Saving Energy (refer to pages PPT 50 and PPT 51 for instructions), and continue following the steps
from this location forward.

To Arrange a Slide

The new Slide 2 was inserted directly below Slide 1 because Slide 1 was the selected slide. This duplicate slide
needs to display at the end of the presentation directly after the final title and content slide.

Changing slide order is an easy process and is best performed in the Slides pane. When you click the slide
thumbnail and begin to drag it to a new location, a line indicates the new location of the selected slide. When you
release the mouse button, the slide drops into the desired location. Hence, this process of dragging and then drop-
ping the thumbnail in a new location is called **drag and drop**. You can use the drag-and-drop method to move any
selected item, including text and graphics. The following step moves the new Slide 2 to the end of the presentation
so that it becomes a closing slide.

1

- With Slide 2 selected, drag the Slide 2 slide thumbnail in the Slides pane below the last slide thumbnail (Figure 1–57).

Q&A

The Slide 2 thumbnail is not visible in the Slides pane when I am dragging the thumbnail downward. How do I know it will be positioned in the desired location?

A blue horizontal bar indicates where the slide will move.

Figure 1–57

Other Ways

1. Click slide icon on Outline tab, drag icon to new location

2. Click Slide Sorter (View tab | Presentation Views group), click slide thumbnail, drag thumbnail to new location

Making Changes to Slide Text Content

After creating slides in a presentation, you may find that you want to make changes to the text. Changes may be required because a slide contains an error, the scope of the presentation shifts, or the style is inconsistent. This section explains the types of changes that commonly occur when creating a presentation.

You generally make three types of changes to text in a presentation: additions, replacements, and deletions.

- Additions are necessary when you omit text from a slide and need to add it later. You may need to insert text in the form of a sentence, word, or single character. For example, you may want to add the presenter's middle name on the title slide.

- Replacements are needed when you want to revise the text in a presentation. For example, you may want to substitute the word *their* for the word *there*.

- Deletions are required when text on a slide is incorrect or no longer is relevant to the presentation. For example, a slide may look cluttered. Therefore, you may want to remove one of the bulleted paragraphs to add more space.

Editing text in PowerPoint basically is the same as editing text in a word processing program. The following sections illustrate the most common changes made to text in a presentation.

Replacing Text in an Existing Slide

When you need to correct a word or phrase, you can replace the text by selecting the text to be replaced and then typing the new text. As soon as you press any key on the keyboard, the selected text is deleted and the new text is displayed.

PowerPoint inserts text to the left of the insertion point. The text to the right of the insertion point moves to the right (and shifts downward if necessary) to accommodate the added text.

Deleting Text

You can delete text using one of three methods. One is to use the BACKSPACE key to remove text just typed. The second is to position the insertion point to the left of the text you want to delete and then press the DELETE key. The third method is to drag through the text you want to delete and then press the DELETE or BACKSPACE key. Use the third method when deleting large sections of text.

To Delete Text in a Placeholder

To keep the ending slide clean and simple, you want to delete a few words in the slide show title and subtitle text. The following steps change It Is Easy Being Green to Be Green and then change Saving Energy at Home to Save Energy.

1

- With Slide 5 selected, position the mouse pointer immediately to the left of the first character of the text to be selected (in this case, the I in the word, It).

- Drag the mouse pointer through the last character of the text to be selected (in this case, the space after the y in Easy) (Figure 1–58).

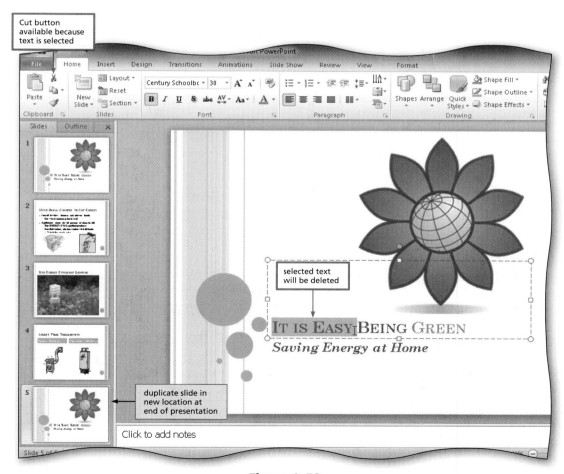

Figure 1–58

• Click the Cut button (Home tab | Clipboard group) to delete all the selected text (Figure 1–59).

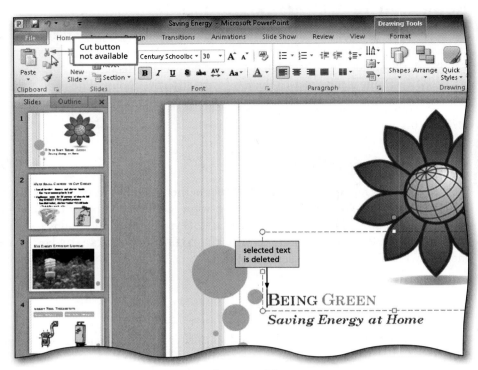

Figure 1–59

• Select the letters, ing, in the word, Being.

• Click the Cut button (Figure 1–60).

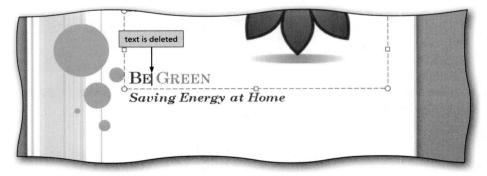

Figure 1–60

• Select the letters, ing, in the word, Saving, and then click the Cut button.

• Type e to change the word to Save (Figure 1–61).

Other Ways
1. Right-click selected text, click Cut on shortcut menu
2. Select text, press DELETE or BACKSPACE key
3. Select text, press CTRL+X

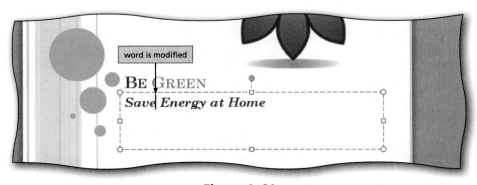

Figure 1–61

Adding a Transition

PowerPoint provides many animation effects to add interest and make a slide show presentation look professional. **Animation** includes special visual and sound effects applied to text or content. A **slide transition** is a special animation effect used to progress from one slide to the next in a slide show. You can control the speed of the transition effect and add a sound.

PowerPoint provides a variety of transitions arranged into three categories that describe the types of effects: Subtle, Exciting, and Dynamic Content.

To Add a Transition between Slides

In this presentation, you apply the Doors transition in the Exciting category to all slides and change the transition speed from 1.40 seconds to 2 seconds. The following steps apply this transition to the presentation.

1
• Click the Transitions tab on the Ribbon and then point to the More button (Transitions tab | Transition to This Slide group) (Figure 1–62).

Q&A
Is a transition applied now?

No. The first slide icon in the Transitions group has an orange border, which indicates no transition has been applied.

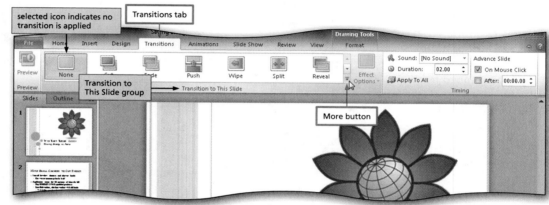

Figure 1–62

2
• Click the More button to expand the Transitions gallery.

• Point to the Doors transition in the Exciting category in the Transitions gallery (Figure 1–63).

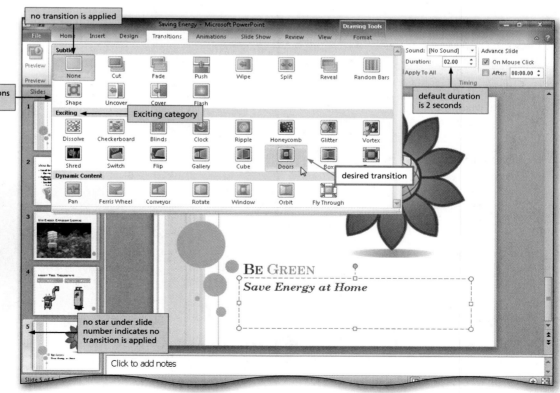

Figure 1–63

- Click Doors in the Exciting category in the Transitions gallery to apply this transition to the closing slide.

Q&A Why does a star appear next to Slide 5 in the Slides tab?

The star indicates that a transition animation effect is applied to that slide.

- Click the Duration up arrow (Transitions tab | Timing group) three times to change the transition speed from 01.40 seconds to 02.00 seconds (Figure 1–64).

Q&A Why did the time change?

Each transition has a default duration time. The Doors transition time is 1:40 seconds.

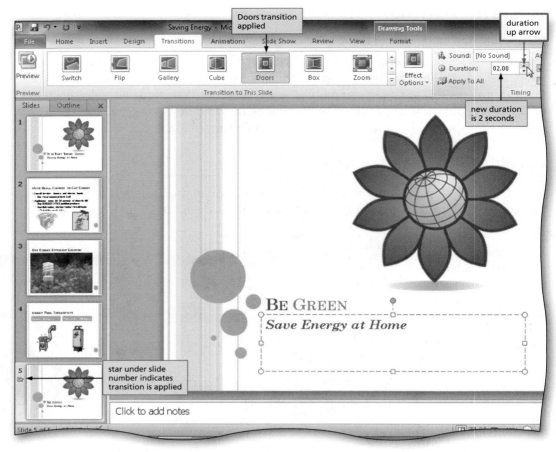

Figure 1–64

- Click the Preview Transitions button (Transitions tab | Preview area) to view the transition and the new transition time (Figure 1–65).

Q&A Can I adjust the duration time I just set?

Yes. Click the Duration up or down arrows or type a speed in the Duration text box and preview the transition until you find the time that best fits your presentation.

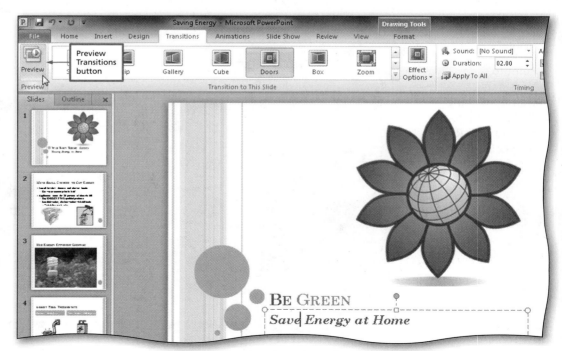

Figure 1–65

5

- Click the Apply To All button (Transitions tab | Timing group) to apply the Doors transition and the increased transition time to Slides 1 through 4 in the presentation (Figure 1–66).

Q&A

What if I want to apply a different transition and duration to each slide in the presentation?

Repeat Steps 2 and 3 for each slide individually.

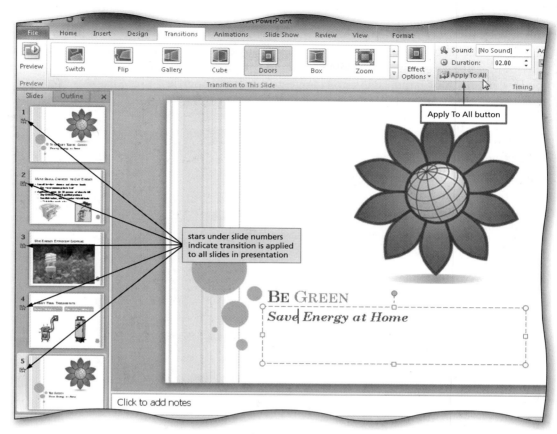

Figure 1–66

Changing Document Properties

PowerPoint helps you organize and identify your files by using **document properties**, which are the details about a file. Document properties, also known as **metadata**, can include information such as the project author, title, subject, and keywords. A **keyword** is a word or phrase that further describes the document. For example, a class name or document topic can describe the file's purpose or content.

Document properties are valuable for a variety of reasons:

- Users can save time locating a particular file because they can view a document's properties without opening the document.
- By creating consistent properties for files having similar content, users can better organize their documents.
- Some organizations require PowerPoint users to add document properties so that other employees can view details about these files.

Five different types of document properties exist, but the more common ones used in this book are standard and automatically updated properties. **Standard properties** are associated with all Microsoft Office documents and include author, title, and subject. **Automatically updated properties** include file system properties, such as the date you create or change a file, and statistics, such as the file size.

To Change Document Properties

The **Document Information Panel** contains areas where you can view and enter document properties. You can view and change information in this panel at any time while you are creating a document. Before saving the presentation again, you want to add your name and course information as document properties. The following steps use the Document Information Panel to change document properties.

1

- Click File on the Ribbon to open the Backstage view.

- If necessary, click the Info tab in the Backstage view to display the Info gallery (Figure 1–67).

Q&A How do I close the Backstage view?

Click File on the Ribbon or click the preview of the document in the Info gallery to return to the PowerPoint document window.

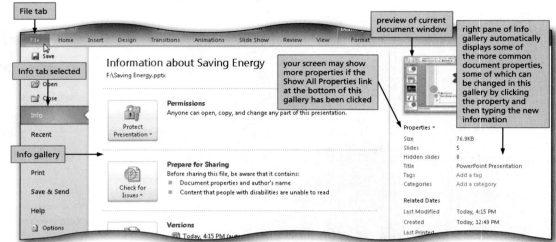

Figure 1–67

2

- Click the Properties button in the right pane of the Info gallery to display the Properties menu (Figure 1–68).

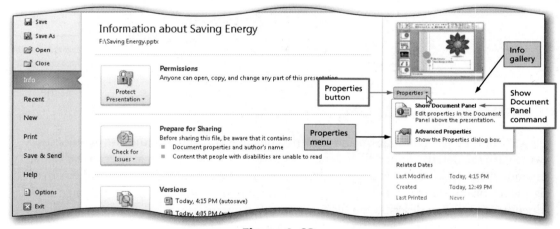

Figure 1–68

3

- Click Show Document Panel on the Properties menu to close the Backstage view and display the Document Information Panel in the PowerPoint document window (Figure 1–69).

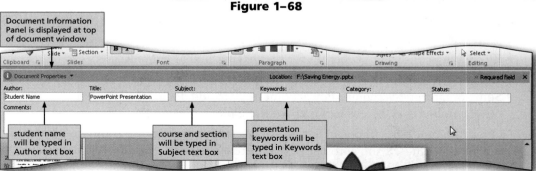

Figure 1–69

Q&A Why are some of the document properties in my Document Information Panel already filled in?

The person who installed Microsoft Office 2010 on your computer or network may have set or customized the properties.

- Click the Author text box, if necessary, and then type your name as the Author property. If a name already is displayed in the Author text box, delete it before typing your name.

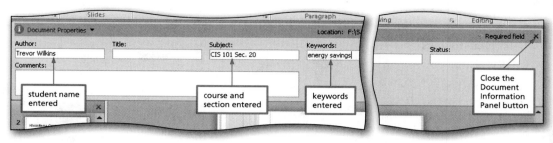

Figure 1–70

- Click the Subject text box, if necessary delete any existing text, and then type your course and section as the Subject property.

- If an AutoComplete dialog box appears, click its Yes button.

- Click the Keywords text box, if necessary delete any existing text, and then type **energy savings** as the Keywords property (Figure 1–70).

Q&A What types of document properties does PowerPoint collect automatically?

PowerPoint records details such as time spent editing a document, the number of times a document has been revised, and the fonts and themes used in a document.

Other Ways

1. Click File on Ribbon, click Info in Backstage view, if necessary click Show All Properties link in Info gallery, click property to change and type new information, close Backstage view

- Click the Close the Document Information Panel button so that the Document Information Panel no longer is displayed.

To Save an Existing Presentation with the Same File Name

You have made several modifications to the presentation since you last saved it. Thus, you should save it again. The following step saves the document again. For an example of the step listed below, refer to the Office 2010 and Windows 7 chapter at the beginning of this book.

 Click the Save button on the Quick Access Toolbar to overwrite the previously saved file.

BTW

Saving in a Previous PowerPoint Format
To ensure that your presentation will open in PowerPoint 2003 or older versions of this software, you must save your file in PowerPoint 97-2003 format. These files will have the .ppt extension.

Viewing the Presentation in Slide Show View

The Slide Show button, located in the lower-right corner of the PowerPoint window above the status bar, allows you to show a presentation using a computer. The computer acts like a slide projector, displaying each slide on a full screen. The full-screen slide hides the toolbars, menus, and other PowerPoint window elements.

To Start Slide Show View

When making a presentation, you use **Slide Show view**. You can start Slide Show view from Normal view or Slide Sorter view. Slide Show view begins when you click the Slide Show button in the lower-right corner of the PowerPoint window above the status bar. PowerPoint then shows the current slide on the full screen without any of the PowerPoint window objects, such as the menu bar or toolbars. The following steps start Slide Show view.

1

- Click the Slide 1 thumbnail in the Slides pane to select and display Slide 1.

- Point to the Slide Show button in the lower-right corner of the PowerPoint window on the status bar (Figure 1–71).

Q&A

Why did I need to select Slide 1?

When you run a slide show, PowerPoint begins the show with the currently displayed slide. If you had not selected Slide 1, then only Slide 5 would have displayed in the slide show.

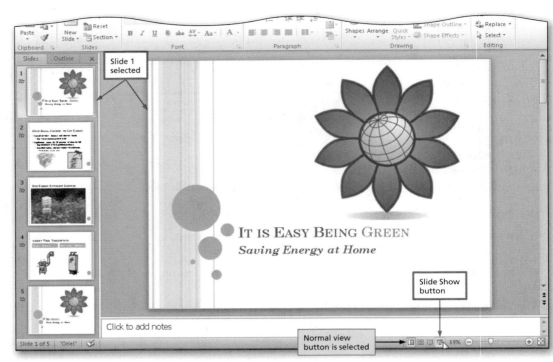

Figure 1–71

2

- Click the Slide Show button to display the title slide (Figure 1–72).

Q&A

Where is the PowerPoint window?

When you run a slide show, the PowerPoint window is hidden. It will reappear once you end your slide show.

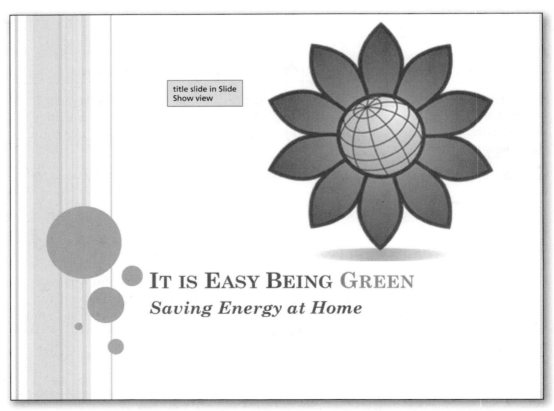

Figure 1–72

Other Ways

1. Click Slide Show From Beginning button (Slide Show tab | Start Slide Show group)
2. Press F5

To Move Manually through Slides in a Slide Show

After you begin Slide Show view, you can move forward or backward through the slides. PowerPoint allows you to advance through the slides manually or automatically. During a slide show, each slide in the presentation shows on the screen, one slide at a time. Each time you click the mouse button, the next slide appears. The following steps move manually through the slides.

- Click each slide until Slide 5 (Be Green) is displayed (Figure 1–73).

Q&A I see a small toolbar in the lower-left corner of my slide. What is this toolbar?

The Slide Show toolbar appears when you begin running a slide show and then move the mouse pointer. The buttons on this toolbar allow you to navigate to the next slide, the previous slide, to mark up the current slide, or to change the current display.

Figure 1–73

- Click Slide 5 so that the black slide appears with a message announcing the end of the slide show (Figure 1–74).

Q&A How can I end the presentation at this point?

Click the black slide to return to Normal view in the PowerPoint window or press the ESC key.

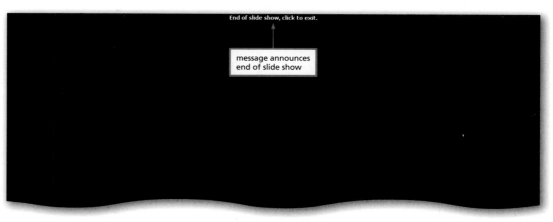

Figure 1–74

Other Ways		
1. Press PAGE DOWN to advance one slide at a time, or press PAGE UP to go back one slide at a time	2. Press RIGHT ARROW or DOWN ARROW to advance one slide at a time, or press LEFT ARROW or UP ARROW to go back one slide at a time	3. If Slide Show toolbar is displayed, click Next Slide or Previous Slide button on toolbar

To Quit PowerPoint

This project now is complete. The following steps quit PowerPoint. For a detailed example of the procedure summarized below, refer to the Office 2010 and Windows 7 chapter at the beginning of this book.

1 If you have one PowerPoint presentation open, click the Close button on the right side of the title bar to close the document and quit PowerPoint; or if you have multiple PowerPoint presentations open, click File on the Ribbon to open the Backstage view and then click Exit in the Backstage view to close all open documents and quit PowerPoint.

2 If a Microsoft PowerPoint dialog box appears, click the Save button to save any changes made to the document since the last save.

BTW

Certification
The Microsoft Office Specialist (MOS) program provides an opportunity for you to obtain a valuable industry credential — proof that you have the PowerPoint 2010 skills required by employers. For more information, visit the PowerPoint 2010 Certification Web page (scsite.com/ppt2010/cert).

To Start PowerPoint

Once you have created and saved a document, you may need to retrieve it from your storage medium. For example, you might want to revise the presentation or print it. The following steps, which assume Windows 7 is running, start PowerPoint so that you can open and modify the presentation. You may need to ask your instructor how to start PowerPoint for your computer. For a detailed example of the procedure summarized below, refer to the Office 2010 and Windows 7 chapter at the beginning of this book.

1 Click the Start button on the Windows 7 taskbar to display the Start menu.

2 Type **Microsoft PowerPoint** as the search text in the 'Search programs and files' text box and watch the search results appear on the Start menu.

3 Click Microsoft PowerPoint 2010 in the search results on the Start menu to start PowerPoint and display a new blank document in the PowerPoint window.

4 If the PowerPoint window is not maximized, click the Maximize button next to the Close button on its title bar to maximize the window.

To Open a Document from PowerPoint

Earlier in this chapter you saved your project on a USB flash drive using the file name, Saving Energy. The following steps open the Saving Energy file from the PowerPoint folder in the CIS 101 folder on the USB flash drive. For a detailed example of the procedure summarized below, refer to the Office 2010 and Windows 7 chapter at the beginning of this book.

1 With your USB flash drive connected to one of the computer's USB ports, click File on the Ribbon to open the Backstage view.

2 Click Open in the Backstage view to display the Open dialog box.

3 Navigate to the location of the file to be opened (in this case, the USB flash drive, then to the CIS 101 folder [or your class folder], and then to the PowerPoint folder).

4 Click Saving Energy to select the file to be opened.

5 Click the Open button (Open dialog box) to open the selected file and display the opened document in the PowerPoint window.

Printing a Presentation

After creating a presentation, you may want to print the slides. Printing a presentation enables you to distribute the document to others in a form that can be read or viewed but typically not edited. It is a good practice to save a presentation before printing it, in the event you experience difficulties printing.

Determine the best method for distributing the presentation.
The traditional method of distributing a presentation uses a printer to produce a hard copy. A **hardcopy** or **printout** is information that exists on a physical medium such as paper. For users who can receive fax documents, you can elect to print a hard copy on a remote fax machine. Hard copies can be useful for the following reasons:

- Many people prefer proofreading a hard copy of a document rather than viewing it on the screen to check for errors and readability.

- Hard copies can serve as reference material if your storage medium is lost or becomes corrupted and you need to recreate the document.

    Instead of distributing a hard copy of a presentation slides, users can choose to distribute the presentation as an electronic image that mirrors the original document's appearance. The electronic image of the document can be e-mailed, posted on a Web site, or copied to a portable storage medium such as a USB flash drive. Two popular electronic image formats, sometimes called fixed formats, are PDF by Adobe Systems and XPS by Microsoft. In PowerPoint, you can create electronic image files through the Print tab in the Backstage view, the Save & Send tab in the Backstage view, and the Save As dialog box. Electronic images of documents, such as PDF and XPS, can be useful for the following reasons.

- Users can view electronic images of documents without the software that created the original document (e.g., PowerPoint). Specifically, to view a PDF file, you use a program called Acrobat Reader, which can be downloaded free from Adobe's Web site. Similarly, to view an XPS file, you use a program called an XPS Viewer, which is included in the latest versions of Windows and Internet Explorer.

- Sending electronic documents saves paper and printer supplies. Society encourages users to contribute to **green computing**, which involves reducing the environmental waste generated when using a computer.

Plan Ahead

To Print a Presentation

With the completed presentation saved, you may want to print it. If copies of the presentation are being distributed to audience members, you will print a hard copy of each individual slide on a printer. The following steps print a hard copy of the contents of the saved Saving Energy presentation.

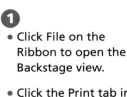

1

- Click File on the Ribbon to open the Backstage view.

- Click the Print tab in the Backstage view to display the Print gallery (Figure 1–75).

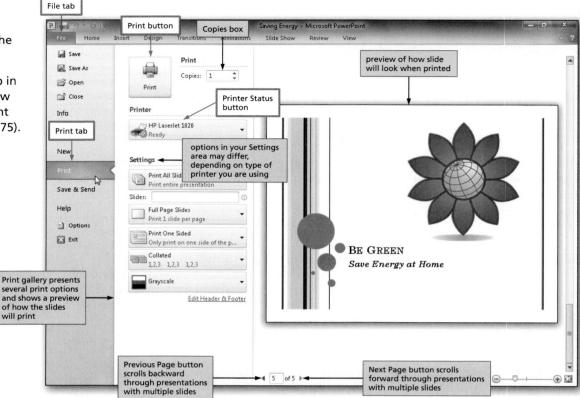

Figure 1–75

Q&A How do I preview Slides 2 through 5?

Click the Next Page button in the Print gallery to scroll forward through pages in the document; similarly, click the Previous Page button to scroll backward through pages.

Q&A How can I print multiple copies of my slides?

Increase the number in the Copies box in the Print gallery.

Q&A What if I decide not to print the document at this time?

Click File on the Ribbon to close the Backstage view and return to the PowerPoint document window.

2

- Verify the printer name that appears on the Printer box Status button will print a hard copy of the document. If necessary, click the Printer Status button to display a list of available printer options and then click the desired printer to change the currently selected printer.

BTW **Quick Reference**
For a table that lists how to complete the tasks covered in this book using the mouse, Ribbon, shortcut menu, and keyboard, see the Quick Reference Summary at the back of this book, or visit the PowerPoint 2010 Quick Reference Web page (scsite.com/ppt2010/qr).

3

- Click the Print button in the Print gallery to print the document on the currently selected printer.

- When the printer stops, retrieve the hard copy (Figure 1–76).

Q&A

Do I have to wait until my document is complete to print it?

No, you can follow these steps to print a document at any time while you are creating it.

Q&A

What if I want to print an electronic image of a document instead of a hard copy?

You would click the Printer Status button in the Print gallery and then select the desired electronic image option such as a Microsoft XPS Document Writer, which would create an XPS file.

(a) Slide 1

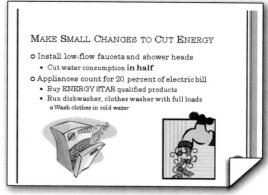

(b) Slide 2

(c) Slide 3

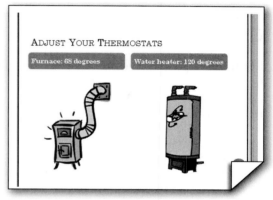

(d) Slide 4

(e) Slide 5

Figure 1–76

Other Ways

1. Press CTRL+P, press ENTER

To Quit PowerPoint

The project now is complete. The following steps quit PowerPoint. For a detailed example of the procedure summarized below, refer to the Office 2010 and Windows 7 chapter at the beginning of this book.

1 If you have one PowerPoint document open, click the Close button on the right side of the title bar to close the document and quit PowerPoint; or if you have multiple PowerPoint documents open, click File on the Ribbon to open the Backstage view and then click Exit in the Backstage view to close all open documents and quit PowerPoint.

2 If a Microsoft Office PowerPoint dialog box appears, click the Save button to save any changes made to the document since the last save.

Chapter Summary

In this chapter you have learned how to apply a document theme, create a title slide and text slides with a bulleted list, clip art, and a photograph, size and move clip art and a photograph, format and edit text, add a slide transition, view the presentation in Slide Show view, and print slides as handouts. The items listed below include all the new PowerPoint skills you have learned in this chapter.

1. Start PowerPoint (PPT 4)
2. Choose a Document Theme (PPT 5)
3. Enter the Presentation Title (PPT 7)
4. Enter the Presentation Subtitle Paragraph (PPT 9)
5. Select a Paragraph (PPT 10)
6. Italicize Text (PPT 11)
7. Increase Font Size (PPT 11)
8. Select a Word (PPT 12)
9. Change the Text Color (PPT 13)
10. Save a Presentation (PPT 14)
11. Add a New Text Slide with a Bulleted List (PPT 14)
12. Enter a Slide Title (PPT 16)
13. Select a Text Placeholder (PPT 16)
14. Type a Multi-Level Bulleted List (PPT 17)
15. Select a Group of Words (PPT 19)
16. Bold Text (PPT 19)
17. Add a Slide with the Title Only Layout (PPT 21)
18. Add a New Slide and Enter a Slide Title and Headings (PPT 23)
19. Move to Another Slide in Normal View (PPT 25)
20. Insert a Clip from the Clip Organizer into the Title Slide (PPT 27)
21. Insert a Clip from the Clip Organizer into a Content Placeholder (PPT 30)
22. Insert a Photograph from the Clip Organizer into a Slide without a Content Placeholder (PPT 32)
23. Resize Clip Art (PPT 33)
24. Move Clips (PPT 36)
25. Duplicate a Slide (PPT 38)
26. Arrange a Slide (PPT 39)
27. Delete Text in a Placeholder (PPT 41)
28. Add a Transition between Slides (PPT 43)
29. Change Document Properties (PPT 46)
30. Save an Existing Presentation with the Same File Name (PPT 47)
31. Start Slide Show View (PPT 47)
32. Move Manually through Slides in a Slide Show (PPT 49)
33. Quit PowerPoint (PPT 50)
34. Open a Document from PowerPoint (PPT 50)
35. Print a Presentation (PPT 51)

If you have a SAM 2010 user profile, your instructor may have assigned an autogradable version of this assignment. If so, log into the SAM 2010 Web site at www.cengage.com/sam2010 to download the instruction and start files.

Learn It Online

Test your knowledge of chapter content and key terms.

Instructions: To complete the Learn It Online exercises, start your browser, click the Address bar, and then enter the Web address **scsite.com/ppt2010/learn**. When the PowerPoint 2010 Learn It Online page is displayed, click the link for the exercise you want to complete and then read the instructions.

Chapter Reinforcement TF, MC, and SA
A series of true/false, multiple choice, and short answer questions that test your knowledge of the chapter content.

Flash Cards
An interactive learning environment where you identify chapter key terms associated with displayed definitions.

Practice Test
A series of multiple choice questions that test your knowledge of chapter content and key terms.

Who Wants To Be a Computer Genius?
An interactive game that challenges your knowledge of chapter content in the style of a television quiz show.

Wheel of Terms
An interactive game that challenges your knowledge of chapter key terms in the style of the television show *Wheel of Fortune*.

Crossword Puzzle Challenge
A crossword puzzle that challenges your knowledge of key terms presented in the chapter.

Apply Your Knowledge

Reinforce the skills and apply the concepts you learned in this chapter.

Modifying Character Formats and Paragraph Levels and Moving a Clip
Note: To complete this assignment, you will be required to use the Data Files for Students. See the inside back cover of this book for instructions on downloading the Data Files for Students, or contact your instructor for information about accessing the required files.

Instructions: Start PowerPoint. Open the presentation, Apply 1-1 Flu Season, from the Data Files for Students.

The two slides in the presentation discuss ways to avoid getting or spreading the flu. The document you open is an unformatted presentation. You are to modify the document theme, indent the paragraphs, resize and move the clip art, and format the text so the slides look like Figure 1–77 on the next page.

Continued >

Apply Your Knowledge *continued*

Perform the following tasks:

1. Change the document theme to Urban. On the title slide, use your name in place of Student Name and bold and italicize your name. Increase the title text font size to 60 point. Resize and position the clip as shown in Figure 1–77a.

2. On Slide 2, increase the indent of the second, third, and fifth paragraphs (Cover mouth and nose with a tissue; No tissue? Use your elbow or sleeve; Use soap, warm water for 20 seconds) to second-level paragraphs. Then combine paragraphs six and seven (Drink fluids; Get plenty of rest) to read, Drink fluids and get plenty of rest, as shown in Figure 1–77b.

3. Change the document properties, as specified by your instructor. Save the presentation using the file name, Apply 1–1 Avoid the Flu. Submit the revised document in the format specified by your instructor.

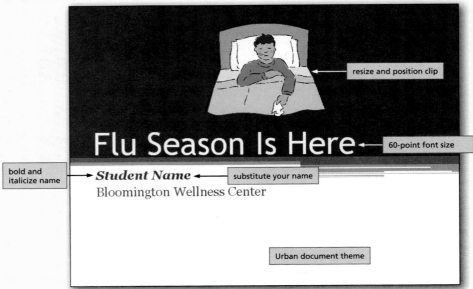

(a) Slide 1 (Title Slide with Clip Art)

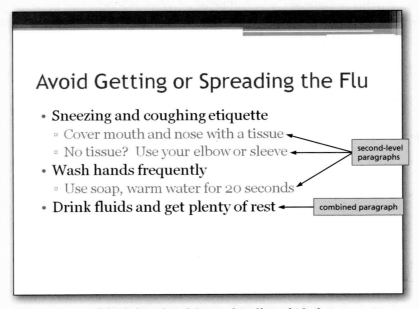

(b) Slide 2 (Multi-Level Bulleted List)

Figure 1–77

Extend Your Knowledge

Extend the skills you learned in this chapter and experiment with new skills. You may need to use Help to complete the assignment.

Changing Slide Theme, Layout, and Text

Note: To complete this assignment, you will be required to use the Data Files for Students. See the inside back cover of this book for instructions on downloading the Data Files for Students, or contact your instructor for information about accessing the required files.

Instructions: Start PowerPoint. Open the presentation that you are going to prepare for your dental hygiene class, Extend 1–1 Winning Smile, from the Data Files for Students.
    You will choose a theme, format slides, and create a closing slide.

Perform the following tasks:
1. Apply an appropriate document theme.
2. On Slide 1, use your name in place of Student Name. Format the text on this slide using techniques you learned in this chapter, such as changing the font size and color and also bolding and italicizing words.
3. On Slide 2, change the slide layout and adjust the paragraph levels so that the lines of text are arranged under two headings: Discount Dental and Dental Insurance (Figure 1–78).
4. On Slide 3, create paragraphs and adjust the paragraph levels to create a bulleted list. Edit the text so that the slide meets the 7 × 7 rule, which states that each line should have a maximum of seven words, and each slide should have a maximum of seven lines.
5. Create an appropriate closing slide using the title slide as a guide.
6. The slides contain a variety of clips downloaded from the Microsoft Clip Organizer. Size and move them when necessary.
7. Apply an appropriate transition to all slides.
8. Change the document properties, as specified by your instructor. Save the presentation using the file name, Extend 1–1 Dental Plans.
9. Submit the revised document in the format specified by your instructor.

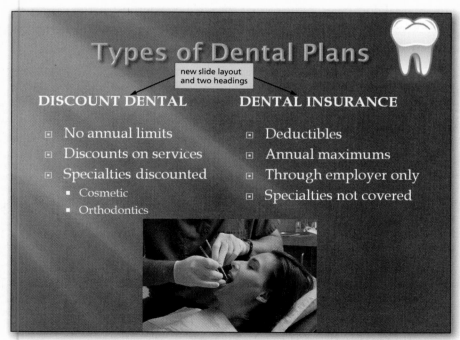

Figure 1–78

Make It Right

Analyze a presentation and correct all errors and/or improve the design.

Correcting Formatting and List Levels

Note: To complete this assignment, you will be required to use the Data Files for Students. See the inside back cover of this book for instructions on downloading the Data Files for Students, or contact your instructor for information about accessing the required files.

Instructions: Start PowerPoint. Open the presentation, Make It Right 1–1 Air Ducts, from the Data Files for Students.

Members of your homeowners' association are having their semiannual meeting, and each member of the board is required to give a short presentation on the subject of energy savings. You have decided to discuss the energy-saving benefits of maintaining the air ducts in your home. Correct the formatting problems and errors in the presentation while keeping in mind the guidelines presented in this chapter.

Perform the following tasks:

1. Change the document theme from Origin, shown in Figure 1–79, to Module.
2. On Slide 1, replace the words, Student Name, with your name. Format your name so that it displays prominently on the slide.
3. Increase the size of the clip on Slide 1 and move it to the upper-right corner.
4. Move Slide 2 to the end of the presentation so that it becomes the new Slide 3.
5. On Slide 2, correct the spelling errors and then increase the font size of the Slide 2 title text, Check Hidden Air Ducts, to 54 point. Increase the size of the clip and move it up to fill the white space on the right of the bulleted list.
6. On Slide 3, correct the spelling errors and then change the font size of the title text, Energy Savings, to 54 point. Increase the indent levels for paragraphs 2 and 4. Increase the size of the clips. Center the furnace clip at the bottom of the slide.
7. Change the document properties, as specified by your instructor. Save the presentation using the file name, Make It Right 1–1 Ducts Presentation.
8. Apply the same transition and duration to all slides.
9. Submit the revised document in the format specified by your instructor.

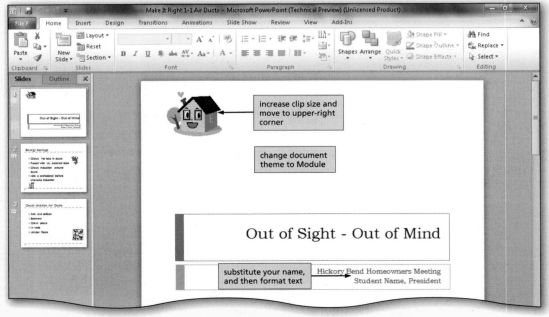

Figure 1–79

In the Lab

Design and/or create a presentation using the guidelines, concepts, and skills presented in this chapter. Labs 1, 2, and 3 are listed in order of increasing difficulty.

Lab1: Creating a Presentation with Bulleted Lists, a Closing Slide, and Clips

Problem: You are working with upper-level students to host a freshmen orientation seminar. When you attended this seminar, you received some helpful tips on studying for exams. Your contribution to this year's seminar is to prepare a short presentation on study skills. You develop the outline shown in Figure 1–80 and then prepare the PowerPoint presentation shown in Figures 1–81a through 1–81d.

Studying for an Exam
Freshmen Orientation Seminar
Sarah Jones

Prepare in Advance
　Location
　　　Quiet, well-lit
　Timing
　　　15-minute breaks every hour
　Material
　　　Quiz yourself

Exam Time
　Day of Exam
　　　Rest properly
　　　Eat a good meal
　　　Wear comfy clothes
　　　Be early
　　　Be confident

Figure 1–80

Perform the following tasks:

1. Create a new presentation using the Aspect document theme.

2. Using the typed notes illustrated in Figure 1–80, create the title slide shown in Figure 1–81a, using your name in place of Sarah Jones. Italicize your name and increase the font size to 24 point. Increase the font size of the title text paragraph, Hit the Books, to 48 point. Increase the font size of the first paragraph of the subtitle text, Studying for an Exam, to 28 point.

(a) Slide 1 (Title Slide)
Figure 1–81

Continued >

In the Lab *continued*

3. Using the typed notes in Figure 1–80, create the two text slides with bulleted lists and find and insert clips from the Microsoft Clip Organizer, as shown in Figures 1–81b and 1–81c.

4. Create a closing slide by duplicating Slide 1, deleting your name, replacing the photograph with the photograph shown in Figure 1–81d, and moving the slide to the end of the presentation.

5. On Slide 3, change the font color of the words, Be confident, to Yellow (fourth color in the Standard Colors row).

6. Apply the Uncover transition in the Subtle category to all slides. Change the duration to 1.25 seconds.

7. Drag the scroll box to display Slide 1. Click the Slide Show button to start Slide Show view. Then click to display each slide.

8. Change the document properties, as specified by your instructor. Save the presentation using the file name, Lab 1–1 Study Skills.

9. Submit the document in the format specified by your instructor.

(b) Slide 2

(c) Slide 3

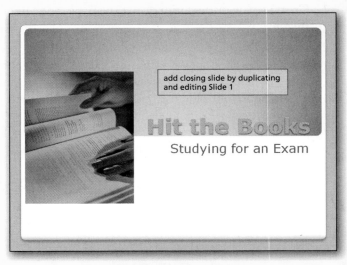

(d) Slide 4 (Closing Slide)

Figure 1–81 (continued)

In the Lab

Lab 2: Creating a Presentation with Bulleted Lists and Clips

Problem: Your health class instructor has assigned every student a different vitamin to research. She hands you the outline shown in Figure 1–82 and asks you to create the presentation about Vitamin D shown in Figures 1–83a through 1–83d on pages PPT 62 and PPT 63.

Vitamin D

The Sunshine Vitamin
Are You D-ficient?
Presented by Jim Warner

Why Is Vitamin D Important?
    We need Vitamin D
        Vital to our bodies
                Promotes absorption of calcium and magnesium
                    For healthy teeth and bones
                Maintains calcium and phosphorus in blood

    Daily Requirements
        How much do we need?
            Child: 5 mcg (200 IU)
            Adult: 10-20 mcg (400-600 IU)

Vitamin D Sources
    Sunshine
        Is our primary source
                Vitamin manufactured by our body after exposure
                    Three times a week
                    For 10-15 minutes
    Foods and Supplements
        Contained in few foods
                Some fish liver oils
                Flesh of fatty fish
        Fortified products
                Milk and cereals
        Available as supplement

Vitamin D History
    Research began in 1924
        Found to prevent rickets
    United States and Canada
        Instituted policy of fortifying foods with Vitamin D
                Milk — food of choice
    Other countries
        Fortified cereal, bread, margarine

Figure 1–82

Continued >

In the Lab *continued*

Perform the following tasks:

1. Create a new presentation using the Solstice document theme.

2. Using the typed notes illustrated in Figure 1–82, create the title slide shown in Figure 1–83a, using your name in place of Jim Warner. Italicize the title, The Sunshine Vitamin, and increase the font size to 48 point. Change the font size of the first line of the subtitle text, Are You D-ficient?, to 36 point. Change the font color of the title text to Orange (third color in the Standard Colors row) and both lines of the subtitle text to Light Blue (seventh color in the Standard Colors row).

3. Using the typed notes in Figure 1–82, create the three text slides with bulleted lists shown in Figures 1–83b through 1–83d. Change the color of the title text on all slides and the text above the bulleted lists on Slides 2 and 3 to Orange.

4. Add the photographs and clip art shown in Figures 1–83a through 1–83d from the Microsoft Clip Organizer. Adjust the clip sizes when necessary.

5. Apply the Ripple transition in the Exciting category to all slides. Change the duration to 2.00 seconds.

6. Drag the scroll box to display Slide 1. Click the Slide Show button to start Slide Show view. Then click to display each slide.

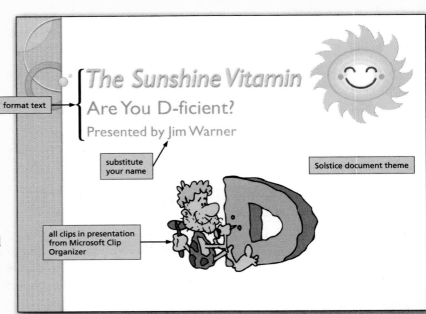

(a) Slide 1 (Title Slide)

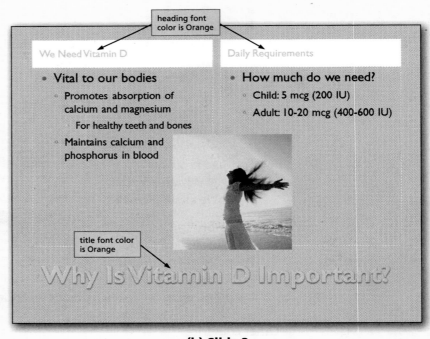

(b) Slide 2

Figure 1–83

7. Change the document properties, as specified by your instructor. Save the presentation using the file name, Lab 1–2 Vitamin D.

8. Submit the revised document in the format specified by your instructor.

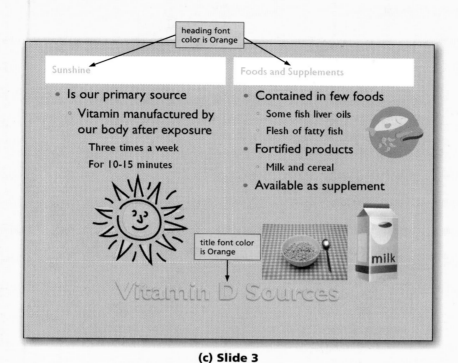

(c) Slide 3

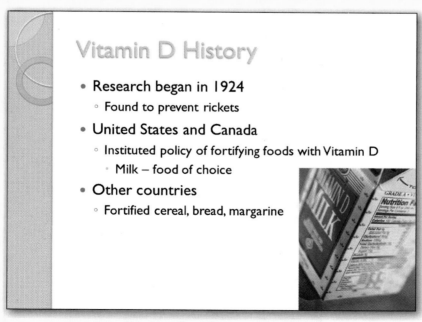

(d) Slide 4
Figure 1–83 (continued)

In the Lab

Lab 3: Creating and Updating Presentations with Clip Art

Problem: You are employed part time at your health club, and the Child Care Center director has asked you to put together a presentation for her to use at the next open house. The club has a large playroom that is perfect for children's parties.

Instructions Part 1: Using the outline in Figure 1–84, create the presentation shown in Figure 1–85. Use the Office Theme document theme. On the title slide shown in Figure 1–85a, increase the font size of the title paragraph, Make It a Party!, to 48, change the font color to Red, and change the text font style to italic. Decrease the font size of the entire subtitle paragraph to 28, and change the font color to Blue.

Make It a Party!
    Host Your Child's
    Next Birthday Party
    At The Oaks Health Club

We Do the Work
You Enjoy the Moment
    Two-hour party
    Two chaperones
    Lunch & cake provided
    Game or craft activity available
    Decorations

Two Party Packages
    Package No. 1 - $8/child
        Lunch
            Hot Dogs
            Pizza
    Package No. 2 - $12/child
        Lunch including beverage
            Hot Dogs
            Pizza
        Game
        Craft (age appropriate)

Reserve Your Party Date
    Reserve 2 weeks in advance
    Deposit required
    Party room can hold 20 children
    Sign up in the Child Care Center

Figure 1–84

Create the three text slides with multi-level bulleted lists, photographs, and clip art shown in Figures 1–85b through 1–85d on the next page. Adjust the clip sizes when necessary. Apply the Vortex transition in the Exciting category to all slides and decrease the duration to 3.00 seconds. Change the document properties, as specified by your instructor. Save the presentation using the file name, Lab 1–3 Part One Child Party.

(a) Slide 1 (Title Slide)

(b) Slide 2
Figure 1–85

Continued >

In the Lab *continued*

Two Party Packages

Package No. 1 - $8/child

- Lunch
  - Hot Dogs
  - Pizza

Package No. 2 - $12/child

- Lunch including beverage
  - Hot Dogs
  - Pizza
- Game
- Craft (age appropriate)

(c) Slide 3

Reserve Your Party Date

- Reserve 2 weeks in advance
- Deposit required
- Party room can hold 20 children
- Sign up in the Child Care Center

(d) Slide 4
Figure 1–85 (continued)

Instructions Part 2:   The children's parties have proved to be a great perk for members of the health club. A large group of older adults work out at the club and also meet socially once a month. These members have asked about renting the playroom to hold a retirement party for some of their friends. You decide to modify the children's party presentation to promote retirement parties. Use the outline in Figure 1–86 to modify the presentation created in Part 1 to create the presentation shown in Figure 1–87 on the next page. Required changes are indicated by a yellow highlight.

To begin, save the current presentation with the new file name, Lab 1–3 Part Two Retirement Party. Change the document theme to Flow. On Slide 3, change the pianist's name from Ms. Winn to your name. Apply the Fade transition in the Subtle category to all slides and change the duration speed to 2.25 seconds. View the slide show. Change the document properties, as specified by your instructor. Submit both Part One and Part Two documents in the format specified by your instructor.

Make It a Party!
Host Your
Retirement Party
At The Oaks Health Club

We Do the Work
You Enjoy the Moment
Two-hour party

Lunch & cake provided

Decorations
Music

Two Party Packages
Package No. 1 - $9/person
Lunch
Lasagna
Salad & bread
Package No. 2 - $20/person
Lunch including beverage
Lasagna
Salad & bread
Ms. Winn on piano
Photo booth

Reserve Your Party Date
Reserve 2 weeks in advance
Deposit required
Party room can hold 15 adults
Sign up at the main desk

Figure 1–86

Continued >

In the Lab *continued*

(a) Slide 1 (Title Slide)

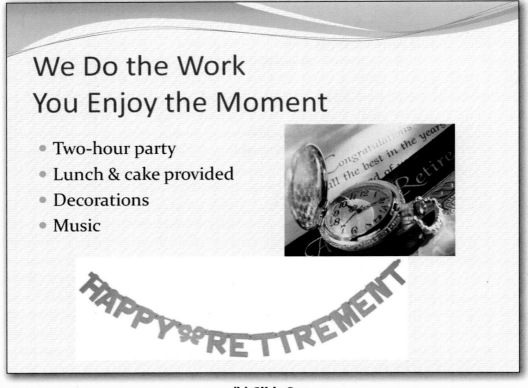

(b) Slide 2
Figure 1–87

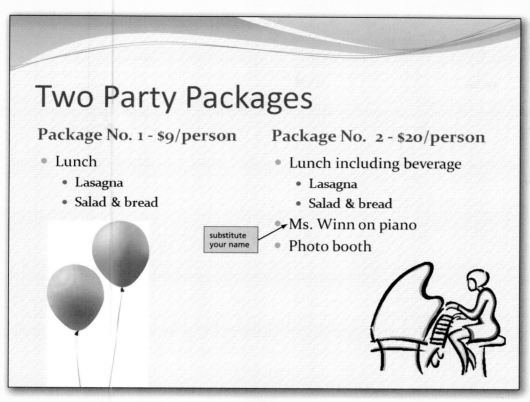

(c) Slide 3

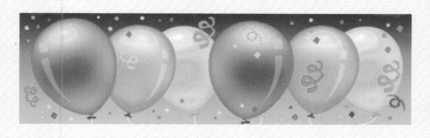

(d) Slide 4
Figure 1–87 (continued)

Cases and Places

Apply your creative thinking and problem-solving skills to design and implement a solution.

Note: To complete these assignments, you may be required to use the Data Files for Students. See the inside back cover of this book for instructions on downloading the Data Files for Students, or contact your instructor for information about accessing the required files.

As you design the presentations, remember to use the 7 × 7 rule: a maximum of seven words on a line and a maximum of seven lines on one slide.

1: Design and Create a Presentation about Galileo

Academic

Italian-born Galileo is said to be the father of modern science. After the invention of the telescope by a Dutch eyeglass maker named Hans Lippershey, Galileo made his own telescope and made many discoveries. You decide to prepare a PowerPoint presentation to accompany a speech that is required in your Astronomy class. You create the outline shown in Figure 1–88 about Galileo. Use this outline, along with the concepts and techniques presented in this chapter, to develop and format a slide show with a title slide and three text slides with bulleted lists. Add photographs and clip art from the Microsoft Clip Organizer and apply a transition. Submit your assignment in the format specified by your instructor.

Galileo Galilei
　　Father of Modern Science
　　Astronomy 201
　　Sandy Wendt

Major Role in Scientific Revolution
February 15, 1564 - January 8, 1642
　　Physicist
　　Mathematician
　　Astronomer
　　Philosopher

Galileo's Research Years
　　1581 - Studied medicine
　　1589-1592 - Studied math and physics
　　1592-1607 - Padua University
　　　　Developed Law of Inertia
　　1609 - Built telescope
　　　　Earth's moon
　　　　Jupiter's moons

Galileo's Later Years
　　Dialogue - Two Chief World Systems
　　　　Controversy develops
　　1633 - Rome
　　　　Heresy trial
　　　　Imprisoned
　　1642 - Dies

Figure 1–88

2: Design and Create a Presentation Promoting Hiking for Family Fitness

Personal

A great way for the entire family to get exercise is by participating in a hiking adventure. Employees at the local forest preserve district near your home have remodeled the nature center, and you have volunteered to give a presentation at the open house to help families plan their hikes. Use the outline shown in Figure 1–89 and then create an accompanying PowerPoint presentation. Use the concepts and techniques presented in this chapter to develop and format this slide show with a title slide, three text slides with bulleted lists, and clip art. Add photographs and clip art from the Microsoft Clip Organizer and apply a transition. Submit your assignment in the format specified by your instructor.

Take a Hike
> An Adventure with Kids
> Presented by Joshua Lind
> Pines Nature Center

Planning the Adventure
> Trail length – varies by child's age
>> Ages 2 to 4: 1 to 2 miles
>> Ages 5 to 7: 3 to 4 miles
>> Ages 8 to 12: 5 to 7 miles
> Backpack – limit to 20 percent of child's weight

Packing Supplies
> Snacks and Drinks
>> Child's favorite healthy foods
>>> Fruit and nuts
>> Water
> Miscellaneous
>> Sunscreen
>> Insect repellent
>> First-aid kit

Wearing the Right Clothes
> Dress in layers
>> Children get cold quicker than adults
> Wear long pants and long-sleeved shirt
>> Protect against insects and cuts
> Wear a hat and comfortable shoes
>> Keep body warm

Figure 1–89

Continued >

Cases and Places *continued*

3: Design and Create a Landscaping Service Presentation

Professional

The home and garden center where you work is hosting weekend clinics for customers. The owner asks you to give a presentation about the center's new landscaping division and hands you the outline shown in Figure 1–90. Use the concepts and techniques presented in this chapter to develop and format a PowerPoint presentation with a title slide, three text slides with bulleted lists, and clip art. Add photographs and clip art from the Microsoft Clip Organizer and apply a transition. Submit your assignment in the format specified by your instructor.

Barry's Landscaping Service
Bensenville, Indiana

Full-Service Landscaping
Initial design
Installation
Maintenance

Scope of Services
Landscape design
Irrigation
Lighting
Lawn-care programs
Tree/shrub maintenance
Masonry, carpentry
Water features

Our Promise to You
Deliver on-time service
Provide highest level of workmanship
Give maximum value for your dollar
Install high-quality plants and materials
Respond quickly to your needs

Figure 1–90

2 | Enhancing a Presentation with Pictures, Shapes, and WordArt

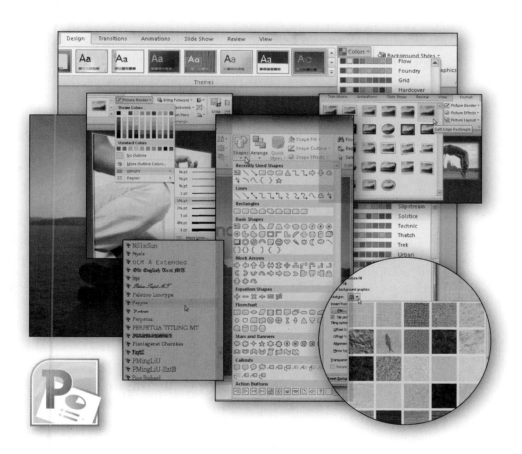

Objectives

You will have mastered the material in this chapter when you can:

- Change theme colors
- Insert a picture to create a background
- Format slide backgrounds
- Insert and size a shape
- Add text to a shape

- Apply effects to a shape
- Change the font and add a shadow
- Format pictures
- Apply a WordArt style
- Format WordArt
- Format text using the Format Painter

2 | Enhancing a Presentation with Pictures, Shapes, and WordArt

Introduction

In our visually oriented culture, audience members enjoy viewing effective graphics. Whether reading a document or viewing a PowerPoint presentation, people increasingly want to see photographs, artwork, graphics, and a variety of typefaces. Researchers have known for decades that documents with visual elements are more effective than those that consist of only text because the illustrations motivate audiences to study the material. People remember at least one-third more information when the document they are seeing or reading contains visual elements. These graphics help clarify and emphasize details, so they appeal to audience members with differing backgrounds, reading levels, attention spans, and motivations.

Project — Presentation with Pictures, Shapes, and WordArt

BTW

Yoga's Origins
The term, yoga, is derived from the Sanskrit word yuj, meaning to join or unite. Yogis have been practicing this system of exercises and philosophy of mental control for more than 26,000 years.

The project in this chapter follows graphical guidelines and uses PowerPoint to create the presentation shown in Figure 2–1. This slide show, which discusses yoga and meditation, has a variety of illustrations and visual elements. For example, pictures have particular shapes and effects. The enhanced type has a style that blends well with the background and illustrations. Pictures and type are formatted using Quick Styles and WordArt, which give your presentation a professional look.

Overview

As you read through this chapter, you will learn how to create the presentation shown in Figure 2–1 by performing these general tasks:

- Format slide backgrounds.
- Insert and format pictures by applying styles and effects.
- Insert and format shapes.
- Format text using WordArt.
- Print a handout of your slides.

(a) Slide 1 (Title Slide with Picture Background and Shapes)

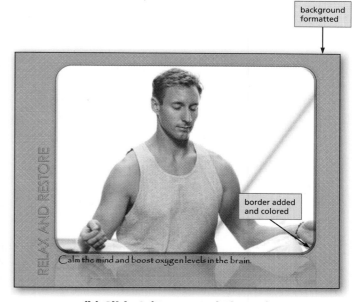

(b) Slide 2 (Formatted Picture)

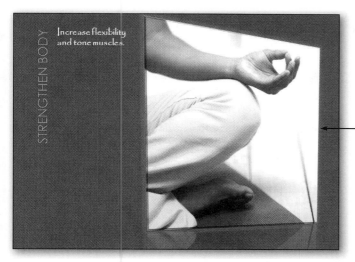

(c) Slide 3 (Formatted Picture)

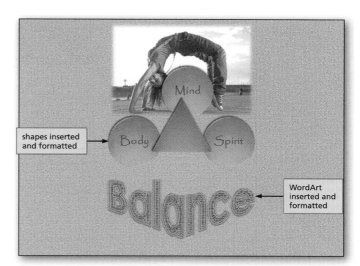

(d) Slide 4 (Inserted and Formatted Shapes)

Figure 2–1

Plan Ahead

General Project Guidelines

When creating a PowerPoint presentation, the actions you perform and decisions you make will affect the appearance and characteristics of the finished document. As you create a presentation with illustrations, such as the project shown in Figure 2–1, you should follow these general guidelines:

1. **Focus on slide text content.** Give some careful thought to the words you choose. Some graphic designers advise starting with a blank screen so that the document theme does not distract from or influence the words.

2. **Apply style guidelines.** Many organizations and publishers establish guidelines for writing styles. These rules apply to capitalization, punctuation, word usage, and document formats. Ask your instructor or manager for a copy of these guidelines or use popular writing guides, such as the *The Chicago Manual of Style*, *The Associated Press Stylebook*, and *The Elements of Style*.

3. **Use color effectively.** Your audience's eyes are drawn to color on a slide. Used appropriately, color can create interest by emphasizing material and promoting understanding. Be aware of symbolic meanings attached to colors, such as red generally representing danger, electricity, and heat.

4. **Adhere to copyright regulations.** Copyright laws apply to printed and electronic materials. You can copy an existing photograph or artwork if it is in the public domain, if your company owns the graphic, or if you have obtained permission to use it. Be certain you have the legal right to use a desired graphic in your presentation.

5. **Consider graphics for multicultural audiences.** In today's intercultural society, your presentation might be viewed by people whose first language is different from yours. Some graphics have meanings specific to a culture, so be certain to learn about your intended audience and their views.

6. **Use WordArt in moderation.** Used correctly, the graphical nature of WordArt can add interest and set a tone. Format text with a WordArt style only when needed for special emphasis.

When necessary, more specific details concerning the above guidelines are presented at appropriate points in the chapter. The chapter also will identify the actions you perform and decisions made regarding these guidelines during the creation of the presentation shown in Figure 2–1.

Starting PowerPoint

Chapter 1 introduced you to starting PowerPoint, selecting a document theme, creating slides with clip art and a bulleted list, and printing a presentation. The following steps, which assume Windows 7 is running, start PowerPoint. You may need to ask your instructor how to start PowerPoint for your computer. For a detailed example of the procedure summarized on the next page, refer to pages OFF 33 through OFF 35 in the Office 2010 and Windows 7 chapter.

For an introduction to Windows 7 and instruction about how to perform basic Windows 7 tasks, read the Office 2010 and Windows 7 chapter at the beginning of this book, where you can learn how to resize windows, change screen resolution, create folders, move and rename files, use Windows Help, and much more.

To Start PowerPoint and Apply a Document Theme

1 Click the Start button on the Windows 7 taskbar to display the Start menu.

2 Type `Microsoft PowerPoint` as the search text in the 'Search programs and files' text box.

3 Click Microsoft PowerPoint 2010 in the search results on the Start menu to start PowerPoint and display a new blank document.

4 If the PowerPoint window is not maximized, click the Maximize button.

5 Apply the Verve document theme.

Focus on slide text content.
Once you have researched your presentation topic, many methods exist to begin developing slide content.

- Select a document theme and then enter text, illustration, and tables.

- Open an existing presentation and modify the slides and theme.

- Import an outline created in Microsoft Word.

- Start with a blank presentation that uses the default Office Theme. Consider this practice similar to an artist who begins creating a painting with a blank, white canvas.

Experiment using different methods of developing the initial content for slides. Experienced PowerPoint users sometimes find one technique works better than another to stimulate creativity or help them organize their ideas in a particular circumstance.

Plan Ahead

For an introduction to Office 2010 and instruction about how to perform basic tasks in Office 2010 programs, read the Office 2010 and Windows 7 chapter at the beginning of this book, where you can learn how to start a program, use the Ribbon, save a file, open a file, quit a program, use Help, and much more.

Creating Slides and Changing Font Colors and Background Style

In Chapter 1, you selected a document theme and then typed the content for the title and text slides. In this chapter, you will type the slide content for the title and text slides, select a background, insert and format pictures and shapes, and then insert and format WordArt. To begin creating the four slides in this presentation, you will enter text in four different layouts, change the theme colors, and then change the background style.

Apply style guidelines.
A good stylebook is useful to decide when to use numerals or words to represent numbers, as in the sentence, More than 25 students are waiting for the bus to arrive. Stylebooks also offer rules on forming possessives, capitalizing titles, and using commas. Once you decide on a style to use in your presentation, apply it consistently throughout your presentation.

Plan Ahead

To Create a Title Slide

Recall from Chapter 1 that the title slide introduces the presentation to the audience. In addition to introducing the presentation, this project uses the title slide to capture the audience's attention by using title text and a background picture. The following steps create the slide show's title slide.

1 Type **Yoga and Meditation** in the title text placeholder.

2 Type **Unify Your Mind,** in the subtitle text placeholder.

3 Press the ENTER key and then type **Body,** as the second line in the subtitle text placeholder.

4 Press the ENTER key and then type **and Spirit** as the third line in the subtitle text placeholder. Change the capital letter 'A' in the word, And, at the beginning of this line to a lowercase 'a' (Figure 2–2).

Q&A Some stylebooks recommend using lowercase letters when using coordinating conjunctions (for, and, nor, but, or, yet, so) and also when using articles (a, an, the). Why is the case of the word, and, changed in the subtitle text?

By default, PowerPoint capitalizes the first word of each paragraph. For consistency, you can decide to lowercase this word to apply a particular style rule so that the word, and, is lowercase in both the title and subtitle text.

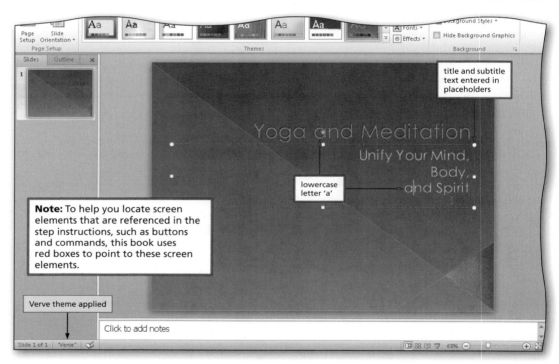

Figure 2–2

To Create the First Text Slide

The first text slide you create in Chapter 2 emphasizes the relaxation and restoration benefits derived from practicing yoga and meditation. The following steps add a new slide (Slide 2) and then create a text slide using the Picture with Caption layout.

1 Click Home on the Ribbon to display the Home tab, click the New Slide button arrow, and then click Picture with Caption in the Layout gallery to add a new slide with this layout.

2 Type **Relax and Restore** in the title text placeholder.

3 Press CTRL+ENTER to move to the caption placeholder and then type **Calm the mind and boost oxygen levels in the brain.** in this placeholder (Figure 2–3).

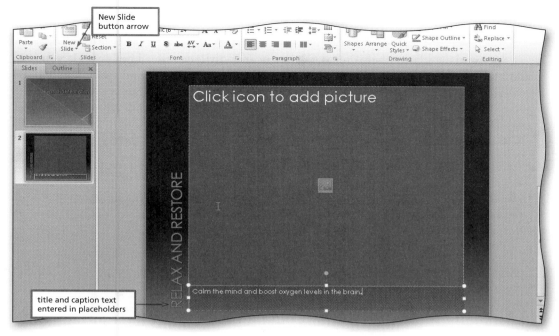

Figure 2–3

To Create the Second Text Slide

The second text slide you create stresses the fact that yoga and meditation strengthen the body in multiple ways. The following steps add a new text slide (Slide 3) that uses the Content with Caption layout.

1 Click the New Slide button arrow and then click Content with Caption in the Layout gallery to add a new slide with this layout.

2 Type **Strengthen Body** in the title text placeholder.

3 Press CTRL+ENTER and then type **Increase flexibility and tone muscles.** in the caption placeholder (Figure 2–4).

Q&A Why does the text display with capital letters despite the fact I am typing uppercase and lowercase letters?

The Verve theme uses the All Caps effect for the title text. This effect converts lowercase letters to uppercase.

BTW

BTWs
For a complete list of the BTWs found in the margins of this book, visit the PowerPoint 2010 BTW Web page (scsite.com/ppt2010/btw).

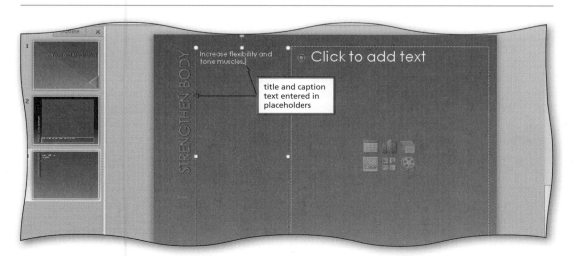

Figure 2–4

To Create the Third Text Slide

Yoga and meditation help create balance in an individual's life. The last slide you create uses graphics to depict the connection among the mind, body, and spirit. You will insert symbols later in this project to create this visual element. For now, you want to create the basic slide. The following step adds a new text slide (Slide 4) that uses the Blank layout.

1 Click the New Slide button arrow and then click Blank in the Layout gallery. (Figure 2–5).

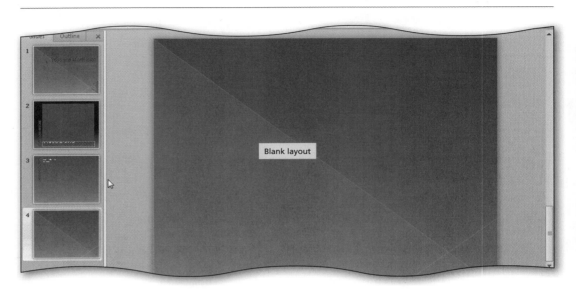

Figure 2–5

Presentation Template Color Scheme

Each presentation template has 12 complementary colors, which collectively are called the **color scheme**. You can apply these colors to all slides, an individual slide, notes pages, or audience handouts. A color scheme consists of four colors for a background and text, six accent colors, and two hyperlink colors. The Theme Colors button on the Design tab contains a square with four colors; the top two colors indicate the primary text and background colors, and the bottom two colors indicate the accent colors. You also can customize the theme colors to create your own set and give them a unique name. Table 2–1 explains the components of a color scheme.

Table 2–1 Color Scheme Components

Component	Description
Background color	The background color is the fundamental color of a PowerPoint slide. For example, if the background color is black, you can place any other color on top of it, but the fundamental color remains black. The black background shows everywhere you do not add color or other objects.
Text color	The text color contrasts with the background color of the slide. As a default, the text border color is the same as the text color. Together with the background color, the text and border colors set the tone for a presentation. For example, a gray background with black text and border sets a dramatic tone. In contrast, a red background with yellow text and border sets a vibrant tone.
Accent colors	Accent colors are designed as colors for secondary features on a slide. They often are used as fill colors on graphs and as shadows.
Hyperlink colors	The default hyperlink color is set when you type the text. When you click the hyperlink text during a presentation, the color changes to the Followed Hyperlink color.

To Change the Presentation Theme Colors

The first modification to make is to change the color scheme throughout the presentation. The following steps change the color scheme for the template from a gray title slide background with pink text and accents to a blue background with pink and orange accents.

1

- Click Design on the Ribbon and then click the Theme Colors button (Design tab | Themes group) to display the Theme Colors gallery.

- Scroll down and then point to the Oriel built-in theme to display a live preview of this color scheme (Figure 2–6).

 Experiment

- Point to various themes in the Theme Colors gallery and watch the colors change on Slide 4.

 Why does a gold line surround the Verve color scheme in the Theme Colors gallery?

It shows the Verve document theme is applied, and those eight colors are associated with that theme.

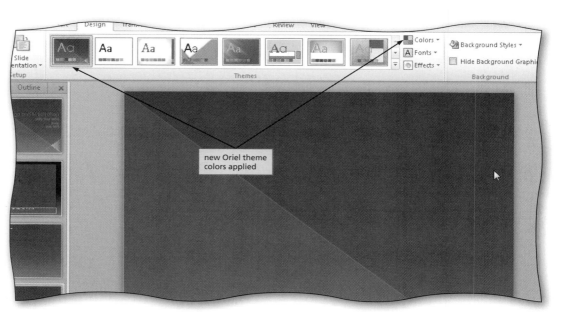

Figure 2–6

2

- Click Oriel in the Theme Colors gallery to change the presentation theme colors to Oriel (Figure 2–7).

Q&A What if I want to return to the original theme color?

You would click the Theme Colors button and then click Verve in the Theme Colors gallery.

Figure 2–7

To Save a Presentation

You have performed many tasks while creating this slide and do not want to risk losing work completed thus far. Accordingly, you should save the document.

The following steps assume you already have created folders for storing your files, for example, a CIS 101 folder (for your class) that contains a PowerPoint folder (for your assignments). Thus, these steps save the document in the PowerPoint folder in the CIS 101 folder on a USB flash drive using the file name, Yoga. For a detailed example of the procedure summarized below, refer to pages OFF 27 through OFF 29 in the Office 2010 and Windows 7 chapter at the beginning of this book.

1 With a USB flash drive connected to one of the computer's USB ports, click the Save button on the Quick Access Toolbar to display the Save As dialog box.

2 Type **Yoga** in the File name text box to change the file name. Do not press the ENTER key after typing the file name because you do not want to close the dialog box at this time.

3 Navigate to the desired save location (in this case, the PowerPoint folder in the CIS 101 folder [or your class folder] on the USB flash drive).

4 Click the Save button (Save As dialog box) to save the document in the selected folder on the selected drive with the entered file name.

Inserting and Formatting Pictures in a Presentation

With the text entered and background formatted in the presentation, the next step is to insert digital pictures into the placeholders on Slides 2 and 3 and then format the pictures. These graphical images draw the viewers' eyes to the slides and help them retain the information presented.

In the following pages, you will perform these tasks:

1. Insert the first digital picture into Slide 3.
2. Insert the second digital picture into Slide 2.
3. Change the look of the first picture.
4. Change the look of the second picture.
5. Resize the second picture.
6. Insert a digital picture into the Slide 1 background.
7. Format slide backgrounds.

Adhere to copyright regulations.
You have permission to use the clips from the Microsoft Clip Organizer. If you want to use a clip from another source, be certain you have the legal right to insert this file in your presentation. Read the copyright notices that accompany the clip and are posted on the Web site. The owners of these images and files often ask you to give them credit for using their work, which may be satisfied by stating where you obtained the images.

**Plan
Ahead**

To Insert a Picture

The next step in creating the presentation is to insert one of the digital yoga pictures in the picture placeholder in Slide 3. The picture is available on the Data Files for Students. See the inside back cover of this book for instructions on downloading the Data Files for Students, or contact your instructor for information about accessing the required files.

The following steps insert a picture, which, in this example, is located in the PowerPoint Chapter 02 folder on the same USB flash drive that contains the saved presentation, into Slide 3.

1
- With your USB flash drive connected to one of the computer's USB ports, click the Previous Slide button to display Slide 3.

- Click the Insert Picture from File icon in the content placeholder to display the Insert Picture dialog box.

2
- If Computer is not displayed in the navigation pane, drag the navigation pane scroll bar (Insert Picture dialog box) until Computer appears.

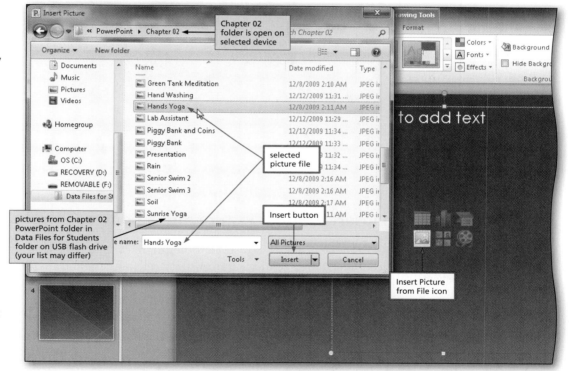

Figure 2 – 8

- Click Computer in the navigation pane to display a list of available storage devices in the Insert Picture dialog box. If necessary, scroll through the dialog box until your USB flash drive appears in the list of available storage devices.

- Double-click your USB flash drive in the list of available storage devices to display a list of files and folders on the selected USB flash drive. Double-click the Data Files for Students folder, double-click the PowerPoint folder, and then double-click the Chapter 02 folder to display a list of files in that folder.

- Scroll down and then click Hands Yoga to select the file name (Figure 2–8).

Q&A What if the picture is not on a USB flash drive?
Use the same process, but select the drive containing the picture.

3

- Click the Insert button (Insert Picture dialog box) to insert the picture into the content placeholder in Slide 3 (Figure 2–9).

Q&A

What are the symbols around the picture?

A selected graphic appears surrounded by a **selection rectangle**, which has small squares and circles, called **sizing handles**, at each corner and middle location.

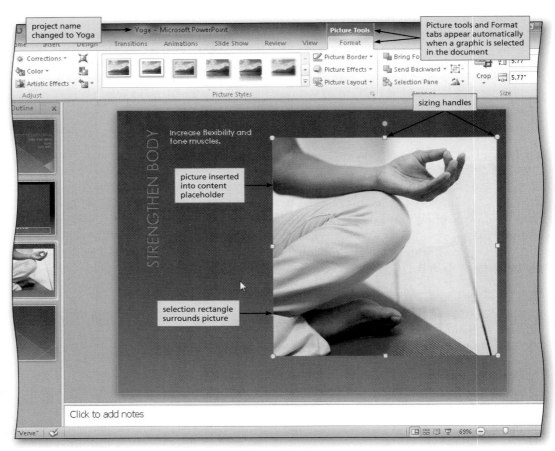

Figure 2 – 9

To Insert Another Picture into a Content Placeholder

Modernism's Effect on Graphic Design
The modernist movement of the late nineteenth and twentieth centuries influenced the design principles in use today. Artists and architects of that era simplified the world in terms of legible fonts, abstract shapes, and balanced layouts. Modernists sought to create works independent of language so their message could reach people throughout the world.

The next step is to insert another digital yoga picture into the Slide 2 content placeholder. This second picture also is available on the Data Files for Students. See the inside back cover of this book for instructions on downloading the Data Files for Students, or contact your instructor for information about accessing the required files.

The following steps insert a picture into Slide 2.

1 Click the Previous Slide button to display Slide 2.

2 With your USB flash drive connected to one of the computer's USB ports, click the Insert Picture from File icon in the content placeholder to display the Insert Picture dialog box.

3 If the list of files and folders on the selected USB flash drive are not displayed in the Insert Picture dialog box, double-click your USB flash drive to display them and then navigate to the PowerPoint Chapter 02 folder.

4 Scroll down and then click Green Tank Meditation to select the file name.

5 Click the Insert button (Insert Picture dialog box) to insert the picture into the Slide 2 content placeholder (Figure 2–10).

picture inserted into content placeholder

Figure 2–10

To Insert a Picture into a Slide without a Content Placeholder

In Chapter 1, you inserted a clip into a slide without a content placeholder. You also can insert a picture into a slide that does not have a content placeholder. The picture for Slide 4 is available on the Data Files for Students. See the inside back cover of this book for instructions on downloading the Data Files for Students, or contact your instructor for information about accessing the required files. The following steps insert a picture into Slide 4.

1

- Click the Next Slide button two times to display Slide 4.

- With your USB flash drive connected to one of the computer's USB ports, click Insert on the Ribbon (Figure 2–11).

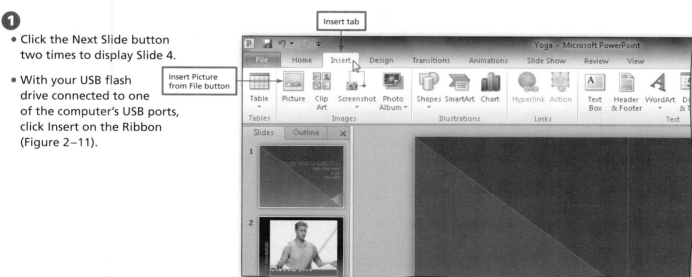

Figure 2–11

2

• Click Insert Picture from File (Insert tab | Images group) to display the Insert Picture dialog box. If the list of files and folders on the selected USB flash drive are not displayed in the Insert Picture dialog box, double-click your USB flash drive to display them and then navigate to the PowerPoint Chapter 02 folder.

• Click Arch Yoga to select the file name (Figure 2–12).

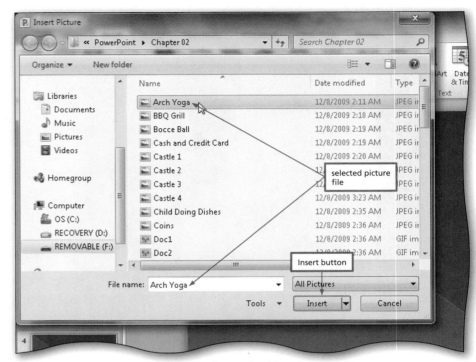

Figure 2–12

3

• Click the Insert button (Insert Picture dialog box) to insert the picture into the Slide 4 content placeholder.

• Move the picture so that it displays approximately as shown in Figure 2–13.

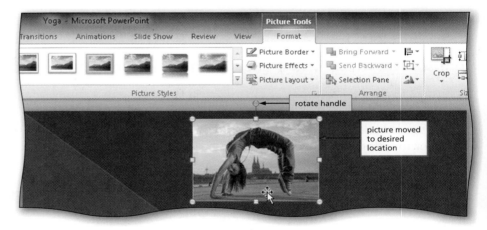

Figure 2–13

Q&A

What is the green circle attached to the selected graphic?

The green circle is a rotate handle. When you drag a graphic's rotate handle, the graphic moves in either a clockwise or counter clockwise direction.

To Correct a Picture

A photograph's color intensity can be modified by changing the brightness and contrast. **Brightness** determines the overall lightness or darkness of the entire image, whereas **contrast** is the difference between the darkest and lightest areas of the image. The brightness and contrast are changed in predefined percentage increments. The following step increases the brightness and decreases the contrast to intensify the picture colors.

1

- With the Arch Yoga picture on Slide 4 still selected, click the Corrections button (Picture Tools Format tab | Adjust group) to display the Corrections gallery.

- Point to Brightness: +20% Contrast: −40% (fourth picture in first row of Brightness and Contrast area) to display a live preview of these corrections on the picture (Figure 2–14).

Experiment

- Point to various pictures in the Brightness and Contrast area and watch the brightness and contrast change on the picture in Slide 4.

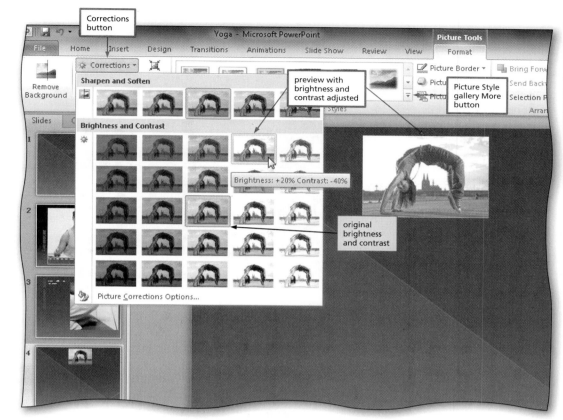

Figure 2–14

Q&A | Why is a yellow border surrounding the picture in the center of the gallery?

The image on Slide 4 currently has normal brightness and contrast (0%), which is represented by this center image in the gallery.

- Click Brightness: +20% Contrast: −40% to apply this correction to the yoga picture.

Q&A | How can I remove all effects from the picture?

Click the Reset Picture button (Picture Tools Format tab | Adjust group).

Other Ways
1. Click Picture Corrections Options, move Brightness or Contrast sliders or enter number in box next to slider (Format Picture dialog box)

To Apply a Picture Style

The pictures on Slides 2, 3, and 4 grasp the audience's attention, but you can increase their visual appeal by applying a style. A **style** is a named group of formatting characteristics. PowerPoint provides more than 25 picture styles that enable you easily to change a picture's look to a more visually appealing style, including a variety of shapes, angles, borders, and reflections. The photos in Slides 2, 3, and 4 in this chapter use styles that apply soft edges, reflections, or angled perspectives to the pictures. The following steps apply a picture style to the Slide 4 picture.

- With the Slide 4 picture selected, click the Picture Tools Format tab and then click the More button in the Picture Styles gallery (Picture Tools Format tab | Picture Styles group) (shown in Figure 2–14 on the previous page) to expand the gallery.

- Point to Soft Edge Rectangle in the Picture Styles gallery to display a live preview of that style applied to the picture in the document (Figure 2–15).

Experiment

- Point to various picture styles in the Picture Styles gallery and watch the style of the picture change in the document window.

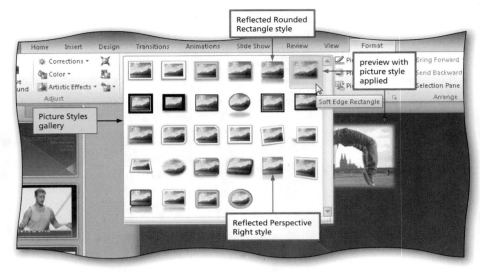

Figure 2–15

- Click Soft Edge Rectangle in the Picture Styles gallery to apply the style to the selected picture (Figure 2–16).

Figure 2–16

To Apply Other Picture Styles

The next step is to apply picture styles to the yoga pictures in Slides 3 and 2. To provide continuity, both of these styles will have a reflection. The following steps apply other picture styles to the Slide 3 and Slide 2 pictures.

1. Click the Previous Slide button to display Slide 3.

2. Click the Slide 3 picture to select it, click the Picture Tools Format tab, and then click the More button in the Picture Styles gallery to expand the gallery.

3. Click Reflected Perspective Right in the Picture Styles gallery to apply this style to the picture in Slide 3.

4. Click the Previous Slide button to display Slide 2.

5. Click the Slide 2 picture to select it, click the Picture Tools Format tab, and then click the More button in the Picture Styles gallery to expand the gallery.

6. Click Reflected Rounded Rectangle in the Picture Styles gallery to apply this style to the picture in Slide 2 (Figure 2–17).

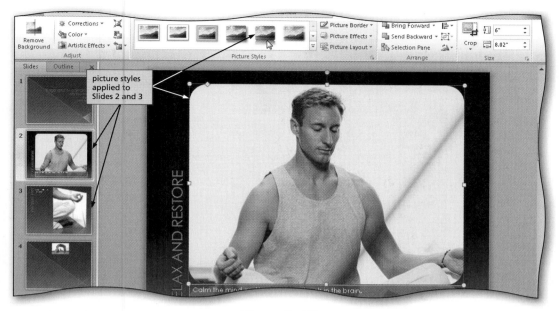

Figure 2–17

To Apply Picture Effects

PowerPoint provides a variety of picture effects so that you can further customize a picture. Effects include shadows, reflections, glow, soft edges, bevel, and 3-D rotation. The difference between the effects and the styles is that each effect has several options, providing you with more control over the exact look of the image.

In this presentation, the photos on Slides 2 and 3 have an orange glow effect and have a bevel applied to their edges. The following steps apply picture effects to the selected picture.

1

- With the Slide 2 picture selected, click the Picture Effects button (Picture Tools Format tab | Picture Styles group) to display the Picture Effects menu.

Q&A

What if the Picture Tools Format tab no longer is displayed on my Ribbon?

Double-click the picture to display the Picture Tools and Format tabs.

- Point to Glow on the Picture Effects menu to display the Glow gallery.

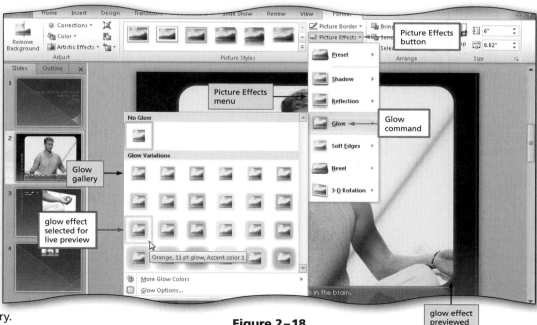

Figure 2–18

- Point to Orange, 11 pt glow, Accent color 1 in the Glow Variations area (leftmost glow in third row) to display a live preview of the selected glow effect applied to the picture in the document window (Figure 2–18).

Experiment

- Point to various glow effects in the Glow gallery and watch the picture change in the document window.

2

- Click Orange, 11 pt glow, Accent color 1 in the Glow gallery to apply the selected picture effect.

3

- Click the Picture Effects button (Picture Tools Format tab | Picture Styles group) to display the Picture Effects menu again.

- Point to Bevel on the Picture Effects menu to display the Bevel gallery.

- Point to Angle (leftmost bevel in second row) to display a live preview of the selected bevel effect applied to the Slide 2 picture (Figure 2–19).

🔎 **Experiment**

- Point to various bevel effects in the Bevel gallery and watch the picture change in the slide.

4

- Click Angle in the Bevel gallery to apply the selected picture effect.

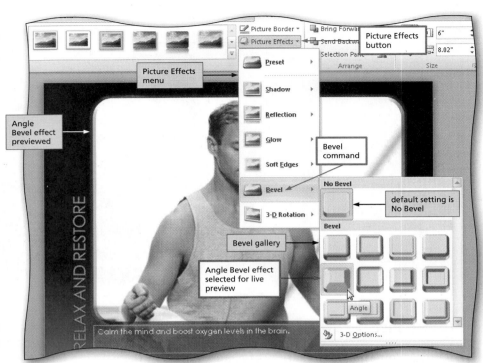

Figure 2–19

Other Ways

1. Right-click picture, click Format Picture on shortcut menu, select desired options (Format Picture dialog box), click Close button

2. Click Format Shape dialog box launcher (Picture

Tools Format tab | Picture Styles group), select desired options (Format Picture dialog box), click Close button

To Apply a Picture Style and Effect to Another Picture

In this presentation, the Slide 3 picture also has orange glow and bevel effects. The following steps apply the picture style and picture effects to the picture.

1 Click the Next Slide button to display Slide 3 and then click the picture to select it.

2 Click the Picture Effects button (Picture Tools Format tab | Picture Styles group) to display the Picture Effects menu and then point to Glow on the Picture Effects menu to display the Glow gallery.

3 Click Orange, 11 pt glow, Accent color 1 (leftmost glow in third row) in the Glow gallery to apply the picture effect to the picture.

4 Click the Picture Effects button (Picture Tools Format tab | Picture Styles group) to display the Picture Effects menu again and then point to Bevel on the Picture Effects menu to display the Bevel gallery.

5 Click Convex (third bevel in second row) in the Bevel area to apply the picture effect to the selected picture (Figure 2–20).

Figure 2–20

To Add a Picture Border

The next step is to add a small border to the Slide 3 picture. Some picture styles provide a border, but the Reflected Rounded Rectangle style you applied to this picture does not. The following steps add a border to the Slide 3 picture.

1

- With the Slide 3 picture still selected, click the Picture Border button (Picture Tools Format tab | Picture Styles group) to display the Picture Border gallery.

Q&A What if the Picture Tools Format tab no longer is displayed on my Ribbon?

Double-click the picture to display the Picture Tools and Format tabs.

2

- Point to Weight on the Picture Border gallery to display the Weight list.

- Point to 1½ pt to display a live preview of this line weight on the picture (Figure 2–21).

🔍 **Experiment**

- Point to various line weights in the Weight list and watch the line thickness change.

Q&A Can I make the line width more than 6 pt?

Yes. Click More Lines and then increase the amount in the Width box.

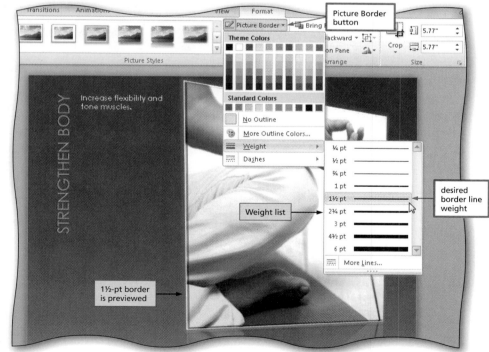

Figure 2–21

3

- Click 1½ pt to add this line weight to the picture.

To Change a Picture Border Color

The default color for the border you added to the Slide 3 picture is White. Earlier in this chapter, you changed the color scheme to Oriel. To coordinate the border color with the title text color and other elements of this theme, you will use a shade of red in the Oriel color scheme. Any color galleries you display show colors defined in this current color scheme. The following steps change the Slide 3 picture border color.

1

- With the Slide 3 photo still selected, click the Picture Border button (Picture Tools Format tab | Picture Styles group) to display the Picture Border gallery.

Q&A

What if the Picture Tools Format tab no longer is displayed on my Ribbon?

Double-click the picture to display the Picture Tools and Format tabs.

2

- Point to Red, Accent 3 (seventh theme color from left in first row) in the Picture Border gallery to display a live preview of that border color on the picture (Figure 2–22).

Experiment

- Point to various colors in the Picture Border gallery and watch the border on the picture change in the slide.

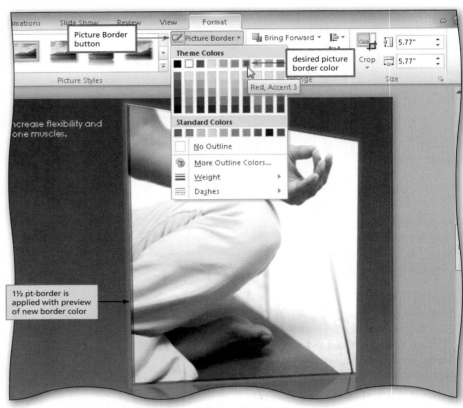

Figure 2–22

3

- Click Red, Accent 3 in the Picture Border gallery to change the picture border color.

To Add a Picture Border and Color to Another Picture

In this presentation, the Slide 2 picture does not have a border as part of the Reflected Perspective Right picture style. The following steps add a border to Slide 2 and change the color.

1 Click the Previous Slide button to display Slide 2 and then click the picture to select it.

2 Click the Picture Border button (Picture Tools Format tab | Picture Styles group) to display the Picture Border gallery.

3 Point to Weight on the Picture Border gallery to display the Weight list and then point to 1½ pt to display a live preview of this line weight on the picture.

4 Click 1½ pt to add this line weight to the picture.

5 Click the Picture Border button (Picture Tools Format tab | Picture Styles group) to display the Picture Border gallery again and then click Red, Accent 3 in the Picture Border gallery to change the picture border color (Figure 2–23).

1½ pt border is applied with new border color

Figure 2–23

To Resize a Graphic by Entering Exact Measurements

The next step is to resize the Slide 3 picture so that it fills much of the empty space in the slide. In Chapter 1, you resized clips by dragging the sizing handles. This technique also applies to changing the size of photos. You also can resize graphics by specifying exact height and width measurements. The yoga picture can be enlarged so that its height and width measurements are 6.0". When a graphic is selected, its height and width measurements show in the Size group of the Picture Tools Format tab. The following steps resize the Slide 3 picture by entering its desired exact measurements.

1

- Click the Next Slide button to display Slide 3 and then select the picture. Click the Shape Height text box (Picture Tools Format tab | Size group) to select the contents in the text box and then type   6 as the height (Figure 2–24).

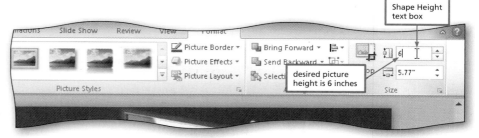

Shape Height text box

desired picture height is 6 inches

Figure 2–24

Q&A | What if the contents of the Shape Height text box are not selected?
Triple-click the Shape Height text box.

Q&A | Why did the width size also change?
PowerPoint kept the photo in proportion so that the width changed the same amount as the height changed.

2

- Click the Shape Width text box (Picture Tools Format tab | Size group) to select the contents in the text box and then type   6   as the width if this number does not display automatically.

- If necessary, move the photo to the location shown in Figure 2–25.

Q&A

What if I want to return a graphic to its original size and start again?

With the graphic selected, click the Size and Position dialog box launcher (Picture Tools Format tab | Size group), if necessary click the Size tab (Format Picture dialog box), click the Reset button, and then click the Close button.

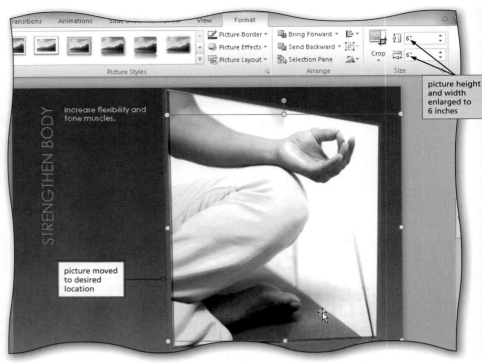

Figure 2–25

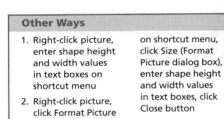

Other Ways

1. Right-click picture, enter shape height and width values in text boxes on shortcut menu
   on shortcut menu, click Size (Format Picture dialog box), enter shape height and width values in text boxes, click Close button

2. Right-click picture, click Format Picture

To Resize Another Graphic Using Exact Measurements

The Arch Yoga picture on Slide 4 also can be enlarged to fill space at the top of the slide. The yoga picture can be enlarged so that its height and width measurements are 3" and 4.48", respectively. The following steps resize the Slide 4 picture.

1 Click the Next Slide button to display Slide 4 and then select the picture. Click the Shape Height text box (Picture Tools Format tab | Size group) to select the contents in the text box and type   3   as the height.

2 Move the photo to the location shown in Figure 2–26.

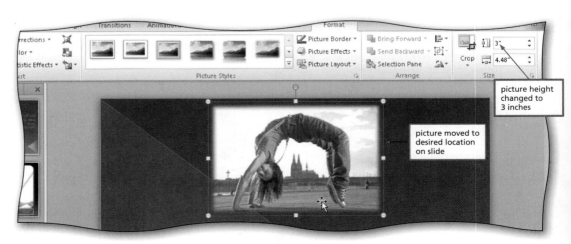

Figure 2–26

To Save an Existing Document with the Same File Name

You have made several modifications to the document since you last saved it. Thus, you should save it again. The following step saves the document again. For an example of the step listed below, refer to page OFF 51 in the Office 2010 and Windows 7 chapter at the beginning of this book.

 Click the Save button on the Quick Access Toolbar to overwrite the previously saved file.

Break Point: If you wish to take a break, this is a good place to do so. You can quit PowerPoint now. To resume at a later time, start PowerPoint, open the file called Yoga, and continue following the steps from this location forward.

Formatting Slide Backgrounds

A slide's background is an integral part of a presentation because it can generate audience interest. Every slide can have the same background, or different backgrounds can be used in a presentation. This background is considered **fill**, which is the content that makes up the interior of a shape, line, or character. Three fills are available: solid, gradient, and picture or texture. **Solid fill** is one color used throughout the entire slide. **Gradient fill** is one color shade gradually progressing to another shade of the same color or one color progressing to another color. **Picture or texture fill** uses a specific file or an image that simulates a material, such as cork, granite, marble, or canvas.

Once you add a fill, you can adjust its appearance. For example, you can adjust its **transparency**, which allows you to see through the background, so that any text on the slide is visible. You also can select a color that is part of the theme or a custom color. You can use **offsets**, another background feature, to move the background from the slide borders in varying distances by percentage. **Tiling options** repeat the background image many times vertically and horizontally on the slide; the smaller the tiling percentage, the greater the number of times the image is repeated.

BTW

Resetting Backgrounds
If you have made many changes to the background and want to start the process over, click the Reset Background button in the Format Background dialog box.

To Insert a Texture Fill

A wide variety of texture fills are available to give your presentation a unique look. The 24 pictures in the Textures gallery give the appearance of a physical object, such as water drops, sand, tissue paper, and a paper bag. You also can use your own texture pictures for custom backgrounds. When you insert a fill, PowerPoint assumes you want this custom background on only the current slide displayed. To make this background appear on all slides in the presentation, click the Apply to All button in the Format Background dialog box. The following steps insert the Sand fill on Slide 4 in the presentation.

1

- Right-click anywhere on the Slide 4 blue background to display the shortcut menu (Figure 2–27).

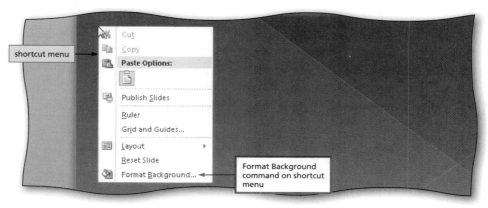

Figure 2–27

2

- Click Format Background on the shortcut menu to display the Format Background dialog box.

- With the Fill pane displaying, click 'Picture or texture fill' to expand the fill options (Figure 2–28).

Q&A Why did the background change to a yellow texture?

This texture is the Papyrus background, which is the default texture fill.

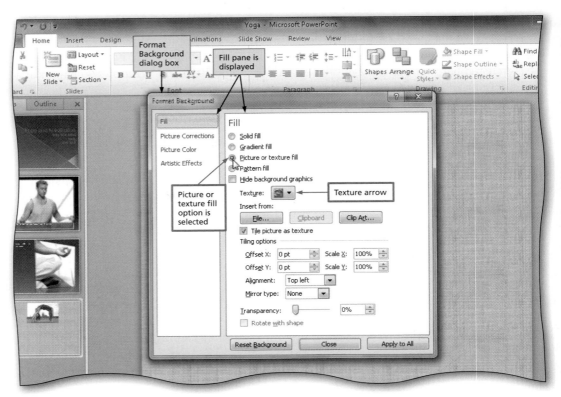

Figure 2–28

3

- Click the Texture arrow to display the Texture gallery (Figure 2–29).

Q&A Is a live preview available to see the various textures on this slide?

No. Live preview is not an option with the background textures and fills.

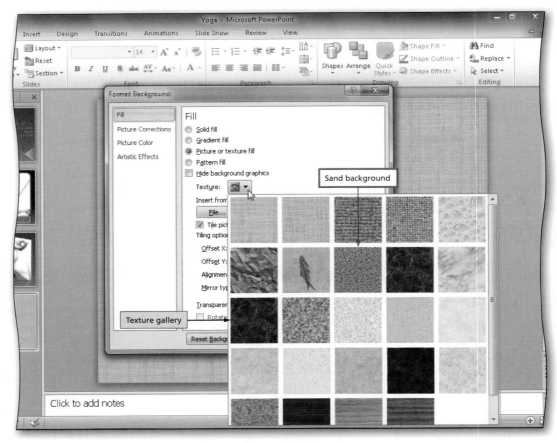

Figure 2–29

4

• Click the Sand background (third texture in second row) to insert this background on Slide 4 (Figure 2–30).

Q&A

The Format Background dialog box is covering part of the slide. Can I move this box?

Yes. Click the dialog box title and drag it to a different location so that you can view the slide.

Q&A

Could I insert this background on all four slides simultaneously?

Yes. You would click the Apply to All button to insert the Sand background on all slides.

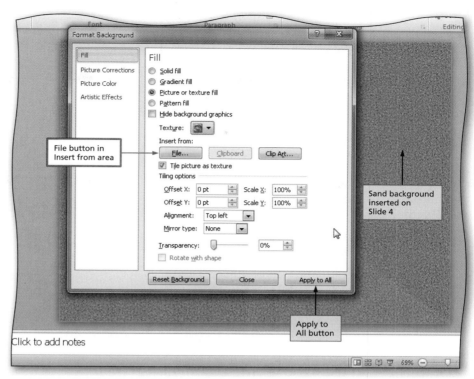

Other Ways

1. Click Design tab, Background Styles, click Format Background (Design tab | Background group)

Figure 2–30

To Insert a Picture to Create a Background

For variety and interest, you want to use another yoga picture as the Slide 1 background. This picture is stored on the Data Files for Students. PowerPoint will stretch the height and width of this picture to fill the slide area. The following steps insert the picture, Sunrise Yoga, on only Slide 1.

1

• Click the Previous Slide button three times to display Slide 1.

• With the Fill pane displaying (Format Background dialog box), click 'Picture or texture fill'.

• Click the File button in the Insert from area (shown in Figure 2–30) to display the Insert Picture dialog box.

• If necessary, double-click your USB flash drive in the list of available storage devices to display a list of files and folders on the selected USB flash drive and then navigate to the PowerPoint Chapter 02 folder.

• Scroll down and then click Sunrise Yoga to select the file name (Figure 2–31).

Q&A

What if the picture is not on a USB flash drive?

Use the same process, but select the drive containing the picture.

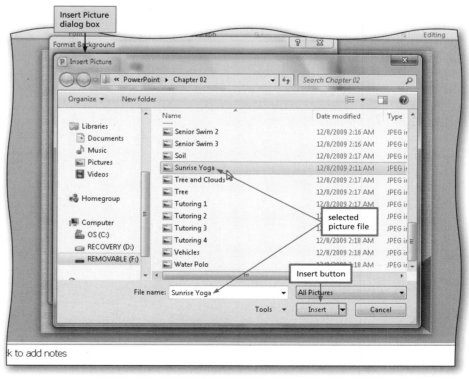

Figure 2–31

2

- Click the Insert button (Insert Picture dialog box) to insert the Sunrise Yoga picture as the Slide 1 background (Figure 2–32).

Q&A
What if I do not want to use this picture?

Click the Undo button on the Quick Access Toolbar.

Q&A
Why do the Left and Right offsets in the Stretch options area show a –6% value?

PowerPoint automatically reduced the photograph slightly so that it fills the entire slide.

Q&A
Can I move the Format Background dialog box to the left so that I can see more of the subtitle text?

Yes. Click the dialog box title and then drag the box to the desired location on the slide.

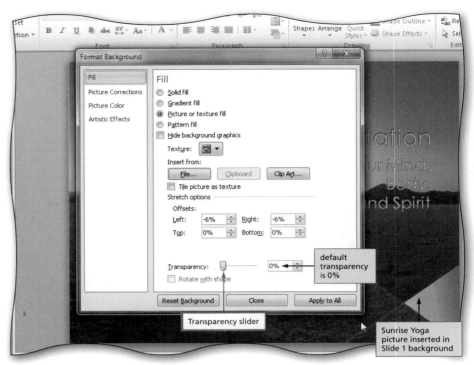

Figure 2–32

To Format the Background Picture Fill Transparency

The Sunrise Yoga picture on Slide 1 is a rich color and conflicts with the title and subtitle text. One method of reducing this richness is to change the transparency. The **Transparency slider** indicates the amount of opaqueness. The default setting is 0, which is fully opaque. The opposite extreme is 100%, which is fully transparent. To change the transparency, you can move the Transparency slider or enter a number in the text box next to the slider. The following step adjusts the transparency to 10%.

1

- Click the Transparency slider and drag it to the right until 10% is displayed in the Transparency text box (Figure 2–33).

Q&A
Can I move the slider in small increments so that I can get a precise percentage easily?

Yes. Press the RIGHT ARROW or LEFT ARROW key to move the slider in one-percent increments.

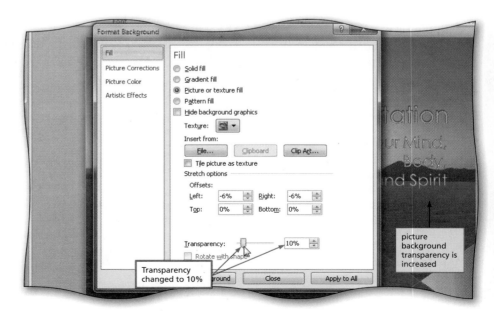

Figure 2–33

To Format the Background Texture Fill Transparency

The Sand texture on Slide 4 is dark and may not offer sufficient contrast with the symbols and text you are going to insert on this slide. You can adjust the transparency of slide texture in the same manner that you change a picture transparency. The following steps adjust the texture transparency to 50%.

1

- Click the Next Slide button three times to display Slide 4.

- Click the Transparency slider and drag it to the right until 50% is displayed in the Transparency text box (Figure 2–34).

2

- Click the Close button (Format Background dialog box).

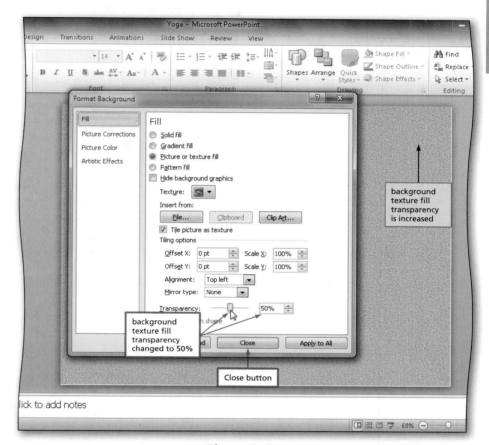

Figure 2–34

To Choose a Background Style

Now that the backgrounds for Slides 1 and 4 are set, and the title and text paragraphs for the presentation have been entered, you need to make design decisions for Slides 2 and 3. In this project, you will choose a background for these slides. For each theme, PowerPoint provides 12 **background styles** with designs that may include color, shading, patterns, and textures. **Fill effects** add pattern and texture to a background, which add depth to a slide. The following steps add a background style to Slides 2 and 3 in the presentation.

- Click the Previous Slide button once to display Slide 3 and then click the Design tab on the Ribbon.

- Click the Background Styles button (Design tab | Background group) to display the Background Styles gallery.

- Right-click Style 11 (third style in third row) to display the shortcut menu (Figure 2–35).

Experiment

- Point to various styles themes in the Background Styles gallery and watch the backgrounds change on the slide.

Q&A Are the backgrounds displayed in a specific order?

Yes. They are arranged in order from light to dark running from left to right. The first row has solid backgrounds; the middle row has darker fills at the top and bottom; the bottom row has fill patterns. If you point to a background, a ScreenTip with the background's name appears on the screen.

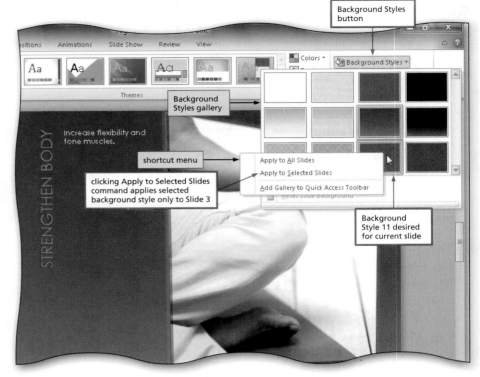

Figure 2–35

- Click Apply to Selected Slides to apply Style 11 to Slide 3 (Figure 2–36).

Q&A If I decide later that this background style does not fit the theme of my presentation, can I apply a different background?

Yes. You can repeat these steps at any time while creating your presentation.

Q&A What if I want to apply this background style to all slides in the presentation?

Click the desired style or click Apply to All Slides in the shortcut menu.

Other Ways

1. Click Background Styles, right-click desired background, press s

Figure 2–36

To Choose Another Background Style

In this presentation, the Slide 2 background can have a coordinating background to complement the yoga picture. The following steps add a background to Slide 2.

1 Click the Previous Slide button to display Slide 2. Click the Background Styles button (Design tab | Background group) and then right-click Style 10 (second style in third row) to display the shortcut menu.

2 Click Apply to Selected Slides to apply this background style to Slide 2 (Figure 2–37).

Background Style 10 applied to Slide 2

RELAX AND RESTORE

Calm the mind and boost oxygen levels in the brain.

Figure 2–37

Formatting Title and Content Text

Choosing well-coordinated colors and styles for text and objects in a presentation is possible. Once you select a particular Quick Style and make any other font changes, you then can copy these changes to other text using the **Format Painter**. The Format Painter allows you to copy all formatting changes from one object to another.

BTW

Introducing the Presentation
Before your audience enters the room, start the presentation and then display Slide 1. This slide should be visually appealing and provide general interest in the presentation. An effective title slide gives a good first impression.

To Change the Subtitle and Caption Font

The default Verve theme heading, subtitle, and caption text font is Century Gothic. To draw more attention to subtitle and caption text and to help differentiate these slide elements from the title text, you want to change the font from Century Gothic to Papyrus. To change the font, you must select the letters you want to format. In Chapter 1, you selected a paragraph and then formatted the characters. To format the text in multiple paragraphs quickly and simultaneously, you can select all the paragraphs to be formatted and then apply formatting changes. The following steps change the subtitle and caption font.

1
- Click the Previous Slide button to display Slide 1. Move the mouse pointer to the left of the first subtitle paragraph, Unify Your Mind, until the mouse pointer changes to an I-beam (Figure 2–38).

Figure 2–38

2
- Drag downward to select all three subtitle lines that will be formatted (Figure 2–39).

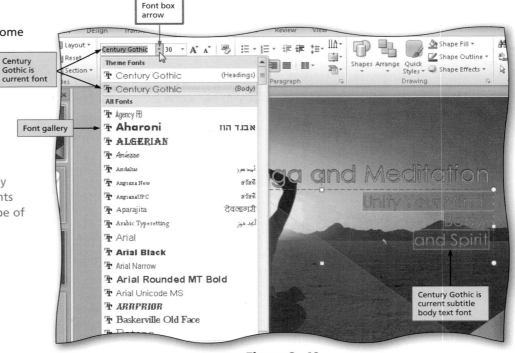

Figure 2–39

3
- With the text selected, click Home on the Ribbon and then click the Font box arrow (Home tab | Font group) to display the Font gallery (Figure 2–40).

Q&A

Will the fonts in my Font gallery be the same as those shown in Figure 2–40?

Your list of available fonts may differ, depending on what fonts you have installed and the type of printer you are using.

Figure 2–40

4

- Scroll through the Font gallery and then point to Papyrus (or a similar font) to display a live preview of the title text in the Papyrus font (Figure 2–41).

 Experiment

- Point to various fonts in the Font gallery and watch the subtitle text font change in the slide.

- Click Papyrus (or a similar font) to change the font of the selected text to Papyrus.

Figure 2–41

Other Ways		
1. Click Font box arrow on Mini toolbar, click desired font in Font gallery	Font tab, select desired font in Font list, click OK button	desired font in Font list, click OK button
2. Right-click selected text, click Font on shortcut menu (Font dialog box), click	3. Click Font dialog box launcher (Home tab | Font group), click Font tab (Font dialog box), select	4. Press CTRL+SHIFT+F, click Font tab (Font dialog box), select desired font in the Font list, click OK button

To Shadow Text

A **shadow** helps letters display prominently by adding a shadow behind the text. The following step adds a shadow to the selected subtitle text, Unify Your Mind, Body, and Spirit.

1

- With the subtitle text selected, click the Text Shadow button (Home tab \| Font group) to add a shadow to the selected text (Figure 2–42).

Q&A

How would I remove a shadow?

You would click the Shadow button a second time, or you immediately could click the Undo button on the Quick Access Toolbar.

Figure 2–42

To Format the Subtitle Text

To increase readability, you can format the Slide 1 subtitle text by bolding the characters and changing the font color to yellow. The following steps format the Slide 1 subtitle text.

1 With the subtitle text selected, click the Bold button (Home tab | Font group) to bold the text.

2 Click the Font Color arrow and change the color to Light Yellow, Text 2 (fourth color in first row) (Figure 2–43).

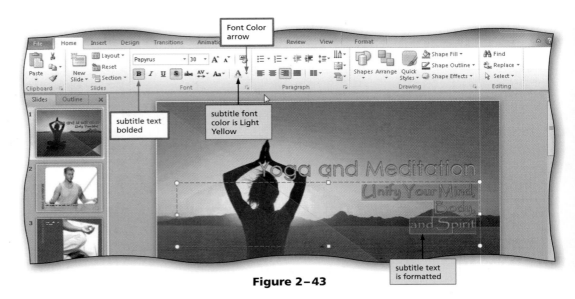

Figure 2–43

To Format the Slide 2 Caption

The caption on a slide should be large enough for audience members to read easily and should coordinate with the font styles in other parts of the presentation. The caption on Slide 2 can be enhanced by changing the font, the font color, and the font size. The following steps format the Slide 2 caption text.

1 Click the Next Slide button to display Slide 2. Triple-click the caption text to select all the characters, click the Font box arrow on the Mini toolbar, and then scroll down and click Papyrus.

2 Click the Increase Font Size button on the Mini toolbar three times to increase the font size to 20 point.

3 Click the Bold button on the Mini toolbar to bold the text (Figure 2–44).

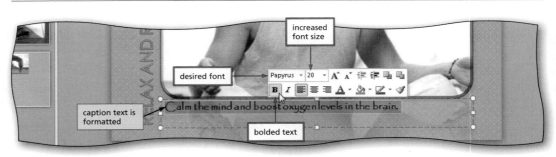

Figure 2–44

Format Painter

To save time and avoid formatting errors, you can use the Format Painter to apply custom formatting to other places in your presentation quickly and easily. You can use this feature in three ways:

- To copy only character attributes, such as font and font effects, select text that has these qualities.
- To copy both paragraph attributes, such as alignment and indentation and character attributes, select the entire paragraph.
- To apply the same formatting to multiple words, phrases, or paragraphs, double-click the Format Painter button and then select each item you want to format. You then can press the ESC key or click the Format Painter button to turn off this feature.

To Format Text Using the Format Painter

To save time and duplicated effort, you quickly can use the Format Painter to copy formatting attributes from the Slide 2 caption text and apply them to Slide 3. The following steps use the Format Painter to copy formatting features.

1
- With the Slide 2 caption text still selected, double-click the Format Painter button (Home tab | Clipboard group).

- Move the mouse pointer off the Ribbon (Figure 2–45).

Q&A
Why did my mouse pointer change shape?

The mouse pointer changed shape by adding a paintbrush to indicate that the Format Painter function is active.

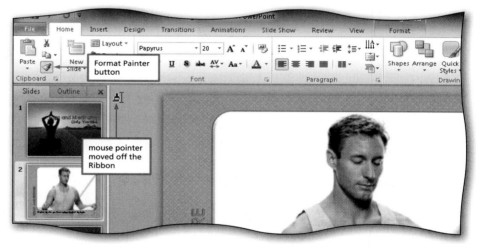

Figure 2–45

2
- Click the Next Slide button to display Slide 3. Triple-click the caption placeholder to apply the format to all the caption text (Figure 2–46).

- Press the ESC key to turn off the Format Painter feature.

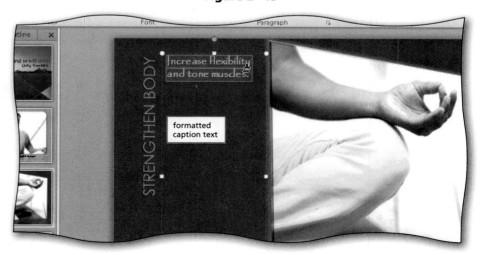

Other Ways

1. Click Format Painter button on Mini toolbar

Figure 2–46

Break Point: If you wish to take a break, this is a good place to do so. Be sure to save the Yoga file again and then you can quit PowerPoint. To resume at a later time, start PowerPoint, open the file called Yoga, and continue following the steps from this location forward.

Sizing Shapes
PowerPoint's Shapes gallery provides a wide variety of symbols that can help emphasize your major points on each slide. As you select the shapes and then size them, keep in mind that your audience will focus on the largest shapes first. The most important information, therefore, should be placed in or near the shapes with the most visual size.

Adding and Formatting a Shape

One method of getting the audience's attention and reinforcing the major concepts being presented is to have graphical elements on the title slide. PowerPoint provides a wide variety of predefined shapes that can add visual interest to a slide. Shape elements include lines, basic geometrical shapes, arrows, equation shapes, flowchart symbols, stars, banners, and callouts. After adding a shape to a slide, you can change its default characteristics by adding text, bullets, numbers, and styles. You also can combine multiple shapes to create a more complex graphic.

Slides 1 and 4 in this presentation are enhanced in a variety of ways. First, a sun shape is added to the Slide 1 title text in place of the letter o. Then a circle shape is inserted on Slide 4 and copied twice, and text is added to each circle and then formatted. Finally, a triangle is inserted on top of the three circle shapes on Slide 4.

To Add a Shape

Many of the shapes included in the Shapes gallery can direct the viewer to important aspects of the presentation. For example, the sun shape helps emphasize the presentation's theme of practicing yoga and meditation, and it complements the Sunrise Yoga background picture. The following steps add the Sun shape to Slide 1.

1
- Click the Previous Slide button two times to display Slide 1. Click the Shapes button (Home tab | Drawing group) to display the Shapes gallery (Figure 2–47).

Figure 2–47

Q&A

I do not see a Shapes button in the Drawing group. Instead, I have three rows of the shapes I have used recently in presentations. Why?

Monitor dimensions and resolution affect how buttons display on the Ribbon. Click the Shapes More button to display the entire Shapes gallery.

2

- Click the Sun shape in the Basic Shapes area of the Shapes gallery.

Q&A Why did my pointer change shape?

The pointer changed to a plus shape to indicate the Sun shape has been added to the Clipboard.

- Position the mouse pointer (a crosshair) above the person's hands in the picture, as shown in Figure 2–48.

Figure 2–48

3

- Click Slide 1 to insert the Sun shape (Figure 2–49).

Figure 2–49

Other Ways
1. Click More button (Drawing Tools Format tab | Insert Shapes group)

To Resize a Shape

The next step is to resize the Sun shape. The shape should be reduced so that it is approximately the same size as the letter o in the words Yoga and Meditation. The following steps resize the selected Sun shape.

1

- With the mouse pointer appearing as two-headed arrow, drag a corner sizing handle on the picture diagonally inward until the Sun shape is resized approximately as shown in Figure 2–50.

Q&A What if my shape is not selected?

To select a shape, click it.

Q&A What if the shape is the wrong size?

Repeat Steps 1 and 2.

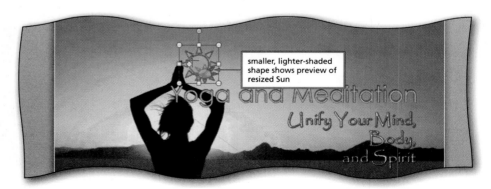

Figure 2–50

2

- Release the mouse button to resize the shape.

- Drag the Sun shape on top of the letter o in the word, Yoga (Figure 2–51).

Q&A What if I want to move the shape to a precise location on the slide?

With the shape selected, press the ARROW keys or the CTRL+ARROW keys to move the shape to the desired location.

Figure 2–51

Other Ways

1. Enter shape height and width in Height and Width text boxes (Drawing Tools Format tab | Size group)

2. Click Size and Position dialog box launcher

(Drawing Tools Format tab | Size group), click Size tab, enter desired height and width values in text boxes, click Close button

---

To Copy and Paste a Shape

The next step is to copy the Sun shape. The duplicate shape will be placed over the letter 'o' in the word, Meditation. The following steps copy and move the identical second Sun shape.

1

- With the Sun shape still selected, click the Copy button (Home tab | Clipboard group) (Figure 2–52).

Q&A What if my shape is not selected?

To select a shape, click it.

Figure 2–52

②

- Click the Paste button on the Home tab to insert a duplicate Sun shape on Slide 1.

- Drag the Sun shape on top of the letter o in the word, Meditation, and release the mouse button when a dashed line connects this Sun shape to the Sun shape that is displaying in the word, Yoga (Figure 2–53).

Figure 2–53

Q&A
What does the dashed line represent?

PowerPoint displays this Smart Guide when two shapes are aligned precisely. In this case, the two Sun shapes are centered horizontally.

Other Ways

1. Right-click selected shape, click Copy on shortcut menu, right-click, click Paste on shortcut menu

2. Select shape, press CTRL+C, press CTRL+V

To Add Other Shapes

Circles, squares, and triangles are among the geometric shapes included in the Shapes gallery. These shapes can be combined to show relationships among the elements, and they can help illustrate the basic concepts presented in your slide show. The following steps add the Oval and Isosceles Triangle shapes to Slide 4.

①

- Click the Next Slide button three times to display Slide 4 and then click the Shapes button (Home tab | Drawing group) to display the Shapes gallery (Figure 2–54).

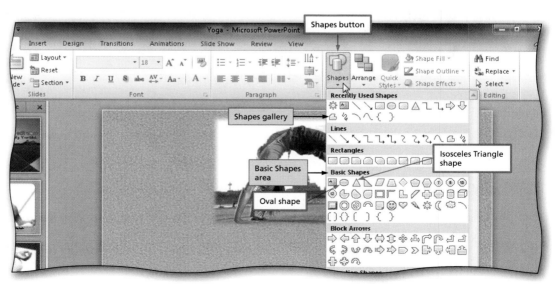

Figure 2–54

- Click the Oval shape in the Basic Shapes area of the Shapes gallery.

- Position the mouse pointer in the center of Slide 4 and then click to insert the Oval shape.

- Press and hold down the SHIFT key and then drag a corner sizing handle until the Oval shape forms a circle and is the size shown in Figure 2–55.

Q&A Why did I need to press the SHIFT key while enlarging the shape?

Holding down the SHIFT key while dragging draws a perfect circle.

- Move the shape so it is positioned approximately as shown in the figure.

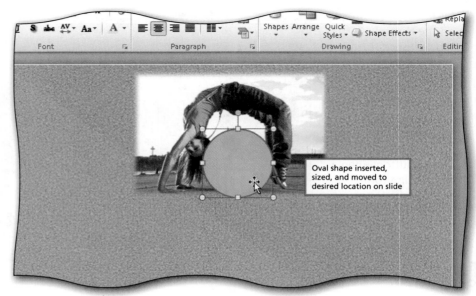

Oval shape inserted, sized, and moved to desired location on slide

Figure 2–55

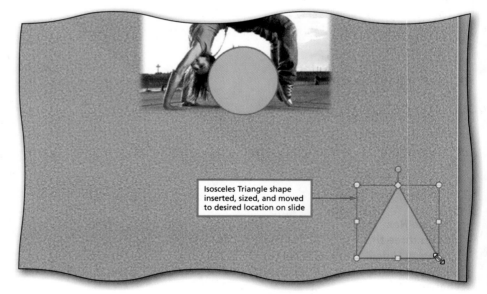

- Click the Shapes button (Home tab | Drawing group) and then click the Isosceles Triangle shape in the Basic Shapes area of the Shapes gallery.

- Position the mouse pointer in the right side of Slide 4 and then click to insert the Isosceles Triangle shape.

- Resize the shape so that it displays approximately as shown in Figure 2–56.

Isosceles Triangle shape inserted, sized, and moved to desired location on slide

Figure 2–56

To Apply a Shape Style

Formatting text in a shape follows the same techniques as formatting text in a placeholder. You can change font, font color and size, and alignment. The next step is to apply a shape style to the oval so that it appears to have depth. The Shape Styles gallery has a variety of styles that change depending upon the theme applied to the presentation. The following steps apply a style to the Oval shape.

- Click the Oval shape to select it and then display the Drawing Tools Format tab (Figure 2–57).

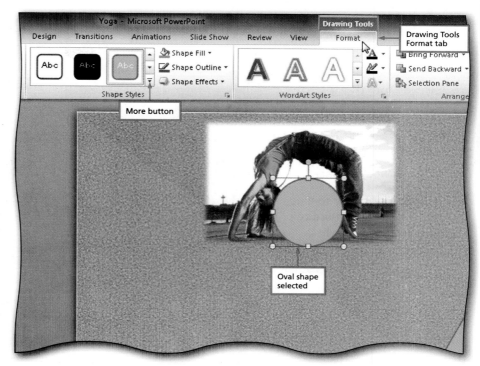

Figure 2–57

- Click the More button in the Shape Styles gallery (Drawing Tools Format tab | Shape Styles group) to expand the Shape Styles gallery.

- Point to Intense Effect – Orange, Accent 1 in the Shape Styles gallery (second shape in last row) to display a live preview of that style applied to the shape in the slide (Figure 2–58).

 **Experiment**

- Point to various styles in the Shape Styles gallery and watch the style of the shape change.

❸

- Click Intense Effect – Orange, Accent 1 in the Shape Styles gallery to apply the selected style to the Oval shape.

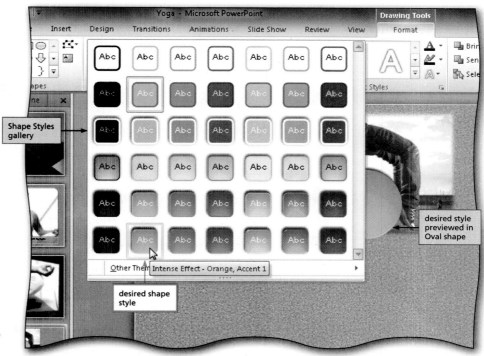

Figure 2–58

Other Ways
1. Click Format Shape dialog box launcher (Drawing Tools Format tab | Shape Styles group), select desired colors (Format Shape dialog box), click Close button 2. Right-click shape, click Format Shape on shortcut menu, select desired colors (Format Shape dialog box), click Close button

To Add Formatted Text to a Shape

Formatting text in a shape follows the same techniques as formatting text in a placeholder. You can change font, font color and size, and alignment. The next step is to add the word, Mind, to the shape, change the font to Papyrus and the font color to Blue-Gray, center and bold the text, and increase the font size to 24 point. The following step adds text to the Oval shape.

 1

- With the Oval shape selected, type **Mind** in the shape.

- Change the font to Papyrus.

- Change the font color to Blue-Gray, Background 2 (third color in first Theme Colors row).

- Change the font size to 24 point and bold the text (Figure 2–59).

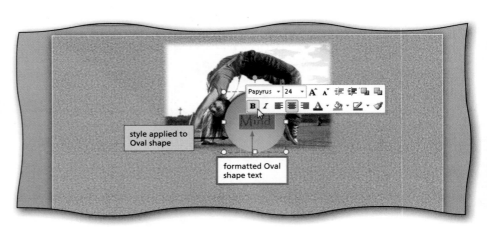

Figure 2–59

BTW

Drawing a Square
Holding down the SHIFT key while dragging a Rectangle shape draws a square.

To Copy a Shape

Your presentation emphasizes that mind, body, and spirit are equal components in finding balance in life. Each of these elements can be represented by an oval. The following steps copy the Oval shape.

1 Click Home on the Ribbon. Click the edge of the Oval shape so that it is a solid line.

2 Click the Copy button (Home tab | Clipboard group).

3 Click the Paste button (Home tab | Clipboard group) two times to insert two duplicate Oval shapes on Slide 4.

4 Move the Oval shapes so they appear approximately as shown in Figure 2–60.

5 In the left oval, select the word, Mind, and then type the word, **Body**, in the oval.

6 In the right oval, select the word, Mind, and then type the word, **Spirit**, in the oval (Figure 2–60). You may need to enlarge the size of the oval shapes slightly so that each word is displayed on one line.

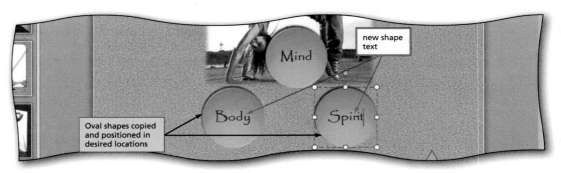

Figure 2–60

To Apply Another Style

The triangle shape helps show the unity among body, mind, and spirit. You can apply a coordinating shape style to the isosceles triangle and then place it on top of the three ovals. The following steps apply a style to the Isosceles Triangle shape.

1 Display the Drawing Tools Format tab. Click the Isosceles Triangle shape on Slide 4 to select it.

2 Click the More button in the Shape Styles gallery (Drawing Tools Format tab | Shape Styles group) to expand the Shape Styles gallery and then click Intense Effect – Blue, Accent 2 (third style in last row) to apply that style to the triangle.

3 Move the triangle shape to the center of the Ovals.

4 Click the Bring Forward button twice (Drawing Tools Format tab | Arrange group) to display the triangle on top of the ovals. Resize the triangle if necessary so that it displays as shown in Figure 2–61.

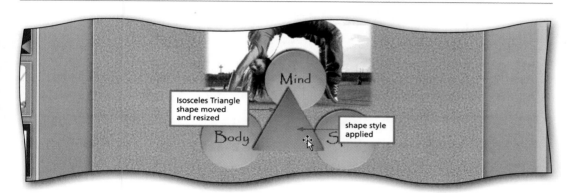

Figure 2–61

Break Point: If you wish to take a break, this is a good place to do so. Be sure to save the Yoga file again and then you can quit PowerPoint. To resume at a later time, start PowerPoint, open the file called Yoga, and continue following the steps from this location forward.

Using WordArt

One method of adding appealing visual elements to a presentation is by using **WordArt** styles. This feature is found in other Microsoft Office applications, including Word and Excel. This gallery of decorative effects allows you to type new text or convert existing text to WordArt. You then can add elements such as fills, outlines, and effects.

As with slide backgrounds, WordArt fill in the interior of a letter can consist of a solid color, texture, picture, or gradient. The WordArt **outline** is the exterior border surrounding each letter or symbol. PowerPoint allows you to change the outline color, weight, and style. You also can add an **effect**, which helps add emphasis or depth to the characters. Some effects are shadows, reflections, glows, bevels, and 3-D rotations.

Use WordArt in moderation.
Some WordArt styles are bold and detailed, and they can detract from the message you are trying to present if not used carefully. Select a WordArt style when needed for special emphasis, such as a title slide that audience members will see when they enter the room. WordArt can have a powerful effect, so do not overuse it.

**Plan
Ahead**

To Insert WordArt

Yoga and meditation can help individuals find balance among the mind, body, and spirit. The symbols on Slide 4 emphasize this relationship, and you want to call attention to the concept. You quickly can add a visual element to the slide by selecting a WordArt style from the WordArt Styles gallery and then applying it to a word. The following steps insert WordArt.

1

- With Slide 4 displaying, click Insert on the Ribbon.

- Click the WordArt button (Insert tab | Text group) to display the WordArt gallery (Figure 2–62).

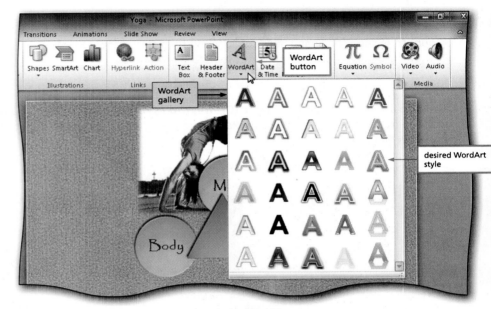

Figure 2–62

2

- Click Fill – Blue, Accent 2, Double Outline – Accent 2 (last letter A in third row) to display the WordArt text box (Figure 2–63).

Q&A What is a matte bevel style that is part of some of the styles in the gallery?

A matte finish gives a dull and rough effect. A bevel edge is angled or sloped and gives the effect of a three-dimensional object.

Figure 2–63

3

- Type **Balance** in the text box, as the WordArt text (Figure 2–64).

Q&A Why did the Format tab appear automatically in the Ribbon?

It appears when you select text to which you could add a WordArt style or other effect.

Figure 2–64

To Change the WordArt Shape

The WordArt text is useful to emphasize the harmony among the mind, body, and spirit. You can further emphasize this word by changing its shape. PowerPoint provides a variety of graphical shapes that add interest to text. The following steps change the WordArt to Triangle Down shape.

1

- With the Slide 4 text still selected, click the Text Effects button (Drawing Tools Format tab | WordArt Styles group) to display the Text Effects menu (Figure 2–65).

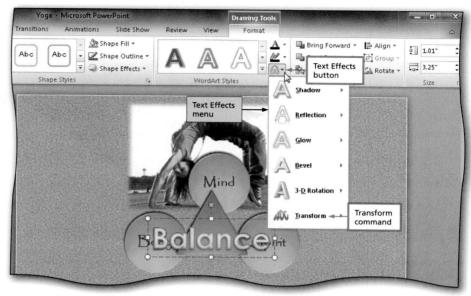

Figure 2–65

2

- Point to Transform in the Text Effects menu to display the WordArt Transform gallery (Figure 2–66).

 **Experiment**

- Point to various styles in the Transform gallery and watch the format of the text and borders change.

Q&A

How can I see the preview of a Transform effect if the gallery is overlaying the WordArt letters?

Move the WordArt text box to the left or right side of the slide and then repeat Steps 1 and 2.

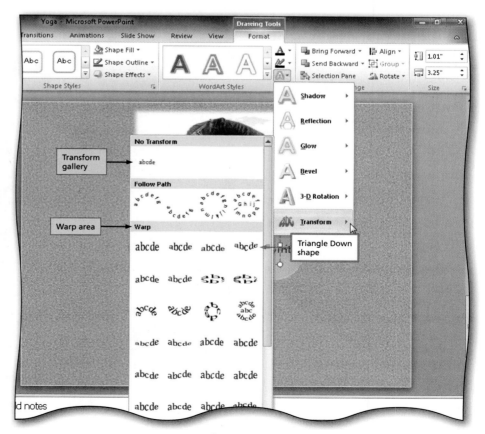

Figure 2–66

3

- Click the Triangle Down shape in the Warp area to apply the Triangle Down shape to the WordArt text (Figure 2–67).

Q&A Can I change the shape I applied to the WordArt?

Yes. Position the insertion point in the text box and then repeat Steps 1 and 2.

Figure 2–67

4

- Drag the WordArt downward until it is positioned approximately as shown in Figure 2–68.

- Drag a corner sizing handle diagonally outward until the WordArt is resized approximately as shown in the figure.

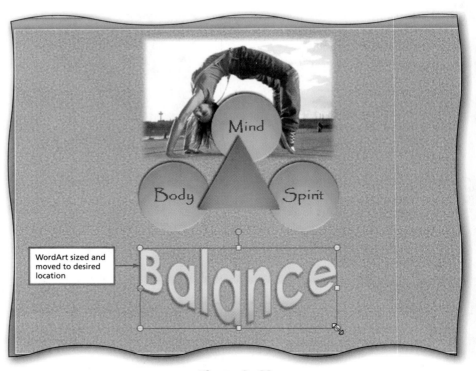

Figure 2–68

To Apply a WordArt Text Fill

The Slide 4 background has a Sand texture for the background, and you want to coordinate the WordArt fill with a similar texture. The following steps add the Denim texture as a fill for the WordArt characters.

1

- With the WordArt text selected, click the Text Fill button arrow (Drawing Tools Format tab | WordArt Styles group) to display the Text Fill gallery.

Q&A The Text Fill gallery did not display. Why not?

Be sure you click the Text Fill button arrow, which is to the right of the Text Fill button. If you mistakenly click the Text Fill button, PowerPoint places the default fill in the WordArt instead of displaying the Text Fill gallery.

- Point to Texture in the Text Fill gallery to display the Texture gallery (Figure 2–69).

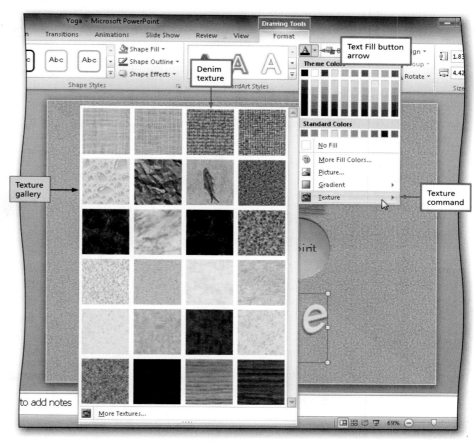

Figure 2–69

Experiment

- Point to various styles in the Text Fill gallery and watch the fill change.

Q&A How can I see the preview of a fill if the gallery is overlaying the WordArt letters?

Move the WordArt text box to the left or right side of the slide and then repeat Step 1.

2

- Click the Denim texture (third texture in first row) to apply this texture as the fill for the WordArt.

Q&A Can I apply this texture simultaneously to text that appears in more than one place on my slide?

Yes. Select one area of text, press and then hold the CTRL key while you select the other text, and then apply the texture.

To Change the Weight of the WordArt Outline

The letters in the WordArt style applied have a double outline around the edges. To emphasize this characteristic, you can increase the width of the lines. As with font size, lines also are measured in point size, and PowerPoint gives you the option to change the line **weight**, or thickness, starting with ¼ point (pt) and increasing in one-fourth–point increments. Other outline options include modifying the color and the line style, such as changing to dots or dashes or a combination of dots and dashes. The following steps change the WordArt outline weight to 6 pt.

 1

- With the WordArt still selected, click the Text Outline button arrow (Drawing Tools Format tab | WordArt Styles group) to display the Text Outline gallery.

- Point to Weight in the gallery to display the Weight list.

- Point to 6 pt to display a live preview of this line weight on the WordArt text outline (Figure 2–70).

Experiment

- Point to various line weights in the Weight list and watch the line thickness change.

Q&A Can I make the line width more than 6 pt?

Yes. Click More Lines and increase the amount in the Width box.

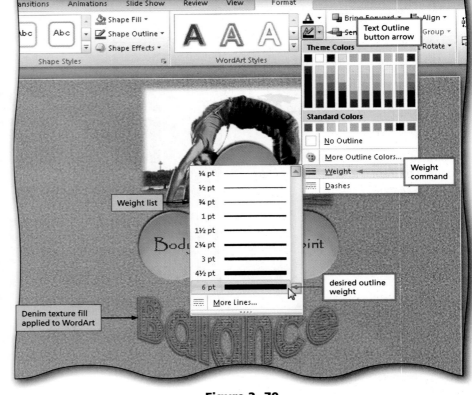

Figure 2–70

 2

- Click 6 pt to apply this line weight to the title text outline.

Q&A Must my text have an outline?

No. To delete the outline, click No Outline in the Text Outline gallery.

To Change the Color of the WordArt Outline

The WordArt outline color is similar to the Denim fill color. To add variety, you can change the outline color. The following steps change the WordArt outline color.

1

- With the WordArt still selected, click the Text Outline button arrow (Drawing Tools Format tab | WordArt Styles group) to display the Text Outline gallery.

- Point to Orange, Accent 1 (fifth color in first row) to display a live preview of this outline color (Figure 2–71).

🔎 **Experiment**

- Point to various colors in the gallery and watch the outline colors change.

2

- Click Orange, Accent 1 to apply this color to the WordArt outline.

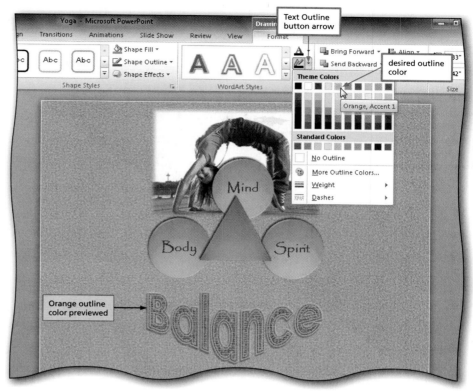

Figure 2–71

To Add a Transition between Slides

A final enhancement you will make in this presentation is to apply the Rotate transition in the Dynamic Content category to all slides and change the transition speed to Slow. The following steps apply this transition to the presentation.

1 Click Transitions on the Ribbon. Click the More button (Transitions tab | Transition to This Slide group) to expand the Transitions gallery.

2 Click the Rotate transition in the Dynamic Content category to apply this transition to Slide 4.

3 Click the Duration up arrow in the Timing group four times to change the transition speed from 02.00 to 03.00.

4 Click the Preview Transitions button (Transitions tab | Preview area) to view the new transition time.

5 Click the Apply To All button (Transitions tab | Timing group) to apply this transition and speed to all four slides in the presentation (Figure 2–72 on the next page).

BTW

Selecting Effect Options
Many PowerPoint transitions have options that you can customize to give your presentation a unique look. When you click the Effect Options button (Transitions tab | Transition to This Slide group), you can, for example, select the option to have a slide appear on the screen from the left or the right, or the screen can fade to black before the next slide is displayed.

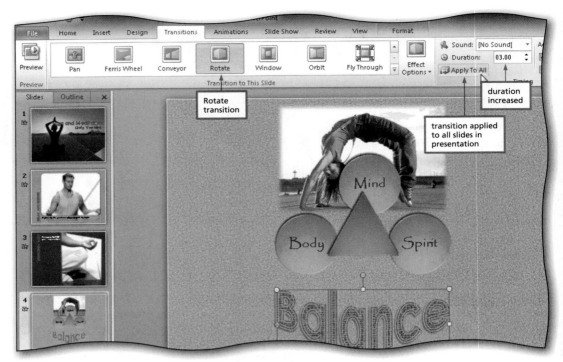

Figure 2–72

To Change Document Properties

Before saving the presentation again, you want to add your name, class name, and some keywords as document properties. The following steps use the Document Information Panel to change document properties.

1 Click File on the Ribbon to open the Backstage view. If necessary, click the Info tab.

2 Click the Properties button in the right pane of the Info gallery.

3 Click Show Document Panel on the Properties menu to close the Backstage view and display the Document Information Panel.

4 Click the Author box, if necessary, and then type your name as the Author property.

5 Click the Subject text box and then type your course and section as the Subject property.

6 Click the Keywords text box and then type `yoga, meditation` as the Keywords property.

7 Click the Close the Document Information Panel button so that the Document Information Panel no longer is displayed.

BTW

Certification
The Microsoft Office Specialist (MOS) program provides an opportunity for you to obtain a valuable industry credential — proof that you have the PowerPoint 2010 skills required by employers. For more information, visit the PowerPoint 2010 Certification Web page (scsite.com/ppt2010/cert).

To Print a Presentation

With the completed presentation saved, you may want to print it. If copies of the presentation are being distributed to audience members, you will print a hard copy of each individual slide on a printer. The following steps print a hard copy of the contents of the saved Yoga presentation.

1 Click File on the Ribbon to open the Backstage view. Click the Print tab in the Backstage view to display the Print gallery.

2 Verify the printer name in the Printer box will print a hard copy of the document. If necessary, click the Printer box arrow to display a list of available Printer options and then click the desired printer to change the currently selected printer.

3 Click the Print button in the Print gallery to print the document on the currently selected printer. When the printer stops, retrieve the hard copy (Figure 2–73).

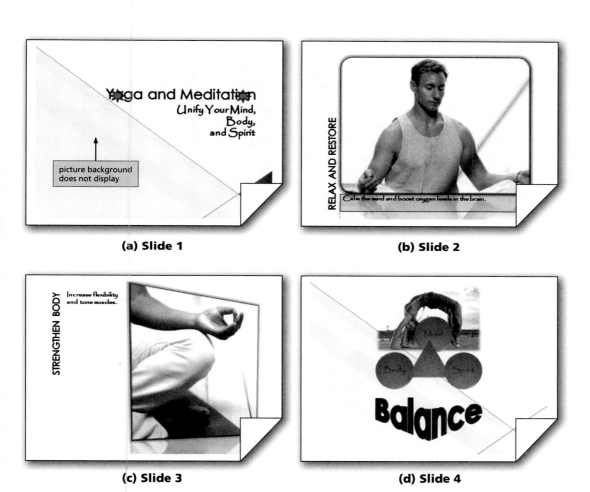

(a) **Slide 1**

(b) **Slide 2**

(c) **Slide 3**

(d) **Slide 4**

Figure 2–73 (Handouts printed using a black-and-white printer)

To Save an Existing Presentation with the Same File Name

You have made several changes to the presentation since you last saved it. Thus, you should save it again. The following step saves the document again.

1 Click the Save button on the Quick Access Toolbar to overwrite the previously saved file.

BTW

Quick Reference
For a table that lists how to complete the tasks covered in this book using the mouse, Ribbon, shortcut menu, and keyboard, see the Quick Reference Summary at the back of this book, or visit the PowerPoint 2010 Quick Reference Web page (scsite.com/ppt2010/qr).

To Run an Animated Slide Show

All changes are complete, and the presentation is saved. You now can view the Yoga presentation. The following steps start Slide Show view.

1 Click the Slide 1 thumbnail in the Slides tab to select and display Slide 1.

2 Click the Slide Show button to display the title slide and then click each slide to view the transition effect and slides.

To Quit PowerPoint

This project is complete. The following steps quit PowerPoint.

1 If you have one PowerPoint document open, click the Close Button on the right side of the title bar to close the document and then quit PowerPoint; or if you have multiple PowerPoint documents open, click File on the Ribbon to open the Backstage view and then click Exit in the Backstage view to close all open documents and quit PowerPoint.

2 If a Microsoft PowerPoint dialog box appears, click the Save button to save any changes made to the presentation since the last save.

Chapter Summary

In this chapter you have learned how to add a background style, insert and format pictures, add shapes, size graphic elements, apply styles, and insert WordArt. The items listed below include all the new PowerPoint skills you have learned in this chapter.

1. Change the Presentation Theme Colors (PPT 81)
2. Insert a Picture (PPT 83)
3. Insert a Picture into a Slide without a Content Placeholder (PPT 85)
4. Correct a Picture (PPT 86)
5. Apply a Picture Style (PPT 87)
6. Apply Picture Effects (PPT 89)
7. Add a Picture Border (PPT 91)
8. Change a Picture Border Color (PPT 92)
9. Resize a Graphic by Entering Exact Measurements (PPT 93)
10. Insert a Texture Fill (PPT 95)
11. Insert a Picture to Create a Background (PPT 97)
12. Format the Background Picture Fill Transparency (PPT 98)
13. Format the Background Texture Fill Transparency (PPT 99)
14. Choose a Background Style (PPT 99)
15. Change the Subtitle and Caption Font (PPT 101)
16. Shadow Text (PPT 103)
17. Format Caption Text Using the Format Painter (PPT 105)
18. Add a Shape (PPT 106)
19. Resize a Shape (PPT 107)
20. Copy and Paste a Shape (PPT 108)
21. Add Other Shapes (PPT 109)
22. Apply a Shape Style (PPT 110)
23. Add Formatted Text to a Shape (PPT 112)
24. Insert WordArt (PPT 114)
25. Change the WordArt Shape (PPT 115)
26. Apply a WordArt Text Fill (PPT 117)
27. Change the Weight of the WordArt Outline (PPT 118)
28. Change the Color of the WordArt Outline (PPT 118)

Learn It Online

Test your knowledge of chapter content and key terms.

Instructions: To complete the Learn It Online exercises, start your browser, click the Address bar, and then enter the Web address **scsite.com/ppt2010/learn**. When the PowerPoint 2010 Learn It Online page is displayed, click the link for the exercise you want to complete and then read the instructions.

Chapter Reinforcement TF, MC, and SA
A series of true/false, multiple choice, and short answer questions that test your knowledge of the chapter content.

Flash Cards
An interactive learning environment where you identify chapter key terms associated with displayed definitions.

Practice Test
A series of multiple choice questions that test your knowledge of chapter content and key terms.

Who Wants To Be a Computer Genius?
An interactive game that challenges your knowledge of chapter content in the style of a television quiz show.

Wheel of Terms
An interactive game that challenges your knowledge of chapter key terms in the style of the television show *Wheel of Fortune*.

Crossword Puzzle Challenge
A crossword puzzle that challenges your knowledge of key terms presented in the chapter.

Apply Your Knowledge

Reinforce the skills and apply the concepts you learned in this chapter.

Changing the Background and Adding Photographs, WordArt, and a Shape Quick Style
Note: To complete this assignment, you will be required to use the Data Files for Students. See the inside back cover of this book for instructions on downloading the Data Files for Students, or contact your instructor for information about accessing the required files.

Instructions: Start PowerPoint. Open the presentation, Apply 2-1 Lab Procedures, from the Data Files for Students.

The four slides in the presentation present laboratory safety procedures for your chemistry class. The document you open is an unformatted presentation. You are to add pictures, which are available on the Data Files for Students. You also will change the background style, change slide layouts, apply a transition, and use the Format Painter so the slides look like Figure 2–74.

Perform the following tasks:

1. Change the background style to Style 5 (row 2, column 1).

2. On the title slide (Figure 2–74a), create a background by inserting the picture called Lab Assistant. Change the transparency to 30%.

3. Apply the WordArt style, Fill – Red, Accent 2, Matte Bevel (row 6, column 3) to the title text and increase the font size to 54 point. Also, apply the WordArt Transform text effect, Chevron Up (row 2, column 1 in the Warp area) to this text.

4. In the Slide 1 subtitle area, replace the words, Student Name, with your name. Bold and italicize your name and the words, Presented by, and then apply the WordArt style, Fill – Red, Accent 2, Warm Matte Bevel (row 5, column 3). Position this subtitle text and the title text as shown in Figure 2–74a.

Continued >

Apply Your Knowledge *continued*

5. On Slide 2, change the layout to Two Content and insert the pictures shown in Figure 2–74b called Female in Lab Coat and Female with Goggles. In the left placeholder, apply the Rotated, White picture style to the inserted picture. In the right placeholder, apply the Reflected Bevel, Black picture style to the inserted picture and then change the picture border color to Purple.

6. On Slide 3, change the layout to Two Content and insert the Fire Extinguisher picture shown in Figure 2–74c. Apply the Soft Edge Oval picture style and change the picture brightness to +20% (row 3, column 4 in the Brightness and Contrast area).

7. On Slide 4, change the layout to Picture with Caption and then insert the picture, Hand Washing shown in Figure 2–74d. Increase the subtitle text font size to 18 point. Change the title text font size to 28 point, add a shadow, change font to Algerian, and change the font color to Purple.

(a) Slide 1

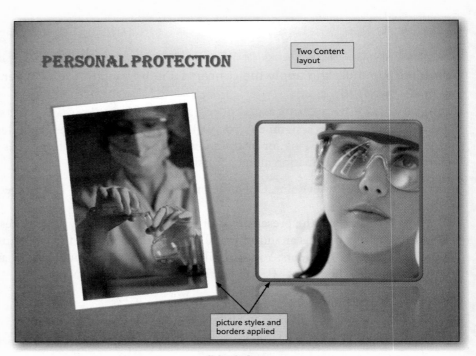

(b) Slide 2

Figure 2–74

8. Use the Format Painter to format the title text on Slides 2 and 3 with the same features as the title text on Slide 4.

9. Apply the Wipe transition in the Subtle category to all slides. Change the duration to 2.00 seconds.

10. Change the document properties, as specified by your instructor. Save the presentation using the file name, Apply 2-1 Chemistry Lab Safety. Submit the revised document in the format specified by your instructor.

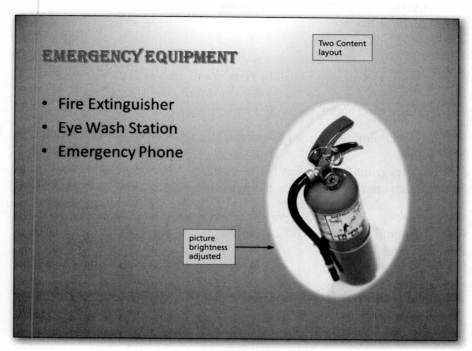

(c) Slide 3

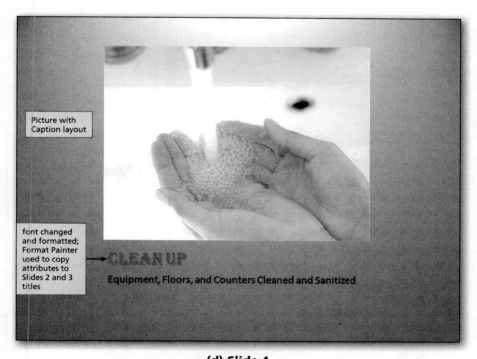

(d) Slide 4

Figure 2 – 74 (Continued)

Extend Your Knowledge

Extend the skills you learned in this chapter and experiment with new skills. You may need to use Help to complete the assignment.

Changing Slide Backgrounds and Picture Contrast, and Inserting Shapes and WordArt

Note: To complete this assignment, you will be required to use the Data Files for Students. See the inside back cover of this book for instructions on downloading the Data Files for Students, or contact your instructor for information about accessing the required files.

Instructions: Start PowerPoint. Open the presentation, Extend 2-1 Smith Family Reunion, from the Data Files for Students.

You will create backgrounds including inserting a picture to create a background, apply a WordArt Style and Effect, and add shapes to create the presentation shown in Figure 2–75.

Perform the following tasks:

1. Change the background style to Denim (row 1, column 3) and change the transparency to 48%. On Slides 2 through 5, change the title text to bold.

2. On the title slide (Figure 2–75a), create a background by inserting the picture called Tree, which is available on the Data Files for Students. Change the transparency to 40%.

3. Apply the WordArt style, Gradient Fill – Blue, Accent 1, to the title text and increase the font size to 66 point. Also, apply the WordArt Transform text effect, Arch Up (row 1, column 1 in the Follow Path area), to this text.

4. In the Slide 1 subtitle area, insert the Wave shape in the Stars and Banners area. Also, apply the Shape Style, Subtle Effect – Orange, Accent 6 to the Wave shape. Type **Highlights From Our Last Reunion** and increase the font size to 40 point, change the text to bold italic and change the color to Green. Position the shape as shown in Figure 2–75a.

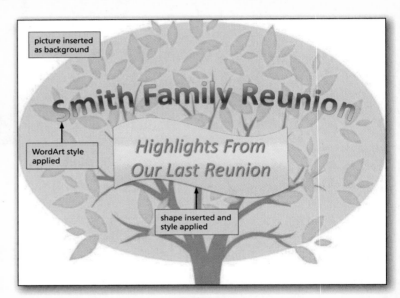

(a) Slide 1

(b) Slide 2

Figure 2–75

5. On Slide 2, change the layout to Two Content and insert the pictures shown in Figure 2–75b. The pictures to be inserted are called Bocce Ball and Frisbee Catcher and are available on the Data Files for Students. In the left placeholder, apply the Rotated White picture style to the inserted picture and change the picture border to Light Green. In the right placeholder, apply the Beveled Oval Black picture style to the inserted picture.

6. Insert the Plaque shape in the Basic Shapes area. Also, apply the Shape Style, Subtle Effect, Olive Green, Accent 3 and apply the Shape Effect, 3-D Rotation, Parallel, Off Axis 1 Right. Type **Cousin Tom & His Frisbee Moves** and increase the font size to 28 point. Move the shape as shown in Figure 2–75b.

(c) Slide 3

7. On Slide 3, change the layout to Picture with Caption and insert the picture shown in Figure 2–75c. The picture to be inserted is called BBQ Grill. Increase the title font size to 44 point. Also, increase the subtitle font size to 32 point, and then bold and italicize this text.

8. On Slide 4, change the layout to Two Content and insert the pictures shown in Figure 2–75d. The pictures to be inserted are called Reunion Boys and Reunion Toddler. In the left placeholder, apply the Rotated, White picture effect to the picture. In the right placeholder, apply the Bevel Perspective picture effect. Move the pictures as shown in Figure 2–75d.

(d) Slide 4

Figure 2–75 (Continued)

Continued >

Extend Your Knowledge *continued*

9. On Slide 5, change the layout to Title and Content and insert the picture shown in Figure 2–75e. The picture to be inserted is called Reunion. Enlarge the picture as shown.

10. Insert the Oval Callout and Cloud Callout shapes in the Callouts area. In the Oval Callout shape, type **I hope Grandma makes cookies!** and change the font size to 24 point bold italic. Also add a Shape Style, Moderate Effect – Olive Green Accent 3 to this shape. In the Cloud Callout shape, type **I'm looking forward to our next reunion!** and change the font size to 24 point and the style to bold italic. Move the shapes as shown in Figure 2–75e. Use the adjustment handles (the yellow diamond below each shape) to move the callout arrows as shown in Figure 2–75e. You may need to use Help to learn how to move these arrows.

11. On Slide 6, change the layout to Picture with Caption and insert the picture shown in Figure 2–75f and change the picture contrast to +20. The picture to be inserted is called Reunion Tree.

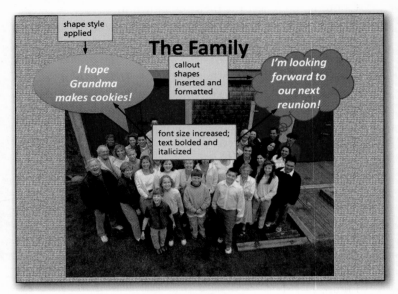

(e) Slide 5

(f) Slide 6

Figure 2–75 (Continued)

12. Insert the Up Ribbon shape in the Stars and Banners area and type the words **Announcing Our Next Reunion**. Change the font color to Green, the font size to 32 point, and the style to bold italic. Also, apply the Shape Style, Subtle Effect – Orange Accent 6. In the title placeholder, type **Save the date – June 20, 2012** and change the font size to 28 point. Bold this text.

13. Add the Orbit transition under the Dynamic Content section to Slide 6 only. You may need to use Help to learn how to apply the transition to only one slide. Change the duration to 2.00 seconds.

14. Change the document properties, as specified by your instructor. Save the presentation using the file name, Extend 2-1 Smith Reunion.

15. Submit the revised document in the format specified by your instructor.

Make It Right

Analyze a presentation and correct all errors and/or improve the design.

Changing a Theme and Background Style

Note: To complete this assignment, you will be required to use the Data Files for Students. See the inside back cover of this book for instructions on downloading the Data Files for Students, or contact your instructor for information about accessing the required files.

Instructions: Start PowerPoint. Open the presentation, Make It Right 2-1 New Aerobics Classes, from the Data Files for Students.

Correct the formatting problems and errors in the presentation while keeping in mind the guidelines presented in this chapter.

Perform the following tasks:

1. Change the document theme from Flow, shown in Figure 2–76, to Waveform. Apply the Background Style 10 (row 3, column 2) to Slide 5 only.

2. On the title slide, change the title from New Aerobics Classes to New Pool Programs. Type your name in place of Northlake Fitness Center and change the font to bold italic.

3. Move Slide 2 to the end of the presentation so that it becomes the new Slide 5.

4. Adjust the picture sizes, font sizes, and shapes so they do not overlap text and are the appropriate dimensions for the slide content.

5. Apply the Ripple transition to all slides. Change the duration to 02.00.

6. Change the document properties, as specified by your instructor. Save the presentation using the file name, Make It Right 2-1 New Pool Programs.

7. Submit the revised document in the format specified by your instructor.

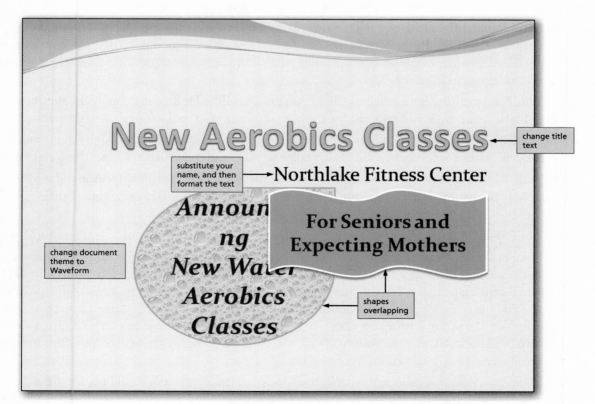

Figure 2–76

In the Lab

Design and/or create a presentation using the guidelines, concepts, and skills presented in this chapter. Labs 1, 2, and 3 are listed in order of increasing difficulty.

Lab 1: Creating a Presentation Inserting Pictures and Applying Picture Styles

Problem: You are studying German operas in your Music Appreciation class. Wilhelm Richard Wagner (pronounced 'va:gner') lived from 1813 to 1883 and was a composer, conductor, theatre director, and essayist known for his operas. Wagner wrote and composed many operas, and King Ludwig II of Bavaria was one of his biggest supporters. Because you recently visited southern Germany and toured King Ludwig's castles, you decide to create a PowerPoint presentation with some of your photos to accompany your class presentation. These pictures are available on the Data Files for Students. Create the slides shown in Figure 2–77 from a blank presentation using the Office Theme document theme.

Note: To complete this assignment, you will be required to use the Data Files for Students. See the inside back cover of this book for instructions on downloading the Data Files for Students, or contact your instructor for information about accessing the required files.

Instructions: Perform the following tasks:

1. On Slide 1, create a background by inserting the picture called Castle 1, which is available on the Data Files for Students.

2. Type **Fairy Tale Trip to Germany** as the Slide 1 title text. Apply the WordArt style, Fill – Tan, Text 2, Outline – Background 2, and increase the font size to 60 point. Change the text fill to the Papyrus texture, and then change the text outline weight to 1½ pt. Also, apply the Transform text effect, Arch Up (in the Follow Path area), to this text. Position this WordArt as shown in Figure 2–77a.

3. Type the title and content for the four text slides shown in Figure 2–77. Apply the Two Content layout to Slides 2 and 3 and the Picture with Caption layout to Slides 4 and 5.

4. On Slide 2, insert the picture called Castle 2 from the Data Files for Students in the right placeholder. Apply the Bevel Perspective picture style. Resize the picture so that it is approximately 4.5" × 6", change the border color to Purple, change the border weight to 6 pt, and then move the picture, as shown in Figure 2–77b.

5. On Slide 3, insert the picture called Castle 3 from the Data Files for Students. Apply the Reflected Bevel, Black picture style and then change the border color to Green. Do not change the border weight.

6. On Slide 4, insert the picture called Castle 4 from the Data Files for Students. Apply the Beveled Oval, Black picture style, change the border color to Blue, and then change the border weight to 6 pt.

7. On Slide 5, insert the picture called Castle 5 from the Data Files for Students. Apply the Moderate Frame, Black picture style, change the border color to Purple, and then change the border weight to 6 pt.

8. For both Slides 4 and 5, increase the title text size to 28 point and the caption text size to 24 point.

9. On Slide 2, change the title text font to Algerian, change the color to purple, and bold this text. Use the Format Painter to apply these formatting changes to the Slide 3 title text. In Slide 3, insert the Vertical Scroll shape located in the Stars and Banners area, apply the Subtle Effect – Purple, Accent 4 shape style, and change the shape outline weight to 3 pt. Type the text, **Inspiration for Disney's Sleeping Beauty Castle**, and then change the font to Curlz MT, or a similar font. Bold this text, change the color to Dark Blue, and then change the size to 28 point. Increase the scroll shape size, as shown in Figure 2–77c.

10. On Slides 2, 3, 4, and 5, change the background style to the White marble fill texture (row 2, column 5) and change the transparency to 35%. Apply the Glitter transition to all slides. Change the duration to 04.50.

11. Change the document properties, as specified by your instructor. Save the presentation using the file name, Lab 2-1 Trip to Germany.

12. Submit the revised document in the format specified by your instructor.

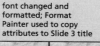

picture inserted as background

WordArt style, texture fill, and effect applied

(a) Slide 1

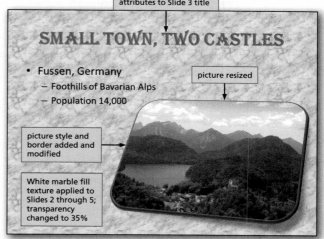

font changed and formatted; Format Painter used to copy attributes to Slide 3 title

picture resized

picture style and border added and modified

White marble fill texture applied to Slides 2 through 5; transparency changed to 35%

(b) Slide 2

picture style applied and border color changed to Green

shape inserted and formatted

font changed to Curlz MT and formatted

(c) Slide 3

picture style applied and border color and weight changed

Ludwig's Homage to Wagner

font size increased

(d) Slide 4

picture style applied and border color and weight changed

Hohenschwangau Castle

font size increased

(e) Slide 5

Figure 2–77

In the Lab

Lab 2: Creating a Presentation with a Shape and with WordArt

Problem: With the economy showing some improvement, many small businesses are approaching lending institutions for loans to expand their businesses. You work part-time for Loans Are Us, and your manager asked you to prepare a PowerPoint presentation for the upcoming Small Business Fair in your community. The pictures for this presentation are available on the Data Files for Students.

Note: To complete this assignment, you will be required to use the Data Files for Students. See the inside back cover of this book for instructions on downloading the Data Files for Students, or contact your instructor for information about accessing the required files.

Instructions: Perform the following tasks:

1. Create a new presentation using the Austin document theme.

2. Type the title and content for the title slide and the three text slides shown in Figure 2–78a–d. Apply the Title Only layout to Slide 2, the Two Content layout to Slide 3, and the Picture with Caption layout to Slide 4.

3. On both Slides 2 and 4, create a background by inserting the picture called Money. Change the transparency to 35%.

4. On Slide 1, insert the picture called Meeting. Apply the Reflected Bevel, White picture style. Resize the picture so that it is approximately 3.76" × 4.7", change the border color to Dark Blue, change the border weight to 3 pt, and then move the picture, as shown in Figure 2–78a. Increase the title text font size to 60 point, and then apply the WordArt style, Fill – Orange, Accent 6, Warm Matte Bevel.

5. Increase the subtitle text, Loans Are Us, font size to 28 point and then bold and italicize this text. Apply the WordArt style, Fill – Green, Accent 1, Metal Bevel, Reflection.

6. On Slide 2, bold the title text. Insert the pictures called Doc1, Doc2, and Doc3. Resize these pictures so they are approximately 3" x 2.7" and then move them to the locations shown in Figure 2–78b. Insert the Flowchart: Decision shape located in the Flowchart area, apply the Subtle Effect – Orange, Accent 6 shape style, and then resize the shape so that it is approximately 1.5" × 5.83". Change the shape outline weight to 6 pt. Type **Assets, Liabilities & Sales Reports** as the shape text, change the font to Aharoni, or a similar font, change the color to Dark Blue, and then change the size to 24 point.

7. On Slide 3, bold the title text. Insert the picture called Presentation into the right placeholder, apply the Beveled Oval, Black shape picture style, resize the picture so that it is approximately 3.5" × 5.25", and then sharpen the picture 50%.

8. On Slide 4, insert the picture called Cash and Credit Card. Change the title text font size to 36 point and bold this text. Change the subtitle text font size to 24 point and then bold and italicize these words.

9. Apply the Shape transition to all slides. Change the duration to 01.25.

10. Change the document properties, as specified by your instructor. Save the presentation using the file name, Lab 2-2 Small Business Loans.

11. Submit the document in the format specified by your instructor.

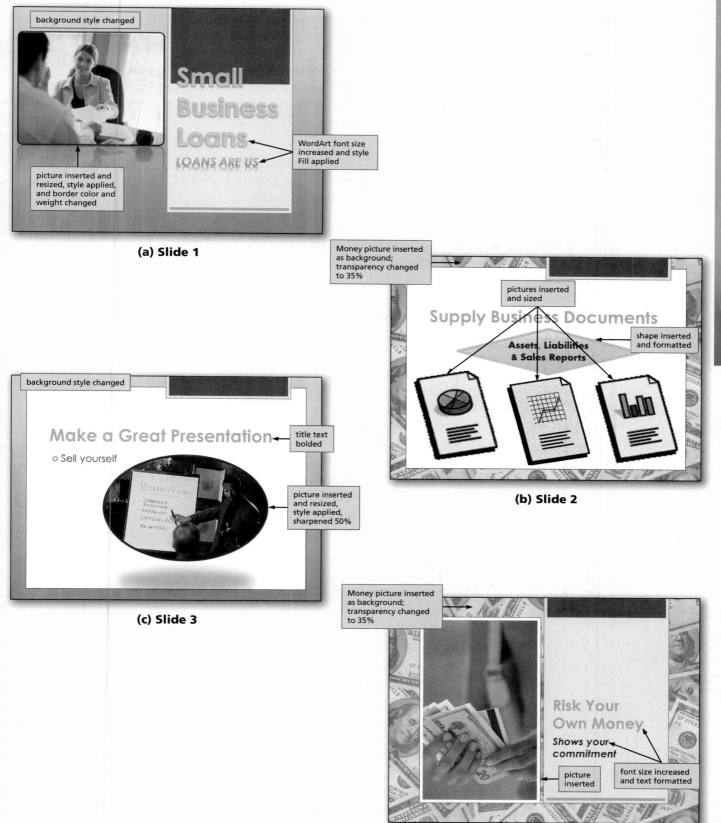

Figure 2–78

In the Lab

Lab 3: Creating a Presentation with Pictures and Shapes

Problem: One of your assignments in your child development class is to give a speech about teaching children the value of money, so you decide to create a PowerPoint presentation to add a little interest to your speech. Prepare the slides shown in Figures 2–79a through 2–79e. The pictures for this presentation are available on the Data Files for Students.

Note: To complete this assignment, you will be required to use the Data Files for Students. See the inside back cover of this book for instructions on downloading the Data Files for Students, or contact your instructor for information about accessing the required files.

Instructions: Perform the following tasks:

1. Create a new presentation using the Median document theme, and then change the presentation theme colors to Flow. This presentation should have five slides; apply the Title Slide layout to Slide 1, the Picture with Caption layout to Slides 2 and 5, the Comparison layout to Slide 3, and the Blank layout to Slide 4.

2. Type the title and content text for the title slide and the four text slides shown in Figure 2–79a–d.

3. On Slide 1, change the title text font size to 54 point. To make the letter 's' appear smaller than the other letters in the first word of the title slide title text placeholder, change the font size of this letter to 44 point. Insert the Oval shape, resize it so that it is approximately 0.5" × 0.5", and change the shape fill to white, which is the second color in the first row of the Theme Colors gallery. Type **$**, increase the font size to 48 point, change the color to green, and bold this dollar sign. Cover the letter 'o' in the word, Do, with this shape.

4. Insert the picture called Piggy Bank. Apply the Rounded Diagonal Corner, White picture style. Resize the picture so that it is approximately 4.4" × 5.03", change the border color to Light Blue, change the border weight to 3 pt, and then move the picture, as shown in Figure 2–79a. Change the subtitle font size to 32 point and then bold this text.

5. On Slide 2, insert the picture called Child Doing Dishes and then decrease the picture's contrast to −20%. Change the title text size to 36 point and bold this text. Change the caption text size to 32 point.

6. On Slide 3, change the background style to Style 6. Bold the title text. Change the heading title text size in both placeholders to 32 point. In the right placeholder, insert the picture called Father and Daughter and then apply the Reflected Bevel, White picture style. Resize the picture so that it is approximately 3" × 4", change the border color to Light Blue, and then change the border weight to 3 pt, as shown in Figure 2–79c.

7. On Slide 4, create a background by inserting the picture called Piggy Bank and Coins. Insert the Cloud shape located in the Basic Shapes area and then increase the cloud shape size so that it is approximately 3" × 5.6". Change the shape outline color to Yellow and then change the shape outline weight to 3 pt. Type **Teach your children to save for a big purchase.** as the shape text, and then change the font to Comic Sans MS. Bold and italicize this text and then change the font size to 32 point.

8. On Slide 5, create a background by inserting the picture called Coins. Insert the picture called Father and Child Shopping and then decrease the picture's brightness to −20%. Change the title text font size to 36 point and bold this text.

9. Apply the Box transition to all slides. Change the duration to 02.00. Check the spelling and correct any errors.

10. Change the document properties, as specified by your instructor. Save the presentation using the file name, Lab 2-3 ABCs of Money.

11. Submit the revised document in the format specified by your instructor.

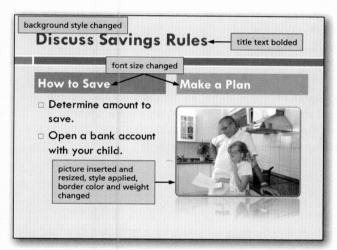

(a) Slide 1

(b) Slide 2

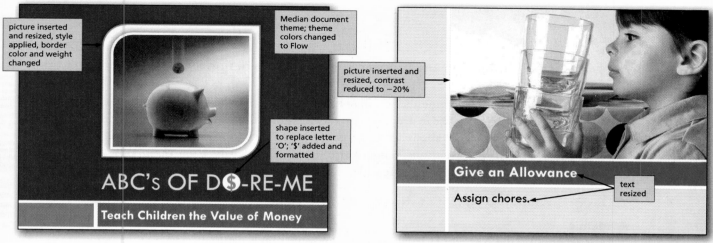

(c) Slide 3

(d) Slide 4

(e) Slide 5

Figure 2–79

Cases and Places

Apply your creative thinking and problem-solving skills to design and implement a solution.

Note: To complete these assignments, you may be required to use the Data Files for Students. See the inside back cover of this book for instructions on downloading the Data Files for Students, or contact your instructor for information about accessing the required files.

As you design the presentations, remember to use the 7 × 7 rule: a maximum of seven words on a line and a maximum of seven lines on one slide.

1: Design and Create a Presentation about Acid Rain

Academic

Nature depends on the correct pH balance. Although some rain is naturally acidic with a pH level of around 5.0, human activities have increased the amount of acid in this water. Burning fossil fuels, including coal, oil, and natural gas, produces sulfur dioxide. Exhaust from vehicles releases nitrogen oxides. Both of these gases, when released into the atmosphere, mix with water droplets, forming acid rain. In your science class, you are studying about the causes and effects of acid rain. Create a presentation to show what causes acid rain and what effects it can have on humans, animals, plant life, lakes, and rivers. The presentation should contain at least three pictures appropriately resized. The Data Files for Students contains five pictures called Factory, Rain, Soil, Tree and Clouds, and Vehicles; you can use your own digital pictures or pictures from Office.com if they are appropriate for this topic. These pictures also should have appropriate styles and border colors. Use shapes such as arrows to show what gases are released into the atmosphere. Apply at least three objectives found at the beginning of this chapter to develop the presentation. Add a title slide with a shape and a closing slide. Be sure to check spelling.

2: Design and Create a Presentation about Tutoring

Personal

You have been helping some of your classmates with their schoolwork, and you have decided that you should start a small tutoring business. In the student center, there is a kiosk where students can find out about programs and activities on campus. The student center manager gave you permission to submit a short PowerPoint presentation promoting your tutoring business; this presentation will be added to the kiosk. The presentation should contain pictures appropriately resized. The Data Files for Students contains four pictures called Tutoring 1, Tutoring 2, Tutoring 3, and Tutoring 4, or you can use your own digital pictures or pictures from Office.com if they are appropriate for this topic. Change the contrast and brightness for at least one picture. Insert shapes and WordArt to enhance your presentation. Apply a transition in the Subtle area to all slides and increase the duration. Be sure to check spelling.

3: Design and Create a Presentation on Setting Up Children's Fish Tanks

Professional

Fish make great pets for young children, but there is a lot to learn before they can set up a fish tank properly. The owner of the pet store where you work has asked you to create a presentation for the store to give parents an idea of what they need to purchase and consider when setting up a fish tank. He would like you to cover the main points such as the appropriate size bowl or tank, setup procedures, filtration, water quality, types of fish, care, and feeding. The presentation should contain pictures appropriately resized. The Data Files for Students contains five pictures called Fish 1, Fish 2, Fish 3, Fish 4, and Fish 5, or you can use your own digital pictures or pictures from Office.com if they are appropriate for this topic. Add a title slide and closing slide to complete your presentation. Format the title slide with a shape and change the theme color scheme. Change the title text font on the title slide. Format the background with at least one picture and apply a background texture to at least one slide. This presentation is geared to parents of young children, so keep it colorful, simple, and fun.

1 Creating a Worksheet and an Embedded Chart

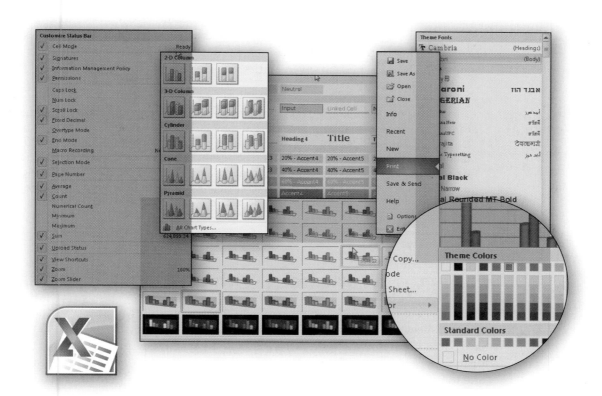

Objectives

You will have mastered the material in this chapter when you can:

- Describe the Excel worksheet
- Enter text and numbers
- Use the Sum button to sum a range of cells
- Copy the contents of a cell to a range of cells using the fill handle
- Apply cell styles
- Format cells in a worksheet

- Create a Clustered Cylinder chart
- Change a worksheet name and worksheet tab color
- Change document properties
- Preview and print a worksheet
- Use the AutoCalculate area to display statistics
- Correct errors on a worksheet

1 | Creating a Worksheet and an Embedded Chart

Introduction

Almost any organization collects vast amounts of data. Often, data is consolidated into a summary so that people in the organization better understand the meaning of the data. An Excel worksheet allows data easily to be summarized and charted. A chart conveys a visual representation of data. In this chapter, you will create a worksheet that includes a chart. The data in the worksheet and chart includes data for donations made to a not-for-profit organization that operates in several cities.

Project Planning Guidelines

> The process of developing a worksheet that communicates specific information requires careful analysis and planning. As a starting point, establish why the worksheet is needed. Once the purpose is determined, analyze the intended users of the worksheet and their unique needs. Then, gather information about the topic and decide what to include in the worksheet. Finally, determine the worksheet design and style that will be most successful at delivering the message. Details of these guidelines are provided in Appendix A. In addition, each project developed in this book provides practical applications of these planning considerations.

Project — Worksheet with an Embedded Chart

The project in this chapter follows proper design guidelines and uses Excel to create the worksheet shown in Figure 1–1. The worksheet contains fundraising data for the Save Sable River Foundation. The Save Sable River Foundation raises funds to care for the environment and preserve the usability of a river that flows through six cities. The foundation raises funds by using five different fundraising activities. Through a concentrated marketing campaign and providing visible results to the communities, the Save Sable River Foundation quickly became a popular local institution. After several years of successful fundraising, senior management requested an easy-to-read worksheet that shows lifetime fundraising amounts for each fundraising technique by city. In addition, they asked for a chart showing lifetime fundraising amounts because the president of the foundation likes to have a graphical representation that allows him quickly to identify stronger and weaker fundraising activities by city.

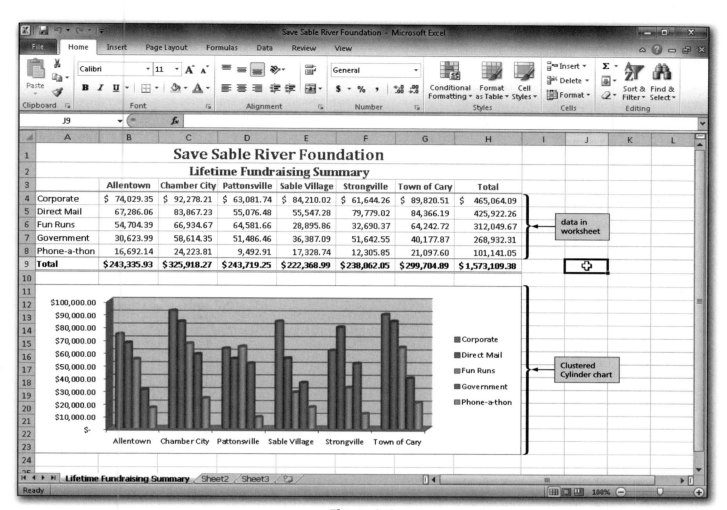

Figure 1–1

The first step in creating an effective worksheet is to make sure you understand what is required. The person or persons requesting the worksheet should supply their requirements in a requirements document. A **requirements document** includes a needs statement, a source of data, a summary of calculations, and any other special requirements for the worksheet, such as charting and Web support. Figure 1–2 on the following page shows the requirements document for the new workbook to be created in this chapter.

requirements document

REQUEST FOR NEW WORKBOOK

Date Submitted:	March 22, 2012
Submitted By:	Kevin Li
Worksheet Title:	Save Sable River Foundation Lifetime Fundraising Summary
Needs:	An easy-to-read worksheet that shows a summary of the Save Sable River Foundation's lifetime fundraising efforts for each city in which we operate (Allentown, Chamber City, Pattonsville, Sable Village, Strongville, and the Town of Cary). The worksheet also should include total funds raised for each city, total funds raised for each fundraising activity, and total lifetime funds raised.
Source of Data:	The data for the worksheet is available from the chief financial officer (CFO) of the Save Sable River Foundation.
Calculations:	The following calculations must be made for the worksheet: (a) total lifetime funds raised for each of the six cities; (b) total lifetime funds raised for each of the five fundraising activities; and (c) total lifetime funds raised for the organization.
Chart Requirements:	Below the data in the worksheet, construct a Clustered Cylinder chart that compares the total funds raised for each city within each type of fundraising activity.

Approvals

Approval Status:	X	Approved
		Rejected
Approved By:	Marsha Davis	
Date:	March 29, 2012	
Assigned To:	J. Quasney, Spreadsheet Specialist	

Figure 1–2

Overview

As you read this chapter, you will learn how to create the worksheet shown in Figure 1–1 on the previous page by performing these general tasks:

- Enter text in the worksheet
- Total data in the worksheet
- Format the text in the worksheet
- Insert a chart into the worksheet
- Identify the worksheet with a worksheet name
- Preview and print the worksheet

Plan Ahead

General Project Guidelines
While creating an Excel worksheet, you need to make several decisions that will determine the appearance and characteristics of the finished worksheet. As you create the worksheet shown in Figure 1–1, you should follow these general guidelines:

1. **Select titles and subtitles for the worksheet.** Follow the *less is more* guideline. The less text in the titles and subtitles, the more impact the titles and subtitles will have. Use the fewest words possible to specify the information presented in the worksheet to the intended audience.

(continued)

(continued)

2. **Determine the contents for rows and columns.** Rows typically contain information that is analogous to items in a list, such as the fundraising techniques used by an organization. Columns typically contain descriptive information about items in rows or contain information that helps to group the data in the worksheet, such as the locations in which the organization operates. Row headings and column headings are usually placed in alphabetical sequence, unless an alternative order is recommended in the requirements document.

3. **Determine the calculations that are needed.** You can decide to total data in a variety of ways, such as across rows or in columns. You also can include a grand total.

4. **Determine where to save the workbook.** You can store a workbook permanently, or **save** it, on a variety of storage media including a hard disk, USB flash drive, CD, or DVD. You also can indicate a specific location on the storage media for saving the workbook.

5. **Identify how to format various elements of the worksheet.** The overall appearance of a worksheet significantly affects its ability to communicate clearly. Examples of how you can modify the appearance, or format, of text include changing its shape, size, color, and position on the worksheet.

6. **Decide on the type of chart needed.** Excel can create many different types of charts, such as cylinder charts and pie charts. Each type of chart relays a different message about the data in the worksheet. Choose a type of chart that relays the message that you want to convey.

7. **Establish where to position and how to format the chart.** The position and format of the chart should command the attention of the intended audience. If possible, position the chart so that it prints with the worksheet data on a single page.

8. **Choose a name for the worksheet.** Each worksheet in a workbook should be named to clarify its purpose. A good worksheet name is succinct, unique to the workbook, and meaningful to any user of the workbook.

9. **Determine the best method for distributing the workbook.** Workbooks and worksheets can be distributed on paper or electronically. The decision regarding how to distribute workbooks and worksheets greatly depends on your intended audience. For example, a worksheet may be printed for inclusion in a report, or a workbook may be distributed using e-mail if the recipient intends to update the workbook.

When necessary, more specific details concerning the above guidelines are presented at appropriate points in the chapter. The chapter also will identify the actions performed and decisions made regarding these guidelines during the creation of the worksheet shown in Figure 1–1 on page EX 3.

Plan Ahead

BTW

Worksheet Development
The key to developing a useful worksheet is careful planning. Careful planning can reduce your effort significantly and result in a worksheet that is accurate, easy to read, flexible, and useful. When analyzing a problem and designing a worksheet solution, you should follow these steps: (1) define the problem, including need, source of data, calculations, charting, and Web or special requirements; (2) design the worksheet; (3) enter the data and formulas; and (4) test the worksheet.

After carefully reviewing the requirements document (Figure 1–2) and making the necessary decisions, the next step is to design a solution or draw a sketch of the worksheet based on the requirements, including titles, column and row headings, the location of data values, and the Clustered Cylinder chart, as shown in Figure 1–3 on the following page. The dollar signs, 9s, and commas that you see in the sketch of the worksheet indicate formatted numeric values.

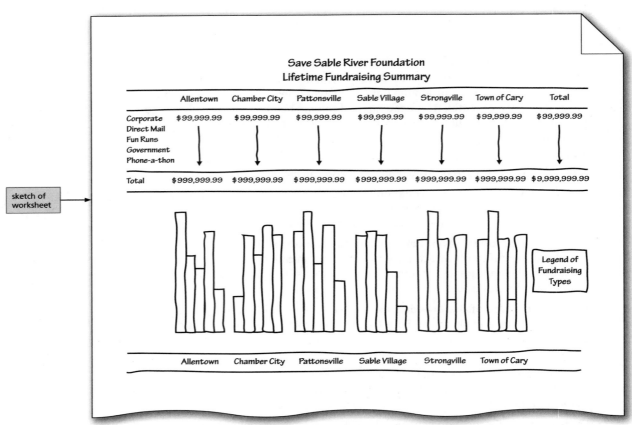

Figure 1–3

BTW

With a good understanding of the requirements document, an understanding of the necessary decisions, and a sketch of the worksheet, the next step is to use Excel to create the worksheet and chart.

To Start Excel

If you are using a computer to step through the project in this chapter and you want your screens to match the figures in this book, you should change your screen's resolution to 1024 × 768. For information about how to change a computer's resolution, refer to the Office 2010 and Windows 7 chapter at the beginning of this book.

The following steps, which assume Windows 7 is running, start Excel based on a typical installation. You may need to ask your instructor how to start Excel for your computer. For a detailed example of the procedure summarized below, refer to the Office 2010 and Windows 7 chapter.

① Click the Start button on the Windows 7 taskbar to display the Start menu.

② Type **Microsoft Excel** as the search text in the 'Search programs and files' text box and watch the search results appear on the Start menu.

③ Click Microsoft Excel 2010 in the search results on the Start menu to start Excel and display a new blank workbook in the Excel window.

④ If the Excel window is not maximized, click the Maximize button next to the Close button on its title bar to maximize the window.

Selecting a Cell

To enter data into a cell, you first must select it. The easiest way **to select a cell** (make it active) is to use the mouse to move the block plus sign mouse pointer to the cell and then click.

     An alternative method is to use the arrow keys that are located just to the right of the alphanumeric keys on a standard keyboard. An arrow key selects the cell adjacent to the active cell in the direction of the arrow on the key.

     You know a cell is selected, or active, when a heavy border surrounds the cell and the active cell reference appears in the Name box on the left side of the formula bar. Excel also changes the active cell's column heading and row heading to a gold color.

For an introduction to Office 2010 and instruction about how to perform basic tasks in Office 2010 programs, read the Office 2010 and Windows 7 chapter at the beginning of this book, where you can learn how to start a program, use the Ribbon, save a file, open a file, quit a program, use Help, and much more.

Entering Text

In Excel, any set of characters containing a letter, hyphen (as in a telephone number), or space is considered text. **Text** is used to place titles, such as worksheet titles, column titles, and row titles, on the worksheet.

Select titles and subtitles for the worksheet.
Worksheet titles and subtitles should be as brief and meaningful as possible. A worksheet title could include the name of the organization, department, or a description of the content of the worksheet. A worksheet subtitle, if included, could include a more detailed description of the content of the worksheet. Examples of worksheet titles are December 2010 Payroll and Year 2011 Projected Budget, and examples of subtitles are Marketing Department and Rent and Utilities, respectively.

Plan Ahead

Determine the contents of rows and columns.
As shown in Figure 1–4, data in a worksheet often is identified by row and column titles so that the user of a worksheet easily can identify the meaning of the data. Rows typically contain information that is similar to items in a list. Columns typically contain descriptive information about items in rows or contain information that helps to group the data in the worksheet. Examples of row titles are Product and Total, and examples of column titles are Name and Address.

Plan Ahead

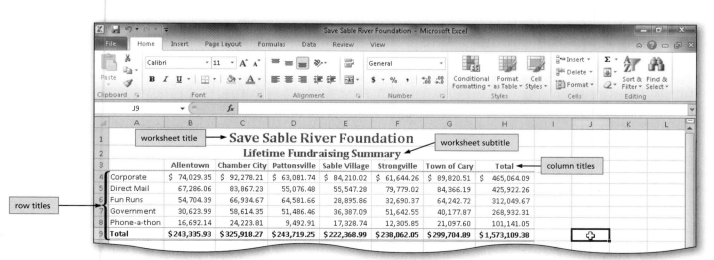

Figure 1–4

To Enter the Worksheet Titles

As shown in Figure 1–4 on the previous page, the worksheet title, Save Sable River Foundation, identifies the organization for which the worksheet is being created in Chapter 1. The worksheet subtitle, Lifetime Fundraising Summary, identifies the type of report.

The following steps enter the worksheet titles in cells A1 and A2. Later in this chapter, the worksheet titles will be formatted so they appear as shown in Figure 1–4.

1

- If necessary, click cell A1 to make cell A1 the active cell (Figure 1–5).

Q&A What if I make a mistake while typing?

If you type the wrong letter and notice the error before clicking the Enter box or pressing the ENTER key, use the BACKSPACE key to delete all the characters back to and including the incorrect letter. To cancel the entire entry before entering it into the cell, click the Cancel box in the formula bar or press the ESC key. If you see an error in a cell after entering the text, select the cell and retype the entry.

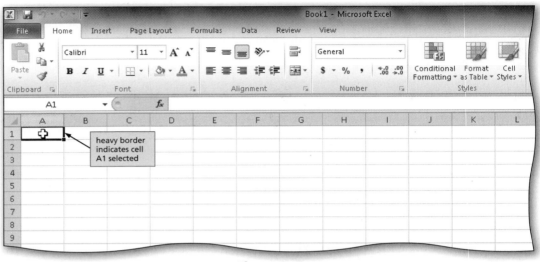

Figure 1–5

2

- Type **Save Sable River Foundation** in cell A1 and then point to the Enter box in the formula bar to prepare to enter text in the active cell (Figure 1–6).

Q&A Why did the appearance of the formula bar change?

Excel displays the title in the formula bar and in cell A1. When you begin typing a cell entry, Excel displays two additional boxes in the formula bar:

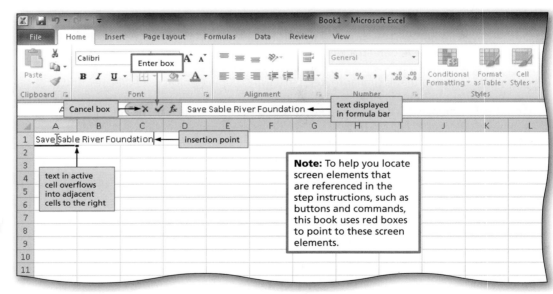

Figure 1–6

the Cancel box and the Enter box. Clicking the **Enter box** completes an entry. Clicking the **Cancel box** cancels an entry.

Q&A What is the vertical line in cell A1?

The text in cell A1 is followed by the insertion point. The **insertion point** is a blinking vertical line that indicates where the next typed character will appear.

3

• Click the Enter box to complete the entry and enter a worksheet title (Figure 1–7).

Q&A

Why does the entered text appear in three cells?

When the text is longer than the width of a column, Excel displays the overflow characters in adjacent cells to the right as long as those adjacent cells contain no data. If the adjacent cells contain data, Excel would hide the overflow characters. Excel displays the overflow characters in the formula bar whenever that cell is the active cell.

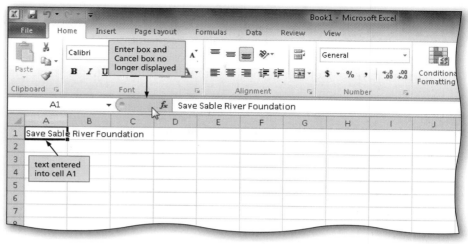

Figure 1–7

4

• Click cell A2 to select it.

• Type **Lifetime Fundraising Summary** as the cell entry.

• Click the Enter box to complete the entry and enter a worksheet subtitle (Figure 1–8).

Q&A

What happens when I click the Enter box?

When you complete an entry by clicking the Enter box, the insertion point disappears and the cell in which the text is entered remains the active cell.

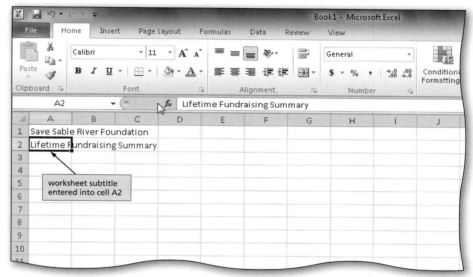

Figure 1–8

Other Ways
1. To complete entry, click any cell other than active cell
2. To complete entry, press ENTER
3. To complete entry, press HOME, PAGE UP, PAGE DOWN, or END
4. To complete entry, press UP ARROW, DOWN ARROW, LEFT ARROW, or RIGHT ARROW.

AutoCorrect

The **AutoCorrect feature** of Excel works behind the scenes, correcting common mistakes when you complete a text entry in a cell. AutoCorrect makes three types of corrections for you:

1. Corrects two initial capital letters by changing the second letter to lowercase.
2. Capitalizes the first letter in the names of days.
3. Replaces commonly misspelled words with their correct spelling. For example, it will change the misspelled word *recieve* to *receive* when you complete the entry. AutoCorrect will correct the spelling of hundreds of commonly misspelled words automatically.

BTW

Q&As
For a complete list of the Q&As found in many of the step-by-step sequences in this book, visit the Excel 2010 Q&A Web page (scsite.com/ex2010/qa).

To Enter Column Titles

The column titles in row 3 (Allentown, Chamber City, Pattonsville, Sable Village, Strongville, Town of Cary, and Total) identify the numbers in each column. In the case of the Save the Sable River Foundation data, the cities identify the funds raised using each fundraising type. The cities, therefore, are placed in columns. To enter the column titles in row 3, select the appropriate cell and then enter the text. The following steps enter the column titles in row 3.

1

• Click cell B3 to make it the active cell (Figure 1–9).

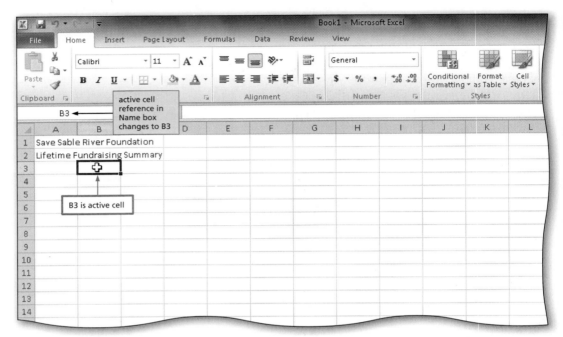

Figure 1–9

2

• Type **Allentown** to begin entry of a column title in the active cell (Figure 1–10).

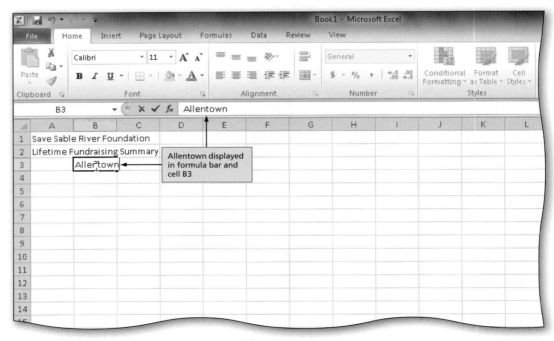

Figure 1–10

3

- Press the RIGHT ARROW key to enter a column title and make the cell to the right the active cell (Figure 1–11).

Q&A

Why is the RIGHT ARROW key used to complete the entry in the cell?

If the next entry you want to enter is in an adjacent cell, use the arrow keys to complete the entry in a cell. When you press an arrow key to complete an entry, the adjacent cell in the direction of the arrow (up, down, left, or right) becomes the active cell. If the next entry

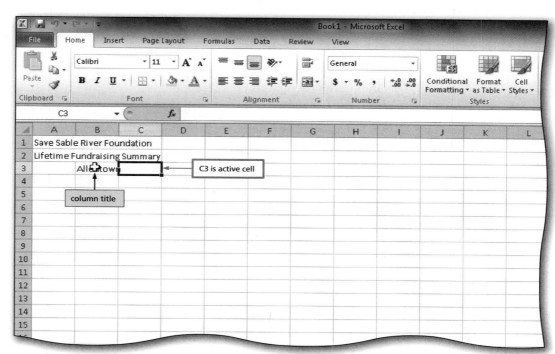

Figure 1–11

is in a nonadjacent cell, complete the current entry by clicking the next cell in which you plan to enter data. You also can click the Enter box or press the ENTER key and then click the appropriate cell for the next entry.

4

- Repeat Steps 2 and 3 to enter the remaining column titles; that is, enter **Chamber City** in cell C3, **Pattonsville** in cell D3, **Sable Village** in cell E3, **Strongville** in cell F3, **Town of Cary** in cell G3, and **Total** in cell H3 (complete the last entry in cell H3 by clicking the Enter box in the formula bar) (Figure 1–12).

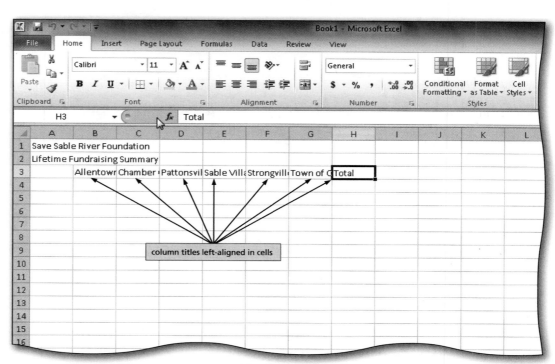

Figure 1–12

To Enter Row Titles

The next step in developing the worksheet for this project is to enter the row titles in column A. For the Save Sable River Foundation data, the list of fundraising activities meets the criterion that information that identifies columns be in a list. It is more likely that in the future, the organization will add more fundraising activities as opposed to more cities. Each fundraising activity, therefore, should be placed in its own row. The row titles in column A (Corporate, Direct Mail, Fun Runs, Government, Phone-a-thon, and Total) identify the numbers in each row.

This process for entering row titles is similar to the process for entering column titles. The following steps enter the row titles in the worksheet.

1

- Click cell A4 to select it.

- Type **Corporate** and then press the DOWN ARROW key to enter a row title and to make the cell below the current cell the active cell (Figure 1–13).

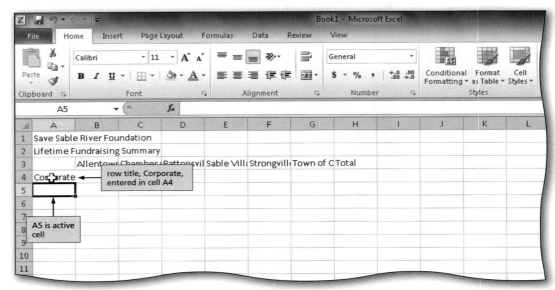

Figure 1–13

2

- Repeat Step 1 to enter the remaining row titles in column A; that is, enter **Direct Mail** in cell A5, **Fun Runs** in cell A6, **Government** in cell A7, **Phone-a-thon** in cell A8, and **Total** in cell A9 (Figure 1–14).

Q&A

Why is the text left-aligned in the cells?

When you enter text, Excel automatically left-aligns the text in the cell. Excel treats any combination of numbers, spaces, and nonnumeric characters as text. For example, Excel recognizes the following entries as text: 401AX21, 921–231, 619 321, 883XTY

You can change the text alignment in a cell by realigning it. Other alignment techniques are discussed later in this chapter.

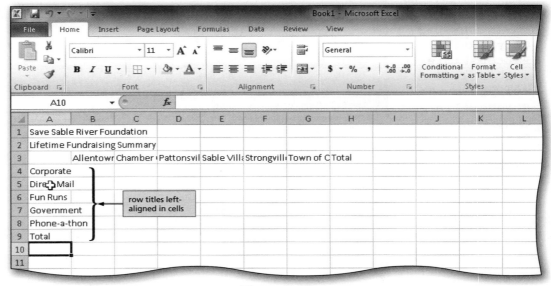

Figure 1–14

Entering Numbers

In Excel, you can enter numbers into cells to represent amounts. A **number** can contain only the following characters:

0 1 2 3 4 5 6 7 8 9 + - ( ) , / . $ % E e

If a cell entry contains any other keyboard character (including spaces), Excel interprets the entry as text and treats it accordingly. The use of the special characters is explained when they are used in this book.

BTW

Numeric Limitations
In Excel, a number can be between approximately −1 $\times 308^{10}$ and 1 $\times 308^{10}$. This means it can be between a negative 1 followed by 308 zeros and a positive 1 followed by 308 zeros. To enter a number such as 6,000,000,000,000,000, you can type 6,000,000,000,000,000, or you can type 6E15, which translates to 6 $\times$ 1015.

To Enter Numbers

The Save Sable River Foundation Lifetime Fundraising Summary numbers used in Chapter 1 are summarized in Table 1–1. These numbers, which represent lifetime fundraising amounts for each of the fundraising activities and cities, must be entered in rows 4, 5, 6, 7, and 8.

Table 1–1 Save Sable River Foundation Lifetime Fundraising Summary						
	Allentown	**Chamber City**	**Pattonsville**	**Sable Village**	**Strongville**	**Town of Cary**
Corporate	74029.35	92278.21	63081.74	84210.02	61644.26	89820.51
Direct Mail	67286.06	83867.23	55076.48	55547.28	79779.02	84366.19
Fun Runs	54704.39	66934.67	64581.66	28895.86	32690.37	64242.72
Government	30623.99	58614.35	51486.46	36387.09	51642.55	40177.87
Phone-a-thon	16692.14	24223.81	9492.91	17328.74	12305.85	21097.60

The following steps enter the numbers in Table 1–1 one row at a time.

1

- Click cell B4 to select it.

- Type 74029.35 and then press the RIGHT ARROW key to enter the data in the selected cell and make the cell to the right the active cell (Figure 1–15).

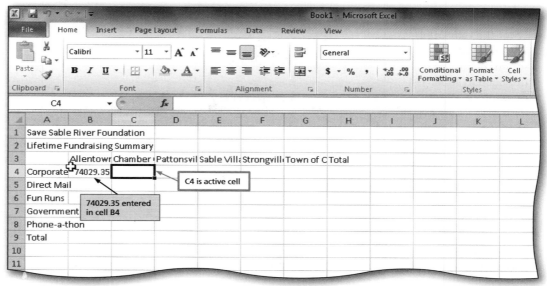

Figure 1–15

Q&A

Do I need to enter dollar signs, commas, or trailing zeros for the fundraising summary amounts?

You are not required to type dollar signs, commas, or trailing zeros. When you enter a dollar value that has cents, however, you must add the decimal point and the numbers representing the cents. Later in this chapter, the numbers will be formatted to use dollar signs, commas, and trailing zeros to improve the appearance and readability of the numbers.

2

- Enter 92278.21 in cell C4, 63081.74 in cell D4, 84210.02 in cell E4, 61644.26 in cell F4, and 89820.51 in cell G4 to complete the first row of numbers in the worksheet (Figure 1–16).

Q&A

Why are the numbers right-aligned?

When you enter numeric data in a cell, Excel recognizes the values as numbers and right-aligns the values in order to properly vertically align decimal and integer values. For example, values entered below those entered in this step automatically will be right-aligned as well so that the decimals of the values properly align.

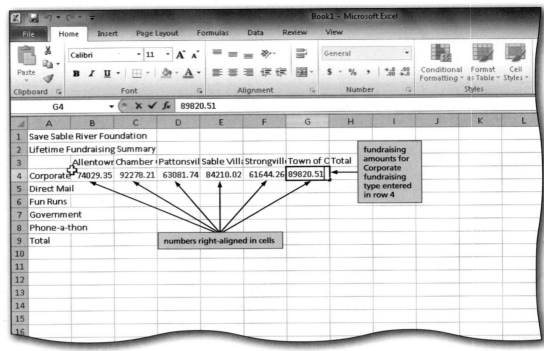

Figure 1–16

3

- Click cell B5 to select it and complete the entry in the previously selected cell.

- Enter the remaining lifetime fundraising summary numbers provided in Table 1–1 on page EX 13 for each of the four remaining fundraising activities in rows 5, 6, 7, and 8 to finish entering numbers in the worksheet (Figure 1–17).

Q&A

Why did clicking cell B5 complete the entry in cell G4?

Selecting another cell completes the entry in the previously selected cell in the same way as pressing the ENTER key, pressing an arrow key, or clicking the Enter box on the formula bar. In the next set of steps, the entry of the number in cell G4 will be completed by selecting another cell.

Figure 1–17

Calculating a Sum

The next step in creating the worksheet is to perform any necessary calculations, such as calculating the column and row totals.

To Sum a Column of Numbers

As stated in the requirements document in Figure 1–2 on page EX 4, totals are required for each city, each fundraising activity, and the organization. The first calculation is to determine the fundraising total for the fundraising activities in the city of Allentown in column B. To calculate this value in cell B9, Excel must add, or sum, the numbers in cells B4, B5, B6, B7, and B8. Excel's **SUM function**, which adds all of the numbers in a range of cells, provides a convenient means to accomplish this task.

A **range** is a series of two or more adjacent cells in a column or row or a rectangular group of cells. For example, the group of adjacent cells B4, B5, B6, B7, and B8 is called a range. Many Excel operations, such as summing numbers, take place on a range of cells.

After the total lifetime fundraising amount for the fundraising activities in the city of Allentown in column B is determined, the totals for the remaining cities and totals for each fundraising activity will be determined. The following steps sum the numbers in column B.

1

- Click cell B9 to make it the active cell and complete the entry in the previously selected cell.

- Click the Sum button (Home tab | Editing group) to display a formula in the formula bar and in the active cell (Figure 1–18).

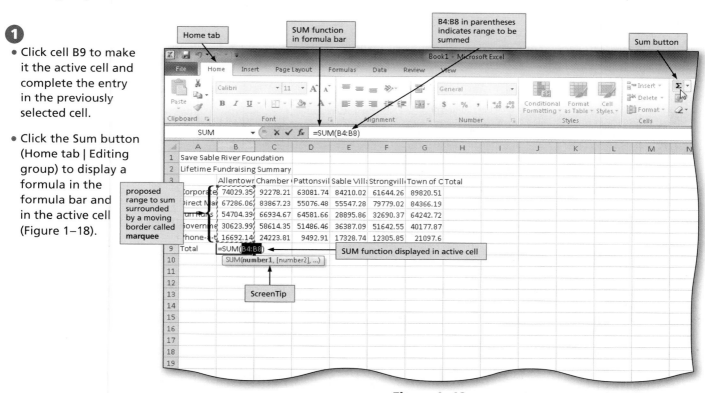

Figure 1–18

How does Excel know which cells to sum?

When you enter the SUM function using the Sum button, Excel automatically selects what it considers to be your choice of the range to sum. When proposing the range to sum, Excel first looks for a range of cells with numbers above the active cell and then to the left. If Excel proposes the wrong range, you can correct it by dragging through the correct range before pressing the ENTER key. You also can enter the correct range by typing the beginning cell reference, a colon (:), and the ending cell reference.

Calculating Sums
Excel calculates sums for a variety of data types. For example, Boolean values, such as TRUE and FALSE, can be summed. Excel treats the value of TRUE as 1 and the value of FALSE as 0. Times also can be summed. For example, Excel treats the sum of 1:15 and 2:45 as 4:00.

2

- Click the Enter box in the formula bar to enter a sum in the active cell (Figure 1–19).

What is the purpose of the Sum button arrow?

If you click the Sum button arrow on the right side of the Sum button (Home tab | Editing group) (Figure 1–19), Excel displays a list of often used functions from which you can choose. The list includes functions that allow you to determine the average, the number of items in the selected range, the maximum value, or the minimum value of a range of numbers.

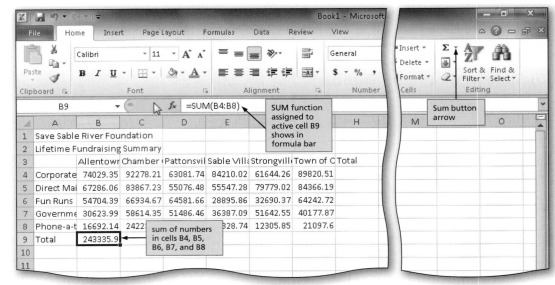

Figure 1–19

Other Ways

1. Click Insert Function button in the formula bar, select SUM in Select a function list, click OK button, select range, click OK button

2. Click Sum button arrow (Home tab | Editing group), click More Functions, select SUM (Insert Function dialog box), click OK button, select range, click OK button

3. Type = S in cell, select SUM from list, select range

4. Press ALT + EQUAL SIGN (=) twice

Entering Numbers as Text
Sometimes, you will want Excel to treat numbers, such as postal codes and telephone numbers, as text. To enter a number as text, start the entry with an apostrophe (').

Using the Fill Handle to Copy a Cell to Adjacent Cells

Excel also must calculate the totals for Chamber City in cell C9, Pattonsville in cell D9, Sable Village in cell E9, Strongville in cell F9, and the Town of Cary in cell G9. Table 1–2 illustrates the similarities between the entry in cell B9 and the entries required to sum the totals in cells C9, D9, E9, F9 and G9.

Table 1–2 Sum Function Entries in Row 9		
Cell	**Sum Function Entries**	**Remark**
B9	=SUM(B4:B8)	Sums cells B4, B5, B6, B7, and B8
C9	=SUM(C4:C8)	Sums cells C4, C5, C6, C7, and C8
D9	=SUM(D4:D8)	Sums cells D4, D5, D6, D7, and D8
E9	=SUM(E4:E8)	Sums cells E4, E5, E6, E7, and E8
F9	=SUM(F4:F8)	Sums cells F4, F5, F6, F7, and F8
G9	=SUM(G4:G8)	Sums cells G4, G5, G6, G7, and G8

To place the SUM functions in cells C9, D9, E9, F9, and G9, you could follow the same steps shown previously in Figures 1–18 on page EX 15 and 1–19. A second, more efficient method, however, is to copy the SUM function from cell B9 to the range C9:G9. The cell being copied is called the **source area** or **copy area**. The range of cells receiving the copy is called the **destination area** or **paste area**.

Although the SUM function entries in Table 1–2 are similar, they are not exact copies. The range in each SUM function entry uses cell references that are one column to the right of the previous column. When you copy formulas that include cell references, Excel automatically adjusts them for each new position, resulting in the SUM function entries illustrated in Table 1–2. Each adjusted cell reference is called a **relative reference**.

To Copy a Cell to Adjacent Cells in a Row

The easiest way to copy the SUM formula from cell B9 to cells C9, D9, E9, F9, and G9 is to use the fill handle. The **fill handle** is the small black square located in the lower-right corner of the heavy border around the active cell. The following steps use the fill handle to copy cell B9 to the adjacent cells C9:G9.

1

- With cell B9 active, point to the fill handle to activate it (Figure 1–20).

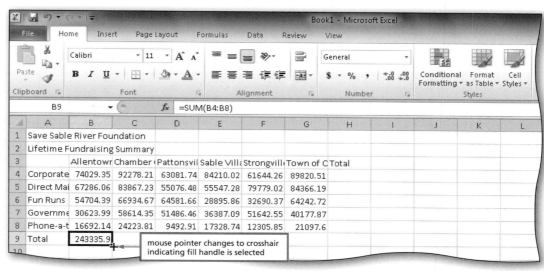

Figure 1–20

2

- Drag the fill handle to select the destination area, range C9:G9, to display a shaded border around the source area and the destination area (Figure 1–21). Do not release the mouse button.

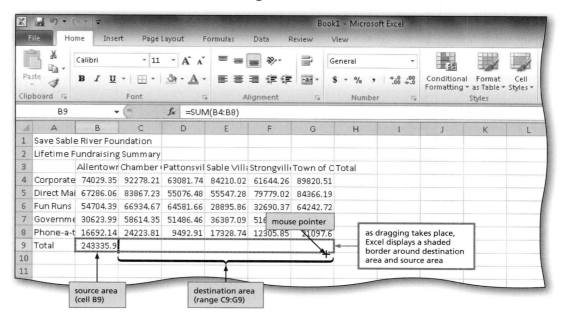

Figure 1–21

3

- Release the mouse button to copy the SUM function from the active cell to the destination area and calculate the sums (Figure 1–22).

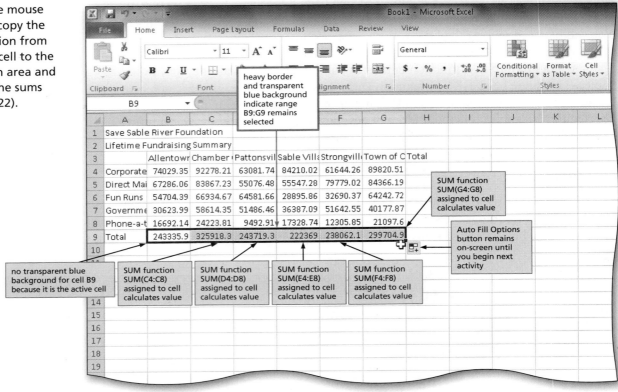

Figure 1–22

Q&A

What is the purpose of the Auto Fill Options button?

When you copy one range to another, Excel displays an Auto Fill Options button (Figure 1–22). The Auto Fill Options button allows you to choose whether you want to copy the values from the source area to the destination area with formatting, do so without formatting, or copy only the format. To view the available fill options, click the Auto Fill Options button. The Auto Fill Options button disappears when you begin another activity in Excel, such as typing data in another cell or applying formatting to a cell or range of cells.

Other Ways
1. Select source area, click Copy button (Home tab | Clipboard group), select destination area, click Paste button (Home tab | Clipboard group)
2. Right-click source area, click Copy on shortcut menu, right-click destination area, click Paste on shortcut menu
3. Select source area and then point to border of range; while holding down CTRL, drag source area to destination area

To Determine Multiple Totals at the Same Time

The next step in building the worksheet is to determine the lifetime fundraising totals for each fundraising activity and total lifetime fundraising for the organization in column H. To calculate these totals, you can use the SUM function much as it was used to total the lifetime fundraising amounts by city in row 9. In this example, however, Excel will determine totals for all of the rows at the same time. The following steps sum multiple totals at once.

1

- Click cell H4 to make it the active cell (Figure 1–23).

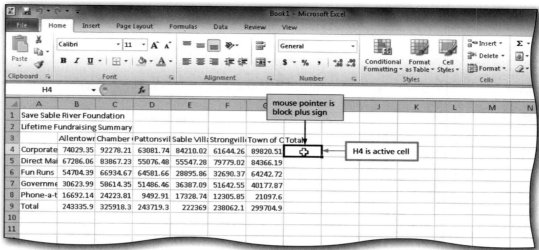

Figure 1–23

2

- With the mouse pointer in cell H4 and in the shape of a block plus sign, drag the mouse pointer down to cell H9 to highlight the range with a transparent view (Figure 1–24).

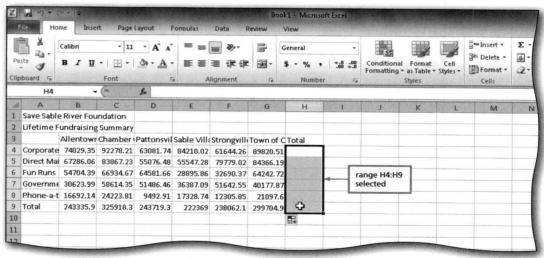

Figure 1–24

3

- Click the Sum button (Home tab | Editing group) to calculate and display the sums of the corresponding rows (Figure 1–25).

- Select cell A10 to deselect the selected range.

Q&A How does Excel create unique totals for each row?

If each cell in a selected range is next to a row of numbers, Excel assigns the SUM function to each cell when you click the Sum button.

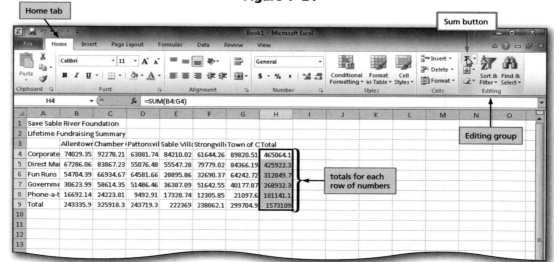

Figure 1–25

BTW

Organizing Files and Folders
You should organize and store files in folders so that you easily can find the files later. For example, if you are taking an introductory computer class called CIS 101, a good practice would be to save all Excel files in an Excel folder in a CIS 101 folder. For a discussion of folders and detailed examples of creating folders, refer to the Office 2010 and Windows 7 chapter at the beginning of this book.

To Save a Workbook

You have performed many tasks while creating this workbook and do not want to risk losing work completed thus far. Accordingly, you should save the workbook.

The following steps assume you already have created folders for storing your files, for example, a CIS 101 folder (for your class) that contains an Excel folder (for your assignments). Thus, these steps save the workbook in the Excel folder in the CIS 101 folder on a USB flash drive using the file name, Save Sable River Foundation. For a detailed example of the procedure summarized below, refer to the Office 2010 and Windows 7 chapter at the beginning of this book.

1 With a USB flash drive connected to one of the computer's USB ports, click the Save button on the Quick Access Toolbar to display the Save As dialog box.

2 Type `Save Sable River Foundation` in the File name text box to change the file name. Do not press the ENTER key after typing the file name because you do not want to close the dialog box at this time.

3 Navigate to the desired save location (in this case, the Excel folder in the CIS 101 folder [or your class folder] on the USB flash drive).

4 Click the Save button (Save As dialog box) to save the document in the selected folder on the selected drive with the entered file name.

Break Point: If you wish to take a break, this is a good place to do so. You can quit Excel. To resume at a later time, start Excel, open the file called Save Sable River Foundation, and continue following the steps from this location forward.

Formatting the Worksheet

The text, numeric entries, and functions for the worksheet now are complete. The next step is to format the worksheet. You **format** a worksheet to emphasize certain entries and make the worksheet easier to read and understand.

Figure 1–26a shows the worksheet before formatting. Figure 1–26b shows the worksheet after formatting. As you can see from the two figures, a worksheet that is formatted not only is easier to read but also looks more professional.

Plan Ahead

> **Identify how to format various elements of the worksheet.**
> By formatting the contents of the worksheet, you can improve its overall appearance. When formatting a worksheet, consider the following formatting suggestions:
>
> • **Increase the font size of cells.** An increased font size gives more impact to the text in a cell. In order to indicate their relative importance, worksheet titles should have the largest font size, followed by worksheet subtitles, and then column and row headings.
>
> • **Change the font color of cells.** Different cell colors help the reader of a worksheet quickly differentiate between the sections of a worksheet. Worksheet titles and subtitles easily should be identifiable from column and row headings. The overuse of too many colors, however, may be distracting to the reader of a worksheet.
>
> • **Center the worksheet titles, subtitles, and column headings.** Centering text in worksheet titles and subtitles over the portion of the worksheet that they represent helps the reader of a worksheet quickly to identify the information that is of interest to them.
>
> *(continued)*

(continued)

- **Modify column widths to best fit text in cells.** Make certain that text in a cell does not overflow into another cell. A column's width should be adjusted to accommodate the largest amount of text used in a cell in the column. Columns that contain data that is similar in nature to other columns should share the same column width.

- **Change the font style of cells.** Use a bold font style to make worksheet titles, worksheet subtitles, column headings, row heading, and totals stand out. Use italics and underline font styles judiciously, as specific rules of grammar apply to their use.

Plan
Ahead

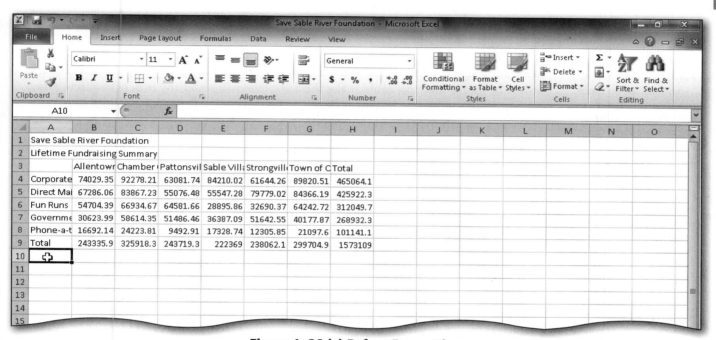

Figure 1–26 (a) Before Formatting

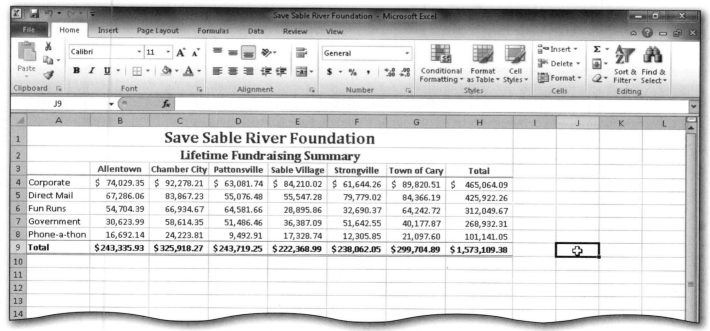

Figure 1–26 (b) After Formatting

To change the unformatted worksheet in Figure 1–26a on the previous page to the formatted worksheet in Figure 1–26b on the previous page, the following tasks must be completed:

1. Change the font, change the font style to bold, increase the font size, and change the font color of the worksheet titles in cells A1 and A2.
2. Center the worksheet titles in cells A1 and A2 across columns A through H.
3. Format the body of the worksheet. The body of the worksheet, range A3:H9, includes the column titles, row titles, and numbers. Formatting the body of the worksheet changes the numbers to use a dollars-and-cents format, with dollar signs in the first row (row 4) and the total row (row 9); adds underlining that emphasizes portions of the worksheet; and modifies the column widths to fit the text in the columns and make the text and numbers readable.

The remainder of this section explains the process required to format the worksheet. Although the formatting procedures are explained in the order described above, you should be aware that you could make these format changes in any order. Modifying the column widths, however, usually is done last because other formatting changes may affect the size of data in the cells in the column.

BTW

Fonts
In general, use no more than two font types in a worksheet because the use of more fonts can make a worksheet difficult to read.

BTW

Fonts and Themes
Excel uses default recommended fonts based on the workbook's theme. A theme is a collection of fonts and color schemes. The default theme is named Office, and the two default fonts for the Office theme are Calibri and Cambria. Excel, however, allows you to apply any font to a cell or range as long as the font is installed on your computer.

Font, Style, Size, and Color

The characters that Excel displays on the screen are a specific font, style, size, and color. The **font**, or font face, defines the appearance and shape of the letters, numbers, and special characters. Examples of fonts include Calibri, Cambria, Times New Roman, Arial, and Courier. **Font style** indicates how the characters are emphasized. Common font styles include regular, bold, underline, and italic. The **font size** specifies the size of the characters on the screen. Font size is gauged by a measurement system called points. A single point is about 1/72 of one inch in height. Thus, a character with a **point size** of 10 is about 10/72 of one inch in height. The **font color** defines the color of the characters. Excel can display characters in a wide variety of colors, including black, red, orange, and blue.

When Excel begins, the preset font for the entire workbook is Calibri, with a font size, font style, and font color of 11–point regular black. Excel allows you to change the font characteristics in a single cell, a range of cells, the entire worksheet, or the entire workbook.

To Change a Cell Style

Excel includes the capability of changing several characteristics of a cell, such the font, font size, and font color, all at once by assigning a predefined cell style to a cell. Using the predefined styles that Excel includes provides a consistent appearance to common portions of your worksheets, such as worksheet titles, worksheet subtitles, column headings, and total rows. The following steps assign the Title cell style to the worksheet title in cell A1.

1

- Click cell A1 to make cell A1 the active cell.

- Click the Cell Styles button (Home tab | Styles group) to display the Cell Styles gallery (Figure 1–27).

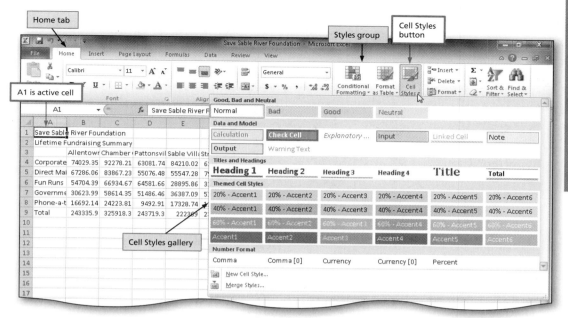

Figure 1–27

2

- Point to the Title cell style in the Titles and Headings area of the Cell Styles gallery to see a live preview of the cell style in the active cell (Figure 1–28).

Experiment

- Point to several other cell styles in the Cell Styles gallery to see a live preview of other cell styles in cell A1.

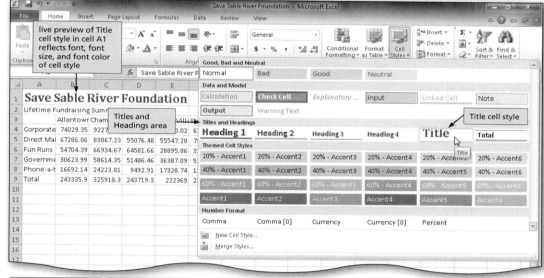

Figure 1–28

3

- Click the Title cell style to apply the cell style to the active cell (Figure 1–29).

Q&A

Why do several items in the Font group on the Ribbon change?

The changes to the Font box, Bold button, and Font Size box indicate the font changes applied to the active cell, cell A1, as a result of applying the Title cell style.

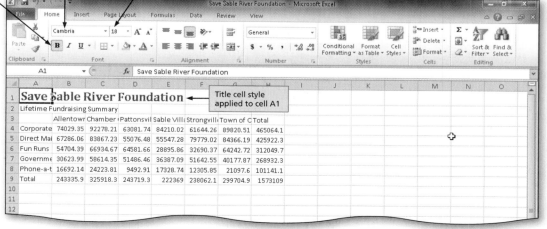

Figure 1–29

To Change the Font

Different fonts often are used in a worksheet to make it more appealing to the reader and to relate or distinguish data in the worksheet. The following steps change the worksheet subtitle's fonts from Calibri to Cambria.

1

- Click cell A2 to make it the active cell.

- Click the Font box arrow (Home tab | Font group) to display the Font gallery (Figure 1–30).

Q&A

Which fonts are displayed in the Font gallery?

Because many programs supply additional fonts beyond what comes with the Windows 7 operating system, the number of fonts available on your computer will depend on the programs installed. This book uses only fonts that come with the Windows 7 operating system and Microsoft Office 2010.

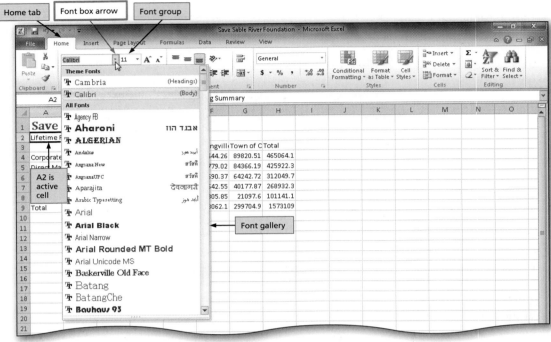

Figure 1–30

2

- Point to Cambria in the Theme Fonts area of the Font gallery to see a live preview of the selected font in the active cell (Figure 1–31).

Experiment

- Point to several other fonts in the Font gallery to see a live preview of other fonts in the selected cell.

Q&A

What is the Theme Fonts area?

Excel applies the same default theme to any new workbook that you start. A **theme** is a collection of cell styles and other styles that have common characteristics, such as a color scheme and font. The default theme for an Excel workbook is the Office theme. The Theme Fonts area of the Font gallery includes the fonts included in the default Office theme. Cambria is recommended for headings and Calibri is recommended by Microsoft for cells in the body of the worksheet (Figure 1–31).

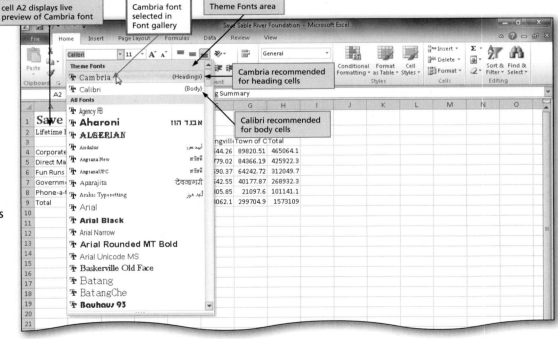

Figure 1–31

3

- Click Cambria in the Theme Fonts area to change the font of the worksheet subtitle to Cambria (Figure 1–32).

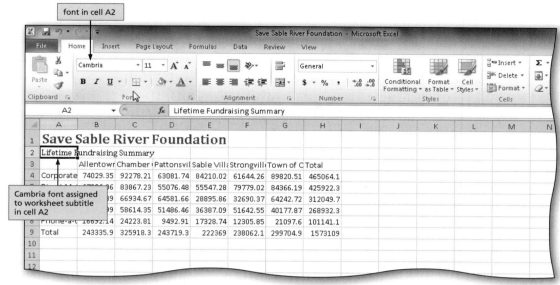

font in cell A2

Cambria font assigned to worksheet subtitle in cell A2

Figure 1–32

Other Ways

1. Click Font box arrow on Mini toolbar, click desired font in Font gallery

2. Right-click cell, click Format Cells on shortcut

   menu, click Font tab (Format Cells dialog box), click desired font, click OK button

To Bold a Cell

You **bold** an entry in a cell to emphasize it or make it stand out from the rest of the worksheet. The following step bolds the worksheet subtitle in cell A2.

1

- With cell A2 active, click the Bold button (Home tab | Font group) to change the font style of the active cell to bold (Figure 1–33).

Q&A What if a cell already includes a bold style?

If the active cell is already bold, then Excel displays the Bold button with a transparent orange background.

Q&A How do I remove the bold style from a cell?

Clicking the Bold button (Home tab | Font group) a second time removes the bold font style.

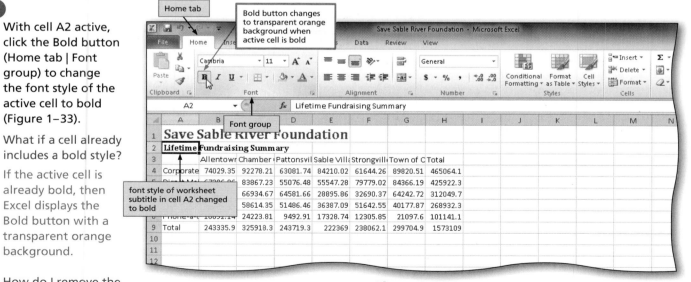

Home tab

Bold button changes to transparent orange background when active cell is bold

Font group

font style of worksheet subtitle in cell A2 changed to bold

Figure 1–33

Other Ways

1. Click Bold button on Mini toolbar

2. Right-click cell, click Format Cells on shortcut menu, click Font tab

   (Format Cells dialog box), click Bold, click OK button

3. Press CTRL+B

To Increase the Font Size of a Cell Entry

Increasing the font size is the next step in formatting the worksheet subtitle. You increase the font size of a cell so that the entry stands out and is easier to read. The following steps increase the font size of the worksheet subtitle in cell A2.

- With cell A2 selected, click the Font Size box arrow (Home tab | Font group) to display the Font Size list.

- Point to 14 in the Font Size list to see a live preview of the active cell with the selected font size (Figure 1–34).

 **Experiment**

- Point to several other font sizes in the Font Size list to see a live preview of other font sizes in the selected cell.

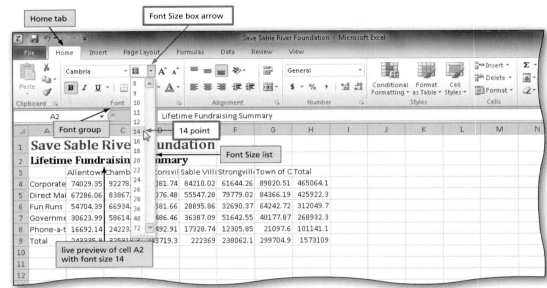

Figure 1–34

- Click 14 in the Font Size list to change the font size in the active cell (Figure 1–35).

Q&A

Can I assign a font size that is not in the Font Size list?

Yes. An alternative to clicking a font size in the Font Size list is to click the Font Size box (Home tab | Font group), type the font size, and then press the ENTER key. This procedure allows you to assign a font size not available in the Font Size list to a selected cell entry.

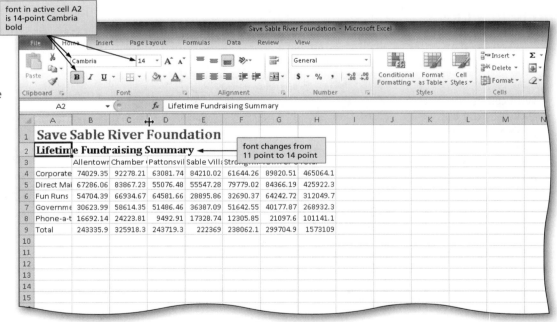

Figure 1–35

Other Ways

1. Click Increase Font Size button (Home tab | Font group) or Decrease Font Size button (Home tab | Font group)

2. Click Font Size box arrow on Mini toolbar, click desired font size in Font Size gallery

3. Right-click cell, click Format Cells on shortcut menu, click Font tab (Format Cells dialog box), select font size in Size box, click OK button

To Change the Font Color of a Cell Entry

The next step is to change the color of the font in cell A2 from black to dark blue. The following steps change the font color of a cell entry.

1

- With cell A2 selected, click the Font Color button arrow (Home tab | Font group) to display the Font Color gallery.

- Point to Dark Blue, Text 2 (dark blue color in column 4, row 1) in the Theme Colors area of the Font Color gallery to see a live preview of the font color in the active cell (Figure 1–36).

Experiment

- Point to several other colors in the Font Color gallery to see a live preview of other font colors in the active cell.

Q&A Which colors does Excel make available on the Font Color gallery?

You can choose from more than 60 different font colors on the Font Color gallery (Figure 1–36). Your Font Color gallery may have more or fewer colors, depending on color settings of your operating system. The Theme Colors area includes colors that are included in the current workbook's theme.

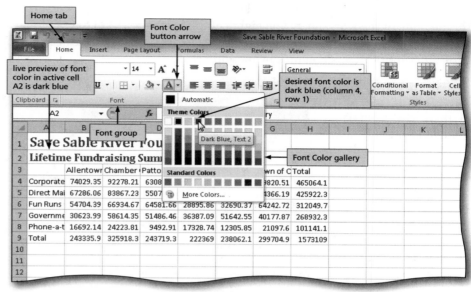

Figure 1–36

2

- Click Dark Blue, Text 2 (column 4, row 1) on the Font Color gallery to change the font of the worksheet subtitle in the active cell (Figure 1–37).

Q&A Why does the Font Color button change after I select the new font color?

When you choose a color on the Font Color gallery, Excel changes the Font Color button (Home tab | Font group) to the chosen color. Thus, to change the font color of the cell entry in another cell to the same color, you need only to select the cell and then click the Font Color button (Home tab | Font group).

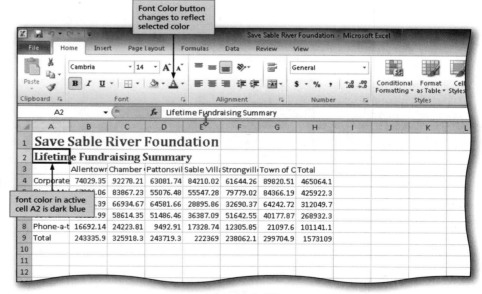

Figure 1–37

Other Ways

1. Click Font Color box arrow on Mini toolbar, click desired font color in the Font Color gallery

2. Right-click cell, click Format Cells on shortcut menu, click Font tab (Format Cells dialog box), select color in Font Color gallery, click OK button

To Center Cell Entries Across Columns by Merging Cells

The final step in formatting the worksheet title and subtitle is to center them across columns A through H. Centering a title across the columns used in the body of the worksheet improves the worksheet's appearance. To do this, the eight cells in the range A1:H1 are combined, or merged, into a single cell that is the width of the columns in the body of the worksheet. The eight cells in the range A2:H2 are merged in a similar manner. **Merging cells** involves creating a single cell by combining two or more selected cells. The following steps center the worksheet title and subtitle across columns by merging cells.

1
- Select cell A1 and then drag to cell H1 to highlight the range to be merged and centered (Figure 1–38).

Q&A What if a cell in the range B1:H1 contains data?

For the Merge & Center button (Home tab | Alignment group) to work properly, all the cells except the leftmost cell in the selected range must be empty.

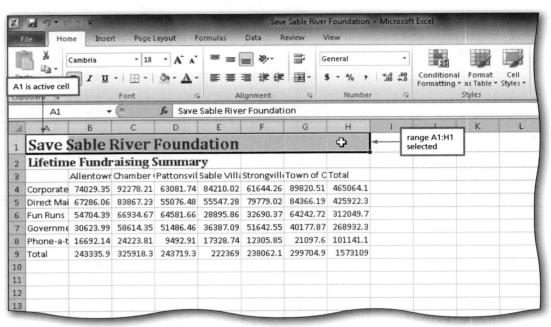

Figure 1–38

2
- Click the Merge & Center button (Home tab | Alignment group) to merge cells A1 through H1 and center the contents of the leftmost cell across the selected columns (Figure 1–39).

Q&A What happened to cells B1 through H1?

After the merge, cells B1 through H1 no longer exist. The new cell A1 now extends across columns A through H.

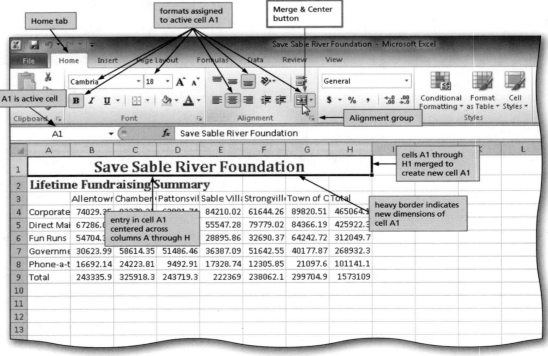

Figure 1–39

3

- Repeat Steps 1 and 2 to merge and center the worksheet subtitle across cells A2 through H2 (Figure 1–40).

Q&A

Are cells B1 through H1 and B2 through H2 lost forever?

No. The opposite of merging cells is **splitting a merged cell.** After you have merged multiple cells to create one merged cell, you can unmerge, or split, the merged cell to display the original cells on the worksheet. You split a merged cell by selecting it and clicking the Merge & Center button. For example, if you click the Merge & Center button a second time in Step 2, it will split the merged cell A1 into cells A1, B1, C1, D1, E1, F1, G1, and H1.

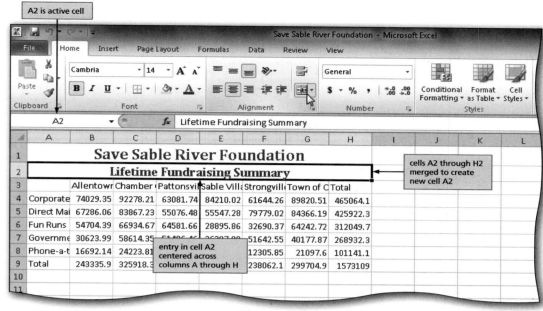

Figure 1–40

Other Ways
1. Right-click selection, click Merge & Center button on Mini toolbar 2. Right-click selection, click Format Cells on shortcut	menu, click Alignment tab (Format Cells dialog box), select Center Across Selection in Horizontal list, click OK button

To Format Column Titles and the Total Row

The next step to format the worksheet is to format the column titles in row 3 and the total values in row 9. Column titles and the total row should be formatted so anyone who views the worksheet quickly can distinguish the column titles and total row from the data in the body of the worksheet. The following steps format the column titles and total row using cell styles in the default worksheet theme.

1

- Click cell A3 and then drag the mouse pointer to cell H3 to select a range (Figure 1–41).

Q&A

Why is cell A3 selected in the range for the column headings?

The style to be applied to the column headings includes an underline that will help to distinguish the column headings from the rest of the worksheet. Including cell A3 in the range ensures that the cell will include the underline, which is visually appealing and further helps to separate the data in the worksheet.

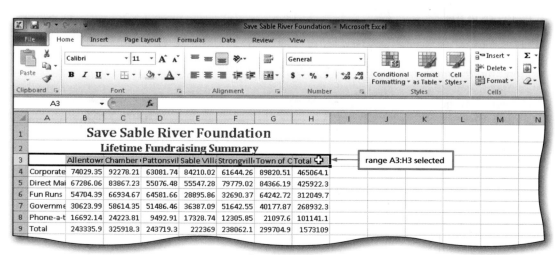

Figure 1–41

2

- Click the Cell Styles button (Home tab | Styles group) to display the Cell Styles gallery.

- Point to the Heading 3 cell style in the Titles and Headings area of the Cell Styles gallery to see a live preview of the cell style in the selected range (Figure 1–42).

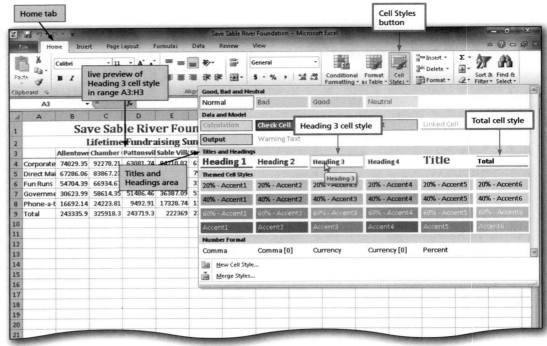

Figure 1–42

 Experiment

- Point to other cell styles in the Titles and Headings area of the Cell Styles gallery to see a live preview of other cell styles in the selected range, A3:H3.

3

- Click the Heading 3 cell style to apply the cell style to the selected range.

- Click the Center button (Home tab | Alignment group) to center the column headings in the selected range.

- Click cell A9 and then drag the mouse pointer to cell H9 to select a range (Figure 1–43).

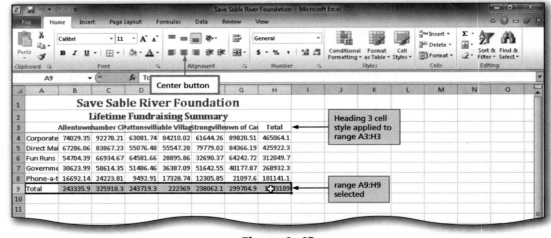

Figure 1–43

Q&A | Why should I choose Heading 3 instead of another heading cell style?

Excel includes many types of headings, such as Heading 1 and Heading 2, because worksheets often include many levels of headings above columns. In the case of the worksheet created for this project, the Heading 3 title includes formatting that makes the column titles' font size smaller than the title and subtitle and makes the column titles stand out from the data in the body of the worksheet.

4

- Click the Cell Styles button (Home tab | Styles group) to display the Cell Styles gallery and then click the Total cell style in the Titles and Headings area to apply the selected cell style to the cells in the selected range.

- Click cell A11 to select it (Figure 1–44).

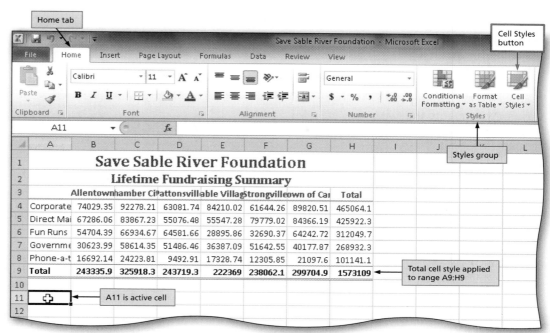

Figure 1–44

To Format Numbers in the Worksheet

As previously noted, the numbers in the worksheet should be formatted to use a dollar-and-cents format, with dollar signs in the first row (row 4) and the total row (row 9). Excel allows you to format numbers in a variety of ways, and these methods are discussed in other chapters in this book. The following steps use buttons on the Ribbon to format the numbers in the worksheet.

1

- Select cell B4 and drag the mouse pointer to cell H4 to select a range (Figure 1–45).

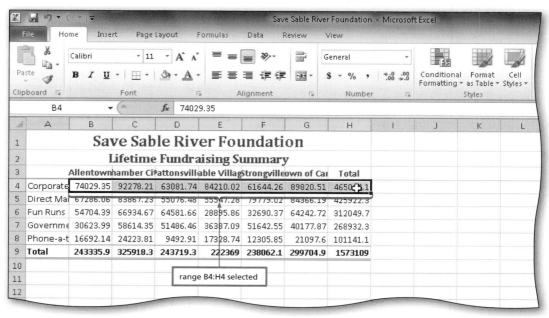

Figure 1–45

2

- Click the Accounting Number Format button (Home tab | Number group) to apply the Accounting Number format to the cells in the selected range.

- Select the range B5:H8 (Figure 1–46).

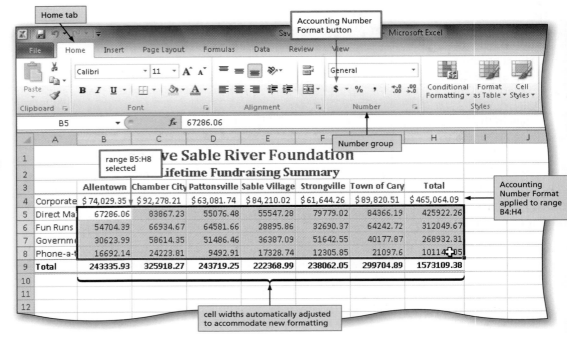

Figure 1–46

Q&A

What effect does the Accounting Number format have on the selected cells?

The Accounting Number format causes the cells to be displayed with two decimal places so that decimal places in cells below the selected cells align vertically. Cell widths are adjusted automatically to accommodate the new formatting.

3

- Click the Comma Style button (Home tab | Number group) to apply the Comma Style format to the selected range.

- Select the range B9:H9 to make it the active range (Figure 1–47).

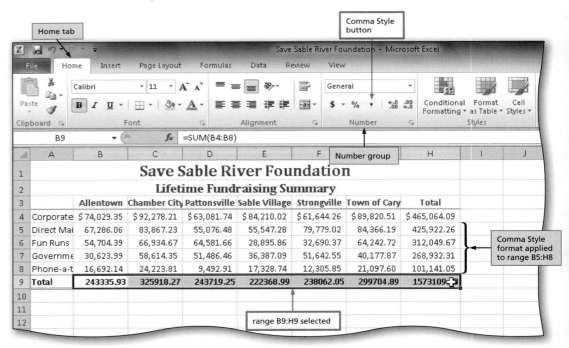

Figure 1–47

Q&A

What effect does the Comma Style format have on the selected cells?

The Comma Style format causes the cells to be displayed with two decimal places and commas as thousands separators.

4

- Click the Accounting Number Format button (Home tab | Number group) to apply the Accounting Number format to the cells in the selected range.

- Select cell A11 (Figure 1–48).

Q&A

Why did the column widths automatically adjust again?

Because the total row contains larger numbers, the Accounting Number format again causes the cell widths automatically to adjust to accommodate the new formatting just as occurred in Step 2.

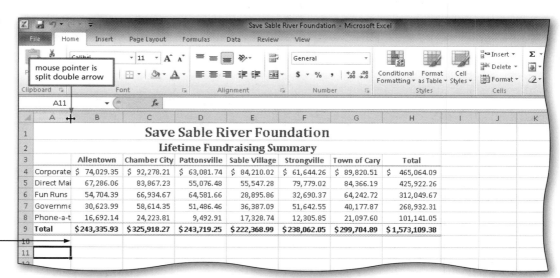

Figure 1–48

Other Ways

1. Click Accounting Number Format or Comma Style button on Mini toolbar

2. Right-click selection, click Format Cells on the shortcut menu, click

Number tab (Format Cells dialog box), select Accounting in Category list or select Number and click Use 1000 Separator, click OK button

To Adjust the Column Width

The last step in formatting the worksheet is to adjust the width of column A so that the word Phone-a-thon in cell A8 is shown in its entirety in the cell. Excel includes several methods for adjusting cell widths and row heights, and these methods are discussed later in this book. The following steps adjust the width of column A so that the contents of cell A8 are displayed in the cell.

1

- Point to the boundary on the right side of the column A heading above row 1 to change the mouse pointer to a split double arrow (Figure 1–49).

Figure 1–49

2

- Double-click on the boundary to adjust the width of the column to the width of the largest item in the column (Figure 1–50).

Q&A

What if none of the items in column A extends through the entire width of the column?

If all of the items in column A were shorter in length than the width of the column when you double-click the right side of the column A heading, then Excel still would adjust the column width to the largest item in the column. That is, Excel would reduce the width of the column to the largest item.

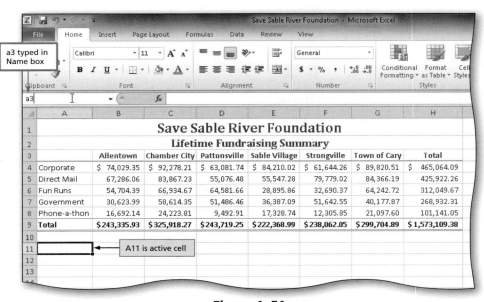

Figure 1–50

Using the Name Box to Select a Cell

The next step is to chart the lifetime fundraising amounts for the five fundraising activities used by the organization. To create the chart, you first must select the cell in the upper-left corner of the range to chart (cell A3). Rather than clicking cell A3 to select it, the next section describes how to use the Name box to select the cell.

To Use the Name Box to Select a Cell

The Name box is located on the left side of the formula bar. To select any cell, click the Name box and enter the cell reference of the cell you want to select. The following steps select cell A3 using the Name box.

1

- Click the Name box in the formula bar and then type **a3** as the cell you wish to select (Figure 1–51).

Q&A

Why is cell A11 still selected?

Even though cell A11 is the active cell, Excel displays the typed cell reference a3 in the Name box until you press the ENTER key.

Figure 1–51

2

• Press the ENTER key to change the active cell in the Name box (Figure 1–52).

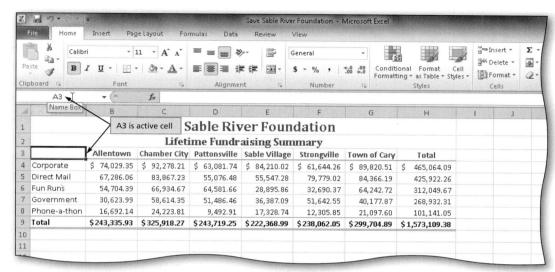

Figure 1–52

Other Ways to Select Cells

As you will see in later chapters, in addition to using the Name box to select any cell in a worksheet, you also can use it to assign names to a cell or range of cells. Excel supports several additional ways to select a cell, as summarized in Table 1–3.

Table 1–3 Selecting Cells in Excel	
Key, Box, or Command	**Function**
ALT+PAGE DOWN	Selects the cell one worksheet window to the right and moves the worksheet window accordingly.
ALT+PAGE UP	Selects the cell one worksheet window to the left and moves the worksheet window accordingly.
ARROW	Selects the adjacent cell in the direction of the arrow on the key.
CTRL+ARROW	Selects the border cell of the worksheet in combination with the arrow keys and moves the worksheet window accordingly. For example, to select the rightmost cell in the row that contains the active cell, press CTRL+RIGHT ARROW. You also can press the END key, release it, and then press the appropriate arrow key to accomplish the same task.
CTRL+HOME	Selects cell A1 or the cell one column and one row below and to the right of frozen titles and moves the worksheet window accordingly.
Find command on Find and Select menu or SHIFT+F5	Finds and selects a cell that contains specific contents that you enter in the Find and Replace dialog box. If necessary, Excel moves the worksheet window to display the cell. You also can press CTRL+F to display the Find dialog box.
Go To command on Find and Select menu or F5	Selects the cell that corresponds to the cell reference you enter in the Go To dialog box and moves the worksheet window accordingly. You also can press CTRL+G to display the Go To dialog box.
HOME	Selects the cell at the beginning of the row that contains the active cell and moves the worksheet window accordingly.
Name box	Selects the cell in the workbook that corresponds to the cell reference you enter in the Name box.
PAGE DOWN	Selects the cell down one worksheet window from the active cell and moves the worksheet window accordingly.
PAGE UP	Selects the cell up one worksheet window from the active cell and moves the worksheet window accordingly.

Break Point: If you wish to take a break, this is a good place to do so. Be sure to save the Save Sable River Foundation file again and then you can quit Excel. To resume at a later time, start Excel, open the file called Save Sable River Foundation, and continue following the steps from this location forward.

Adding a Clustered Cylinder Chart to the Worksheet

As outlined in the requirements document in Figure 1–2 on page EX 4, the worksheet should include a Clustered Cylinder chart to graphically represent the lifetime fundraising for each fundraising activity in which the organization engages. The Clustered Cylinder chart shown in Figure 1–53 is called an **embedded chart** because it is drawn on the same worksheet as the data.

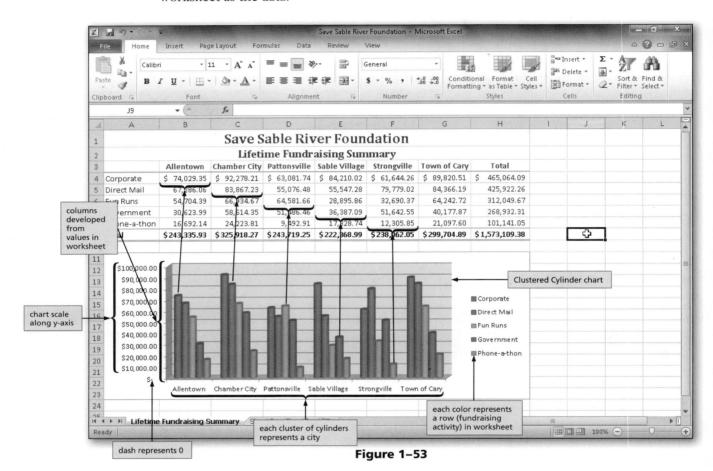

Figure 1–53

Plan Ahead	**Decide on the type of chart needed.**
	Excel includes 11 chart types from which you can choose, including column, line, pie, bar, area, X Y (scatter), stock, surface, doughnut, bubble, and radar. The type of chart you choose depends on the type of data that you have, how much data you have, and the message you want to convey.
	A line chart often is used to illustrate changes in data over time. Pie charts show the contribution of each piece of data to the whole, or total, of the data. Area charts, like line charts, illustrate changes over time, but often are used to compare more than one set of data and the area under the lines is filled in with a different color for each set of data. An X Y (scatter) chart is used much line a line chart, but each piece of data is represented by a dot and is not connected with a line. A stock chart provides a number of methods commonly

(continued)

(continued)

used in the financial industry to show stock market data. A surface chart compares data from three columns and/or rows in a three-dimensional manner. A doughnut chart is much like a pie chart, but a doughnut chart allows for comparing more than one set of data, resulting in a chart that looks like a doughnut, with each subsequent set of data surrounding the previous set. A bubble chart is much like an X Y (scatter) chart, but a third set of data results indicates how large each individual dot, or bubble, is on the chart. A radar chart can compare several sets of data in a manner that resembles a radar screen, with each set of data represented by a different color. A column or cylinder chart is a good way to compare values side by side. A Clustered Cylinder chart can go even further in comparing values across categories.

Establish where to position and how to format the chart.

- When possible, try to position charts so that both the data and chart appear on the screen on the worksheet together and so that the data and chart can be printed in the most readable manner possible.

- When choosing/selecting colors for a chart, consider the color scheme of the rest of the worksheet. The chart should not present colors that are in stark contrast to the rest of the worksheet. If the chart will be printed in color, minimize the amount of dark colors on the chart so that the chart both prints quickly and conserves ink.

Plan Ahead

BTW

Cell Values and Charting
When you change a cell value on which a chart is dependent, Excel redraws the chart instantaneously, unless automatic recalculation is disabled. If automatic recalculation is disabled, then you must press the F9 key to redraw the chart. To enable or disable automatic recalculation, click the Calculations Options button (Formulas tab | Calculation group).

In the case of the Save Sable River Foundation Lifetime Fundraising Summary, comparisons of fundraising activities within each city can be made side by side with a Clustered Cylinder chart. The chart uses differently colored cylinders to represent amounts raised for different fundraising activities. Each city uses the same color scheme for identifying fundraising activities, which allows for easy identification and comparison.

- For the city of Allentown, for example, the dark blue cylinder representing Corporate donations shows lifetime donations of $74,029.35

- For Chamber City, the maroon cylinder representing Direct Mail donations shows lifetime donations of $83,867.23

- For the city of Pattonsville, the lime green cylinder representing donations for Fun Runs shows lifetime donations of $64,581.66

- For Sable Village, the purple cylinder representing Government donations shows lifetime donations of $36,387.09

- For the city of Strongville, the light blue cylinder representing Phone-a-thon donations shows lifetime donations of $12,305.85

Because the same color scheme is used in each city to represent the five fundraising activities, you easily can compare funds raised by each fundraising activity among the cities. The totals from the worksheet are not represented, because the totals are not in the range specified for charting.

Excel derives the chart scale based on the values in the worksheet and then displays the scale along the vertical axis (also called the **y-axis** or **value axis**) of the chart. For example, no value in the range B4:G8 is less than 0 or greater than $100,000.00, so the scale ranges from 0 to $100,000.00. Excel also determines the $10,000.00 increments of the scale automatically. For the numbers along the y-axis, Excel uses a format that includes representing the 0 value with a dash (Figure 1–53).

To Add a Clustered Cylinder Chart to the Worksheet

The area on the worksheet where the chart appears is called the chart location. As shown in Figure 1–53 on page EX 36, the chart location in this worksheet is the range A11:G23; this range is immediately below the worksheet data. Placing the chart below the data on the Save Sable River Foundation Lifetime Fundraising Summary worksheet makes it easier to read the chart along with the data, and the chart and data easily can be printed on one sheet of paper.

The following steps draw a Clustered Cylinder chart that compares the funds raised by fundraising activity for the six cities.

1

- Click cell A3 and then drag the mouse pointer to cell G8 to select the range to be charted (Figure 1–54).

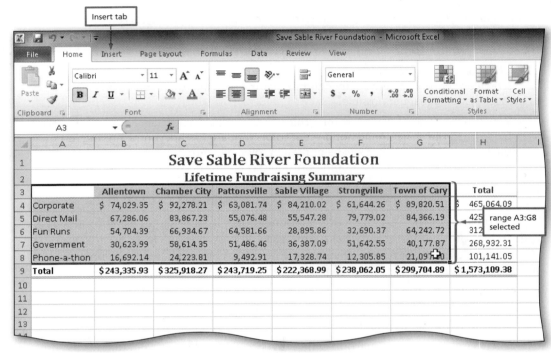

Figure 1–54

2

- Click Insert on the Ribbon to display the Insert tab (Figure 1–55).

Q&A

What tasks can I perform with the Insert tab?

The Insert tab includes commands that allow you to insert various objects, such as shapes, tables, illustrations, and charts, into a worksheet. These objects will be discussed as they are used throughout this book.

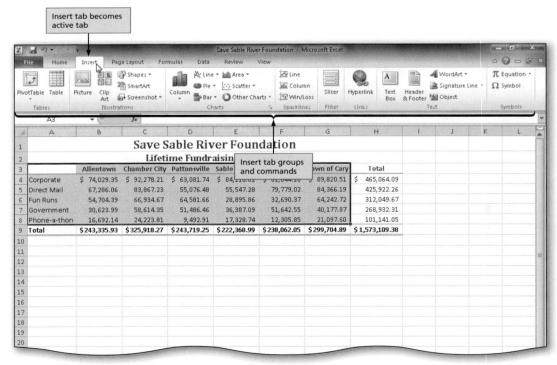

Figure 1–55

3

• Click the Column button (Insert tab | Charts group) to display the Column gallery (Figure 1–56).

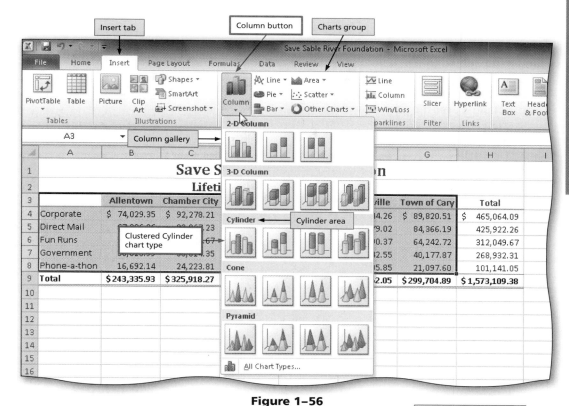

Figure 1–56

4

• Click the Clustered Cylinder chart type in the Cylinder area of the Column gallery to add the selected chart type to the middle of the worksheet in a selection rectangle.

• Press and hold down the mouse button while pointing to the upper-right edge of the selection rectangle to change the mouse pointer to a double two-headed arrow (Figure 1–57).

Q&A

Why is a new tab displayed on the Ribbon?

When you select objects such as shapes or charts, Excel displays contextual tabs that include special commands that are used to work

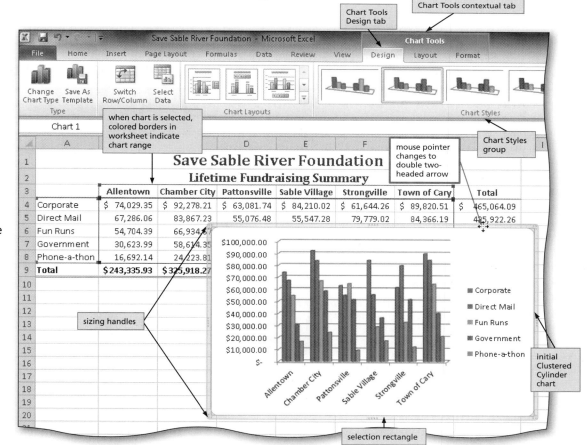

Figure 1–57

with the type of object selected. Because a chart is selected, Excel displays the Chart Tools contextual tab. The three tabs below the Chart Tools contextual tab, Design, Layout, and Format, are tabs that include commands to work with charts.

5

- Drag the chart down and to the left to position the upper-left corner of the dotted line rectangle over the upper-left corner of cell A11.

- Press and hold down the mouse button while pointing to the middle sizing handle on the right edge of the chart (Figure 1–58).

Q&A

How does Excel know which data to use to create the chart?

Excel automatically selects the entries in the topmost row of the chart range (row 3) as the titles for the horizontal axis (also called the **x-axis** or

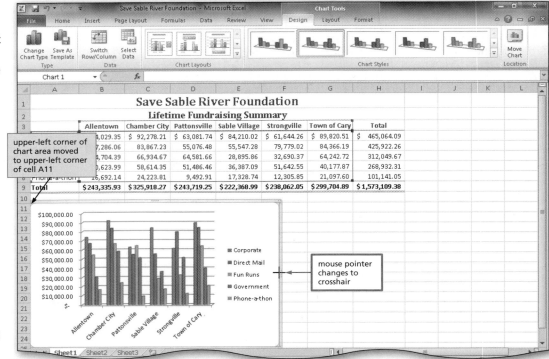

Figure 1–58

category axis) and draws a column for each of the 30 cells in the range containing numbers.

6

- While continuing to hold down the mouse button, press the ALT key and drag the right edge of the chart to the right edge of column H and then release the mouse button to resize the chart.

- Press and hold down the mouse button while pointing to the middle sizing handle on the bottom edge of the selection rectangle and do not release the mouse button (Figure 1–59).

Q&A

Why should I hold the ALT key down while I resize a chart?

Holding down the ALT key while you drag a chart **snaps** (aligns) the edge of the chart

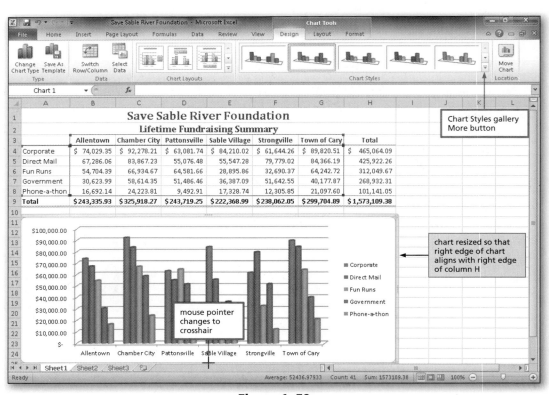

Figure 1–59

area to the worksheet gridlines. If you do not hold down the ALT key, then you can place an edge of a chart in the middle of a column or row.

7

• While continuing to hold down the mouse button, press the ALT key and drag the bottom edge of the chart up to the bottom edge of row 23 and then release the mouse button to resize the chart.

• If necessary, scroll the worksheet so that row 1 displays at the top of the worksheet.

• Click the More button in the Chart Styles gallery (Chart Tools Design tab | Chart Styles group) to expand the gallery (Figure 1–60).

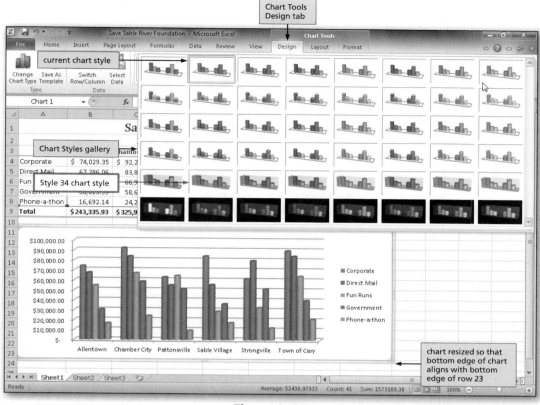

Figure 1–60

8

• Click Style 34 in the Chart Styles gallery (column 2, row 5) to apply the chart style to the chart.

• Click cell J9 to deselect the chart and complete the worksheet (Figure 1–61).

Q&A

What is the purpose of the items on the right side of the chart?

The items to the right of the column chart in Figure 1–61 are the **legend**, which identifies the colors assigned to each bar in the chart. Excel automatically selects the entries in the leftmost column of the chart range (column A) as titles within the legend.

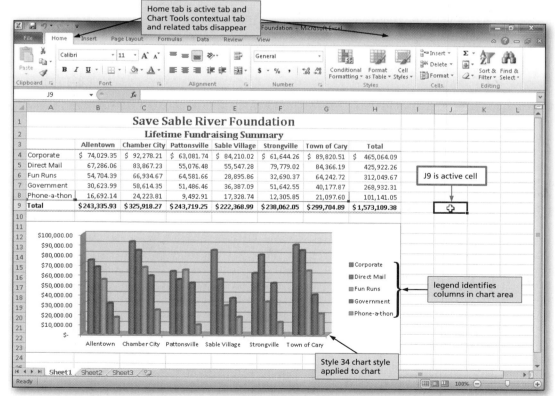

Figure 1–61

Changing the Worksheet Names

The sheet tabs at the bottom of the window allow you to view any worksheet in the workbook. You click the sheet tab of the worksheet you want to view in the Excel window. By default, Excel presets the names of the worksheets to Sheet1, Sheet2, and so on. The worksheet names become increasingly important as you move toward more sophisticated workbooks, especially workbooks in which you reference cells between worksheets.

Plan Ahead	**Choose a name for the worksheet.** Use simple, meaningful names for each worksheet. Worksheet names often match the worksheet title. If a worksheet includes multiple titles in multiple sections of the worksheet, use a name that encompasses the meaning of all of the sections.

To Change the Worksheet Names

Lifetime Fundraising Summary is a meaningful name for the Save Sable River Foundation Lifetime Fundraising Summary worksheet. The following steps rename worksheets by double-clicking the sheet tabs.

1

- Double-click the sheet tab labeled Sheet1 in the lower-left corner of the window.

- Type **Lifetime Fundraising Summary** as the worksheet name and then press the ENTER key to display the new worksheet name on the sheet tab (Figure 1–62).

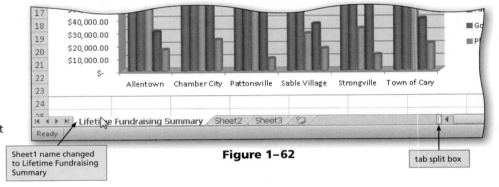

Figure 1–62

Q&A What is the maximum length for a worksheet tab?

Worksheet names can be up to 31 characters (including spaces) in length. Longer worksheet names, however, mean that fewer sheet tabs will show. To view more sheet tabs, you can drag the tab split box (Figure 1–62) to the right. This will reduce the size of the scroll bar at the bottom of the screen. Double-click the tab split box to reset it to its normal position.

2

- Right-click the sheet tab labeled Lifetime Fundraising Summary in the lower-left corner of the window to display a shortcut menu.

- Point to Tab Color on the shortcut menu to display the color gallery (Figure 1–63).

Q&A How can I quickly move between worksheet tabs?

You can use the tab scrolling buttons to the left of the sheet tabs (Figure 1–63) to move between worksheets. The leftmost and rightmost scroll buttons move to the first or last worksheet in the workbook. The two middle scroll buttons move one worksheet to the left or right.

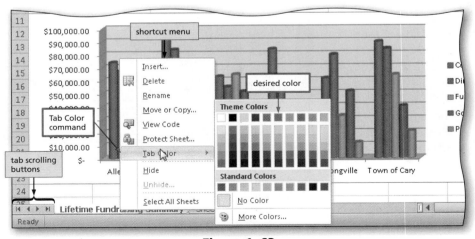

Figure 1–63

3

- Click Red, Accent 2 (column 6, row 1) in the Theme Colors area to change the color of the tab (Figure 1–64)

4

- If necessary, click Home on the Ribbon to display the Home tab.

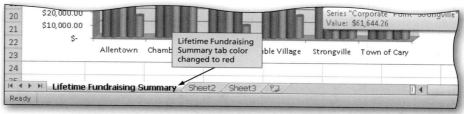

Figure 1–64

Changing Document Properties

Excel helps you organize and identify your files by using **document properties**, which are the details about a file. Document properties, also known as **metadata**, can include information such as the project author, title, subject, and keywords. A **keyword** is a word or phrase that further describes the document. For example, a class name or document topic can describe the file's purpose or content.

Document properties are valuable for a variety of reasons:

- Users can save time locating a particular file because they can view a document's properties without opening the document.
- By creating consistent properties for files having similar content, users can better organize their documents.
- Some organizations require Excel users to add document properties so that other employees can view details about these files.

Five different types of document properties exist, but the more common ones used in this book are standard and automatically updated properties. **Standard properties** are associated with all Microsoft Office documents and include author, title, and subject. **Automatically updated properties** include file system properties, such as the date you create or change a file, and statistics, such as the file size.

To Change Document Properties

The **Document Information Panel** contains areas where you can view and enter document properties. You can view and change information in this panel at any time while you are creating a workbook. Before saving the workbook again, you want to add your name and course information as document properties. The following steps use the Document Information Panel to change document properties.

1

- Click File on the Ribbon to open the Backstage view. If necessary, click the Info tab in the Backstage view to display the Info gallery (Figure 1–65).

Q&A

How do I close the Backstage view?

Click File on the Ribbon or click the preview of the document in the Info gallery to return to the Excel document window.

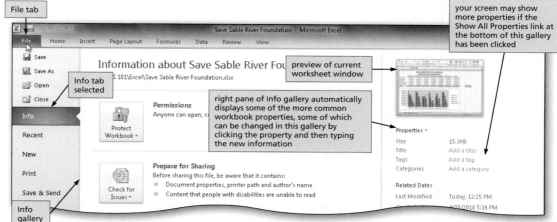

Figure 1–65

2

- Click the Properties button in the right pane of the Info gallery to display the Properties menu (Figure 1–66).

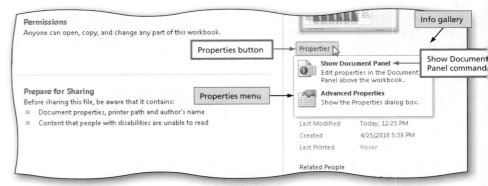

Figure 1–66

3

- Click Show Document Panel on the Properties menu to close the Backstage view and display the Document Information Panel in the Excel workbook window (Figure 1–67).

Q&A

Why are some of the document properties in my Document Information Panel already filled in?

The person who installed Microsoft Office 2010 on your computer or network may have set or customized the properties.

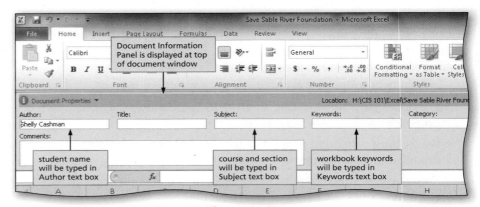

Figure 1–67

4

- Click the Author text box, if necessary, and then type your name as the Author property. If a name already is displayed in the Author text box, delete it before typing your name.

- Click the Subject text box, if necessary delete any existing text, and then type your course and section as the Subject property.

- If an AutoComplete dialog box appears, click its Yes button.

- Click the Keywords text box, if necessary delete any existing text, and then type **Lifetime Fundraising Summary** as the Keywords property (Figure 1–68).

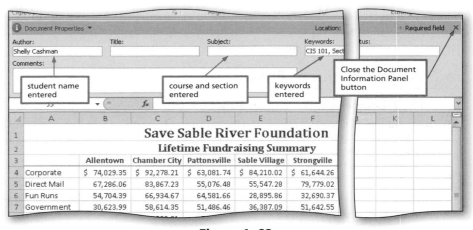

Figure 1–68

Q&A

What types of document properties does Excel collect automatically?

Excel records details such as time spent editing a workbook, the number of times a workbook has been revised, and the fonts and themes used in a workbook.

5

- Click the Close the Document Information Panel button so that the Document Information Panel no longer is displayed. If a dialog box is displayed, click the No button to close it.

Other Ways

1. Click File on Ribbon, click Info in the Backstage view, if necessary click Show All Properties link in Info gallery, click property to change and type new information, close the Backstage view

To Save an Existing Workbook with the Same File Name

You have made several modifications to the workbook since you last saved it. Thus, you should save it again. The following step saves the workbook again. For an example of the step listed below, refer to the Introduction to Office 2010 and Windows 7 chapter at the beginning of this book.

 Click the Save button on the Quick Access Toolbar to overwrite the previously saved file.

Previewing and Printing a Worksheet

After creating a worksheet, you may want to print it. Printing a worksheet enables you to distribute the worksheet to others in a form that can be read or viewed but typically not edited. It is a good practice to save a workbook before printing a worksheet, in the event you experience difficulties printing.

Determine the best method for distributing the worksheet.

The traditional method of distributing a worksheet uses a printer to produce a hard copy. A **hardcopy or printout** is information that exists on a physical medium such as paper. For users that can receive fax documents, you can elect to print a hard copy on a remote fax machine. Hard copies can be useful for the following reasons:

- Many people prefer proofreading a hard copy of a worksheet rather than viewing it on the screen to check for errors and readability.

- Hard copies can serve as reference material if your storage medium is lost or becomes corrupted and you need to re-create the worksheet.

Instead of distributing a hard copy of a worksheet, users can choose to distribute the worksheet as an electronic image that mirrors the original worksheet's appearance. The electronic image of the worksheet can be e-mailed, posted on a Web site, or copied to a portable storage medium such as a USB flash drive. Two popular electronic image formats, sometimes called fixed formats, are PDF by Adobe Systems and XPS by Microsoft. In Excel, you can create electronic image files through the Print tab in the Backstage view, the Save & Send tab in the Backstage view, and the Save As dialog box. Electronic images of worksheets, such as PDF and XPS, can be useful for the following reasons:

- Users can view electronic images of worksheets without the software that created the original worksheet (e.g., Excel). Specifically, to view a PDF file, you use a program called Acrobat Reader, which can be downloaded free from Adobe's Web site. Similarly, to view an XPS file, you use a program called an XPS Viewer, which is included in the latest versions of Windows and Internet Explorer.

- Sending electronic documents saves paper and printer supplies. Society encourages users to contribute to **green computing**, which involves reducing the environmental waste generated when using a computer.

To Preview and Print a Worksheet in Landscape Orientation

With the completed workbook saved, you may want to print it. Because the worksheet is included in a report, you will print a hard copy on a printer. The following steps print a hard copy of the contents of the Save Sable River Foundation Lifetime Fundraising Summary worksheet.

1

● Click File on the Ribbon to open the Backstage view.

● Click the Print tab in the Backstage view to display the Print gallery (Figure 1–69).

Q&A
How can I print multiple copies of my worksheet?

Increase the number in the Copies box in the Print gallery.

Q&A
What if I decide not to print the worksheet at this time?

Click File on the Ribbon to close the Backstage view and return to the Excel workbook window.

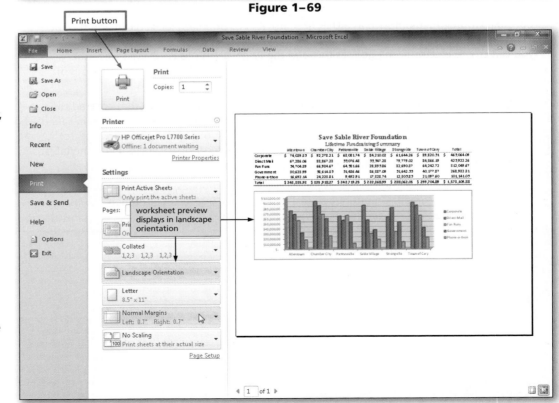

Figure 1–69

2

● Verify the printer name that appears on the Printer Status button will print a hard copy of the document. If necessary, click the Printer Status button to display a list of available printer options and then click the desired printer to change the currently selected printer.

3

● Click the Portrait Orientation button in the Settings area and then select Landscape Orientation to change the orientation of the page to landscape and view the entire worksheet on one page (Figure 1–70).

Figure 1–70

4

● Click the Print button in the Print gallery to print the worksheet in landscape orientation on the currently selected printer.

● When the printer stops, retrieve the hard copy (Figure 1–71).

Q&A Do I have to wait until my worksheet is complete to print it?

No, you can follow these steps to print a document at any time while you are creating it.

Q&A What if I want to print an electronic image of a worksheet instead of a hard copy?

You would click the Printer Status button in the Print gallery and then select the desired electronic image option such as a Microsoft XPS Document Writer, which would create an XPS file.

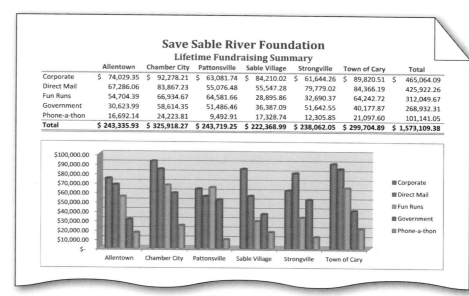

Figure 1–71

Other Ways
1. Press CTRL+P, press ENTER

To Quit Excel

This Save Sable River Foundation workbook now is complete. The following steps quit Excel if only one workbook is open. For a detailed example of the procedure summarized below, refer to the Office 2010 and Windows 7 chapter at the beginning of this book.

1 If you have one Excel workbook open, click the Close button on the right side of the title bar to close the document and quit Excel; or if you have multiple Excel workbooks open, click File on the Ribbon to open the Backstage view and then click the Exit button to close all open workbooks and quit Excel.

2 If a Microsoft Office Excel dialog box appears, click the Save button to save any changes made to the workbook since the last save.

Starting Excel and Opening a Workbook

Once you have created and saved a workbook, you may need to retrieve it from your storage medium. For example, you might want to revise a worksheet or reprint it. Opening a workbook requires that Excel is running on your computer.

To Start Excel

1 Click the Start button on the Windows 7 taskbar to display the Start menu.

2 Type **Microsoft Excel** as the search text in the 'Search programs and files' text box and watch the search results appear on the Start menu.

3 Click Microsoft Excel 2010 in the search results on the Start menu to start Excel and display a new blank workbook in the Excel window.

4 If the Excel window is not maximized, click the Maximize button next to the Close button on its title bar to maximize the window.

To Open a Workbook from Excel

Earlier in this chapter you saved your project on a USB flash drive using the file name, Save Sable River Foundation. The following steps open the Save Sable River Foundation file from the Excel folder in the CIS 101 folder on the USB flash drive. For a detailed example of the procedure summarized below, refer to the Office 2010 and Windows 7 chapter at the beginning of this book.

1 With your USB flash drive connected to one of the computer's USB ports, click File on the Ribbon to open the Backstage view.

2 Click Open in the Backstage view to display the Open dialog box.

3 Navigate to the location of the file to be opened (in this case, the USB flash drive, then to the CIS 101 folder [or your class folder], and then to the Excel folder). For a detailed example of this procedure, refer to Steps 3a–3c in the To Save a File in a Folder section in the Office 2010 and Windows 7 chapter at the beginning of this book.

4 Click Save Sable River Foundation to select the file to be opened.

5 Click the Open button (Open dialog box) to open the selected file and display the opened workbook in the Excel window.

AutoCalculate

You easily can obtain a total, an average, or other information about the numbers in a range by using the **AutoCalculate area** on the status bar. First, select the range of cells containing the numbers you want to check. Next, right-click the AutoCalculate area to display the Status Bar Configuration shortcut menu (Figure 1–72). The check mark to the left of the active functions (Average, Count, and Sum) indicates that the sum, count, and average of the selected range are displayed in the AutoCalculate area on the status bar. The functions of the AutoCalculate commands on the Status Bar Configuration shortcut menu are described in Table 1–4.

BTW

AutoCalculate
Use the AutoCalculate area on the status bar to check your work as you enter data in a worksheet. If you enter large amounts of data, you select a range of data and then check the AutoCalculate area to provide insight into statistics about the data you entered. Often, you will have an intuitive feel for whether the numbers are accurate or if you may have made a mistake while entering the data.

Table 1–4 AutoCalculate Shortcut Menu Commands	
Command	**Function**
Average	AutoCalculate area displays the average of the numbers in the selected range
Count	AutoCalculate area displays the number of nonblank cells in the selected range
Numerical Count	AutoCalculate area displays the number of cells containing numbers in the selected range
Minimum	AutoCalculate area displays the lowest value in the selected range
Maximum	AutoCalculate area displays the highest value in the selected range
Sum	AutoCalculate area displays the sum of the numbers in the selected range

To Use the AutoCalculate Area to Determine a Maximum

The following steps display the largest amounts of funds raised for any city for the Fun Runs fundraising activity.

1

• Select the range B6:G6 and then right-click the AutoCalculate area on the status bar to display the Customize Status Bar shortcut menu (Figure 1–72).

Q&A

What is displayed on the Customize Status Bar shortcut menu?

This shortcut menu includes several commands that allow you to control the items displayed on the Customize Status Bar shortcut menu. The AutoCalculate area includes six commands as well as the result of the associated calculation on the right side of the menu.

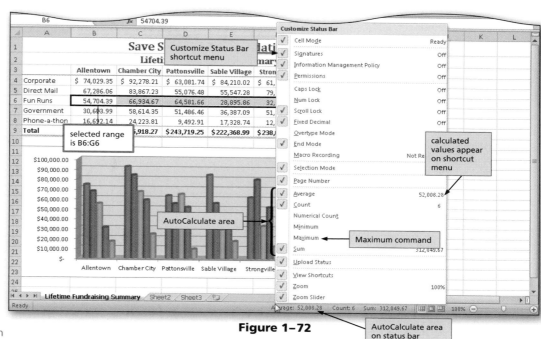

Figure 1–72

2

• Click Maximum on the shortcut menu to display the Maximum value in the range B6:G6 in the AutoCalculate area of the status bar.

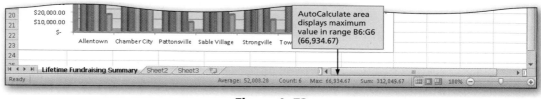

Figure 1–73

• Click anywhere on the worksheet to cause the shortcut menu to disappear (Figure 1–73).

3

• Right-click the AutoCalculate area and then click Maximum on the shortcut menu to cause the Maximum value to no longer appear in the AutoCalculate area.

• Click anywhere on the worksheet to cause the shortcut menu to disappear.

Correcting Errors

You can correct errors on a worksheet using one of several methods. The method you choose will depend on the extent of the error and whether you notice it while typing the data or after you have entered the incorrect data into the cell.

Correcting Errors While You Are Typing Data into a Cell

If you notice an error while you are typing data into a cell, press the BACKSPACE key to erase the incorrect characters and then type the correct characters. If the error is a major one, click the Cancel box in the formula bar or press the ESC key to erase the entire entry and then reenter the data from the beginning.

Correcting Errors After Entering Data into a Cell

If you find an error in the worksheet after entering the data, you can correct the error in one of two ways:

1. If the entry is short, select the cell, retype the entry correctly, and then click the Enter box or press the ENTER key. The new entry will replace the old entry.

2. If the entry in the cell is long and the errors are minor, using Edit mode may be a better choice than retyping the cell entry. Use the Edit mode as described below.

   a. Double-click the cell containing the error to switch Excel to Edit mode. In **Edit mode**, Excel displays the active cell entry in the formula bar and a flashing insertion point in the active cell (Figure 1–74). With Excel in Edit mode, you can edit the contents directly in the cell — a procedure called **in-cell editing**.

   b. Make changes using in-cell editing, as indicated below.

      (1) To insert new characters between two characters, place the insertion point between the two characters and begin typing. Excel inserts the new characters at the location of the insertion point.

      (2) To delete a character in the cell, move the insertion point to the left of the character you want to delete and then press the DELETE key or place the insertion point to the right of the character you want to delete and then press the BACKSPACE key. You also can use the mouse to drag through the character or adjacent characters you want to delete and then press the DELETE key or click the Cut button (Home tab | Clipboard group).

      (3) When you are finished editing an entry, click the Enter box or press the ENTER key.

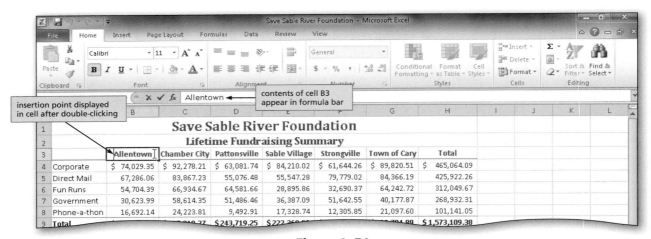

Figure 1–74

When Excel enters the Edit mode, the keyboard usually is in Insert mode. In **Insert mode**, as you type a character, Excel inserts the character and moves all characters to the right of the typed character one position to the right. You can change to Overtype mode by pressing the INSERT key. In **Overtype mode**, Excel overtypes, or replaces, the character to the right of the insertion point. The INSERT key toggles the keyboard between Insert mode and Overtype mode.

While in Edit mode, you may have reason to move the insertion point to various points in the cell, select portions of the data in the cell, or switch from inserting characters to overtyping characters. Table 1–5 summarizes the more common tasks performed during in-cell editing.

Table 1–5 Summary of In-Cell Editing Tasks

	Task	Mouse	Keyboard
1	Move the insertion point to the beginning of data in a cell.	Point to the left of the first character and click.	Press HOME
2	Move the insertion point to the end of data in a cell.	Point to the right of the last character and click.	Press END
3	Move the insertion point anywhere in a cell.	Point to the appropriate position and click the character.	Press RIGHT ARROW or LEFT ARROW
4	Highlight one or more adjacent characters.	Drag the mouse pointer through adjacent characters.	Press SHIFT+RIGHT ARROW or SHIFT+LEFT ARROW
5	Select all data in a cell.	Double-click the cell with the insertion point in the cell if there are no spaces in the data in the cell.	
6	Delete selected characters.	Click the Cut button (Home tab | Clipboard group)	Press DELETE
7	Delete characters to the left of the insertion point.		Press BACKSPACE
8	Delete characters to the right of the insertion point.		Press DELETE
9	Toggle between Insert and Overtype modes.		Press INSERT

BTW

Excel Help
At any time while using Excel, you can find answers to questions and display information about various topics through Excel Help. Used properly, this form of assistance can increase your productivity and reduce your frustrations by minimizing the time you spend learning how to use Excel. For instruction about Excel Help and exercises that will help you gain confidence in using it, read the Office 2010 and Windows 7 chapter at the beginning of this book.

Undoing the Last Cell Entry

Excel provides the Undo command on the Quick Access Toolbar (Figure 1–75), which allows you to erase recent cell entries. Thus, if you enter incorrect data in a cell and notice it immediately, click the Undo button and Excel changes the cell entry to what it was prior to the incorrect data entry.

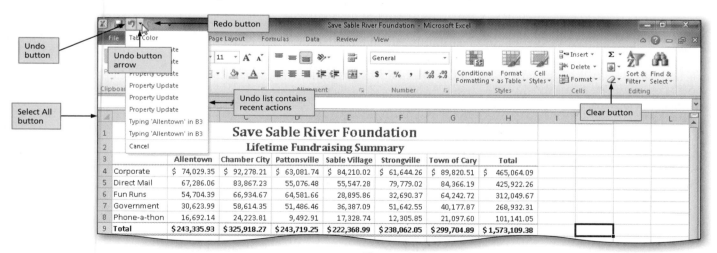

Figure 1–75

Excel remembers the last 100 actions you have completed. Thus, you can undo up to 100 previous actions by clicking the Undo button arrow to display the Undo list and then clicking the action to be undone (Figure 1–75). You can drag through several actions in the Undo list to undo all of them at once. If no actions are available for Excel to undo, then the Undo button is dimmed and inoperative.

The Redo button, next to the Undo button on the Quick Access Toolbar, allows you to repeat previous actions.

Clearing a Cell or Range of Cells

If you enter data into the wrong cell or range of cells, you can erase, or clear, the data using one of the first four methods listed below. The fifth method clears the formatting from the selected cells.

TO CLEAR CELL ENTRIES USING THE FILL HANDLE

1. Select the cell or range of cells and then point to the fill handle so the mouse pointer changes to a crosshair.
2. Drag the fill handle back into the selected cell or range until a shadow covers the cell or cells you want to erase. Release the mouse button.

TO CLEAR CELL ENTRIES USING THE SHORTCUT MENU

1. Select the cell or range of cells to be cleared.
2. Right-click the selection.
3. Click Clear Contents on the shortcut menu.

TO CLEAR CELL ENTRIES USING THE DELETE KEY

1. Select the cell or range of cells to be cleared.
2. Press the DELETE key.

TO CLEAR CELL ENTRIES AND FORMATTING USING THE CLEAR BUTTON

1. Select the cell or range of cells to be cleared.
2. Click the Clear button (Home tab | Editing group) (Figure 1–75 on the previous page).
3. Click Clear Contents on the menu.

TO CLEAR FORMATTING USING THE CELL STYLES BUTTON

1. Select the cell or range of cells from which you want to remove the formatting.
2. Click the Cell Styles button (Home tab | Styles group) and point to Normal.
3. Click Normal in the Cell Styles Gallery.

The Clear button (Home tab | Editing group) is the only command that clears both the cell entry and the cell formatting. As you are clearing cell entries, always remember that you should *never press the* SPACEBAR *to clear a cell.* Pressing the SPACEBAR enters a blank character. A blank character is text and is different from an empty cell, even though the cell may appear empty.

Clearing the Entire Worksheet

If the required worksheet edits are extremely extensive, you may want to clear the entire worksheet and start over. To clear the worksheet or delete an embedded chart, you would use the following steps.

TO CLEAR THE ENTIRE WORKSHEET

1. Click the Select All button on the worksheet (Figure 1–75).
2. Click the Clear button (Home tab | Editing group) and then click Clear All on the Clear menu to delete both the entries and formats.

The Select All button selects the entire worksheet. Instead of clicking the Select All button, you can press CTRL+A. To clear an unsaved workbook, click the workbook's Close Window button or click the Close button in the Backstage view. Click the No button if the Microsoft Excel dialog box asks if you want to save changes. To start a new, blank workbook, click the New button in the Backstage view.

BTW

Getting Back to Normal
If you accidentally assign unwanted formats to a range of cells, you can use the Normal cell style selection in the Cell Styles gallery. Click Cell Styles (Home tab | Styles group) and then click Normal in the Cell Styles gallery. Doing so changes the format to Normal style. To view the characteristics of the Normal style, right-click the style in the Cell Styles gallery and then click Modify or press ALT+APOSTROPHE (').

BTW

Certification
The Microsoft Office Specialist (MOS) program provides an opportunity for you to obtain a valuable industry credential — proof that you have the Excel 2010 skills required by employers. For more information, visit the Excel 2010 Certification Web page (scsite.com/ex2010/cert).

To delete an embedded chart, you would complete the following steps.

TO DELETE AN EMBEDDED CHART

1. Click the chart to select it.
2. Press the DELETE key.

To Quit Excel

The project now is complete. The following steps quit Excel. For a detailed example of the procedure summarized below, refer to the Office 2010 and Windows 7 chapter at the beginning of this book.

1 If you have one Excel workbook open, click the Close button on the right side of the title bar to close the document and quit Excel; or if you have multiple Excel workbooks open, click File on the Ribbon to open the Backstage view and then click Exit in the Backstage view to close all open workbooks and quit Excel.

2 If a Microsoft Office Excel dialog box appears, click the Save button to save any changes made to the document since the last save.

BTW

Quitting Excel
Do not forget to remove your USB flash drive from the USB port after quitting Excel, especially if you are working in a laboratory environment. Nothing can be more frustrating than leaving all of your hard work behind on a USB flash drive for the next user.

Chapter Summary

In this chapter you have learned how to enter text and numbers to create a worksheet, how to select a range, how to use the Sum button, format cells, insert a chart, and preview and print a worksheet. The items listed below include all the new Excel skills you have learned in this chapter.

1. To Start Excel (EX 6)
2. Enter the Worksheet Titles (EX 8)
3. Enter Column Titles (EX 10)
4. Enter Row Titles (EX 12)
5. Enter Numbers (EX 13)
6. Sum a Column of Numbers (EX 15)
7. Copy a Cell to Adjacent Cells in a Row (EX 17)
8. Determine Multiple Totals at the Same Time (EX 18)
9. Save a Workbook (EX 20)
10. Change a Cell Style (EX 22)
11. Change the Font (EX 24)
12. Bold a Cell (EX 25)
13. Increase the Font Size of a Cell Entry (EX 26)
14. Change the Font Color of a Cell Entry (EX 27)
15. Center Cell Entries Across Columns by Merging Cells (EX 28)
16. Format Column Titles and the Total Row (EX 29)
17. Format Numbers in the Worksheet (EX 31)
18. Adjust the Column Width (EX 33)
19. Use the Name Box to Select a Cell (EX 34)
20. Add a Clustered Cylinder Chart to the Worksheet (EX 38)
21. Change the Worksheet Names (EX 42)
22. Change Document Properties (EX 43)
23. Save an Existing Workbook with the Same File Name (EX 45)
24. Preview and Print a Worksheet in Landscape Orientation (EX 46)
25. Quit Excel (EX 47)
26. Start Excel (EX 47)
27. Open a Workbook from Excel (EX 48)
28. Use the AutoCalculate Area to Determine a Maximum (EX 49)
29. Clear Cell Entries Using the Fill Handle (EX 52)
30. Clear Cell Entries Using the Shortcut Menu (EX 52)
31. Clear Cell Entries Using the DELETE Key (EX 52)
32. Clear Cell Entries and Formatting Using the Clear Button (EX 52)
33. Clear Formatting Using the Cell Styles Button (EX 52)
34. Clear the Entire Worksheet (EX 52)
35. Delete an Embedded Chart (EX 53)

If you have a SAM 2010 user profile, your instructor may have assigned an autogradable version of this assignment. If so, log into the SAM 2010 Web site at www.cengage.com/sam2010 to download the instruction and start files.

Learn It Online

Test your knowledge of chapter content and key terms.

Instructions: To complete the Learn It Online exercises, start your browser, click the Address bar, and then enter the Web address **scsite.com/ex2010/learn**. When the Excel 2010 Learn It Online page is displayed, click the link for the exercise you want to complete and then read the instructions.

Chapter Reinforcement TF, MC, and SA
A series of true/false, multiple choice, and short answer questions that test your knowledge of the chapter content.

Flash Cards
An interactive learning environment where you identify chapter key terms associated with displayed definitions.

Practice Test
A series of multiple choice questions that test your knowledge of chapter content and key terms.

Who Wants To Be a Computer Genius?
An interactive game that challenges your knowledge of chapter content in the style of a television quiz show.

Wheel of Terms
An interactive game that challenges your knowledge of chapter key terms in the style of the television show *Wheel of Fortune*.

Crossword Puzzle Challenge
A crossword puzzle that challenges your knowledge of key terms presented in the chapter.

Apply Your Knowledge

Reinforce the skills and apply the concepts you learned in this chapter.

Changing the Values in a Worksheet
Instructions: Start Excel. Open the workbook Apply 1–1 Clothes Campus Third Quarter Expenses (Figure 1–76a). See the inside back cover of this book for instructions for downloading the Data Files for Students, or see your instructor for information on accessing the files required in this book.

1. Make the changes to the worksheet described in Table 1–6 so that the worksheet appears as shown in Figure 1–76b. As you edit the values in the cells containing numeric data, watch the totals in row 7, the totals in column F, and the chart change.

2. Change the worksheet title in cell A1 to the Title cell style and then merge and center it across columns A through F. Use buttons in the Font group on the Home tab on the Ribbon to change the worksheet subtitle in cell A2 to 16-point Cambria red, bold font and then center it across columns A through F. Use the Red, Accent 2 theme color (column 6, row 1 on the Font gallery) for the red font color.

3. Apply the worksheet name, Third Quarter Expenses, to the sheet tab and apply the Red, Accent 2 theme color to the sheet tab.

4. Change the document properties as specified by your instructor. Save the workbook using the file name, Apply 1–1 Clothed for Campus Third Quarter Expenses. Submit the revised workbook as specified by your instructor.

Table 1–6 New Worksheet Data	
Cell	**Change Cell Contents To**
A1	Clothed for Campus
B4	7829.50
C4	19057.83
D5	24217.92
E5	25859.62
E6	35140.84

(a) Before

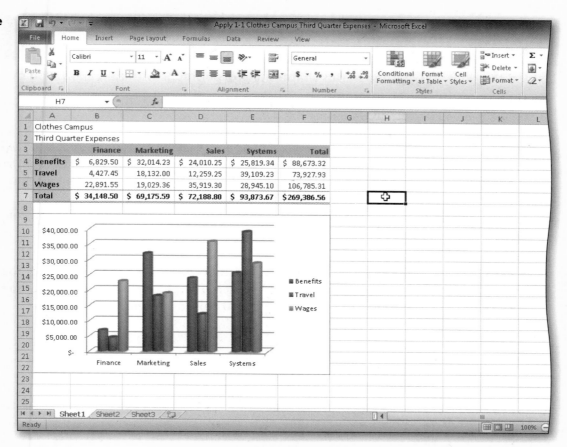

(b) After

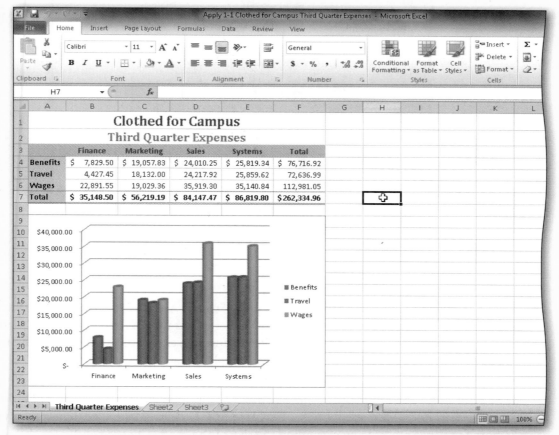

Figure 1–76

Extend Your Knowledge

Extend the skills you learned in this chapter and experiment with new skills. You may need to use Help to complete the assignment.

Formatting a Worksheet and Adding Additional Charts

Instructions: Start Excel. Open the workbook Extend 1–1 Pack Right Moving Supplies. See the inside back cover of this book for instructions for downloading the Data Files for Students, or see your instructor for information on accessing the files required in this book. Perform the following tasks to format cells in the worksheet and to add two charts to the worksheet.

1. Use the commands in the Font group on the Home tab on the Ribbon to change the font of the title in cell A1 to 22-point Arial Black, green, bold, and the subtitle of the worksheet to 14-point Arial, red, bold.

2. Select the range A3:G8, click the Insert tab on the Ribbon, and then click the Dialog Box Launcher in the Charts group on the Ribbon to open the Insert Chart dialog box. If necessary, drag the lower-right corner of the Insert Chart dialog box to expand it (Figure 1–77).

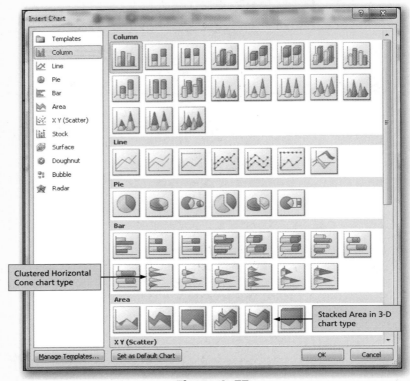

Figure 1–77

3. Insert a Stacked Area in 3-D chart by clicking the Stacked Area in 3-D chart in the gallery and then clicking the OK button. You may need to use the scroll box on the right side of the Insert Chart dialog box to view the Area charts in the gallery. Move the chart either below or to the right of the data in the worksheet. Click the Design tab and apply a chart style of your choice to the chart.

4. Deselect the chart and reselect the range A3:G8, and then follow Step 3 above to insert a Clustered Horizontal Cone chart in the worksheet. Move the chart either below or to the right of the data so that each chart does not overlap the Stacked Area in 3-D chart. Make sure to make the values on the horizontal axis readable by expanding the size of the chart. Choose a different chart style for this chart than the one you selected for the Stacked Area in 3-D chart.

5. Resize each chart so that each snaps to the worksheet gridlines. You may need to scroll the worksheet to resize and view the charts. Preview the worksheet.

6. Apply a worksheet name to the sheet tab and apply a color of your choice to the sheet tab.

7. Change the document properties as specified by your instructor. Save the workbook using the file name, Extend 1–1 Pack Right Moving Supplies Charts. Submit the revised workbook as specified by your instructor.

Make It Right

Analyze a workbook and correct all errors and/or improve the design.

Fixing Formatting Problems and Data Errors in a Worksheet

Instructions: Start Excel. Open the workbook Make It Right 1–1 Pets. See the inside back cover of this book for instructions for downloading the Data Files for Students, or see your instructor for information on accessing the files required for this book. Correct the following formatting problems and data errors (Figure 1–78) in the worksheet, while keeping in mind the guidelines presented in this chapter.

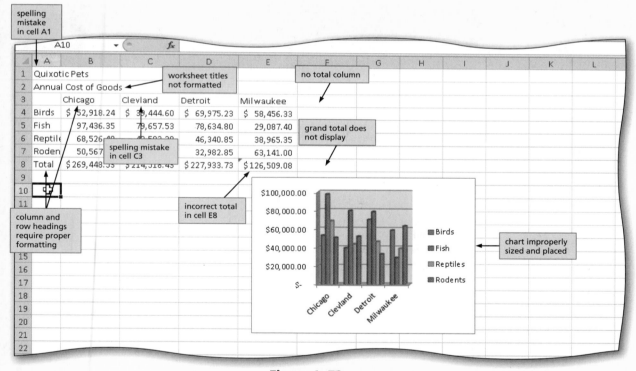

Figure 1–78

1. Merge and center the worksheet title and subtitle appropriately.

2. Format the worksheet title with a cell style appropriate for a worksheet title.

3. Format the subtitle using commands in the Font group on the Home tab on the Ribbon and apply the Red, Accent 2 color to the subtitle.

4. Correct the spelling mistake in cell A1 by changing Quixotic to Exotic. Correct the spelling mistake in cell C3 by changing Clevland to Cleveland.

Continued >

Make It Right *continued*

5. Add a column header for totals in column F and create the necessary totals in row 8.

6. Apply proper formatting to the column headers and total row, including centering the column headers.

7. Adjust the column sizes so that all data in each column is visible.

8. Create the grand total for the annual cost of goods.

9. The SUM function in cell E8 does not sum all of the numbers in the column. Correct this error by editing the range for the SUM function in the cell.

10. Resize and move the chart so that it is below the worksheet data and does not extend past the right edge of the worksheet data. Be certain to snap the chart to the worksheet gridlines by holding down the ALT key as you resize the chart to the right edge of column F and the bottom of row 22.

11. Apply a worksheet name to the sheet tab and apply the Aqua, Accent 5 color to the sheet tab.

12. Change the document properties as specified by your instructor. Save the workbook using the file name, Make It Right 1–1 Exotic Pets Annual Cost of Goods. Submit the revised workbook as specified by your instructor.

In the Lab

Design and/or create a workbook using the guidelines, concepts, and skills presented in this chapter. Labs 1, 2, and 3 are listed in order of increasing difficulty.

Lab 1: Annual Revenue Analysis Worksheet

Problem: You work as a spreadsheet specialist for A Healthy Body Shop, a high-end total fitness center franchise. Your manager has asked you to develop an annual revenue analysis worksheet similar to the one shown in Figure 1–79.

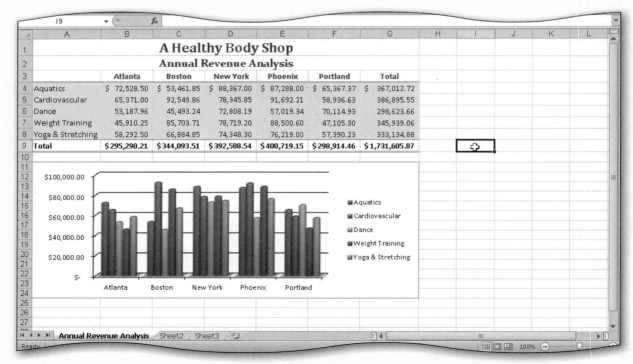

Figure 1–79

Instructions: Perform the following tasks.

1. Start Excel. Enter the worksheet title, A Healthy Body Shop, in cell A1 and the worksheet subtitle, Annual Revenue Analysis, in cell A2. Beginning in row 3, enter the franchise locations, fitness activities, and annual revenues shown in Table 1–7.

Table 1–7 A Healthy Body Shop Annual Revenues

	Atlanta	Boston	New York	Phoenix	Portland
Aquatics	72528.50	53461.85	88367.00	87288.00	65367.37
Cardiovascular	65371.00	92549.86	78345.85	91692.21	58936.63
Dance	53187.96	45493.24	72808.19	57019.34	70114.93
Weight Training	45910.25	85703.71	78719.20	88500.60	47105.30
Yoga & Stretching	58292.50	66884.85	74348.30	76219.00	57390.23

2. Create totals for each franchise location, fitness activity, and company grand total.

3. Format the worksheet title with the Title cell style. Center the title across columns A through G. Do not be concerned if the edges of the worksheet title are not displayed.

4. Format the worksheet subtitle to 14-point Constantia dark blue, bold font, and center it across columns A through G.

5. Use Cell Styles to format the range A3:G3 with the Heading 3 cell style, the range A4:G8 with the 40% - Accent 6 cell style, and the range A9:G9 with the Total cell style. Center the column headers in row 3. Apply the Accounting Number format to the range B4:G4 and the range B9:G9. Apply the Comma Style to the range B5:G8. Adjust any column widths to the widest text entry in each column.

6. Select the range A3:F8 and then insert a Clustered Cylinder chart. Apply the Style 26 chart style to the chart. Move and resize the chart so that it appears in the range A11:G24. If the labels along the horizontal axis (x-axis) do not appear as shown in Figure 1–79, then drag the right side of the chart so that it is displayed in the range A11:G24.

7. Apply the worksheet name, Annual Revenue Analysis, to the sheet tab and apply the Orange, Accent 6, Darker 25% color to the sheet tab. Change the document properties, as specified by your instructor.

8. Save the workbook using the file name Lab 1-1 A Healthy Body Shop Annual Revenue Analysis.

9. Preview and print the worksheet in landscape orientation.

10. Make the following two corrections to the sales amounts: 62,675.45 for New York Weight Training (cell D7), 67,238.56 for Portland Cardiovascular (cell F5). After you enter the corrections, the company totals in cell G8 should equal $1,723,864.05.

11. Preview and print the revised worksheet in landscape orientation. Close the workbook without saving the changes.

12. Submit the assignment as specified by your instructor.

In the Lab

Lab 2: Semiannual Sales Analysis Worksheet

Problem: As the chief accountant for Play 'em Again, a reseller of cell phones, DVDs, electronic games, MP3 players, and accessories, you have been asked by the vice president to create a worksheet to analyze the semiannual sales for the company by products across sales channels (Figure 1–80 on the following page). The sales channels and corresponding revenue by product for the year are shown in Table 1–8.

Continued >

In the Lab *continued*

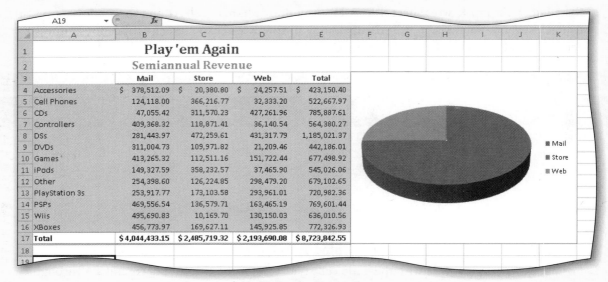

Figure 1–80

Instructions: Perform the following tasks.

1. Create the worksheet shown in Figure 1–80 using the data in Table 1–8.

2. Use the SUM function to determine total revenue for the three sales channels, the totals for each product, and the company total. Add column and row headings for the totals row and totals column, as appropriate.

Table 1–8 Play 'em Again Semiannual Revenue			
	Mail	Store	Web
Accessories	378512.09	20380.80	24257.51
Cell Phones	124118.00	366216.77	32333.20
CDs	47055.42	311570.23	427261.96
Controllers	409368.32	118871.41	36140.54
DSs	281443.97	472259.61	431317.79
DVDs	311004.73	109971.82	21209.46
Games	413265.32	112511.16	151722.44
iPods	149327.59	358232.57	37465.90
Other	254398.60	126224.85	298479.20
PlayStation 3s	253917.77	173103.58	293961.01
PSPs	469556.54	136579.71	163465.19
Wiis	495690.83	10169.70	130150.03
XBoxes	456773.97	169627.11	145925.85

3. Format the worksheet title with the Title cell style and center it across columns A through E. Use the Font group on the Ribbon to format the worksheet subtitle to 16-point Cambria red, bold font. Center the title across columns A through E.

4. Format the range B3:E3 with the Heading 3 cell style and center the text in the cells. Format the range A4:E16 with the 20% - Accent 4 cell style, and the range B9:E9 with the Total cell style. Format cells B4:E4 and B17:E17 with the Accounting Number Format and cells B5:E16 with the Comma Style numeric format.

5. Create a pie chart that shows the revenue contributions of each sales channel. Chart the sales channel names (B3:D3) and corresponding totals (B17:D17). That is, select the range B3:D3, and then while holding down the CTRL key, select the range B17:D17. Insert the Pie in 3-D chart, as shown in Figure 1–80, by using the Pie button (Insert tab | Charts group). Use the chart location F3: K17.

6. Apply the worksheet name, Semiannual Revenue, to the sheet tab and apply the Purple, Accent 4, Lighter 80% color to the sheet tab. Change the document properties, as specified by your instructor.

7. Save the workbook using the file name, Lab 1-2 Play 'em Again Semiannual Revenue. Print the worksheet in landscape orientation.

8. Two corrections to the figures were sent in from the accounting department. The correct revenue is $118,124.45 for Cell Phones sold through the mail (cell B5) and $43,573.67 for iPods sold over the Web (cell D11). After you enter the two corrections, the company total in cell E17 should equal $8,723,956.77. Print the revised worksheet in landscape orientation.

9. Use the Undo button to change the worksheet back to the original numbers in Table 1–8. Use the Redo button to change the worksheet back to the revised state.

10. Close Excel without saving the latest changes. Start Excel and open the workbook saved in Step 7. Double-click cell E6 and use in-cell editing to change the PSPs revenue (cell C14) to $128,857.32. Write the company total in cell E17 at the top of the first printout. Click the Undo button.

11. Click cell A1 and then click the Merge & Center button on the Home tab on the Ribbon to split cell A1 into cells A1, B1, C1, D1, and E1. To merge the cells into one again, select the range A1:E1 and then click the Merge & Center button.

12. Close the workbook without saving the changes. Submit the assignment as specified by your instructor.

In the Lab

Lab 3: Projected College Cash Flow Analysis Worksheet

Problem: Attending college is an expensive proposition and your resources are limited. To plan for your four-year college career, you have decided to organize your anticipated resources and expenses in a worksheet. The data required to prepare your worksheet is shown in Table 1–9.

Table 1–9 College Cost and Resources

Resources	Freshman	Sophomore	Junior	Senior
529 Plans	2700.00	2889.00	3091.23	3307.62
Financial Aid	5250.00	5617.50	6010.73	6431.48
Job	3100.00	3317.00	3549.19	3797.63
Parents	3700.00	3959.00	4236.13	4532.66
Savings	4250.00	4547.50	4865.83	5206.43
Other	1100.00	1177.00	1259.39	1347.55
Expenses	**Freshman**	**Sophomore**	**Junior**	**Senior**
Activities Fee	500.00	535.00	572.45	612.52
Books	650.00	695.50	744.19	796.28
Clothes	750.00	802.50	858.68	918.78
Entertainment	1650.00	1765.50	1889.09	2021.32
Room & Board	7200.00	7704.00	8243.28	8820.31
Tuition	8250.00	8827.50	9445.43	10106.60
Miscellaneous	1100.00	1177.00	1259.39	1347.55

Continued >

In the Lab *continued*

Instructions Part 1: Using the numbers in Table 1–9, create the worksheet shown in columns A through F in Figure 1–81. Format the worksheet title as Calibri 24-point bold purple. Merge and center the worksheet title in cell A1 across columns A through F. Format the worksheet subtitles in cells A2 and A11 as Calibri 16-point bold red. Format the ranges A3:F3 and A12:F12 with the Heading 2 cell style and center the text in the cells. Format the ranges A4:F9 and A13:F19 with the 20% - Accent 2 cell style, and the ranges A10:F10 and A20:F20 with the Total cell style.

Change the name of the sheet tab and apply the Purple color from the Standard Colors area to the sheet tab. Update the document properties, including the addition of at least one keyword to the properties, and save the workbook using the file name, Lab 1-3 Part 1 College Resources and Expenses. Print the worksheet. Submit the assignment as specified by your instructor.

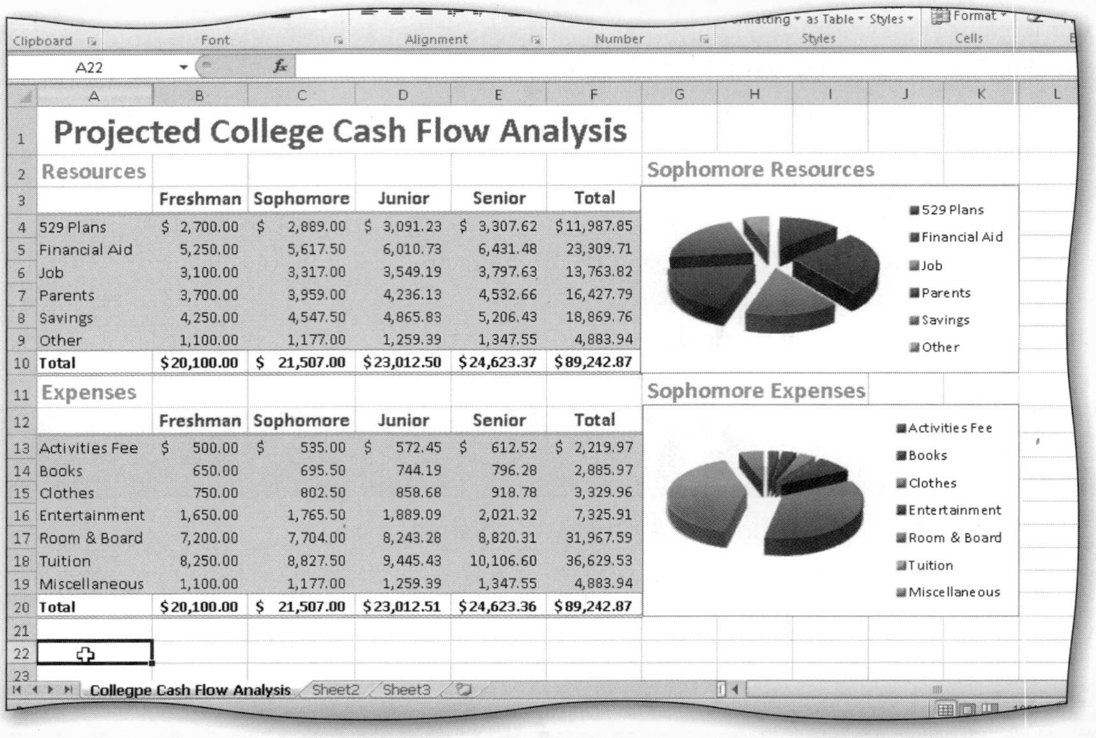

Figure 1–81

After reviewing the numbers, you realize you need to increase manually each of the Sophomore-year expenses in column C by $400, except for the Activities Fee. Change the Sophomore-year expenses to reflect this change. Manually change the Parents resources for the Sophomore year by the amount required to cover the increase in costs. The totals in cells F10 and F20 should equal $91,642.87. Print the worksheet. Close the workbook without saving changes.

Instructions Part 2: Open the workbook Lab 1-3 Part 1 College Resources and Expenses and then save the workbook using the file name, Lab 1-3 Part 2 College Resources and Expenses. Insert an Exploded pie in 3-D chart in the range G3:K10 to show the contribution of each category of resources for the Freshman year. Chart the range A4:B9 and apply the Style 26 chart style to the chart. Add the Pie chart title as shown in cell G2 in Figure 1–81. Insert an Exploded pie in 3-D chart in the range G12:K20 to show the contribution of each category of expenses for the Freshman year. Chart the range A13:B19 and apply the Style 26 chart style to the chart. Add the Pie chart title shown in cell G11 in Figure 1–81. Save the workbook. Print the worksheet in landscape orientation. Submit the assignment as specified by your instructor.

Instructions Part 3: Open the workbook Lab 1-3 Part 2 College Resources and Expenses and then save the workbook using the file name, Lab 1-3 Part 3 College Resources and Expenses. A close inspection of Table 1–9 shows that both cost and financial support figures increase 7% each year. Use Excel Help to learn how to enter the data for the last three years using a formula and the Copy and Paste buttons (Home tab | Clipboard group). For example, the formula to enter in cell C4 is =B4*1.07. Enter formulas to replace all the numbers in the range C4:E9 and C13:E19. If necessary, reformat the tables, as described in Part 1. The worksheet should appear as shown in Figure 1–81, except that some of the totals will be off by approximately 0.01 due to rounding errors. Save the workbook. Submit the assignment as specified by your instructor. Close the workbook without saving changes.

Cases and Places

Apply your creative thinking and problem solving skills to design and implement a solution.

1: Analyzing Quarterly Expenses

Academic

To estimate the funds needed by your school's Travel Club to make it through the upcoming quarter, you decide to create a report for the club itemizing the expected quarterly expenses. The anticipated expenses are listed in Table 1–10. Use the concepts and techniques presented in this chapter to create the worksheet and an embedded Clustered Cylinder chart. Be sure to use an appropriate chart style that compares the quarterly cost of each expense. Total each expense item and each quarter. Include a grand total for all of the expenses. Use the AutoCalculate area to determine the average amount spent per quarter on each expense. Manually insert the averages with appropriate titles in an appropriate area on the worksheet.

Table 1–10 Travel Club Quarterly Expenses				
	1st Quarter	2nd Quarter	3rd Quarter	4th Quarter
Copies and Supplies	75	50	80	150
Meeting Room Rent	400	425	400	425
Miscellaneous	150	100	175	70
Refreshments	130	155	150	225
Speaker Fees	200	200	400	500
Travel	450	375	500	375

2: Create an Exploded Pie in 3-D Chart to Summarize Property Values

Personal

Your wealthy Aunt Nicole owns several properties of varying value. She would like to see the values of the properties in a worksheet and chart that helps her to better understand her investments. She has asked you to develop a worksheet totaling the values of the properties and also to include other relevant statistics. The property values are: Property 1, $56,671.99; Property 2, $82,276.58; Property 3, $60,135.45; Property 4, $107,373.39; and Property 5, $87,512.82. Create an Exploded pie in 3-D chart to illustrate the relative property values. Use the AutoCalculate area to find the average, maximum, and minimum property values and manually enter them and their corresponding identifiers in an appropriate area of the worksheet. Use the Sum button to total the property values.

Continued >

Cases and Places *continued*

3: Analyzing Historical Yearly Sales

Business

You are working part-time for Noble's Mobile Services. Your manager has asked you to prepare a worksheet to help her analyze historical yearly sales by type of product (Table 1–11). Use the concepts and techniques presented in this chapter to create the worksheet and an embedded 3-D Clustered Column chart that includes proper numerical formatting, totaling, and formatting of the worksheet.

Table 1–11 Noble's Mobile Services Historical Yearly Sales				
	2008	2009	2010	2011
Camera Phones	92598	10487	136791	176785
Headsets	9035	8909	4886	6512
Music Phones	57942	44923	54590	67696
Other Accessories	27604	38793	24483	33095
Satellite Radios	17161	19293	30763	44367
Standard Mobile Phones	8549	9264	7600	6048
Wireless PDAs	57963	68059	103025	87367

2 | Formulas, Functions, and Formatting

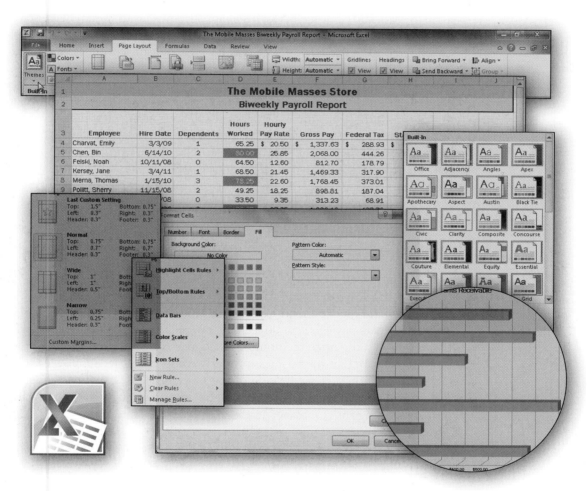

Objectives

You will have mastered the material in this chapter when you can:

- Enter formulas using the keyboard
- Enter formulas using Point mode
- Apply the AVERAGE, MAX, and MIN functions
- Verify a formula using Range Finder
- Apply a theme to a workbook
- Apply a date format to a cell or range

- Add conditional formatting to cells
- Change column width and row height
- Check the spelling in a worksheet
- Set margins, headers, and footers in Page Layout view
- Preview and print versions of a worksheet

2 | Formulas, Functions, and Formatting

Introduction

In Chapter 1, you learned how to enter data, sum values, format a worksheet to make it easier to read, and draw a chart. This chapter continues to highlight these topics and presents some new ones.

The new topics covered in this chapter include using formulas and functions to create a worksheet. A **function** is a prewritten formula that is built into Excel. Other new topics include option buttons, verifying formulas, applying a theme to a worksheet, adding borders, formatting numbers and text, using conditional formatting, changing the widths of columns and heights of rows, spell checking, using alternative types of worksheet displays and printouts, and adding page headers and footers to a worksheet. One alternative worksheet display and printout shows the formulas in the worksheet instead of the values. When you display the formulas in the worksheet, you see exactly what text, data, formulas, and functions you have entered into it.

Project — Worksheet with Formulas and Functions

The project in this chapter follows proper design guidelines and uses Excel to create the worksheet shown in Figure 2–1. The Mobile Masses Store opened its doors when consumer demand for mobile devices, such as mobile phones and PDAs, had just begun. The store's owners pay each employee on a biweekly basis. Before the owners pay the employees, they summarize the hours worked, pay rate, and tax information for each employee to ensure that the business properly compensates its employees. This summary includes information such as the employee names, hire dates, number of dependents, hours worked, hourly pay rate, net pay, and tax information. As the complexity of the task of creating the summary increases, the owners want to use Excel to create a biweekly payroll report.

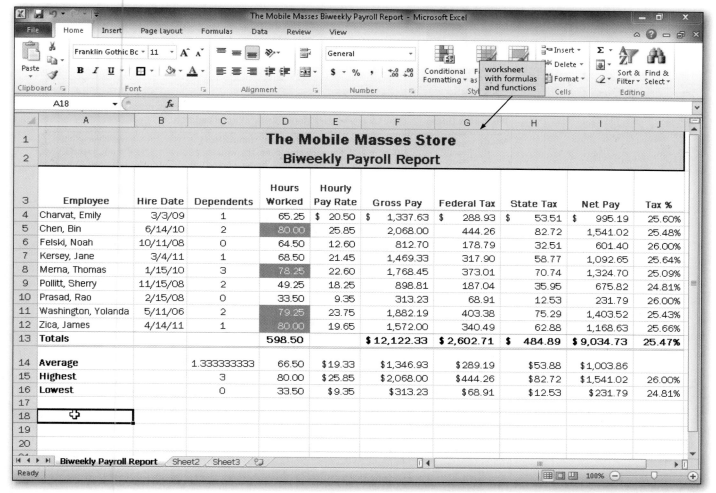

The Mobile Masses Biweekly Payroll Report - Microsoft Excel

	A	B	C	D	E	F	G	H	I	J
1					**The Mobile Masses Store**					
2					**Biweekly Payroll Report**					
3	**Employee**	**Hire Date**	**Dependents**	**Hours Worked**	**Hourly Pay Rate**	**Gross Pay**	**Federal Tax**	**State Tax**	**Net Pay**	**Tax %**
4	Charvat, Emily	3/3/09	1	65.25	$ 20.50	$ 1,337.63	$ 288.93	$ 53.51	$ 995.19	25.60%
5	Chen, Bin	6/14/10	2	80.00	25.85	2,068.00	444.26	82.72	1,541.02	25.48%
6	Felski, Noah	10/11/08	0	64.50	12.60	812.70	178.79	32.51	601.40	26.00%
7	Kersey, Jane	3/4/11	1	68.50	21.45	1,469.33	317.90	58.77	1,092.65	25.64%
8	Merna, Thomas	1/15/10	3	78.25	22.60	1,768.45	373.01	70.74	1,324.70	25.09%
9	Pollitt, Sherry	11/15/08	2	49.25	18.25	898.81	187.04	35.95	675.82	24.81%
10	Prasad, Rao	2/15/08	0	33.50	9.35	313.23	68.91	12.53	231.79	26.00%
11	Washington, Yolanda	5/11/06	2	79.25	23.75	1,882.19	403.38	75.29	1,403.52	25.43%
12	Zica, James	4/14/11	1	80.00	19.65	1,572.00	340.49	62.88	1,168.63	25.66%
13	**Totals**			**598.50**		**$ 12,122.33**	**$ 2,602.71**	**$ 484.89**	**$ 9,034.73**	**25.47%**
14	**Average**		1.333333333	66.50	$19.33	$1,346.93	$289.19	$53.88	$1,003.86	
15	**Highest**		3	80.00	$25.85	$2,068.00	$444.26	$82.72	$1,541.02	26.00%
16	**Lowest**		0	33.50	$9.35	$313.23	$68.91	$12.53	$231.79	24.81%

Figure 2–1

Recall that the first step in creating an effective worksheet is to make sure you understand what is required. The people who will use the worksheet usually provide the requirements. The requirements document for The Mobile Masses Store Biweekly Payroll Report worksheet includes the following needs: source of data, summary of calculations, and other facts about its development (Figure 2–2 on the following page).

REQUEST FOR NEW WORKSHEET

Date Submitted:	April 16, 2012
Submitted By:	Samuel Snyder
Worksheet Title:	The Mobile Masses Store Biweekly Payroll Report
Needs:	An easy-to-read worksheet that summarizes the company's biweekly payroll (Figure 2-3). For each employee, the worksheet is to include the employee's name, hire date, dependents, hours worked, hourly pay rate, gross pay, federal tax, state tax, net pay, and total tax percent. The worksheet also should include totals and the average, highest value, and lowest value for column of numbers specified below.
Source of Data:	The data supplied by Samuel includes the employee names, hire dates, hours worked, and hourly pay rates. This data is shown in Table 2-1 on page EX 72.
Calculations:	The following calculations must be made for each of the employees: 1. Gross Pay = Hours Worked × Hourly Pay Rate 2. Federal Tax = 0.22 × (Gross Pay − Dependents * 24.32) 3. State Tax = 0.04 × Gross Pay 4. Net Pay = Gross Pay − (Federal Tax + State Tax) 5. Tax % = (Federal Tax + State Tax) / Gross Pay 6. Compute the totals for hours worked, gross pay, federal tax, state tax, and net pay. 7. Compute the total tax percent. 8. Use the AVERAGE function to determine the average for dependents, hours worked, hourly pay rate, gross pay, federal tax, state tax, and net pay. 9. Use the MAX and MIN functions to determine the highest and lowest values for dependents, hours worked, hourly pay rate, gross pay, federal tax, state tax, net pay, and total tax percent.

Approvals

Approval Status:	X	Approved
		Rejected
Approved By:	Julie Adams	
Date:	April 23, 2012	
Assigned To:	J. Quasney, Spreadsheet Specialist	

Figure 2–2

Overview

As you read this chapter, you will learn how to create the worksheet shown in Figure 2–1 by performing these general tasks:

- Enter formulas and apply functions in the worksheet
- Add conditional formatting to the worksheet
- Apply a theme to the worksheet
- Set margins, and add headers and footers to a worksheet
- Work with the worksheet in Page Layout view
- Change margins on the worksheet
- Print a section of the worksheet

Plan
Ahead

General Project Decisions

While creating an Excel worksheet, you need to make several decisions that will determine the appearance and characteristics of the finished worksheet. As you create the worksheet necessary to meet the requirements shown in Figure 2–2, you should follow these general guidelines:

1. **Plan the layout of the worksheet.** Rows typically contain items analogous to items in a list. A name could serve as an item in a list, and, therefore, each name could be placed in a row. As a list grows, such as a list of employees, the number of rows in the worksheet will increase. Information about each item in the list and associated calculations should appear in columns.

2. **Determine the necessary formulas and functions needed.** Calculations result from known values. Formulas for such calculations should be known in advance of creating a worksheet. Values such as the average, highest, and lowest values can be calculated using Excel functions as opposed to relying on complex formulas.

3. **Identify how to format various elements of the worksheet.** The appearance of the worksheet affects its ability to express information clearly. Numeric data should be formatted in generally accepted formats, such as using commas as thousands separators and parentheses for negative values.

4. **Establish rules for conditional formatting.** Conditional formatting allows you to format a cell based on the contents of the cell. Decide under which circumstances you would like a cell to stand out from related cells and determine in what way the cell will stand out.

5. **Specify how the hard copy of a worksheet should appear.** When it is possible that a person will want to create a hard copy of a worksheet, care should be taken in the development of the worksheet to ensure that the contents can be presented in a readable manner. Excel prints worksheets in landscape or portrait orientation, and margins can be adjusted to fit more or less data on each page. Headers and footers add an additional level of customization to the printed page.

When necessary, more specific details concerning the above guidelines are presented at appropriate points in the chapter. The chapter also will identify the actions performed and decisions made regarding these guidelines during the creation of the worksheet shown in Figure 2–1 on page EX 67.

In addition, using a sketch of the worksheet can help you visualize its design. The sketch for The Mobile Masses Store Biweekly Payroll Report worksheet includes a title, a subtitle, column and row headings, and the location of data values (Figure 2–3 on the following page). It also uses specific characters to define the desired formatting for the worksheet, as follows:

1. The row of Xs below the leftmost column defines the cell entries as text, such as employee names.

2. The rows of Zs and 9s with slashes, dollar signs, decimal points, commas, and percent signs in the remaining columns define the cell entries as numbers. The Zs indicate that the selected format should instruct Excel to suppress leading 0s. The 9s indicate that the selected format should instruct Excel to display any digits, including 0s.

3. The decimal point means that a decimal point should appear in the cell entry and indicates the number of decimal places to use.

4. The slashes in the second column identify the cell entry as a date.

5. The dollar signs that are not adjacent to the Zs in the first row below the column headings and in the total row signify a fixed dollar sign. The dollar signs that are adjacent to the Zs below the total row signify a floating dollar sign, or one that appears next to the first significant digit.

BTW

Aesthetics versus Function
The function, or purpose, of a worksheet is to provide a user with direct ways to accomplish tasks. In designing a worksheet, functional considerations should come before visual aesthetics. Avoid the temptation to use flashy or confusing visual elements within the worksheet. One exception to this guideline occurs when you may need to draw the user's attention to an area of a worksheet that will help the user more easily complete a task.

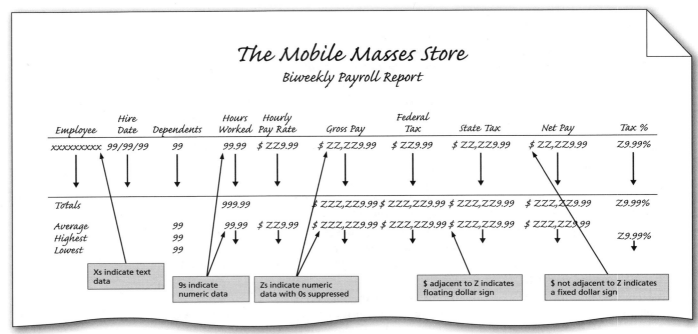

Figure 2–3

6. The commas indicate that the selected format should instruct Excel to display a comma separator only if the number has enough digits to the left of the decimal point.

7. The percent sign (%) in the far-right column indicates a percent sign should appear after the number.

With a good comprehension of the requirements document, an understanding of the necessary decisions, and a sketch of the worksheet, the next step is to use Excel to create the worksheet.

To Start Excel

If you are using a computer to step through the project in this chapter and you want your screens to match the figures in this book, you should change your screen's resolution to 1024 × 768. For information about how to change a computer's resolution, refer to the Office 2010 and Windows 7 chapter at the beginning of this book.

The following steps, which assume Windows 7 is running, start Excel based on a typical installation. You may need to ask your instructor how to start Excel for your computer. For a detailed example of the procedure summarized below, refer to the Office 2010 and Windows 7 chapter.

1 Click the Start button on the Windows 7 taskbar to display the Start menu.

2 Type **Microsoft Excel** as the search text in the 'Search programs and files' text box, and watch the search results appear on the Start menu.

3 Click Microsoft Excel 2010 in the search results on the Start menu to start Excel and display a new blank workbook in the Excel window.

4 If the Excel window is not maximized, click the Maximize button next to the Close button on its title bar to maximize the window.

Entering the Titles and Numbers into the Worksheet

The first step in creating the worksheet is to enter the titles and numbers into the worksheet. The following sets of steps enter the worksheet title and subtitle and then the biweekly payroll report data shown in Table 2–1.

For an introduction to Office 2010 and instruction about how to perform basic tasks in Office 2010 programs, read the Office 2010 and Windows 7 chapter at the beginning of this book, where you can learn how to start a program, use the Ribbon, save a file, open a file, quit a program, use Help, and much more.

To Enter the Worksheet Title and Subtitle

The following steps enter the worksheet title and subtitle into cells A1 and A2.

1 If necessary, select cell A1. Type **The Mobile Masses Store** in the selected cell and then press the DOWN ARROW key to enter the worksheet title.

2 Type **Biweekly Payroll Report** in cell A2 and then press the DOWN ARROW key to enter the worksheet subtitle (Figure 2–4 on page 73).

The employee names and the row titles Totals, Average, Highest, and Lowest in the leftmost column begin in cell A4 and continue down to cell A16. The employee data is entered into rows 4 through 12 of the worksheet. The remainder of this section explains the steps required to enter the column titles, payroll data, and row titles, as shown in Figure 2–4, and then save the workbook.

To Enter the Column Titles

BTW

The Ribbon and Screen Resolution
Excel may change how the groups and buttons within the groups appear on the Ribbon, depending on the computer's screen resolution. Thus, your Ribbon may look different from the ones in this book if you are using a screen resolution other than 1024 × 768.

The column titles in row 3 begin in cell A3 and extend through cell J3. Some of the column titles in Figure 2–3 include multiple lines of text, such as Hours Worked in cell D3. To start a new line in a cell, press ALT+ENTER after each line, except for the last line, which is completed by clicking the Enter box, pressing the ENTER key, or pressing one of the arrow keys. When you see ALT+ENTER in a step, press the ENTER key while holding down the ALT key and then release both keys. The following steps enter the column titles.

1 With cell A3 selected, type **Employee** and then press the RIGHT ARROW key to enter the column heading.

2 Type **Hire Date** in cell B3 and then press the RIGHT ARROW key to enter the column heading.

3 Type **Dependents** and then press the RIGHT ARROW key to enter the column heading.

4 In cell D3, type **Hours** and then press ALT+ENTER to enter the first line of the column heading. Type **Worked** and then press the RIGHT ARROW key to enter the column heading.

5 Type **Hourly** and then press ALT+ENTER to begin a new line in the cell. Type **Pay Rate** and then press the RIGHT ARROW key to enter the column heading.

6 Type **Gross Pay** in cell F3 and then press the RIGHT ARROW key to enter the column heading.

7 Type **Federal Tax** in cell G3 and then press the RIGHT ARROW key to enter the column heading.

8 Type **State Tax** in cell H3 and then press the RIGHT ARROW key to enter the column heading.

9 Type **Net Pay** in cell I3 and then press the RIGHT ARROW key to enter the column heading.

10 Type **Tax %** in cell J3 to enter the column heading.

BTW

BTWs
For a complete list of the BTWs found in the margins of this book, visit the Excel 2010 BTW Web page (scsite.com/ex2010/btw).

To Enter the Biweekly Payroll Data

The biweekly payroll data in Table 2–1 includes a hire date for each employee. Excel considers a date to be a number and, therefore, it displays the date right-aligned in the cell. The following steps enter the data for each employee: name, hire date, dependents, hours worked, and hourly pay rate.

1 Select cell A4, type **Charvat, Emily,** and then press the RIGHT ARROW key to enter the employee name.

2 Type **3/3/09** in cell B4 and then press the RIGHT ARROW key to enter a date in the selected cell.

3 Type **1** in cell C4 and then press the RIGHT ARROW key to enter a number in the selected cell.

4 Type **65.25** in cell D4 and then press the RIGHT ARROW key to enter a number in the selected cell.

5 Type **20.50** in cell E4 and then click cell A5 to enter a number in the selected cell.

6 Enter the payroll data in Table 2–1 for the eight remaining employees in rows 5 through 12 (Figure 2–4).

Q&A

In step 2, why did the date that was entered change from 3/3/09 to 3/3/2009?

When Excel recognizes that you entered a date in mm/dd/yy format, it automatically formats the date as mm/dd/yyyy for you. Most professionals prefer to view dates in mm/dd/yyyy format as opposed to mm/dd/yy format because the latter can cause confusion regarding the intended year. For example, a date displayed as 3/3/50 could imply a date of 3/3/1950 or 3/3/2050. The use of a four-digit year eliminates this confusion.

Table 2–1 The Mobile Masses Store Biweekly Payroll Report Data				
Employee	**Hire Date**	**Dependents**	**Hours Worked**	**Hourly Pay Rate**
Charvat, Emily	3/3/09	1	65.25	20.50
Chen, Bin	6/14/10	2	80.00	25.85
Felski, Noah	10/11/08	0	64.50	12.60
Kersey, Jane	3/4/11	1	68.50	21.45
Merna, Thomas	1/15/10	3	78.25	22.60
Pollitt, Sherry	11/15/08	2	49.25	18.25
Prasad, Rao	2/15/08	0	33.50	9.35
Washington, Yolanda	5/11/06	2	79.25	23.75
Zica, James	4/14/11	1	80.00	19.65

To Enter the Row Titles

The following steps add row titles for the rows that will contain the totals, average, highest, and lowest amounts.

1 Select cell A13. Type **Totals** and then press the DOWN ARROW key to enter a row header.

2 Type **Average** in cell A14 and then press the DOWN ARROW key to enter a row header.

3 Type **Highest** in cell A15 and then press the DOWN ARROW key to enter a row header.

4 Type **Lowest** in cell A16 and then press the ENTER key to enter a row header. Select cell F4 to prepare to enter a formula in the cell (Figure 2–4).

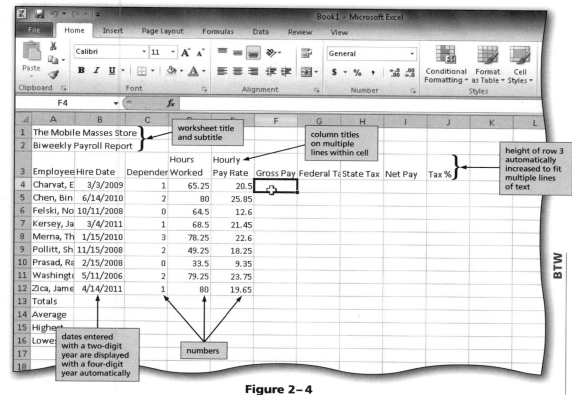

Figure 2–4

To Change Document Properties

As discussed in Chapter 1, the first time you save a workbook, you should change the document properties. The following steps change the document properties.

1 Click File on the Ribbon to open the Backstage view. If necessary, click the Info tab in the Backstage view to display the Info gallery.

2 Click the Properties button in the right pane of the Info gallery to display the Properties menu.

3 Click Show Document Panel on the Properties menu to close the Backstage view and display the Document Information Panel in the Excel workbook window.

4 Click the Author text box, if necessary, and then type your name as the Author property. If a name already is displayed in the Author text box, delete it before typing your name.

5 Click the Subject text box, if necessary delete any existing text, and then type your course and section as the Subject property.

6 If an AutoComplete dialog box appears, click its Yes button.

7 Click the Keywords text box, if necessary delete any existing text, and then type **Biweekly Payroll Report** as the Keywords property.

8 If an AutoComplete dialog box appears, click its Yes button.

9 Click the Close the Document Information Panel button so that the Document Information Panel no longer is displayed.

To Change the Sheet Name and Save the Workbook

The following steps change the sheet name to Biweekly Payroll Report, change the sheet tab color, and save the workbook on a USB flash drive in the Excel folder (for your assignments) using the file name, The Mobile Masses Biweekly Payroll Report.

1 Double-click the Sheet1 tab and then enter `Biweekly Payroll Report` as the sheet name and then press the ENTER key.

2 Right-click the tab to display the shortcut menu and then click Tab Color on the shortcut menu to display the Color gallery. Click Blue, Accent 1, Darker 25% (column 5, row 5) in the Theme Colors area to apply a new color to the sheet tab.

3 With a USB flash drive connected to one of the computer's USB ports, click the Save button on the Quick Access Toolbar to display the Save As dialog box.

4 Type `The Mobile Masses Biweekly Payroll Report` in the File name text box to change the file name. Do not press the ENTER key after typing the file name because you do not want to close the dialog box at this time.

5 Navigate to the desired save location (in this case, the Excel folder in the CIS 101 folder [or your class folder] on the USB flash drive).

6 Click the Save button (Save As dialog box) to save the document in the selected folder on the selected drive with the entered file name.

BTW

Entering Numbers in a Range
An efficient way to enter data into a range of cells is to select a range and then enter the first number in the upper-left cell of the range. Excel responds by accepting the value and moving the active cell selection down one cell. When you enter the last value in the first column, Excel moves the active cell selection to the top of the next column.

Entering Formulas

One of the reasons Excel is such a valuable tool is that you can assign a **formula** to a cell, and Excel will calculate the result. Consider, for example, what would happen if you had to multiply 65.25 by 20.5 and then manually enter the product for Gross Pay, 1,337.625, in cell F4. Every time the values in cells D4 or E4 changed, you would have to recalculate the product and enter the new value in cell F4. By contrast, if you enter a formula in cell F4 to multiply the values in cells D4 and E4, Excel recalculates the product whenever new values are entered into those cells and displays the result in cell F4.

Plan Ahead

> **Determine the formulas and functions needed.**
> As you have learned, formulas and functions simplify the creation and maintenance of worksheets because Excel performs calculations for you. When formulas and functions are used together properly, the amount of data that a user manually must enter in a worksheet greatly can be diminished:
>
> - **Utilize proper algebraic notation.** Most Excel formulas are the result of algebraic calculations. A solid understanding of algebraic operators and the order of operations is important to writing sound formulas.
>
> - **Utilize the fill handle and copy and paste operations to copy formulas.** The fill handle and the Excel copy and paste functionality help to minimize errors caused by retyping formulas. When possible, if a similar formula will be used repeatedly in a worksheet, avoid retyping the formula and instead use the fill handle.
>
> - **Be careful about using invalid and circular cell references.** An invalid reference occurs when Excel does not understand a cell reference used in a formula, resulting in Excel displaying a #REF! error message in the cell.
>
> *(Continued)*

(Continued)

A formula in a cell that contains a reference back to itself is called a **circular reference**. Excel often warns you when you create a circular reference. In almost all cases, circular references are the result of an incorrect formula. A circular reference can be direct or indirect. For example, placing the formula =A1 in cell A1 results in a direct circular reference. An indirect circular reference occurs when a formula in a cell refers to another cell or cells that include a formula that refers back to the original cell.

- **Employ the Excel built-in functions whenever possible.** Excel includes prewritten formulas called **functions** to help you compute a range of values and statistics. A function takes a value or values, performs an operation, and returns a result to the cell. The values that you use with a function are called **arguments**. All functions begin with an equal sign and include the arguments in parentheses after the function name. For example, in the function =AVERAGE(C4:C12), the function name is AVERAGE, and the argument is the range C4:C12. Become familiar with the extensive number of built-in functions. When you have the choice, always use built-in functions instead of writing and typing a formula version of your mathematical expression. Such a practice reduces the possibility of errors and simplifies the formula used in a cell, resulting in improved readability.

Plan Ahead

BTW

Automatic Recalculation
Every time you enter a value into a cell in the worksheet, Excel automatically recalculates all formulas. You can change to manual recalculation by clicking the Calculation Options button (Formulas tab | Calculation group) and then clicking Manual. In manual calculation mode, pressing the F9 key instructs Excel to recalculate all formulas.

To Enter a Formula Using the Keyboard

The formulas needed in the worksheet are noted in the requirements document as follows:

1. Gross Pay (column F) = Hours Worked × Hourly Pay Rate
2. Federal Tax (column G) = 0.22 × (Gross Pay − Dependents × 24.32)
3. State Tax (column H) = 0.04 × Gross Pay
4. Net Pay (column I) = Gross Pay − (Federal Tax + State Tax)
5. Tax% (column J) = (Federal Tax + State Tax) / Gross Pay

The gross pay for each employee, which appears in column F, is equal to hours worked in column D times hourly pay rate in column E. Thus, the gross pay for Emily Charvat in cell F4 is obtained by multiplying 65.25 (cell D4) by 20.50 (cell E4) or =D4*E4. The following steps enter the initial gross pay formula in cell F4 using the keyboard.

1

- With cell F4 selected, type **=d4*e4** in the cell to display the formula in the formula bar and in the current cell and to display colored borders around the cells referenced in the formula (Figure 2–5).

Q&A What occurs on the worksheet as I enter the formula?

The **equal sign** (=) preceding d4*e4 alerts Excel that you are entering a formula or function and not text. Because the most common error when entering a formula is to reference the wrong cell in a formula mistakenly, Excel colors the borders of the cells referenced in the formula. The coloring helps in the reviewing process to ensure the cell references are correct.

The **asterisk** (*) following d4 is the arithmetic operator that directs Excel to perform the multiplication operation.

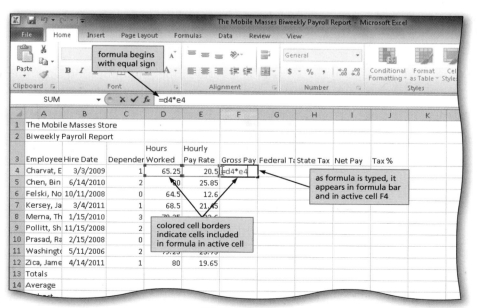

Figure 2–5

2

- Press the RIGHT ARROW key to complete the arithmetic operation indicated by the formula, to display the result in the worksheet, and to select the cell to the right (Figure 2–6). The number of decimal places shown in cell F4 may be different, but these values will be adjusted later in this chapter.

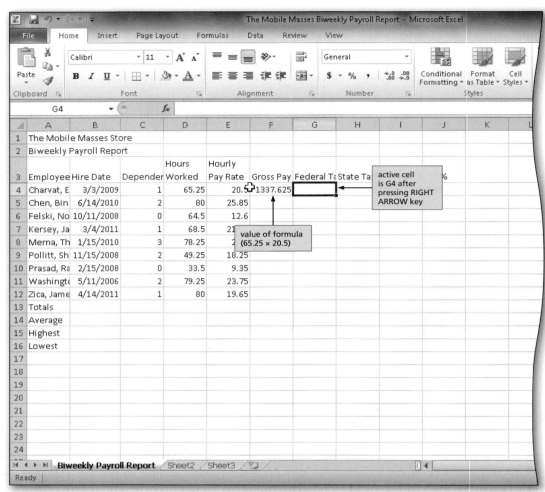

Figure 2–6

Arithmetic Operations

Table 2–2 describes multiplication and other valid Excel arithmetic operators.

Table 2–2 Summary of Arithmetic Operators			
Arithmetic Operator	Meaning	Example of Usage	Meaning
–	Negation	–78	Negative 78
%	Percentage	=23%	Multiplies 23 by 0.01
^	Exponentiation	=3 ^ 4	Raises 3 to the fourth power
*	Multiplication	=61.5 * C5	Multiplies the contents of cell C5 by 61.5
/	Division	=H3 / H11	Divides the contents of cell H3 by the contents of cell H11
+	Addition	=11 + 9	Adds 11 and 9
–	Subtraction	=22 – F15	Subtracts the contents of cell F15 from 22

Order of Operations

When more than one arithmetic operator is involved in a formula, Excel follows the same basic order of operations that you use in algebra. Moving from left to right in a formula, the **order of operations** is as follows: first negation (−), then all percentages (%), then all exponentiations (^), then all multiplications (*) and divisions (/), and finally, all additions (+) and subtractions (−).

As in algebra, you can use parentheses to override the order of operations. For example, if Excel follows the order of operations, 8 * 3 + 2 equals 26. If you use parentheses, however, to change the formula to 8 * (3 + 2), the result is 40, because the parentheses instruct Excel to add 3 and 2 before multiplying by 8. Table 2−3 illustrates several examples of valid Excel formulas and explains the order of operations.

BTW

Troubling Formulas
If Excel does not accept a formula, remove the equal sign from the left side and complete the entry as text. Later, after you have entered additional data in the cells reliant on the formula or determined the error, reinsert the equal sign to change the text back to a formula and edit the formula as needed.

Table 2−3 Examples of Excel Formulas

Formula	Meaning
=G15	Assigns the value in cell G15 to the active cell.
=2^4 + 7	Assigns the sum of 16 + 7 (or 23) to the active cell.
=100 + D2 or =D2 +100 or =(100 + D2)	Assigns 100 plus the contents of cell D2 to the active cell.
=25% * 40	Assigns the product of 0.25 times 40 (or 10) to the active cell.
− (K15 * X45)	Assigns the negative value of the product of the values contained in cells K15 and X45 to the active cell. You do not need to type an equal sign before an expression that begins with minus signs, which indicates a negation.
=(U8 − B8) * 6	Assigns the product of the difference between the values contained in cells U8 and B8 times 6 to the active cell.
=J7 / A5 + G9 * M6 − Z2 ^ L7	Completes the following operations, from left to right: exponentiation (Z2 ^ L7), then division (J7 / A5), then multiplication (G9 * M6), then addition (J7 / A5) + (G9 * M6), and finally subtraction (J7 / A5 + G9 * M6) − (Z2 ^ L7). If cells A5 = 6, G9 = 2, J7 = 6, L7 = 4, M6 = 5, and Z2 = 2, then Excel assigns the active cell the value −5; that is, 6 / 6 + 2 * 5 − 2 ^ 4 = −5.

To Enter Formulas Using Point Mode

The sketch of the worksheet in Figure 2−3 on page EX 70 calls for the federal tax, state tax, net pay, and tax % for each employee to appear in columns G, H, I, and J, respectively. All four of these values are calculated using formulas in row 4:

Federal Tax (cell G4) = 0.22 × (Gross Pay − Dependents × 24.32) or =0.22*(F4−C4*24.32)
State Tax (cell H4) = 0.04 × Gross Pay or = 0.04* F4
Net Pay (cell I4) = Gross Pay − (Federal Tax + State Tax) or =F4-(G4+H4)
Tax % (cell J4) = (Federal Tax + State Tax) / Gross Pay or =(G4+H4)/F4

An alternative to entering the formulas in cells G4, H4, I4, and J4 using the keyboard is to enter the formulas using the mouse and Point mode. **Point mode** allows you to select cells for use in a formula by using the mouse. The steps on the following pages enter formulas using Point mode.

1

- With cell G4 selected type `=0.22*(` to begin the formula and then click cell F4 to add a cell reference in the formula (Figure 2–7).

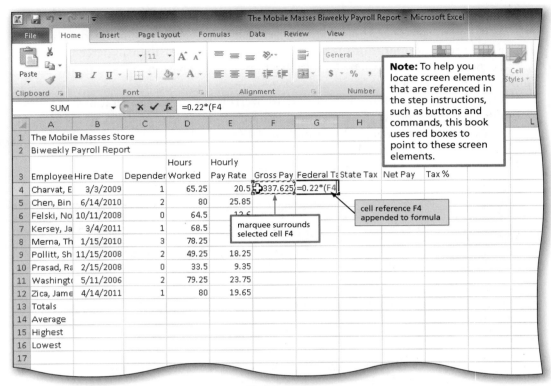

Figure 2–7

2

- Type – (minus sign) and then click cell C4 to add a subtraction operator and a reference to another cell to the formula.

- Type `*24.32)` to complete the formula (Figure 2–8).

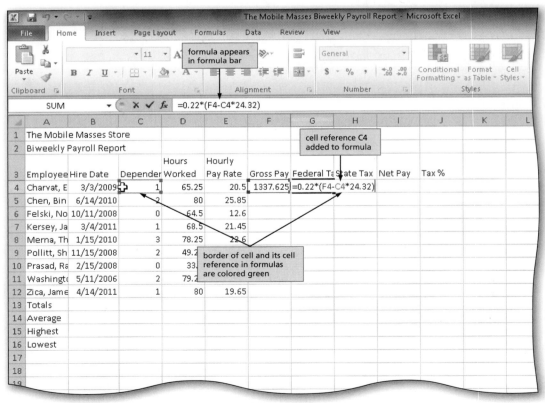

Figure 2–8

3

- Click the Enter box in the formula bar and then select cell H4 to prepare to enter the next formula.

- Type **=0.04*** and then click cell F4 to add a cell reference to the formula (Figure 2–9).

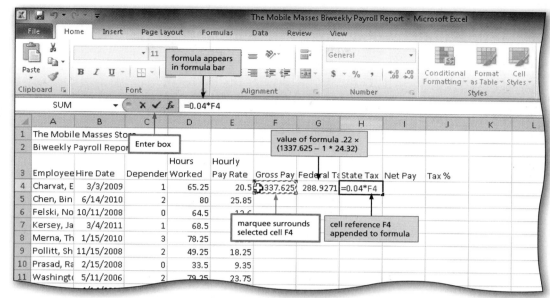

Figure 2–9

Q&A

Why should I use Point mode to enter formulas?

Using Point mode to enter formulas often is faster and more accurate than using the keyboard to type the entire formula when the cell you want to select does not require you to scroll. In many instances, as in these steps, you may want to use both the keyboard and mouse when entering a formula in a cell. You can use the keyboard to begin the formula, for example, and then use the mouse to select a range of cells.

4

- Click the Enter box in the formula bar and then select cell I4 to prepare to enter the next formula.

- Type **=** (equal sign) and then click cell F4 to begin the formula and add a cell reference to the formula.

- Type **–(** (minus sign followed by an open parenthesis) and then click cell G4 to add a subtraction operator, open parenthesis, and cell reference to the formula.

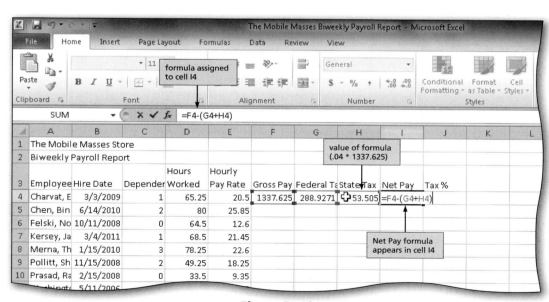

Figure 2–10

- Type **+** (plus sign) and then click cell H4 to add an addition operator and cell reference to the formula.

- Type **)** (close parenthesis) to complete the formula (Figure 2–10).

5

- Click the Enter box in the formula bar to enter the formula in cell I4.

- Select cell J4. Type = ((equal sign followed by an open parenthesis) and then click cell G4 to add a reference to the formula.

- Type + (plus sign) and then click cell H4 to add a cell reference to the formula.

- Type) / (close parenthesis followed by a forward slash), and then click cell F4 to add a cell reference to the formula.

- Click the Enter box in the formula bar to enter the formula in cell J4 (Figure 2–11).

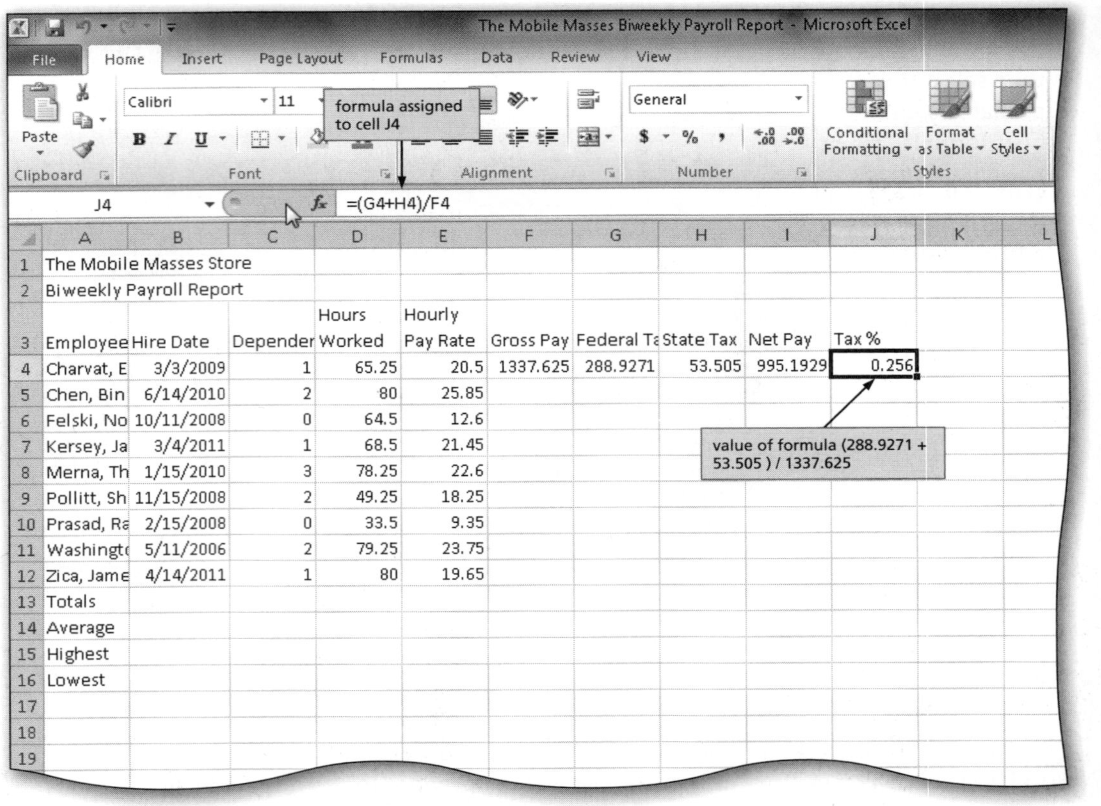

Figure 2–11

Q&A

Why do three decimal places show in cell J4?

The actual value assigned by Excel to cell J4 from the division operation in step 5 is 0.256000075. While not all the decimal places appear in Figure 2–11, Excel maintains all of them for computational purposes. Thus, if referencing cell J4 in a formula, the value used for computational purposes is 0.256000075, not 0.256. The cell formatting is set to display six digits after the decimal point, but the formatting also suppresses trailing zeroes. If the cell formatting were set to display six digits and show trailing zeroes, then Excel would display 0.256000 in cell J4. If you change the cell formatting of column J to display nine digits after the decimal point, then Excel displays the true value 0.256000075.

To Copy Formulas Using the Fill Handle

The five formulas for Emily Charvat in cells F4, G4, H4, I4, and J4 now are complete. You could enter the same five formulas one at a time for the eight remaining employees. A much easier method of entering the formulas, however, is to select the formulas in row 4 and then use the fill handle to copy them through row 12. When performing copying operations in Excel, the source area is the cell, or range, from which data or formulas are being copied. When a range is used as a source, sometimes it is called the source range. The destination area is the cell, or range, to which data or formulas are being copied. When a range is used as a destination, sometimes it is called the destination range. Recall from Chapter 1 that the fill handle is a small rectangle in the lower-right corner of the active cell or active range. The following steps copy the formulas using the fill handle.

1

- Select the source range, F4:J4 in this case, and then point to the fill handle.

- Drag the fill handle down through cell J12 and continue to hold the mouse button to select the destination range (Figure 2–12).

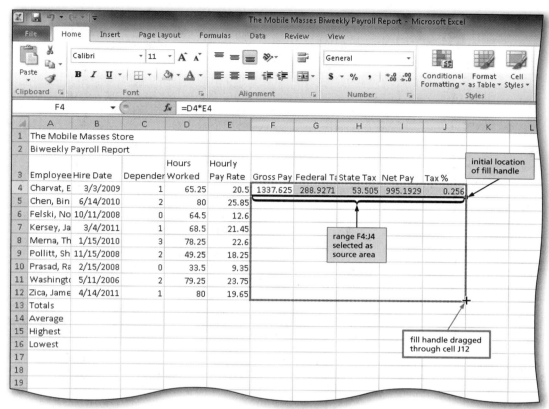

Figure 2–12

2

- Release the mouse button to copy the formulas to the destination range (Figure 2–13).

Q&A

How does Excel adjust the cell references in the formulas in the destination area?

Recall that when you copy a formula, Excel adjusts the cell references so that the new formulas

	Employee	Hire Date	Dependen	Hours Worked	Hourly Pay Rate	Gross Pay	Federal Ta	State Tax	Net Pay	Tax %
3	Employee	Hire Date	Dependen	Worked	Pay Rate	Gross Pay	Federal Ta	State Tax	Net Pay	Tax %
4	Charvat, E	3/3/2009	1	65.25	20.5	1337.625	288.9271	53.505	995.1929	0.256
5	Chen, Bin	6/14/2010	2	80	25.85	2068	444.2592	82.72	1541.021	0.254826
6	Felski, No	10/11/2008			12.6	812.7	178.794	32.508	601.398	0.26
7	Kersey, Ja	3/4/2011			21.45	1469.325	317.9011	58.773	1092.651	0.256359
8	Merna, Th	1/15/2010			22.6	1768.45	373.0078	70.738	1324.704	0.250924
9	Pollitt, Sh	11/15/2008			18.25	898.8125	187.038	35.9525	675.8221	0.248095
10	Prasad, Ra	2/15/2008			9.35	313.225	68.9095	12.529	231.7865	0.26
11	Washingto	5/11/2006	2	79.25	23.75	1882.188	403.3805	75.2875	1403.52	0.254315
12	Zica, Jame	4/14/2011	1	80	19.65	1572	340.4896	62.88	1168.63	0.256596
13	Totals									
14	Average									
15	Highest									

gross pay, federal tax, state tax, net pay, and tax % formulas in range F4:J4 copied to range F5:J12

Auto Fill Options button appears after copying the range F4:J4 to range F5:J12

Figure 2–13

contain references corresponding to the new location and perform calculations using the appropriate values. Thus, if you copy downward, Excel adjusts the row portion of cell references. If you copy across, then Excel adjusts the column portion of cell references. These cell references are called **relative cell references**.

Other Ways

1. Select source area, click Copy button (Home tab | Clipboard group), select destination area, click Paste button (Home tab | Clipboard group)

2. Right-click source area, click Copy on shortcut menu, right-click destination area, click Paste icon on shortcut menu

3. Select source area and then point to border of range; while holding down CTRL, drag source area to destination area

Option Buttons

Excel displays Option buttons in a workbook while you are working on it to indicate that you can complete an operation using automatic features such as AutoCorrect, Auto Fill, error checking, and others. For example, the Auto Fill Options button shown in Figure 2–13 appears after a fill operation, such as dragging the fill handle. When an error occurs in a formula in a cell, Excel displays the Trace Error button next to the cell and identifies the cell with the error by placing a green triangle in the upper left of the cell.

Table 2–4 summarizes the Option buttons available in Excel. When one of these buttons appears on your worksheet, click the button arrow to produce the list of options for modifying the operation or to obtain additional information.

BTW

The Paste Options Button
The Paste Options button provides powerful functionality. When performing copy and paste operations, the button allows you great freedom in specifying what it is you want to paste. For example, you could choose to paste an exact copy of what you copied, including the cell contents and formatting. You also could copy just formulas, just formatting, just the cell values, a combination of these options, or a picture of what you copied.

Table 2–4 Options Buttons in Excel		
Button	**Name**	**Menu Function**
	Auto Fill Options	Gives options for how to fill cells following a fill operation, such as dragging the fill handle.
	AutoCorrect Options	Undoes an automatic correction, stops future automatic corrections of this type, or causes Excel to display the AutoCorrect Options dialog box.
	Insert Options	Lists formatting options following an insertion of cells, rows, or columns.
(Ctrl)	Paste Options	Specifies how moved or pasted items should appear (for example, with original formatting, without formatting, or with different formatting).
	Trace Error	Lists error-checking options following the assignment of an invalid formula to a cell.

BTW

Selecting a Range
You can select a range using the keyboard. Press the F8 key and then use the arrow keys to select the desired range. After you are finished, make sure to press the F8 key to turn off the selection process or you will continue to select ranges.

To Determine Totals Using the Sum Button

The next step is to determine the totals in row 13 for the hours worked in column D, gross pay in column F, federal tax in column G, state tax in column H, and net pay in column I. To determine the total hours worked in column D, the values in the range D4 through D12 must be summed. To do so, enter the function =sum(d4:d12) in cell D13 or select cell D13, click the Sum button (Home tab | Editing group), and then press the ENTER key. Recall that a function is a prewritten formula that is built into Excel. Similar SUM functions can be used in cells F13, G13, H13, and I13 to total gross pay, federal tax, state tax, and net pay, respectively. The following steps determine totals in cell D13 and the range F13:I13.

1 Select cell to contain the sum, cell D13 in this case. Click the Sum button (Home tab | Editing group) to sum the contents of the range D4:D12 in cell D13 and then click the Enter box to display a total in the selected cell.

2 Select the range to contain the sums, range F13:I13 in this case. Click the Sum button (Home tab | Editing group) to display totals in the selected range (Figure 2–14).

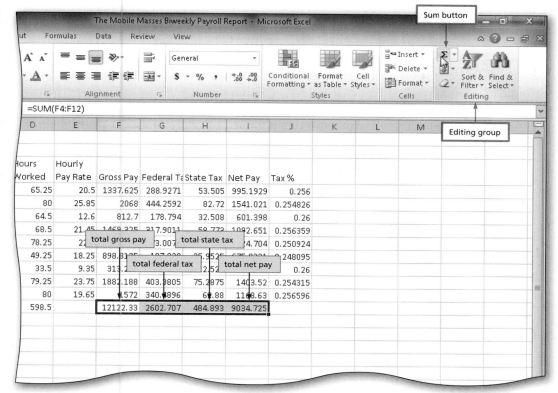

Figure 2-14

To Determine the Total Tax %

With the totals in row 13 determined, the next step is to copy the tax % formula in cell J12 to cell J13 as performed in the following steps.

1 Select the cell to be copied, J12 in this case, and then point to the fill handle.

2 Drag the fill handle down through cell J13 to copy the formula (Figure 2–15).

Q&A Why was the formula I13/F13 not copied to cell J13 earlier?

The formula, I13/F13, was not copied to cell J13 when cell J4 was copied to the range J5:J12 because both cells involved in the computation (I13 and F13) were blank, or zero, at the time. A **blank cell** in Excel has a numerical value of zero, which would have resulted in an error message in cell J13. Once the totals were determined, both cells I13 and F13 (especially F13, because it is the divisor) had nonzero numerical values.

ersey, Ja	3/4/2011	1	68.5	21.45	1469.325	317.9011	58.773	1092.651	0.256359
lerna, Th	1/15/2010	3	78.25	22.6	1768.45	373.0078	70		0.250924
ollitt, Sh	11/15/2008	2	49.25	18.25	898.8125	187.038	35.		0.248095
rasad, Ra	2/15/2008	0	33.5	9.35	313.225	68.9095	12		0.26
Vashingto	5/11/2006	2	79.25	23.75	1882.188	403.3805	75.2875	1403.52	0.254315
ca, Jame	4/14/2011	1	80	19.65	1572	340.489		1168.63	0.256596
otals			598.5		12122.33	2602.70		034.735	0.254704
verage									
ighest									

formula is =(G12+H12)/F12

formula is =(G13+H13)/F13

Auto Fill Options button appears after copying cell J12 to cell J13

Figure 2-15

Using the AVERAGE, MAX, and MIN Functions

The next step in creating The Mobile Masses Biweekly Payroll Report worksheet is to compute the average, highest value, and lowest value for the number of dependents listed in the range C4:C12 using the AVERAGE, MAX, and MIN functions in the range C14:C16. Once the values are determined for column C, the entries can be copied across to the other columns.

With Excel, you can enter functions using one of five methods: (1) the keyboard or mouse, (2) the Insert Function box in the formula bar, (3) the Sum menu, (4) the Sum command (Formulas tab | Function Library group), and (5) the Name box area in the formula bar (Figure 2–16). The method you choose will depend on your typing skills and whether you can recall the function name and required arguments.

In the following pages, each of the first three methods will be used. The keyboard and mouse method will be used to determine the average number of dependents (cell C14). The Insert Function button in the formula bar method will be used to determine the highest number of dependents (cell C15). The Sum menu method will be used to determine the lowest number of dependents (cell C16).

BTW

Statistical Functions
Excel usually considers a blank cell to be equal to 0. The statistical functions, however, ignore blank cells. Excel thus calculates the average of three cells with values of 10, blank, and 8 to be 9 [(10 + 8) / 2] and not 6 [(10 + 0 + 8) / 3].

To Determine the Average of a Range of Numbers Using the Keyboard and Mouse

The **AVERAGE function** sums the numbers in the specified range and then divides the sum by the number of cells with numeric values in the range. The following steps use the AVERAGE function to determine the average of the numbers in the range C4:C12.

- Select the cell to contain the average, cell C14 in this case.

- Type **=av** in the cell to display the Formula AutoComplete list. Press the DOWN ARROW key to highlight the required formula (Figure 2–16).

Q&A

What is happening as I type?

As you type the equal sign followed by the characters in the name of a function, Excel displays the Formula AutoComplete list. This list contains those functions that alphabetically match the letters you have typed. Because you typed =av, Excel displays all the functions that begin with the letters av.

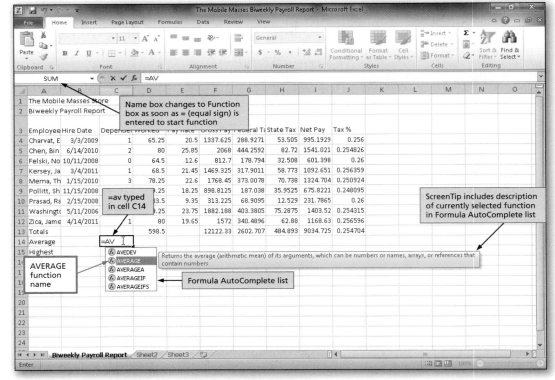

Figure 2–16

2

- Double-click AVERAGE in the Formula AutoComplete list to select the function.

- Select the range to be averaged, C4:C12 in this case, to insert the range as the argument to the function (Figure 2–17).

Q&A As I drag, why does the function in cell C14 change?

When you click cell C4, Excel appends cell C4 to the left parenthesis in the formula bar and surrounds cell C4 with a marquee. When you begin dragging, Excel appends to the argument a colon (:) and the cell reference of the cell where the mouse pointer is located.

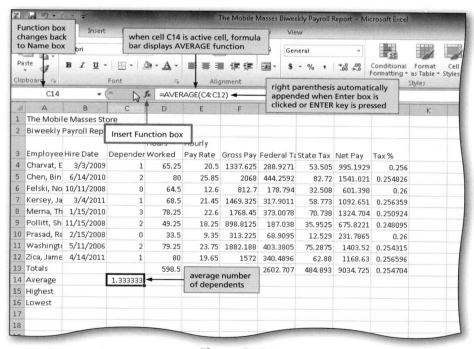

Figure 2–17

3

- Click the Enter box to compute the average of the numbers in the selected range and display the result in the selected cell (Figure 2–18).

Q&A Can I use the arrow keys to complete the entry instead?

No. When you use Point mode you cannot use the arrow keys to complete the entry. While in Point mode, the arrow keys change the selected cell reference in the range you are selecting.

Q&A What is the purpose of the parentheses in the function?

The AVERAGE function requires that the argument (in this case, the range C4:C12) be included within parentheses following the function name. Excel automatically appends the right parenthesis to complete the AVERAGE function when you click the Enter box or press the ENTER key.

Figure 2–18

Other Ways

1. Click Insert Function box in the formula bar, click AVERAGE

2. Click Sum button arrow (Home tab | Editing group), click Average

3. Click Sum button arrow (Formulas tab | Function Library group), click Average

To Determine the Highest Number in a Range of Numbers Using the Insert Function Box

The next step is to select cell C15 and determine the highest (maximum) number in the range C4:C12. Excel includes a function called the **MAX function** that displays the highest value in a range. Although you could enter the MAX function using the keyboard and Point mode as described in the previous steps, an alternative method to entering the function is to use the Insert Function box in the formula bar. The following steps use the Insert Function box in the formula bar to enter the MAX function.

- Select the cell to contain the maximum number, cell C15 in this case.

- Click the Insert Function box in the formula bar to display the Insert Function dialog box.

- Click MAX in the 'Select a function' list (Insert Function dialog box) to select it (Figure 2–19). If the MAX function is not displayed in the 'Select a function' list, scroll the list until the function is displayed.

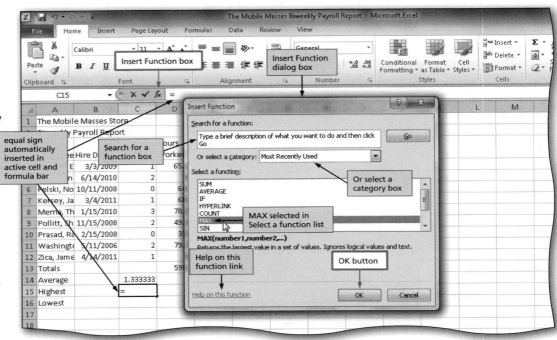

Figure 2–19

- Click the OK button (Insert Function dialog box) to display the Function Arguments dialog box.

- Type **c4:c12** in the Number1 box (Function Arguments dialog box) to enter the first argument of the function (Figure 2–20).

Q&A

Why did numbers appear in the Function Arguments dialog box?

As shown in Figure 2–20, Excel displays the value the MAX function will return to cell C15 in the Function Arguments dialog box. It also lists the first few numbers in the selected range, next to the Number1 box.

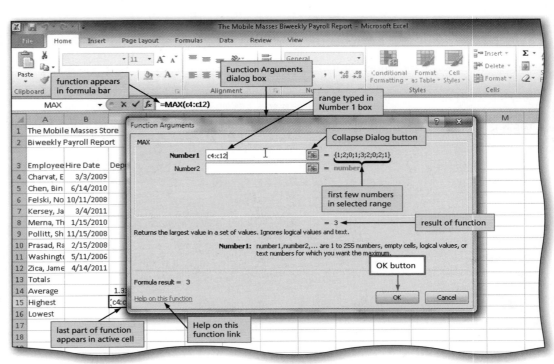

Figure 2–20

3

- Click the OK button (Function Arguments dialog box) to display the highest value in the chosen range in the selected cell (Figure 2–21).

Q&A

Why should I not just enter the highest value that I see in the range C4:C12 in cell C15?

In this example, rather than entering the MAX function, you visually could scan the range C4:C12,

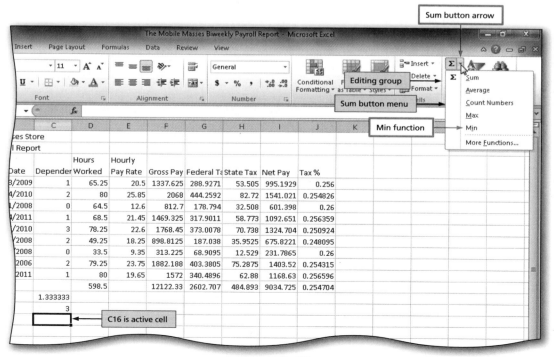

determine that the highest number of dependents is 3, and manually enter the number 3 as a constant in cell C15. Excel would display the number the same as in Figure 2–21. Because it contains a constant, however, Excel will continue to display 3 in cell C15, even if the values in the range C4:C12 change. If you use the MAX function, Excel will recalculate the highest value in the range C4:C12 each time a new value is entered into the worksheet.

Other Ways

1. Click Sum button arrow (Home tab | Editing group), click Max

2. Click Sum button arrow (Formulas tab | Function Library group), click Max

3. Type **=MAX** in cell

To Determine the Lowest Number in a Range of Numbers Using the Sum Menu

The next step is to enter the **MIN function** in cell C16 to determine the lowest (minimum) number in the range C4:C12. Although you can enter the MIN function using either of the methods used to enter the AVERAGE and MAX functions, the following steps perform an alternative using the Sum button (Home tab | Editing group).

1

- Select cell C16 to prepare to enter the next function.

- Click the Sum button arrow (Home tab | Editing group) to display the Sum button menu (Figure 2–22).

Q&A

Why should I use the Sum button menu?

Using the Sum button menu allows you to enter one of five often-used functions easily into a cell, without having to memorize its name or the required arguments.

Figure 2–22

2

- Click Min to display the MIN function in the formula bar and in the active cell (Figure 2–23).

Q&A

Why does Excel select the range C14:C15?

The range C14:C15 automatically selected by Excel is not correct. Excel attempts to guess which cells you want to include in the function by looking for ranges that are adjacent to the selected cell and that contain numeric data.

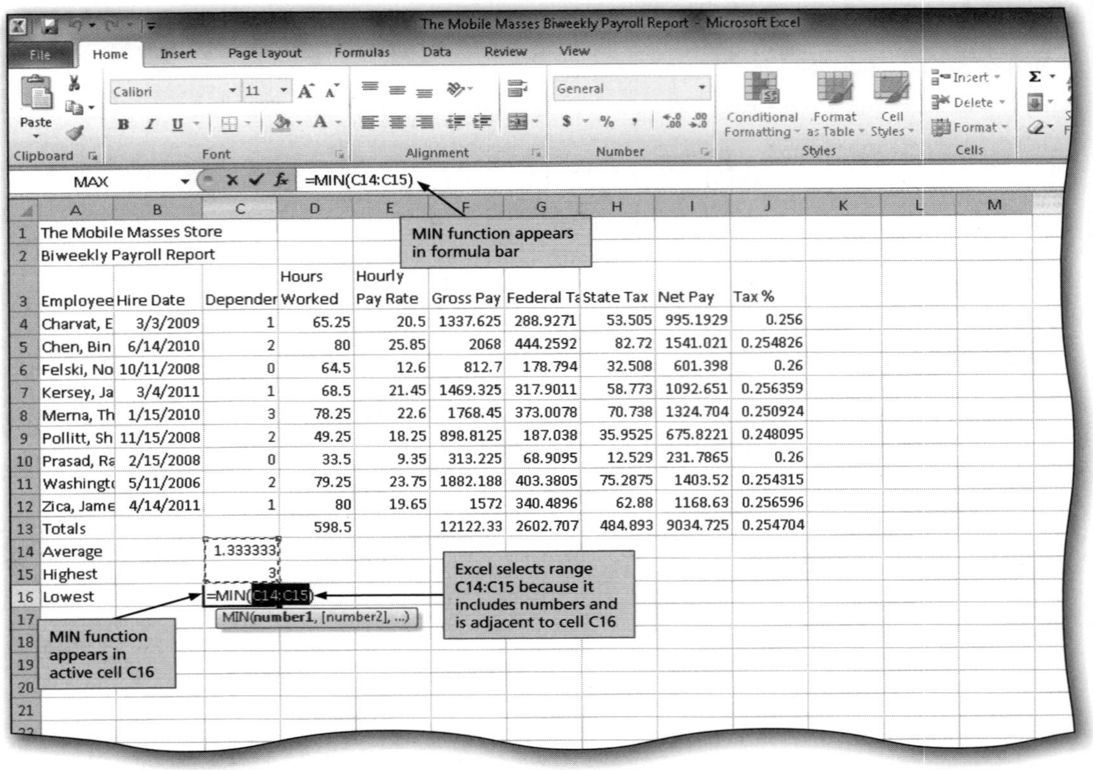

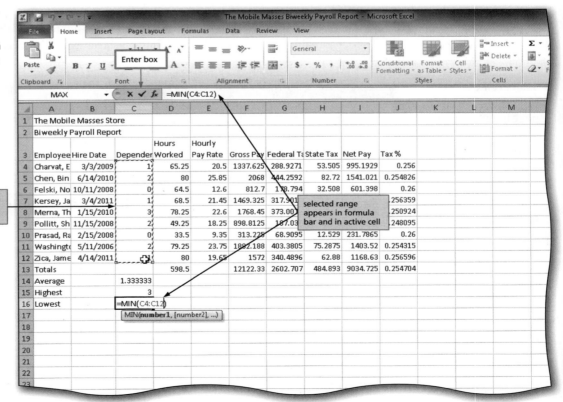

Figure 2–23

3

- Click cell C4 and then drag through cell C12 to display the function with the new range in the formula bar and in the selected cell (Figure 2–24).

Figure 2–24

4

- Click the Enter box to determine the lowest value in the range C4:C12 and display the result in the formula bar and in the selected cell (Figure 2–25).

Q&A

How can I learn about other functions?

Excel has more than 400 additional functions that perform just about every type of calculation you can imagine. These functions are categorized in the Insert Function dialog box shown in Figure 2–19 on page EX 86. To view the

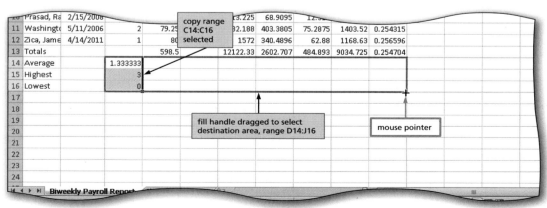

Figure 2–25

categories, click the 'Or select a category' box arrow. To obtain a description of a selected function, select its name in the Insert Function dialog box. Excel displays the description of the function below the Select a function list in the dialog box.

Other Ways
1. Click Insert Function box in the formula bar (if necessary, select Statistical category), click MIN 2. Click Sum button arrow (Formulas tab | Function Library group), click Min 3. Type =MIN in cell

To Copy a Range of Cells Across Columns to an Adjacent Range Using the Fill Handle

The next step is to copy the AVERAGE, MAX, and MIN functions in the range C14:C16 to the adjacent range D14:J16. The following steps use the fill handle to copy the functions.

1

- Select the source range from which to copy the functions, in this case C14:C16.

- Drag the fill handle in the lower-right corner of the selected range through cell J16 and continue to hold down the mouse button to begin a fill operation (Figure 2–26).

Figure 2–26

2

● Release the mouse button to copy the three functions to the selected range (Figure 2–27).

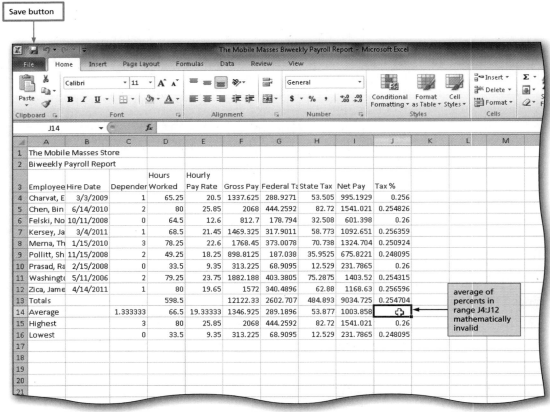

AVERAGE, MAX, and MIN functions in range C14:C16 copied to range D14:J16

9	Pollitt, Sh	11/15/2008						
10	Prasad, Ra	2/15/2008	0	33.5			.529	231.7865	0.26
11	Washingto	5/11/2006	2	79.25	23.75	1882.188	403.3805	75.2875	1403.52	0.254315
12	Zica, Jame	4/14/2011	1	80	19.65	1572	340.4896	62.88	1168.63	0.256596
13	Totals			598.5		12122.33	2602.707	484.893	9034.725	0.254704
14	Average		1.333333	66.5	19.33333	1346.925	289.1896	53.877	1003.858	0.255235
15	Highest		3	80	25.85	2068	444.2592	82.72	1541.021	0.26
16	Lowest		0	33.5	9.35	313.225	68.9095	12.529	231.7865	0.248095

Auto Fill Options button

Figure 2–27

How can I be sure that the function arguments are proper for the cells in range D14:J16?

Remember that Excel adjusts the cell references in the copied functions so that each function refers to the range of numbers above it in the same column. Review the numbers in rows 14 through 16 in Figure 2–27. You should see that the functions in each column return the appropriate values, based on the numbers in rows 4 through 12 of that column.

3

● Select cell J14 and then press the DELETE key to delete the average of the tax % (Figure 2–28).

Why is the formula in cell J14 deleted?

The average of the tax % in cell J14 is deleted because an average of percentages of this type is mathematically invalid.

Save button

	A	B	C	D	E	F	G	H	I	J	K	L	M
1	The Mobile Masses Store												
2	Biweekly Payroll Report												
3	Employee	Hire Date	Depender	Hours Worked	Hourly Pay Rate	Gross Pay	Federal Ta	State Tax	Net Pay	Tax %			
4	Charvat, E	3/3/2009	1	65.25	20.5	1337.625	288.9271	53.505	995.1929	0.256			
5	Chen, Bin	6/14/2010	2	80	25.85	2068	444.2592	82.72	1541.021	0.254826			
6	Felski, No	10/11/2008	0	64.5	12.6	812.7	178.794	32.508	601.398	0.26			
7	Kersey, Ja	3/4/2011	1	68.5	21.45	1469.325	317.9011	58.773	1092.651	0.256359			
8	Merna, Th	1/15/2010	3	78.25	22.6	1768.45	373.0078	70.738	1324.704	0.250924			
9	Pollitt, Sh	11/15/2008	2	49.25	18.25	898.8125	187.038	35.9525	675.8221	0.248095			
10	Prasad, Ra	2/15/2008	0	33.5	9.35	313.225	68.9095	12.529	231.7865	0.26			
11	Washingto	5/11/2006	2	79.25	23.75	1882.188	403.3805	75.2875	1403.52	0.254315			
12	Zica, Jame	4/14/2011	1	80	19.65	1572	340.4896	62.88	1168.63	0.256596			
13	Totals			598.5		12122.33	2602.707	484.893	9034.725	0.254704			
14	Average		1.333333	66.5	19.33333	1346.925	289.1896	53.877	1003.858				
15	Highest		3	80	25.85	2068	444.2592	82.72	1541.021	0.26			
16	Lowest		0	33.5	9.35	313.225	68.9095	12.529	231.7865	0.248095			

average of percents in range J4:J12 mathematically invalid

Figure 2–28

Other Ways

1. Select source area, click Copy button (Home tab | Clipboard group), select destination area, click Paste button (Home tab | Clipboard group)

2. Right-click source area, click Copy on shortcut menu, right-click destination area, click Paste icon on shortcut menu

3. Select source area and then point to border of range; while holding down CTRL, drag source area to destination area

4. Select source area, press CTRL+C, select destination area, press CTRL+V

To Save a Workbook Using the Same File Name

Earlier in this project, an intermediate version of the workbook was saved using the file name, The Mobile Masses Biweekly Payroll Report. The following step saves the workbook a second time, using the same file name.

1 Click the Save button on the Quick Access Toolbar to overwrite the previously saved file.

Break Point: If you wish to take a break, this is a good place to do so. You can quit Excel now. To resume at a later time, start Excel, open the file called Mobile Masses Biweekly Payroll Report, and continue following the steps from this location forward.

Verifying Formulas Using Range Finder

One of the more common mistakes made with Excel is to include a wrong cell reference in a formula. An easy way to verify that a formula references the cells you want it to reference is to use the Excel Range Finder. Use **Range Finder** to check which cells are referenced in the formula assigned to the active cell. Range Finder allows you to make immediate changes to the cells referenced in a formula.

To use Range Finder to verify that a formula contains the intended cell references, double-click the cell with the formula you want to check. Excel responds by highlighting the cells referenced in the formula so that you can check that the cell references are correct.

To Verify a Formula Using Range Finder

The following steps use Range Finder to check the formula in cell J4.

1
- Double-click cell J4 to activate Range Finder (Figure 2–29).

2
- Press the ESC key to quit Range Finder and then click anywhere in the worksheet, such as cell A18, to deselect the current cell.

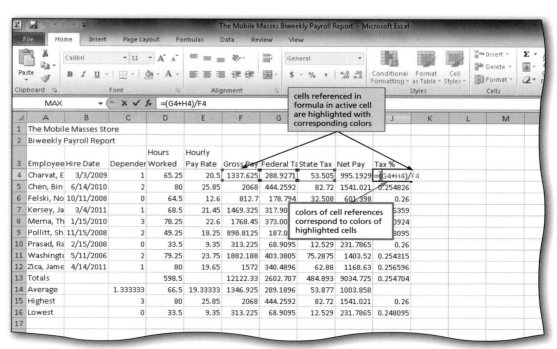

Figure 2–29

Formatting the Worksheet

Although the worksheet contains the appropriate data, formulas, and functions, the text and numbers need to be formatted to improve their appearance and readability.

In Chapter 1, cell styles were used to format much of the worksheet. This section describes how to change the unformatted worksheet in Figure 2–30a to the formatted worksheet in Figure 2–30b using a theme and other commands on the Ribbon. The colors and fonts that are used in the worksheet shown in Figure 2–30b are those that are associated with the Trek theme.

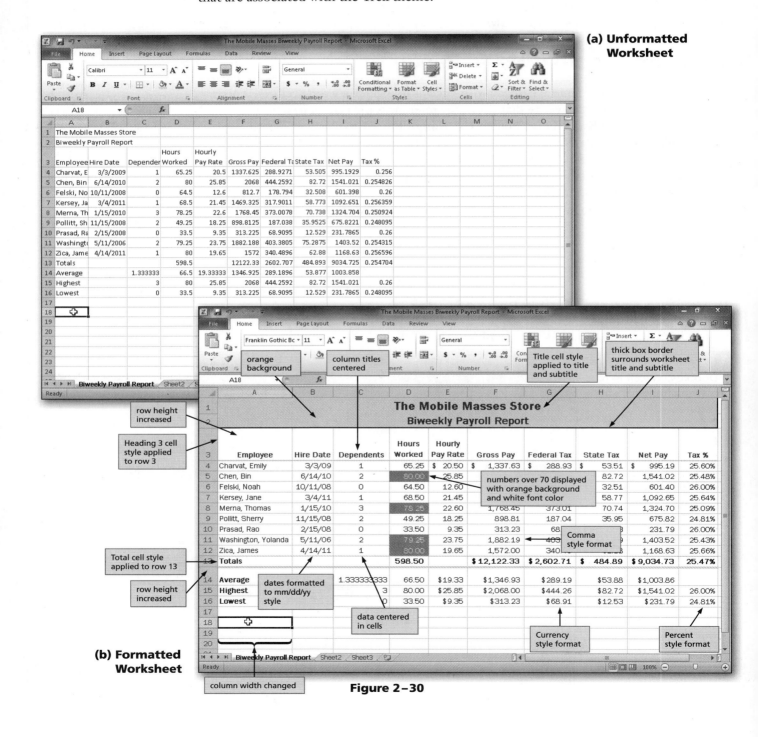

Figure 2–30

Identify how to format various elements of the worksheet.

As you have learned, applying proper formatting to a worksheet improves its appeal and readability. The following list includes additional worksheet formatting considerations.

- **Consider using cell borders and fill colors for various portions of the worksheet.** Cell borders, or box borders, draw a border around a cell or range of cells to set the cell or range off from other portions of the worksheet. For example, worksheet titles often include cell borders. Similarly, the use of a fill color in a cell or range of cells sets off the cell or range from other portions of the worksheet and provides visual impact to draw the user's eye toward the cell or range.

- **Use good judgment when centering values in columns.** If a cell entry is short, such as the dependents in column C, centering the entries within their respective columns improves the appearance of the worksheet.

- **Consider the use of a different theme.** A **theme** is a predefined set of colors, fonts, chart styles, cell styles, and fill effects that can be applied to an entire workbook. Every new workbook that you create is assigned a default theme named Office. Excel, however, includes a variety of other themes that provide a range of visual effects for your workbooks.

- **Apply proper formatting for cells that include dates.** Excel provides a number of date formats so that date values can be formatted to meet your needs. How you decide to format a date depends on a number of factors. For example, dates that include years both before and after the year 2000 should be formatted with a four-digit year. Your organization or department may insist on the use of certain standard date formats. Industry standards also may indicate how you should format date values.

The following outlines the formatting suggested in the sketch of the worksheet in Figure 2–3 on page EX 70.

1. Workbook theme — Trek
2. Worksheet title and subtitle
   a. Alignment — center across columns A through J
   b. Cell style — Title
   c. Font size — title 18; subtitle 16
   d. Background color (range A1:J2) — Orange Accent 1, Lighter 60%
   e. Border — thick box border around range A1:J2
3. Column titles
   a. Cell style — Heading 3
   b. Alignment — center
4. Data
   a. Dates in column B — mm/dd/yy format
   b. Alignment — center data in range C4:C12
   c. Numbers in column D — Comma style and two decimal places; if a cell in range D4:D12 is greater than 70, then cell appears with background color of orange and a font color of white
   d. Numbers in top row (range E4:I4) — Accounting number format
   e. Numbers below top row (range E5:I12) — Comma style and decimal places
5. Total line
   a. Cell style — Total
   b. Numbers — Accounting number format

6. Average, highest, and lowest rows
   a. Font style of row titles in range A14:A16 — bold
   b. Numbers — Currency style with floating dollar sign in the range E14:I16
7. Percentages in column J
   a. Numbers — Percentage style with two decimal places
8. Column widths
   a. Columns A, B, and C — best fit
   b. Column H — 10.22 characters
   c. Column D, E, and J — 7.56 characters
9. Row heights
   a. Row 3 — 48.00 points
   b. Row 14 — 27.00 points
   c. Remaining rows — default

To Change the Workbook Theme

The Trek theme includes fonts and colors that provide the worksheet a professional and subtly colored appearance. The following steps change the workbook theme to the Trek theme.

1

- Display the Page Layout tab.

- Click the Themes button (Page Layout tab | Themes group) to display the Themes gallery.

- Scroll to the bottom of the gallery (Figure 2–31).

🔍 **Experiment**

- Point to several themes in the Themes gallery to see a live preview of the themes.

Q&A Why should I change the theme of a workbook?

A company or department may standardize on a specific theme so that all of their documents have a similar appearance. Similarly, an individual may want to have a theme that sets his or her work apart from the work of others. Other Office programs, such as Word and PowerPoint, include the same themes included with Excel, meaning that all of your Microsoft Office documents can share a common theme.

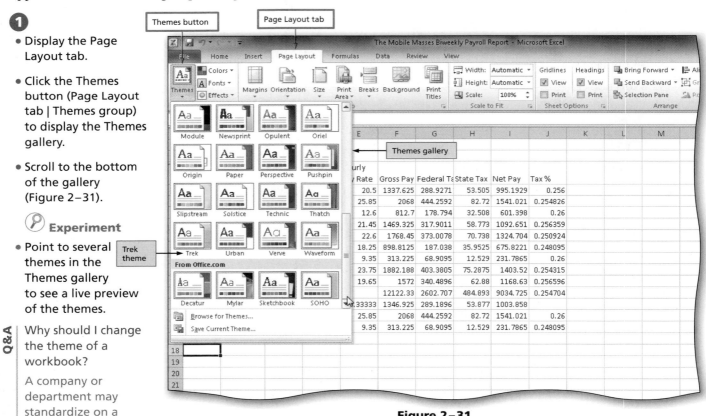

Figure 2–31

2

- Click Trek in the Themes gallery to change the workbook theme (Figure 2–32).

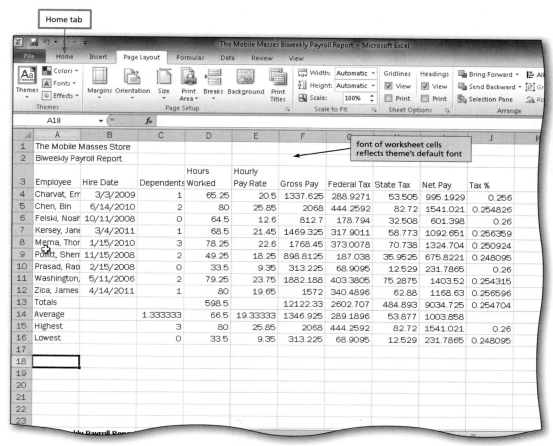

Figure 2–32

Q&A

Why did the cells in the worksheet change?

The cells in the worksheet originally were formatted with the default font for the default Office theme. The default font for the Trek theme is different from that of the default font for the Office theme and, therefore, changed on the worksheet when you changed the theme. If you had modified the font for any of the cells, those cells would not receive the default font for the Trek theme.

To Format the Worksheet Titles

The following steps merge and center the worksheet titles, apply the Title cells style to the worksheet titles, and decrease the font of the worksheet subtitle.

1 Display the Home tab.

2 Select the range to be merged, A1:J1 in this case, and then click the Merge & Center button (Home tab | Alignment group) to merge and center the text in the selected range.

3 Select the range A2:J2 and then click the Merge & Center button (Home tab | Alignment group) to merge and center the text in the selected range.

4 Select the range to contain the Title cell style, in this case A1:A2, click the Cell Styles button (Home tab | Styles group) to display the cell styles gallery, and then click the Title cell style in the Cell Styles gallery to apply the Title cell style to the selected range.

5 Select cell A2 and then click the Decrease Font Size button (Home tab | Font group) to decrease the font size of the selected cell to the next lowest font size (Figure 2–33 on the following page).

What is the effect of clicking the Decrease Font Size button?

When you click the Decrease Font Size button, Excel assigns the next lowest font size in the Font Size gallery to the selected range. The Increase Font Size button works in a similar manner but causes Excel to assign the next highest font size in the Font Size gallery to the selected range.

Color Selection

Knowing how people perceive colors helps you emphasize parts of your worksheet. Warmer colors (red and orange) tend to reach toward the reader. Cooler colors (blue, green, and violet) tend to pull away from the reader. Bright colors jump out of a dark background and are easiest to see. White or yellow text on a dark blue, green, purple, or black background is ideal.

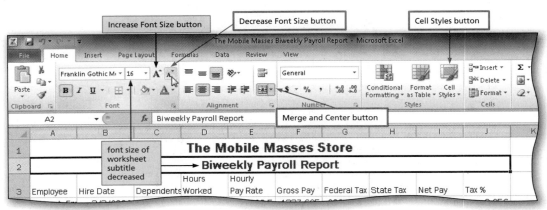

Figure 2–33

To Change the Background Color and Apply a Box Border to the Worksheet Title and Subtitle

The final formats assigned to the worksheet title and subtitle are the orange background color and thick box border (Figure 2–30b on page EX 92). The following steps complete the formatting of the worksheet titles.

- Select the range A1:A2 and then click the Fill Color button arrow (Home tab | Font group) to display the Fill Color gallery (Figure 2–34).

 **Experiment**

- Point to a number of colors in the Fill Color gallery to display a live preview of the color in the range A1:A2.

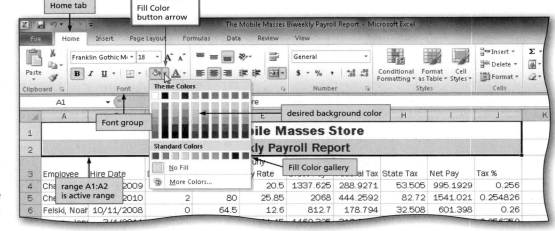

Figure 2–34

- Click Orange, Accent 1, Lighter 60% (column 5, row 3) in the Fill Color gallery to change the background color of the range of cells (Figure 2–35).

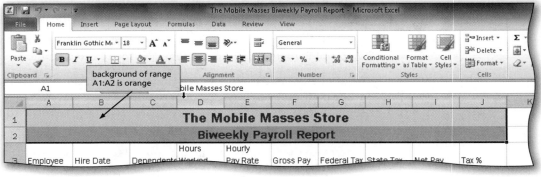

Figure 2–35

3

- Click the Borders button arrow (Home tab | Font group) to display the Borders list (Figure 2–36).

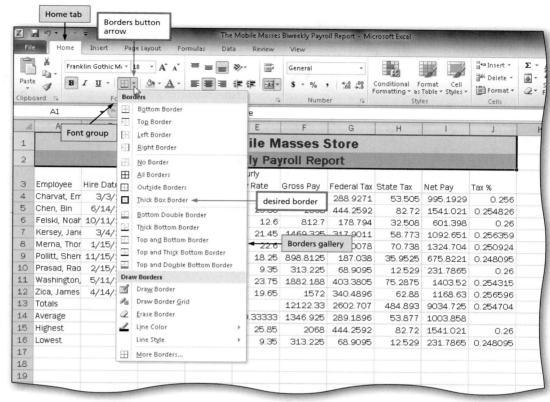

Figure 2–36

4

- Click Thick Box Border in the Borders list to display a thick box border around the selected range.

- Click anywhere in the worksheet, such as cell A18, to deselect the current range (Figure 2–37).

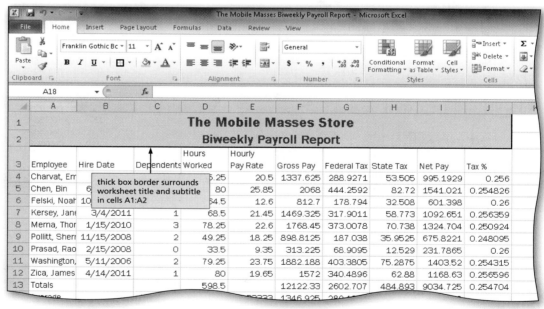

Figure 2–37

Other Ways
1. Click Format Cells Dialog Box Launcher (Home tab | Font group), click appropriate tab (Format Cells dialog box), click desired format, click OK button
2. Right-click range, click Format Cells on shortcut menu, click appropriate tab (Format Cells dialog box), click desired format, click OK button
3. Press CTRL+1, click appropriate tab (Format Cells dialog box), click desired format, click OK button

Background Colors
The most popular background color is blue. Research shows that the color blue is used most often because this color connotes serenity, reflection, and proficiency.

To Apply a Cell Style to the Column Headings and Format the Total Rows

As shown in Figure 2–30b on page EX 92, the column titles (row 3) should have the Heading 3 cell style and the totals row (row 13) should have the Total cell style. The summary information headings in the range A14:A16 should be bold. The following steps assign these styles and formats to row 3 and row 13 and the range A14:A16.

1. Select the range to be formatted, cells A3:J3 in this case.

2. Apply the Heading 3 cell style to the range A3:J3.

3. Click the Center button (Home tab | Alignment group) to center the column headings.

4. Apply the Total cell style to the range A13:J13.

5. Bold the range A14:A16 (Figure 2–38).

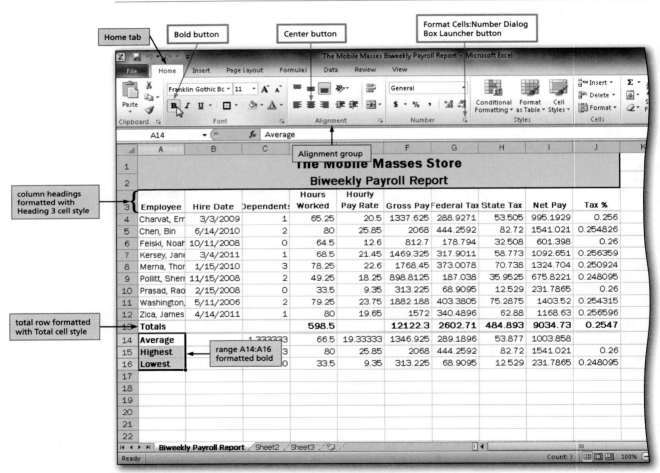

Figure 2–38

To Format Dates and Center Data in Cells

With the column titles and total rows formatted, the next step is to format the dates in column B and center the dependents in column C. The following steps format the dates in the range B4:B12 and center the data in the range C4:C12.

1

- Select the range to contain the new date format, cells B4:B12 in this case.

- Click the Format Cells: Number Dialog Box Launcher (Home tab | Number group) to display the Format Cells dialog box.

- If necessary, click the Number tab (Format Cells dialog box), click Date in the Category list, and then click 3/14/01 in the Type list to choose the format for the selected range (Figure 2–39).

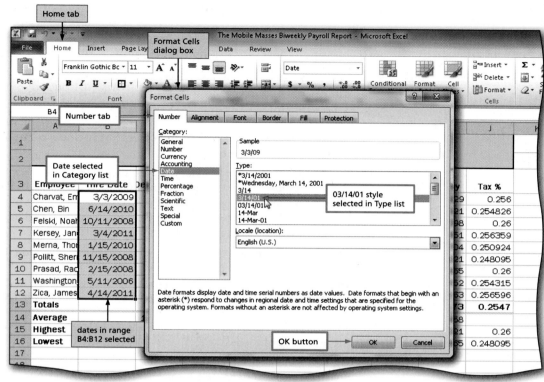

Figure 2–39

2

- Click the OK button (Format Cells dialog box) to format the dates in the current column using the selected date format style.

3

- Select the range C4:C12 and then click the Center button (Home tab | Alignment group) to center the data in the selected range.

- Select cell E4 to deselect the selected range (Figure 2–40).

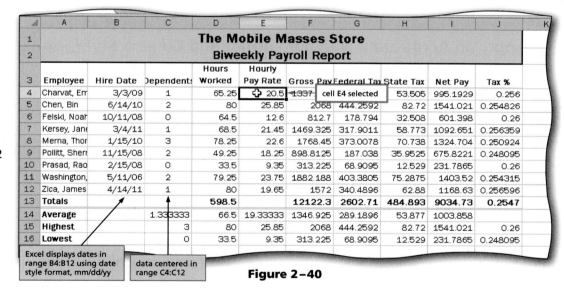

Figure 2–40

Q&A

Can I format an entire column at once?

Yes. Rather than selecting the range B4:B12 in Step 1, you could have clicked the column B heading immediately above cell B1, and then clicked the Center button (Home tab | Alignment group). In this case, all cells in column B down to the last cell in the worksheet would have been formatted to use center alignment. This same procedure could have been used to format the dates in column C.

Other Ways

1. Right-click range, click Format Cells on shortcut menu, click appropriate tab (Format Cells dialog box), click desired format, click OK button

2. Press CTRL+1, click appropriate tab (Format Cells dialog box), click desired format, click OK button

Formatting Numbers Using the Ribbon

As shown in Figure 2–30b on page EX 92, the worksheet is formatted to resemble an accounting report. For example, in columns E through I, the numbers in the first row (row 4), the totals row (row 13), and the rows below the totals (rows 14 through 16) have dollar signs, while the remaining numbers (rows 5 through 12) in column E through column I do not.

Plan Ahead

Determine proper formatting for cells that include currency and other numeric amounts.

- To append a dollar sign to a number, you should use the Accounting number format. Excel displays numbers using the **Accounting number format** with a dollar sign to the left of the number, inserts a comma every three positions to the left of the decimal point, and displays numbers to the nearest cent (hundredths place). Clicking the Accounting Number Format button (Home tab | Number group) assigns the desired Accounting number format.

- When you use the Accounting Number Format button to assign the Accounting number format, Excel displays a **fixed dollar sign** to the far left in the cell, often with spaces between it and the first digit. To assign a **floating dollar sign** that appears immediately to the left of the first digit with no spaces, use the Currency style (Format Cells dialog box). Whether you use the Accounting number format or the Currency style format depends on a number of factors, including the preference of your organization, industry standards, and the aesthetics of the worksheet.

- The Comma style format is used to instruct Excel to display numbers with commas and no dollar signs. The **Comma style format**, which can be assigned to a range of cells by clicking the Comma Style button (Home tab | Number group), inserts a comma every three positions to the left of the decimal point and causes numbers to be displayed to the nearest hundredths.

To Apply an Accounting Number Format and Comma Style Format Using the Ribbon

The following steps assign formats using the Accounting Number Format button and the Comma Style button (Home tab | Number group). The Accounting Number format is applied to the currency amounts in rows 4 and 13. The Comma style is applied to the range E4:I12 and to column D (Hours Worked).

1

- Select the range to contain the Accounting Number Format, cells E4:I4 in this case.

- While holding down the CTRL key, select the range F13:I13 to select the nonadjacent range.

- Click the Accounting Number Format button (Home tab | Number group) to apply the Accounting number format with fixed dollar signs to the selected nonadjacent ranges (Figure 2–41).

Q&A

What is the effect of applying the Accounting number format?

The Accounting Number Format button assigns a fixed dollar sign to the numbers in the ranges E4:I4 and F13:I13. In each cell in these ranges, Excel displays the dollar sign to the far left with spaces between it and the first digit in the cell.

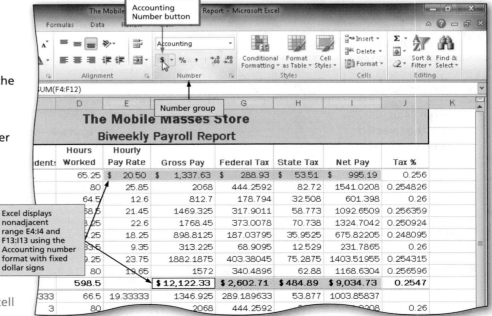

Figure 2–41

2

- Select the range to contain the Comma style format, cells E5:I12 in this case.

- Click the Comma Style button (Home tab | Number group) to assign the Comma style format to the selected range (Figure 2–42).

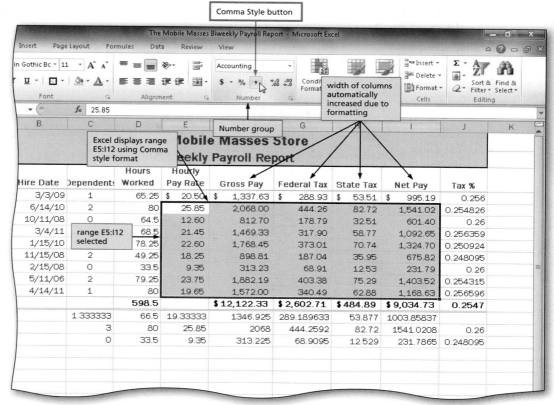

Figure 2–42

3

- Select the range to contain the Comma style format, cells D4:D16 in this case.

- Click the Comma Style button (Home tab | Number group) to assign the Comma style format to the selected range (Figure 2–43).

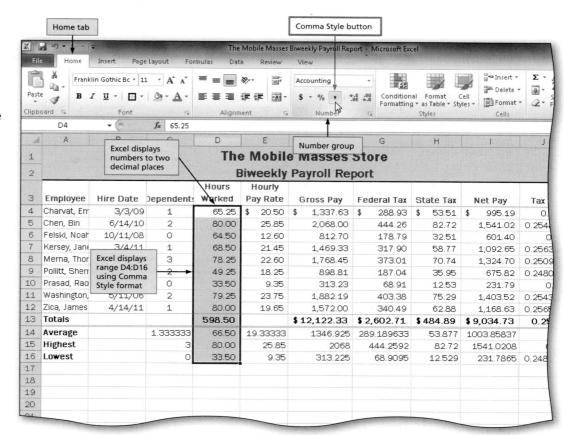

Figure 2–43

To Apply a Currency Style Format with a Floating Dollar Sign Using the Format Cells Dialog Box

The following steps use the Format Cells dialog box to apply the Currency style format with a floating dollar sign to the numbers in the range E14:I16.

1

- Select the range E14:I16 and then click the Format Cells: Number Dialog Box Launcher (Home tab | Number group) to display the Format Cells dialog box.

- If necessary, click the Number tab (Format Cells dialog box) to display the Number tab (Format Cells dialog box) (Figure 2–44).

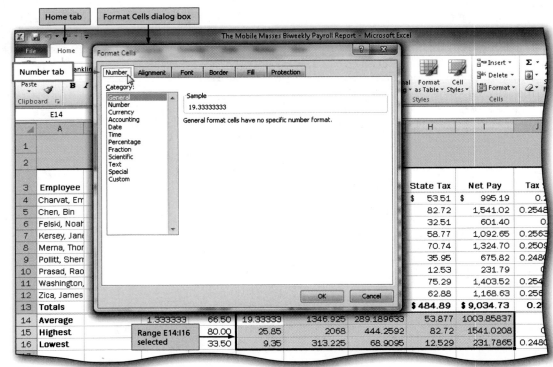

Figure 2–44

2

- Click Currency in the Category list to select the necessary number format category, and then click the third style ($1,234.10) in the Negative numbers list (Format Cells dialog box) to select the desired currency format for negative numbers (Figure 2–45).

 How do I select the proper format?

You can choose from 12 categories of formats. Once you select a category, you can select the number of decimal places, whether or not a dollar sign should be displayed, and how

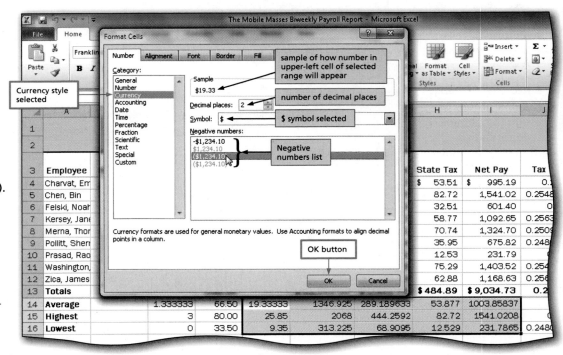

Figure 2–45

negative numbers should appear. Selecting the appropriate negative numbers format is important, because doing so adds a space to the right of the number in order to align the numbers in the worksheet on the decimal points. Some of the available negative number formats do not align the numbers in the worksheet on the decimal points.

3

- Click the OK button (Format Cells dialog box) to assign the Currency style format with a floating dollar sign to the selected range (Figure 2–46).

Q&A What is the difference between using the Accounting Number style and Currency style?

When using the Accounting Number Style button, recall that a floating dollar sign always appears immediately to the left of the first digit, and the fixed dollar sign always appears on the left side of the cell. Cell E4, for example, has a fixed dollar sign, while cell E14 has a floating dollar sign. The Currency style was assigned to cell E14 using the Format Cells dialog box and the result is a floating dollar sign.

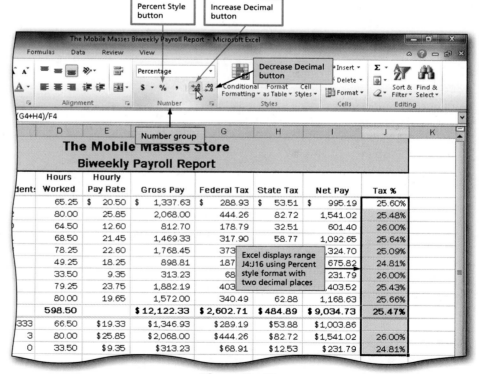

Figure 2–46

Other Ways

1. Press CTRL+1, click Number tab (Format Cells dialog box), click Currency

   in Category list, select format, click OK button

2. Press CTRL+SHIFT+DOLLAR SIGN ($)

To Apply a Percent Style Format and Use the Increase Decimal Button

The next step is to format the tax % in column J. Currently, Excel displays the numbers in column J as a decimal fraction (for example, 0.256 in cell J4). The following steps format the range J4:J16 to the Percent style format with two decimal places.

1

- Select the range to format, cell J4:J16 in this case.

- Click the Percent Style button (Home tab | Number group) to display the numbers in the selected range as a rounded whole percent.

Q&A What is the result of clicking the Percent Style button?

The Percent Style button instructs Excel to display a value as a percentage, determined by multiplying the cell entry by 100, rounding the result to the nearest percent, and adding a percent sign. For example, when cell J4 is formatted using the Percent Style buttons, Excel displays the actual value 0.256 as 26%.

2

- Click the Increase Decimal button (Home tab | Number group) two times to display the numbers in the selected range with two decimal places (Figure 2–47).

Figure 2–47

Other Ways

1. Right-click range, click Format Cells on shortcut menu, click Number tab (Format Cells dialog box), click Percentage

   in Category list, select format, click OK button

2. Press CTRL+1, click Number tab (Format Cells dialog box), click Percentage

   in Category list, select format, click OK button

3. Press CTRL+SHIFT+ percent sign (%)

Conditional Formatting

The next step is to emphasize the values greater than 70 in column D by formatting them to appear with an orange background and white font color (Figure 2–48).

Plan Ahead

Establish rules for conditional formatting.

- Excel lets you apply formatting that appears only when the value in a cell meets conditions that you specify. This type of formatting is called **conditional formatting**. You can apply conditional formatting to a cell, a range of cells, the entire worksheet, or the entire workbook. Usually, you apply conditional formatting to a range of cells that contains values you want to highlight, if conditions warrant.

- A **condition**, which is made up of two values and a relational operator, is true or false for each cell in the range. If the condition is true, then Excel applies the formatting. If the condition is false, then Excel suppresses the formatting. What makes conditional formatting so powerful is that the cell's appearance can change as you enter new values in the worksheet.

- As with worksheet formatting, follow the less-is-more rule when considering conditional formatting. Use conditional formatting to make cells and ranges stand out and raise attention. Too much conditional formatting can result in confusion for the reader of the worksheet.

BTW

Conditional Formatting You can assign any format to a cell, a range of cells, a worksheet, or an entire workbook conditionally. If the value of the cell changes and no longer meets the specified condition, Excel suppresses the conditional formatting.

To Apply Conditional Formatting

The following steps assign conditional formatting to the range D4:D12, so that any cell value greater than 70 will cause Excel to display the number in the cell with an orange background and a white font color.

1

- Select the range D4:D12.

- Click the Conditional Formatting button (Home tab | Styles group) to display the Conditional Formatting list (Figure 2–48).

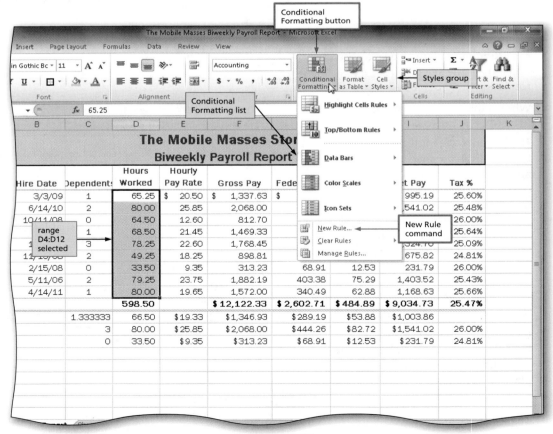

Figure 2–48

2

- Click New Rule in the Conditional Formatting list to display the New Formatting Rule dialog box.

- Click 'Format only cells that contain' in the Select a Rule Type area (New Formatting Rule dialog box) to change the 'Edit the Rule Description' area.

- In the 'Edit the Rule Description' area, click the box arrow in the relational operator box (second text box) to display a list of relational operators, and then select greater than to select the desired operator.

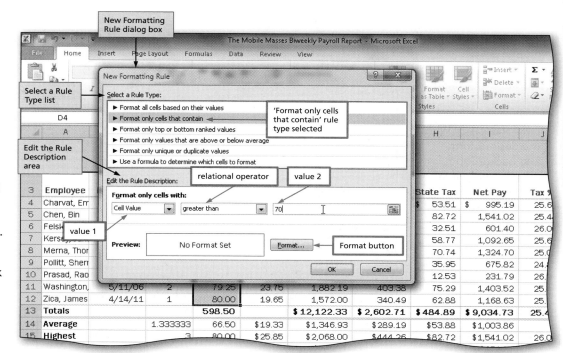

Figure 2–49

- Select the rightmost box, and then type 70 in the box in the 'Edit the Rule Description' area to enter the second value of the rule description (Figure 2–49).

Q&A | What do the changes in the 'Edit the Rule Description' indicate?

The 'Edit the Rule Description' area allows you to view and edit the rules for the conditional format. In this case, reading the area indicates that Excel should conditionally format only cells with cell values greater than 70.

3

- Click the Format button (New Formatting Rule dialog box) to display the Format Cells dialog box.

- If necessary, click the Font tab. Click the Color box arrow (Format Cells dialog box) to display the Color gallery and then click White, Background 1 (column 1, row 1) in the Color gallery to select the font color.

- Click the Fill tab (Format Cells dialog box) to display the Fill sheet and then click the orange color in column 5, row 5 to select the background color (Figure 2–50).

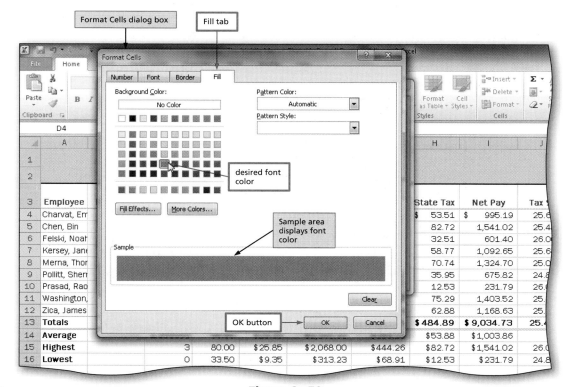

Figure 2–50

4

- Click the OK button (Format Cells dialog box) to close the Format Cells dialog box and display the New Formatting Rule dialog box with the desired font and background colors displayed in the Preview box (Figure 2–51).

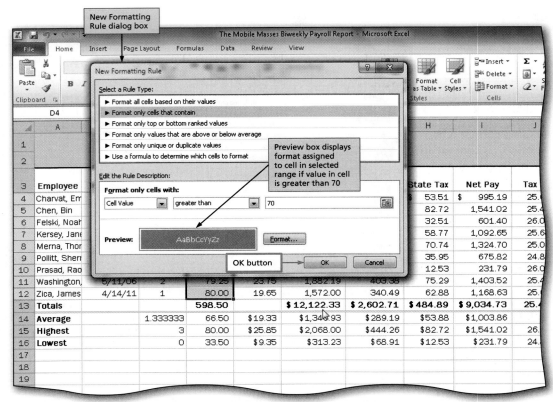

Figure 2–51

5

- Click the OK button to assign the conditional format to the selected range.

- Click anywhere in the worksheet, such as cell A18, to deselect the current range (Figure 2–52).

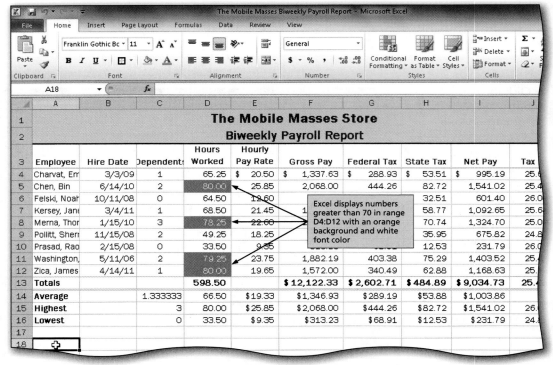

Figure 2–52

Conditional Formatting Operators

As shown in Figure 2–49 on page EX 105, the second text box in the New Formatting Rule dialog box allows you to select a relational operator, such as less than, to use in the condition. The eight different relational operators from which you can choose for conditional formatting in the New Formatting Rule dialog box are summarized in Table 2–5.

Table 2–5 Summary of Conditional Formatting Relational Operators	
Relational Operator	**Description**
between	Cell value is between two numbers.
not between	Cell value is not between two numbers.
equal to	Cell value is equal to a number.
not equal to	Cell value is not equal to a number.
greater than	Cell value is greater than a number.
less than	Cell value is less than a number.
greater than or equal to	Cell value is greater than or equal to a number.
less than or equal to	Cell value is less than or equal to a number.

Changing the Widths of Columns and Heights of Rows

When Excel starts and displays a blank worksheet on the screen, all of the columns have a default width of 8.43 characters, or 64 pixels. These values may change depending on the theme applied to the workbook. For example, in this chapter, the Trek theme was applied to the workbook, resulting in columns having a default width of 8.11 characters. A character is defined as a letter, number, symbol, or punctuation mark in 11-point Calibri font, the default font used by Excel. An average of 8.43 characters in 11-point Calibri font will fit in a cell.

Another measure of the height and width of cells is pixels, which is short for picture element. A **pixel** is a dot on the screen that contains a color. The size of the dot is based on your screen's resolution. At the resolution of 1024 × 768 used in this book, 1024 pixels appear across the screen and 768 pixels appear down the screen for a total of 786,432 pixels. It is these 786,432 pixels that form the font and other items you see on the screen.

The default row height in a blank worksheet is 15 points (or 20 pixels). Recall from Chapter 1 that a point is equal to 1/72 of an inch. Thus, 15 points is equal to about 1/5 of an inch. You can change the width of the columns or height of the rows at any time to make the worksheet easier to read or to ensure that Excel displays an entry properly in a cell.

BTW

Hidden Rows and Columns
For some people, trying to unhide a range of columns using the mouse can be frustrating. An alternative is to use the keyboard: select the columns to the right and left of the hidden columns and then press CTRL+SHIFT+) (RIGHT PARENTHESIS). To use the keyboard to hide a range of columns, press CTRL+0 (ZERO). You also can use the keyboard to unhide a range of rows by selecting the rows immediately above and below the hidden rows and then pressing CTRL+SHIFT+((LEFT PARENTHESIS). To use the keyboard to hide a range of rows, press CTRL+9.

To Change the Widths of Columns

When changing the column width, you can set the width manually or you can instruct Excel to size the column to best fit. **Best fit** means that the width of the column will be increased or decreased so that the widest entry will fit in the column. Sometimes, you may prefer more or less white space in a column than best fit provides. To change the white space, Excel allows you to change column widths manually.

When the format you assign to a cell causes the entry to exceed the width of a column, Excel automatically changes the column width to best fit. If you do not assign a format to a cell or cells in a column, the column width will remain 8.43 characters. To set a column width to best fit, double-click the right boundary of the column heading above row 1.

The steps on the following pages change the column widths: column A, B, and C to best fit; column H to 10.22 characters; and columns D, E, and J to 7.56 characters.

1

- Drag through column headings A, B, and C above row 1 to select the columns.

- Point to the boundary on the right side of column heading C to cause the mouse pointer to become a split double arrow (Figure 2–53).

Q&A

What if I want to make a large change to the column width?

If you want to increase or decrease column width significantly, you can right-click a column heading and then use the Column Width command on the shortcut menu to change the column's width. To use this command, however, you must select one or more entire columns.

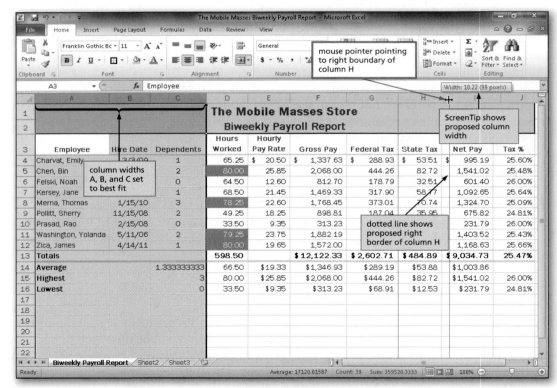

Figure 2–53

2

- Double-click the right boundary of column heading C to change the width of the selected columns to best fit.

- Point to the boundary on the right side of the column H heading above row 1.

- When the mouse pointer changes to a split double arrow, drag until the ScreenTip indicates Width: 10.22 (99 pixels). Do not release the mouse button (Figure 2–54).

Q&A

What happens if I change the column width to zero (0)?

If you decrease the column width to 0, the column is hidden. **Hiding cells** is a technique you can use to hide data that might not be relevant to a particular report or sensitive data that you do not want others to see. To instruct Excel to display a hidden column, position the mouse pointer to the right of the column heading boundary where the hidden column is located and then drag to the right.

Figure 2–54

3

- Release the mouse button to change the column width.

- Click the column D heading above row 1 to select the column.

- While holding down the CTRL key, click the column E heading and then the column J heading above row 1 so that nonadjacent columns are selected (Figure 2–55).

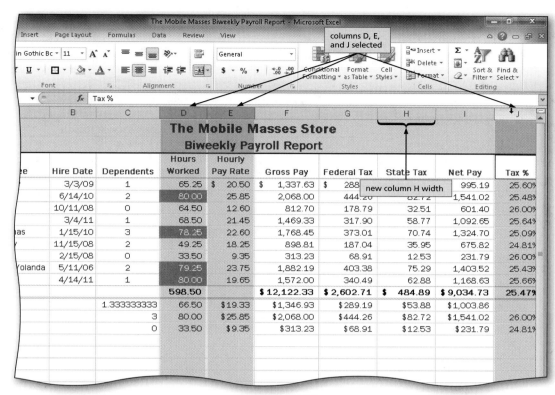

Figure 2–55

4

- If necessary, scroll the worksheet to the right so that the right border of column J is visible. Point to the boundary on the right side of the column J heading above row 1.

- Drag until the ScreenTip indicates Width: 7.56 (75 pixels). Do not release the mouse button (Figure 2–56).

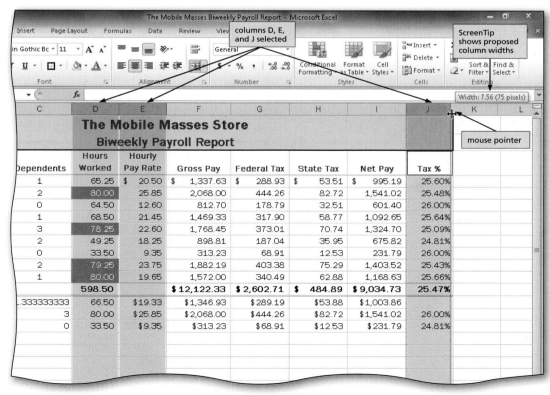

Figure 2–56

- Release the mouse button to change the column widths.

- If necessary, scroll the worksheet to the left so that the left border of column A is visible.

- Click anywhere in the worksheet, such as cell A18, to deselect the columns (Figure 2–57).

Other Ways

1. Right-click column heading or drag through multiple column headings and right-click, click Column Width on shortcut menu, enter desired column width, click OK button

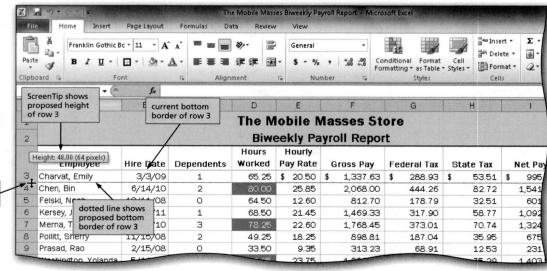

Figure 2–57

To Change the Heights of Rows

When you increase the font size of a cell entry, such as the title in cell A1, Excel automatically increases the row height to best fit so that it can display the characters properly. Recall that Excel did this earlier when multiple lines were entered in a cell in row 3, and when the cell style of the worksheet title and subtitle was changed.

You also can increase or decrease the height of a row manually to improve the appearance of the worksheet. The following steps improve the appearance of the worksheet by increasing the height of row 3 to 48.00 points and increasing the height of row 14 to 27.00 points.

- Point to the boundary below row heading 3.

- Drag down until the ScreenTip indicates Height: 48.00 (64 pixels). Do not release the mouse button (Figure 2–58).

Figure 2–58

2

- Release the mouse button to change the row height.

- Point to the boundary below row heading 14.

- Drag down until the ScreenTip indicates Height: 27.00 (36 pixels). Do not release the mouse button (Figure 2–59).

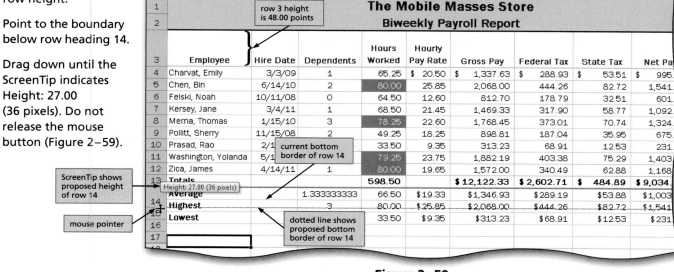

Figure 2–59

3

- Release the mouse button to change the row height.

- Click anywhere in the worksheet, such as cell A18, to deselect the current cell (Figure 2–60).

Q&A

Can I hide a row?

Yes. As with column widths, when you decrease the row height to 0, the row is hidden. To instruct Excel to display a hidden row, position the mouse pointer just below the row heading boundary where the row is hidden and then drag down. To set a row height to best fit, double-click the bottom boundary of the row heading.

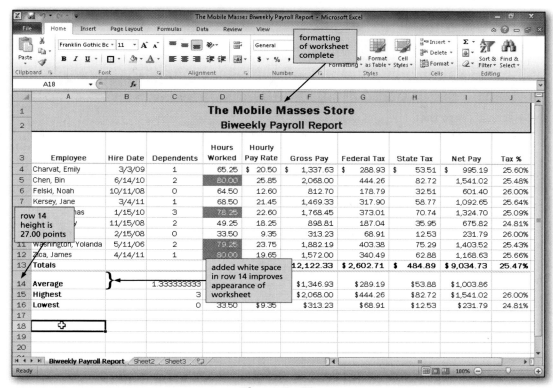

Figure 2–60

Other Ways
1. Right-click row heading or drag through multiple row headings and right-click, click Row Height   on shortcut menu, enter desired row height, click OK button

Break Point: If you wish to take a break, this is a good place to do so. Be sure to save the The Mobile Masses Biweekly Payroll Report file again and then you can quit Excel. To resume at a later time, start Excel, open the file called The Mobile Masses Biweekly Payroll Report and continue following the steps from this location forward.

BTW

Spell Checking
While Excel's spell checker is a valuable tool, it is not infallible. You should proofread your workbook carefully by pointing to each word and saying it aloud as you point to it. Be mindful of misused words such as its and it's, through and though, and to and too. Nothing undermines a good impression more than a professional looking report with misspelled words.

Checking Spelling

Excel includes a **spell checker** you can use to check a worksheet for spelling errors. The spell checker looks for spelling errors by comparing words on the worksheet against words contained in its standard dictionary. If you often use specialized terms that are not in the standard dictionary, you may want to add them to a custom dictionary using the Spelling dialog box.

When the spell checker finds a word that is not in either dictionary, it displays the word in the Spelling dialog box. You then can correct it if it is misspelled.

To Check Spelling on the Worksheet

To illustrate how Excel responds to a misspelled word, the following steps misspell purposely the word, Employee, in cell A3 as the word, Empolyee, as shown in Figure 2–61.

1

- Click cell A3 and then type **Empolyee** to misspell the word Employee.

- Select cell A1 so that the spell checker begins checking at the selected cell.

- Click Review on the Ribbon to display the Review tab.

- Click the Spelling button (Review tab | Proofing group) to run the spell checker and display the misspelled word in the Spelling dialog box (Figure 2–61).

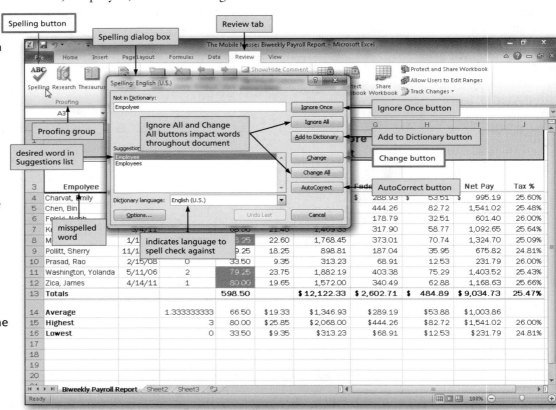

Figure 2–61

Q&A

What happens when the spell checker finds a misspelled word?

When the spell checker identifies that a cell contains a word not in its standard or custom dictionary, it selects that cell as the active cell and displays the Spelling dialog box. The Spelling dialog box lists the word not found in the dictionary and a list of suggested corrections (Figure 2–61).

2

- Click the Change button (Spelling dialog box) to change the misspelled word to the correct word (Figure 2–62).

- Click the Close button (Spelling dialog box) to close the Spelling dialog box.

- If the Microsoft Excel dialog box is displayed, click the OK button.

3

- Click anywhere in the worksheet, such as cell A18, to deselect the current cell.

- Display the Home tab.

- Click the Save button on the Quick Access Toolbar to save the workbook.

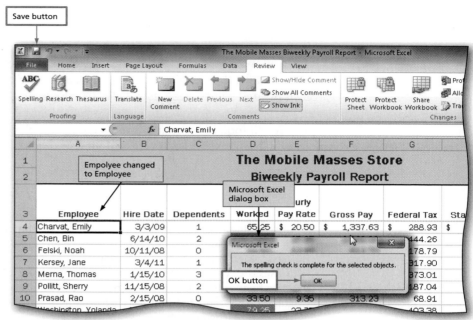

Figure 2–62

What other actions can I take in the Spelling dialog box?

If one of the words in the Suggestions list is correct, click it and then click the Change button. If none of the suggestions is correct, type the correct word in the Not in Dictionary text box and then click the Change button. To change the word throughout the worksheet, click the Change All button instead of the Change button. To skip correcting the word, click the Ignore Once button. To have Excel ignore the word for the remainder of the worksheet, click the Ignore All button.

Other Ways

1. Press F7

Additional Spell Checker Considerations

Consider these additional guidelines when using the spell checker:

- To check the spelling of the text in a single cell, double-click the cell to make the formula bar active and then click the Spelling button (Review tab | Proofing group).

- If you select a single cell so that the formula bar is not active and then start the spell checker, Excel checks the remainder of the worksheet, including notes and embedded charts.

- If you select a cell other than cell A1 before you start the spell checker, Excel will display a dialog box when the spell checker reaches the end of the worksheet, asking if you want to continue checking at the beginning.

- If you select a range of cells before starting the spell checker, Excel checks the spelling of the words only in the selected range.

- To check the spelling of all the sheets in a workbook, right-click any sheet tab, click Select All Sheets on the sheet tab shortcut menu, and then start the spell checker.

- To add words to the dictionary such as your last name, click the Add to Dictionary button in the Spelling dialog box (Figure 2–61) when Excel identifies the word as not in the dictionary.

- Click the AutoCorrect button (Spelling dialog box) to add the misspelled word and the correct version of the word to the AutoCorrect list. For example, suppose that you misspell the word, do, as the word, dox. When the spell checker displays the Spelling dialog box with the correct word, do, in the Change to box, click the AutoCorrect button. Then, anytime in the future that you type the word dox, Excel automatically will change it to the word, do.

BTW

Error Checking
Always take the time to check the formulas of a worksheet before submitting it to your supervisor. You can check formulas by clicking the Error Checking button (Formulas tab | Formula Auditing group). You also should test the formulas by employing data that tests the limits of formulas. Experienced spreadsheet specialists spend as much time testing a workbook as they do creating it, and they do so before placing the workbook into production.

Preparing to Print the Worksheet

Excel allows for a great deal of customization in how a worksheet appears when printed. For example, the margins on the page can be adjusted. A header or footer can be added to each printed page as well. Excel also has the capability to work on the worksheet in Page Layout view. **Page Layout view** allows you to create or modify a worksheet while viewing how it will look in printed format. The default view that you have worked in up until this point in the book is called **Normal view**.

Plan Ahead

Specify how the printed worksheet should appear.

Before printing a worksheet, you should consider how the worksheet will appear when printed. In order to fit as much information on the printed page as possible, the margins of the worksheet should be set to a reasonably small width and height. While the current version of a worksheet may print on one page, you may add more data in the future that causes the worksheet to extend to multiple pages. It is, therefore, a good idea to add a page header to the worksheet that prints in the top margin of each page. A **header** is common content that prints on every page of a worksheet. Landscape orientation is a good choice for large worksheets because the printed worksheet's width is greater than its length.

To Change the Worksheet's Margins, Header, and Orientation in Page Layout View

The following steps change to Page Layout view, narrow the margins of the worksheet, change the header of the worksheet, and set the orientation of the worksheet to landscape. Often, you may want to reduce margins so that the printed worksheet better fits the page. **Margins** are those portions of a printed page outside the main body of the printed document and always are blank when printed. Recall that in Chapter 1, the worksheet was printed in landscape orientation. The current worksheet also is too wide for a single page and requires landscape orientation to fit on one page in a readable manner.

- Click the Page Layout button on the status bar to view the worksheet in Page Layout view (Figure 2–63).

Q&A

What are some key features of Page Layout view?

Page Layout view shows the worksheet divided into pages. A gray background separates each page. The white areas surrounding each page indicate the print margins. The top of each page includes a Header area, and the bottom of each page includes a Footer area. Page Layout view also includes a ruler at the top of the page that assists you in placing objects on the page, such as charts and pictures.

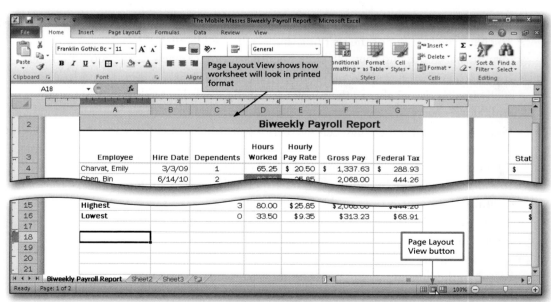

Figure 2–63

2

- Display the Page Layout tab.

- Click the Margins button (Page Layout tab | Page Setup group) to display the Margins gallery (Figure 2–64).

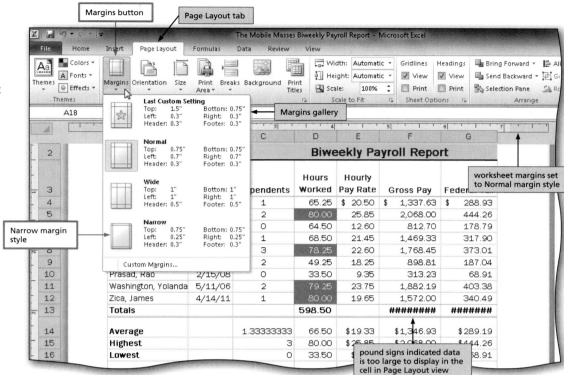

Figure 2–64

3

- Click Narrow in the Margins gallery to change the worksheet margins to the Narrow margin style.

- Drag the scroll bar on the right side of the worksheet to the top so that row 1 of the worksheet is displayed.

- Click above the worksheet title in cell A1 in the center area of the Header area.

- Type **Samuel Snyder** and then press the ENTER key. Type **Chief Financial Officer** to complete the worksheet header (Figure 2–65).

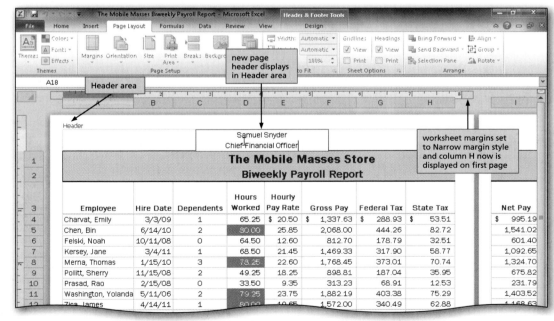

Figure 2–65

Q&A

What else can I place in a header?

You can add text, page number information, date and time information, the file path of the workbook, the file name of the workbook, the sheet name of the workbook, and pictures to a header.

4

- Select cell B16 to deselect the header. Click the Orientation button (Page Layout tab | Page Setup group) to display the Orientation gallery (Figure 2–66).

Q&A

Why do I need to deselect the header?

Excel disables almost all of the buttons on the Ribbon as you edit a header or footer. In addition to the commands on the Design tab (Figure 2–65 on the previous page), only a few commands remain available on the Home tab on the Ribbon. To continue working in Excel, therefore, you should select a cell in the worksheet so that all of the commands on the Ribbon are available for your use.

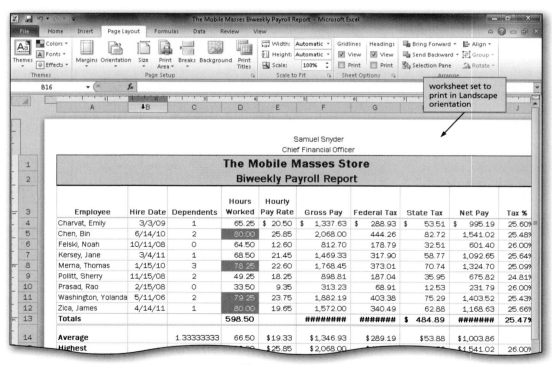

Figure 2–66

5

- Click Landscape in the Orientation gallery to change the worksheet's orientation to landscape (Figure 2–67).

Q&A

Do I need to change the orientation every time I want to print the worksheet?

No. Once you change the orientation and save the workbook, Excel will save the orientation setting for that workbook until you change it. When you open a new workbook, Excel sets the orientation to portrait.

Figure 2–67

Other Ways

1. Click Page Setup Dialog Box Launcher (Page Layout tab | Page Setup group), click Page tab
   (Page Setup dialog box), click Portrait or Landscape, click OK button

Printing the Worksheet

Excel provides other options for printing a worksheet. The following sections print the worksheet and print a section of the worksheet.

To Print a Worksheet

The following steps print the worksheet.

1 Click File on the Ribbon to open the Backstage view.

2 Click the Print tab in the Backstage view to display the Print gallery.

3 If necessary, click the Printer Status button in the Print gallery to display a list of available Printer options and then click the desired printer to change the currently selected printer.

4 Click the Print button in the Print gallery to print the worksheet in landscape orientation on the currently selected printer.

5 When the printer stops, retrieve the hard copy (Figure 2–68).

BTW

Conserving Ink and Toner
If you want to conserve ink or toner, you can instruct Excel to print draft quality documents by clicking File on the Ribbon to open the Backstage view, clicking Options in the Backstage view to display the Excel Options dialog box, clicking Advanced in the left pane (Excel Options dialog box), scrolling to the Print area in the right pane, placing a check mark in the 'Use draft quality' check box, and then clicking the OK button. Then, use the Backstage view to print the document as usual.

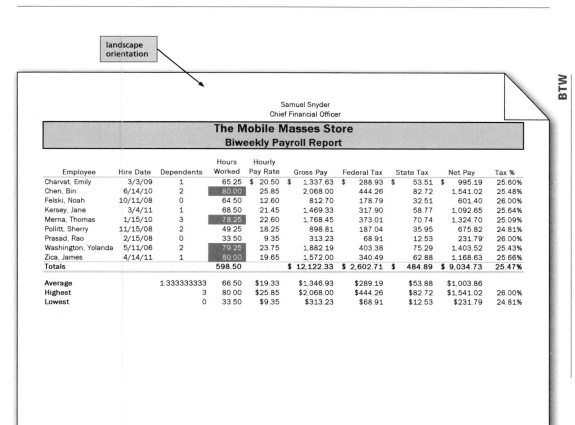

landscape orientation

Samuel Snyder
Chief Financial Officer

The Mobile Masses Store
Biweekly Payroll Report

Employee	Hire Date	Dependents	Hours Worked	Hourly Pay Rate	Gross Pay	Federal Tax	State Tax	Net Pay	Tax %
Charvat, Emily	3/3/09	1	65.25	$ 20.50	$ 1,337.63	$ 288.93	$ 53.51	$ 995.19	25.60%
Chen, Bin	6/14/10	2	80.00	25.85	2,068.00	444.26	82.72	1,541.02	25.48%
Felski, Noah	10/11/08	0	64.50	12.60	812.70	178.79	32.51	601.40	26.00%
Kersey, Jane	3/4/11	1	68.50	21.45	1,469.33	317.90	58.77	1,092.65	25.64%
Merna, Thomas	1/15/10	3	78.25	22.60	1,768.45	373.01	70.74	1,324.70	25.09%
Pollitt, Sherry	11/15/08	2	49.25	18.25	898.81	187.04	35.95	675.82	24.81%
Prasad, Rao	2/15/08	0	33.50	9.35	313.23	68.91	12.53	231.79	26.00%
Washington, Yolanda	5/11/06	2	79.25	23.75	1,882.19	403.38	75.29	1,403.52	25.43%
Zica, James	4/14/11	1	80.00	19.65	1,572.00	340.49	62.88	1,168.63	25.66%
Totals			598.50		$ 12,122.33	$ 2,602.71	$ 484.89	$ 9,034.73	25.47%
Average		1.333333333	66.50	$19.33	$1,346.93	$289.19	$53.88	$1,003.86	
Highest		3	80.00	$25.85	$2,068.00	$444.26	$82.72	$1,541.02	26.00%
Lowest		0	33.50	$9.35	$313.23	$68.91	$12.53	$231.79	24.81%

Figure 2–68

BTW

Printing Document Properties
To print document properties, click File on the Ribbon to open the Backstage view, click the Print tab in the Backstage view to display the Print gallery, click the first button in the Settings area to display a list of options specifying what you can print, click Document Properties in the list to specify you want to print the document properties instead of the actual document, and then click the Print button in the Print gallery to print the document properties on the currently selected printer.

To Print a Section of the Worksheet

You might not always want to print the entire worksheet. You can print portions of the worksheet by selecting the range of cells to print and then clicking the Selection option button in the Print what area in the Print dialog box. The following steps print the range A3:F16.

- Select the range to print, cells A3:F16 in this case.

- Click File on the Ribbon to open the Backstage view.

- Click the Print tab to display the Print gallery.

- Click Print Active Sheets in the Settings area (Print tab | Print gallery) to display a list of options that determine what Excel should print (Figure 2–69).

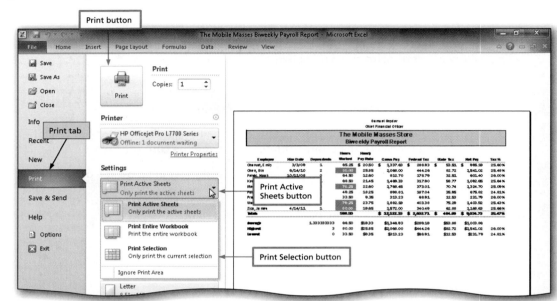

Figure 2–69

- Click Print Selection to instruct Excel to print only the selected range.

- Click the Print button in the Print gallery to print the selected range of the worksheet on the currently selected printer (Figure 2–70).

- Click the Normal button on the status bar to return to Normal view.

- Click cell A18 to deselect the range A3:F16.

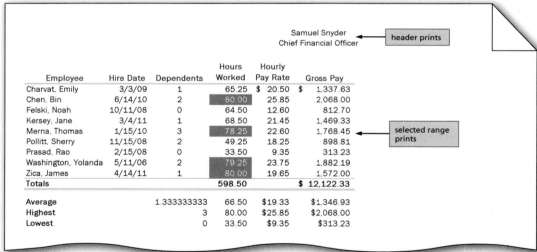

Samuel Snyder
Chief Financial Officer ← header prints

Employee	Hire Date	Dependents	Hours Worked	Hourly Pay Rate	Gross Pay
Charvat, Emily	3/3/09	1	65.25	$ 20.50	$ 1,337.63
Chen, Bin	6/14/10	2	80.00	25.85	2,068.00
Felski, Noah	10/11/08	0	64.50	12.60	812.70
Kersey, Jane	3/4/11	1	68.50	21.45	1,469.33
Merna, Thomas	1/15/10	3	78.25	22.60	1,768.45
Pollitt, Sherry	11/15/08	2	49.25	18.25	898.81
Prasad, Rao	2/15/08	0	33.50	9.35	313.23
Washington, Yolanda	5/11/06	2	79.25	23.75	1,882.19
Zica, James	4/14/11	1	80.00	19.65	1,572.00
Totals			598.50		$ 12,122.33
Average		1.333333333	66.50	$19.33	$1,346.93
Highest		3	80.00	$25.85	$2,068.00
Lowest		0	33.50	$9.35	$313.23

selected range prints →

Figure 2–70

Q&A

What are my options for telling Excel what to print?

Excel includes three options to allow you to determine what should be printed (Figure 2–69). As shown in the previous steps, the Print Selection button instructs Excel to print the selected range. The Print Active Sheets button instructs Excel to print the active worksheet (the worksheet currently on the screen) or the selected worksheets. Finally, the Print Entire Workbook button instructs Excel to print all of the worksheets in the workbook.

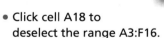

Other Ways

1. Select range, click Print Area button (Page Layout tab | Page Setup group), click Set Print Area, click Quick Print button on Quick Access Toolbar, click Print Area, click Clear Print Area
2. Select range, click Print Area button (Page Layout tab | Page Setup group), click Set Print Area, click File tab to open Backstage view, click Print tab, click Print button

Displaying and Printing the Formulas Version of the Worksheet

BTW

Values versus Formulas
When completing class assignments, do not enter numbers in cells that require formulas. Most instructors will check both the values version and formulas version of your worksheets. The formulas version verifies that you entered formulas, rather than numbers, in formula-based cells.

Thus far, you have been working with the **values version** of the worksheet, which shows the results of the formulas you have entered, rather than the actual formulas. Excel also can display and print the **formulas version** of the worksheet, which shows the actual formulas you have entered, rather than the resulting values.

The formulas version is useful for debugging a worksheet. **Debugging** is the process of finding and correcting errors in the worksheet. Viewing and printing the formulas version instead of the values version makes it easier to see any mistakes in the formulas.

When you change from the values version to the formulas version, Excel increases the width of the columns so that the formulas and text do not overflow into adjacent cells on the right. The formulas version of the worksheet, thus, usually is significantly wider than the values version. To fit the wide printout on one page, you can use landscape orientation, which has already been selected for the workbook, and the Fit to option in the Page sheet in the Page Setup dialog box.

To Display the Formulas in the Worksheet and Fit the Printout on One Page

The following steps change the view of the worksheet from the values version to the formulas version of the worksheet and then print the formulas version on one page.

1

- Press CTRL+ACCENT MARK (`) to display the worksheet with formulas.

- Click the right horizontal scroll arrow until column J appears (Figure 2–71).

2

- Click the Page Setup Dialog Box Launcher (Page Layout tab | Page Setup group) to display the Page Setup dialog box.

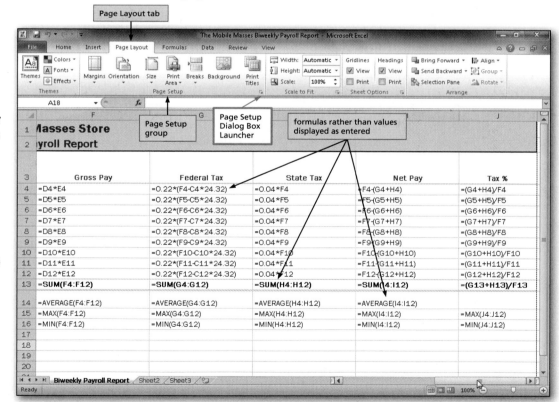

Figure 2–71

3

- If necessary, click Landscape in the Orientation area to select it.

- If necessary, click Fit to in the Scaling area to select it.

- Click the Print button (Page Setup dialog box) to print the formulas in the worksheet on one page in landscape orientation (Figure 2–72). If necessary, in the Backstage view, select the Print Active Sheets option in the Settings area of the Print gallery.

- When Excel displays the Backstage view, click the Print button to print the worksheet.

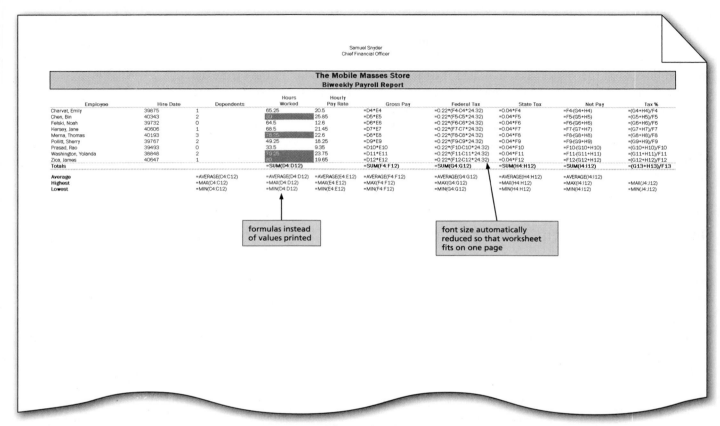

Figure 2–72

5

- After viewing and printing the formulas version, press CTRL+ACCENT MARK (`) to instruct Excel to display the values version.

- Click the left horizontal scroll arrow until column A appears.

To Change the Print Scaling Option Back to 100%

Depending on your printer, you may have to change the Print Scaling option back to 100% after using the Fit to option. Doing so will cause the worksheet to print at the default print scaling of 100%. The following steps reset the Print Scaling option so that future worksheets print at 100%, instead of being resized to print on one page.

1 If necessary, display the Page Layout tab and then click the Page Setup Dialog Box Launcher (Page Layout tab | Page Setup group) to display the Page Setup dialog box.

2 Click Adjust to in the Scaling area to select the Adjust to setting.

3 If necessary, type 100 in the Adjust to box to adjust the print scaling to a new percentage.

4 Click the OK button (Page Setup dialog box) to set the print scaling to normal.

5 Display the Home tab.

Q&A What is the purpose of the Adjust to box in the Page Setup dialog box?

The Adjust to box allows you to specify the percentage of reduction or enlargement in the printout of a worksheet. The default percentage is 100%. When you click the Fit to option, this percentage automatically changes to the percentage required to fit the printout on one page.

To Save the Workbook and Quit Excel

With the workbook complete, the following steps save the workbook and quit Excel.

1 Click the Save button on the Quick Access Toolbar.

2 Click the Close button on the upper-right corner of the title bar.

Chapter Summary

In this chapter you have learned how to enter formulas, calculate an average, find the highest and lowest numbers in a range, verify formulas using Range Finder, added borders, align text, format numbers, change column widths and row heights, and add conditional formatting to a range of numbers. In addition, you learned to spell check a worksheet, print a section of a worksheet, and display and print the formulas version of the worksheet using the Fit to option. The items listed below include all the new Excel skills you have learned in this chapter.

1. Enter a Formula Using the Keyboard (EX 75)
2. Enter Formulas Using Point Mode (EX 77)
3. Copy Formulas Using the Fill Handle (EX 80)
4. Determine the Average of a Range of Numbers Using the Keyboard and Mouse (EX 84)
5. Determine the Highest Number in a Range of Numbers Using the Insert Function Box (EX 86)
6. Determine the Lowest Number in a Range of Numbers Using the Sum Menu (EX 87)
7. Copy a Range of Cells Across Columns to an Adjacent Range Using the Fill Handle (EX 89)
8. Verify a Formula Using Range Finder (EX 91)
9. Change the Workbook Theme (EX 94)
10. Change the Background Color and Apply a Box Border to the Worksheet Title and Subtitle (EX 96)
11. Format Dates and Center Data in Cells (EX 98)
12. Apply an Accounting Number Format and Comma Style Format Using the Ribbon (EX 100)
13. Apply a Currency Style Format with a Floating Dollar Sign Using the Format Cells Dialog Box (EX 102)
14. Apply a Percent Style Format and Use the Increase Decimal Button (EX 103)
15. Apply Conditional Formatting (EX 104)
16. Change the Widths of Columns (EX 107)
17. Change the Heights of Rows (EX 110)
18. Check Spelling on the Worksheet (EX 112)
19. Change the Worksheet's Margins, Header, and Orientation in Page Layout View (EX 114)
20. Print a Section of the Worksheet (EX 118)
21. Display the Formulas in the Worksheet and Fit the Printout on One Page (EX 119)

Learn It Online

Test your knowledge of chapter content and key terms.

Instructions: To complete the Learn It Online exercises, start your browser, click the Address bar, and then enter **scsite.com/ex2010/learn** as the Web address. When the Excel 2010 Learn It Online page is displayed, click the link for the exercise you want to complete and then read the instructions.

Chapter Reinforcement TF, MC, and SA
A series of true/false, multiple choice, and short answer questions that test your knowledge of the chapter content.

Flash Cards
An interactive learning environment where you identify chapter key terms associated with displayed definitions.

Practice Test
A series of multiple choice questions that test your knowledge of chapter content and key terms.

Who Wants To Be a Computer Genius?
An interactive game that challenges your knowledge of chapter content in the style of a television quiz show.

Wheel of Terms
An interactive game that challenges your knowledge of chapter key terms in the style of the television show *Wheel of Fortune*.

Crossword Puzzle Challenge
A crossword puzzle that challenges your knowledge of key terms presented in the chapter.

Apply Your Knowledge

Reinforce the skills and apply the concepts you learned in this chapter.

Profit Analysis Worksheet

Instructions: The purpose of this exercise is to open a partially completed workbook, enter formulas and functions, copy the formulas and functions, and then format the worksheet titles and numbers. As shown in Figure 2–73, the completed worksheet analyzes the costs associated with a police department's fleet of vehicles.

	A	B	C	D	E	F	G
1			**Village of Scott Police Department**				
2			**Monthly Vehicle Cost-per-Mile Summary**				
3	Vehicle ID	Miles Driven	Cost per Mile	Maintenance Cost	Mileage Cost	Total Cost	Total Cost per Mile
4	670543	2,007	$ 0.49	$ 242.80	$ 983.43	$ 1,226.23	$ 0.61
5	979253	3,192	0.48	446.37	1,532.16	1,978.53	0.62
6	948173	3,802	0.65	472.47	2,471.30	2,943.77	0.77
7	837625	2,080	0.62	432.25	1,289.60	1,721.85	0.83
8	824664	2,475	0.56	369.88	1,386.00	1,755.88	0.71
9	655385	3,294	0.50	352.05	1,647.00	1,999.05	0.61
10	836417	3,640	0.70	417.80	2,548.00	2,965.80	0.81
11	993617	3,395	0.70	390.39	2,376.50	2,766.89	0.81
12	779468	4,075	0.55	442.17	2,241.25	2,683.42	0.66
13	**Totals**	**27,960**		$ 3,566.18	$ 16,475.24	$ 20,041.42	$ 0.72
14	**Highest**	4,075	$0.70	$472.47	$2,548.00	$2,965.80	$0.83
15	**Lowest**	2,007	$0.48	$242.80	$983.43	$1,226.23	$0.61
16	**Average**	3,107	$0.58	$396.24	$1,830.58	$2,226.82	$0.72

Figure 2–73

1. Start Excel. Open the workbook Apply 2-1 Village of Scott Police Department. See the inside back cover of this book for instructions for downloading the Data Files for Students or see your instructor for information on accessing the files required in this book.

2. Use the following formulas in cells E4, F4, and G4:

   Mileage Cost (cell E4) = Miles Driven * Cost per Mile or = B4 * C4

   Total Cost (cell F4) = Maintenance Cost + Mileage Cost or = D4 + E4

   Total Cost per Mile (cell G4) = Total Cost / Miles Driven or = F4 / B4

   Use the fill handle to copy the three formulas in the range E4:G4 to the range E5:G12.

3. Determine totals for the miles driven, maintenance cost, mileage cost, and total cost in row 13. Copy the formula in cell G12 to G13 to assign the formula in cell G12 to G13 in the total line. If necessary, reapply the Total cell style to cell G13.

4. In the range B14:B16, determine the highest value, lowest value, and average value, respectively, for the values in the range B4:B12. Use the fill handle to copy the three functions to the range C14:G16.

5. Format the worksheet as follows:

   a. change the workbook theme to Foundry by using the Themes button (Page Layout tab | Themes group)

   b. cell A1 — change to Title cell style

   c. cell A2 — change to a font size of 16

   d. cells A1:A2 — Rose background color and a thick box border

   e. cells C4:G4 and D13:G13 — Accounting number format with two decimal places and fixed dollar signs by using the Accounting Number Format button (Home tab | Number group)

   f. cells C5:G12 — Comma style format with two decimal places by using the Comma Style button (Home tab | Number group)

   g. cells B4:B16 — Comma style format with no decimal places

   h. cells C14:G16 — Currency style format with floating dollar signs by using the Format Cells: Number Dialog Box Launcher (Home tab | Number group)

   i. cells G4:G12 — apply conditional formatting so that cells with a value greater than 0.80 appear with a rose background color

6. Switch to Page Layout View and delete any current text in the Header area. Enter your name, course, laboratory assignment number, and any other information, as specified by your instructor, in the Header area. Preview and print the worksheet in landscape orientation. Change the document properties, as specified by your instructor. Save the workbook using the file name, Apply 2-1 Village of Scott Police Department Complete.

7. Use Range Finder to verify the formula in cell G13.

Continued >

Apply Your Knowledge *continued*

8. Print the range A3:D16. Press CTRL+ACCENT MARK (`) to change the display from the values version of the worksheet to the formulas version. Print the formulas version in landscape orientation on one page (Figure 2–74) by using the Fit to option in the Page sheet in the Page Setup dialog box. Press CTRL+ACCENT MARK (`) to change the display of the worksheet back to the values version. Close the workbook without saving it.

9. Submit the workbook and results as specified by your instructor.

Jeff Quasney
Apply 2-1 Village of Scott Police Department

Village of Scott Police Department
Monthly Vehicle Cost-per-Mile Summary

Vehicle ID	Miles Driven	Cost per Mile	Maintenance Cost	Mileage Cost	Total Cost	Total Cost per Mile
670543	2007	0.49	242.8	=B4*C4	=D4+E4	=F4/B4
979253	3192	0.48	446.37	=B5*C5	=D5+E5	=F5/B5
948173	3802	0.65	472.47	=B6*C6	=D6+E6	=F6/B6
837625	2080	0.62	432.25	=B7*C7	=D7+E7	=F7/B7
824664	2475	0.56	369.88	=B8*C8	=D8+E8	=F8/B8
655385	3294	0.5	352.05	=B9*C9	=D9+E9	=F9/B9
836417	3640	0.7	417.8	=B10*C10	=D10+E10	=F10/B10
993617	3395	0.7	390.39	=B11*C11	=D11+E11	=F11/B11
779468	4075	0.55	442.17	=B12*C12	=D12+E12	=F12/B12
Totals	=SUM(B4:B12)		=SUM(D4:D12)	=SUM(E4:E12)	=SUM(F4:F12)	=F13/B13
Highest	=MAX(B4:B12)	=MAX(C4:C12)	=MAX(D4:D12)	=MAX(E4:E12)	=MAX(F4:F12)	=MAX(G4:G12)
Lowest	=MIN(B4:B12)	=MIN(C4:C12)	=MIN(D4:D12)	=MIN(E4:E12)	=MIN(F4:F12)	=MIN(G4:G12)
Average	=AVERAGE(B4:B12)	=AVERAGE(C4:C12)	=AVERAGE(D4:D12)	=AVERAGE(E4:E12)	=AVERAGE(F4:F12)	=AVERAGE(G4:G12)

Figure 2–74

Extend Your Knowledge

Extend the skills you learned in this chapter and experiment with new skills. You may need to use Help to complete the assignment.

Applying Conditional Formatting to Cells

Instructions: Start Excel. Open the workbook Extend 2-1 State Wildlife Department Employee Ratings. See the inside back cover of this book for instructions for downloading the Data Files for Students, or see your instructor for information on accessing the files required in this book. Perform the following tasks to apply three types of conditional formatting to cells in a worksheet:

1. Select the range C4:C18. Click the Conditional Formatting button (Home tab | Styles group) and then click New Rule in the Conditional Formatting list. Select 'Format only top or bottom ranked values' in the Select a Rule Type area (Conditional Formatting Rules Manager dialog box), as shown in Figure 2–75. Enter any value between 10 and 25 in the text box in the Edit the Rule Description (New Formatting Rule dialog box) area, and click the '% of the selected range' check box to select it. Click the Format button, and choose a blue background to assign this conditional format. Click the OK button in each dialog box and view the worksheet.

2. With range C4:C18 selected, apply a conditional format to the range that uses a green background color to highlight cells with scores that are below average.

3. With range D4:D18 selected, apply a conditional format to the range that uses an orange background to highlight cells that contain Exemplary or Exceeds Requirements.

4. With range B4:B18 selected, apply a conditional format to the range that uses a red background color to highlight cells with duplicate student names.

5. Change the document properties as specified by your instructor. Save the workbook using the file name, Extend 2-1 State Wildlife Department Employee Ratings Complete. Submit the revised workbook as specified by your instructor.

Figure 2–75

Make It Right

Analyze a workbook and correct all errors and/or improve the design.

Correcting Formatting, Functions, and Formulas in a Worksheet

Instructions: Start Excel. Open the workbook Make It Right 2-1 Dion Designwear Profit Analysis. See the inside back cover of this book for instructions for downloading the Data Files for Students, or see your instructor for information on accessing the files required for this book.

In this exercise you will learn how to correct formatting, functions, and formula problems in a worksheet (Figure 2–76).

	A	B	C	D	E	F	G	H
1				**Dion Designwear**				
2				Profit Anaylsis				
3	**Product**	**Desciption**	**Cost**	**Profit**	**Units Sold**	**Total Sales**	**Total Profit**	**% Profit**
4	4835	Coat	$247.63	$144.83	95,159	$37,346,101.14	$13,781,877.97	36.903%
5	7563	Custom	210.08	142.18	75,762	26,687,922.12	10,771,841.16	40.362%
6	8191	Dress	186.53	99.48	69,297	19,819,634.97	6,893,665.56	34.782%
7	8409	Hat	146.82	59.97	39,164	8,098,723.56	2,348,665.08	29.000%
8	5677	Jacket	140.68	85.63	38,261	8,658,846.91	3,276,289.43	37.837%
9	8985	Shirt	68.38	8.15	42,420	3,246,402.60	345,723.00	10.649%
10	5871	Slacks	144.54	30.44	68,536	11,992,429.28	2,086,235.84	17.396%
11	7796	Sleepwear	93.74	11.80	77,413	8,170,168.02	913,473.40	11.181%
12	7777	Suit	305.91	126.00	19,999	8,637,768.09	2,519,874.00	29.173%
13	8178	Sweater	112.21	9.24	61,257	7,439,662.65	566,014.68	7.608%
14	**Totals**				**587,268**	**$140,097,659.34**	**$43,503,660.12**	**31.052%**
15	Lowest		$68.38	$8.15	19,999	$3,246,402.60	$345,723.00	7.608%
16	Highest		$305.91	$144.83	95,159	$37,346,101.14	$13,781,877.97	40.362%
17	Average		$156.54	$71.77	54,679	$14,009,765.93	$3,302,420.24	25.489%
18								
19								

Figure 2–76

Continued >

Make It Right *continued*

Perform the following tasks:

1. Add a thick box border around the title and subtitle so that they appear more separated from the rest of the worksheet.

2. Adjust the width of column D to 8.11 pixels so that the word in the column header does not wrap. Adjust the column widths of columns F and G to best fit.

3. Spell check the worksheet and correct any spelling mistakes that are found, but ignore any spelling mistakes found with the worksheet title and the product descriptions.

4. Center the values in the Product column.

5. The averages in several columns do not include the product in row 4. Adjust the functions in these cells so that all products are included in the calculation.

6. The total sales calculations should be:

   Total Sales = Units Sold * (Cost + Profit)

   Adjust the formulas in the range F4:F13 so that the correct formula is used.

7. The value for the lowest value in column E was entered as a number rather than as a function. Replace the value with the appropriate function.

8. The currency values in rows 4 and 14 should be formatted with the Accounting Number Format button (Home tab | Number group). They are currently formatted with the Currency format (floating dollar sign). The Accounting number format displays a fixed dollar sign.

9. Delete the function in the cell containing the average of % Profit because it is mathematically invalid.

10. Change the document properties as specified by your instructor. Save the workbook using the file name, Make It Right 2–1 Dion Designwear Profit Analysis Corrected. Submit the revised workbook as specified by your instructor.

In the Lab

Design and/or create a workbook using the guidelines, concepts, and skills presented in this chapter. Labs 1, 2, and 3 are listed in order of increasing difficulty.

Lab 1: Accounts Receivable Balance Worksheet

Problem: You are a part-time assistant in the accounting department at Aficionado Guitar Parts, a Chicago-based supplier of custom guitar parts. You have been asked to use Excel to generate a report that summarizes the monthly accounts receivable balance (Figure 2–77). A chart of the balances also is desired. The customer data in Table 2–6 is available for test purposes.

Table 2–6 Aficionado Guitar Parts Accounts Receivable Data				
Customer	**Beginning Balance**	**Credits**	**Payments**	**Purchases**
Cervantes, Katriel	803.01	56.92	277.02	207.94
Cummings, Trenton	285.05	87.41	182.11	218.22
Danielsson, Oliver	411.45	79.33	180.09	364.02
Kalinowski, Jadwiga	438.37	60.90	331.10	190.39
Lanctot, Royce	378.81	48.55	126.15	211.38
Raglow, Dora	710.99	55.62	231.37	274.71
Tuan, Lin	318.86	85.01	129.67	332.89

Instructions Part 1: Create a worksheet similar to the one shown in Figure 2–77. Include the five columns of customer data in Table 2–6 in the report, plus two additional columns to compute a service charge and a new balance for each customer. Assume no negative unpaid monthly balances.

	A	B	C	D	E	F	G
1		**Aficionado Guitar Parts**					
2		**Monthy Accounts Receivable Balance Report**					
3	Customer	Beginning Balance	Credits	Payments	Purchases	Service Charge	New Balance
4	Cervantes, Katriel	$803.01	$56.92	$277.02	$207.94	$15.24	$692.25
5	Cummings, Trenton	285.05	87.41	182.11	218.22	0.50	234.25
6	Danielsson, Oliver	411.45	79.33	180.09	364.02	4.94	520.99
7	Kalinowski, Jadwiga	438.37	60.90	331.10	190.39	1.51	238.27
8	Lanctot, Royce	378.81	48.55	126.15	211.38	6.63	422.12
9	Raglow, Dora	710.99	55.62	231.37	274.71	13.78	712.49
10	Tuan, Lin	318.86	85.01	129.67	332.89	3.39	440.46
11	Totals	$3,346.54	$473.74	$1,457.51	$1,799.55	$46.00	$3,260.84
12	Highest	$803.01	$87.41	$331.10	$364.02	$15.24	$712.49
13	Lowest	$285.05	$48.55	$126.15	$190.39	$0.50	$234.25
14	Average	$478.08	$67.68	$208.22	$257.08	$6.57	$465.83
15							
16							

Figure 2–77

Perform the following tasks:

1. Enter and format the worksheet title **Aficionado Guitar Parts** and worksheet subtitle **Monthly Accounts Receivable Balance Report** in cells A1 and A2. Change the theme of the worksheet to the Trek theme. Apply the Title cell style to cells A1 and A2. Change the font size in cell A1 to 28 points. Merge and center the worksheet title and subtitle across columns A through G. Change the background color of cells A1 and A2 to the Red standard color. Change the font color of cells A1 and A2 to the White theme color. Draw a thick box border around the range A1:A2.

2. Change the width of column A to 20.00 points. Change the widths of columns B through G to 12.00 points. Change the heights of row 3 to 36.00 points and row 12 to 30.00 points.

3. Enter the column titles in row 3 and row titles in the range A11:A14, as shown in Figure 2–77. Center the column titles in the range A3:G3. Apply the Heading 3 cell style to the range A3:G3. Apply the Total cell style to the range A11:G11. Bold the titles in the range A12:A14. Change the font size in the range A3:G14 to 12 points.

4. Enter the data in Table 2–6 in the range A4:E10.

5. Use the following formulas to determine the service charge in column F and the new balance in column G for the first customer. Copy the two formulas down through the remaining customers.

   a. Service Charge (cell F4) = 3.25% * (Beginning Balance – Payments – Credits)

   b. New Balance (G4) = Beginning Balance + Purchases – Credits – Payments + Service Charge

6. Determine the totals in row 11.

7. Determine the maximum, minimum, and average values in cells B12:B14 for the range B4:B10, and then copy the range B12:B14 to C12:G14.

Continued >

In the Lab continued

8. Format the numbers as follows: (a) assign the Currency style with a floating dollar sign to the cells containing numeric data in the ranges B4:G4 and B11:G14, and (b) assign a number style with two decimal places and a thousand's separator (currency with no dollar sign) to the range B5:G10.

9. Use conditional formatting to change the formatting to white font on a red background in any cell in the range F4:F10 that contains a value greater than 10.

10. Change the worksheet name from Sheet1 to Accounts Receivable and the sheet tab color to the Red standard color. Change the document properties, as specified by your instructor. Change the worksheet header with your name, course number, and other information as specified by your instructor.

11. Spell check the worksheet. Preview and then print the worksheet in landscape orientation. Save the workbook using the file name, Lab 2-1 Part 1 Aficionado Guitar Parts Accounts Receivable Balance Report.

12. Print the range A3:D14. Print the formulas version on another page. Close the workbook without saving the changes. Submit the assignment as specified by your instructor.

Instructions Part 2: In this part of the exercise, you will create a 3-D Bar chart on a new worksheet in the workbook (Figure 2–78). If necessary, use Excel Help to obtain information on inserting a chart on a separate sheet in the workbook.

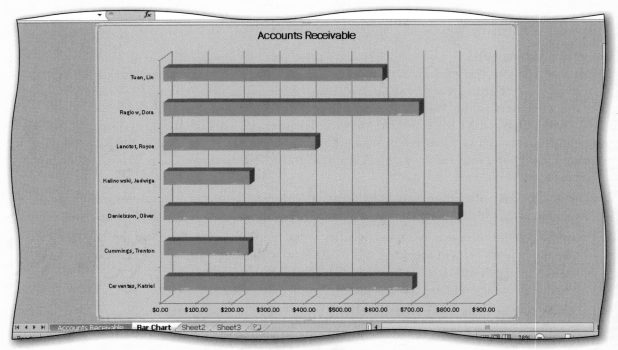

Figure 2–78

1. Open the workbook Lab 2-1 Part 1 Aficionado Guitar Parts Accounts Receivable Balance Report workbook created in Part 1. Save the workbook using the file name, Lab 2-1 Part 2 Aficionado Guitar Parts Accounts Receivable Balance Report.

2. Use the CTRL key and mouse to select the nonadjacent chart ranges A4:A10 and G4:G10. That is, select the range A4:A10 and while holding down the CTRL key, select the range G4:G10.

3. Click the Bar button (Insert tab | Charts group) and then select Clustered Bar in 3-D in the 3-D Bar area. When the chart is displayed on the worksheet, click the Move Chart button (Chart Tools Design tab | Location group). When the Move Chart dialog box appears, click New sheet and then type Bar Chart for the sheet name. Click the OK button (Move Chart dialog box). Change the sheet tab color to the Green standard color.

4. When the chart is displayed on the new worksheet, click the Series 1 series label and then press the DELETE key to delete it. Click the chart area, which is a blank area near the edge of the chart, click the Shape Fill button (Chart Tools Format tab | Shape Styles group), and then select Orange, Accent 1, Lighter 60% in the gallery (column 5, row 3). Click one of the bars in the chart. Click the Shape Fill button (Chart Tools Format tab | Shape Styles group) and then select the Green standard color. Click the Chart Title button (Chart Tools Layout tab | Labels group) and then select Above Chart in the Chart Title gallery. If necessary, use the scroll bar on the right side of the worksheet to scroll to the top of the chart. Click the edge of the chart title to select it and then type `Accounts Receivable` as the chart title.

5. Drag the Accounts Receivable tab at the bottom of the worksheet to the left of the Bar Chart tab to reorder the sheets in the workbook. Preview and print the chart.

6. Click the Accounts Receivable sheet tab. Change the following beginning balances: customer Oliver Danielsson to $702.13 and customer Lin Tuan to $482.74. The company also decided to change the service charge from 3.25% to 2.75% for all customers. After copying the adjusted formula in cell F4 to the range F5:F10, click the Auto Fill Options button and then click Fill without Formatting to maintain the original formatting in the range F5:F10. The total new balance in cell G11 should equal $3,720.82.

7. Select both sheets by holding down the SHIFT key and then clicking the Bar Chart tab. Preview and print the selected sheets. Save the workbook. Submit the assignment as specified by your instructor.

In the Lab

Lab 2: Sales Summary Worksheet

Problem: You have been asked to build a worksheet for a start-up company, Electry Auto, that analyzes the financing needs for the company's first six months in business. The company plans to begin operations in January with an initial investment of $500,000.00. The expected revenue and costs for the company's first six months are shown in Table 2–7. The desired worksheet is shown in Figure 2–79 on the following page. The initial investment is shown at the starting balance for January (cell B4). The amount of financing required by the company is shown as the lowest ending balance (cell F12).

Table 2–7 Electry Auto Start-Up Financing Needs Data

Month	Revenue	Costs
January	105000	220000
February	82000	260000
March	200000	255000
April	250000	320000
May	325000	420000
June	510000	540000

Continued >

Instructions Part 1: Perform the following tasks to build the worksheet shown in Figure 2–79.

	A	B	C	D	E	F
1			**Electry Auto**			
2			**Start-Up Financing Needs**			
3	*Month*	*Starting Balance*	*Revenue*	*Costs*	*Net Income*	*Ending Balance*
4	January	$ 500,000.00	$ 105,000.00	$ 220,000.00	$ (115,000.00)	$ 385,000.00
5	February	385,000.00	82,000.00	260,000.00	(178,000.00)	207,000.00
6	March	207,000.00	200,000.00	255,000.00	(55,000.00)	152,000.00
7	April	152,000.00	250,000.00	320,000.00	(70,000.00)	82,000.00
8	May	82,000.00	325,000.00	420,000.00	(95,000.00)	(13,000.00)
9	June	(13,000.00)	510,000.00	540,000.00	(30,000.00)	(43,000.00)
10	*Average*	$218,833.33	$245,333.33	$335,833.33	($90,500.00)	$128,333.33
11	*Highest*	$500,000.00	$510,000.00	$540,000.00	($30,000.00)	$385,000.00
12	*Lowest*	($13,000.00)	$82,000.00	$220,000.00	($178,000.00)	($43,000.00)
13						
14						
15						
16						
17						
18						

Figure 2–79

1. Start Excel. Apply the Concourse theme to a new workbook.

2. Increase the width of column A to 10.00 and the width of columns B through F to 14.00.

3. Enter the worksheet title **Electry Auto** in cell A1 and the worksheet subtitle **Start-Up Financing Needs** in cell A2. Enter the column titles in row 3, as shown in Figure 2–79. In row 3, use ALT+ENTER to start a new line in a cell.

4. Enter the start-up financing needs data described in Table 2–7 in columns A, C, and D in rows 4 through 9. Enter the initial starting balance (cell B4) of 500000.00. Enter the row titles in the range A10:A12, as shown in Figure 2–79.

5. For the months of February through March, the starting balance is equal to the previous month's ending balance. Obtain the starting balance for February by setting the starting balance of February to the ending balance of January. Use a cell reference rather than typing in the data. Copy the formula for February to the remaining months.

6. Obtain the net income amounts in column E by subtracting the costs in column D from the revenues in column C. Enter the formula in cell E4 and copy it to the range E5:E9. Obtain the ending balance amounts in column F by adding the starting balance in column B to the net income in column F. Enter the formula in cell F4 and copy it to the range F5:F9.

7. In the range B10:B12, use the AVERAGE, MAX, and MIN functions to determine the average value, highest value, and lowest value in the range B4:B9. Copy the range B10:B12 to the range C10:F12.

8. One at a time, merge and center the worksheet title and subtitle across columns A through F. Select cells A1 and A2 and change the background color to light blue (column 7 in the Standard Colors area in the Fill Color gallery). Apply the Title cell style to cells A1 and A2. Change the worksheet title in cell A1 to 28-point white (column 1, row 1 on the Font Color gallery). Change the worksheet subtitle to the same color. Assign a thick box border to the range A1:A2.

9. Center the titles in row 3, columns A through F. Apply the Heading 3 cell style to the range A3:F3. Use the Italic button (Home tab | Font group) to italicize the column titles in row 3 and the row titles in the range A10:A12.

10. Assign a thick box border to the range A10:F12. Change the background and font color for cell F12 to the same colors applied to the worksheet title in Step 8.

11. Change the row heights of row 3 to 36.00 points and row 10 to 30.00 points.

12. Assign the Accounting number format to the range B4:F4. Assign the Comma style format to the range B5:F9. Assign a Currency format with a floating dollar sign to the range B10:F12.

13. Rename the sheet tab as Start-Up Financing Needs. Apply the Light Blue color to the sheet tab. Change the document properties, as specified by your instructor. Change the worksheet header with your name, course number, and other information as specified by your instructor. Save the workbook using the file name Lab 2-1 Part 1 Electry Auto Start-Up Financing Needs. Print the entire worksheet in landscape orientation. Next, print only the range A3:B9.

14. Display the formulas version by pressing CTRL+ACCENT MARK (`). Print the formulas version using the Fit to option button in the Scaling area on the Page tab in the Page Setup dialog box. After printing the worksheet, reset the Scaling option by selecting the Adjust to option button on the Page tab in the Page Setup dialog box and changing the percent value to 100%. Change the display from the formulas version to the values version by pressing CTRL+ACCENT MARK (`). Do not save the workbook.

15. Submit the revised workbook as requested by your instructor.

Instructions Part 2: In this part of the exercise, you will change the revenue amounts until the lowest ending balance is greater than zero, indicating that the company does not require financing in its first six months of operation. Open the workbook created in Part 1 and save the workbook as Lab 2-1 Part 2 Electry Auto Start-Up Financing Needs. Manually increment each of the six values in the revenue column by $1,000.00 until the lowest ending balance in cell F12 is greater than zero. The value of cell F12 should equal $5,000.00 All six values in column C must be incremented the same number of times. Update the worksheet header and save the workbook. Print the worksheet. Submit the assignment as specified by your instructor.

Instructions Part 3: In this part of the exercise, you will change the monthly costs until the lowest ending balance is greater than zero, indicating that the company does not require financing in its first six months of operation. Open the workbook created in Part 1 and then save the workbook as Lab 2-1 Part 3 Electry Auto Start-Up Financing Needs. Manually decrement each of the six values in the costs column by $1,000.00 until the lowest ending balance in cell F12 is greater than zero. Decrement all six values in column C the same number of times. Your worksheet is correct when the lowest ending balance in cell F12 is $5,000.00. Update the worksheet header and save the workbook. Print the worksheet. Submit the assignment as specified by your instructor.

In the Lab

Lab 3: Stock Club Investment Analysis

Problem: Several years ago, you and a large group of friends started a stock club. Each year every member invests more money per month. You have decided to create a portfolio worksheet (Figure 2–80) that summarizes the club's current stock holdings so that you can share the information with your group of friends. The club's portfolio is summarized in Table 2–8. Table 2–8 also shows the general layout of the worksheet to be created.

	A	B	C	D	E	F	G	H	I	J
1					**Sock-It-Away Stock Club**					
2					Summary of Investments					
3	Company	Stock Symbol	Purchase Date	Shares	Initial Price per Share	Initial Cost	Current Price per Share	Current Value	Gain/Loss	Percent Gain/Loss
4	Apple	AAPL	3/3/2007	250	$ 86.17	$ 21,542.50	$ 75.32	$ 18,830.00	$ (2,712.50)	-12.59%
5	Caterpillar	CAT	6/14/2008	200	81.74	16,348.00	69.02	13,804.00	(2,544.00)	-15.56%
6	Disney	DIS	10/11/2006	300	31.06	9,318.00	37.38	11,214.00	1,896.00	20.35%
7	General Electric	GE	3/4/2009	500	7.24	3,620.00	9.39	4,695.00	1,075.00	29.70%
8	MetLife	MET	1/15/2008	200	60.92	12,184.00	77.09	15,418.00	3,234.00	26.54%
9	Microsoft	MSFT	11/15/2006	500	29.20	14,600.00	36.30	18,150.00	3,550.00	24.32%
10	PepsiCo	PEP	2/15/2006	350	57.86	20,251.00	70.65	24,727.50	4,476.50	22.11%
11	Target	TGT	5/11/2004	450	44.11	19,849.50	44.02	19,809.00	(40.50)	-0.20%
12	Wal-Mart	WMT	4/14/2009	250	50.81	12,702.50	57.20	14,300.00	1,597.50	12.58%
13	Totals					$ 130,415.50		$ 140,947.50	$ 10,532.00	8.08%
14	Average			333.3333	$49.90	$14,490.61	$52.93	$15,660.83	$1,170.22	
15	Highest			500	$86.17	$21,542.50	$77.09	$24,727.50	$4,476.50	29.70%
16	Lowest			200	$7.24	$3,620.00	$9.39	$4,695.00	($2,712.50)	-15.56%

Figure 2–80

Table 2–8 Sock-It-Away Stock Club

Company	Stock Symbol	Purchase Date	Shares	Initial Price per Share	Initial Cost	Current Price per Share	Current Value	Gain/ Loss	Percent Gain/ Loss
Apple	AAPL	3/3/2007	250	86.17	Formula A	75.32	Formula B	Formula C	Formula D
Caterpillar	CAT	6/14/2008	200	81.74		69.02			
Disney	DIS	10/11/2006	300	31.06		37.38			
General Electric	GE	3/4/2009	500	7.24		9.39			
MetLife	MET	1/15/2008	200	60.92		77.09			
Microsoft	MSFT	11/15/2006	500	29.20		36.30			
PepsiCo	PEP	2/15/2006	350	57.86		70.65			
Target	TGT	5/11/2004	450	44.11		44.02			
Wal-Mart	WMT	4/14/2009	250	50.81		57.20			
Totals			Formula E						
Average			Formula F						
Highest			Formula G						
Lowest			Formula H						

Instructions: Perform the following tasks:

1. Start Excel. Enter the worksheet titles Sock-It-Away Stock Club in cell A1 and Summary of Investments in cell A2.

2. Enter the column titles and data in Table 2–8 beginning in row 3.

3. Change the column widths and row heights as follows: column A — 11.78; column C — 10.00; columns E and G — 7.44; columns F, H, and I — 13.00; column J — 8.22; row 3 — 56.25 points; row 14 — 27.00 points.

4. Enter the following formulas in row 4 and then copy them down through row 12:

   a. Enter Formula A in cell F4: Initial Cost = Shares × Initial Price per Share

   b. Enter Formula B in cell H4: Current Value = Shares × Current Price Per Share

   c. Enter Formula C in cell I4: Gain/Loss = Current Value – Initial Cost

   d. Enter Formula D in cell J4: Percent Gain/Loss = Gain/Loss / Initial Cost

5. Compute the totals for initial cost, current value, gain/loss, and percent gain loss. For the percent gain/loss in cell J13, copy cell J12 to J13 using the fill handle.

6. In cells D14, D15, and D16, enter Formulas E, F, and G using the AVERAGE, MAX, and MIN functions. Copy the three functions across through the range J14:J16. Delete the invalid formula in cell J14.

7. Format the worksheet as follows:

   a. Apply the Trek theme to the worksheet.

   b. Format the worksheet title with Title cell style. Merge and center across columns A through J.

   c. Format the worksheet subtitle with Franklin Gothic Book font, 16 point font size, Black, Text 1 theme font color. Merge and Center across columns A through J.

   d. Format the worksheet title and subtitle background with Orange, Accent 1, Lighter 60% theme color and a thick box border.

   e. Format row 3 with the Heading 3 cell style and row 13 with the Total cell style.

   f. Format the data in rows 4 through 12: center data in column B; format dates in column C to the mm/dd/yy date format; range E4:I4 — Accounting number format style with fixed dollar sign; range E5:I12 — Comma style; range J4:J13 — Percent style with two decimal places; cells F13, H13, and I13 — Accounting Number format with fixed dollar sign.

   g. Format E14:I16 — Currency format with floating decimal places; J15:J16 — Percent style with two decimal places.

   h. Format J4:J12 — apply conditional formatting so that if a cell in range is less than 0, then cell appears with a pink background color.

8. Spell check the worksheet. Change the name of the sheet tab to Summary of Investments and apply the Orange, Accent 1, Darker 25% theme color to the sheet tab. Update the document properties, and save the workbook using the file name, Lab 2-3 Sock-It-Away Stock Club Summary of Investments. Print the worksheet in landscape orientation. Print the formulas version on one page. Close the workbook without saving changes. Submit the assignment as specified by your instructor.

Cases and Places

Apply your creative thinking and problem-solving skills to design and implement a solution.

1: Analyzing Emergency Student Loans

Academic

The Student Assistance office at your school provides emergency loans at simple interest. The data obtained from six types of loans and the desired report format are shown in Table 2–9. The required formulas are shown in Table 2–10. Use the concepts and techniques presented in this chapter to create and format the worksheet. Include total, average, maximum, and minimum values for Principal, Interest, and Amount Due.

Table 2–9 Emergency Student Loan Data and Worksheet Layout			
Loan Type	Principal	Rate	Time in Years
Academic Supplies	$40,000	7.5%	.4
Medical Emergency	$25,500	12%	.33
Personal Emergency	$12,750	8.25%	.5
Room and Board	$27,000	6.5%	1
Travel Expenses	$4,550	12%	.5
Tuition Reimbursement	$107,000	6%	1

Table 2–10 Emergency Student Loan Formulas
Interest = Principal × Rate × Time
Amount Due = Principal + Interest
Average = AVERAGE function
Minimum = MIN function
Maximum = MAX function

2: Analyzing Energy Consumption

Personal

Your parents believe that your late night studying sessions and household appliance usage contribute to excessive electricity bills. You have decided to try to prove them wrong by analyzing your daily and monthly electricity consumption. You research the energy consumption of your personal items and appliance usage to obtain consumption costs per hour for each item. Table 2–11 contains the data and format for the report you want to create.

Use the concepts and techniques presented in this project to create and format the worksheet. Include an embedded 3-D Pie chart that shows the cost per month. Use Microsoft Excel Help to create a professional looking 3-D Pie chart with title and data labels.

Table 2–11 Appliance Electricity Usage Costs

Appliance	Cost per Hour	Hours Used Daily	Total Cost Per Day	Total Cost per Month (30 Days)
Clothes dryer	$0.325	1		
Computer	$0.02	6		
DVD player	$0.035	1		
Light bulbs	$0.043	8		
Refrigerator	$0.035	24		
Stereo	$0.02	5		
Television	$0.04	4		
Washing machine	$0.03	2		

3: Analyzing Profit Potential

Professional

You work for HumiCorp, an online retailer of home humidifiers. Your manager wants to know the profit potential of their inventory based on the items in inventory listed in Table 2–12. Table 2–12 contains the format of the desired report. The required formulas are shown in Table 2–13. Use the concepts and techniques developed in this chapter to create and format the worksheet. The company just received 67 additional desk-sized humidifiers and shipped out 48 room-sized humidifiers. Update the appropriate cells to reflect the change in inventory.

Table 2–12 HumiCorp Inventory Profit Potential Data and Worksheet Layout

Item	Units on Hand	Unit Cost	Total Cost	Unit Price	Total Value	Potential Profit
Desk	187	27.58	Formula A	Formula B	Formula C	Formula D
Filtered home-sized	42	324.14				
Filtered room-sized	118	86.55				
Home-sized	103	253.91				
Room-sized	97	53.69				
Total	—	—	—	—	—	—
Average	Formula E					
Lowest	Formula F					
Highest	Formula G					

Table 2–13 HumiCorp Inventory Profit Potential Formulas

Formula A = Units on Hand × Unit Cost

Formula B = Unit Cost × (1 / (1 − .66))

Formula C = Units on Hand × Unit Price

Formula D = Total Value − Total Cost

Formula E = AVERAGE function

Formula F = MIN function

Formula G = MAX function

1 | Databases and Database Objects: An Introduction

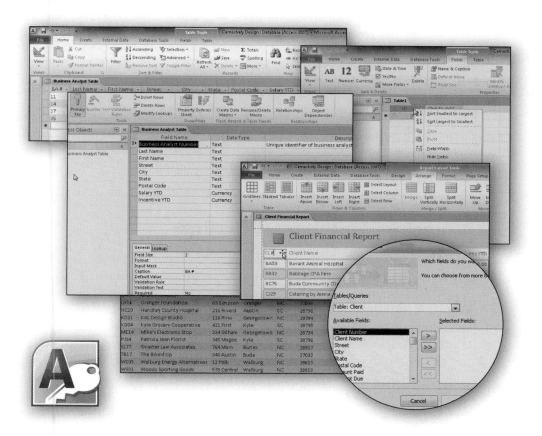

Objectives

You will have mastered the material in this chapter when you can:

- Design a database to satisfy a collection of requirements
- Describe the features of the Access window
- Create a database
- Create tables in Datasheet and Design views
- Add records to a table

- Close a database
- Open a database
- Print the contents of a table
- Create and use a query
- Create and use a form
- Create and print custom reports
- Modify a report in Layout view

1 | Databases and Database Objects: An Introduction

Introduction

The term **database** describes a collection of data organized in a manner that allows access, retrieval, and use of that data. Microsoft Access 2010, usually referred to as simply Access, is a database management system. A **database management system**, such as Access, is software that allows you to use a computer to create a database; add, change, and delete data in the database; ask and answer questions concerning the data in the database; and create forms and reports using the data in the database.

The process of developing a database that communicates specific information requires careful analysis and planning. As a starting point, establish why the database is needed. Once the purpose is determined, analyze the intended users of the database and their unique needs. Then, gather information about the topic and decide what to include in the database. Finally, determine the database design and style that will be most successful at delivering the message. Details of these guidelines are provided in Appendix A. In addition, each project in this book provides practical applications of these planning considerations.

Project — Database Creation

Camashaly Design Group is a small company that provides custom marketing solutions for the service, nonprofit, and retail sectors. Alyssa Morgan, Camden Scott, and Ashton James started the business after they graduated from a local university. The three owners, all computer graphics design majors and business minors, worked on a service learning project during college that produced a Web site for a nonprofit organization. Alyssa, Camden, and Ashton worked well together. Upon researching the local area for competing businesses, they decided to form their own company. The company specializes in designing and maintaining Web sites and using social networking Web sites for online marketing. They also conduct market research and develop printed media. Camashaly already has received one award for its design work. Camashaly is also recognized for its efforts in providing work opportunities to individuals who want flexible schedules and to student interns.

Camashaly uses business analysts to work collaboratively with clients. Business analysts are employees who translate business requirements into marketing specifications and serve as the interface between clients and Camashaly. Business analysts are paid a base salary and can earn incentive pay for maintaining and expanding client relationships.

Camashaly charges a one-time fee for Web site development. Clients can pay for Web site maintenance by contracting for a specified number of hours or can pay for maintenance on an hour-by-hour basis. Other fees vary depending on the specific scope of work.

To ensure that operations run smoothly, Camashaly organizes data on its clients and business analysts in a database managed by Access. In this way, Camashaly keeps its data current and accurate while the owners can analyze the data for trends and produce a variety of useful reports. In this chapter, you will create the Camashaly database.

In a **relational database** such as those maintained by Access, a database consists of a collection of tables, each of which contains information on a specific subject. Figure 1–1 shows the database for Camashaly Design. It consists of two tables: the Client table (Figure 1–1a) contains information about the clients to whom Camashaly provides services, and the Business Analyst table (Figure 1–1b) contains information about the business analysts to whom these clients are assigned.

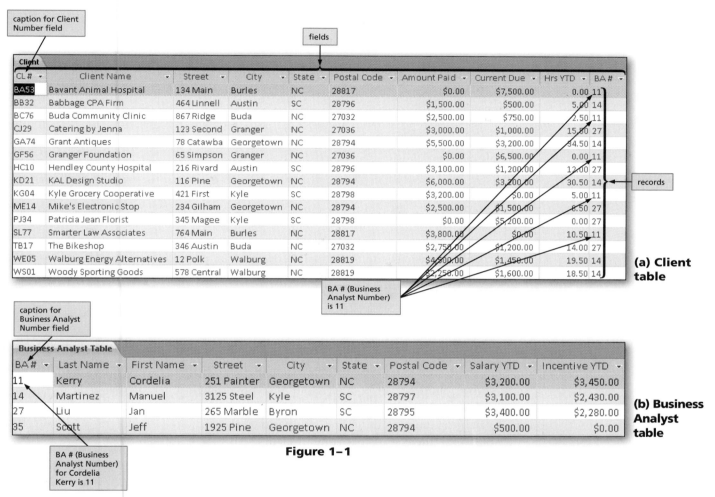

Figure 1–1

The rows in the tables are called **records**. A record contains information about a given person, product, or event. A row in the Client table, for example, contains information about a specific client, such as the client's name, address information, and other data.

The columns in the tables are called fields. A **field** contains a specific piece of information within a record. In the Client table, for example, the fourth field, City, contains the name of the city where the client is located.

The first field in the Client table is CL #, which is an abbreviation for Client Number. Camashaly Design assigns each client a client number. As is common to the way in which many organizations format client numbers, Camashaly Design calls it a number, although it actually contains letters. The Camashaly client numbers consist of two uppercase letters followed by a two-digit number.

The client numbers are unique; that is, no two clients are assigned the same number. Such a field can be used as a **unique identifier**. A unique identifier, as its name suggests, is a way of uniquely identifying each record in the database. A given client number will appear only in a single record in the table. Only one record exists, for example, in which the client number is BB32. A unique identifier also is called a **primary key**. Thus, the Client Number field is the primary key for the Client table.

The next eight fields in the Client table are Client Name, Street, City, State, Postal Code, Amount Paid, Current Due, and Hrs YTD, which is an abbreviation for Contract Hours YTD. YTD is an abbreviation for year to date. The Amount Paid column contains the amount that the client has paid Camashaly Design YTD prior to the current period. The Current Due column contains the amount due to Camashaly for the current period. The Hrs YTD column contains the number of hours the client has contracted for Web site maintenance so far this year. For example, client BB32 is Babbage CPA Firm. The address is 464 Linnell in Austin, South Carolina. The postal code is 28796. The client has paid $1,500.00 for services so far this year. The amount due for the current period is $500.00. The client has contracted for 5.00 hours of Web site maintenance.

Camashaly assigns a single business analyst to work with each client. The last column in the Client table, BA #, which is an abbreviation for Business Analyst Number, gives the number of the client's business analyst.

The first field in the Business Analyst table is also BA #, an abbreviation for Business Analyst Number. The business analyst numbers are unique, so the Business Analyst Number field is the primary key of the Business Analyst table.

The other fields in the Business Analyst table are Last Name, First Name, Street, City, State, Postal Code, Salary YTD, and Incentive YTD. The Salary YTD field gives the salary paid to the analyst thus far this year. The Incentive YTD gives the incentive for which the analyst qualified thus far this year. For example, business analyst 14 is Manuel Martinez. His address is 3125 Steel in Kyle, South Carolina. The Postal Code is 28797. So far this year, he has been paid $3,100.00 in salary. He has earned $2,430.00 in incentive pay.

The business analyst number appears in both the Client table and the Business Analyst table, and relates clients and business analysts. For example, in the Client table, you see that the business analyst number for client Babbage CPA Firm is 14. To find the name of this business analyst, look for the row in the Business Analyst table that contains 14 in the BA # column. After you have found it, you know the client is assigned to Manuel Martinez. To find all the clients assigned to Cordelia Kerry, you would first look in the Business Analyst table to find that her number is 11. You would then look through the Client table for all the clients that contain 11 in the BA # column. Her clients are BA53 (Bavant Animal Hospital), BC76 (Buda Community Clinic), GF56 (Granger Foundation), KG04 (Kyle Grocery Cooperative), and SL77 (Smarter Law Associates).

The last business analyst in the Business Analyst table, Jeff Scott, has not been assigned any clients yet; therefore, his business analyst number, 35, does not appear on any row in the Client table.

Overview

As you read this chapter, you will learn how to create the database shown in Figure 1–1 by performing these general tasks:

- Design the database.
- Create a new blank database.
- Create a table and add the records.
- Preview and print the contents of a table.
- Create a second table and import the records.
- Create a simple query.
- Create a simple form.
- Create and modify a report.

Database Design Guidelines

Database design refers to the arrangement of data into tables and fields. In the example in this chapter, the design is specified, but in many cases, you will have to determine the design based on what you want the system to accomplish.

Plan
Ahead

When designing a database to satisfy a given set of requirements, the actions you take and the decisions you make will determine the tables and fields that will be included in the database. As you create a database, such as the one shown in Figure 1–1 on page AC 3, you should follow these general guidelines:

1. **Identify the tables.** Examine the requirements for the database to identify the main objects that are involved. There will be a table for each object you identify.

   In one database, for example, the main objects might be departments and employees. Thus, there would be two tables: one for departments and the other for employees. In another database, the main objects might be clients and business analysts. In this case, there also would be two tables: one for clients and the other for business analysts. In still another database, the main objects might be books, publishers, and authors. This database would require three tables: one for books, a second for publishers, and a third for authors.

2. **Determine the primary keys.** Recall that the primary key is the unique identifier for records in the table. For each table, determine the unique identifier. In a Department table, for example, the unique identifier might be the Department Code. For a Book table, the unique identifier might be the ISBN.

3. **Determine the additional fields.** The primary key will be a field or combination of fields in a table. A table typically will contain many additional fields, each of which contains a type of data. Examine the project requirements to determine these additional fields. For example, in an Employee table, the additional fields might include such fields as Employee Name, Street Address, City, State, Postal Code, Date Hired, Salary, and so on.

4. **Determine relationships between the tables.** Examine the list of tables you have created to see which tables are related. When you determine that two tables are related, include matching fields in the two tables. For example, in a database containing employees and departments, there is a relationship between the two tables because one department can have many employees assigned to it. Department Code could be the matching field in the two tables.

5. **Determine data types for the fields.** For each field, determine the type of data the field can contain. One field, for example, might contain only numbers. Another field might contain currency amounts, while a third field might contain only dates. Some fields contain text data, meaning any combination of letters, numbers, and special characters (!, ;, ', &, and so on). For example, in an Employee table, the Date Hired field would contain dates, the Salary field would contain currency amounts, and the Hours Worked field would contain numbers. The other fields in the Employee table would contain text data, such as Employee Name and Department Code.

6. **Identify and remove any unwanted redundancy.** Redundancy is the storing of a piece of data in more than one place. Redundancy usually, but not always, causes problems, such as wasted space, difficulties with update, and possible data inconsistency. Examine each table you have created to see if it contains redundancy and, if so, determine whether the redundancy causes the problems described. If it does, remove the redundancy by splitting the table into two tables. For example, you might have a single table of employees. In addition to typical employee data (name, address, earnings, and so on), the table might contain Department Number and Department Name. If so, the Department Name could repeat multiple times. Every employee whose department number is 12, for example, would have the same department name. It would be better to split the table into two tables: one for Employees and one for Department. In the Department table, the Department Name is stored only once.

7. **Determine a storage location for the database.** The database you have designed will be stored in a single file. You need to determine a location in which to store the file.

8. **Determine additional properties for fields.** Before creating the database, determine any other properties you should specify for the fields. These could include a field size, which is

(continued)

Plan Ahead

(continued)

the maximum number of characters that can be stored in the field. If you want something other than the field name to appear at the top of a column (such as an abbreviation), you can change the caption to the desired heading. You also can add a description, which is a message that appears on the screen concerning a field whenever the field is selected.

9. **Determine the best method for distributing the database objects.** The traditional method of distributing database objects uses a printer to produce a hard copy of a table or report on paper. You also can distribute the table as an electronic image that mirrors the original table's appearance.

When necessary, more specific details concerning the above guidelines are presented at appropriate points in the chapter. The chapter also will identify the actions performed and decisions made regarding these guidelines during the creation of the database shown in Figure 1–1 on page AC 3.

Designing a Database

This section illustrates the database design process by showing how you would design the database for Camashaly Design from a set of requirements. In this section, you will use commonly accepted shorthand to represent the tables and fields that make up the database as well as the primary keys for the tables. For each table, you give the name of the table followed by a set of parentheses. Within the parentheses is a list of the fields in the table separated by columns. You underline the primary key. For example,

Product (<u>Product Code</u>, Description, On Hand, Price)

represents a table called Product. The Product table contains four fields: Product Code, Description, On Hand, and Price. The Product Code field is the primary key.

Database Requirements

The Camashaly Design database must maintain information on both clients and business analysts. The business currently keeps this data in two Word tables and two Excel workbooks, as shown in Figure 1–2. They use Word tables for address information and Excel workbooks for financial information.

Client Number	Client Name	Street	City	State	Postal Code
BA53	Bavant Animal Hospital	134 Main	Burles	NC	28817
BB32	Babbage CPA Firm	464 Linnell	Austin	SC	28796
BC76	Buda Community Clinic	867 Ridge	Buda	NC	27032
CJ29	Catering by Jenna	123 Second	Granger	NC	27036
GA74	Grant Antiques	78 Catawba	Georgetown	NC	28794
GF56	Granger Foundation	65 Simpson	Granger	NC	27036
HC10	Hendley County Hospital	216 Rivard	Austin	SC	28796
KD21	KAL Design Studio	116 Pine	Georgetown	NC	28794
KG04	Kyle Grocery Cooperative	421 First	Kyle	SC	28798
ME14	Mike's Electronic Stop	234 Gilham	Georgetown	NC	28794
PJ34	Patricia Jean Florist	345 Magee	Kyle	SC	28798
SL77	Smarter Law Associates	764 Main	Burles	NC	28817
TB17	The Bikeshop	346 Austin	Buda	NC	27032
WE05	Walburg Energy Alternatives	12 Polk	Walburg	NC	28819
WS01	Woody Sporting Goods	578 Central	Walburg	NC	28819

Figure 1–2   (a) Client Address Information (Word Table)

	A	B	C	D	E	F	G	H
1	Client Number	Client Name	Amount Paid	Current Due	Contract Hours YTD			
2	BA53	Bavant Animal Hospital	0.00	7,500.00	0			
3	BB32	Babbage CPA Firm	1,500.00	500.00	5			
4	BC76	Buda Community Clinic	2,500.00	750.00	2.5			
5	CJ29	Catering by Jenna	3,000.00	1,000.00	15.5			
6	GA74	Grant Antiques	5,500.00	3,200.00	34.5			
7	GF56	Granger Foundation	0.00	6,500.00	0			
8	HC10	Hendley County Hospital	3,100.00	1,200.00	12			
9	KD21	KAL Design Studio	6,000.00	3,200.00	30.5			
10	KG04	Kyle Grocery Cooperative	3,200.00	0.00	5			
11	ME14	Mike's Electronic Stop	2,500.00	1,500.00	8.5			
12	PJ34	Patricia Jean Florist	0.00	5,200.00	0			
13	SL77	Smarter Law Associates	3,800.00	0.00	10.5			
14	TB17	The Bikeshop	2,750.00	1,200.00	14			
15	WE05	Walburg Energy Alternatives	4,500.00	1,450.00	19.5			
16	WS01	Woody Sporting Goods	2,250.00	1,600.00	18.5			

Figure 1–2   (b) Client Financial Information (Excel Worksheet)

Business Analyst Number	Last Name	First Name	Street	City	State	Postal Code
11	Kerry	Cordelia	251 Painter	Georgetown	NC	28794
14	Martinez	Manuel	3125 Steel	Kyle	SC	28797
27	Liu	Jan	265 Marble	Byron	SC	28795
35	Scott	Jeff	1925 Pine	Georgetown	NC	28794

Figure 1–2   (c) Business Analyst Address Information (Word Table)

	A	B	C	D	E	F	G	H	I
1	Business Analyst Number	Last Name	First Name	Salary YTD	Incentive YTD				
2	11	Kerry	Cordelia	3,200.00	3,450.00				
3	14	Martinez	Manuel	3,100.00	2,430.00				
4	27	Liu	Jan	3,400.00	2,280.00				
5	35	Scott	Jeff	500.00	0.00				

Figure 1–2   (d) Business Analyst Financial Information (Excel Worksheet)

For clients, Camashaly needs to maintain address data. It currently keeps this address data in a Word table (Figure 1–2a). It also maintains financial data for each client. This includes the amount paid, current amount due, and contract hours YTD for the client. It keeps these amounts, along with the client name and number, in the Excel workbook shown in Figure 1–2b.

Camashaly keeps business analyst address data in a Word table, as shown in Figure 1–2c. Just as with clients, it keeps financial data for business analysts, including their salary YTD and incentive YTD, in a separate Excel workbook, as shown in Figure 1–2d.

Finally, it keeps track of which clients are assigned to which business analysts. Each client is assigned to a single business analyst, but each business analyst might be assigned many clients. Currently, for example, clients BA53 (Bavant Animal Hospital), BC76 (Buda Community Clinic), GF56 (Granger Foundation), KG04 (Kyle Grocery Cooperative), and SL77 (Smarter Law Associates) are assigned to business analyst 11 (Cordelia Kerry). Clients BB32 (Babbage CPA Firm), GA74 (Grant Antiques), KD21 (KAL Design Studio), WE05 (Walburg Energy Alternatives), and WS01 (Woody Sporting Goods) are assigned to business analyst 14 (Manuel Martinez). Clients CJ29 (Catering by Jenna), HC10 (Hendley County Hospital), ME14 (Mike's Electronic Stop), PJ34 (Patricia Jean Florist), and TB17 (The Bikeshop) are assigned to business analyst 27 (Jan Liu). Camashaly has an additional business analyst, Jeff Scott, whose number has been assigned as 35, but who has not yet been assigned any clients.

BTW

Additional Data for Camashaly
There are many other types of data that Camashaly could include in a database. For example, they might keep all employee information in a database as well as information on client contracts and an inventory of hardware and software.

Naming Tables and Fields

BTW

Naming Files
The following characters cannot be used in a file name: question mark (?), quotation mark ("), slash (/), backslash (\ ), colon (:), asterisk (*), vertical bar (|), greater than symbol (>), and less than symbol (<).

In designing your database, you must name the tables and fields. Thus, before beginning the design process, you must understand the rules Access applies to table and field names. These rules are:

1. Names can be up to 64 characters in length.
2. Names can contain letters, digits, and spaces, as well as most of the punctuation symbols.
3. Names cannot contain periods (.), exclamation points (!), accent graves (`), or square brackets ([ ]).
4. The same name cannot be used for two different fields in the same table.

The approach to naming tables and fields used in this text is to begin the names with an uppercase letter and to use lowercase for the other letters. In multiple-word names, each word begins with an uppercase letter, and there is a space between words (for example, Client Number). You should know that other approaches exist, all of which are acceptable in Access. Some people omit the space (ClientNumber). Still others use an underscore in place of the space (Client_Number). Finally, some use an underscore in place of a space, but use the same case for all letters (CLIENT_NUMBER or client_number).

Identifying the Tables

BTW

Naming Fields
Access 2010 has a number of reserved words, words that have a special meaning to Access. You cannot use these reserved words as field names. For example, Name is a reserved word and could not be used in the Client table to describe a client's name. For a complete list of reserved words in Access 2010, consult Access Help.

Now that you know the rules for naming tables and fields, you are ready to begin the design process. The first step is to identify the main objects involved in the requirements. For the Camashaly Design database, the main objects are clients and business analysts. This leads to two tables, which you must name. Reasonable names for these two tables are:

Client

Business Analyst

Determining the Primary Keys

The next step is to identify the fields that will be the unique identifiers, or primary keys. Client numbers uniquely identify clients, and business analyst numbers uniquely identify business analysts. Thus, the primary key for the Client table is the client number, and the primary key for the Business Analyst table is the business analyst number. Reasonable names for these fields would be Client Number and Business Analyst Number, respectively. Adding these primary keys to the tables gives:

Client (<u>Client Number</u>)
Business Analyst (<u>Business Analyst Number</u>)

Determining Additional Fields

After identifying the primary keys, you need to determine and name the additional fields. In addition to the client number, the Client Address Information shown in Figure 1–2a on page AC 6 contains the client name, street, city, state, and postal code. These would be fields in the Client table. The Client Financial Information shown in Figure 1–2b also contains the client number and client name, which are already included in the Client table. The financial information also contains the amount paid, current due, and contract hours YTD. Adding the amount paid, current due, and contract hours YTD fields to those already identified in the Client table and assigning reasonable names gives:

Client (<u>Client Number</u>, Client Name, Street, City, State, Postal Code,
    Amount Paid, Current Due, Contract Hours YTD)

Similarly, examining the Business Analyst Address Information in Figure 1–2c adds the last name, first name, street, city, state, and postal code fields to the Business Analyst table. In addition to the business analyst number, last name, and first name, the Business Analyst Financial Information in Figure 1–2d would add the salary YTD and Incentive YTD. Adding these fields to the Business Analyst table and assigning reasonable names gives:

Business Analyst (<u>Business Analyst Number</u>, Last Name, First Name, Street, City,
State, Postal Code, Salary YTD, Incentive YTD)

Determining and Implementing Relationships Between the Tables

**Plan
Ahead**

> **Determine relationships between the tables.**
> The most common type of relationship you will encounter between tables is the **one-to-many relationship**. This means that each row in the first table may be associated with many rows in the second table, but each row in the second table is associated with only one row in the first. The first table is called the "one" table and the second is called the "many" table. For example, there may be a relationship between departments and employees, in which each department can have many employees, but each employee is assigned to only one department. In this relationship, there would be two tables, Department and Employee. The Department table would be the "one" table in the relationship. The Employee table would be the "many" table.
> To determine relationships between tables, you can follow these general guidelines:
>
> * Identify the "one" table.
> * Identify the "many" table.
> * Include the primary key from the "one" table as a field in the "many" table.

According to the requirements, each client has one business analyst, but each business analyst can have many clients. Thus, the Business Analyst table is the "one" table, and the Client table is the "many" table. To implement this one-to-many relationship between business analysts and clients, add the Business Analyst Number field (the primary key of the Business Analyst table) to the Client table. This produces:

Client (<u>Client Number</u>, Client Name, Street, City, State, Postal Code, Amount Paid,
Current Due, Contract Hours YTD, Business Analyst Number)
Business Analyst (<u>Business Analyst Number</u>, Last Name, First Name, Street, City,
State, Postal Code, Salary YTD, Incentive YTD)

BTW

Database Design Language (DBDL) DBDL is a commonly accepted shorthand representation for showing the structure of a relational database. You write the name of the table and then within parentheses you list all the columns in the table. If the columns continue beyond one line, indent the subsequent lines.

Determining Data Types for the Fields

Each field has a **data type**. This indicates the type of data that can be stored in the field. Three of the most commonly used data types are:

1. **Text** — The field can contain any characters. A maximum number of 255 characters is allowed in a field whose data type is Text.

2. **Number** — The field can contain only numbers. The numbers either can be positive or negative. Fields are assigned this type so they can be used in arithmetic operations. Fields that contain numbers but will not be used for arithmetic operations (such as postal codes) usually are assigned a data type of Text.

3. **Currency** — The field can contain only monetary data. The values will appear with currency symbols, such as dollar signs, commas, and decimal points, and with two digits following the decimal point. Like numeric fields, you can use currency fields in arithmetic operations. Access assigns a size to currency fields automatically.

Table 1–1 shows the other data types that are available in Access.

Table 1–1 Additional Data Types

Data Type	Description
Memo	Field can store a variable amount of text or combinations of text and numbers where the total number of characters may exceed 255.
Date/Time	Field can store dates and times.
AutoNumber	Field can store a unique sequential number that Access assigns to a record. Access will increment the number by 1 as each new record is added.
Yes/No	Field can store only one of two values. The choices are Yes/No, True/False, or On/Off.
OLE Object	Field can store an OLE object, which is an object linked to or embedded in the table.
Hyperlink	Field can store text that can be used as a hyperlink address.
Attachment	Field can contain an attached file. Images, spreadsheets, documents, charts, and so on can be attached to this field in a record in the database. You can view and edit the attached file.
Calculated	Field specified as a calculation based on other fields. The value is not actually stored.

In the Client table, because the Client Number, Client Name, Street, City, and State can all contain letters, their data types should be Text. The data type for Postal Code is Text instead of Number because postal codes are not used in arithmetic operations; you do not add postal codes or find an average postal code, for example. The Amount Paid and Current Due fields both contain monetary data, so their data types should be Currency. The Contract Hours YTD field contains a number that is not a currency amount, so its data type should be Number.

Similarly, in the Business Analyst table, the data type for the Business Analyst Number, Last Name, First Name, Street, City, State, and Postal Code fields all should be Text. The Salary YTD and Incentive YTD fields both contain monetary amounts, so their data types should be Currency.

Fields whose data type is Number often require you to change the field size, which is the storage space assigned to the field by Access. Table 1–2 shows the possible field sizes for Number fields. If the size were Byte, Integer, or Long Integer, for example, only integers could be stored. If you try to store a value that has decimal places, such as 2.50, the portion to the right of the decimal point would be removed, giving a result of 2. To address this problem, you would change to a size such as Single.

Table 1–2 Field Sizes for Number Fields

Field Size	Description
Byte	Integer value in the range of 0 to 255
Integer	Integer value in the range of –32,768 to 32,767
Long Integer	Integer value in the range of –2,147,483,648 to 2,147,483,647
Single	Numeric values with decimal places to seven significant digits — requires 4 bytes of storage
Double	Numeric values with decimal places to more accuracy than Single — requires 8 bytes of storage
Replication ID	Special identifier required for replication
Decimal	Numeric values with decimal places to more accuracy than Single or Double — requires 12 bytes of storage.

Identifying and Removing Redundancy

Redundancy means storing the same fact in more than one place. It usually results from placing too many fields in a table — fields that really belong in separate tables — and often causes serious problems. If you had not realized there were two objects, clients and business analysts, for example, you might have placed all the data in a single Client table. Figure 1–3 shows an example of a table that includes both client and business analyst information. Notice that the data for a given business analyst (number, name, address, and so on) occurs on more than one record. The data for analyst 11, Cordelia Kerry, is repeated in the figure.

Client Table

Client Number	Client Name	Street	...	Business Analyst Number	Last Name	First Name	...
BA53	Bavant Animal Hospital	134 Main	...	11	Kerry	Cordelia	...
BB32	Babbage CPA Firm	464 Linnell	...	14	Martinez	Manuel	...
BC76	Buda Community Clinic	867 Ridge	...	11	Kerry	Cordelia	...
...	...	...	...	...	...	...	...

business analyst numbers are 11

name of business analyst 11 appears more than once

Figure 1–3

Storing this data on multiple records is an example of redundancy, which causes several problems, including:

1. Wasted storage space. The name of business analyst 11, Cordelia Kerry, for example, should be stored only once. Storing this fact several times is wasteful.

2. More difficult database updates. If, for example, Cordelia Kerry's name is spelled wrong and needs to be changed in the database, her name would need to be changed in several different places.

3. A possibility of inconsistent data. Nothing prohibits the business analyst's last name from being Kerry on client BA53's record and Bronson on client BC76's record. The data would be inconsistent. In both cases, the business analyst number is 11, but the last names are different.

The solution to the problem is to place the redundant data in a separate table, one in which the data no longer will be redundant. If, for example, you place the data for business analysts in a separate table (Figure 1–4), the data for each business analyst will appear only once.

Client Table

Client Number	Client Name	Street	...	Business Analyst Number
BA53	Bavant Animal Hospital	134 Main	...	11
BB32	Babbage CPA Firm	464 Linnell	...	14
BC76	Buda Community Clinic	867 Ridge	...	11
...	...	...		

business analyst numbers are 11

Business Analyst Table

Business Analyst Number	Last Name	First Name	...
11	Kerry	Cordelia	...
14	Martinez	Manuel	...
...	...		...

name of business analyst 11 appears only once

Figure 1–4

BTW

Postal Codes
Some organizations with customers throughout the country have a separate table of postal codes, cities, and states. When placing an order, you typically are asked for your postal code (or ZIP code), rather than city, state, and postal code. You then are asked to confirm that the city and state correspond to that postal code.

Notice that you need to have the business analyst number in both tables. Without it, there would be no way to tell which business analyst is associated with which client. The remaining business analyst data, however, was removed from the Client table and placed in the Business Analyst table. This new arrangement corrects the problems of redundancy in the following ways:

1. Because the data for each business analyst is stored only once, space is not wasted.

2. Changing the name of a business analyst is easy. You have only to change one row in the Business Analyst table.

3. Because the data for a business analyst is stored only once, inconsistent data cannot occur. Designing to omit redundancy will help you to produce good and valid database designs.

You should always examine your design to see if it contains redundancy. If it does, you should decide whether you need to remove the redundancy by creating a separate table.

If you examine your design, you'll see that there is one area of redundancy (see the data in Figure 1–1 on page AC 3). Cities and states are both repeated. Every client whose postal code is 28794, for example, has Georgetown as the city and NC as the state. To remove this redundancy, you would create a table whose primary key is Postal Code and that contains City and State as additional fields. City and State would be removed from the Client table. Having City, State, and Postal Code in a table is very common, however, and usually you would not take such action. No other redundancy exists in your tables.

To Start Access

For an introduction to Windows 7 and instruction about how to perform basic Windows 7 tasks, read the Office 2010 and Windows 7 chapter at the beginning of this book, where you can learn how to resize windows, change screen resolution, create folders, move and rename files, use Windows Help, and much more.

If you are using a computer to step through the project in this chapter and you want your screens to match the figures in this book, you should change your screen's resolution to 1024 × 768. For information about how to change a computer's resolution, refer to the Office 2010 and Windows 7 chapter at the beginning of this book.

The following steps, which assume Windows 7 is running, start Access based on a typical installation. You may need to ask your instructor how to start Access for your computer. For a detailed example of the procedure summarized below, refer to the Office 2010 and Windows 7 chapter.

1 Click the Start button on the Windows 7 taskbar to display the Start menu.

2 Type `Microsoft Access` as the search text in the 'Search programs and files' text box and watch the search results appear on the Start menu.

3 Click Microsoft Access 2010 in the search results on the Start menu to start Access and display the Backstage view for Access.

4 If the Access window is not maximized, click the Maximize button next to the Close button on its title bar to maximize the window.

Creating a Database

In Access, all the tables, reports, forms, and queries that you create are stored in a single file called a database. Thus, you first must create the database to hold the tables, reports, forms, and queries. You can use either the Blank database option or a template to create a new database. If you already know the tables and fields you want in your database, you would use the Blank database option. If not, you can use a template. Templates can guide you by suggesting some commonly used databases.

Determine a storage location for the database.
When creating a database, you must decide which storage medium to use.

If you always work on the same computer and have no need to transport your database to a different location, then your computer's hard drive will suffice as a storage location. It is a good idea, however, to save a backup copy of your database on a separate medium in case the file becomes corrupted or the computer's hard drive fails.

If you plan to work on your database in various locations or on multiple computers, then you can consider saving your projects on a portable medium, such as a USB flash drive or CD. The projects in this book are stored on a USB flash drive, which saves files quickly and reliably and can be reused. CDs are easily portable and serve as good backups for the final versions of projects because they generally can save files only one time.

Plan Ahead

For an introduction to Office 2010 and instruction about how to perform basic tasks in Office 2010 programs, read the Office 2010 and Windows 7 chapter at the beginning of this book, where you can learn how to start a program, use the Ribbon, save a file, open a file, quit a program, use Help, and much more.

To Create a Database

Because you already know the tables and fields you want in the Camashaly Design database, you would use the Blank database option rather than using a template. The following steps assume you already have created folders for storing your files, for example, a CIS 101 folder (for your class) that contains an Access folder (for your assignments). Thus, these steps save the document in the Access folder in the CIS 101 folder on a USB flash drive using the file name, Camashaly Design. For a detailed example of the procedure summarized below, refer to the Office 2010 and Windows 7 chapter at the beginning of this book.

BTW

Q&As
For a complete list of the Q&As found in many of the step-by-step sequences in this book, visit the Access 2010 Q&A Web page (scsite.com/ac2010/qa).

1 With a USB flash drive connected to one of the computer's USB ports, ensure the New tab is selected in the Backstage view and that Blank database is selected in the New gallery.

2 Click the Browse button in the right pane of the New gallery to display the File New Database dialog box.

3 Type **Camashaly Design** in the File New Database dialog box to change the file name. Do not press the ENTER key after typing the file name.

4 Navigate to the desired save location (in this case, the Access folder in the CIS 101 folder [or your class folder] on the USB flash drive).

5 Click the OK button, which returns you to the New gallery. (Your screen may show Camashaly Design.accdb.)

6 Click the Create button in the right pane of the New gallery to create the database on the selected drive with the entered file name (Figure 1–5).

The title bar for my Navigation Pane contains All Tables rather than All Access Objects, as in the figure. Is that a problem?

It is not a problem. The title bar indicates how the Navigation Pane is organized. You can carry out the steps in the text with either organization. To make your screens match the ones in the text, click the Navigation Pane arrow and then click Object Type.

I do not have the Search bar that appears on the figure. Is that a problem?

It is not a problem. If your Navigation Pane does not display a Search bar and you want your screens to match the ones in the text, right-click the Navigation Pane title bar arrow to display a shortcut menu, and then click Search Bar.

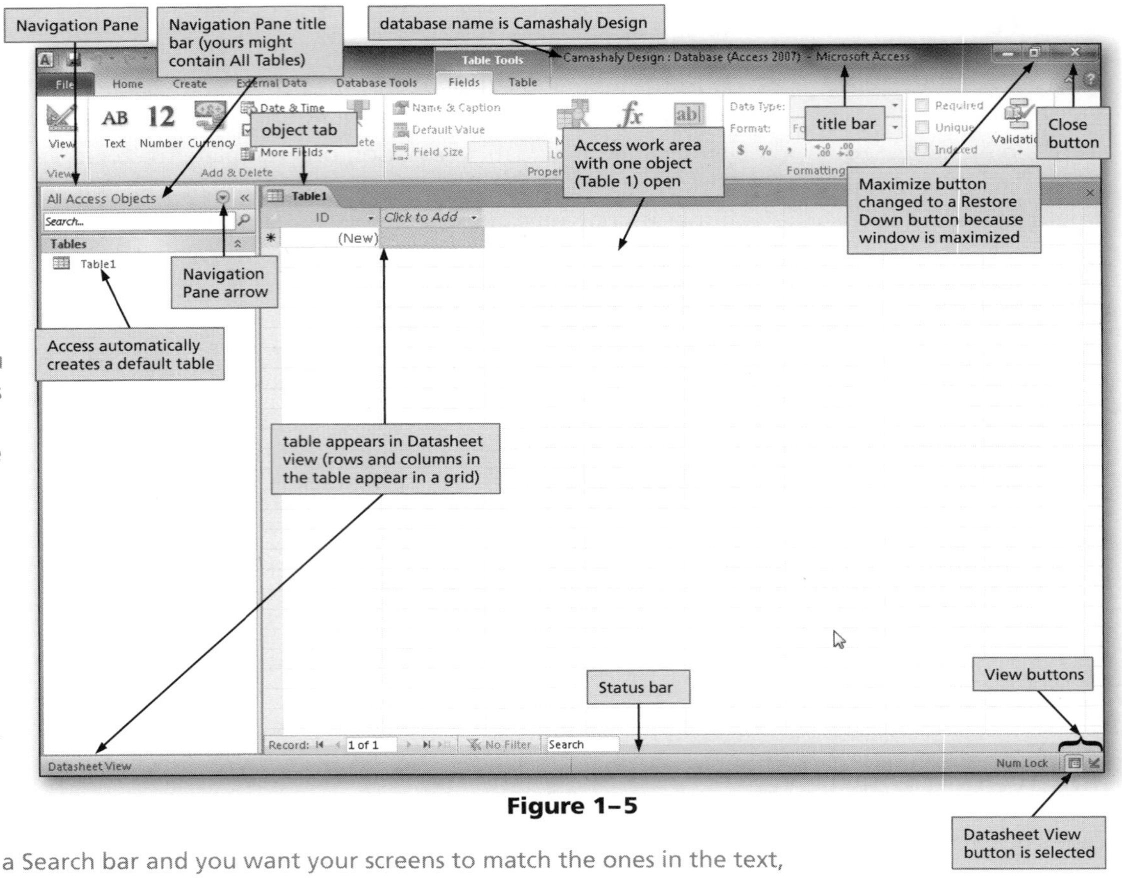

Figure 1–5

TO CREATE A DATABASE USING A TEMPLATE

Available Templates The Blank web database button on the New tab in the Backstage view allows you to create a database that you can publish to a SharePoint server running Access Services. Access 2010 also includes five Web-based templates. To display previously used templates, click the My templates button.

Ideally, you will design your own database, create a blank database, and then create the tables you have determined that your database should contain. If you are not sure what database design you will need, you could use a template. Templates can guide you by suggesting some commonly used databases. To create a database using a template, you would use the following steps.

1. After starting Access, be sure the Backstage view is open. If it is not, click File on the Ribbon to open it.

2. Click the New tab if it is not already selected.

3. Click Sample templates to display a list of templates stored locally or search Microsoft Office online for additional templates.

4. Click the template you want to use.

5. Enter a file name (or accept the suggested file name) and select a location for the database.

6. Click the Create button to create the database or the Download button to download the database and create the database, if necessary.

The Access Window

The Access window consists of a variety of components to make your work more efficient and documents more professional. These include the Navigation Pane, Access work area, Ribbon, shortcut menus, and Quick Access Toolbar. Some of these components are common to other Microsoft Office 2010 programs; others are unique to Access.

Navigation Pane and Access Work Area

You work on objects such as tables, forms, and reports in the **Access work area**. In the work area in Figure 1–5, a single table, Table1, is open in the work area. **Object tabs** for the open objects appear at the top of the work area. If you have multiple objects open at the same time, you can select one of the open objects by clicking its tab. To the left of the work area is the Navigation Pane. The **Navigation Pane** contains a list of all the objects in the database. You use this pane to open an object. You also can customize the way objects are displayed in the Navigation Pane.

The **Status bar**, located at the bottom of the Access window, presents information about the database object, the progress of current tasks, and the status of certain commands and keys; it also provides controls for viewing the object. As you type text or perform certain commands, various indicators may appear on the Status bar. The left edge of the Status bar in Figure 1–5 shows that the table object is open in Datasheet view. Toward the right edge are View buttons, which you can use to change the view that currently is displayed.

Creating a Table

To create a table, you must describe the structure of the table to Access. That is, you must describe all the fields that make up the table and their characteristics. You must also indicate the primary key.

In Access, you can use two different views to create a table: Datasheet view and Design view. In **Datasheet view**, the data in the table is presented in rows and columns, similar to a spreadsheet. Although the main reason to use Datasheet view is to add or update records in a table, you can also use it to create a table or to later modify its structure. The other view, **Design view**, is only used to create a table or to modify the structure of the table.

As you might expect, Design view has more functionality for creating a table than Datasheet view. That is, there are certain actions that can only be performed in Design view. If creating your table requires such actions, you must use Design view. If not, you can choose either view. In this chapter, you will create the first table, the Business Analyst table, in Datasheet view. You will create the second table, the Client table, in Design view.

Whichever view you choose to use, before creating the table, you need to determine the names and data types of the fields that will make up the table. You already have determined the types for the Camashaly fields. You also need to determine additional properties for the fields.

BTW

The Ribbon and Screen Resolution
Access may change how the groups and buttons within the groups appear on the Ribbon, depending on the computer's screen resolution. Thus, your Ribbon may look different from the ones in this book if you are using a screen resolution other than 1024 × 768.

<table>
<tr><td>Plan
Ahead</td><td>

Determine additional properties for fields.

- **Determine if a special caption is warranted.** Normally, the field name will appear as the label for a field on a form or report and as the column name in Datasheet view. If you would rather have a different name appear, you can change the field's caption to the desired name. One common use of captions is to shorten the column heading. If the data in a column is considerably shorter than the column heading, you could change the caption to a shorter heading. This would enable you to reduce the width of the column and yet still be able to see the entire column heading.

- **Determine if a special description is warranted.** Determine whether to include a description that would appear in the Status bar whenever the field is selected.

- **Determine field sizes.** For Text fields, determine the field size; that is, the maximum number of characters that can be entered in the field. Users will be prohibited from entering a value that has more characters than the field size.

- **Determine formats.** Determine whether the data in the field should be formatted in any particular way. You could, for example, specify that a number field is to be formatted with precisely two decimal places.

</td></tr>
</table>

BTW

Naming Tables
Database users typically have their own guidelines for naming tables. Some use the singular version of the object being described while others use the prefix tbl with a table name. This book uses the singular version of the object (Client, Business Analyst) but adds the word Table to the name for the Business Analyst table to illustrate another possible approach. Including the word Table can assist visually impaired users when viewing the Navigation Pane.

The results of these decisions for the fields in the Business Analyst table are shown in Table 1–3. The table also shows the data types and field sizes of the fields as well as any special properties that need to be changed. The Business Analyst Number field has a caption of BA #, enabling the width of the Business Analyst Number column to be reduced in the datasheet.

Table 1–3 Structure of Business Analyst Table

Field Name	Data Type	Field Size	Description
Business Analyst Number	Text	2	**Primary Key** **Description:** Business Analyst Number **Caption:** BA #
Last Name	Text	15	
First Name	Text	15	
Street	Text	15	
City	Text	15	
State	Text	2	
Postal Code	Text	5	
Salary YTD	Currency		
Incentive YTD	Currency		

To Modify the Primary Key

When you first create your database, Access automatically creates a table for you. You can immediately begin defining the fields. If, for any reason, you do not have this table or inadvertently delete it, you can create the table by clicking Create on the Ribbon and then clicking the Table button (Create tab | Tables group). In either case, you are ready to define the fields.

The following steps define the first field, the Business Analyst Number field, which is the primary key. Access has already created a primary key field, which it has named ID. Thus, the steps will change the name, data type, and other properties of this field to match the Business Analyst field in Table 1–3.

1

- Right-click the column heading for the ID field to display a shortcut menu (Figure 1–6).

Why does my shortcut menu look different?

You right-clicked within the column instead of right-clicking the column heading.

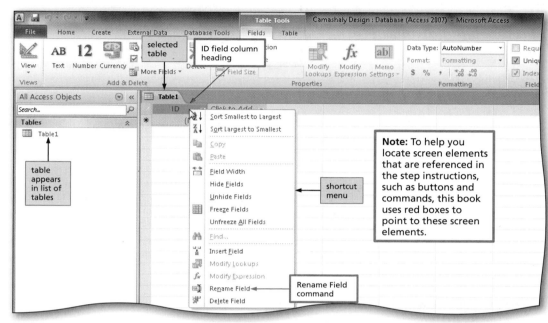

Figure 1–6

2

- Click Rename Field on the shortcut menu to highlight the current name.

- Type **Business Analyst Number** to assign a name to the new field.

- Click the white space immediately below the field name to complete the addition of the field (Figure 1–7).

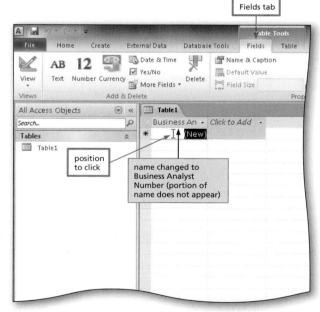

Figure 1–7

Why doesn't the whole name appear?

The default column size is not large enough for Business Analyst Number to appear in its entirety. You will address this issue in later steps.

- Because the data type needs to be changed from AutoNumber to Text, click the Data Type box arrow (Table Tools Fields tab | Formatting group) to display a menu of available data types (Figure 1–8).

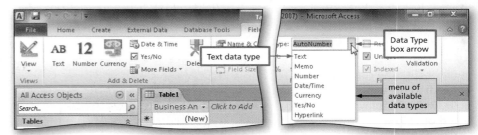

Figure 1–8

④

- Click Text to select the data type for the field (Figure 1–9).

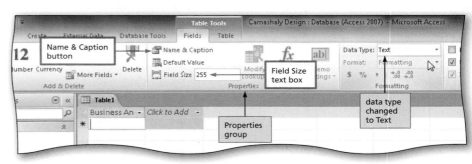

Figure 1–9

⑤

- Click the Field Size text box (Table Tools Fields tab | Properties group) to select the current field size, use either the DELETE or BACKSPACE keys to erase the current field size, and then type **2** as the new field size.

- Click the Name & Caption button (Table Tools Fields tab | Properties group) to display the Enter Field Properties dialog box.

- Click the Caption text box (Enter Field Properties dialog box), and then type **BA #** as the caption.

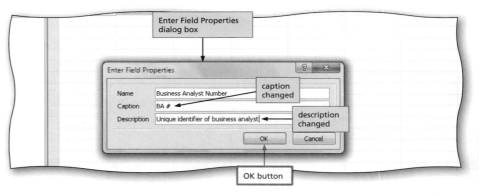

Figure 1–10

- Click the Description text box, and then type **Unique identifier of business analyst** as the description (Figure 1–10).

⑥

- Click the OK button (Enter Field Properties dialog box) to change the caption and description (Figure 1–11).

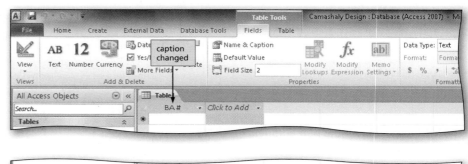

Figure 1–11

To Define the Remaining Fields in a Table

To define an additional field, you click the Click to Add column heading, select the data type, and then type the field name. This is different from the process you used to modify the ID field, which was an existing field. The following steps define the remaining fields shown in Table 1–3 on page AC 16.

1

- Click the Click to Add column heading to display a menu of available data types (Figure 1–12).

Q&A Why don't I rename the field like I renamed the ID field?

The ID field was an existing field, created automatically by Access. For a new field, you need to click the Click to Add heading.

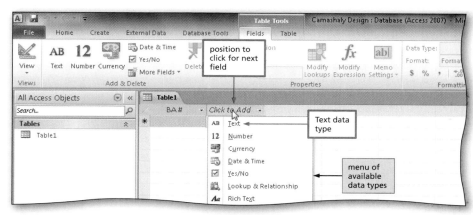

Figure 1–12

2

- Click Text in the menu of available data types to select the Text data type.

- Type Last Name to enter a field name.

- Click the white space below the field name to complete the change of the name. Click the white space a second time to select the field (Figure 1–13).

Q&A I realized after I entered the field name that I selected the wrong data type. How can I correct it?

Click the Data Type box arrow and then select the correct type.

Q&A I inadvertently clicked the white space before entering the field name. How can I correct the name?

Right-click the field name, click Rename Field on the shortcut menu, and then type the new name.

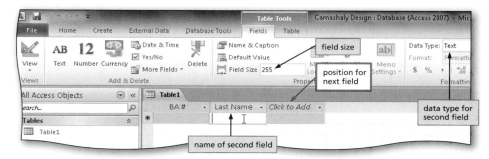

Figure 1–13

3

- Change the field size to 15 just as you changed the field size of the Business Analyst Number field.

- Using the same technique, add the remaining fields in the Business Analyst table. For the First Name, Street, City, State, and Postal Code fields, the Text data type is correct, but you will need to change the field size to match Table 1–3. For the Salary YTD and Incentive YTD fields, you need to change the data type to Currency. Before defining the Incentive YTD field, you may need to click the right scroll arrow to bring the column for the field to the screen (Figure 1–14).

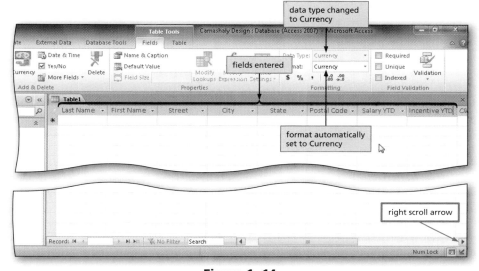

Figure 1–14

Q&A

Why does Currency appear twice?

The second Currency is the format, which indicates how the data will be displayed. For the Currency data type, Access automatically sets the format to Currency, which is usually what you would want. You could change it to something else, if desired, by clicking the arrow and selecting the desired format.

Q&A

I have an extra row between the row containing the field names and the row that begins with the asterisk. What happened? Is this a problem? If so, how do I fix it?

You inadvertently added a record to the table by pressing some key. Even pressing the SPACEBAR would add a record. You now have a record you do not want. To fix it, you need to delete the record, which you will do in Step 4.

- If you have an additional record between the field names and the asterisk, click the record selector (the box at the beginning of the record), press the DELETE key, and then click the Yes button when Access asks you if you want to delete the record.

Making Changes to the Structure

When creating a table, check the entries carefully to ensure they are correct. If you discover a mistake while still typing the entry, you can correct the error by repeatedly pressing the BACKSPACE key until the incorrect characters are removed. Then, type the correct characters. If you do not discover a mistake until later, you can use the following techniques to make the necessary changes to the structure:

BTW

Currency Symbols
To show the symbol for the Euro (€) instead of the dollar sign, change the Format property for the field whose data type is currency. To change the default symbols for currency, change the settings in the operating system using the control panel.

- To undo your most recent change, click the Undo button on the Quick Access Toolbar. If there is nothing that Access can undo, this button will be dim, and clicking it will have no effect.
- To delete a field, right-click the column heading for the field (the position containing the field name), and then click Delete Field on the shortcut menu.
- To change the name of a field, right-click the column heading for the field, click Rename Field on the shortcut menu, and then type the desired field name.
- To insert a field as the last field, click the Click to Add column heading, click the appropriate data type on the menu of available data types, type the desired field name, and, if necessary, change the field size.
- To insert a field between existing fields, right-click the column heading for the field that will follow the new field, and then click Insert Field on the shortcut menu. Right-click the column heading for the field, click Rename Field on the shortcut menu, and then type the desired field name.
- To move a field, click the column heading for the field to be moved to select the field, and then drag the field to the desired position.

As an alternative to these steps, you may want to start over. To do so, click the Close button for the table, and then click the No button in the Microsoft Access dialog box. Click Create on the Ribbon and then click the Table button to create a table. You then can repeat the process you used earlier to define the fields in the table.

To Save a Table

The Business Analyst table structure now is complete. The final step is to save the table within the database. As part of the process, you will give the table a name. The following steps save the table, giving it the name, Business Analyst Table.

1

- Click the Save button on the Quick Access Toolbar to display the Save As dialog box (Figure 1–15).

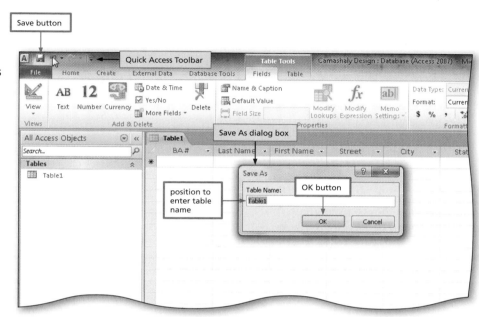

Figure 1–15

2

- Type **Business Analyst Table** to change the name to be assigned to the table.

- Click the OK button (Save As dialog box) to save the table (Figure 1–16).

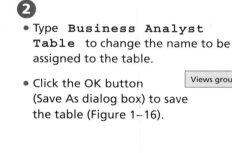

Other Ways

1. Click File on the Ribbon, click Save in the Backstage view
2. Right-click tab for table, click Save on shortcut menu
3. Press CTRL+S

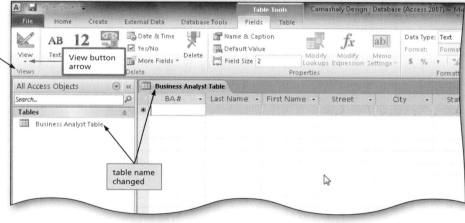

Figure 1–16

To View the Table in Design View

Even when creating a table in Datasheet view, Design view can be helpful. You should view the fields, data types, and properties to ensure you have entered them correctly. This viewing is easier to do in Design view. It is also easier to determine the primary key in Design view. The following steps view the structure of the Business Analyst Table in Design view so that you can verify the design is correct.

1

• Click the View button arrow (Table Tools Fields tab | Views group) to display the View button menu (Figure 1–17).

Could I just click the View button rather than the arrow?

Yes. Clicking the button is equivalent to clicking the command represented by the icon currently appearing on the button. Because the icon on the button in Figure 1–17 is the icon for Design view, clicking the button would display the table in Design view. If you are uncertain, you can always click the arrow and select from the menu.

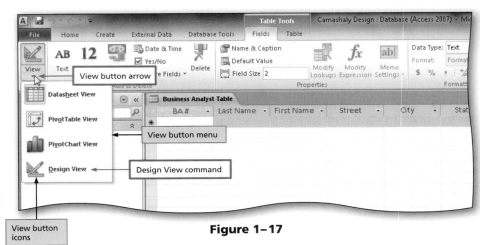

Figure 1–17

2

• Click Design View on the View button menu to view the table in Design view (Figure 1–18).

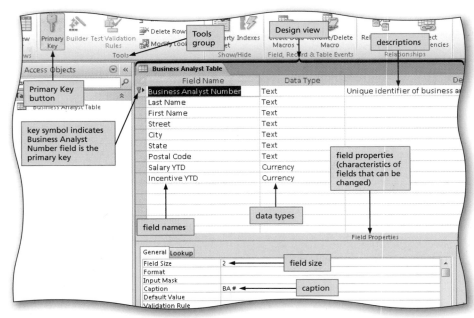

Figure 1–18

Other Ways

1. Click Design View button on Status bar

Checking the Structure in Design View

You should use Design view to carefully check the entries you have made. In Figure 1–18, for example, you can see that the Business Analyst Number field is the primary key of the Business Analyst Table by the key symbol in front of the field name. If your table does not have a key symbol, you can click the Primary Key button (Table Tools Design tab | Tools group) to designate the field as the primary key. You also can check that the data type, the description, the field size, and the caption are all correct.

For the other fields, you can see the field name, data type, and description without taking any special action. To see the field size and/or caption for a field, click the field's **row selector**, the small box that precedes the field. Clicking the row selector for the Last Name field, for example, displays the field properties for the field (Figure 1–19). You then can check to see that the field size is correct. In addition, if the field has a caption, you can check to see if that is correct as well. If you find any mistakes, you can make the necessary corrections on this screen. When you have finished, you would click the Save button to save your changes.

To Close the Table

Once you are sure that your entries are correct and you have saved your changes, you can close the table.

1

• Click the Close button for the Business Analyst Table to close the table (Figure 1–19).

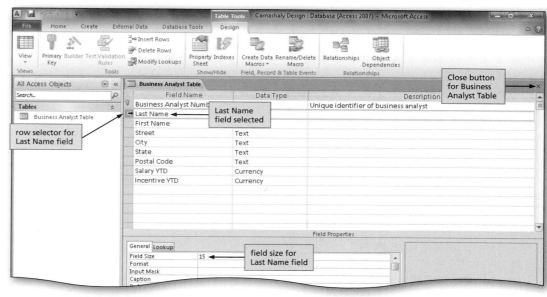

Figure 1–19

Other Ways

1. Right-click tab for table, click Close on shortcut menu

To Add Records to a Table

Creating a table by building the structure and saving the table is the first step in a two-step process. The second step is to add records to the table. To add records to a table, the table must be open. When making changes to tables, you work in Datasheet view. In Datasheet view, the table is represented as a collection of rows and columns called a **datasheet**.

You often add records in phases. For example, you might not have enough time to add all the records in one session. The following steps open the Business Analyst Table in Datasheet view and then add the first two records in the Business Analyst Table (Figure 1–20).

BA #	Last Name	First Name	Street	City	State	Postal Code	Salary YTD	Incentive YTD
11	Kerry	Cordelia	251 Painter	Georgetown	NC	28794	$3,200.00	$3,450.00
14	Martinez	Manuel	3125 Steel	Kyle	SC	28797	$3,100.00	$2,430.00

Figure 1–20

1

• Right-click the Business Analyst Table in the Navigation Pane to display the shortcut menu (Figure 1–21).

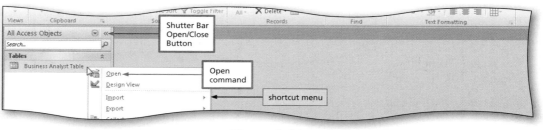

Figure 1–21

2

- Click Open on the shortcut menu to open the table in Datasheet view.

Q&A

What if I want to return to Design view?

You can open Design view by clicking Design View on the shortcut menu.

- Click the Shutter Bar Open/Close Button to close the Navigation Pane (Figure 1–22).

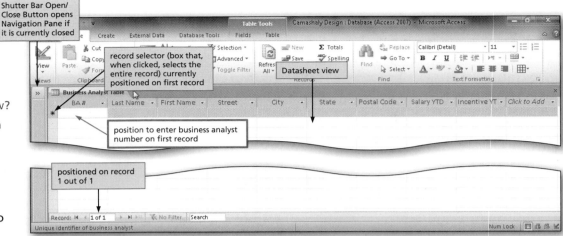

Figure 1–22

3

- Click the BA # field if necessary to display an insertion point, and type 11 to enter the first business analyst number (Figure 1–23).

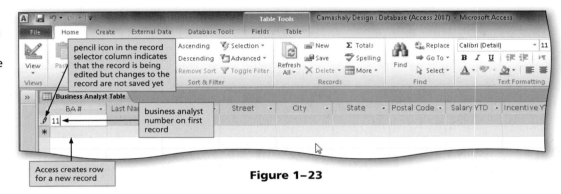

Figure 1–23

4

- Press the TAB key to move to the next field.

- Enter the last name, first name, street, city, state, and postal code by typing the following entries, pressing the TAB key after each one: **Kerry** as the last name, **Cordelia** as the first name, **251 Painter** as the street, **Georgetown** as the city, **NC** as the state, and **28794** as the postal code.

- Type **3200** in the Salary YTD field (Figure 1–24).

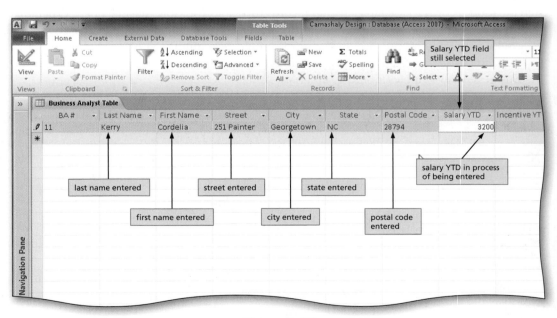

Figure 1–24

Q&A

Do I need to type a dollar sign?

You do not need to type dollar signs or commas. In addition, because the digits to the right of the decimal point are both zeros, you do not need to type either the decimal point or the zeros.

5

- Press the TAB key to complete the entry for the field.

- Type 3450 in the Incentive YTD field, and then press the TAB key to complete the entry of the first record (Figure 1–25).

How and when do I save the record?

As soon as you have entered or modified a record and moved to another record, the original record is saved. This is different from other applications. The rows entered in an Excel worksheet, for example, are not saved until the entire worksheet is saved.

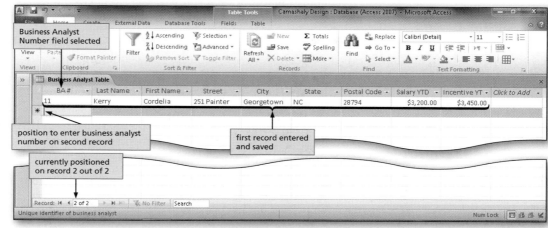

Figure 1–25

6

- Use the techniques shown in Steps 3 through 5 to enter the data for the second record (Figure 1–26).

Experiment

- Click the Salary YTD field on either of the records. Be sure the Table Tools Fields tab is selected. Click the Format box arrow and then click each of the

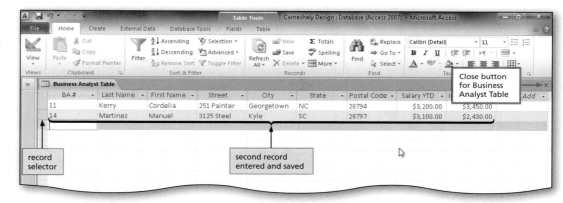

Figure 1–26

formats in the Format box menu to see the effect on the values in the Salary YTD field. When finished, click Currency in the Format box menu.

Making Changes to the Data

As you enter data, check your entries carefully to ensure they are correct. If you make a mistake and discover it before you press the TAB key, correct it by pressing the BACKSPACE key until the incorrect characters are removed, and then type the correct characters. If you do not discover a mistake until later, you can use the following techniques to make the necessary corrections to the data:

- To undo your most recent change, click the Undo button on the Quick Access Toolbar. If there is nothing that Access can undo, this button will be dimmed, and clicking it will have no effect.

- To add a record, click the New (blank) record button, click the position for the Business Analyst Number field on the first open record, and then add the record. Do not worry about it being in the correct position in the table. Access will reposition the record based on the primary key, in this case, the Business Analyst Number.

BTW

Adding Records
You can add records in any order. When you close a table and re-open it, the records will be in order by primary key.

- To delete a record, click the record selector, shown in Figure 1–26, for the record to be deleted. Then press the DELETE key to delete the record, and click the Yes button when Access asks you to verify that you do indeed want to delete the record.

- To change the contents of one or more fields in a record, the record must be on the screen. If it is not, use any appropriate technique, such as the UP ARROW and DOWN ARROW keys or the vertical scroll bar, to move to it. If the field you want to correct is not visible on the screen, use the horizontal scroll bar along the bottom of the screen to shift all the fields until the one you want appears. If the value in the field is currently highlighted, you can simply type the new value. If you would rather edit the existing value, you must have an insertion point in the field. You can place the insertion point by clicking in the field or by pressing F2. You then can use the arrow keys, the DELETE key, and the BACKSPACE key for making the correction. You also can use the INSERT key to switch between Insert and Overtype mode. When you have made the change, press the TAB key to move to the next field.

If you cannot determine how to correct the data, you may find that you are "stuck" on the record, in which case Access neither allows you to move to another record nor allows you to close the table until you have made the correction. If you encounter this situation, simply press the ESC key. Pressing the ESC key will remove from the screen the record you are trying to add. You then can move to any other record, close the table, or take any other action you desire.

To Close a Table

Now that you have created and saved the Business Analyst Table, you can close it. The following step closes the table.

1 Click the Close button for the Business Analyst Table, shown in Figure 1–26, to close the table (Figure 1–27).

Figure 1–27

To Quit Access

The following steps quit Access. For a detailed example of the procedure summarized below, refer to the Office 2010 and Windows 7 chapter at the beginning of this book.

1 Click the Close button on the right side of the title bar to quit Access.

2 If a Microsoft Access dialog box appears, click the Save button to save any changes made to the object since the last save.

Break Point: If you wish to take a break, this is a good place to do so. To resume at a later time, continue following the steps from this location forward.

Starting Access and Opening a Database

Once you have created and later closed a database, you will need to open it in the future in order to use it. Opening a database requires that Access is running on your computer.

To Start Access

1 Click the Start button on the Windows 7 taskbar to display the Start menu.

2 Type `Microsoft Access` as the search text in the 'Search programs and files' text box and watch the search results appear on the Start menu.

3 Click Microsoft Access 2010 in the search results on the Start menu to start Access.

To Open a Database from Access

Earlier in this chapter, you saved your database on a USB flash drive using the file name, Camashaly Design. The following steps open the Camashaly Design database from the Access folder in the CIS 101 folder on the USB flash drive. For a detailed example of the procedure summarized below, refer to the Office 2010 and Windows 7 chapter at the beginning of this book.

BTW

Organizing Files and Folders
You should organize and store files in folders so that you easily can find the files later. For a discussion of folders and detailed examples of creating folders, refer to the Office 2010 and Windows 7 chapter at the beginning of this book.

1 With your USB flash drive connected to one of the computer's USB ports, click File on the Ribbon to open the Backstage view, if necessary.

2 Click Open in the Backstage view to display the Open dialog box.

3 Navigate to the location of the file to be opened (in this case, the USB flash drive, then to the CIS 101 folder [or your class folder], and then to the Access folder).

4 Click Camashaly Design to select the file to be opened.

5 Click the Open button (Open dialog box) to open the selected file and display the opened database in the Access window.

6 If a Security Warning appears, click the Enable Content button (Figure 1–28).

Q&A

When would I not want to enable the content?

You would want to disable the content if you suspected that your database might contain harmful content or damaging macros. Because you are the one who created the database and no one else has used it, you should have no such suspicions.

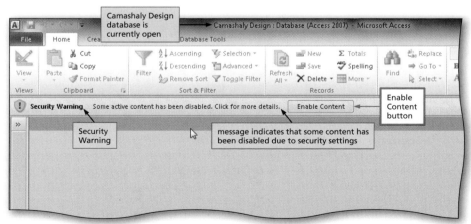

Figure 1–28

Other Ways

1. Click File on the Ribbon, click Recent in the Backstage view, click file name

To Add Additional Records to a Table

You can add records to a table that already contains data using a process almost identical to that used to add records to an empty table. The only difference is that you place the insertion point after the last record before you enter the additional data. To do so, use the **Navigation buttons**, which are buttons used to move within a table, found near the lower-left corner of the screen when a table is open. The purpose of each of the Navigation buttons is described in Table 1–4.

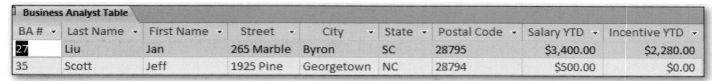

Table 1–4 Navigation Buttons in Datasheet View	
Button	**Purpose**
First record	Moves to the first record in the table
Previous record	Moves to the previous record
Next record	Moves to the next record
Last record	Moves to the last record in the table
New (blank) record	Moves to the end of the table to a position for entering a new record

The following steps add the remaining records (Figure 1–29) to the Business Analyst table.

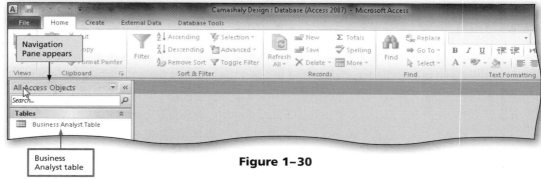

Figure 1–29

1

- If the Navigation Pane is closed, click the Shutter Bar Open/ Close Button, shown in Figure 1–27, to open the Navigation Pane (Figure 1–30).

Figure 1–30

2

- Right-click the Business Analyst table in the Navigation Pane to display a shortcut menu.

- Click Open on the short-cut menu to open the table in Datasheet view.

- Close the Navigation Pane by clicking the Shutter Bar Open/Close Button (Figure 1–31).

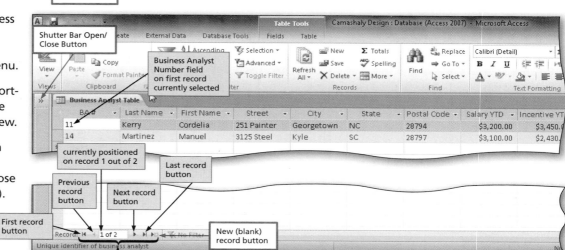

Figure 1–31

- Click the New (blank) record button to move to a position to enter a new record (Figure 1–32).

Q&A

Could you just click the Business Analyst Number (BA #) on the first open record and then add the record?

Yes, but it's a good habit to use the New (blank) Record button. Once a table contains more records than will fit on the screen, it is easier to click the New (blank) record button.

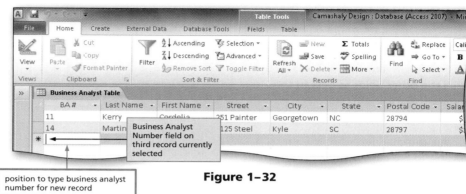

Figure 1–32

- Add the records shown in Figure 1–29, using the same techniques you used to add the first two records (Figure 1–33).

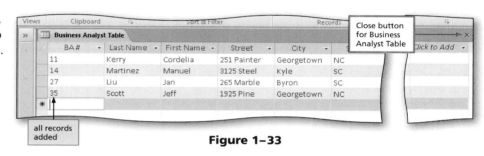

Figure 1–33

Other Ways

1. Click New button (Home tab | Records group)
2. Press CTRL+PLUS SIGN (+)

To Resize Columns in a Datasheet

Access assigns default column sizes, which do not always allow all the data in the field to appear. In some cases, the data might appear but not the entire field name. You can correct this problem by **resizing** the column (changing its size) in the datasheet. In some instances, you may want to reduce the size of a column. The State field, for example, is short enough that it does not require all the space on the screen that is allotted to it. Changing a column width changes the **layout**, or design, of a table.

The following steps resize the columns in the Business Analyst table and save the changes to the layout.

1

- Point to the right boundary of the field selector for the Business Analyst (BA #) field (Figure 1–34) so that the mouse pointer becomes a two-headed arrow.

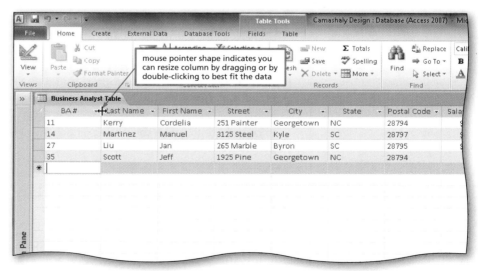

Figure 1–34

2

- Double-click the right boundary of the field selector to resize the field so that it best fits the data.

- Use the same technique to resize all the other fields to best fit the data (Figure 1–35).

3

- Save the changes to the layout by clicking the Save button on the Quick Access Toolbar (Figure 1–35).

- Click the table's Close button (shown in Figure 1–33) to the table.

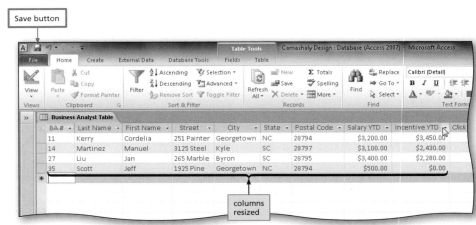

Figure 1–35

Q&A

What if I closed the table without saving the layout changes?

You would be asked if you want to save the changes.

Other Ways

1. Right-click field name, click Field Width

Plan Ahead

Determine the best method for distributing the database objects.

The traditional method of distributing database objects uses a printer to produce a hard copy of a table. A **hard copy** or **printout** is information that exists on a physical medium such as paper. For users who can receive fax documents, you can elect to print a hard copy on a remote fax machine. Hard copies can be useful for the following reasons:

- Many people prefer proofreading a hard copy of a document rather than viewing it on the screen to check for errors and readability.

- Hard copies can serve as reference material if your storage medium is lost or becomes corrupted and you need to re-create the document.

Instead of distributing a hard copy, users can choose to distribute the document as an electronic image that mirrors the original document's appearance. The electronic image of the document can be e-mailed, posted on a Web site, or copied to a portable medium such as a USB flash drive. Two popular electronic image formats, sometimes called fixed formats, are PDF by Adobe Systems and XPS by Microsoft. In Access, you can create PDF and XPS files through the External Data tab on the Ribbon. Electronic images of documents, such as PDF and XPS, can be useful for the following reasons:

- Users can view electronic images of documents without the software that created the original document (i.e., Access). Specifically, to view a PDF file, you use a program called Acrobat Reader, which can be downloaded free from Adobe's Web site. Similarly, to view an XPS file, you use a program called an XPS Viewer, which is included in the latest versions of Windows and Internet Explorer.

- Sending electronic documents saves paper and printer supplies. Society encourages users to contribute to **green computing**, which involves reducing the environmental waste generated when using a computer.

BTW

Changing Printers
To change the default printer that appears in the Print dialog box, click File on the Ribbon, click the Print tab in the Backstage view, click Print in the Print gallery, then click the Name box arrow and select the desired printer.

Previewing and Printing the Contents of a Table

When working with a database, you often will need to print a copy of the table contents. Figure 1–36 shows a printed copy of the contents of the Business Analyst table. (Yours may look slightly different, depending on your printer.) Because the Business Analyst table is substantially wider than the screen, it also will be wider than the normal printed page in portrait orientation. **Portrait orientation** means the printout is across the width of the page. **Landscape orientation** means the printout is across the height of the page. Thus, to print the wide database table, you might prefer to use landscape orientation. A convenient way to change to landscape orientation is to preview what the printed copy will look like by using Print Preview. This allows you to determine whether landscape orientation is necessary and, if it is, to change the orientation easily to landscape. In addition, you also can use Print Preview to determine whether any adjustments are necessary to the page margins.

BA #	Last Name	First Name	Street	City	State	Postal Code	Salary YTD	Incentive YTD
11	Kerry	Cordelia	251 Painter	Georgetown	NC	28794	$3,200.00	$3,450.00
14	Martinez	Manuel	3125 Steel	Kyle	SC	28797	$3,100.00	$2,430.00
27	Liu	Jan	265 Marble	Byron	SC	28795	$3,400.00	$2,280.00
35	Scott	Jeff	1925 Pine	Georgetown	NC	28794	$500.00	$0.00

Business Analyst Table   4/12/2012

Figure 1–36

To Preview and Print the Contents of a Table

The following steps use Print Preview to preview and then print the contents of the Business Analyst table.

1

- If the Navigation Pane is closed, open the Navigation Pane by clicking the Shutter Bar Open/Close Button.

- Be sure the Business Analyst table is selected.

Q&A

Why do I have to be sure the Business Analyst table is selected? It is the only object in the database.

When the database contains only one object, you don't have to worry about selecting the object. Ensuring that the correct object is selected is a good habit to form, however, to make sure that the object you print is the one you want.

- Click File on the Ribbon to open the Backstage view.

- Click the Print tab in the Backstage view to display the Print gallery (Figure 1–37).

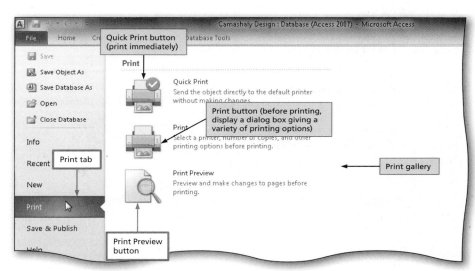

Figure 1–37

2

- Click the Print Preview button in the Print gallery to display a preview of what the table will look like when printed.

- Close the Navigation Pane to free up more of the screen for the preview (Figure 1–38).

Q&A

I can't read the table. Can I magnify a portion of the table?

Yes. Point the mouse pointer, whose shape will change to a magnifying glass, at the portion of the table that you want to magnify, and then click. You can return the view of the table to the one shown in the figure by clicking a second time.

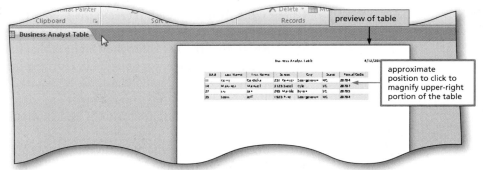

Figure 1–38

3

- Click the mouse pointer in the position shown in Figure 1–38 to magnify the upper-right section of the table (Figure 1–39).

My table was already magnified in a different area. How can I see the area shown in the figure?

One way is to use the scroll bars to move to the desired portion of the table. You also can click the mouse pointer anywhere in the table to produce a screen like the one in Figure 1–38, and then click in the location shown in the figure.

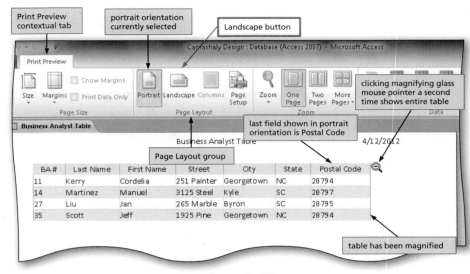

Figure 1–39

4

- Click the Landscape button to change to landscape orientation (Figure 1–40).

- Click the Print button (Print Preview tab | Print group) to display the Print dialog box.

- Click the OK button (Print dialog box) to print the table.

- When the printer stops, retrieve the hard copy of the Business Analyst Table.

- Click the Close Print Preview button (Print Preview tab | Close Preview group) to close the Print Preview window.

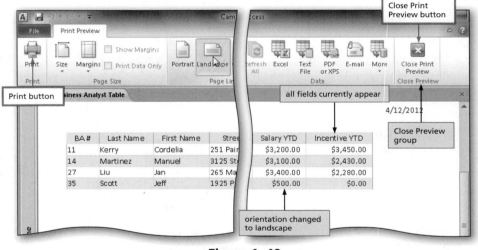

Figure 1–40

Other Ways

1. Press CTRL+P, click OK button (Print dialog box)

Creating Additional Tables

The Camashaly Design database contains two tables, the Business Analyst table and the Client table. You still need to create the Client table and add records to it. You created the Business Analyst table in Datasheet view. You will create the Client table in Design view.

Recall that the fields for the Client table are Client Number, Client Name, Street, City, State, Postal Code, Amount Paid, Current Due, Contract Hours YTD, and Business Analyst Number. The details that must be entered for these fields are shown in Table 1–5. The Client Number is the primary key. The Client Number field and the Business Analyst Number fields have both descriptions and captions. The Contract Hours YTD has a caption.

Because the values in the Contract Hours YTD field have decimal places, only Single, Double, or Decimal would be possible field size choices. (See Table 1–2 on Page AC 10 for a description of the possible field sizes for Number fields.) The difference between these choices concerns the amount of accuracy. Double is more accurate than Single, for example, but requires more storage space. Because the rates are only two decimal places, Single is a perfectly acceptable choice.

In addition to changing the field size for the Contract Hours YTD, you will also change the format to Fixed (a fixed number of decimal places) and the number of decimal places to 2.

Table 1–5 Structure of Client Table			
Field Name	**Data Type**	**Field Size**	**Notes**
Client Number	Text	4	**Primary Key** **Description:** Client Number (two uppercase letters followed by 2-digit number) **Caption:** CL #
Client Name	Text	30	
Street	Text	15	
City	Text	15	
State	Text	2	
Postal Code	Text	5	
Amount Paid	Currency		
Current Due	Currency		
Contract Hours YTD	Number	Single	**Caption:** Hrs YTD **Format:** Fixed **Decimal Places:** 2
Business Analyst Number	Text	2	**Caption:** BA # **Description:** Business Analyst Number (number of business analyst for client)

To Create a Table in Design View

The next step in creating the table is to define the fields by specifying the required details in Design view. You will make entries in the Field Name, Data Type, and Description columns and enter additional information in the Field Properties box in the lower portion of the Table window. As you define the fields, the row selector (Figure 1–19 on page AC 23) indicates the field you currently are describing. Clicking the row selector selects the entire row. It is positioned on the first field, indicating Access is ready for you to enter the name of the first field in the Field Name column.

The following steps use Design view to define the fields in the table.

- Open the Navigation Pane.

- Click Create on the Ribbon to display the Create tab (Figure 1–41).

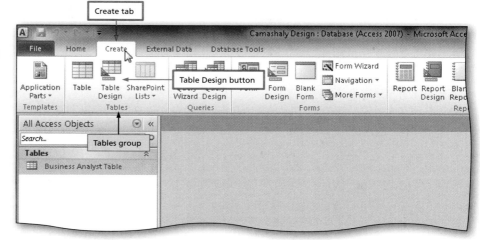

Figure 1–41

2

- Click the Table Design button (Create tab | Tables group) to create a new table in Design view (Figure 1–42).

Q&A

Could I save the table now so I can assign it the name I want, rather than Table1?

You certainly could. Be aware, however, that you will still need to save it again once you have added all your fields.

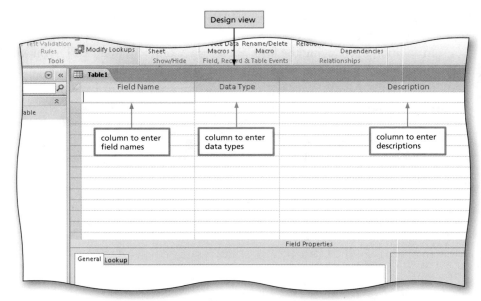

Figure 1–42

3

- Type **Client Number** (the name of the first field) in the Field Name column and then press the TAB key to accept the field name and move to the Data Type column (Figure 1–43).

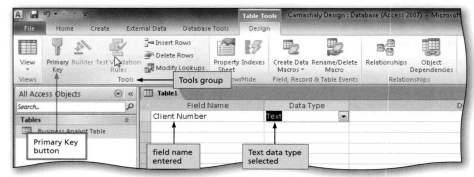

Figure 1–43

4

- Click the Primary Key button (Table Tools Design tab | Tools group) to designate the Client Number field as the primary key (Figure 1–44).

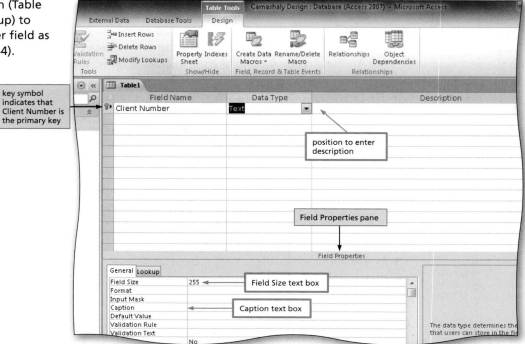

Figure 1–44

5

- Press the TAB key to move to the Description column, and then type `Client Number (two uppercase letters followed by a two-digit number)` as the description.

- Click the Field Size text box in the Field Properties pane to produce an insertion point, use either the BACKSPACE or DELETE key as necessary to erase the current entry (255), and then type `4` to change the field size.

- Click the Caption text box to produce an insertion point, and then type `CL #` to enter a caption (Figure 1–45).

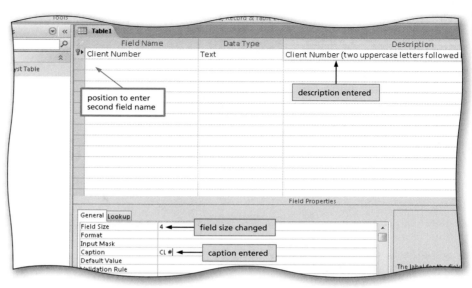

Figure 1–45

6

- Click the Field Name column on the second row to produce an insertion point and then make the entries for the Client Name field.

- Use the techniques illustrated in Steps 1 through 5 to make the entries for the remaining fields in the Client table structure, shown in Table 1–5 on page AC 33, up through and including the name of the Amount Paid field.

- Click the Data Type box arrow to display a menu of available data types (Figure 1–46).

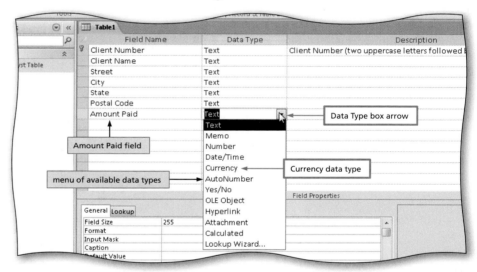

Figure 1–46

7

- Click Currency to select the data type.

- Enter the Current Due field and select the Currency data type.

- Enter the Contract Hours YTD field and select the Number data type (Figure 1–47).

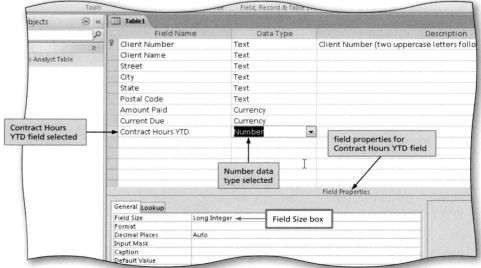

Figure 1–47

8

- Click the Field Size box to display the Field Size box arrow.

- Click the Field Size box arrow to display the Field Size box menu (Figure 1–48).

Q&A What would happen if I left the field size set to Integer?

If the field size is Integer, no decimal places can be stored. Thus a value of 2.50 would be stored as 2.

If you enter your hours and none of the values have decimal places, probably you did not change the field size.

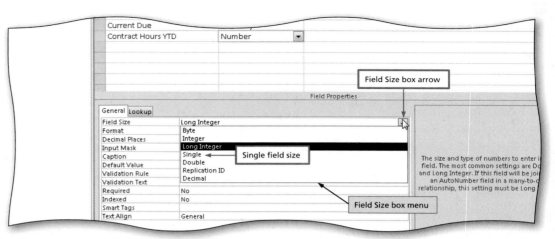

Figure 1–48

9

- Click Single to select single precision as the field size.

- Click the Format box to display the Format box arrow.

- Click the Format box arrow to display the Format box menu (Figure 1–49).

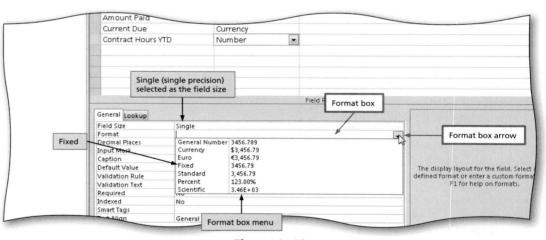

Figure 1–49

10

- Click Fixed to select fixed as the format.

- Click the Decimal Places box to display the Decimal Places box arrow.

- Click the Decimal Places box arrow to enter the number of decimal places.

- Click 2 to select 2 as the number of decimal places.

- Click the Caption text box to produce an insertion point, and then type **Hrs YTD** to enter a caption (Figure 1–50).

Figure 1–50

11

- Enter the Business Analyst Number field from Table 1–5. Be sure to change the description, field size, and caption to the ones shown in the table.

- Click the Save button on the Quick Access Toolbar to display the Save As dialog box, type Client as the name of the table, and then click the OK button (Save As dialog box) to save the table (Figure 1–51).

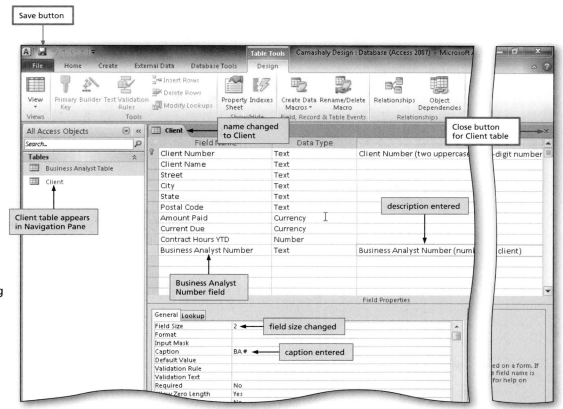

Figure 1–51

Other Ways

1. Press F6 to move between the upper pane and the lower pane in the Table Design window

Correcting Errors in the Structure

When creating a table, check the entries carefully to ensure they are correct. If you make a mistake and discover it before you press the TAB key, you can correct the error by repeatedly pressing the BACKSPACE key until the incorrect characters are removed. Then, type the correct characters. If you do not discover a mistake until later, you can click the entry, type the correct value, and then press the ENTER key. You can use the following techniques to make changes to the structure:

- If you accidentally add an extra field to the structure, select the field by clicking the row selector (the leftmost column on the row that contains the field to be deleted). Once you have selected the field, press the DELETE key. This will remove the field from the structure.

- If you forget to include a field, select the field that will follow the field you want to add by clicking the row selector, and then press the INSERT key. The remaining fields move down one row, making room for the missing field. Make the entries for the new field in the usual manner.

- If you made the wrong field a primary key field, click the correct primary key entry for the field and then click the Primary Key button (Table Tools Design tab | Tools group).

- To move a field, click the row selector for the field to be moved to select the field, and then drag the field to the desired position.

As an alternative to these steps, you may want to start over. To do so, click the Close button for the window containing the table, and then click the No button in the Microsoft Access dialog box. Click Create on the Ribbon and then click the Table Design button to create a table. You then can repeat the process you used earlier to define the fields in the table.

BTW

AutoCorrect Feature
The AutoCorrect feature of Access corrects common mistakes when entering text in a cell. AutoCorrect corrects two capital letters by changing the second letter to lowercase and capitalizes the first letter in the names of days. It also corrects more than 400 commonly misspelled words.

BTW

Other AutoCorrect Options
Using the Office AutoCorrect feature, you can create entries that will replace abbreviations with spelled-out names and phrases automatically. To specify AutoCorrect rules, click File to open the Backstage view, click Options, and then click Proofing in the Access Options dialog box.

To Close the Table

Now that you have completed and saved the Client table, you can close it. The following step closes the table.

1 Click the Close button for the Client table (see Figure 1–51) to close the table.

Importing Data from Other Applications to Access

Now that you have created the Client table, you could add the records to it just as you did with the Business Analyst table. Access provides an alternative, however, that is available because Camashaly Design has already stored the necessary data in an Excel workbook (Figure 1–52). The data is stored in the form of an Excel **list**; that is, the first row contains column headings describing the data in each of the columns, and the remaining rows contain the data. Camashaly can **import** the data, which means to make a copy of the data in a table in the Access database.

When importing data, you have two choices. You can create a new table, in which case the column headings in the worksheet become the field names in the table. Access will attempt to assign appropriate data types. You would need to review the data types, adjust field sizes, captions, descriptions, and formats after the data was imported. The other option is to add the records to an existing table. This method is appropriate if you have already created the table, provided the column headings in the worksheet match the field names in the table, as they do in the case of the Client table.

	A	B	C	D	E	F	G	H	I	J	K
1	Client Number	Client Name	Street	City	State	Postal Code	Amount Paid	Current Due	Contract Hours YTD	Business Analyst Number	
2	BA53	Bavant Animal Hospital	134 Main	Burles	NC	28817	$0.00	$7,500.00	0.00	11	
3	BB32	Babbage CPA Firm	464 Linnell	Austin	SC	28796	$1,500.00	$500.00	5.00	14	
4	BC76	Buda Community Clinic	867 Ridge	Buda	NC	27032	$2,500.00	$750.00	2.50	11	
5	CJ29	Catering by Jenna	123 Second	Granger	NC	27036	$3,000.00	$1,000.00	15.50	27	
6	GA74	Grant Antiques	78 Catawba	Georgetown	NC	28794	$5,500.00	$3,200.00	34.50	14	
7	GF56	Granger Foundation	65 Simpson	Granger	NC	27036	$0.00	$6,500.00	0.00	11	
8	HC10	Hendley County Hospital	216 Rivard	Austin	SC	28796	$3,100.00	$1,200.00	12.00	27	
9	KD21	KAL Design Studio	116 Pine	Georgetown	NC	28794	$6,000.00	$3,200.00	30.50	14	
10	KG04	Kyle Grocery Cooperative	421 First	Kyle	SC	28798	$3,200.00	$0.00	5.00	11	
11	ME14	Mike's Electronic Stop	234 Gilham	Georgetown	NC	28794	$2,500.00	$1,500.00	8.50	27	
12	PJ34	Patricia Jean Florist	345 Magee	Kyle	SC	28798	$0.00	$5,200.00	0.00	27	
13	SL77	Smarter Law Associates	764 Main	Burles	NC	28817	$3,800.00	$0.00	10.50	11	
14	TB17	The Bikeshop	346 Austin	Buda	NC	27032	$2,750.00	$1,200.00	14.00	27	
15	WE05	Walburg Energy Alternatives	12 Polk	Walburg	NC	28819	$4,500.00	$1,450.00	19.50	14	
16	WS01	Woody Sporting Goods	578 Central	Walburg	NC	28819	$2,250.00	$1,600.00	18.50	14	
17											

Figure 1–52

The process of importing into an Access database uses a wizard. Specifically, if the data is imported from an Excel worksheet, the process will use the Import Spreadsheet Wizard. The wizard takes you through some basic steps, asking a few simple questions. After you have answered the questions, the wizard will import or link the data.

To Import an Excel Worksheet

To import the data in the Camashaly Client Data workbook, you use the Import Spreadsheet Wizard to place the rows from an Excel worksheet into an existing table. The following steps import the Camashaly Client Data Excel workbook, which is provided as a data file. See the inside back cover of this book for instructions on downloading the Data Files for Students, or contact your instructor for more information about accessing the required files.

1

- Click External Data on the Ribbon to display the External Data tab (Figure 1–53).

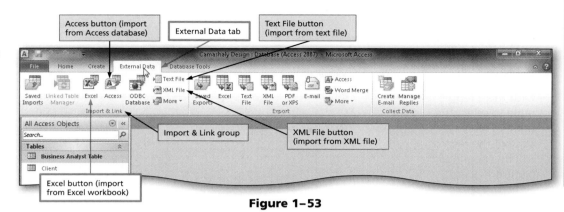

Figure 1–53

2

- Click the Excel button (External Data tab | Import & Link group) to display the Get External Data – Excel Spreadsheet dialog box.

- Click the Browse button (Get External Data – Excel Spreadsheet dialog box) to display the File Open dialog box.

- Navigate to the USB flash drive (or the location of your data files).

- Double-click your USB flash drive, and then click Camashaly Client Data to select the file to be opened.

- Click the Open button (File Open dialog box), which will return you to the Get External Data dialog box with the Camashaly Client Data workbook selected.

3

- Click the option button to append a copy of records to a table (Figure 1–54).

Q&A

What happens if I select the option button to import records into a new table?

Instead of the records being added to an existing table, they will be placed in a new table. Access will assign all the data types. You would then need to ensure they are correct. You also would need to change any field sizes, descriptions, captions, formats, or number of decimal places to the ones you want.

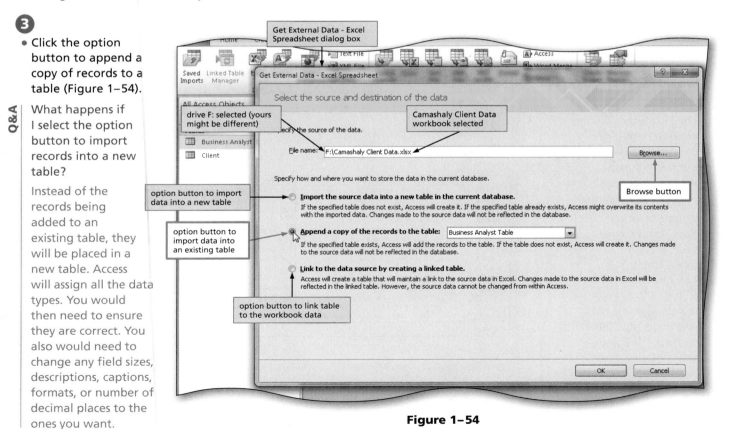

Figure 1–54

4
- Click the arrow to produce a menu of available tables.

- Click the Client table to select the table to which a copy of the records will be appended (Figure 1–55).

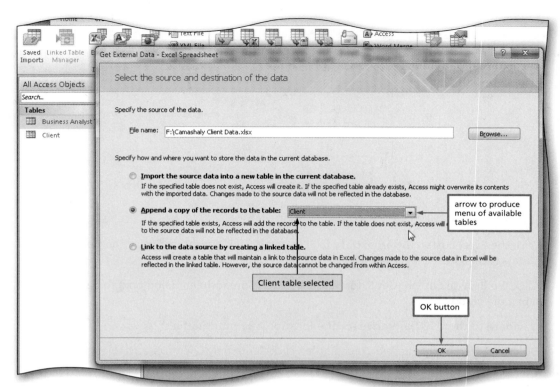

Figure 1–55

5
- Click the OK button to move to the next Import Spreadsheet Wizard screen (Figure 1–56).

Q&A

The First Row Contains Column Headings check box is checked, but it is dimmed. What if I want to remove the check mark?

When you are appending records to an existing table, the first row must contain column headings. If instead you were creating a new table, the first row might not contain column headings. In that case, you would have control over this check box.

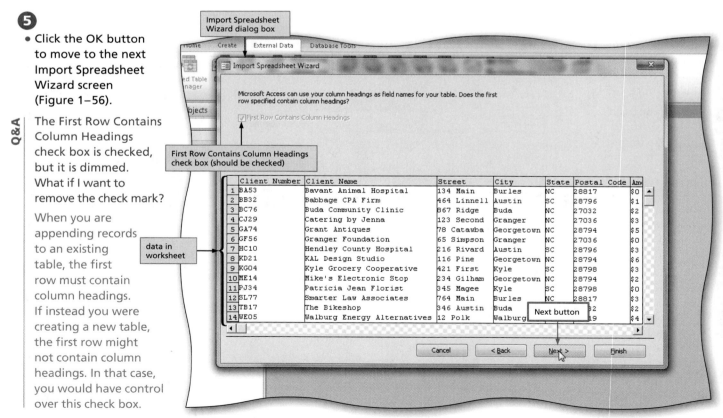

Figure 1–56

6

- Click the Next button to move to the next Import Spreadsheet Wizard screen (Figure 1–57).

Q&A What happens if I later realize I have selected the wrong table?

If you have not yet clicked the Finish button, you can click the Back button to return to the screen where you selected the table, and then select the correct table.

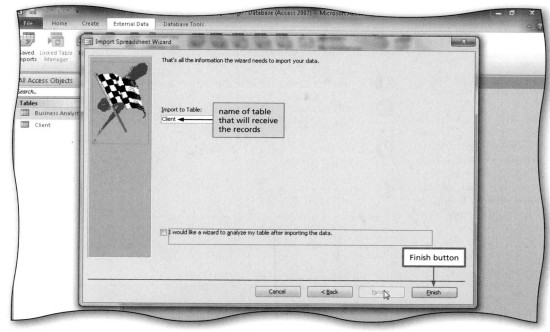

Figure 1–57

7

- Because the table name is correct, click the Finish button to import the data (Figure 1–58).

Q&A I got an error message that stated that a particular field did not exist in the Client table. What did I do wrong? How do I fix it?

When you created the table, you did not name that particular field correctly. Open the table in Design view and change the field name to the correct name. Check other field names as well. When you are done, save and close the table. Then, repeat the import process.

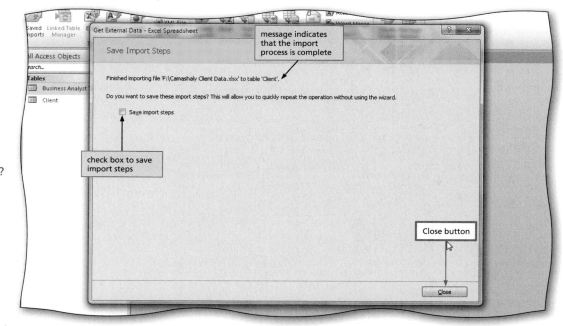

Figure 1–58

8

- Because you will not save the import steps, click the Close button.

Q&A When would I save the import steps?

If you think you might need to repeat these steps in the future, you can save time by saving the steps.

Other Ways
1. Right-click table in Navigation Pane, click Import on shortcut menu.

To Resize Columns in a Datasheet

You can resize the columns in the datasheet for the Client table just as you resized the columns in the datasheet for the Business Analyst table. The following steps resize the columns in the Client table to best fit the data.

BTW

Resizing Columns
To resize all columns in a datasheet to best fit simultaneously, select the column heading for the first column, hold down the SHIFT key and select the last column in the datasheet. Then, double-click the right boundary of any field selector.

1 Open the Client table in Datasheet view and then close the Navigation Pane.

2 Double-click the right boundary of the field selectors of each of the fields to resize the columns so that they best fit the data.

3 Save the changes to the layout by clicking the Save button on the Quick Access Toolbar (Figure 1–59).

4 Close the table.

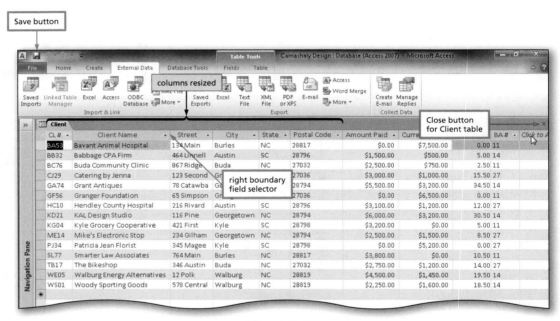

Figure 1–59

Break Point: If you wish to take a break, this is a good place to do so. You can quit Access now. To resume at a later time, start Access, open the database called Camashaly Design, and continue following the steps from this location forward.

Additional Database Objects

A computerized database such as Access contains many types of objects. Tables are the objects you use to store and manipulate data. Access supports other important types of objects as well; each of these objects has a specific purpose that assists in maximizing the benefits of a database. Through queries (questions), Access makes it possible to ask complex questions concerning the data in the database and then receive instant answers. Access also allows the user to produce attractive and useful forms for viewing and updating data. Additionally, Access includes report creation tools that make it easy to produce sophisticated reports for presenting data.

To Use the Simple Query Wizard to Create a Query

Queries are simply questions, the answers to which are in the database. Access contains a powerful query feature that helps you find the answers to a wide variety of questions. Once you have examined the question you want to ask to determine the fields involved in the question, you can begin creating the query. If there are no restrictions involved in the query, nor any special order or calculations, you can use the Simple Query Wizard.

The following steps use the Simple Query Wizard to create a query that Camashaly Design might use to obtain financial information on its clients. The query displays the number, name, amount paid, current due, contract hours YTD, and business analyst number of all clients.

1

- If the Navigation Pane is closed, click the Shutter Bar Open/Close Button to open the Navigation Pane.

- Be sure the Client table is selected.

- Click Create on the Ribbon to display the Create tab.

- Click the Query Wizard button (Create tab | Queries group) to display the New Query dialog box (Figure 1–60).

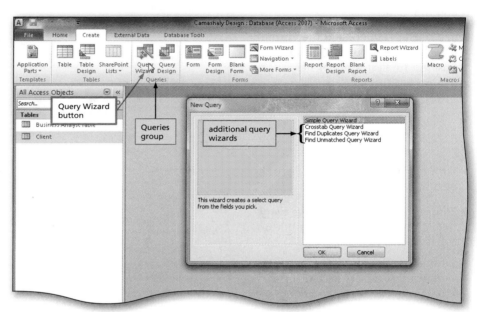

Figure 1–60

2

- Be sure Simple Query Wizard is selected, and then click the OK button (New Query dialog box) to display the Simple Query Wizard dialog box (Figure 1–61).

Q&A What would happen if the Business Analyst Table were selected instead of the Client table?

The list of available fields would contain fields from the Business Analyst Table rather than the Client table.

Q&A If the list contained Business Analyst Table fields, how could I make it contain Client table fields?

Click the arrow in the Tables/Queries box and then click the Client table in the list that appears.

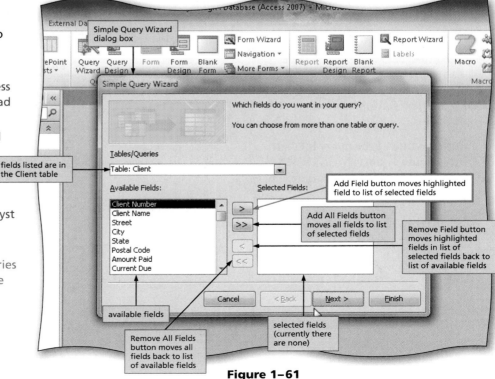

Figure 1–61

3

- With the Client Number field selected, click the Add Field button to add the field to the query.

- With the Client Name field selected, click the Add Field button a second time to add the field.

- Click the Amount Paid field, and then click the Add Field button to add the field.

- In a similar fashion, add the Current Due, Contract Hours YTD, and Business Analyst Number fields (Figure 1–62).

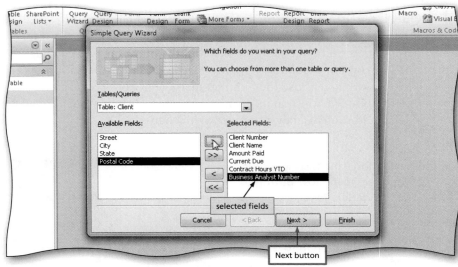

Figure 1–62

4

- Click the Next button to move to the next screen.

- Ensure that the Detail (shows every field of every record) option button is selected (Figure 1–63).

Q&A

What is the difference between Detail and Summary?

Detail shows all the records and fields. Summary only shows computations (for example, the total amount paid).

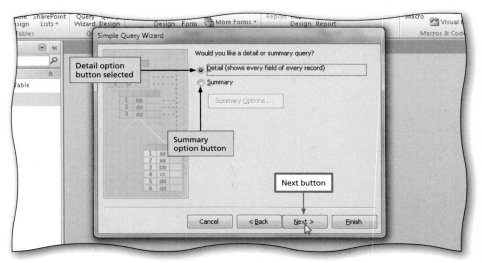

Figure 1–63

5

- Click the Next button to move to the next screen.

- Ensure the title of the query is Client Query (Figure 1–64).

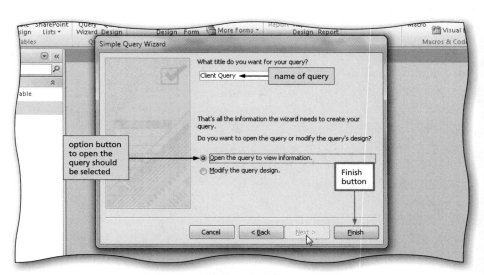

Figure 1–64

6

- Click the Finish button to create the query (Figure 1–65).

- Click the Close button for the Client Query to remove the query results from the screen.

Q&A

If I want to use this query in the future, do I need to save the query?

Normally you would. The one exception is a query created by the wizard. The wizard automatically saves the query it creates.

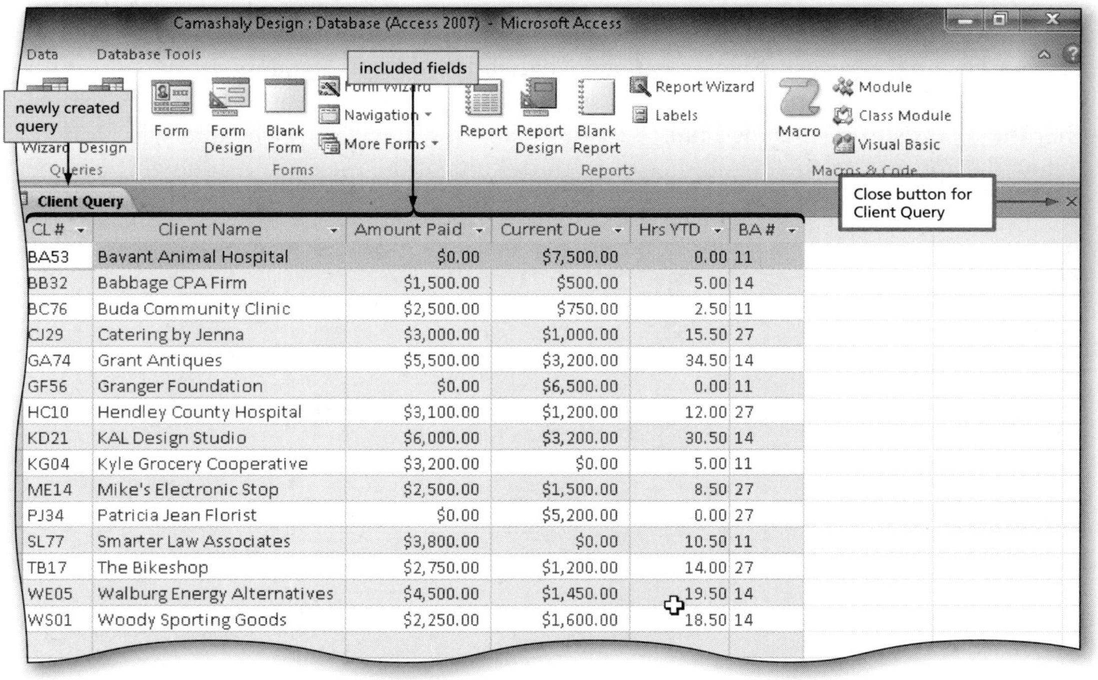

Figure 1–65

Using Queries

After you have created and saved a query, Access stores it as a database object and makes it available for use in a variety of ways:

- To view the results of the query, open it by right-clicking the query in the Navigation Pane and clicking Open on the shortcut menu.

- To print the results with the query open, click File on the Ribbon, click the Print tab, and then click either Print or Quick Print.

- If you want to change the design of the query, right-click the query in the Navigation Pane and then click Design View on the shortcut menu to open the query in Design view.

- To print the query without first opening it, be sure the query is selected in the Navigation Pane and click File on the Ribbon, click the Print tab, and then click either Print or Quick Print.

You can switch between views of a query using the View button (Home tab | Views group). Clicking the arrow in the bottom of the button produces the View button menu. You then click the desired view in the menu. The two query views you will use in this chapter are Datasheet view (see the results) and Design view (change the design). You also can click the top part of the View button, in which case, you will switch to the view identified by the icon on the button. In the figure, the button contains the icon for Design view, so clicking the button would change to Design view. For the most part, the icon on the button represents the view you want, so you can usually simply click the button.

To Use a Criterion in a Query

After you have determined the fields to be included in a query, you will determine whether there are any restrictions on the records that are to be included. For example, you might only want to include those clients whose business analyst number is 14. In such a case, you need to enter the 14 as a **criterion**, which is a condition that the records to be included must satisfy. To do so, you will open the query in Design view, enter the criterion below the appropriate field, and then view the results of the query. The following steps enter a criterion to include only the clients of business analyst 14 and then view the query results.

- Right-click the Client Query in the Navigation Pane to produce a shortcut menu (Figure 1–66).

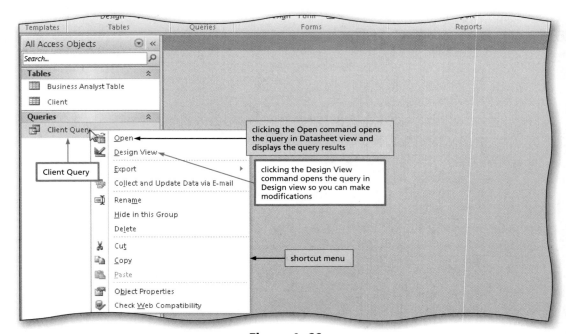

Figure 1–66

2

- Click Design View on the shortcut menu to open the query in Design view (Figure 1–67).

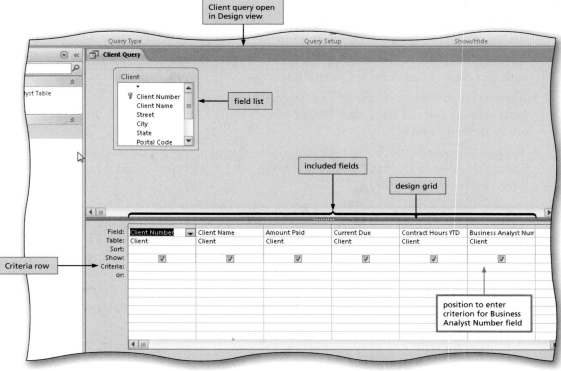

Figure 1–67

3

- Click the Criteria row in the Business Analyst Number column of the grid, and then type **14** as the criterion (Figure 1–68).

Q&A The Business Analyst Number field is a text field. Do I need to enclose the value for a text field in quotation marks?

You could, but it is not necessary, because Access inserts the quotation marks for you automatically.

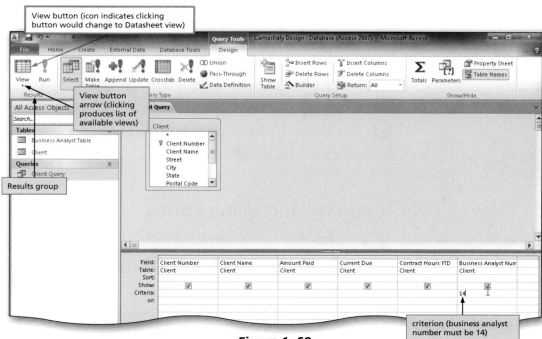

Figure 1–68

4

- Click the View button to display the query results in Datasheet view (Figure 1–69).

Q&A Could I click the View button arrow and then click Datasheet view?

Yes, if the icon representing the view you want appears on the View button; however, it is easier just to click the button.

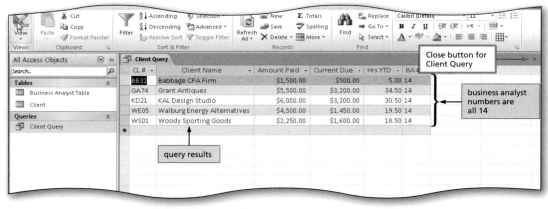

Figure 1–69

5

- Click the Close button for the Client Query to close the query.

- When asked if you want to save your changes, click the No button.

Q&A If I saved the query, what would happen the next time I ran the query?

You would see only clients of business analyst 14.

Q&A Could I save the query with another name?

Yes. To save the query with another name, click File on the Ribbon, click Save Object As, enter a new file name in the Save As dialog box and click OK (Save As dialog box).

Other Ways

1. Click Run button (Query Tools Design tab | Results group)
2. Click Datasheet View button on Status bar

To Print the Results of a Query

The following steps print the results of a saved query.

1 With the Client Query selected in the Navigation Pane, click File on the Ribbon to open the Backstage view.

2 Click the Print tab in the Backstage view to display the Print gallery.

3 Click the Quick Print button to print the query.

Creating and Using Forms

In Datasheet view, you can view many records at once. If there are many fields, however, only some of the fields in each record might be visible at a time. In **Form view**, where data is displayed in a form on the screen, you usually can see all the fields, but only for one record.

To Create a Form

Like a paper form, a **form** in a database is a formatted document with fields that contain data. Forms allow you to view and maintain data. Forms also can be used to print data, but reports are more commonly used for that purpose. The simplest type of form in Access is one that includes all the fields in a table stacked one above the other. The following steps create a form, use the form to view records, and then save the form.

- Select the Client table in the Navigation Pane.

- If necessary, click Create on the Ribbon to display the Create tab (Figure 1–70).

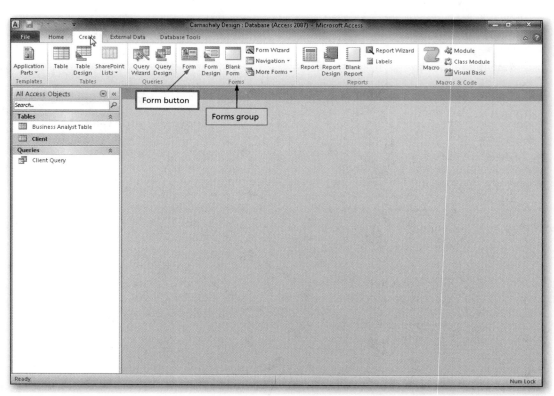

Figure 1–70

2

• Click the Form button (Create tab | Forms group) to create a simple form (Figure 1–71).

Q&A A Field list appeared on my screen. What should I do?

Click the Add Existing Fields button (Form Layout Tools Design tab | Tools group) to remove the Field list from the screen.

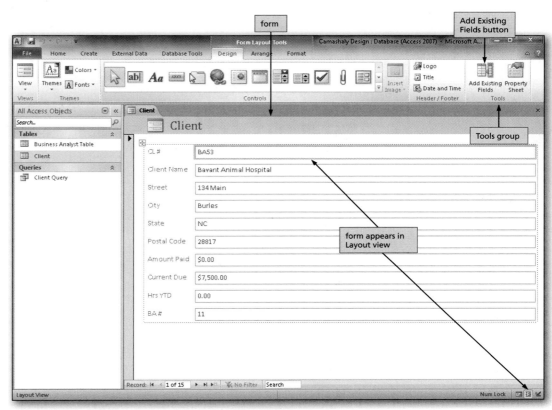

Figure 1–71

3

• If the form appears in Layout view, click the Form View button on the Access Status bar to display the form in Form view.

Q&A How can I recognize Layout view?

Access identifies Layout view in three ways. The left side of the Status bar will contain the words Layout View; there will be shading around the outside of the selected field in the form; and the Layout View button will be selected on the right side of the Status bar.

• Click the Next Record button three times to move to record 4 (Figure 1–72).

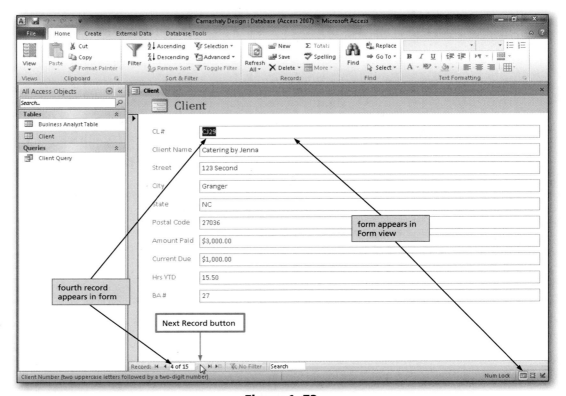

Figure 1–72

4

- Click the Save button on the Quick Access Toolbar to display the Save As dialog box (Figure 1–73).

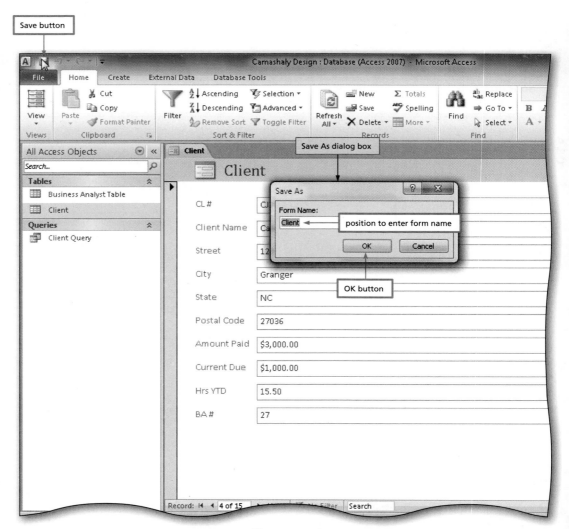

Figure 1–73

Q&A

Did I have to click the Next Record button before saving?

No. The only reason you were asked to click the button was so that you could experience navigation within the form.

5

- Type **Client Form** as the form name, and then click the OK button to save the form.

- Click the Close button for the form to close the form.

Other Ways

1. Click View button (Form Layout Tools Design tab | Views group)

Using a Form

After you have saved a form, you can use it at anytime by right-clicking the form in the Navigation Pane and then clicking Open in the shortcut menu. In addition to viewing data in the form, you can also use it to enter or update data, a process that is very similar to updating data using a datasheet. If you plan to use the form to enter or revise data, you must ensure you are viewing the form in Form view.

Break Point: If you wish to take a break, this is a good place to do so. You can quit Access now. To resume at a later time, start Access, open the database called Camashaly Design, and continue following the steps from this location forward.

Creating and Printing Reports

Camashaly Design wants to create the Client Financial Report shown in Figure 1–74. Just as you can create a form containing all fields by clicking a single button, you can click a button to create a report containing all the fields. Doing so will not match the report shown in Figure 1–74, however, which does not contain all the fields. Some of the column headings are different. In addition, some of the headings in the report in Figure 1–74 are split over multiple lines, whereas the ones in the report created by clicking the button will not be split. Fortunately, you can later modify the report design to make it precisely match the figure. To do so, you use Layout view for the report.

Client Financial Report

Thursday, April 12, 2012
5:17:00 PM

Client Number	Client Name	Amount Paid	Current Due	Hrs YTD	Business Analyst Number
BA53	Bavant Animal Hospital	$0.00	$7,500.00	0.00	11
BB32	Babbage CPA Firm	$1,500.00	$500.00	5.00	14
BC76	Buda Community Clinic	$2,500.00	$750.00	2.50	11
CJ29	Catering by Jenna	$3,000.00	$1,000.00	15.50	27
GA74	Grant Antiques	$5,500.00	$3,200.00	34.50	14
GF56	Granger Foundation	$0.00	$6,500.00	0.00	11
HC10	Hendley County Hospital	$3,100.00	$1,200.00	12.00	27
KD21	KAL Design Studio	$6,000.00	$3,200.00	30.50	14
KG04	Kyle Grocery Cooperative	$3,200.00	$0.00	5.00	11
ME14	Mike's Electronic Stop	$2,500.00	$1,500.00	8.50	27
PJ34	Patricia Jean Florist	$0.00	$5,200.00	0.00	27
SL77	Smarter Law Associates	$3,800.00	$0.00	10.50	11
TB17	The Bikeshop	$2,750.00	$1,200.00	14.00	27
WE05	Walburg Energy Alternatives	$4,500.00	$1,450.00	19.50	14
WS01	Woody Sporting Goods	$2,250.00	$1,600.00	18.50	14
		$40,600.00	$34,800.00	176.00	

Figure 1–74

To Create a Report

You will first create a report containing all fields. The following steps create and save the initial report. They also modify the report title.

- Be sure the Client table is selected in the Navigation Pane.

- Click Create on the Ribbon to display the Create tab (Figure 1–75).

Q&A Why do I need to select the Client table prior to clicking Create on the Ribbon?

You don't need to select it at that point. You do need to select it prior to clicking the Report button at the next step because Access will include all the fields in whichever table or query is currently selected.

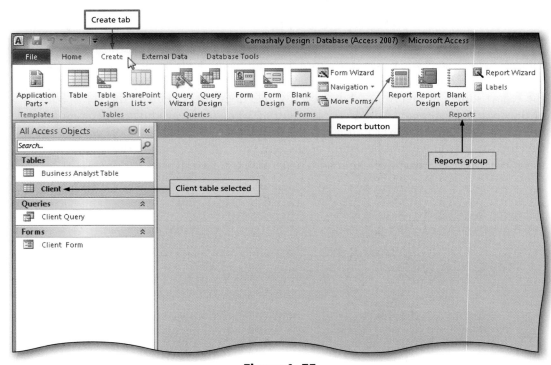

Figure 1–75

- Click the Report button (Create tab | Reports group) to create the report (Figure 1–76).

Q&A Why is the report title Client?

Access automatically assigns the name of the table or query as the title. It also automatically includes the date. You can change either of these later.

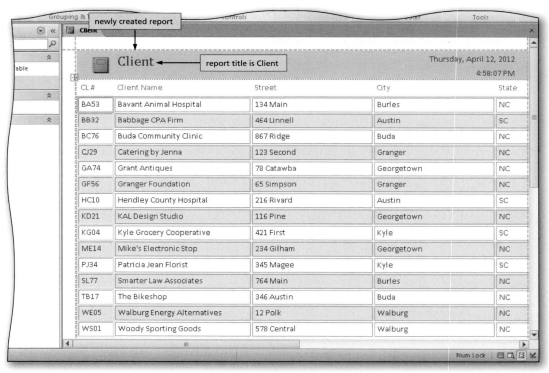

Figure 1–76

3

- Click the Save button on the Quick Access Toolbar to display the Save As dialog box and then type **Client Financial Report** as the name of the report (Figure 1–77).

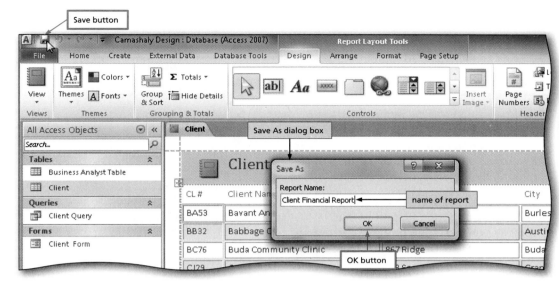

Figure 1–77

4

- Click the OK button (Save As dialog box) to save the report (Figure 1–78).

The name of the report changed. Why didn't the report title also change?

The report title just happens to begin with the same name as the report. If you change the name of the report, Access will not change the report title. You can change it at any time to any title you like.

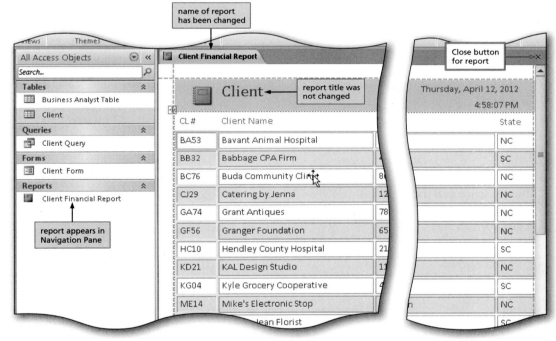

Figure 1–78

5

- Close the report by clicking its Close button.

Using Layout View in a Report

When working with a report in Access, there are four different ways to view the report. They are Report view, Print Preview, Layout view, and Design view. Report view shows the report on the screen. Print Preview shows the report as it will appear when printed. Layout view is similar to Report view in that it shows the report on the screen, but it also allows you to make changes to the report. It is usually the easiest way to make such changes. Design view also allows you to make changes, but it does not show you the actual report. It is most useful when the changes you need to make are especially complex. In this chapter, you will use Layout view to modify the report.

To Modify Column Headings and Resize Columns

To make the report match the one in Figure 1–74, you need to change the title, remove some columns, modify the column headings, and also resize the columns. The following steps use Layout view to make the necessary modifications to the report.

1

- Right-click Client Financial Report in the Navigation Pane, and then click Layout View on the shortcut menu to open the report in Layout view.

- If a Field list appears, click the Add Existing Fields button (Report Layout Tools Design tab | Tools group) to remove the Field list from the screen.

- Close the Navigation Pane.

- Click the report title once to select it.

- Click the report title a second time to produce an insertion point (Figure 1–79).

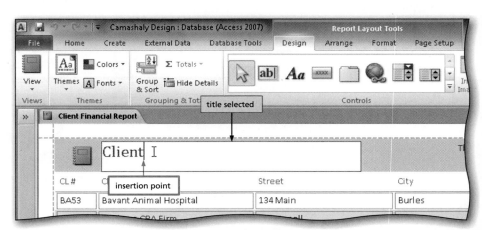

Figure 1–79

Q&A I clicked at a different position in the title and my insertion point is in the middle of Client. How do I produce an insertion point at the position shown in the figure?

You can use the RIGHT ARROW key to move the insertion point to the position in the figure or you can click the desired position.

2

- Press the SPACEBAR to insert a space and then type **Financial Report** to complete the title.

- Click the column heading for the Street field to select it.

- Hold the SHIFT key down and then click the column headings for the City field, the State field, and the Postal Code fields to select multiple column headings.

Q&A What happens if I don't hold the SHIFT key down?

As soon as you click the column heading, it will be the only one that is selected. To select multiple objects, you need to hold the SHIFT key down for every object after the first one.

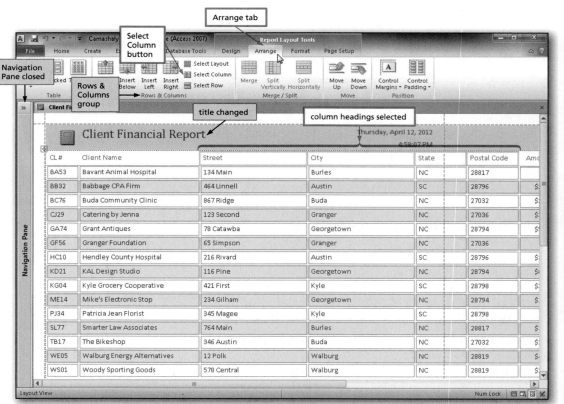

Figure 1–80

Q&A

I selected the wrong collection of objects. What should I do?

You can click somewhere else on the report so that the objects you want are not selected, and then begin the process again. Alternatively, you can repeatedly click the Undo button on the Quick Access Toolbar to undo your selections. Once you have done so, you can select the objects you want.

- Click Arrange on the Ribbon to display the Arrange tab (Figure 1–80).

3

- Click the Select Column button (Report Layout Tools Arrange tab | Rows & Columns group) to select the entire columns corresponding to the column headings you selected in the previous step.

- Press the DELETE key to delete the columns.

- Click the column heading for the Client Number field twice, once to select it and the second time to produce an insertion point (Figure 1–81).

Q&A

I inadvertently selected the wrong field. What should I do?

Click somewhere outside the various fields to deselect the one you have selected. Then, click the Client Number field twice.

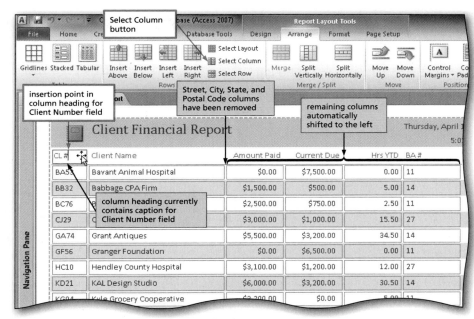

Figure 1–81

4

- Use the DELETE or BACKSPACE keys as necessary to erase the current entry and then type `Client Number` as the new entry.

- Click the heading for the Business Analyst Number field twice, erase the current entry, and then type `Business Analyst Number` as the new entry.

- Click the Client Number field heading to select it, point to the lower boundary of the heading for the Client Number field so that the mouse pointer changes to a two-headed arrow and then drag the lower boundary to the approximate position shown in Figure 1–82 to expand the column headings.

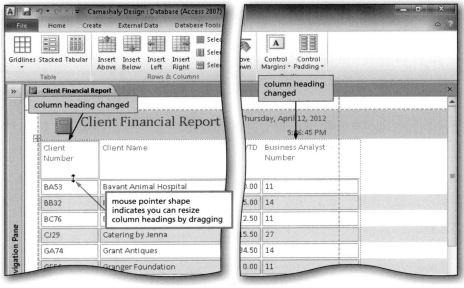

Figure 1–82

Q&A

Do I have to be exact?

No. If you are in a slightly different position, your report would look a little different from the one in the figure, but the difference would not be significant.

5

- Point to the right boundary of the heading for the Client Number field so that the mouse pointer changes to a two-headed arrow and then drag the right boundary to the approximate position shown in Figure 1–83 to reduce the width of the column.

Q&A

Do I have to be exact?

No. Again, if you are in a slightly different position, the difference between your report and the one in the figure would not be significant.

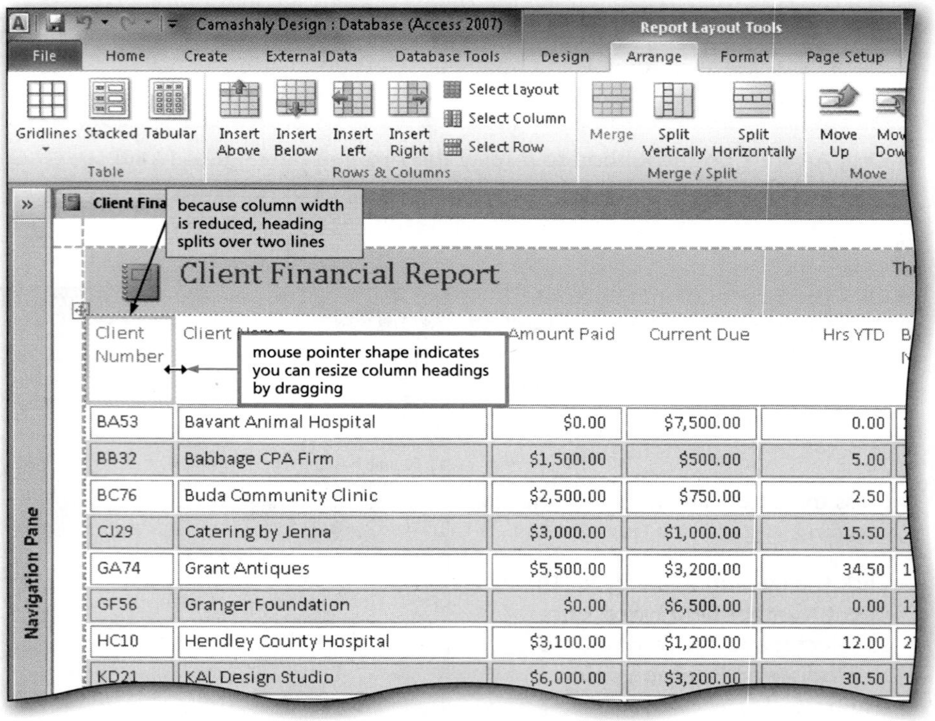

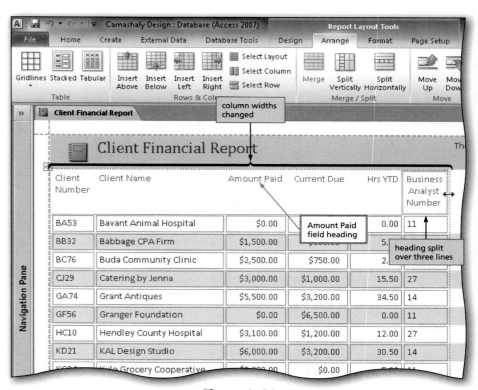

Figure 1–83

6

- Using the same technique, resize the other columns to the sizes shown in Figure 1–84.

Figure 1–84

To Add Totals to a Report

The report in Figure 1–74 contains totals for the Amount Paid, Current Due, and Hrs YTD columns. You can use Layout view to add these totals. The following steps use Layout view to include totals for these three columns.

1

- Click the Amount Paid field heading (shown in Figure 1–84) to select the field.

Q&A   Do I have to click the heading? Could I click the field on one of the records?

You do not have to click the heading. You also could click the Amount Paid field on any record.

- Click Design on the Ribbon to display the Design tab.

- Click the Totals button (Report Layout Tools Design tab | Grouping & Totals group) to display the list of available calculations (Figure 1–85).

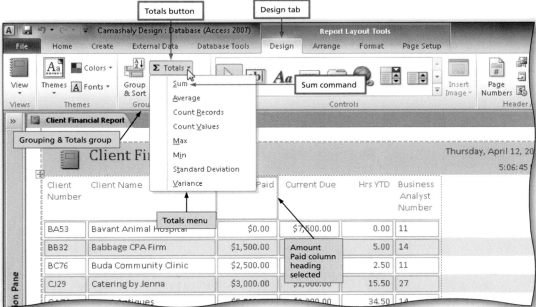

Figure 1–85

2

- Click Sum to calculate the sum of the amount of paid values.

Q&A   Is Sum the same as Total?

Yes.

- Using the same technique, add totals for the Current Due and Hrs YTD columns.

- Scroll down to the bottom of the report to verify that the totals are included. If necessary, expand the size of the total controls so they appear completely.

- Click the Page number to select it and then drag it to the approximate position shown in Figure 1–86.

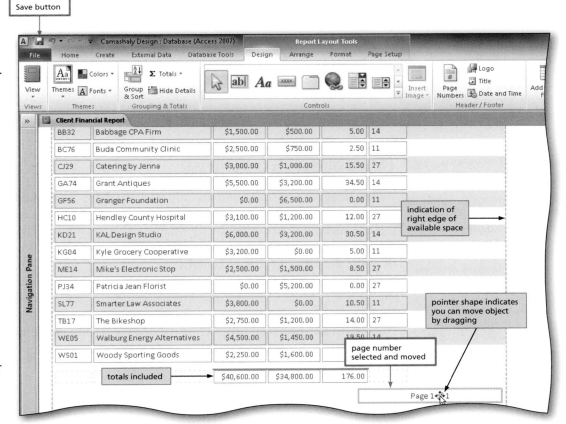

Figure 1–86

Q&A Why did I need to move the page number?

The dotted line near the right-hand edge of the screen indicates the right-hand border of the available space on the printed page, based on whatever margins and orientation are currently selected. A portion of the page number extends beyond this border. By moving the page number, it no longer extends beyond the border.

3

- Click the Save button on the Quick Access Toolbar to save your changes to the report layout.

- Close the report.

To Print a Report

The following steps print the report.

1 With the Client Financial Report selected in the Navigation Pane, click File on the Ribbon to open the Backstage view.

2 Click the Print tab in the Backstage view to display the Print gallery.

3 Click the Quick Print button to print the report.

Q&A How can I print multiple copies of my report?

Click File on the Ribbon to open the Backstage view. Click the Print tab, click Print in the Print gallery to display the Print dialog box, increase the number in the Number of Copies box, and then click the OK button (Print dialog box).

Q&A How can I print a range of pages rather than printing the whole report?

Click File on the Ribbon to open the Backstage view. Click the Print tab, click Print in the Print gallery to display the Print dialog box, click the Pages option button in the Print Range area, enter the desired page range, and then click the OK button (Print dialog box).

BTW

Tabbed Documents Versus Overlapping Windows
By default, Access 2010 displays database objects in tabbed documents instead of overlapping windows. If your database is in overlapping windows mode, click File on the Ribbon, click Options in the Backstage view, click Current Database in the Access Options dialog box, and select the Display Document Tabs check box and the Tabbed Documents option button.

Database Properties

Access helps you organize and identify your databases by using **database properties**, which are the details about a file. Database properties, also known as **metadata**, can include such information as the file's author, title, or subject. **Keywords** are words or phrases that further describe the database. For example, a class name or database topic can describe the file's purpose or content.

Five different types of document properties exist, but the more common ones used in this book are standard and automatically updated properties. **Standard properties** are associated with all Microsoft Office documents and include author, title, and subject. **Automatically updated properties** include file system properties, such as the date you create or change a file, and statistics, such as the file size.

To Change Database Properties

The Database Properties dialog box contains areas where you can view and enter database properties. You can view and change information in this dialog box at anytime while you are working on your database. It is a good idea to add your name and class name as database properties. You also can add keywords that further describe your database. The following steps use the Properties dialog box to change database properties.

1

- Click File on the Ribbon to open the Backstage view.

- If necessary, click the Info tab in the Backstage view to display the Information gallery (Figure 1–87).

Q&A

How do I close the Backstage view?

Click File on the Ribbon or click the preview of the document in the Information gallery to return to the Access database window.

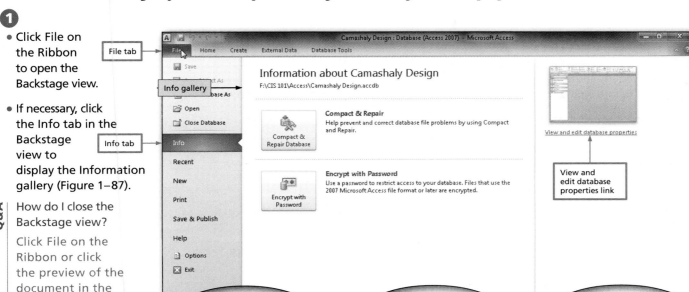

Figure 1–87

2

- Click the 'View and edit database properties' link in the right pane of the Info gallery to display the Camashaly Design.accdb Properties dialog box (Figure 1–88).

Q&A

Why are some of the database properties in my Properties dialog box already filled in?

The person who installed Microsoft Office 2010 on your computer or network may have set or customized the properties.

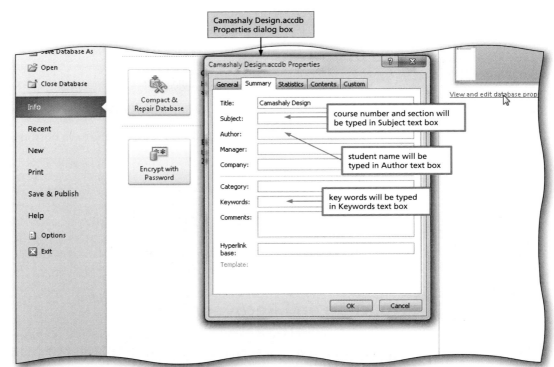

Figure 1–88

3

- If necessary, click the Summary tab.

- Click the Subject text box, if necessary delete any existing text, and then type **CIS 101, Section 20** as the Subject property.

- Click the Author text box and then type **Trevor Wilkins** as the Author property. If a name already is displayed in the Author text box, delete it before typing the new name.

- Click the Keywords text box, if necessary delete any existing text, and then type **online marketing, Web site design** as the Keywords property (Figure 1–89).

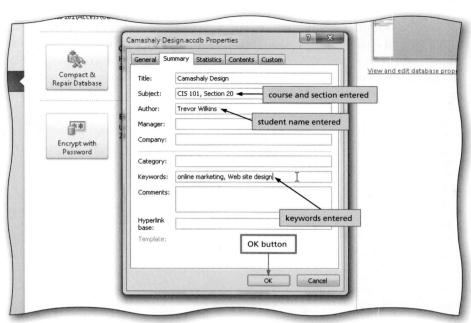

Figure 1–89

 Q&A

What types of properties does Access collect automatically?

Access records such details as when the database was created, when it was last modified, total editing time, and the various objects contained in the database.

4

- Click the OK button to save your changes and remove the Camashaly Design.accdb Properties dialog box from the screen.

To Quit Access

The following steps quit Access.

1 Click the Close button on the right side of the title bar to quit Access.

2 If a Microsoft Access dialog box appears, click the Save button to save any changes made to the object since the last save.

Special Database Operations

The special operations involved in maintaining a database are backup, recovery, compacting a database, and repairing a database.

Backup and Recovery

It is possible to damage or destroy a database. Users can enter data that is incorrect; programs that are updating the database can end abnormally during an update; a hardware problem can occur; and so on. After any such event has occurred, the database may contain invalid data. It even might be totally destroyed.

Obviously, you cannot allow a situation in which data has been damaged or destroyed to go uncorrected. You must somehow return the database to a correct state. This process is called recovery; that is, you **recover** the database.

The simplest approach to recovery involves periodically making a copy of the database (called a **backup copy** or a **save copy**). This is referred to as **backing up** the database. If a problem occurs, you correct the problem by copying this backup copy over the actual database, often referred to as the **live database**.

To back up the database that is currently open, you use the Back Up Database command on the Save & Publish tab in the Backstage view. In the process, Access suggests a name that is a combination of the database name and the current date. For example, if you back up the Camashaly Design database on April 20, 2012, Access will suggest the name, Camashaly Design_2012-04-20. You can change this name if you desire, although it is a good idea to use this name. By doing so, it will be easy to distinguish between all the backup copies you have made to determine which is the most recent. In addition, if you discover that a critical problem occurred on April 18, 2012, you may want to go back to the most recent backup before April 18. If, for example, the database was not backed up on April 17 but was backed up on April 16, you would use Camashaly Design_2012-04-16.

To Back Up a Database

You would use the following steps to back up a database to a file on a hard disk or high-capacity removable disk.

1. Open the database to be backed up.
2. Click File on the Ribbon to open the Backstage view, and then click the Save & Publish tab.
3. With Save Database As selected in the File Types area, click Back Up Database in the Save Database As area, and then click the Save As button.
4. Selected the desired location in the Save As box. If you do not want the name Access has suggested, enter the desired name in the File name text box.
5. Click the Save button to back up the database.

Access creates a backup copy with the desired name in the desired location. Should you ever need to recover the database using this backup copy, you can simply copy it over the live version.

Compacting and Repairing a Database

As you add more data to a database, it naturally grows larger. When you delete an object (records, tables, forms, or queries), the space previously occupied by the object does not become available for additional objects. Instead, the additional objects are given new space; that is, space that was not already allocated. To remove this wasted space from the database, you must **compact** the database. The same option that compacts the database also repairs problems that might have occurred in the database.

To Compact and Repair a Database

You would use the following steps to compact and repair a database.

1. Open the database to be compacted.
2. Click File on the Ribbon to open the Backstage view, and then, if necessary, select the Info tab.
3. Click the Compact & Repair Database button in the Information gallery to compact and repair the database.

The database now is the compacted form of the original.

BTW

Access Help
At any time while using Access, you can find answers to questions and display information about various topics through Help. Used properly, this form of assistance can increase your productivity and reduce your frustrations by minimizing the time you spend learning how to use Access. For instruction about Access Help and exercises that will help you gain confidence in using it, read the Office 2010 and Windows 7 chapter at the beginning of this book.

BTW

Certification
The Microsoft Office Specialist (MOS) program provides an opportunity for you to obtain a valuable industry credential — proof that you have the Access 2010 skills required by employers. For more information, visit the Access 2010 Certification Web page (scsite.com/ ac2010/cert).

BTW

Quick Reference
For a table that lists how to complete the tasks covered in this book using the mouse, Ribbon, shortcut menu, and keyboard, see the Quick Reference Summary at the back of this book, or visit the Access 2010 Quick Reference Web page (scsite.com/ac2010/qr).

Additional Operations

Additional special operations include opening another database, closing a database without exiting Access, and saving a database with another name. They also include deleting a table (or other object) as well as renaming an object. Finally, you can change properties of a table or other object, such as the object's description.

When you open another database, Access will automatically close the database that previously was open. Before deleting or renaming an object, you should ensure that the object has no dependent objects; that is, other objects that depend on the object you want to delete.

TO OPEN ANOTHER DATABASE

To open another database, you would use the following steps.

1. Click File on the Ribbon to open the Backstage view.
2. Click Open.
3. Select the database to be opened.
4. Click the Open button.

TO CLOSE A DATABASE WITHOUT EXITING ACCESS

You would use the following steps to close a database without quitting Access.

1. Click File on the Ribbon to open the Backstage view.
2. Click Close Database.

TO SAVE A DATABASE WITH ANOTHER NAME

To save a database with another name, you would use the following steps.

1. Click File on the Ribbon to open the Backstage view, and then select the Save & Publish tab.
2. With Save Database As selected in the File Types area and Access Database selected in the Save Database As area, click the Save As button.
3. Enter a name and select a location for the new version.
4. Click the Save button.

TO DELETE A TABLE OR OTHER OBJECT IN THE DATABASE

You would use the following steps to delete a database object.

1. Right-click the object in the Navigation Pane.
2. Click Delete on the shortcut menu.
3. Click the Yes button in the Microsoft Access dialog box.

TO RENAME AN OBJECT IN THE DATABASE

You would use the following steps to rename a database object.

1. Right-click the object in the Navigation Pane.
2. Click Rename on the shortcut menu.
3. Type the new name and press the ENTER key.

Chapter Summary

In this chapter you have learned to design a database, create an Access database, create tables and add records to them, print the contents of tables, create queries, create forms, and create reports. You also have learned how to change database properties. The items listed below include all the new Access skills you have learned in this chapter.

1. Start Access (AC 12)
2. Create a Database (AC 13)
3. Create a Database Using a Template (AC 14)
4. Modify the Primary Key (AC 16)
5. Define the Remaining Fields in a Table (AC 19)
6. Save a Table (AC 21)
7. View the Table in Design View (AC 21)
8. Close the Table (AC 23)
9. Add Records to a Table (AC 23)
10. Quit Access (AC 26)
11. Open a Database from Access (AC 27)
12. Add Additional Records to a Table (AC 28)
13. Resize Columns in a Datasheet (AC 29)
14. Preview and Print the Contents of a Table (AC 31)
15. Create a Table in Design View (AC 33)
16. Import an Excel Worksheet (AC 38)
17. Use the Simple Query Wizard to Create a Query (AC 43)
18. Use a Criterion in a Query (AC 46)
19. Print the Results of a Query (AC 48)
20. Create a Form (AC 48)
21. Create a Report (AC 52)
22. Modify Column Headings and Resize Columns (AC 54)
23. Add Totals to a Report (AC 57)
24. Change Database Properties (AC 59)
25. Back Up a Database (AC 61)
26. Compact and Repair a Database (AC 61)
27. Open Another Database (AC 62)
28. Close a Database without Exiting Access (AC 62)
29. Save a Database with Another Name (AC 62)
30. Delete a Table or Other Object in the Database (AC 62)
31. Rename an Object in the Database (AC 62)

If you have a SAM 2010 user profile, your instructor may have assigned an autogradable version of this assignment. If so, log into the SAM 2010 Web site at www.cengage.com/sam2010 to download the instruction and start files.

Learn It Online

Test your knowledge of chapter content and key terms.

Instructions: To complete the Learn It Online exercises, start your browser, click the Address bar, and then enter the Web address **scsite.com/ac2010/learn**. When the Access 2010 Learn It Online page is displayed, click the link for the exercise you want to complete and then read the instructions.

Chapter Reinforcement TF, MC, and SA
A series of true/false, multiple choice, and short answer questions that test your knowledge of the chapter content.

Flash Cards
An interactive learning environment where you identify chapter key terms associated with displayed definitions.

Practice Test
A series of multiple choice questions that test your knowledge of chapter content and key terms.

Who Wants To Be a Computer Genius?
An interactive game that challenges your knowledge of chapter content in the style of a television quiz show.

Wheel of Terms
An interactive game that challenges your knowledge of chapter key terms in the style of the television show *Wheel of Fortune*.

Crossword Puzzle Challenge
A crossword puzzle that challenges your knowledge of key terms presented in the chapter.

Apply Your Knowledge

Reinforce the skills and apply the concepts you learned in this chapter.

Adding a Caption, Creating a Query, Creating a Form, and Creating a Report

Instructions: Start Access. Open the Babbage CPA Firm database. See the inside back cover of this book for instructions for downloading the Data Files for Students, or see your instructor for information on accessing the files required in this book.

The Babbage CPA Firm employs bookkeepers who maintain the books for those clients who need bookkeeping services. The Babbage CPA Firm has a database that keeps track of its bookkeepers and clients. Each client is assigned to a single bookkeeper, but each bookkeeper may be assigned many clients. The database has two tables. The Client table contains data on the clients who use the bookkeeping services of the Babbage CPA Firm. The Bookkeeper table contains data on the bookkeepers employed by Babbage CPA Firm.

Perform the following tasks:

1. Open the Bookkeeper table in Design view and add BKR # as the caption for Bookkeeper Number. Save the changes to the table.

2. Open the Bookkeeper table in Datasheet view and resize all columns to best fit the data. Save the changes to the layout of the table.

3. Use the Simple Query Wizard to create a query for the Client table that contains the Client Number, Client Name, Amount Paid, and Balance Due. Use the name, Client Query, for the query.

4. Create a simple form for the Bookkeeper table. Use the name, Bookkeeper, for the form.

5. Close the Bookkeeper form.

6. Create the report shown in Figure 1–90 for the Client table. The report includes totals for both the Amount Paid and Balance Due fields. Be sure the totals appear completely. You might need to expand the size of the controls. Move the page number so that it is within the margins.

7. Compact the database.

8. Back up the database.

9. Change the database properties, as specified by your instructor. Submit the revised database in the format specified by your instructor.

Client Financial Report				Thursday, April 12, 2012 8:38:16 PM
Client Number	Client Name	Amount Paid	Balance Due	Bookkeeper Number
A54	Afton Mills	$575.00	$315.00	22
A62	Atlas Suppliers	$250.00	$175.00	24
B26	Blake-Scripps	$875.00	$250.00	24
D76	Dege Grocery	$1,015.00	$325.00	22
G56	Grand Cleaners	$485.00	$165.00	24
H21	Hill Shoes	$0.00	$285.00	34
J77	Jones Plumbing	$685.00	$0.00	22
M26	Mohr Crafts	$125.00	$185.00	24
S56	SeeSaw Industries	$1,200.00	$645.00	22
T45	Tate Repair	$345.00	$200.00	34
W24	Woody Sporting Goods	$975.00	$0.00	34
C29	Catering by Jenna	$0.00	$250.00	34
		$6,530.00	$2,795.00	

Figure 1–90

Extend Your Knowledge

Extend the skills you learned in this chapter and experiment with new skills. You may need to use Help to complete the assignment.

Using a Database Template to Create a Students Database

Instructions: Access includes a number of templates that you can use to create a beginning database that can be modified to meet your specific needs. You will create a Students database using the Students template. The database includes sample tables, queries, forms, and reports. You will change the database and create the Student Birthdays Query, shown in Figure 1–91.

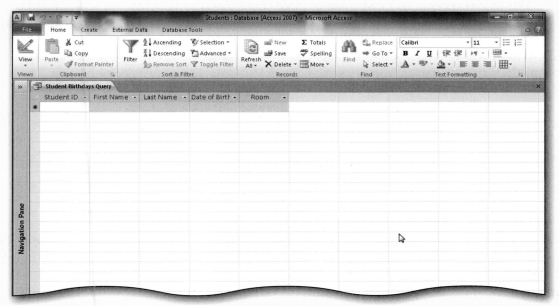

Figure 1–91

Perform the following tasks:

1. Start Access.

2. With a USB flash drive connected to one of the computer's USB ports, ensure the New tab is selected in the Backstage view and select Sample templates in the New gallery.

3. Select the Students template and create a new database on your USB drive with the file name, Students.

4. Close the Student List form and change the organization of the Navigation Pane to Tables and Related Views .

5. Delete the Student Details form.

6. Use the Query Wizard to create the query shown in Figure 1–91. Save the query as Student Birthdays Query.

7. Open the Student Phone List in Layout view and use the tools on the Format tab to make the Student Phone List title bold and change the font size to 24. Delete the control containing the time.

8. Save your changes to the report.

9. Compact the database.

10. Change the database properties, as specified by your instructor. Submit the revised database in the format specified by your instructor.

Make It Right

Analyze a database and correct all errors and/or improve the design.

Correcting Errors in the Table Structure

Instructions: Start Access. Open the Beach Rentals database. See the inside back cover of this book for instructions for downloading the Data Files for Students, or see your instructor for information on accessing the files required in this book.

Beach Rentals is a database containing information on rental properties available at a beach resort. The Rentals table shown in Figure 1–92 contains a number of errors in the table structure. You are to correct these errors before any additional records can be added to the table. The Rental Code field is a Text field that contains a maximum of three characters. The field Address was omitted from the table. The Address field is a Text field with a maximum of 20 characters. It should appear after Rental Code. Only whole numbers should be allowed in the Bedrooms and Bathrooms fields. The column heading Weakly Rental is misspelled, and the field should contain monetary values. The Distance field represents the walking distance from the beach; the field should display two decimal places. The table name should be Rental Units, not Rentals.

Change the database properties, as specified by your instructor. Submit the revised database in the format specified by your instructor.

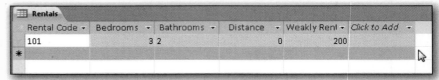

Figure 1–92

In the Lab

Design, create, modify, and/or use a database using the guidelines, concepts, and skills presented in this chapter. Labs are listed in order of increasing difficulty.

Lab 1: Creating Objects for the ECO Clothesline Database

Problem: ECO Clothesline is a local company that designs and manufactures eco-friendly casual wear, yoga clothing, and fitness apparel. All clothes are made from earth-friendly fabrics, such as bamboo, hemp, organic cotton, and natural silk. The company recently decided to store its customer and sales rep data in a database. Each customer is assigned to a single sales rep, but each sales rep may be assigned many customers. The database and the Customer table have been created, but there is no data in the Customer table. The Sales Rep table has not been created. The company plans to import the Customer data from an Excel workbook, shown in Figure 1–93a. The other Excel workbook (Figure 1–93b) contains information on the sales representatives that ECO employs. ECO would like to finish storing this data in a database and has asked for your help.

Instructions: Perform the following tasks: Start Access and open the ECO Clothesline database. See the inside back cover of this book for instructions for downloading the Data Files for Students, or see your instructor for information on accessing the files required in this book.

1. Import the Lab 1-1 Customer Data workbook into the Customer table.

2. Add the captions Cust # to the Customer Number field and SR # to the Sales Rep Number field in the Customer table and save the changes.

3. Open the Customer table in Datasheet view and resize the columns to best fit the data. Save the changes to the layout of the table.

4. Use Datasheet view to create a table in which to store the data related to sales reps. Use the name Sales Rep for the table. The fields and the data for the Sales Rep table are shown in Figure 1–93b.

	A	B		D	E		G	H	I	J	K
1	Customer Number	Customer Name	Street	City	State	Postal Code	Balance	Amount Paid	Sales Rep Number		
2	AM23	Amy's Store	223 Johnson	Oxford	TN	37021	195.00	1,695.00	44		
3	BF34	Barbara's Fashions	1939 Jackson	Lowton	TN	37084	150.00	0.00	51		
4	BL15	Blondie's on Main	3294 Main	Oxford	TN	37021	555.00	1,350.00	49		
5	CM09	Casual by Marie	3140 Halsted	Ashton	VA	20123	295.00	1,080.00	51		
6	CY12	Curlin Yoga Studio	1632 Clark	Georgetown	NC	28794	145.00	710.00	49		
7	DG14	Della's Designs	312 Gilham	Granger	NC	27036	340.00	850.00	44		
8	EC07	Environmentally Casual	1805 Broadway	Pineville	VA	22503	0.00	1,700.00	44		
9	FN19	Fitness Counts	675 Main	Oxford	TN	37021	345.00	1,950.00	51		
10	JN34	Just Natural	2200 Lawrence	Ashton	VA	20123	360.00	700.00	49		
11	LB20	Le Beauty	13 Devon	Lowton	TN	37084	200.00	1,250.00	49		
12	NC25	Nancy's Place	1027 Wells	Walburg	NC	28819	240.00	550.00	44		
13	RD03	Rose's Day Spa	787 Monroe	Pineville	VA	22503	0.00	975.00	51		
14	TT21	Tan and Tone	1939 Congress	Ashton	VA	20123	160.00	725.00	44		
15	TW56	The Workout Place	34 Gilham	Granger	NC	27036	680.00	125.00	51		
16	WS34	Woody's Sporting Goods	578 Central	Walburg	NC	28819	1,235.00	0.00	49		
17											

(a) Customer Data (Excel Workbook)

	A	B	C	D	E	F	G	H	I	J
1	Sales Rep Number	Last Name	First Name	Street	City	State	Postal Code	Base Pay YTD	Comm Rate	
2	44	Jones	Pat	43 Third	Oxford	TN	37021	13,000.00	0.05	
3	49	Gupta	Pinn	678 Hillcrest	Georgetown	NC	28794	15,000.00	0.06	
4	51	Ortiz	Gabe	982 Victoria	Ashton	VA	20123	12,500.00	0.05	
5	55	Sinson	Terry	45 Elm	Walburg	NC	28819	500.00	0.04	
6										

(b) Sales Rep Data (Excel Workbook)

Figure 1–93

The primary key for the Sales Rep table is Sales Rep Number. Assign the caption SR # to the Sales Rep Number field. Comm Rate is a Number field, and Base Pay YTD is a Currency data type. The field size for Sales Rep Number is 2. The State field size is 2, and the Postal Code field size is 5. All other text fields have a field size of 15.

5. Open the Sales Rep table in Design view and change the field size for the Comm Rate field to Single, the format to Fixed, and the Decimal Places to 2.

6. Add the data shown in Figure 1–93b to the Sales Rep table. Resize the columns to best fit the data. Save the changes to the layout of the table.

7. Create a query using the Simple Query Wizard for the Customer table that displays the Customer Number, Customer Name, Balance, Amount Paid, and Sales Rep Number fields. Use the name Customer Query.

8. Create and save the report shown in Figure 1–94 for the Customer table. The report should include Customer Number, Customer Name, Balance, and Sales Rep Number fields. Include a total for the Balance field.

9. Change the database properties, as specified by your instructor. Submit the revised database in the format specified by your instructor.

Customer Balance Report   Thursday, April 12, 2012   8:55:32 PM

Customer Number	Customer Name	Balance	Sales Rep Number
AM23	Amy's Store	$195.00	44
BF34	Barbara's Fashions	$150.00	51
BL15	Blondie's on Main	$555.00	49
CM09	Casual by Marie	$295.00	51
CY12	Curlin Yoga Studio	$145.00	49
DG14	Della's Designs	$340.00	44
EC07	Environmentally Casual	$0.00	44
FN19	Fitness Counts	$345.00	51
JN34	Just Natural	$360.00	49
LB20	Le Beauty	$200.00	49
NC25	Nancy's Place	$240.00	44
RD03	Rose's Day Spa	$0.00	51
TT21	Tan and Tone	$160.00	44
TW56	The Workout Place	$680.00	51
WS34	Woody's Sporting Goods	$1,235.00	49
		$4,900.00	

Figure 1–94

In the Lab

Lab 2: Creating the Walburg Energy Alternatives Database

Problem: Walburg Energy Alternatives is a nonprofit organization that promotes the use of energy alternatives such as solar power and wind power. The organization provides a variety of services and funds itself through donations. Recently, the organization decided to sell a small number of items in its education center to help fund programs. The store purchases the items from vendors that deal in energy-saving products. Currently, the information about the items and vendors is stored in the Excel workbook shown in Figure 1–95. Each item is assigned to a single vendor, but each vendor may be assigned many items. You volunteer part-time at the store, and the store manager has asked you to create a database that will store the item and vendor information. You have already determined that you need two tables in which to store the information: an Item table and a Vendor table.

Instructions: Perform the following tasks:

1. Design a new database in which to store all the objects related to the items for sale. Call the database Walburg Energy Alternatives.

2. Use the information shown in the Excel workbook in Figure 1–95 to determine the primary keys and determine additional fields. Then, determine the relationships between tables, the data types, and the field sizes.

3. Create the Item table using the information shown in Figure 1–95.

4. Create the Vendor table using the information shown in Figure 1–95. Be sure that the field size for the Vendor Code in the Item table is identical to the field size for the Vendor Code in the Vendor table. Add the caption, Phone, for the Telephone Number field.

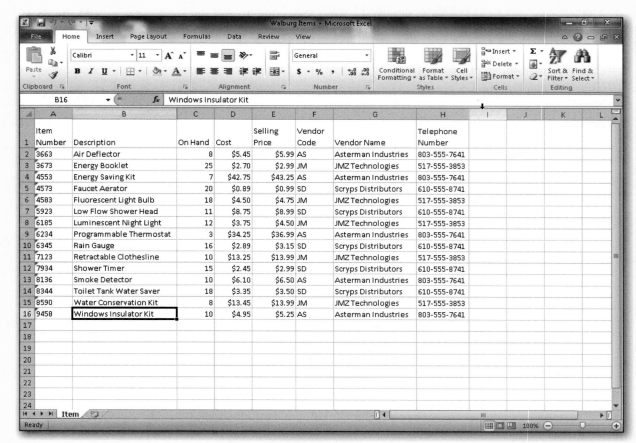

Figure 1–95

5. Add the appropriate data to the Item table. Resize the columns to best fit the data and save the changes to the layout.

6. Add the appropriate data to the Vendor table. Resize the columns to best fit the data and save the changes to the layout.

7. Create a query for the Item table. Include the Item Number, Description, Cost, Selling Price, and Vendor Code in the query. Save the query as Item Query.

8. Open the Item Query and add a criterion to limit retrieval to those items supplied by Scryps Distributors. Save the query as Item-Scryps Query.

9. Create a simple form for the Item table. Use the name, Item, for the form.

10. Create the report shown in Figure 1–96 for the Item table. Do not add any totals.

11. Change the database properties, as specified by your instructor. Submit the database in the format specified by your instructor.

Inventory Status Report

Thursday, April 12, 2012
8:56:19 PM

Item Number	Description	On Hand	Cost
3663	Air Deflector	8	$5.45
3673	Energy Booklet	25	$2.70
4553	Energy Saving Kit	7	$42.75
4573	Faucet Aerator	20	$0.89
4583	Fluorescent Light Bulb	18	$4.50
5923	Low Flow Shower Head	11	$8.75
6185	Luminescent Night Light	12	$3.75
6234	Programmable Thermostat	3	$34.25
6345	Rain Gauge	16	$2.89
7123	Retractable Clothesline	10	$13.25
7934	Shower Timer	15	$2.45
8136	Smoke Detector	10	$6.10
8344	Toilet Tank Water Saver	18	$3.35
8590	Water Conservation Kit	8	$13.45
9458	Windows Insulator Kit	10	$4.95

Figure 1–96

In the Lab

Lab 3: Creating the Philamar Training Database

Problem: Philamar Training provides business processes and information technology training to various companies and organizations. Philamar employs trainers who work with individual companies to determine training needs and then conduct the training. Currently, Philamar keeps data on clients and trainers in two Word documents and two Excel workbooks. Philamar also keeps track of which clients are assigned to which trainers. Each client is assigned to a single trainer, but each trainer might be assigned many clients. Currently, clients BS27, FI28, and MC28 are assigned to trainer 42, Belinda Perry. Clients CE16, CP27, FL93, HN83, and TE26 are assigned to trainer 48, Michael Stevens. Clients EU28 and PS82 are assigned to trainer 53, Manuel Gonzalez. Philamar has an additional trainer, Marty Danville, who has been assigned trainer number 67, but who has not yet been assigned any clients.

Instructions: Using the data shown in Figure 1–97 and the information in the previous paragraph, design the Philamar Training database. The data shown in Figure 1–97 is included in the Data Files for Students in the following files: Lab 1-3a.docx, Lab 1-3b.docx, Lab 1-3c.xlsx, and Lab 1-3d.xlsx. Use the database design guidelines in this chapter to help you in the design process.

Client Number	Client Name	Address	City	State	Postal Code
BS27	Blant and Sons	4806 Park	Kingston	TX	76653
CE16	Center Services	725 Mitchell	San Rita	TX	78364
CP27	Calder Plastics	7300 Cedar	Kingston	TX	76653
EU28	Elba's Furniture	1445 Hubert	Tallmadge	TX	77231
FI28	Farrow-Idsen	829 Wooster	Cedar Ridge	TX	79342
FL93	Fairland Lawn	143 Pangborn	Kingston	TX	76653
HN83	Hurley National	3827 Burgess	Tallmadge	TX	77231
MC28	Morgan-Alyssa	923 Williams	Crumville	TX	76745
PS82	PRIM Staffing	72 Crestview	San Rita	TX	78364
TE26	Telton-Edwards	5672 Anderson	Dunston	TX	77893

(a) Client Address Information (Word Table)

	A	B	C	D	E
1	Client Number	Client Name	Amount Paid	Current Due	
2	BS27	Blant and Sons	$11,876.00	$892.50	
3	CE16	Center Services	$12,512.00	$1,672.00	
4	CP27	Calder Plastics	$5,725.00	$0.00	
5	EU28	Elba's Furniture	$3,245.00	$202.00	
6	FI28	Farrow-Idsen	$8,287.50	$925.50	
7	FL93	Fairland Lawn	$976.00	$0.00	
8	HN83	Hurley National	$0.00	$0.00	
9	MC28	Morgan-Alyssa	$3,456.00	$572.00	
10	PS82	PRIM Staffing	$7,500.00	$485.00	
11	TE26	Telton-Edwards	$6,775.00	$0.00	
12					

(c) Client Financial Information (Excel Workbook)

Trainer Number	Last Name	First Name	Address	City	State	Postal Code
42	Perry	Belinda	261 Porter	Burdett	TX	76734
48	Stevens	Michael	3135 Gill	Rockwood	TX	78884
53	Gonzalez	Manuel	265 Maxwell	Camino	TX	76574
67	Danville	Marty	1827 Maple	Dunston	TX	77893

(b) Trainer Address Information (Word Table)

	A	B	C	D	E
1	Trainer Number	Last Name	First Name	Hourly Rate	YTD Earnings
2	42	Perry	Belinda	$23.00	$17,620.00
3	48	Stevens	Michael	$21.00	$13,567.50
4	53	Gonzalez	Manuel	$24.00	$19,885.00
5	67	Danville	Marty	$20.00	$0.00
6					

(d) Trainer Financial Information (Excel Workbook)

Figure 1–97

When you have completed the database design, create the database, create the tables, and add the data to the appropriate tables. Be sure to determine the correct data types and field sizes.

Finally, prepare the Client Query shown in Figure 1–98 and the Client Status Report shown in Figure 1–99. The report does not include totals. Change the database properties, as specified by your instructor. Submit the database in the format specified by your instructor.

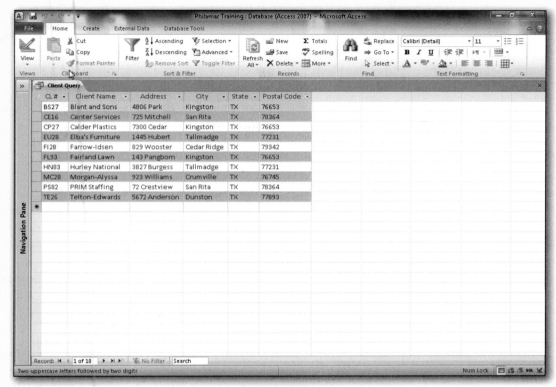

Figure 1–98

Client Status Report

Thursday, April 12, 2012
8:57:10 PM

Client Number	Client Name	Amount Paid	Current Due	Trainer Number
BS27	Blant and Sons	$11,876.00	$892.50	42
CE16	Center Services	$12,512.00	$1,672.00	48
CP27	Calder Plastics	$5,725.00	$0.00	48
EU28	Elba's Furniture	$3,245.00	$202.00	53
FI28	Farrow-Idsen	$8,287.50	$925.50	42
FL93	Fairland Lawn	$976.00	$0.00	48
HN83	Hurley National	$0.00	$0.00	48
MC28	Morgan-Alyssa	$3,456.00	$572.00	42
PS82	PRIM Staffing	$7,500.00	$485.00	53
TE26	Telton-Edwards	$6,775.00	$0.00	48

Figure 1–99

Cases and Places

Apply your creative thinking and problem solving skills to design and implement a solution.

See the inside back cover of this book for instructions for downloading the Data Files for Students, or see your instructor for information on accessing the files required in this book.

1: Design and Create an Advertising Database

Academic

You are a Marketing major currently doing an internship with the Chamber of Commerce in a local city. The Chamber publishes a Newcomer's Guide that contains advertisements from local businesses. Ad reps contact the businesses to arrange for advertising. Each advertiser is assigned to a single ad rep, but each ad rep may be assigned many advertisers. The Chamber would like your help in creating a database of advertisers and advertising representatives.

Based on the information in the Case 1-1 Chamber of Commerce workbook, use the concepts and techniques presented in this chapter to design and create a database to store the data that the Chamber needs. Submit your assignment in the format specified by your instructor.

2: Design and Create a Consignment Database

Personal

You are involved in a volunteer organization that provides clothing and school supplies to needy children. Recently, the Board of Directors decided to open a consignment shop as a way to raise additional funds. In a consignment shop, individuals bring in unwanted items, and the shop sells the items. Proceeds are split between the seller and the shop. The database must keep track of the items for sale in the shop as well as maintain data on the sellers. Each item is assigned to a single seller, but each seller may be assigned many items. The Board has asked you to create a database to store information about the consignment items.

Use the concepts and techniques presented in this chapter to design and create a database to store the consignment data. Then create the necessary tables and enter the data from the Case 1-2 Consignment workbook. Create an Available Items Report that lists the item number, description, price, and seller code. Submit your assignment in the format specified by your instructor.

3: Design and Create a Senior Care Database

Professional

You are co-owner of a company, Senior Care, that provides nonmedical services to older adults who need assistance with daily living. Helpers will drive individuals to appointments, do the grocery shopping, fill prescriptions, help with personal care, and provide companionship. Each client is assigned to a single helper, but each helper may be assigned many clients. The other owners have asked you to create a database of clients and helpers. Use the concepts and techniques presented in this chapter to design and create a database to meet Senior Care needs. Then create the necessary tables and enter the data from the Case 1-3 Senior Care workbook. Create a Client Report that lists each client's client number, client last name, client first name, balance, and helper number. Submit your assignment in the format specified by your instructor.

2 Querying a Database

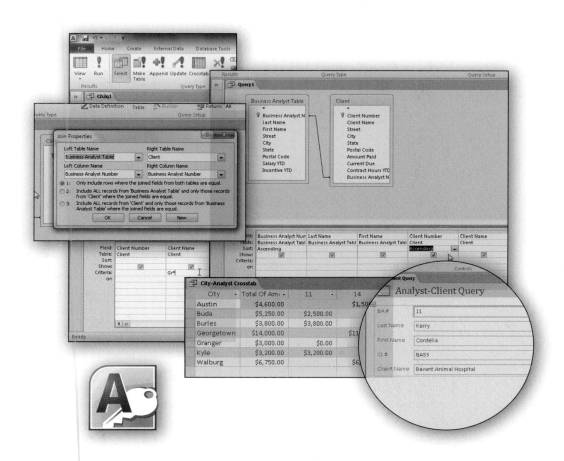

Objectives

You will have mastered the material in this chapter when you can:

- Create queries using Design view
- Include fields in the design grid
- Use text and numeric data in criteria
- Save a query and use the saved query
- Create and use parameter queries
- Use compound criteria in queries
- Sort data in queries
- Join tables in queries

- Create a report and a form from a query
- Export data from a query to another application
- Perform calculations and calculate statistics in queries
- Create crosstab queries
- Customize the Navigation Pane

2 | Querying a Database

Introduction

One of the primary benefits of using a database management system such as Access is the ability to find answers to questions related to data stored in the database. When you pose a question to Access, or any other database management system, the question is called a query. A **query** is simply a question presented in a way that Access can process.

Thus, to find the answer to a question, you first create a corresponding query using the techniques illustrated in this chapter. After you have created the query, you instruct Access to display the query results, that is, to perform the steps necessary to obtain the answer. Access then displays the answer in Datasheet view.

Project — Querying a Database

Organizations and individuals achieve several benefits from storing data in a database and using Access to manage the database. One of the most important benefits is the capability of easily finding the answers to questions and requests such as those shown in Figure 2–1 and the following, which concern the data in the Camashaly Design database:

1. What are the number, name, amount paid, and current due for client BC76?
2. What are the number, name, amount paid, and current due for all clients whose name starts with Gr?
3. Give me the number, name, amount paid, current due, and business analyst number for all clients whose amount paid is more than $3,000 and whose business analyst number is 11.
4. List the client number, name, business analyst number, and amount paid for all clients. Sort the results by business analyst number and amount paid.
5. For each business analyst, list the number, last name, and first name. Also, list the client number and name for each of the business analyst's clients.
6. List the client number, client name, amount paid, current due, and the total amount (amount paid plus current due) for each client.
7. Give me the average amount paid by clients of each business analyst.
8. Summarize the total amount paid by city and by business analyst.

In addition to these questions, Camashaly Design managers need to find information about clients located in a specific city, but they want to enter a different city each time they ask the question. The company can use a parameter query to accomplish this task. Camashaly Design managers also want to summarize data in a specific way, and they can use a crosstab query to present the data in the desired form.

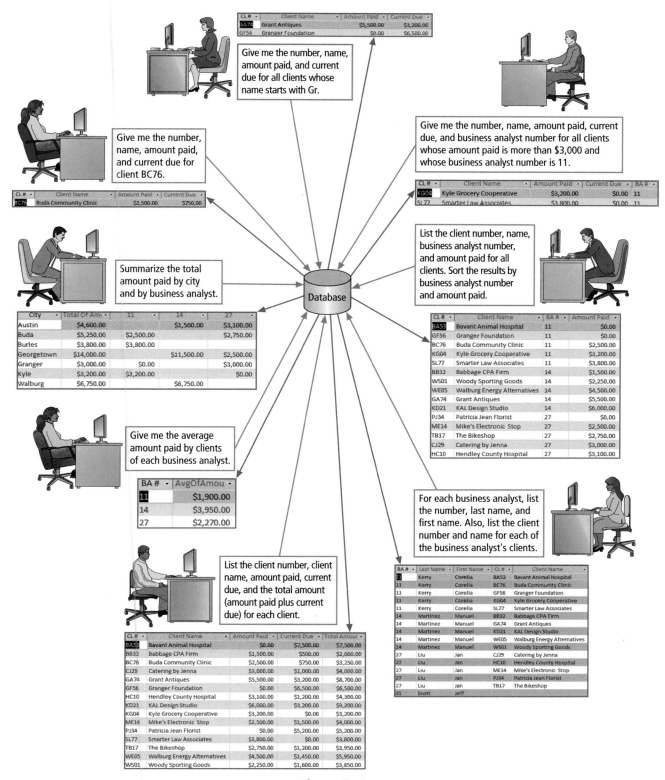

Figure 2–1

Overview

As you read this chapter, you will learn how to query a database by performing these general tasks:

- Create queries using Design view.
- Use criteria in queries.
- Create and use parameter queries.
- Sort data in queries.
- Join tables in queries.
- Create reports and forms from a query.
- Export data from a query.
- Perform calculations in queries.
- Create crosstab queries.

Plan Ahead

> **Query Design Decisions**
>
> When posing a question to Access, you must design an appropriate query. In the process of designing a query, the decisions you make will determine the fields, tables, criteria, order, and special calculations included in the query. To design a query, you can follow these general guidelines:
>
> 1. **Identify the fields.** Examine the question or request to determine which fields from the tables in the database are involved. Examine the contents of these fields to make sure you understand the data type and format for storing the data.
>
> 2. **Identify restrictions.** Unless the question or request calls for the inclusion of all records, determine the restrictions or the conditions records must satisfy to be included in the results.
>
> 3. **Determine whether special order is required.** Examine the question or request to determine whether the results must appear in some specific order.
>
> 4. **Determine whether more than one table is required.** If all the fields identified in Step 1 are in the same table, no special action is required. If this is not the case, identify all tables represented by those fields.
>
> 5. **Determine whether calculations are required.** Examine the question or request to determine whether, in addition to the fields determined in Step 1, calculations must be included. Such calculations include individual record calculations (for example, adding the values in two fields) or group calculations (for example, finding the total of the values in a particular field for all the records).
>
> 6. **If data is to be summarized, determine whether a crosstab query would be appropriate.** If data is to be grouped by two different types of information, you can use a crosstab query. You will need to identify the two types of information. One of the types will form the row headings and the other will form the column headings in the query results.
>
> When necessary, more specific details concerning the decisions and/or actions are presented at appropriate points in the chapter. The chapter also will identify the use of these guidelines in creating queries such as those shown in Figure 2–1.

BTW

Designing Queries
Before creating queries, examine the contents of the tables involved. You need to know the data type for each field and how the data for the field is stored. If a query includes a state, for example, you need to know whether state is stored as the two-character abbreviation or as the full state name.

To Start Access

The following steps, which assume Windows 7 is running, start Access based on a typical installation. You may need to ask your instructor how to start Access for your computer. For a detailed example of the procedure summarized below, refer to the Office 2010 and Windows 7 chapter at the beginning of this book.

1 Click the Start button on the Windows 7 taskbar to display the Start menu.

2 Type **Microsoft Access** as the search text in the 'Search programs and files' text box and watch the search results appear on the Start menu.

3 Click Microsoft Access 2010 in the search results on the Start menu to start Access.

4 If the Access window is not maximized, click the Maximize button next to the Close button on its title bar to maximize the window.

For an introduction to Windows 7 and instruction about how to perform basic Windows 7 tasks, read the Office 2010 and Windows 7 chapter at the beginning of this book, where you can learn how to resize windows, change screen resolution, create folders, move and rename files, use Windows Help, and much more.

To Open a Database from Access

In the previous chapter, you saved your database on a USB flash drive using the file name, Camashaly Design. The following steps open the Camashaly Design database from the Access folder in the CIS 101 folder on the USB flash drive. For a detailed example of the procedure summarized below, refer to the Office 2010 and Windows 7 chapter at the beginning of this book.

1 With your USB flash drive connected to one of the computer's USB ports, click File on the Ribbon to open the Backstage view, if necessary.

2 Click Open in the Backstage view to display the Open dialog box.

3 Navigate to the location of the file to be opened (in this case, the USB flash drive, then to the CIS 101 folder [or your class folder], and then to the Access folder).

4 Click Camashaly Design to select the file to be opened.

5 Click the Open button (Open dialog box) to open the selected file and display the opened database in the Access window.

6 If a Security Warning appears, click the Enable Content option button.

For an introduction to Office 2010 and instruction about how to perform basic tasks in Office 2010 programs, read the Office 2010 and Windows 7 chapter at the beginning of this book, where you can learn how to start a program, use the Ribbon, save a file, open a file, quit a program, use Help, and much more.

Creating Queries

Queries are simply questions, the answers to which are in the database. Access contains a powerful query feature. Through the use of this feature, you can find the answers to a wide variety of complex questions.

BTW

Q&As
For a complete list of the Q&As found in many of the step-by-step sequences in this book, visit the Access 2010 Q&A Web page (scsite.com/ac2010/qa).

> **Note:** In this chapter, you will save each query example. When you use a query for another task, such as to create a form or report, you will assign a specific name to a query; for example, Analyst-Client Query. In situations in which you will not use the query again, you will assign a name using a convention that includes the chapter number and a query number; for example, Ch2q1. Queries are numbered consecutively.

To Create a Query in Design View

Most of the time, you will use Design view to create queries. Once you have created a new query in Design view, you can specify fields, criteria, sorting, calculations, and so on. The following steps create a new query in Design view.

- Close the Navigation Pane.

- Click Create on the Ribbon to display the Create tab.

- Click the Query Design button (Create tab | Queries group) to create a new query (Figure 2–2).

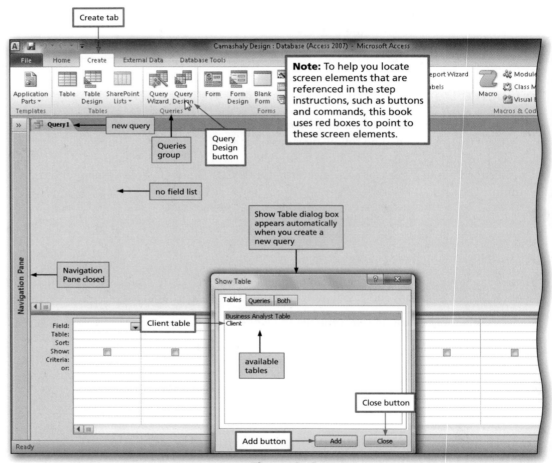

Figure 2–2

Q&A Is it necessary to close the Navigation Pane?

No. It gives you more room for the query, however, so it is usually a good practice to hide it.

2

- Click the Client table (Show Table dialog box) to select the table.

- Click the Add button to add the selected table to the query.

- Click the Close button to remove the dialog box from the screen.

Q&A

What if I inadvertently add the wrong table?

Right-click the table that you added in error and click Remove Table on the shortcut menu. You also can just close the query, indicate that you don't want to save it, and then start over.

- Drag the lower edge of the field list down far enough so all fields in the table appear (Figure 2–3).

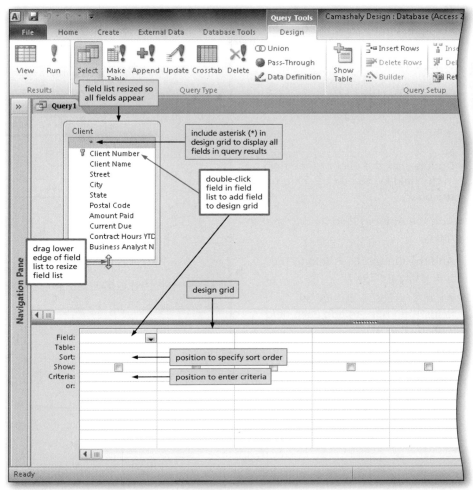

Figure 2–3

Q&A

How do I drag the lower edge?

Point to the lower edge, press and hold the left mouse button, move the mouse pointer to the new position for the lower edge, and then release the left mouse button. While the mouse pointer points to the lower edge of the field list, its shape changes to a two-headed arrow.

Q&A

Is it essential that I resize the field list?

No. You can always scroll through the list of fields using the scroll bar. It is usually more convenient to resize the field list so all fields appear.

To Add Fields to the Design Grid

Once you have a new query displayed in Design view, you are ready to make entries in the design grid, located in the lower pane of the window. You add the fields you want included in the query to the Field row in the grid. Only the fields that appear in the design grid will be included in the results of the query. The following steps begin the creation of a query that Camashaly Design might use to obtain the client number, client name, amount paid, and current due for a particular client. The following step selects the appropriate fields for the query.

①

- Double-click the Client Number field in the field list to add the field to the query.

Q&A

What if I add the wrong field?

Click just above the field name in the design grid to select the column and then press the DELETE key to remove the field.

- Double-click the Client Name field in the field list to add the field to the query.

- Add the Amount Paid field to the query.

- Add the Current Due field to the query (Figure 2–4).

Q&A

What if I want to include all fields? Do I have to add each field individually?

No. Instead of adding individual fields, you can double-click the asterisk (*) to add the asterisk to the design grid. The asterisk is a shortcut indicating all fields are to be included.

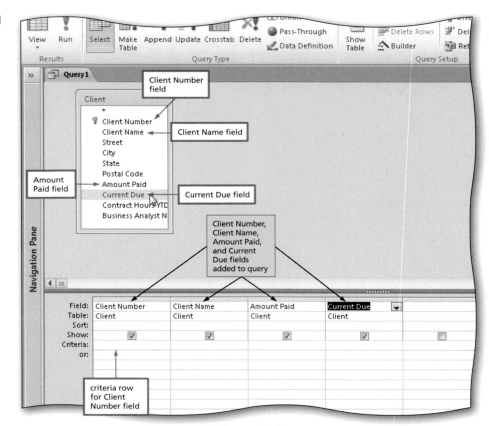

Figure 2–4

BTW

The Ribbon and Screen Resolution

Access may change how the groups and buttons within the groups appear on the Ribbon, depending on the computer's screen resolution. Thus, your Ribbon may look different from the ones in this book if you are using a screen resolution other than 1024 × 768.

Determining Criteria

When you use queries, usually you are looking for those records that satisfy some criterion. In the simple query you created in the previous chapter, for example, you entered a criterion to restrict the records that were included to those on which the business analyst number is 14. In another query, you might want the name, amount paid, and current due amounts of the client whose number is BC76, for example, or of those clients whose names start with the letters, Gr. You enter criteria in the Criteria row in the design grid below the field name to which the criterion applies. For example, to indicate that the client number must be BC76, you first must add the Client Number field to the design grid. You then would type BC76 in the Criteria row below the Client Number field.

To Use Text Data in a Criterion

To use **text data** (data in a field whose data type is Text) in criteria, simply type the text in the Criteria row below the corresponding field name. The following steps finish the creation of a query that Camashaly Design might use to obtain the client number, client name, amount paid, and current due amount of client BC76. These steps add the appropriate criterion so that only the desired client will appear in the results. The steps also save the query.

1

- Click the Criteria row for the Client Number field to produce an insertion point.

- Type **BC76** as the criterion (Figure 2–5).

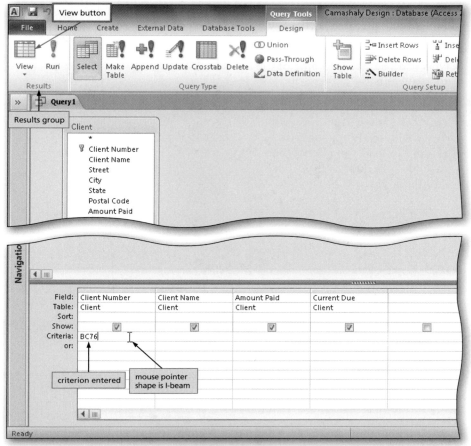

Figure 2–5

2

- Click the View button (Query Tools Design tab | Results group) to display the query results (Figure 2–6).

Q&A

I noticed that there is a View button on both the Home tab and the Design tab. Do they both have the same effect?

Yes. Use whichever one you find most convenient.

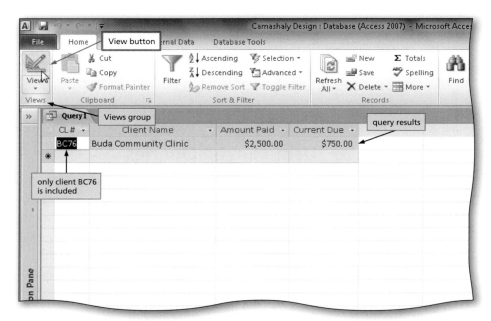

Figure 2–6

3

- Click the Save button on the Quick Access Toolbar to display the Save As dialog box.

- Type **Ch2q1** as the name of the query (Figure 2–7).

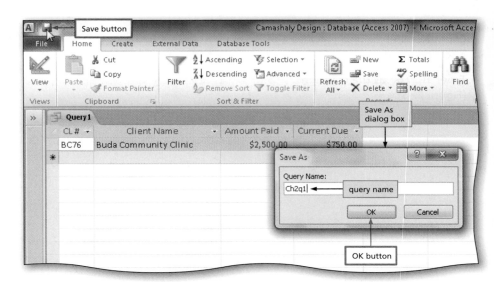

Q&A

Can I also save from Design view?

Yes. You can save the query when you view it in Design view just as you can save the query when you view the query results in Datasheet view.

Figure 2–7

4

- Click the OK button (Save As dialog box) to save the query (Figure 2–8).

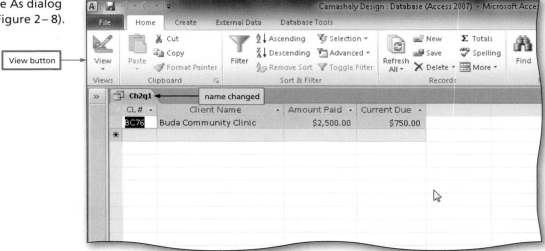

Figure 2–8

Other Ways

1. Right-click query tab, click Save on shortcut menu

Using Saved Queries

After you have created and saved a query, you can use it in a variety of ways:

- To view the results of the query that is not currently open, open it by right-clicking the query in the Navigation Pane and clicking Open on the shortcut menu.

- If you want to change the design of the query that is already open, return to Design view and make the changes.

- If you want to change the design of the query that is not currently open, right-click the query in the Navigation Pane and then click Design View on the shortcut menu to open the query in Design view.

- To print the results with the query open, click File on the Ribbon, click the Print tab in the Backstage view, and then click Quick Print.

- To print the query without first opening it, be sure the query is selected in the Navigation Pane and click File on the Ribbon, click the Print tab in the Backstage view, and then click Quick Print.

- You can switch between views of a query using the View button (Home tab | Views group). Clicking the arrow at the bottom of the button produces the View button menu. You then click the desired view in the menu. The two query views you use in this chapter are Datasheet view (see the results) and Design view (change the design). You can click the top part of the View button, in which case, you will switch to the view identified by the icon on the button. In the figure, the button contains the icon for Design view, so clicking the button would change to Design view. For the most part, the icon on the button represents the view you want, so you can usually simply click the button.

BTW

BTWs
For a complete list of the BTWs found in the margins of this book, visit the Access 2010 BTW Web page (scsite.com/ac2010/btw).

To Use a Wildcard

Microsoft Access supports wildcards. **Wildcards** are symbols that represent any character or combination of characters. One common wildcard, the **asterisk** (*), represents any collection of characters. Thus Gr* represents the letters, Gr, followed by any collection of characters. Another wildcard symbol is the **question mark** (?), which represents any individual character. Thus T?m represents the letter, T, followed by any single character, followed by the letter, m; a search might return the names Tim or Tom.

The following steps modify the previous query so that Camashaly Design can select only those clients whose names begin with Gr. Because you do not know how many characters will follow the Gr, the asterisk wildcard symbol is appropriate. The steps also save the query with a new name using the Save As command.

1

- Click the View button (Home tab | Views group) to return to Design view.

- If necessary, click the Criteria row below the Client Number field to produce an insertion point.

Q&A

The text I entered now has quotation marks surrounding it. What happened?

Criteria for text data needs to be enclosed in quotation marks. You do not have to type the quotation marks; Access adds them automatically.

- Use the DELETE or BACKSPACE key as necessary to delete the current entry.

- Click the Criteria row below the Client Name field to produce an insertion point.

- Type **Gr*** as the criterion (Figure 2–9).

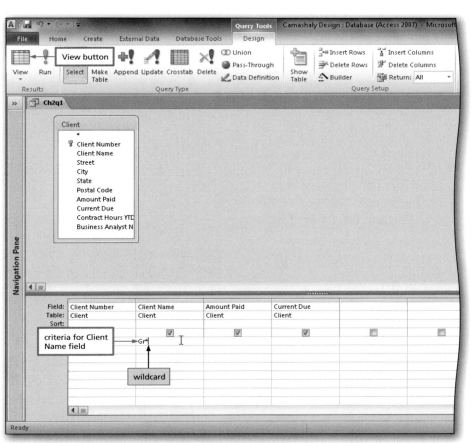

Figure 2–9

2

- View the query results by clicking the View button (Query Tools Design tab | Results group) (Figure 2–10).

🔍 **Experiment**

- Vary the case of the letters in the criteria and view the results to determine whether case makes a difference when entering a wildcard.

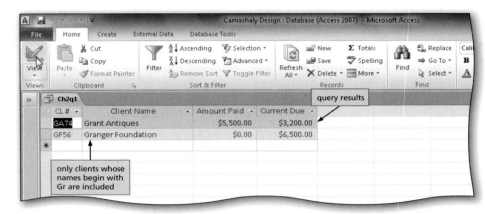

Figure 2–10

3

- Click File on the Ribbon to open the Backstage view (Figure 2–11).

Q&A Why can't I just click the Save button on the Quick Access Toolbar like I did when I saved the previous query?

If you did, you would replace the previous query with the version you just created. Because you want to save both the previous query and the new one, you need to save the new version with a different name. To do so, you must use Save Object As, which is available through the Backstage view.

Figure 2–11

4

- Click Save Object As in the Backstage view to display the Save As dialog box.

- Type **Ch2q2** as the name for the saved query (Figure 2–12).

Q&A The current entry in the As text box is Query. Could I save the query as some other type of object?

Although you usually would want to save the query as another query, you also can save it as a form or report by changing the entry in the As text box. If you do, Access would create either a simple form or a simple report for the query.

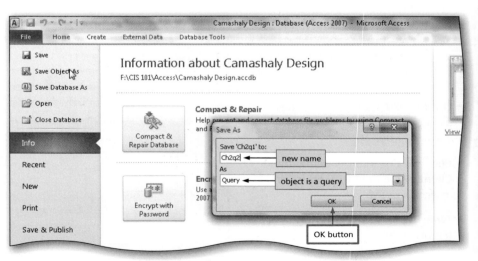

Figure 2–12

⑤

- Click the OK button (Save As dialog box) to save the query with the new name, and then click File on the Ribbon to close the Backstage view (Figure 2–13).

Q&A
How can I tell that the query was saved with the new name?

The new name will appear on the tab.

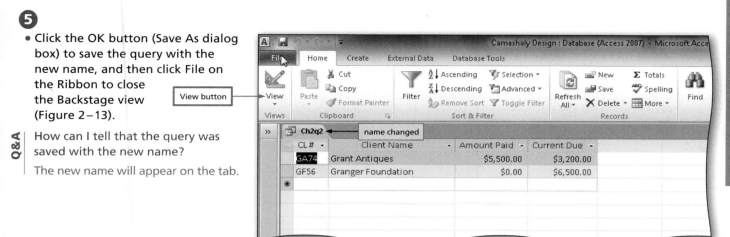

Figure 2–13

To Use Criteria for a Field Not Included in the Results

In some cases, you might require criteria for a particular field that should not appear in the results of the query. For example, you may want to see the client number, client name, address, and amount paid for all clients located in Georgetown. The criteria involve the City field, but you do not want to include the City field in the results.

To enter a criterion for the City field, it must be included in the design grid. Normally, this also would mean it would appear in the results. To prevent this from happening, remove the check mark from its Show check box in the Show row of the grid.

The following steps modify the previous query so that Camashaly Design can select only those clients located in Georgetown. Camashaly does not want the city to appear in the results, however. The steps also save the query with a new name.

❶

- Click the View button (Home tab | Views group), shown in Figure 2–13, to return to Design view.

Q&A
The text I entered is now preceded by the word, Like. What happened?

Criteria including wildcards need to be preceded by the word, Like. You do not have to type the word, Like, however. Access adds it automatically to any criterion involving a wildcard.

- Erase the criterion in the Client Name field.

- Add the City field to the query.

- Type **Georgetown** as the criterion for the City field (Figure 2–14).

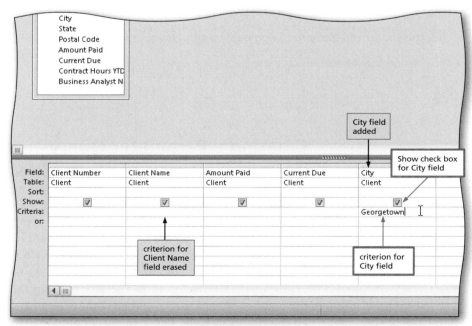

Figure 2–14

2

- Click the Show check box for the City field to remove the check mark (Figure 2–15).

Q&A

Could I have removed the check mark before entering the criterion?

Yes. The order in which you perform the two operations does not matter.

check mark removed from Show check box, indicating that City field will not appear in query results

Access automatically adds quotation marks

Figure 2–15

3

- View the query results (Figure 2–16).

Experiment

- Click the View button to return to Design view, enter a different city name, and view the results. Repeat this process with a variety of city names, including at least one city name that is not in the database. When finished, change the criterion back to Georgetown.

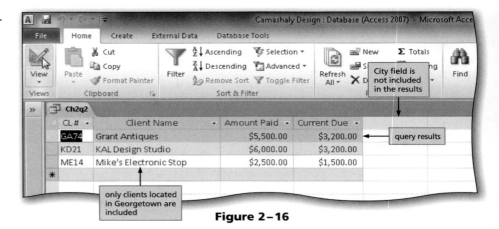

City field is not included in the results

query results

only clients located in Georgetown are included

Figure 2–16

4

- Click File on the Ribbon to open the Backstage view.
- Click Save Object As in the Backstage view to display the Save As dialog box.
- Type **Ch2q3** as the name for the saved query.
- Click the OK button (Save As dialog box) to save the query with the new name.
- Click File on the Ribbon to close the Backstage view.

Creating a Parameter Query

BTW

Queries: Query-by-Example
Query-By-Example, often referred to as QBE, was a query language first proposed in the mid-1970s. In this approach, users asked questions by filling in a table on the screen. The Access approach to queries is based on Query-By-Example.

If you wanted to find clients located in Kyle instead of Georgetown, you would either have to create a new query or modify the existing query by replacing Georgetown with Kyle as the criterion. Rather than giving a specific criterion when you first create the query, on occasion, you may want to be able to enter part of the criterion when you view the query results and then have the appropriate results appear. For example, to include all the clients located in Kyle, you could enter Kyle as a criterion in the City field. From that point on, every time you ran the query, only the clients in Kyle would appear.

A better way is to allow the user to enter the city at the time the user wants to view the results. Thus, a user could view the query results, enter Kyle as the city, and then see all the clients in Kyle. Later, the user could use the same query but enter Georgetown as the city, and then see all the clients in Georgetown.

To enable this flexibility, you create a **parameter query**, which is a query that prompts for input whenever it is used. You enter a parameter (prompt for the user), rather than a specific value as the criterion. You create one by enclosing a value in a criterion in square brackets. It is important that the value in the brackets does not match the name of any field. If you enter a field name in square brackets, Access assumes you want that particular field and does not prompt the user for input. To prompt the user to enter the city name as the input, you could place [Enter City] as the criterion in the City field.

To Create and View a Parameter Query

The following steps create a parameter query that will prompt the users at Camashaly to enter a city, and then display the client number, name, address, and amount paid for all clients located in that city. The steps also save the query with a new name.

1

- Return to Design view.

- Erase the current criterion in the City column, and then type **[Enter City]** as the new criterion (Figure 2–17).

Q&A

What is the purpose of the square brackets?

The square brackets indicate that the text entered is not text that the value in the column must match. Without the brackets, Access would search for records on which the city is Enter City.

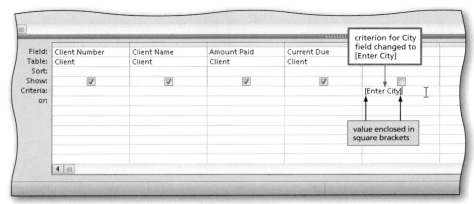

Figure 2–17

Q&A

What if I typed a field name in the square brackets?

Access would simply use the value in that field. To create a parameter query, you must not use a field name in the square brackets.

2

- Click the View button (Query Tools Design tab | Results group) to display the Enter Parameter Value dialog box (Figure 2–18).

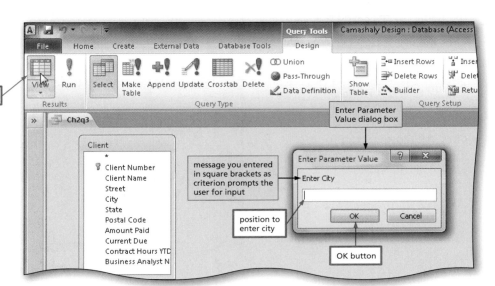

Figure 2–18

3

- Type **Kyle** as the parameter value in the Enter City text box and then click the OK button (Enter Parameter Value dialog box) to close the dialog box and view the query (Figure 2–19).

 Experiment

- Try other characters between the square brackets. In each case, view the results. When finished, change the characters between the square brackets back to Enter City.

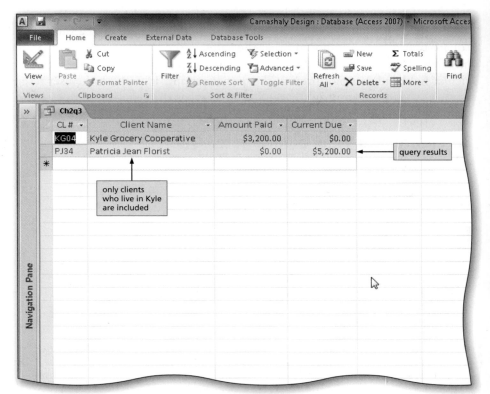

Figure 2–19

4

- Click File on the Ribbon to open the Backstage view.

- Click Save Object As in the Backstage view to display the Save As dialog box.

- Type **Client-City Query** as the name for the saved query.

- Click the OK button (Save As dialog box) to save the query with the new name and then click File on the Ribbon (Figure 2–20).

5

- Click the Close button for the Client-City query to close the query.

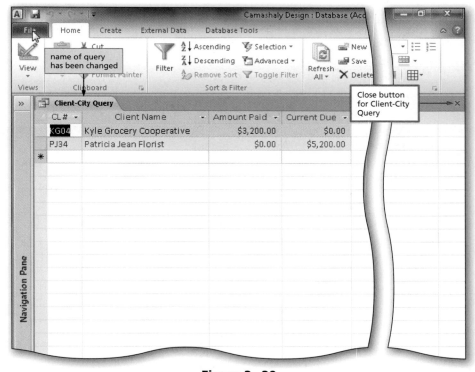

Figure 2–20

Break Point: If you wish to take a break, this is a good place to do so. You can quit Access now. To resume at a later time, start Access, open the database called Camashaly Design, and continue following the steps from this location forward.

To Use a Parameter Query

You use a parameter query like any other saved query. You can open it or you can print the query results. In either case, Access prompts you to supply a value for the parameter each time you use the query. As with other queries, the query always uses the data that is currently in the table. Thus, if changes have been made to the data since the last time you ran the query, the results of the query may be different, even if you enter the same value for the parameter. The following steps use the parameter query named Client-City Query.

1

- Open the Navigation Pane.

- Right-click the Client-City Query to produce a shortcut menu.

- Click Open on the shortcut menu to open the query and display the Enter Parameter Value dialog box (Figure 2–21).

Q&A

The title bar for my Navigation Pane contains Tables and Related Views rather than All Access Objects as it did in Chapter 1. What should I do?

Click the Navigation Pane arrow and then click All Access Objects.

Q&A

I do not have the Search bar at the top of the Navigation Pane that I had in Chapter 1. What should I do?

Right-click the Navigation Pane title bar arrow to display a shortcut menu, and then click Search Bar.

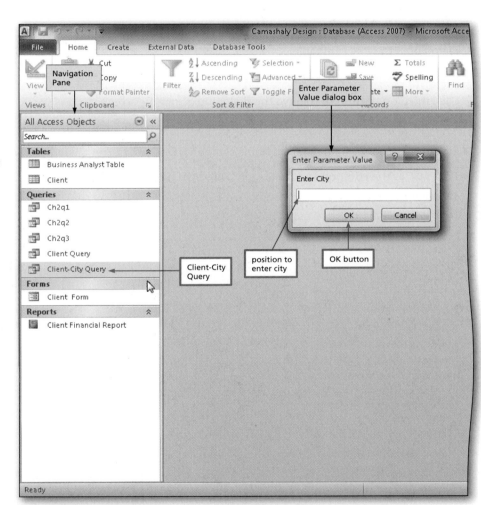

Figure 2–21

2

- Type **Kyle** in the Enter City text box, and then click the OK button (Enter Parameter Value dialog box) to display the results using Kyle as the city, as shown in Figure 2–20.

- Close the query.

To Use a Number in a Criterion

To enter a number in a criterion, type the number without any dollar signs or commas. The following steps create a query that Camashaly Design might use to display all clients whose current due amount is $0. The steps also save the query with a new name.

- Close the Navigation Pane.

- Click Create on the Ribbon to display the Create tab.

- Click the Query Design button (Create tab | Queries group) to create a new query.

- Click the Client table (Show Table dialog box) to select the table.

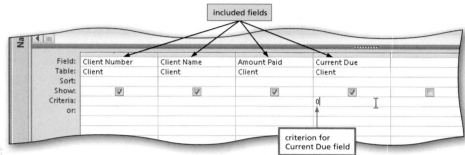

Figure 2–22

- Click the Add button to add the selected table to the query.

- Click the Close button to remove the dialog box from the screen.

- Drag the lower edge of the field list down far enough so all fields in the field list are displayed.

- Include the Client Number, Client Name, Amount Paid, and Current Due fields in the query.

- Type 0 as the criterion for the Current Due field (Figure 2–22).

Q&A Do I need to enter a dollar sign and decimal point?

No. Access will interpret 0 as $0 because the data type for the Current Due field is currency.

❷

- View the query results (Figure 2–23).

Q&A Why did Access display the results as $0.00 when I only entered 0?

Access uses the format for the field to determine how to display the result. In this case, the format indicated that Access should include the dollar sign, decimal point, and two decimal places.

Figure 2–23

❸

- Save the query as Ch2q4.

Q&A How do I know when to use the Save button to save a query or use the Backstage view to perform a Save As?

If you are saving a new query, the simplest way is to use the Save button on the Quick Access Toolbar. If you are saving changes to a previously saved query but do not want to change the name, use the Save button. If you want to save a previously saved query with a new name, you must use the Backstage view and perform a Save Object As.

To Use a Comparison Operator in a Criterion

Unless you specify otherwise, Access assumes that the criteria you enter involve equality (exact matches). In the last query, for example, you were requesting those clients whose current due amount is equal to 0 (zero). If you want something other than an exact match, you must enter the appropriate **comparison operator**. The comparison operators are > (greater than), < (less than), >= (greater than or equal to), <= (less than or equal to), and NOT (not equal to).

The following steps use the > operator to create a query that Camashaly Design might use to find all clients whose amount paid is more than $3,000. The steps also save the query with a new name.

1

- Return to Design view.

- Erase the 0 in the Current Due column.

- Type >3000 as the criterion for the Amount Paid field (Figure 2–24).

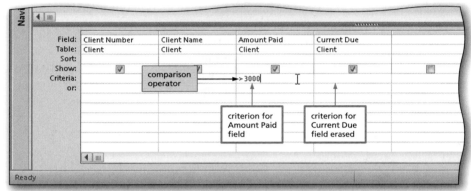

Figure 2–24

2

- View the query results (Figure 2–25).

 Experiment

- Return to Design view. Try a different criterion involving a comparison operator in the Amount Paid field and view the results. When finished, return to Design view, enter the original criterion (>3000) in the Amount Paid field, and view the results.

3

- Save the query as Ch2q5.

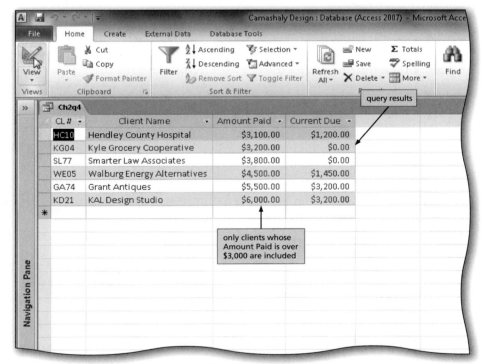

Figure 2–25

Using Compound Criteria

Often you will have more than one criterion that the data for which you are searching must satisfy. This type of criterion is called a **compound criterion**. Two types of compound criteria exist.

In an **AND criterion**, each individual criterion must be true in order for the compound criterion to be true. For example, an AND criterion would allow you to find those clients that have an amount paid greater than $3,000 and whose business analyst is business analyst 11.

Conversely, an **OR criterion** is true provided either individual criterion is true. An OR criterion would allow you to find those clients that have an amount paid greater than $3,000 and also those clients whose business analyst is business analyst 11 — either one criterion or the other is true. In this case, any client whose amount paid is greater than $3,000 would be included in the answer, regardless of whether the client's business analyst is business analyst 11. Likewise, any client whose business analyst is business analyst 11 would be included, regardless of whether the client had an amount paid greater than $3,000.

To Use a Compound Criterion Involving AND

To combine criteria with AND, place the criteria on the same row of the design grid. The following steps use an AND criterion to enable Camashaly to find those clients whose amount paid is greater than $3,000 and whose business analyst is analyst 11. The steps also save the query with a new name.

• Return to Design view.

• Include the Business Analyst Number field in the query.

• Type **11** as the criterion for the Business Analyst Number field (Figure 2–26).

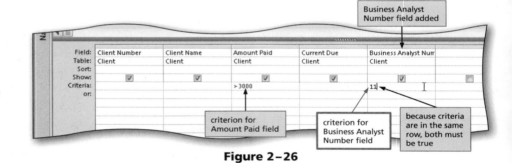

Figure 2–26

• View the query results (Figure 2–27).

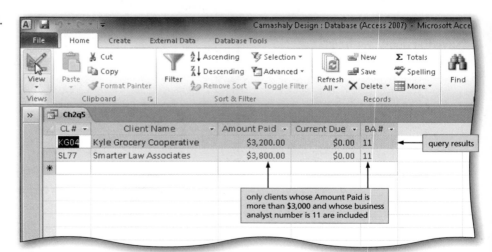

• Save the query as Ch2q6.

Figure 2–27

To Use a Compound Criterion Involving OR

To combine criteria with OR, the criteria must go on separate rows in the Criteria area of the grid. The following steps use an OR criterion to enable Camashaly to find those clients whose amount paid is greater than $3,000 or whose business analyst is analyst 11 (or both). The steps also save the query with a new name.

1

- Return to Design view.

- If necessary, click the Criteria entry for the Business Analyst Number field and then use the BACKSPACE key or the DELETE key to erase the entry ("11").

- Click the or row (the row below the Criteria row) for the Business Analyst Number field and then type   11   as the entry (Figure 2–28).

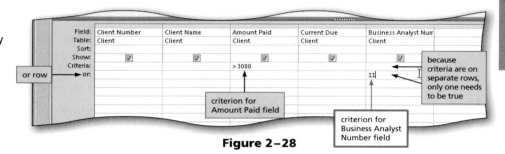

Figure 2–28

2

- View the query results (Figure 2–29).

3

- Save the query as Ch2q7.

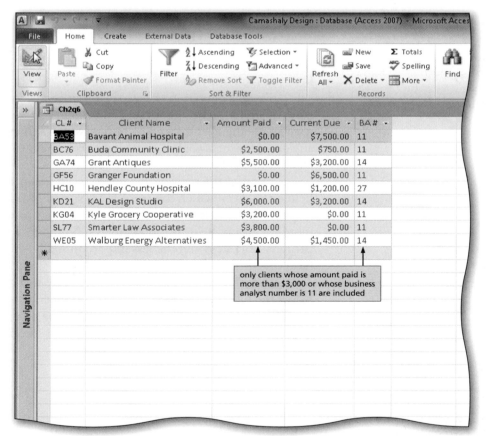

Figure 2–29

Special Criteria

There are three special criteria you can use in queries:

1. If you want to create a criterion involving a range of values in a single field, you can use the **AND operator**. You place the word AND between the individual conditions. For example, if you wanted to find all clients whose amount paid is >= $1,000 and <= $4,000, you would enter `>= 1000 AND <= 4000` as the criterion in the Amount Paid column.

2. You can select values in a given range by using the **BETWEEN operator**. This is often an alternative to the AND operator. For example, to find all clients whose amount paid is between $1,000 and $4,000, inclusive, you would enter `BETWEEN 1000 AND 4000` as the criterion in the Amount Paid column.

3. You can select values in a list by using the **IN operator**. You follow the word IN with the list of values in parentheses. For example, to find clients whose business analyst number is 11 or 14 using the IN operator, you would enter `IN ("11","14")` as the criterion in the Business Analyst Number column. Unlike when you enter a simple criterion, you must enclose text values in quotation marks.

Sorting

In some queries, the order in which the records appear is irrelevant. All you need to be concerned about are the records that appear in the results. It does not matter which one is first or which one is last.

In other queries, however, the order can be very important. You may want to see the cities in which clients are located and would like them arranged alphabetically. Perhaps you want to see the clients listed by business analyst number. Further, within all the clients of any given business analyst, you might want them to be listed by amount paid from largest amount to smallest.

To order the records in a query result in a particular way, you **sort** the records. The field or fields on which the records are sorted is called the **sort key**. If you are sorting on more than one field (such as sorting by amount paid within business analyst number), the more important field (Business Analyst Number) is called the **major key** (also called the **primary sort key**) and the less important field (Amount Paid) is called the **minor key** (also called the **secondary sort key**).

To sort in Microsoft Access, specify the sort order in the Sort row of the design grid below the field that is the sort key. If you specify more than one sort key, the sort key on the left will be the major sort key, and the one on the right will be the minor key.

The following are guidelines related to sorting in queries.

BTW

Sorting Data in a Query
When sorting data in a query, the records in the underlying tables (the tables on which the query is based) are not actually rearranged. Instead, the DBMS determines the most efficient method of simply displaying the records in the requested order. The records in the underlying tables remain in their original order.

**Plan
Ahead**

Determine whether special order is required.
Examine the query or request to see if it contains words, such as order or sort, that would imply that the order of the query results is important. If so, you need to sort the query.

- **Determine the sort key(s).** If sorting is required, identify the field or fields on which the results are to be sorted. In the request, look for language such as ordered by or sort the results by, both of which would indicate that the specified field is a sort key.

- **If using two sort keys, determine major and minor key.** If you are using two sort keys, determine which one is the more important, or the major key. Look for language such as sort by amount paid within business analyst number, which implies that the overall order is by business analyst number. Thus, the Business Analyst Number field would be the major sort key and the Amount Paid field would be the minor sort key.

- **Determine sort order.** Words such as increasing, ascending, or low-to-high imply Ascending order. Words such as decreasing, descending, or high-to-low imply Descending order. Sorting in alphabetical order implies Ascending order. If there are no words to imply a particular order, you would typically use Ascending.

- **Determine restrictions.** Examine the query or request to see if there are any special restrictions. One common restriction is to exclude duplicates. Another common restriction is to list only a certain number of records, for example, to list only the first five records.

To Clear the Design Grid

If the fields you want to include in the next query are different from those in the previous query, it is usually simpler to start with a clear grid, one with no fields already in the design grid. You always can clear the entries in the design grid by closing the query and then starting over. A simpler approach to clearing the entries is to select all the entries and then press the DELETE key. The following steps return to Design view and clear the design grid.

1

- Return to Design view.

- Click just above the Client Number column heading in the grid to select the column.

Q&A
I clicked above the column heading, but the column is not selected. What should I do?

You didn't point to the correct location. Be sure the mouse pointer changes into a down-pointing arrow and then click again.

- Hold the SHIFT key down and click just above the Business Analyst Number column heading to select all the columns (Figure 2–30).

2

- Press the DELETE key to clear the design grid.

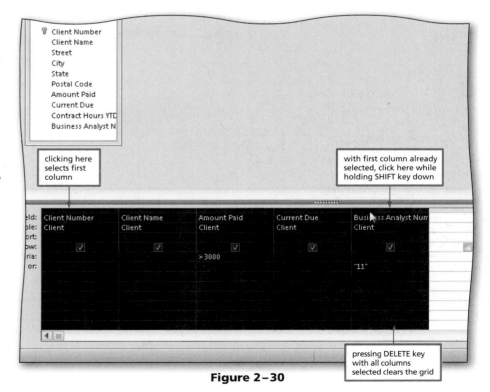

Figure 2–30

To Sort Data in a Query

After determining in the design process that a query is to be sorted, you will need to specify the sort key to Access. The following steps sort the cities in the Client table by indicating that the City field is to be sorted. The steps specify Ascending sort order.

- Include the City field in the design grid.

- Click the Sort row below the City field, and then click the Sort row arrow to display a menu of possible sort orders (Figure 2–31).

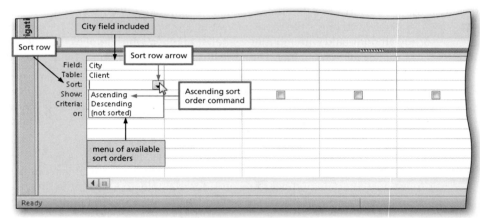

Figure 2–31

- Click Ascending to select the sort order (Figure 2–32).

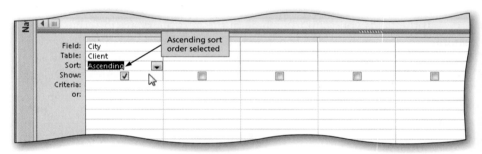

Figure 2–32

- View the query results (Figure 2–33).

 **Experiment**

- Return to Design view and change the sort order to Descending. View the results. Return to Design view and change the sort order back to Ascending. View the results.

 Why do some cities appear more than once?

More than one client is located in those cities.

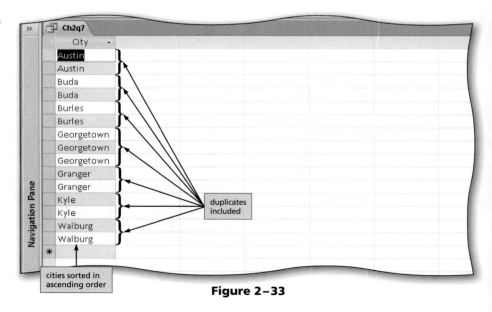

Figure 2–33

To Omit Duplicates

When you sort data, duplicates normally are included. In Figure 2–33, for example, Austin appeared twice, as did Buda, Burles, Granger, Kyle, and Walburg. Georgetown appeared three times. These duplicates do not add any value, so you should eliminate them from the results. To eliminate duplicates, display the query's property sheet. A **property sheet** is a window containing the various properties of the object. To omit duplicates, you will use the property sheet to change the Unique Values property from No to Yes.

The following steps create a query that Camashaly Design might use to obtain a sorted list of the cities in the Client table in which each city is listed only once. The steps also save the query with a new name.

1
- Return to Design view.

- Click the second field (the empty field to the right of City) in the design grid.

- If necessary, click Design on the Ribbon to display the Design tab.

- Click the Property Sheet button (Query Tools Design tab | Show/Hide group) to display the property sheet (Figure 2–34).

Q&A
My property sheet looks different. What should I do?

If your sheet looks different, you clicked the wrong place and will have to close the property sheet and repeat this step.

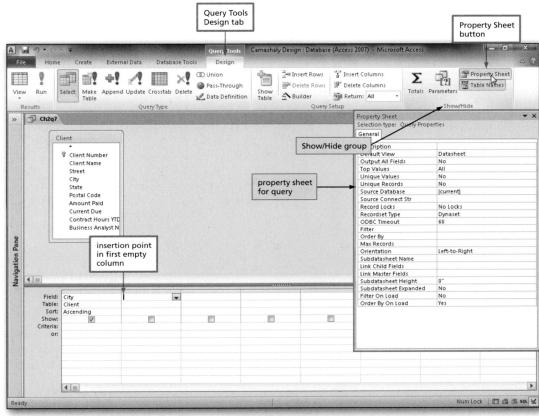

Figure 2–34

2
- Click the Unique Values property box, and then click the arrow that appears to produce a list of available choices (Figure 2–35).

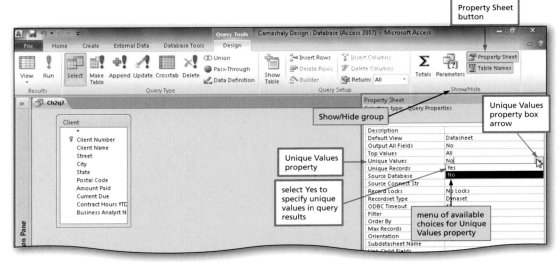

Figure 2–35

● Click **Yes** and then close the Query Properties property sheet by clicking the Property Sheet button (Query Tools Design tab | Show / Hide group) a second time.

● View the query results (Figure 2–36).

● Save the query as **Ch2q8**.

Other Ways

1. Right-click second field in design grid, click Properties on shortcut menu

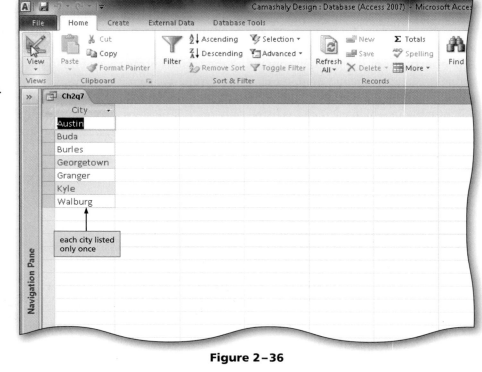

Figure 2–36

To Sort on Multiple Keys

The following steps sort on multiple keys. Specifically, Camashaly needs the data to be sorted by amount paid (low to high) within business analyst number, which means that the Business Analyst Number field is the major key and the Amount Paid field is the minor key. The steps also save the query with a new name.

● Return to Design view. Clear the design grid by clicking the first column in the grid, and then pressing the DELETE key to clear the design grid.

● In the following order, include the Client Number, Client Name, Business Analyst Number, and Amount Paid fields in the query.

● Select Ascending as the sort order for both the Business Analyst Number field and the Amount Paid field (Figure 2–37).

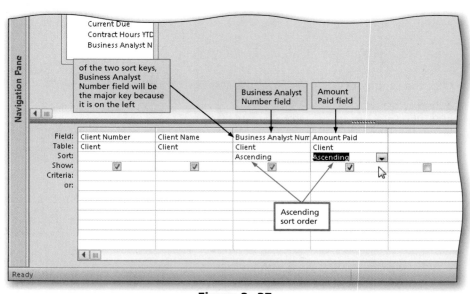

Figure 2–37

2

- View the query results (Figure 2–38).

Experiment

- Return to Design view and try other sort combinations for the Business Analyst Number and Amount Paid fields, such as Ascending for Business Analyst Number and Descending for Amount Paid. In each case, view the results to see the effect of the changes. When finished, select Ascending as the sort order for both fields.

Q&A

What if the Amount Paid field is to the left of the Business Analyst Number field?

It is important to remember that the major sort key must appear to the left of the minor sort key in the design grid. If you attempted to sort by amount paid within business analyst number, but placed the Amount Paid field to the left of the Business Analyst Number field, your results would be incorrect.

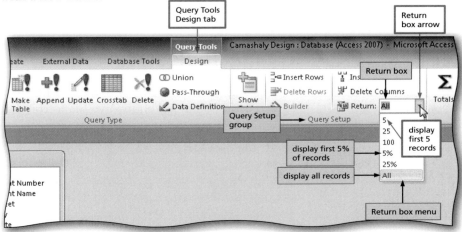

CL #	Client Name	BA #	Amount Paid
BA53	Bavant Animal Hospital	11	$0.00
GF56	Granger Foundation	11	$0.00
BC76	Buda Community Clinic	11	$2,500.00
KG04	Kyle Grocery Cooperative	11	$3,200.00
SL77	Smarter Law Associates	11	$3,800.00
BB32	Babbage CPA Firm	14	$1,500.00
WS01	Woody Sporting Goods	14	$2,250.00
WE05	Walburg Energy Alternatives	14	$4,500.00
GA74	Grant Antiques	14	$5,500.00
KD21	KAL Design Studio	14	$6,000.00
PJ34	Patricia Jean Florist	27	$0.00
ME14	Mike's Electronic Stop	27	$2,500.00
TB17	The Bikeshop	27	$2,750.00
CJ29	Catering by Jenna	27	$3,000.00
HC10	Hendley County Hospital	27	$3,100.00

within group of clients with the same business analyst number, rows are sorted by amount paid in ascending order

overall order is by business analyst number in ascending order

Figure 2–38

3

- Save the query as Ch2q9.

To Create a Top-Values Query

Rather than show all the results of a query, you may want to show only a specified number of records or a percentage of records. Creating a **top-values query** allows you to quantify the results. When you sort records, you can limit results to those records having the highest (descending sort) or lowest (ascending sort) values. To do so, first create a query that sorts the data in the desired order. Next, use the Return box on the Design tab to change the number of records to be included from All to the desired number or percentage. The following steps create a query for Camashaly Design that shows only the first five records that were included in the results of the previous query. The steps also save the resulting query with a new name.

1

- Return to Design view.

- If necessary, click Design on the Ribbon to display the Design tab.

- Click the Return box arrow (Query Tools Design tab | Query Setup group) to display the Return box menu (Figure 2–39).

Query Tools Design tab

Return box arrow

Camashaly Design : Database (Access 2007) - Microsoft Access

Query Tools   Design

External Data   Database Tools   Design

Union   Pass-Through   Data Definition

Make Table   Append   Update   Crosstab   Delete

Insert Rows   Delete Rows   Delete Columns

Return box

Return: All

Show

Builder

Query Setup group

Query Type

Query Setup

Σ Totals

display first 5% of records

display all records

display first 5 records

5
25
100
5%
25%
All

Return box menu

Figure 2–39

2

- Click 5 in the Return box menu to specify that the query results should contain the first five rows.

Q&A

Could I have typed the 5? What about other numbers that do not appear in the list?

Yes, you could have typed the 5. For numbers not appearing in the list, you must type the number.

- View the query results (Figure 2–40).

3

- Save the query as Ch2q10.
- Close the query.

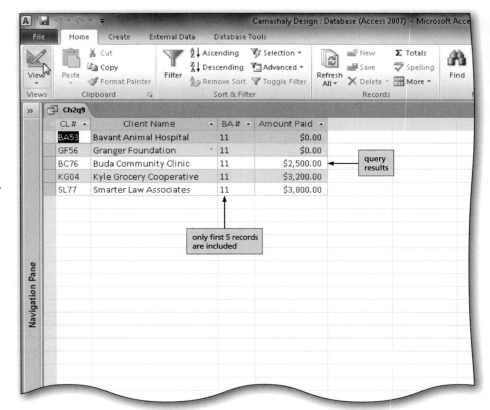

Figure 2–40

Q&A

Do I need to close the query before creating my next query?

Not necessarily. When you use a top-values query, however, it is important to change the value in the Return box back to All. If you do not change the Return value back to All, the previous value will remain in effect. Consequently, you might not get all the records you should in the next query. A good practice whenever you use a top-values query is to close the query as soon as you are done. That way, you will begin your next query from scratch, which guarantees that the value is reset to All.

Break Point: If you wish to take a break, this is a good place to do so. You can quit Access now. To resume at a later time, start Access, open the database called Camashaly Design, and continue following the steps from this location forward.

BTW

Join Line
If you do not get a join line automatically, there may be a problem with one of your table designs. Open each table in Design view and make sure that the data types are the same for the matching field in both tables and that one of the matching fields is the primary key in a table. Correct these errors and create the query again.

Joining Tables

In designing a query, you need to determine whether more than one table is required. If the question being asked involves data from both the Client and Business Analyst tables, for example, both tables are required for the query. For example, a query may require listing the number and name of each client along with the number and name of the client's business analyst. The client's name is in the Client table, whereas the business analyst's name is in the Business Analyst Table. Thus, this query cannot be completed using a single table; both the Client and Business Analyst tables are required. You need to **join** the tables; that is, to find records in the two tables that have identical values in matching fields (Figure 2–41). In this example, you need to find records in the Client table and the Business Analyst table that have the same value in the Business Analyst Number fields.

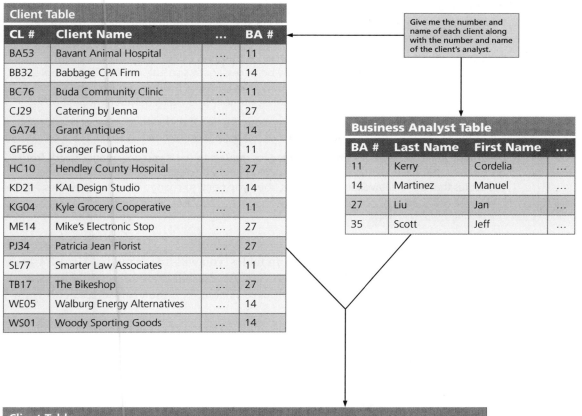

Figure 2–41

BTW

Join Types
The type of join that finds records from both tables that have identical values in matching fields is called an inner join. An inner join is the default join in Access. Outer joins are used to show all the records in one table as well as the common records; that is, the records that share the same value in the join field. In a left outer join, all rows from the table on the left are included. In a right outer join, all rows from the table on the right are included.

The following are guidelines related to joining tables.

Determine whether more than one table is required.
Examine the query or request to see if all the fields involved in the request are in one table. If the fields are in two (or more) tables, you need to join the tables.

- **Determine the matching fields.** If joining is required, identify the matching fields in the two tables that have identical values. Look for the same column name in the two tables or for column names that are similar.

- **Determine whether sorting is required.** Queries that join tables often are used as the basis for a report. If this is the case, it may be necessary to sort the results. For example, the Analyst-Client Report is based on a query that joins the Business Analyst and Client tables. The query is sorted by business analyst number and client number.

- **Determine restrictions.** Examine the query or request to see if there are any special restrictions. For example, the user may only want clients whose current due amount is $0.00.

- **Determine join properties.** Examine the query or request to see if you only want records from both tables that have identical values in matching fields. If you want to see records in one of the tables that do not have identical values, then you need to change the join properties.

To Join Tables

If you have determined in the design process that you need to join tables, you will first bring field lists for both tables to the upper pane of the Query window while working in Design view. Access will draw a line, called a **join line**, between matching fields in the two tables, indicating that the tables are related. You then can select fields from either table. Access joins the tables automatically.

The first step is to create a new query and add the Business Analyst Table to the query. Then, add the Client table to the query. A join line will appear, connecting the Business Analyst Number fields in the two field lists. This join line indicates how the tables are related, that is, linked through these matching fields. If the names of the matching fields differ from one table to the other, Access will not insert the line. You can insert it manually, however, by clicking one of the two matching fields and dragging the mouse pointer to the other matching field.

The following steps create a query that Camashaly Design might use to display information from both the Client table and the Business Analyst Table.

1

- Click Create on the Ribbon to display the Create tab.

- Click the Query Design button (Create tab | Queries group) to create a new query.

- If necessary, click the Business Analyst Table (Show Table dialog box) to select the table.

- Click the Add button (Show Table dialog box) to add a field list for the Business Analyst Table to the query (Figure 2–42).

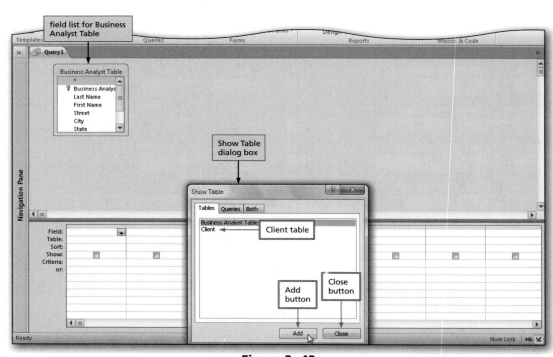

Figure 2–42

2

- Click the Client table (Show Table dialog box).

- Click the Add button (Show Table dialog box) to add a field list for the Client table.

- Close the Show Table dialog box by clicking the Close button.

- Expand the size of the two field lists so all the fields in the Business Analyst and Client tables appear (Figure 2–43).

I didn't get a join line. What should I do?

Ensure that the names of the matching fields are exactly the same, the data types are the same, and the matching field is the primary key in one of the two tables. If all of these are true and you still don't have a join line, you can produce one by pointing to one of the matching fields, pressing the left mouse button, dragging to the other matching field, and releasing the left mouse button.

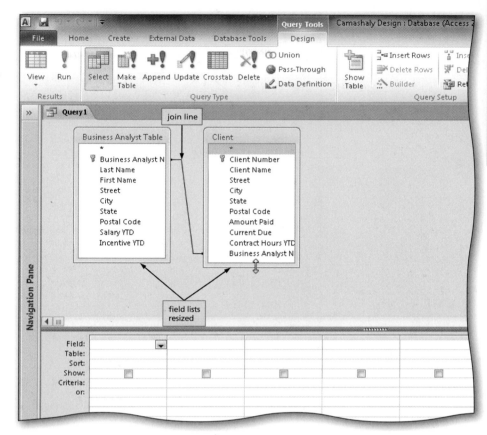

Figure 2–43

3

- In the design grid, include the Business Analyst Number, Last Name, and First Name fields from the Business Analyst Table as well as the Client Number and Client Name fields from the Client table.

- Select Ascending as the sort order for both the Business Analyst Number field and the Client Number field (Figure 2–44).

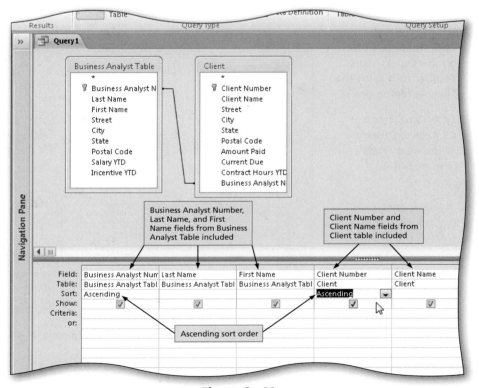

Figure 2–44

4

- View the query results (Figure 2–45).

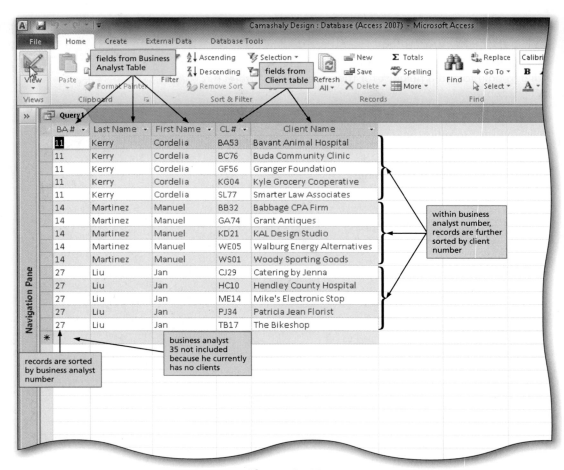

Figure 2–45

5

- Click the Save button on the Quick Access Toolbar to display the Save As dialog box.

- Type **Analyst-Client Query** as the query name (Figure 2–46).

6

- Click the OK button (Save As dialog box) to save the query.

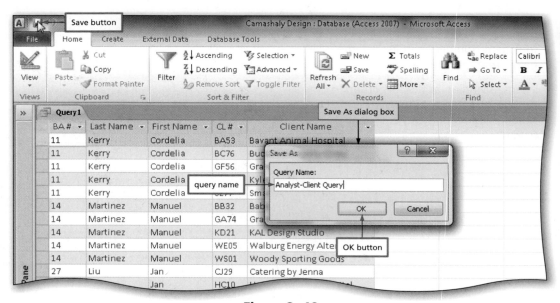

Figure 2–46

To Change Join Properties

Normally, records that do not match do not appear in the results of a join query. For example, a business analyst such as Jeff Scott, for whom no clients currently exist, would not appear in the results. To cause such a record to be displayed, you need to change the **join properties**, which are the properties that indicate which records appear in a join. The following steps change the join properties of the Analyst-Client Query so that Camashaly can include all business analysts in the results, rather than only those analysts who have already been assigned clients.

1

- Return to Design view.

- Right-click the join line to produce a shortcut menu (Figure 2–47).

I don't see Join Properties on my shortcut menu. What should I do?

If Join Properties does not appear on your shortcut menu, you did not point to the appropriate portion of the join line. You will need to point to the correct (middle) portion and right-click again.

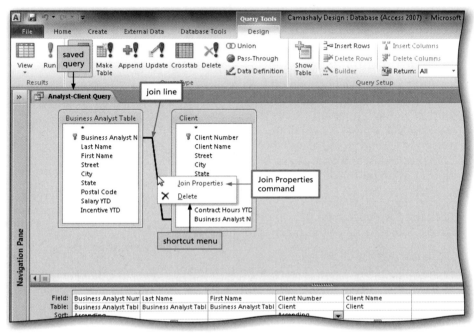

Figure 2–47

2

- Click Join Properties on the shortcut menu to display the Join Properties dialog box (Figure 2–48).

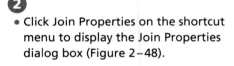

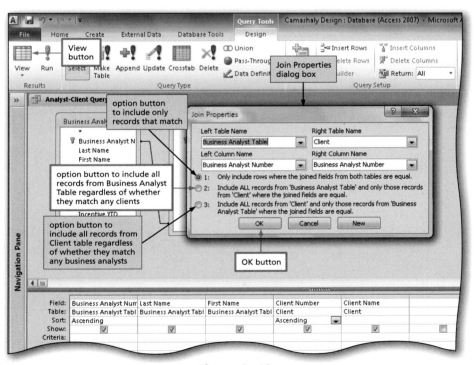

Figure 2–48

3

- Click option button 2 (Join Properties dialog box) to include all records from the Business Analyst Table regardless of whether they match any clients.

- Click the OK button (Join Properties dialog box) to modify the join properties.

- View the query results (Figure 2–49).

 **Experiment**

- Return to Design view, change the Join properties, and select option button 3. View the results to see the effect of this option. When done, return to Design view, change the Join properties, and once again select option button 2.

4

- Click the Save button on the Quick Access Toolbar to save the changes to the query.

- Close the Analyst-Client Query.

Q&A I see a dialog box that asks if I want to save the query. What should I do?

Click the OK button to save the query.

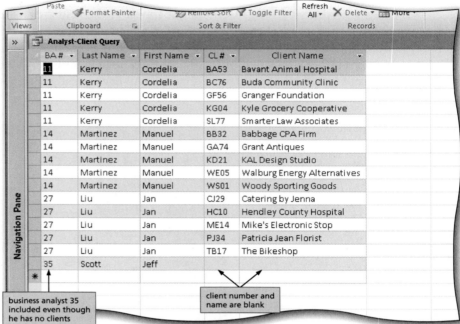

Figure 2–49

To Create a Report Involving a Join

The following steps use the Report Wizard to create the report for Camashaly Design that is shown in Figure 2–50.

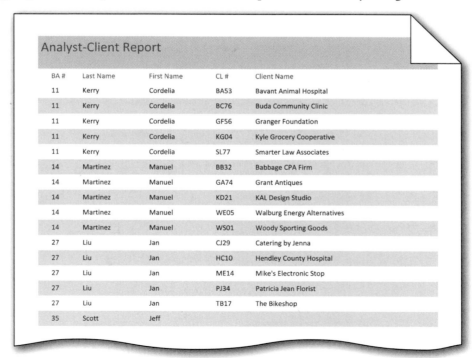

Figure 2–50

1

- Open the Navigation Pane, and then select the Analyst-Client Query in the Navigation Pane.

- Click Create on the Ribbon to display the Create tab.

- Click the Report Wizard button (Create tab | Reports group) to display the Report Wizard dialog box (Figure 2–51).

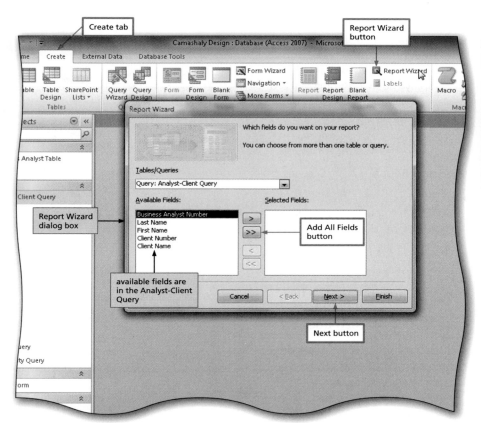

Figure 2–51

2

- Click the Add All Fields button (Report Wizard dialog box) to add all the fields in the Analyst-Client Query.

- Click the Next button to display the next Report Wizard screen (Figure 2–52).

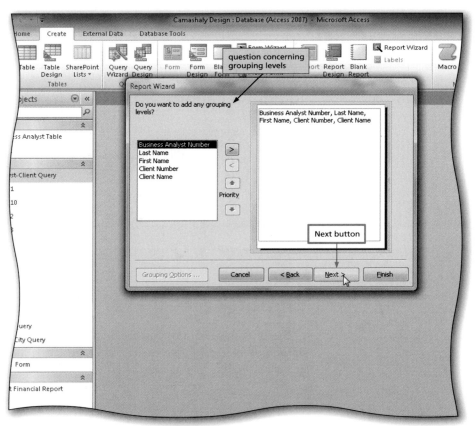

Figure 2–52

3

- Because you will not specify any grouping, click the Next button in the Report Wizard dialog box to display the next Report Wizard screen.

- Because you already specified the sort order in the query, click the Next button again to display the next Report Wizard screen.

- Make sure that Tabular is selected as the Layout and Portrait is selected as the Orientation.

- Click the Next button to display the next Report Wizard screen.

- Erase the current title, and then type **Analyst-Client Report** as the new title.

- Click the Finish button to produce the report (Figure 2–53).

4

- Close the Analyst-Client Report.

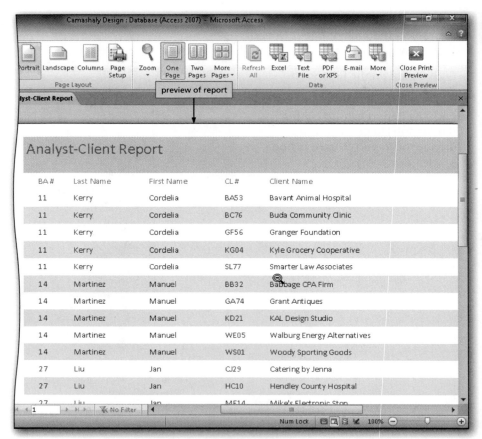

Figure 2–53

To Print a Report

The following steps print a hard copy of the report.

1 With the Analyst-Client Report selected in the Navigation Pane, click File on the Ribbon to open the Backstage view.

2 Click the Print tab in the Backstage view to display the Print gallery.

3 Click the Quick Print button to print the report.

Creating a Form for a Query

In the previous chapter, you created a form for the Client table. You also can create a form for a query. Recall that a **form** in a database is a formatted document with fields that contain data. Forms allow you to view and maintain data.

To Create a Form for a Query

The following steps create a form and then save the form.

1

- If necessary, select the Analyst-Client Query in the Navigation Pane.

- Click Create on the Ribbon to display the Create tab (Figure 2–54).

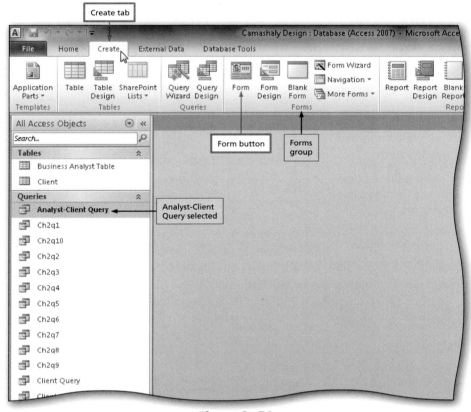

Figure 2–54

2

- Click the Form button (Create tab | Forms group) to create a simple form (Figure 2–55).

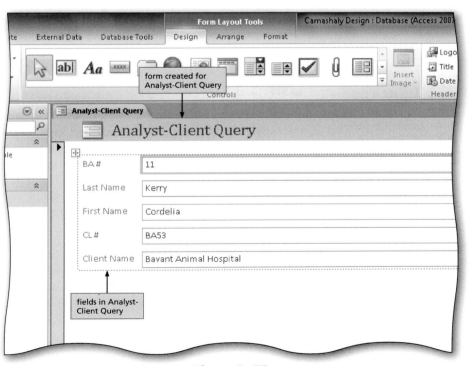

Figure 2–55

3
- Click the Save button on the Quick Access Toolbar to display the Save As dialog box.

- Type **Analyst-Client Form** as the form name (Figure 2–56).

4
- Click the OK button to save the form.

- Click the Close button for the form to close the form.

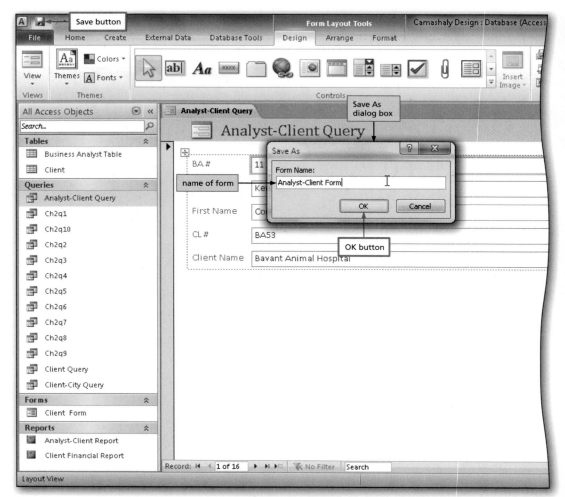

Figure 2–56

Exporting Data
You frequently need to export data so that it can be used in other applications and by other users in an organization. For example, the Accounting department might require financial data in an Excel format to perform certain financial functions. Marketing might require a list of client names and addresses in Word or RTF format for sales purposes.

Using a Form

After you have saved a form, you can use it at any time by right-clicking the form in the Navigation Pane and then clicking Open on the shortcut menu. If you plan to use the form to enter data, you must ensure you are viewing the form in Form view.

Exporting Data from Access to Other Applications

You can **export**, or copy, data from an Access database so that another application (for example, Excel or Word) can use the data. The application that will receive the data determines the export process to be used. You can export to text files in a variety of formats. For applications to which you cannot directly export data, you often can export an appropriately formatted text file that the other application can import. Figure 2–57 shows the Analyst-Client Query exported to Excel.

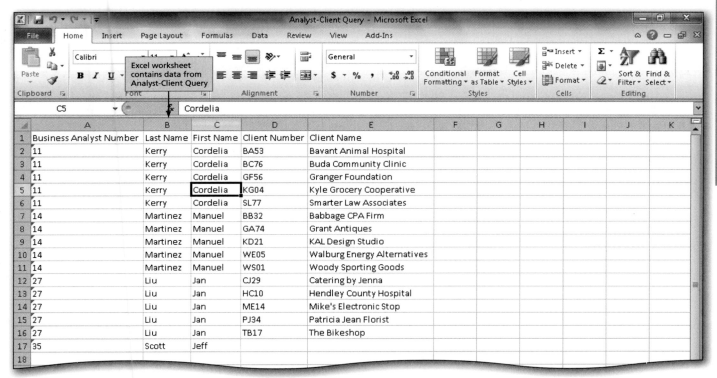

Figure 2–57

To Export Data to Excel

For Camashaly Design to make the Analyst-Client Query available to Excel users, it needs to export the data. To export data to Excel, select the table or query to be exported, and then click the Excel button in the Export group on the External data tab. The following steps export the Analyst-Client Query to Excel and save the export steps. By saving the export steps, you could easily repeat the export process whenever you like without going through all the following steps. You would use the saved steps to export data in the future by clicking the Saved Exports button (External Data tab | Export group) and then selecting the steps you saved.

1

- Click the Analyst-Client Query in the Navigation Pane to select it.

- Click External Data on the Ribbon to display the External Data tab (Figure 2–58).

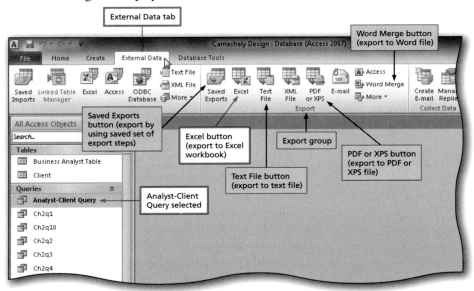

Figure 2–58

2

- Click the Excel button (External Data tab | Export group) to display the Export - Excel Spreadsheet dialog box.

- Click the Browse button (Export - Excel Spreadsheet dialog box) to display the File Save dialog box, and select your USB flash drive as the file location.

- Be sure the file name is Analyst-Client Query and then click the Save button (File Save dialog box) (Figure 2–59).

Q&A Did I need to browse?

No. You could type the appropriate file location.

Q&A Could I change the name of the file?

You could change it. Simply replace the current file name with the one you want.

Q&A What if the file I want to export already exists?

Access will indicate that the file already exists and ask if you want to replace it. If you click the Yes button, the file you export will replace the old file. If you click the No button, you must either change the name of the export file or cancel the process.

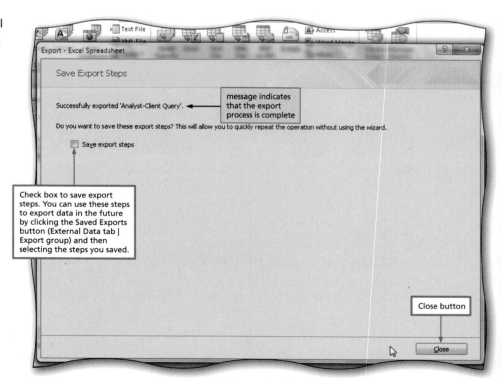

Export - Excel Spreadsheet dialog box

location of workbook to be created

Se____tion for the data you want to export

Specify the destination file name and format.

selected file format (Excel Workbook)

F:\CIS 101\Access\Analyst-Client Query.xlsx ← name of workbook to be created

Browse...

Browse button

File format: Excel Workbook (*.xlsx)   ▼   click arrow if you want to change file format

Specify export options.

check box to include formatting and layout

☐ **Export data with formatting and la**___   __n when exporting a table, query, form, or report.

Select this option to preserve most forma___

check box to open destination file after export is complete

☐ **Open the destination file after the export operation is complete.**

Select this option to view the results of the export operation. This option is available only when you export formatted data.

☐ **Export only the selected records.**

Select this option to export only the selected records. This option is only available when you export formatted data and have records selected.

check box to only export selected records (only valid if you have selected records prior to the export operation)

OK button

OK   Cancel

Figure 2–59

3

- Click the OK button (Export - Excel Spreadsheet dialog box) to export the data (Figure 2–60).

Export - Excel Spreadsheet

Save Export Steps

Successfully exported 'Analyst-Client Query'. ← message indicates that the export process is complete

Do you want to save these export steps? This will allow you to quickly repeat the operation without using the wizard.

☐ Sa_e export steps

Check box to save export steps. You can use these steps to export data in the future by clicking the Saved Exports button (External Data tab | Export group) and then selecting the steps you saved.

Close button

Close

Figure 2–60

④

- Click the 'Save export steps' check box (Export - Excel Spreadsheet dialog box) to display the Save export steps options.

- If necessary, type **Export-Analyst-Client Query** in the Save as text box.

- Type **Export the Analyst-Client Query without formatting** in the Description text box (Figure 2–61).

⑤

- Click the Save Export button (Export - Excel Spreadsheet dialog box) to save the export steps.

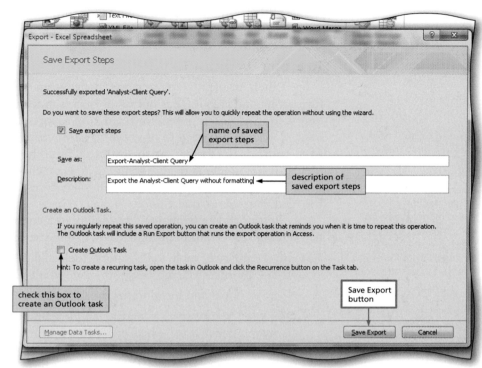

Figure 2–61

Other Ways

1. Right-click database object in Navigation Pane, click Export

To Export Data to Word

It is not possible to export data to the standard Word format. It is possible, however, to export the data as a rich text format (RTF) file, which Word can access. To export data from a query or table to an RTF file, you would use the following steps.

1. With the query or table to be exported selected in the Navigation Pane, click the More button (External Data tab | Export group) and then click Word on the More menu to display the Export - RTF File dialog box.

2. Select the name and location for the file to be created.

3. Click the Save button, and then click the OK button to export the data.

4. Save the export steps if you want, or simply click the Close button in the Export - RTF File dialog box to close the dialog box without saving the export steps.

Text Files

You also can export to text files. Text files contain unformatted characters, including alphanumeric characters, and some special characters, such as tabs, carriage returns, and line feeds.

In **delimited files**, each record is on a separate line, and the fields are separated by a special character, called the **delimiter**. Common delimiters are tabs, semicolons, commas, and spaces. You also can choose any other value that does not appear within the field contents. The comma-separated values (CSV) file often used in Excel is an example of a delimited file.

In **fixed-width files**, the width of any field is the same on every record. For example, if the width of the first field on the first record is 12 characters, the width of the first field on every other record also must be 12 characters.

TO EXPORT DATA TO A TEXT FILE

When exporting data to a text file, you can choose to export the data with formatting and layout. This option preserves much of the formatting and layout in tables, queries, forms, and reports. For forms and reports, this is the only option.

If you do not need to preserve the formatting, you can choose either delimited or fixed-width as the format for the exported file. The most common option, especially if formatting is not an issue, is delimited. You can choose the delimiter and also whether to include field names on the first row. In many cases, delimiting with a comma and including the field names is a good choice.

To export data from a table or query to a comma-delimited file in which the first row contains the column headings, you would use the following steps.

1. With the query or table to be exported selected in the Navigation Pane, click the Text File button (External Data tab | Export group) to display the Export - Text File dialog box.

2. Select the name and location for the file to be created.

3. If you need to preserve formatting and layout, be sure the 'Export data with formatting and layout' check box is checked. If you do not need to preserve formatting and layout, make sure the check box is not checked. Once you have made your selection, click the OK button in the Export - Text File dialog box.

4. To create a delimited file, be sure the Delimited option button is selected in the Export Text Wizard dialog box. To create a fixed-width file, be sure the Fixed Width option button is selected. Once you have made your selection, click the Next button.

5. a. If you are exporting to a delimited file, choose the delimiter that you want to separate your fields, such as a comma. Decide whether to include field names on the first row and, if so, click the Include Field Names on First Row check box. If you want to select a text qualifier, select it in the Text Qualifier list. When you have made your selections, click the Next button.

   b. If you are exporting to a fixed-width file, review the position of the vertical lines that separate your fields. If any lines are not positioned correctly, follow the directions on the screen to reposition them. When you have finished, click the Next button.

6. Click the Finish button to export the data.

7. Save the export steps if you want, or simply click the Close button in the Export - Text File dialog box to close the dialog box without saving the export steps.

BTW

Saving Export Steps
Because query results are based on the data in the underlying tables, a change to an underlying table would result in a new query answer. For example, if the last name for business analyst 11 changed from Kerry to Smith, the change would be made in the Business Analyst Table. If you run the Analyst-Client Query again and export the query using the saved export steps, the Excel workbook would show the changed name.

Adding Criteria to a Join Query

Sometimes you will want to join tables, but you will not want to include all possible records. For example, you would like to create a report showing only those clients whose amount paid is greater than $3,000. In such cases, you will relate the tables and include fields just as you did before. You also will include criteria. To include only those clients whose amount paid is more than $3,000.00, you will include >3000 as a criterion for the Amount Paid field.

To Restrict the Records in a Join

The following steps modify the Analyst-Client Query so that the results for Camashaly Design only include those clients whose amount paid is more than $3,000.

1
- Open the Analyst-Client Query in Design view and close the Navigation Pane.
- Add the Amount Paid field to the query.
- Type **>3000** as the criterion for the Amount Paid field (Figure 2–62).

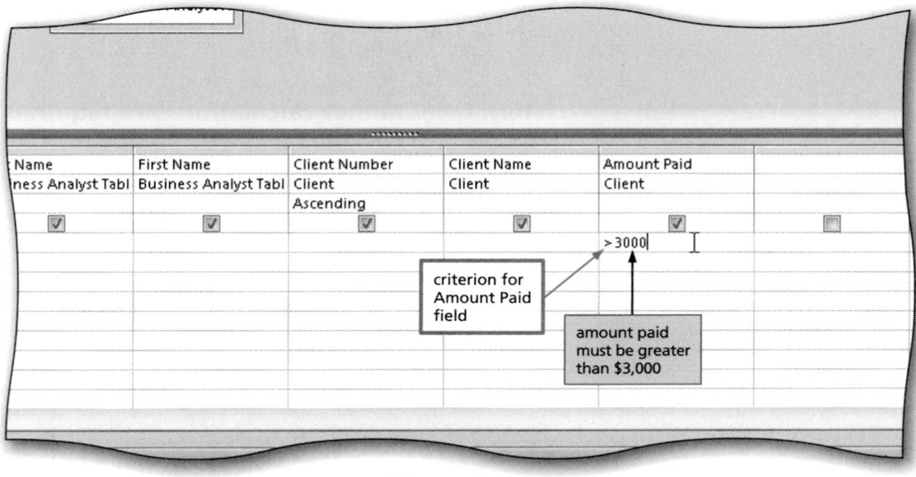

Figure 2–62

2
- View the query results (Figure 2–63).

3
- Close the query.
- When asked if you want to save your changes, click the No button.

Q&A What if I saved the changes?

The next time you used this query, you would only see clients whose amount paid is more than $3,000.

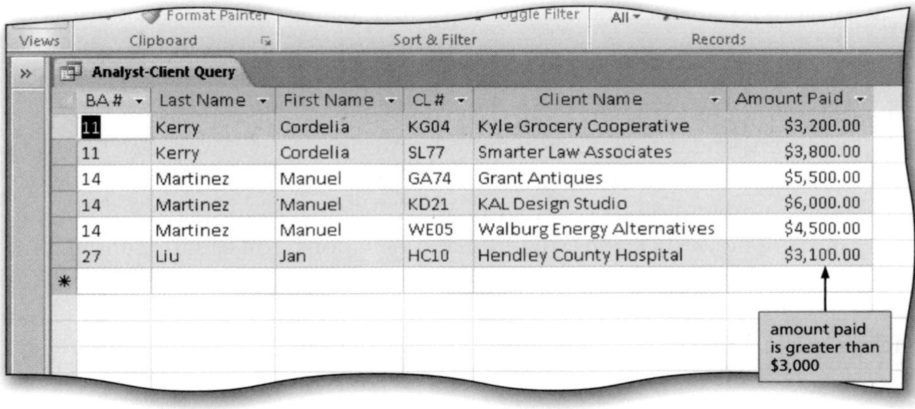

Figure 2–63

Calculations

If you have determined that a special calculation is required for a query, you then need to determine whether the calculation is an individual record calculation (for example, adding the values in two fields) or a group calculation (for example, finding the total of the values in a particular field on all the records).

Camashaly Design may want to know the total amount (amount paid and current due) from each client. This would seem to pose a problem because the Client table does not include a field for total amount. You can calculate it, however, because the total amount is equal to the amount paid plus the current due. A field that can be computed from other fields is called a **calculated field** or a **computed field**. A calculated field is an individual record calculation because each calculation only involves fields in a single record.

BTW

Expression Builder
Access includes a tool to help you create complex expressions. If you click Build on the shortcut menu (see Figure 2–64), Access displays the Expression Builder dialog box, which includes an expression box, operator buttons, and expression elements. You can type parts of the expression directly and paste operator buttons and expression elements into the box. You also can use functions in expressions.

Camashaly also may want to calculate the average amount paid for the clients of each business analyst. That is, they may want the average for the clients of business analyst 11, the average for the clients of business analyst 14, and so on. This type of calculation is called a **group calculation** because each calculation involves groups of records. In this example, the clients of business analyst 11 would form one group, the clients of business analyst 14 would be a second group, and the clients of business analyst 27 would form a third group.

The following are guidelines related to calculations in queries.

<table>
<tr>
<td>

Plan Ahead

</td>
<td>

Determine whether calculations are required.
Examine the query or request to see if there are special calculations to be included. Look for words such as total, sum, compute, or calculate.

• **Determine a name for the calculated field.** If calculations are required, decide on the name for the field. Assign a name that helps identify the contents of the field. For example, if you are adding the cost of a number of items, the name Total Cost would be appropriate. The name, also called an **alias**, becomes the column name when the query is run.

• **Determine the format for the calculated field.** Determine how the calculated field should appear. If the calculation involves monetary amounts, you would use the currency format. If the calculated value contains decimals, determine how many decimal places to display.

</td>
</tr>
</table>

To Use a Calculated Field in a Query

If you have determined that you need a calculated field in a query, you enter a name, or alias, for the calculated field, a colon, and then the calculation in one of the columns in the Field row of the design grid for the query. Any fields included in the expression must be enclosed in square brackets ([ ]). For example, for the total amount, you will type Total Amount:[Amount Paid]+[Current Due] as the expression.

You can type the expression directly into the Field row. You will not be able to see the entire entry, however, because the Field row is not large enough. The preferred way is to select the column in the Field row and then use the Zoom command on its shortcut menu. When Access displays the Zoom dialog box, you can enter the expression.

You are not restricted to addition in calculations. You can use subtraction (−), multiplication (*), or division (/). You also can include parentheses in your calculations to indicate which calculations should be done first.

The following steps create a query that Camashaly Design might use to obtain financial information on its clients, including the total amount (amount paid + current due), which is a calculated field.

• Create a query with a field list for the Client table.

• Add the Client Number, Client Name, Amount Paid, and Current Due fields to the query.

• Right-click the Field row in the first open column in the design grid to display a shortcut menu (Figure 2–64).

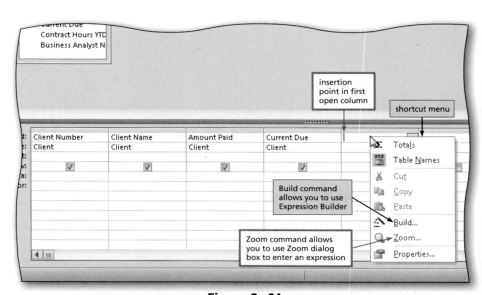

Figure 2–64

2

- Click Zoom on the shortcut menu to display the Zoom dialog box.

- Type **Total Amount: [Amount Paid]+ [Current Due]** in the Zoom dialog box (Figure 2–65).

Do I always need to put square brackets around field names?

If the field name does not contain spaces, square brackets are technically not necessary, although it is still acceptable to use the brackets. It is a good practice, however, to get in the habit of using the brackets.

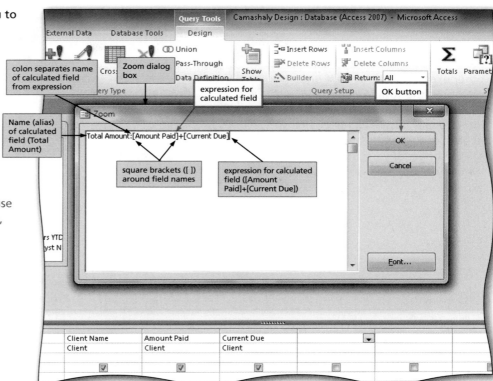

Figure 2–65

3

- Click the OK button (Zoom dialog box) to enter the expression (Figure 2–66).

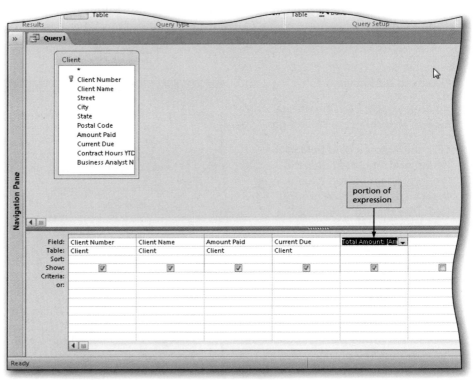

Figure 2–66

4

- View the query results (Figure 2–67).

Experiment

- Return to Design view and try other expressions. In at least one case, omit the Total Amount and the colon. In at least one case, intentionally misspell a field name. In each case, view the results to see the effect of your changes. When finished, reenter the original expression.

CL #	Client Name	Amount Paid	Current Due	Total Amour
BA53	Bavant Animal Hospital	$0.00	$7,500.00	$7,500.00
BB32	Babbage CPA Firm	$1,500.00	$500.00	$2,000.00
BC76	Buda Community Clinic	$2,500.00	$750.00	$3,250.00
CJ29	Catering by Jenna	$3,000.00	$1,000.00	$4,000.00
GA74	Grant Antiques	$5,500.00	$3,200.00	$8,700.00
GF56	Granger Foundation	$0.00	$6,500.00	$6,500.00
HC10	Hendley County Hospital	$3,100.00	$1,200.00	$4,300.00
KD21	KAL Design Studio	$6,000.00	$3,200.00	$9,200.00
KG04	Kyle Grocery Cooperative	$3,200.00	$0.00	$3,200.00
ME14	Mike's Electronic Stop	$2,500.00	$1,500.00	$4,000.00
PJ34	Patricia Jean Florist	$0.00	$5,200.00	$5,200.00
SL77	Smarter Law Associates	$3,800.00	$0.00	$3,800.00
TB17	The Bikeshop	$2,750.00	$1,200.00	$3,950.00
WE05	Walburg Energy Alternatives	$4,500.00	$1,450.00	$5,950.00
WS01	Woody Sporting Goods			$3,850.00

results are calculated by adding the amount paid and the current due

Total Amount field

Figure 2–67

Other Ways

1. Press SHIFT+F2

To Change a Caption

You can change the way items appear in the results of a query by changing their format. You also can change a query result's heading at the top of a column by changing the caption. Just as when you omitted duplicates, you will make this change by using a property sheet. In the property sheet, you can change the desired property, such as the format, the number of decimal places, or the caption. The following steps change the caption of the Amount Paid field to Paid and the caption of the Current Due field to Due. The steps also save the query with a new name.

1

- Return to Design view.

- If necessary, click Design on the Ribbon to display the Design tab.

- Click the Amount Paid field in the design grid, and then click the Property Sheet button (Query Tools Design tab | Show/Hide group) to display the properties for the Amount Paid field.

- Click the Caption box, and then type **Paid** as the caption (Figure 2–68).

Q&A

My property sheet looks different. What should I do?

If your sheet looks different, you clicked the wrong place and will have to close the property sheet and repeat this step.

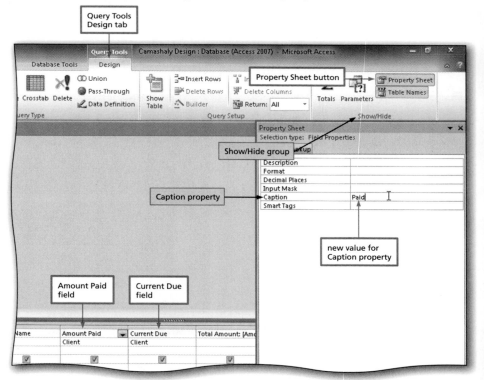

Figure 2–68

2

- Close the property sheet by clicking the Property Sheet button a second time.

- Click the Current Due field in the design grid, and then click the Property Sheet button (Query Tools Design tab | Show/Hide group).

- Click the Caption box, and then type **Due** as the caption.

- Close the Property Sheet by clicking the Property Sheet button a second time.

- View the query results (Figure 2–69).

3

- Save the query as Ch2q11.

- Close the query.

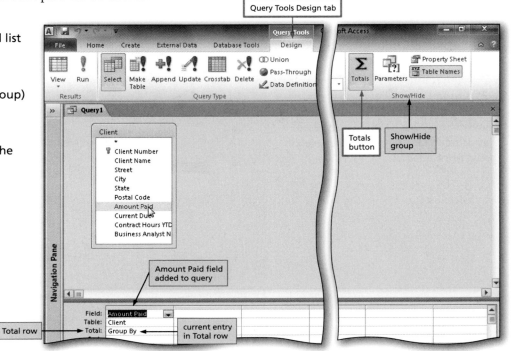

Figure 2–69

Other Ways

1. Right-click field in design grid, click Properties on shortcut menu

To Calculate Statistics

For group calculations, Microsoft Access supports several built-in statistics: COUNT (count of the number of records), SUM (total), AVG (average), MAX (largest value), MIN (smallest value), STDEV (standard deviation), VAR (variance), FIRST (first value), and LAST (last value). These statistics are called aggregate functions. An **aggregate function** is a function that performs some mathematical function against a group of records. To use any of these aggregate functions in a query, you include it in the Total row in the design grid. The Total row usually does not appear in the grid. To include it, click the Totals button on the Design tab.

The following steps create a new query for the Client table. The steps include the Total row in the design grid, and then calculate the average amount paid for all clients.

1

- Create a new query with a field list for the Client table.

- Click the Totals button (Query Tools Design tab | Show/Hide group) to include the Total row in the design grid.

- Add the Amount Paid field to the query (Figure 2–70).

Figure 2–70

2

- Click the Total row in the Amount Paid column to display the Total box arrow.

- Click the Total box arrow to display the Total list (Figure 2–71).

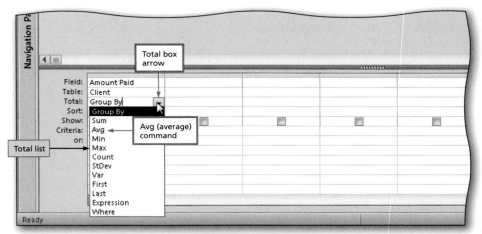

Figure 2–71

3

- Click Avg to select the calculation that Access is to perform (Figure 2–72).

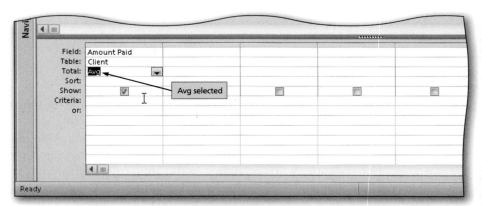

Figure 2–72

4

- View the query results (Figure 2–73).

Experiment

- Return to Design view and try other aggregate functions. In each case, view the results to see the effect of your selection. When finished, select Avg once again.

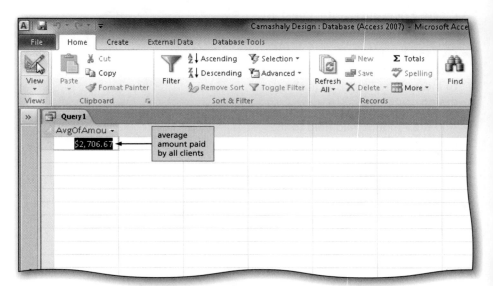

Figure 2–73

To Use Criteria in Calculating Statistics

Sometimes calculating statistics for all the records in the table is appropriate. In other cases, however, you will need to calculate the statistics for only those records that satisfy certain criteria. To enter a criterion in a field, first you select Where as the entry in the Total row for the field, and then enter the criterion in the Criteria row. The following steps use this technique to calculate the average amount paid for clients of business analyst 11. The steps also save the query with a new name.

1

- Return to Design view.

- Include the Business Analyst Number field in the design grid.

- Click the Total box arrow in the Business Analyst Number column to produce a Total list (Figure 2–74).

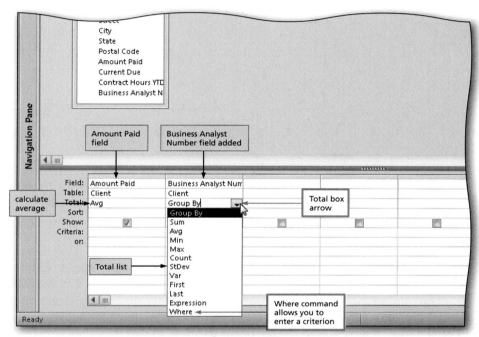

Figure 2–74

2

- Click Where.

- Type **11** as the criterion for the Business Analyst Number field (Figure 2–75).

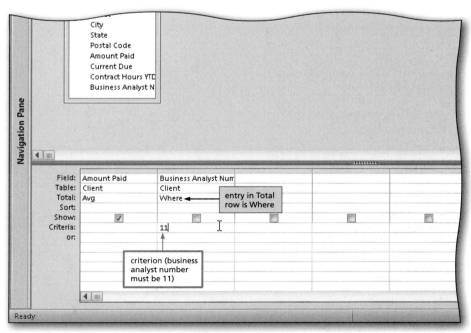

Figure 2–75

3

• View the query results (Figure 2–76).

4

• Save the query as Ch2q12.

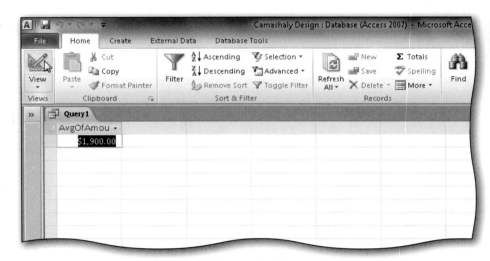

Figure 2–76

To Use Grouping

Another way statistics often are used is in combination with grouping; that is, statistics are calculated for groups of records. You may, for example, need to calculate the average amount paid for the clients of each business analyst. You will want the average for the clients of business analyst 11, the average for clients of business analyst 14, and so on.

Grouping means creating groups of records that share some common characteristic. In grouping by Business Analyst Number, for example, the clients of business analyst 11 would form one group, the clients of business analyst 14 would form a second, and the clients of business analyst 27 would form a third group. The calculations then are made for each group. To indicate grouping in Access, select Group By as the entry in the Total row for the field to be used for grouping.

The following steps create a query that calculates the average amount paid for clients of each business analyst at Camashaly Design. The steps also save the query with a new name.

1

• Return to Design view and clear the design grid.

• Include the Business Analyst Number field in the query.

• Include the Amount Paid field in the query.

• Select Avg as the calculation in the Total row for the Amount Paid field (Figure 2–77).

Q&A

Why didn't I need to change the entry in the Total row for the Business Analyst Number field?

Group By, which is the initial entry in the Total row when you add a field, is correct. Thus, you didn't need to change the entry.

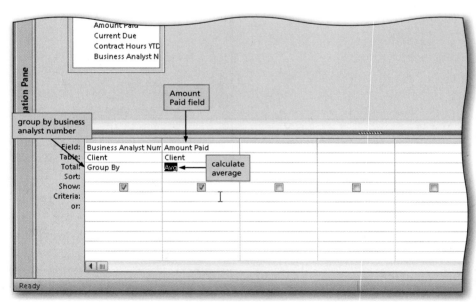

Figure 2–77

2
- View the query results (Figure 2–78).

3
- Save the query as Ch2q13.
- Close the query.

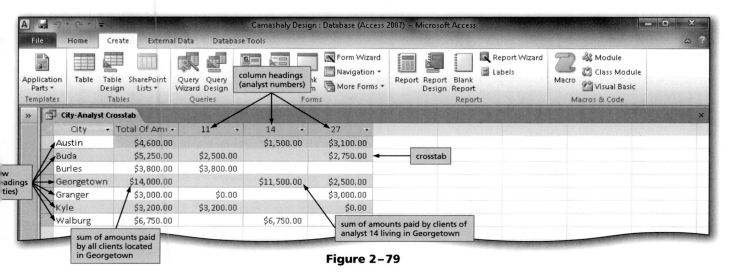

Figure 2–78

Crosstab Queries

A crosstab query calculates a statistic (for example, sum, average, or count) for data that is grouped by two different types of information. One of the types will appear down the side of the resulting datasheet, and the other will appear across the top. Crosstab queries are useful for summarizing data by category or group.

For example, if you have determined that a query must summarize the sum of the amounts paid grouped by both city and business analyst number, you could have cities as the row headings, that is, down the side. You could have business analyst numbers as the column headings, that is, across the top. The entries within the datasheet represent the total of the amounts paid. Figure 2–79 shows a crosstab in which the total of amount paid is grouped by both city and business analyst number with cities down the left side and business analyst numbers across the top. For example, the entry in the row labeled Georgetown and in the column labeled 14 represents the total of the amount paid by all clients of business analyst 14 who are located in Georgetown.

BTW

Certification
The Microsoft Office Specialist (MOS) program provides an opportunity for you to obtain a valuable industry credential — proof that you have the Access 2010 skills required by employers. For more information, visit the Access 2010 Certification Web page (scsite.com/ac2010/cert).

Figure 2–79

To Create a Crosstab Query

The following steps use the Crosstab Query Wizard to create a crosstab query for Camashaly Design that summarizes financial information by city and business analyst.

- Click Create on the Ribbon to display the Create tab.

- Click the Query Wizard button (Create tab | Queries group) to display the New Query dialog box (Figure 2–80).

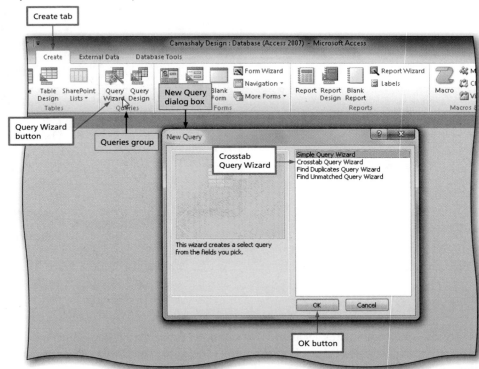

Figure 2–80

- Click Crosstab Query Wizard (New Query dialog box).

- Click the OK button to display the Crosstab Query Wizard dialog box (Figure 2–81).

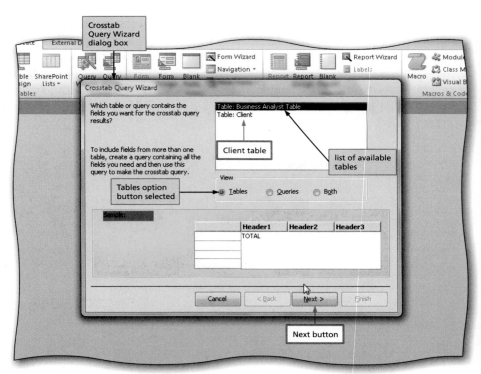

Figure 2–81

3

- With the Tables option button selected, click Table: Client to select the Client table, and then click the Next button to display the next Crosstab Query Wizard screen.

- Click the City field, and then click the Add Field button to select the City field for row headings (Figure 2–82).

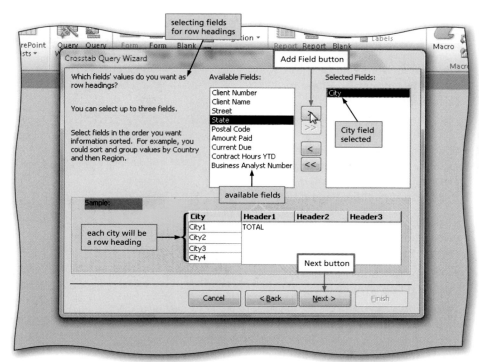

Figure 2–82

4

- Click the Next button to display the next Crosstab Query Wizard screen.

- Click the Business Analyst Number field to select the Business Analyst Number field for column headings (Figure 2–83).

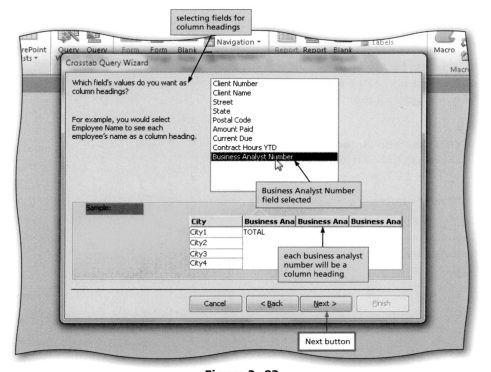

Figure 2–83

5

- Click the Next button to display the next Crosstab Query Wizard screen.

- Click the Amount Paid field to select the Amount Paid field for calculations.

 🔎 **Experiment**

- Click other fields. For each field, examine the list of calculations that are available. When finished, click the Amount Paid field again.

- Click Sum to select Sum as the calculation to be performed (Figure 2–84).

 My list of functions is different. What did I do wrong?

Either you clicked the wrong field, or the Amount Paid field has the wrong data type. For example, if you mistakenly assigned it the Text data type, you would not see Sum in the list of available calculations.

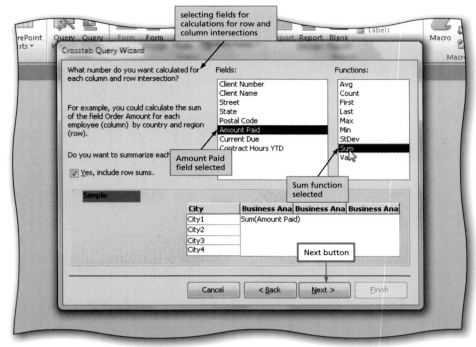

Figure 2–84

6

- Click the Next button to display the next Crosstab Query Wizard screen.

- Type **City-Analyst Crosstab** as the name of the query (Figure 2–85).

7

- Click the Finish button to produce the crosstab shown in Figure 2–79 on Page AC 123.

- Close the query.

 If I want to view the crosstab at some future date, can I just open the query?

Yes.

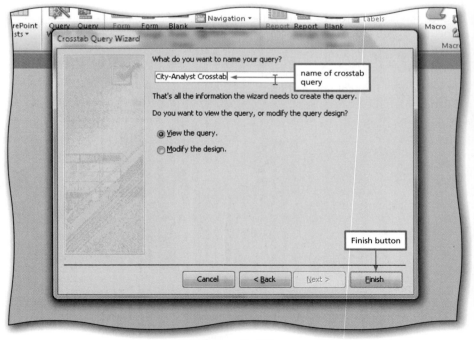

Figure 2–85

To Customize the Navigation Pane

Currently, the entries in the Navigation Pane are organized by object type. That is, all the tables are together, all the queries are together, and so on. You might want to change the way the information is organized. For example, you might want to have the Navigation Pane organized by table, with all the queries, forms, and reports associated with a particular table appearing after the name of the table. You also can use the Search bar to restrict the objects that appear to only those that have a certain collection of characters in their name. For example, if you entered the letters, Cl, only those objects containing Cl somewhere within the name will be included.

The following steps change the organization of the Navigation Pane. They also use the Search bar to restrict the objects that appear.

1
- If necessary, click the Shutter Bar Open/Close Button to open the Navigation Pane.
- Click the Navigation Pane arrow to produce the Navigation Pane menu (Figure 2–86).

2
- Click Tables and Related Views to organize the Navigation Pane by table rather than by the type of object (Figure 2–87).

3
- Click the Navigation Pane arrow to produce the Navigation Pane menu.
- Click Object Type to once again organize the Navigation Pane by object type.

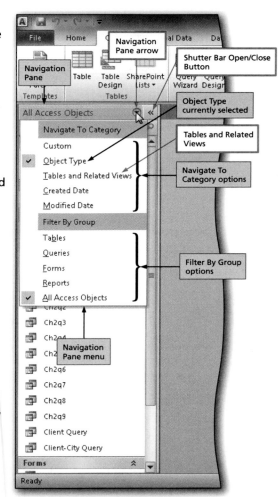

Figure 2–86

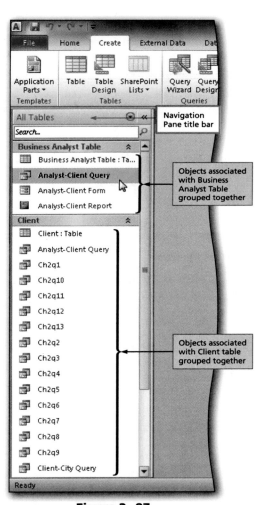

Figure 2–87

Experiment

- Select different Navigate To Category options to see the effect of the option. With each option you select, select different Filter By Group options to see the effect of the filtering. When you have finished experimenting, select the Object Type Navigate To Category option and the All Access Objects Filter By Group option.

- If the Search bar does not appear, right-click the Navigation Pane and click Search Bar on the shortcut menu.

- Click in the Search bar box to produce an insertion point.

- Type **Cl** as the search string to restrict the objects displayed to only those containing the desired string (Figure 2–88).

5

- Click the Clear Search String button to remove the search string and redisplay all objects.

Q&A

Did I have to click the button to redisplay all objects? Couldn't I have simply erased the current string to achieve the same result?

You didn't have to click the button. You could have used the DELETE or BACKSPACE keys to erase the current search string.

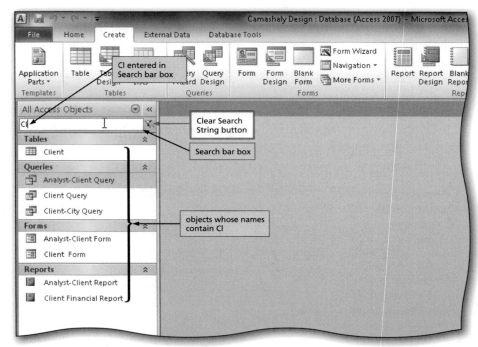

Figure 2–88

BTW

Quick Reference
For a table that lists how to complete the tasks covered in this book using the mouse, Ribbon, shortcut menu, and keyboard, see the Quick Reference Summary at the back of this book, or visit the Access 2010 Quick Reference Web page (scsite.com/ac2010/qr).

To Quit Access

The following steps quit Access.

1 Click the Close button on the right side of the title bar to quit Access.

2 If a Microsoft Access dialog box appears, click the Save button to save any changes made to the object since the last save.

Chapter Summary

In this chapter you have learned to create queries, enter fields, enter criteria, use text and numeric data in queries, use wildcards, use compound criteria, create parameter queries, sort data in queries, join tables in queries, perform calculations in queries, and create crosstab queries. You also learned to create a report and a form that used a query, to export a query, and to customize the Navigation Pane. The items listed below include all the new Access skills you have learned in this chapter.

1. Create a Query in Design View (AC 78)
2. Add Fields to the Design Grid (AC 79)
3. Use Text Data in a Criterion (AC 80)
4. Use a Wildcard (AC 83)
5. Use Criteria for a Field Not Included in the Results (AC 85)
6. Create and View a Parameter Query (AC 87)
7. Use a Parameter Query (AC 89)
8. Use a Number in a Criterion (AC 90)
9. Use a Comparison Operator in a Criterion (AC 91)
10. Use a Compound Criterion Involving AND (AC 92)
11. Use a Compound Criterion Involving OR (AC 93)
12. Clear the Design Grid (AC 95)
13. Sort Data in a Query (AC 96)
14. Omit Duplicates (AC 97)
15. Sort on Multiple Keys (AC 98)
16. Create a Top-Values Query (AC 99)
17. Join Tables (AC 102)
18. Change Join Properties (AC 105)
19. Create a Report Involving a Join (AC 106)

20. Create a Form for a Query (AC 109)
21. Export Data to Excel (AC 111)
22. Export Data to Word (AC 113)
23. Export Data to a Text File (AC 114)
24. Restrict the Records in a Join (AC 115)
25. Use a Calculated Field in a Query (AC 116)

26. Change a Caption (AC 118)
27. Calculate Statistics (AC 119)
28. Use Criteria in Calculating Statistics (AC 121)
29. Use Grouping (AC 122)
30. Create a Crosstab Query (AC 124)
31. Customize the Navigation Pane (AC 127)

 If you have a SAM 2010 user profile, your instructor may have assigned an autogradable version of this assignment. If so, log into the SAM 2010 Web site at www.cengage.com/sam2010 to download the instruction and start files.

Learn It Online

Test your knowledge of chapter content and key terms.

Instructions: To complete the Learn It Online exercises, start your browser, click the Address bar, and then enter the Web address **scsite.com/ac2010/learn**. When the Access 2010 Learn It Online page is displayed, click the link for the exercise you want to complete and then read the instructions.

Chapter Reinforcement TF, MC, and SA
A series of true/false, multiple choice, and short answer questions that test your knowledge of the chapter content.

Flash Cards
An interactive learning environment where you identify chapter key terms associated with displayed definitions.

Practice Test
A series of multiple choice questions that test your knowledge of chapter content and key terms.

Who Wants To Be a Computer Genius?
An interactive game that challenges your knowledge of chapter content in the style of a television quiz show.

Wheel of Terms
An interactive game that challenges your knowledge of chapter key terms in the style of the television show *Wheel of Fortune*.

Crossword Puzzle Challenge
A crossword puzzle that challenges your knowledge of key terms presented in the chapter.

Apply Your Knowledge

Reinforce the skills and apply the concepts you learned in this chapter.

Using Wildcards in a Query, Creating a Parameter Query, Joining Tables, and Creating a Report

Instructions: Start Access. Open the Babbage CPA Firm database that you modified in Apply Your Knowledge in Chapter 1 on page AC 64. (If you did not complete this exercise, see your instructor for a copy of the modified database.)

Perform the following tasks:
1. Create a query for the Client table and add the Client Number, Client Name, City, and Amount Paid fields to the design grid. Find all clients who live in cities that start with Bu. Save the query as Apply 2 Step 1 Query.

Continued >

Apply Your Knowledge *continued*

2. Create a query for the Client table and add the Client Number, Client Name, Bookkeeper Number, and Balance Due fields to the design grid. Sort the records in descending order by Balance Due. Add a criterion for the Bookkeeper Number field that allows the user to enter a different bookkeeper each time the query is run. Save the query as Apply 2 Step 2 Query.

3. Create a query that joins the Bookkeeper and the Client tables. Add the Bookkeeper Number, First Name, and Last Name fields from the Bookkeeper table and the Client Number and Client Name fields from the Client table. Sort the records in ascending order by Bookkeeper Number and Client Number. All bookkeepers should appear in the result, even if they currently have no clients. Save the query as Bookkeeper-Client Query.

4. Create the report shown in Figure 2–89. The report uses the Bookkeeper-Client Query.

Bookkeeper-Client Report

BKR #	First Name	Last Name	CL #	Client Name
22	Johanna	Lewes	A54	Afton Mills
22	Johanna	Lewes	D76	Dege Grocery
22	Johanna	Lewes	J77	Jones Plumbing
22	Johanna	Lewes	S56	SeeSaw Industries
24	Mario	Rodriguez	A62	Atlas Suppliers
24	Mario	Rodriguez	B26	Blake-Scripps
24	Mario	Rodriguez	G56	Grand Cleaners
24	Mario	Rodriguez	M26	Mohr Crafts
34	Choi	Wong	C29	Catering by Jenna
34	Choi	Wong	H21	Hill Shoes
34	Choi	Wong	T45	Tate Repair
34	Choi	Wong	W24	Woody Sporting Goods
38	Theresa	Sinthin		

Figure 2–89

5. Submit the revised database in the format specified by your instructor.

Extend Your Knowledge

Extend the skills you learned in this chapter and experiment with new skills. You may need to use Help to complete the assignment.

Creating Crosstab Queries, Creating Queries Using Criteria, and Exporting a Query

Instructions: Start Access. Open the Natural Earthscapes database. See the inside back cover of this book for instructions for downloading the Data Files for Students, or see your instructor for information on accessing the files required in this book.

Natural Earthscapes is a small landscaping company that specializes in landscaping with native plants. The owners have created an Access database in which to store information about the customers they serve and the workers they employ. You will create the crosstab shown in Figure 2–90. You also will query the database using specified criteria.

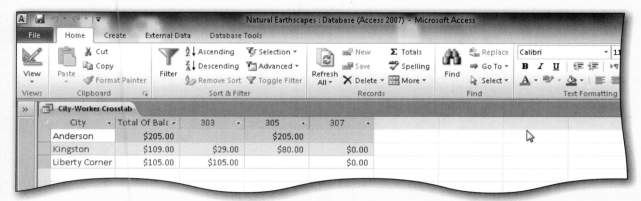

Figure 2–90

Perform the following tasks:

1. Create the crosstab query shown in Figure 2–90. The crosstab query groups the total of customers' balances by city and worker number.

2. Create a query to find all customers who do not live in Kingston. Include the Customer Number, Last Name, Balance, and Amount Paid fields in the design grid. Save the query as Extend 2 Step 2 Query.

3. Create a query to find all customers where the customer's first name is either Frances or Francis. Include the Customer Number, Last Name, First Name, Street, and City fields in the query results. Save the query as Extend 2 Step 3 Query.

4. Create a query to find all customers where the worker number is 303 or 305 and the balance is greater than $40.00. Include the Customer Number, Last Name, First Name, Balance, and Worker Number fields in the design grid. Use the IN operator in your query design. Save the query as Extend 2 Step 4 Query.

5. Export the City-Worker Crosstab as a Word file with the name City-Worker Crosstab.rtf and save the export steps.

6. Open the Customer table and change the balance for AB10 to $90.

7. Use the saved export steps to export the City-Worker Crosstab again. When asked if you want to replace the existing file, click Yes.

8. Change the database properties, as specified by your instructor. Submit the revised database and the exported RTF file in the format specified by your instructor.

Make It Right

Analyze a database and correct all errors and/or improve the design.

Correcting Errors in the Query Design
Instructions: Start Access. Open the Retired Pet Sitters database. See the inside back cover of this book for instructions for downloading the Data Files for Students, or see your instructor for information on accessing the files required in this book.

Continued >

Make It Right *continued*

Retired Pet Sitters is a database maintained by a small pet-sitting business. The queries shown in Figure 2–91 contain a number of errors that need to be corrected before the queries run properly. The query shown in Figure 2–91a displays the query results in the proper order (Last Name, First Name, Balance, Sitter Number), but it is sorted incorrectly. The query results should be sorted by last name within sitter number in ascending order. Also, the caption for the Balance field should be Owed. Save the query with your changes.

When you try to run the query shown in Figure 2–91b, you get 0 results. You are trying to find all customers who live on Magee. Correct the error and save the query with your changes.

Figure 2–91 (a) Incorrect Sort Query

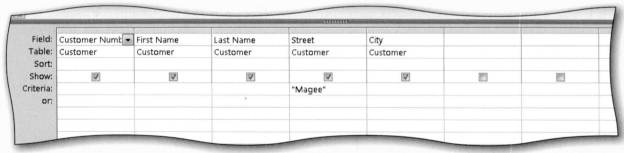

Figure 2–91 (b) Incorrect Criteria Query

Change the database properties, as specified by your instructor. Submit the revised database in the format specified by your instructor.

In the Lab

Design, create, modify, and/or use a database following the guidelines, concepts, and skills presented in this chapter. The assignments are listed in order of increasing difficulty.

Lab 1: Querying the ECO Clothesline Database

Problem: The management of ECO Clothesline has determined a number of questions it wants the database management system to answer. You must obtain answers to the questions posed by management.

Instructions: Use the database modified in the In the Lab 1 of Chapter 1 on page AC 66 for this assignment, or see your instructor for information on accessing the files required for this book.

Perform the following tasks:

1. Open the ECO Clothesline database and create a new query for the Customer table that includes the Customer Number, Customer Name, Amount Paid, and Sales Rep Number fields in the design grid for all customers where the sales rep number is 49. Save the query as Lab 2-1 Step 1 Query.

2. Create a query that includes the Customer Number, Customer Name, and Amount Paid fields for all customers located in Virginia (VA) with a paid amount greater than $1,000.00. Save the query as Lab 2-1 Step 2 Query.

3. Create a query that includes the Customer Number, Customer Name, Street, and City fields for all customers whose names begin with T. Save the query as Lab 2-1 Step 3 Query.

4. Create a query that lists all cities in ascending order. Each city should appear only once. Save the query as Lab 2-1 Step 4 Query.

5. Create a query that allows the user to enter the city to search when the query is run. The query results should display the Customer Number, Customer Name, Balance, and Amount Paid fields. Test the query by searching for those records where the client is located in Ashton. Save the query as Lab 2-1 Step 5 Query.

6. Include the Customer Number, Customer Name, and Balance fields in the design grid. Sort the records in descending order by the Balance field. Display only the top 25 percent of the records in the query result. Save the query as Lab 2-1 Step 6 Query.

7. Join the Sales Rep and the Customer table. Include the Sales Rep Number, First Name, and Last Name fields from the Sales Rep table. Include the Customer Number, Customer Name, and Balance from the Customer table. Sort the records in ascending order by sales rep's last name and customer name. All sales reps should appear in the result even if they currently have no customers. Save the query as Lab 2-1 Step 7 Query.

8. Open the Lab 2-1 Step 7 Query in Design view and remove the Sales Rep table. Add the Amount Paid field to the design grid. Calculate the total of the balance and amount paid amounts. Assign the alias Total Amount to the calculated field. Change the caption for the Balance field to Due. Save the query as Lab 2-1 Step 8 Query.

9. Create a query to display the average balance amount for all customers. Save the query as Lab 2-1 Step 9 Query.

10. Create a query to display the average balance amount for sales rep 51. Save the query as Lab 2-1 Step 10 Query.

11. Create a query to display the average balance amount for each sales rep. Save the query as Lab 2-1 Step 11 Query.

12. Create the crosstab shown in Figure 2–92. The crosstab groups the total of customers' amount paid amounts by state and sales rep number. Save the crosstab as State-Sales Rep Crosstab.

13. Submit the revised database in the format specified by your instructor.

State	Total Of Am...	44	49	51
NC	$2,235.00	$1,400.00	$710.00	$125.00
TN	$6,245.00	$1,695.00	$2,600.00	$1,950.00
VA	$5,180.00	$2,425.00	$700.00	$2,055.00

Figure 2–92

In the Lab

Lab 2: Querying the Walburg Energy Alternatives Database

Problem: The manager of the Walburg Energy Alternatives store has determined a number of questions he wants the database management system to answer. You must obtain answers to the questions posed by the manager.

Instructions: Use the database created in the In the Lab 2 of Chapter 1 on page AC 67 for this assignment, or see your instructor for information on accessing the files required for this book.

Perform the following tasks:

1. Open the Walburg Energy Alternatives database and create a query that includes all fields and all records in the Item table. There should be only one column in the design grid. Name the query Lab 2-2 Step 1 Query.

2. Create a query that includes the Item Number, Description, Cost, and Vendor Code fields for all items where the vendor code is JM. Save the query as Lab 2-2 Step 2 Query.

3. Create a query that includes the Item Number and Description fields for all items where the description starts with the letters, En. Save the query as Lab 2-2 Step 3 Query.

4. Create a query that includes the Item Number and Description fields for all items with a cost less than $4.00. Save the query as Lab 2-2 Step 4 Query.

5. Create a query that includes the Item Number and Description fields for all items with a selling price greater than $20.00. Save the query as Lab 2-2 Step 5 Query.

6. Create a query that includes all fields for all items with a vendor code of AS and where the number on hand is fewer than 10. Save the query as Lab 2-2 Step 6 Query.

7. Create a query that includes all fields for all items that have a selling price greater than $10.00 or a vendor code of JM. Save the query as Lab 2-2 Step 7 Query.

8. Join the Vendor table and the Item table. Include the Vendor Code and Vendor Name fields from the Vendor table and the Item Number, Description, On Hand, and Cost fields from the Item table. Sort the records in ascending order by item number within vendor code. Save the query as Vendor-Item Query.

9. Create the form shown in Figure 2–93. The form uses the Vendor-Item Query.

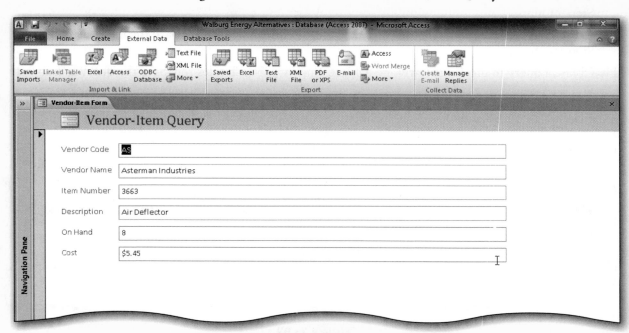

Figure 2–93

10. Create a query that includes the Item Number, Description, On Hand, and Cost fields. Calculate the inventory value (on hand*cost) for all records in the table. Assign the alias Inventory Value to the calculated field. Change the caption for the On Hand column to In Stock. Format the Inventory Value field as currency with two decimal places. Sort the records in descending order by inventory value. Save the query as Lab 2-2 Step 10 Query.

11. Create a query that calculates and displays the average cost of all items. Save the query as Lab 2-2 Step 11 Query.

12. Create a query that calculates and displays the average cost of items grouped by vendor code. Save the query as Lab 2-2 Step 12 Query.

13. Submit the revised database in the format specified by your instructor.

In the Lab

Lab 3: Querying the Philamar Training Database

Problem: The management of Philamar Training has determined a number of questions it wants the database management system to answer. You must obtain answers to the questions posed by management.

Instructions: Use the database created in the In the Lab 3 of Chapter 1 on page AC 70 for this assignment, or see your instructor for information on accessing the files required for this book. For Part 1 and Part 3, save each query using a format similar to the following: Lab 2-3 Part 1a Query, Lab 2-3 Part 3a Query, and so on. Submit the revised database and the Trainer-Client Query.xlsx file in the format specified by your instructor.

Instructions Part 1: Create a new query for the Client table and include the Client Number, Client Name, Amount Paid, and Current Due fields in the design grid. Create queries that answer the following questions: (a) Which clients' names begin with F? (b) Which clients are located in Kingston? (c) Which clients have a current due amount of $0.00? (d) Which clients have an amount paid amount between $5,000.00 and $10,000.00? (e) Which two clients have the highest current due amounts? (f) For each client, what is the total of the current due and amount paid?

Instructions Part 2: Join the Trainer and the Client table. In the design grid, include the Trainer Number, First Name, and Last Name from the Trainer table and the Client Number, Client Name, and Amount Paid from the Client table. Sort the records in ascending order by trainer number and client number. All trainers should appear in the result, even if they currently have no clients. Save the query as Trainer-Client Query. Export the query to Excel and save the export steps.

Instructions Part 3: Create queries to calculate the following statistics: (a) What is the average current due amount for clients assigned to trainer 42? (b) What is the total current due amount for all clients? (c) What is the total amount paid for each trainer?

Cases and Places

Apply your creative thinking and problem solving skills to design and implement a solution.

Note: To complete these assignments, you may be required to use the Data Files for Students. See the inside back cover of this book for instructions on downloading the Data Files for Students, or contact your instructor for information about accessing the required files.

1: Querying the Chamber of Commerce Database

Academic

Use the Chamber of Commerce database you created in Cases and Places 1 in Chapter 1 on page AC 72 for this assignment. Use the concepts and techniques presented in this chapter to create queries for the following:

a. Find the advertiser name and address of all advertisers located on Main.

Continued >

Cases and Places *continued*

b. Find the advertiser number, advertiser name, balance, and amount paid for all advertisers whose balance is greater than $300 or whose amount paid is $0.00.

c. Find the total of the balance and amount paid amounts for each advertiser. Show the advertiser number, advertiser name, and total amount. Sort the results in descending order by total.

d. Find the advertiser number, advertiser name, balance, and amount paid for all advertisers whose balance is between $200 and $500.

e. Create a parameter query for the Advertiser table that will allow the user to enter a different postal code each time the query is run. The user should see all fields in the query result.

f. Find the ad rep for each advertiser. List the ad rep number, last name, first name, advertiser number, advertiser name, and balance. Sort the results in ascending order by ad rep number and advertiser number.

g. Determine the total of the balance amounts and amount paid amounts for all advertisers.

Submit the revised database in the format specified by your instructor.

2: Querying the Consignment Database

Personal

Use the Consignment database you created in Cases and Places 2 in Chapter 1 on page AC 72 for this assignment. Use the concepts and techniques presented in this chapter to create queries for the following:

a. Find the item number and description of all items that contain the word, Table.

b. Find the item number, description, condition, and date of the item that has the earliest posting date.

c. Find the total price (price*quantity) of each item available for sale. Show the item number, item description, and total price.

d. Find the seller of each item. Show the seller's first name and last name as well as the item description, price, quantity, and date posted. Sort the results by item description within seller last name.

e. Create a report based on the query you created in Step d. Include all fields in the report.

f. Modify the query you created in Step d to restrict retrieval to those items with a price greater than $50.00.

g. Find all items posted between March 1, 2012, and March 4, 2012. The user should see all fields in the query result.

Submit the revised database in the format specified by your instructor.

3: Querying the Senior Care Database

Professional

Use the Senior Care database you created in Cases and Places 3 in Chapter 1 on page AC 72 for this assignment. Use the concepts and techniques presented in this chapter to create queries for the following:

a. Find the first name, last name, and address of all clients where the street name begins with the letter U.

b. Find the client number, last name, first name, balance, and amount paid for all clients whose balance is $0.00 or whose amount paid is $0.00.

c. Find the total of the balance and amount paid amounts for each client. Show the client number, client last name, client first name, and total amount. Sort the results in descending order by total.

d. Find the helper for each client. List the helper number, helper last name, helper first name, client number, client last name, and client first name. Sort the results in ascending order by helper number and client number.

e. Create a report for the query created in Step d. Include all fields except the helper first name in the report. Create a form for the query created in Step d.

f. Export the query created in Step d as a text file.

g. Find the highest and lowest balances.

Submit the exported text file and revised database in the format specified by your instructor.

NOTES

NOTES

NOTES

NOTES

Appendix A

Project Planning Guidelines

Using Project Planning Guidelines

The process of communicating specific information to others is a learned, rational skill. Computers and software, especially Microsoft Office 2010, can help you develop ideas and present detailed information to a particular audience.

Using Microsoft Office 2010, you can create projects such as Word documents, PowerPoint presentations, Excel spreadsheets, and Access databases. Productivity software such as Microsoft Office 2010 minimizes much of the laborious work of drafting and revising projects. Some communicators handwrite ideas in notebooks, others compose directly on the computer, and others have developed unique strategies that work for their own particular thinking and writing styles.

No matter what method you use to plan a project, follow specific guidelines to arrive at a final product that presents information correctly and effectively (Figure A–1). Use some aspects of these guidelines every time you undertake a project, and others as needed in specific instances. For example, in determining content for a project, you may decide that a chart communicates trends more effectively than a paragraph of text. If so, you would create this graphical element and insert it in an Excel spreadsheet, a Word document, or a PowerPoint slide.

Determine the Project's Purpose

Begin by clearly defining why you are undertaking this assignment. For example, you may want to track monetary donations collected for your club's fund-raising drive. Alternatively, you may be urging students to vote for a particular candidate in the next election. Once you clearly understand the purpose of your task, begin to draft ideas of how best to communicate this information.

Analyze Your Audience

Learn about the people who will read, analyze, or view your work. Where are they employed? What are their educational backgrounds? What are their expectations? What questions do they have?

PROJECT PLANNING GUIDELINES

1. DETERMINE THE PROJECT'S PURPOSE
Why are you undertaking the project?

2. ANALYZE YOUR AUDIENCE
Who are the people who will use your work?

3. GATHER POSSIBLE CONTENT
What information exists, and in what forms?

4. DETERMINE WHAT CONTENT TO PRESENT TO YOUR AUDIENCE
What information will best communicate the project's purpose to your audience?

Figure A–1

Design experts suggest drawing a mental picture of these people or finding photos of people who fit this profile so that you can develop a project with the audience in mind.

By knowing your audience members, you can tailor a project to meet their interests and needs. You will not present them with information they already possess, and you will not omit the information they need to know.

Example: Your assignment is to raise the profile of your college's nursing program in the community. How much do they know about your college and the nursing curriculum? What are the admission requirements? How many of the applicants admitted complete the program? What percent pass the state board exams?

Gather Possible Content

Rarely are you in a position to develop all the material for a project. Typically, you would begin by gathering existing information that may reside in spreadsheets or databases. Web sites, pamphlets, magazine and newspaper articles, and books could provide insights of how others have approached your topic. Personal interviews often provide perspectives not available by any other means. Consider video and audio clips as potential sources for material that might complement or support the factual data you uncover.

Determine What Content to Present to Your Audience

Experienced designers recommend writing three or four major ideas you want an audience member to remember after reading or viewing your project. It also is helpful to envision your project's endpoint, the key fact you wish to emphasize. All project elements should lead to this ending point.

As you make content decisions, you also need to think about other factors. Presentation of the project content is an important consideration. For example, will your brochure be printed on thick, colored paper or posted on the Web? Will your PowerPoint presentation be viewed in a classroom with excellent lighting and a bright projector, or will it be viewed on a notebook computer monitor? Determine relevant time factors, such as the length of time to develop the project, how long readers will spend reviewing your project, or the amount of time allocated for your speaking engagement. Your project will need to accommodate all of these constraints.

Decide whether a graph, photo, or artistic element can express or emphasize a particular concept. The right hemisphere of the brain processes images by attaching an emotion to them, so audience members are more apt to recall these graphics long term rather than just reading text.

As you select content, be mindful of the order in which you plan to present information. Readers and audience members generally remember the first and last pieces of information they see and hear, so you should place the most important information at the top or bottom of the page.

Summary

When creating a project, it is beneficial to follow some basic guidelines from the outset. By taking some time at the beginning of the process to determine the project's purpose, analyze the audience, gather possible content, and determine what content to present to the audience, you can produce a project that is informative, relevant, and effective.

Appendix B

Publishing Office 2010 Web Pages Online

With Office 2010 programs, you use the Save As command in the Backstage view to save a Web page to a Web site, network location, or FTP site. **File Transfer Protocol (FTP)** is an Internet standard that allows computers to exchange files with other computers on the Internet.

You should contact your network system administrator or technical support staff at your Internet access provider to determine if their Web server supports Web folders, FTP, or both, and to obtain necessary permissions to access the Web server.

Using an Office Program to Publish Office 2010 Web Pages

When publishing online, someone first must assign the necessary permissions for you to publish the Web page. If you are granted access to publish online, you must obtain the Web address of the Web server, a user name, and possibly a password that allows you to connect to the Web server. The steps in this appendix assume that you have access to an online location to which you can publish a Web page.

To Connect to an Online Location

To publish a Web page online, you first must connect to the online location. To connect to an online location using Windows 7, you would perform the following steps.

1. Click the Start button on the Windows 7 taskbar to display the Start menu.
2. Click Computer in the right pane of the Start menu to open the Computer window.
3. Click the 'Map network drive' button on the toolbar to display the Map Network Drive dialog box. (If the 'Map network drive' button is not visible on the toolbar, click the 'Display additional commands' button on the toolbar and then click 'Map network drive' in the list to display the Map Network Drive dialog box.)
4. Click the 'Connect to a Web site that you can use to store your documents and pictures' link (Map Network Drive dialog box) to start the Add Network Location wizard.
5. Click the Next button (Add Network Location dialog box).
6. Click 'Choose a custom network location' and then click the Next button.
7. Type the Internet or network address specified by your network or system administrator in the text box and then click the Next button.
8. Click 'Log on anonymously' to deselect the check box, type your user name in the User name text box, and then click the Next button.
9. If necessary, enter the name you want to assign to this online location and then click the Next button.
10. Click to deselect the Open this network location when I click Finish check box, and then click the Finish button.

11. Click the Cancel button to close the Map Network Drive dialog box.

12. Close the Computer window.

TO SAVE A WEB PAGE TO AN ONLINE LOCATION

The online location now can be accessed easily from Windows programs, including Microsoft Office programs. After creating a Microsoft Office file you wish to save as a Web page, you must save the file to the online location to which you connected in the previous steps. To save a Microsoft Word document as a Web page, for example, and publish it to the online location, you would perform the following steps.

1. Click File on the Ribbon to display the Backstage view and then click Save As in the Backstage view to display the Save As dialog box.

2. Type the Web page file name in the File name text box (Save As dialog box). Do not press the ENTER key because you do not want to close the dialog box at this time.

3. Click the 'Save as type' box arrow and then click Web Page to select the Web Page format.

4. If necessary, scroll to display the name of the online location in the navigation pane.

5. Double-click the online location name in the navigation pane to select that location as the new save location and display its contents in the right pane.

6. If a dialog box appears prompting you for a user name and password, type the user name and password in the respective text boxes and then click the Log On button.

7. Click the Save button (Save As dialog box).

The Web page now has been published online. To view the Web page using a Web browser, contact your network or system administrator for the Web address you should use to connect to the Web page.

Appendix C

Saving to the Web Using Windows Live SkyDrive

Introduction

Windows Live SkyDrive, also referred to as **SkyDrive**, is a free service that allows users to save files to the Web, such as documents, presentations, spreadsheets, databases, videos, and photos. Using SkyDrive, you also can save files in folders, providing for greater organization. You then can retrieve those files from any computer connected to the Internet. Some Office 2010 programs including Word, PowerPoint, and Excel can save files directly to an Internet location such as SkyDrive. SkyDrive also facilitates collaboration by allowing users to share files with other SkyDrive users (Figure C–1).

Figure C–1

Note: An Internet connection is required to perform the steps in this appendix.

To Save a File to Windows Live SkyDrive

You can save files directly to SkyDrive from within Word, PowerPoint, and Excel using the Backstage view. The following steps save an open Word document (Koala Exhibit Flyer, in this case) to SkyDrive. These steps require you to have a Windows Live account. Contact your instructor if you do not have a Windows Live account.

1

- Start Word and then open a document you want to save to the Web (in this case, the Koala Exhibit Flyer).
- Click File on the Ribbon to display the Backstage view (Figure C–2).

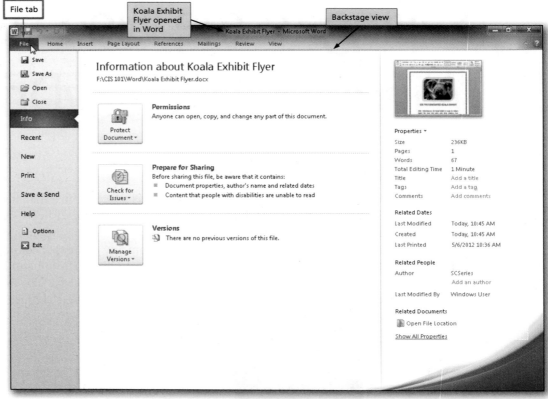

Figure C–2

2

- Click the Save & Send tab to display the Save & Send gallery (Figure C–3).

Figure C–3

3

- Click Save to Web in the Save & Send gallery to display information about saving a file to the Web (Figure C–4).

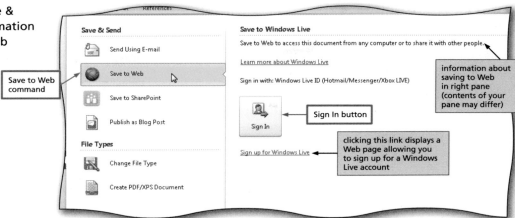

Figure C–4

4

- Click the Sign In button to display a Windows Live login dialog box that requests your e-mail address and password (Figure C–5).

Q&A What if the Sign In button does not appear?

If you already are signed into Windows Live, the Sign In button will not be displayed. Instead, the contents of your Windows Live SkyDrive will be displayed. If you already are signed into Windows Live, proceed to Step 6.

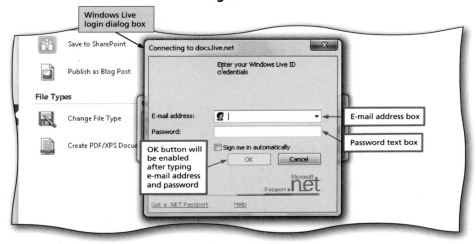

Figure C–5

5

- Enter your Windows Live e-mail address in the E-mail address box (Windows Live login dialog box).

- Enter your Windows Live password in the Password text box.

- Click the OK button to sign into Windows Live and display the contents of your Windows Live SkyDrive in the right pane of the Save & Send gallery.

- If necessary, click the My Documents folder to set the save location for the document (Figure C–6).

Q&A What if the My Documents folder does not exist?

Click another folder to select it as the save location. Record the name of this folder so that you can locate and retrieve the file later in this appendix.

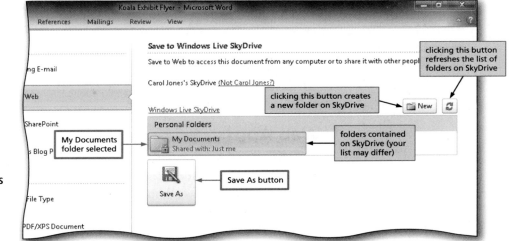

Figure C–6

Q&A My SkyDrive shows personal and shared folders. What is the difference?

Personal folders are private and are not shared with anyone. Shared folders can be viewed by SkyDrive users to whom you have assigned the necessary permissions.

● Click the Save As button in the right pane of the Save & Send gallery to contact the SkyDrive server (which may take some time, depending on the speed of your Internet connection) and then display the Save As dialog box (Figure C–7).

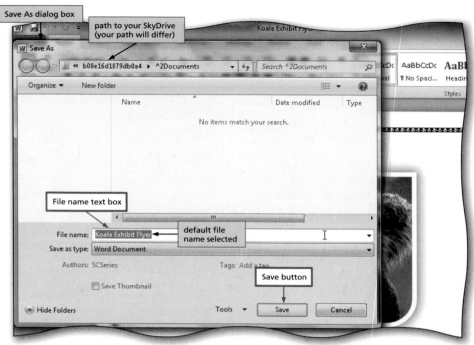

Figure C–7

● Type **Koala Exhibit Web** in the File name text box to enter the file name and then click the Save button (Save As dialog box) to save the file to Windows Live SkyDrive (Figure C–8).

Q&A

Is it necessary to rename the file?

It is good practice to rename the file. If you download the file from SkyDrive to your computer, having a different file name will preserve the original file.

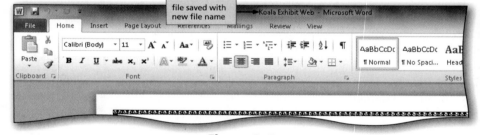

Figure C–8

● If you have one Word document open, click the Close button on the right side of the title bar to close the document and quit Word; or if you have multiple Word documents open, click File on the Ribbon to open the Backstage view and then click Exit in the Backstage view to close all open documents and quit Word.

Web Apps

Microsoft has created a scaled-down, Web-based version of its Microsoft Office suite, called **Microsoft Office Web Apps,** or **Web Apps**. Web Apps contains Web-based versions of Word, PowerPoint, Excel, and OneNote that can be used to view and edit files that are saved to SkyDrive. Web Apps allows users to continue working with their files even while they are not using a computer with Microsoft Office installed. In addition to working with files located on SkyDrive, Web Apps also enables users to create new Word documents, PowerPoint presentations, Excel spreadsheets, and OneNote notebooks. After returning to a computer with the Microsoft Office suite, some users choose to download files from SkyDrive and edit them using the associated Microsoft Office program.

Note: As with all Web applications, SkyDrive and Office Web Apps are subject to change. Consequently, the steps required to perform the actions in this appendix might be different from those shown.

To Download a File from Windows Live SkyDrive

Files saved to SkyDrive can be downloaded from a Web browser using any computer with an Internet connection. The following steps download the Koala Exhibit Web file using a Web browser.

1

- Click the Internet Explorer program button pinned on the Windows 7 taskbar to start Internet Explorer.

- Type **skydrive.live.com** in the Address bar and then press the ENTER key to display a SkyDrive Web page requesting you sign in to your Windows Live account (Figure C–9). (If the contents of your SkyDrive are displayed instead, you already are signed in and can proceed to Step 3 on the next page.)

Q&A Why does the Web address change after I enter it in the Address bar?

The Web address changes because you are being redirected to sign into Windows Live before you can access SkyDrive.

Q&A Can I open the file from Microsoft Word instead of using the Web browser?

If you are opening the file on the same computer from which you saved it to the SkyDrive, click File on the Ribbon to open the Backstage view. Click the Recent tab and then click the desired file name (Koala Exhibit Web, in this case) in the Recent Documents list, or click Open and then navigate to the location of the saved file (for a detailed example of this procedure, refer to the Office 2010 and Windows 7 chapter at the beginning of this book).

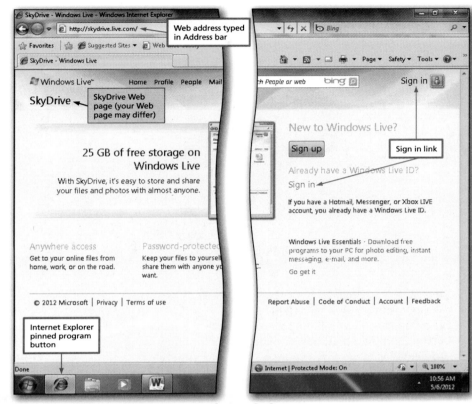

Figure C–9

2

- Click the Sign in link to display the Windows Live ID and Password text boxes (Figure C–10).

Q&A Why can I not locate the Sign in link?

If your computer remembers your Windows Live sign in credentials from a previous session, your e-mail address already may be displayed on the SkyDrive Web page. In this case, point to your e-mail address to display the Sign in button, click the Sign in button, and then proceed to Step 3. If you cannot locate your e-mail address or Sign in link, click the Sign in with a different Windows Live ID link and then proceed to Step 3.

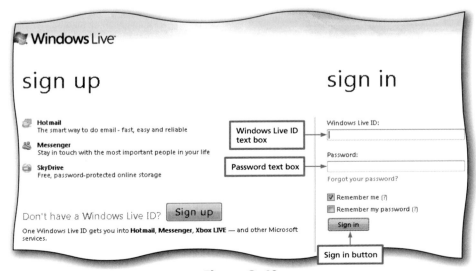

Figure C–10

3

- If necessary, enter your Windows Live ID and password in the appropriate text boxes and then click the Sign in button to sign into Windows Live and display the contents of your SkyDrive (Figure C–11).

Q&A

What if my screen shows the contents of a particular folder, instead of all folders?

To display all folders on your SkyDrive, point to Windows Live in the upper-left corner of the window and then click SkyDrive on the Windows Live menu.

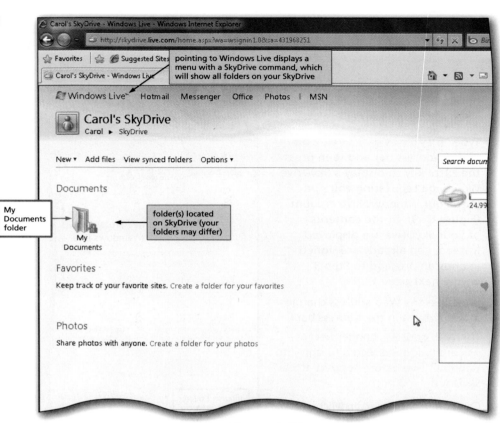

Figure C–11

4

- Click the My Documents folder, or the link corresponding to the folder containing the file you wish to open, to select the folder and display its contents (Figure C–12).

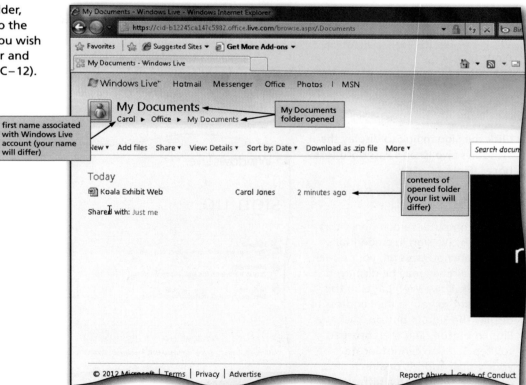

Figure C–12

5
- Point to the Koala Exhibit Web file to select the file and display commands associated with the file.
- Click the More link to display the More menu (Figure C–13).

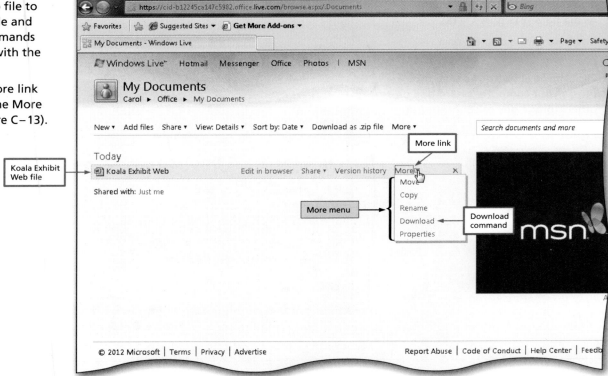

Figure C–13

6
- Click Download on the More menu to display the File Download dialog box (Figure C–14).

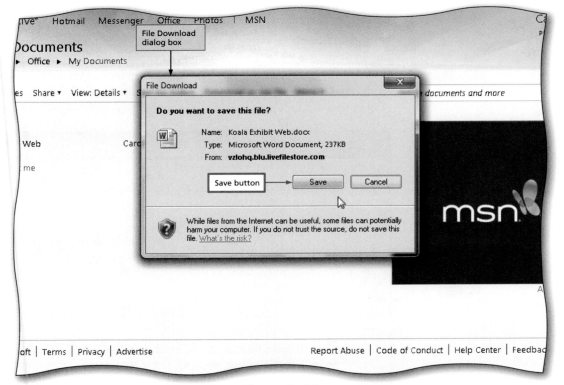

Figure C–14

- Click the Save button (File Download dialog box) to display the Save As dialog box (Figure C–15).

- Navigate to the desired save location.

- Click the Save button to save the file on your computer's hard disk or other storage device connected to the computer.

Figure C–15

Collaboration

In today's workplace, it is common to work with others on projects. Collaborating with the members of your team often requires sharing files. It also can involve multiple people editing and working with a certain set of files simultaneously. Placing files on SkyDrive in a public or shared folder enables others to view or modify the files. The members of the team then can view and edit the files simultaneously using Web Apps, enabling the team to work from one set of files (Figure C–16). Collaboration using Web Apps not only enables multiple people to work together, it also can reduce the amount of time required to complete a project.

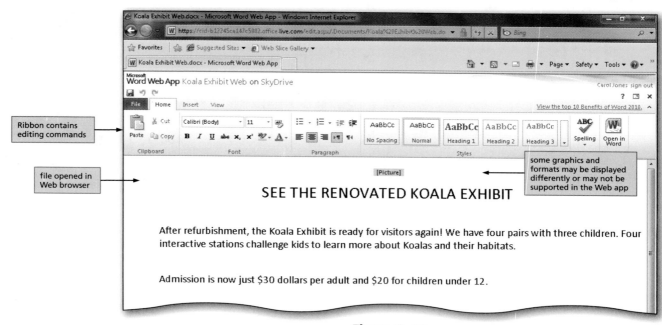

Figure C–16

Index

Quick Reference Summary

Task	Page Number	Mouse	Ribbon	Shortcut Menu	Keyboard Shortcut
All Caps	WD 81		Change Case button (Home tab | Font group), UPPERCASE		CTRL+SHIFT+A
AutoCorrect Entry, Create	WD 86		Options (File tab), Proofing (Word Options dialog box)		
AutoCorrect Options button, Use	WD 85	Point to AutoCorrect Options button in flagged word			
Bibliographical List, Create	WD 108		Bibliography button (References tab | Citations & Bibliography group)		
Bibliography Style, Change	WD 89		Bibliography Style box arrow (References tab | Citations & Bibliography group)		
Bold	WD 28	Bold button on Mini toolbar	Bold button (Home tab | Font group)	Font, Font tab (Font dialog box)	CTRL+B
Bullets, Apply	WD 22		Bullets button (Home tab | Paragraph group)	Bullets	* (ASTERISK), SPACEBAR
Center	WD 14	Center button on Mini toolbar	Center button (Home tab | Paragraph group)	Paragraph, Indents and Spacing tab (Paragraph dialog box)	CTRL+E
Change Case	WD 18		Change Case button (Home tab | Font group)	Font, Font tab (Font dialog box)	SHIFT+F3
Change Spacing before or after Paragraph	WD 43		Spacing Before or Spacing After box arrow (Page Layout tab | Paragraph group)	Paragraph, Indents and Spacing tab (Paragraph dialog box)	
Citation Placeholder, Insert	WD 94		Insert Citation button (References tab | Citations & Bibliography group), Add New Placeholder		
Citation, Edit	WD 91	Click citation, Citations Options box arrow, Edit Citation			
Citation, Insert	WD 90		Insert Citation button (References tab | Citations & Bibliography group), Add New Source		

Table 1: Microsoft Word 2010 Quick Reference Summary *(continued)*

Task	Page Number	Mouse	Ribbon	Shortcut Menu	Keyboard Shortcut
Click and Type	WD 80	Position mouse pointer until desired icon appears, then double-click			
Color Text	WD 25	Font Color button on Mini toolbar	Font Color button arrow (Home tab | Font group)		
Copy	WD 113		Copy button (Home tab | Clipboard group)	Copy	CTRL+C
Count Words	WD 101	Word Count indicator on status bar	Word Count button (Review tab | Proofing group)		CTRL+SHIFT+G
Custom Dictionary, Set Default, View or Modify Entries	WD 120		Options (File tab), Proofing (Word Options dialog box), Custom Dictionaries button		
Document Properties, Change	WD 49		Properties button (File tab | Info tab)		
Document Properties, Print	WD 123		File tab	Print tab, first button in Settings area		
Double-Space	WD 73		Line and Paragraph Spacing button (Home tab | Paragraph group)	Paragraph, Indents and Spacing tab (Paragraph dialog box)	CTRL+2
Double-Underline	WD 81		Underline button arrow (Home tab | Font group)	Font, Font tab (Font dialog box)	CTRL+SHIFT+D
Field, Convert to Regular text	WD 110				Click field, CTRL+SHIFT+F9
Find Text	WD 115	Select Browse Object button on vertical scroll bar, Find button	Find button (Home tab | Editing group)		CTRL+F
Font Size, Change	WD 16	Font Size box arrow on Mini toolbar	Font Size box arrow (Home tab | Font group)	Font, Font tab (Font dialog box)	CTRL+D
Font Size, Decrease	WD 81	Shrink Font button on Mini toolbar	Shrink Font button (Home tab | Font group)		CTRL+SHIFT+<
Font Size, Decrease 1 point	WD 81				CTRL+[
Font Size, Increase 1 point	WD 81				CTRL+]
Font, Change	WD 17	Font box arrow on Mini toolbar	Font box arrow (Home tab | Font group)	Font, Font tab (Font dialog box)	CTRL+D
Footnote, Insert	WD 93		Insert Footnote button (References tab | Footnotes group)		
Formatting Marks	WD 7		Show/Hide ¶ button (Home tab | Paragraph group)		CTRL+SHIFT+*
Go to a Page	WD 117	'Browse the pages in your document' tab in Navigation Pane	Find button arrow (Home tab | Editing group)		CTRL+G
Graphic, Resize	WD 34	Drag sizing handle	Shape Height and Shape Width text boxes (Picture Tools Format tab | Size group)	Size and Position, Size tab (Layout dialog box)	
Hanging Indent, Create	WD 81	Drag Hanging Indent marker on ruler	Paragraph Dialog Box Launcher (Home tab or Page Layout tab | Paragraph group), Indents and Spacing tab (Paragraph dialog box)	Paragraph, Indents and Spacing tab (Paragraph dialog box)	CTRL+T

Table 1: Microsoft Word 2010 Quick Reference Summary *(continued)*

Task	Page Number	Mouse	Ribbon	Shortcut Menu	Keyboard Shortcut
Hanging Indent, Remove	WD 81	Drag Hanging Indent marker on ruler	Paragraph Dialog Box Launcher (Home tab or Page Layout tab | Paragraph group), Indents and Spacing tab (Paragraph dialog box)	Paragraph, Indents and Spacing tab (Paragraph dialog box)	CTRL+SHIFT+T
Header and Footer, Close	WD 78	Double-click dimmed document text	Close Header and Footer button (Header & Footer Tools Design tab | Close group)		
Header, Switch to	WD 75	Double-click dimmed header	Header button (Insert tab | Header & Footer group)		
Indent, Decrease	WD 81	Drag First Line Indent marker on ruler	Decrease Indent button (Home tab | Paragraph group)	Paragraph, Indents and Spacing tab (Paragraph dialog box)	CTRL+SHIFT+M
Indent, First-Line	WD 83	Drag First Line Indent marker on ruler	Paragraph Dialog Box Launcher (Home tab or Page Layout tab | Paragraph group)	Paragraph, Indents and Spacing tab (Paragraph dialog box)	TAB
Indent, Increase	WD 81		Increase Indent button (Home tab | Paragraph group)		CTRL+M
Insertion Point, Move Down/Up One Line	WD 11				DOWN ARROW/ UP ARROW
Insertion Point, Move Down/Up One Paragraph	WD 11				CTRL+DOWN ARROW/ CTRL+UP ARROW
Insertion Point, Move Down/Up One Screen	WD 11				PAGE DOWN/ PAGE UP
Insertion Point, Move Left/ Right One Character	WD 11				LEFT ARROW/ RIGHT ARROW
Insertion Point, Move Left/ Right One Word	WD 11				CTRL+LEFT ARROW/ CTRL+RIGHT ARROW
Insertion Point, Move to Beginning/End of Document	WD 11				CTRL+HOME/ CTRL+END
Insertion Point, Move to Beginning/End of Line	WD 11				HOME/ END
Insertion Point, Move to Bottom of Document Window	WD 11				ALT+CTRL+PAGE DOWN/ ALT+CTRL+PAGE UP
Italicize	WD 24	Italic button on Mini toolbar	Italic button (Home tab | Font group)	Font, Font tab (Font dialog box)	CTRL+I
Justify Paragraph	WD 81		Justify button (Home tab | Paragraph group)	Paragraph, Indents and Spacing tab (Paragraph dialog box)	CTRL+J
Left-Align Paragraph	WD 81		Align Text Left button (Home tab | Paragraph group)	Paragraph, Indents and Spacing tab (Paragraph dialog box)	CTRL+L

Table 1: Microsoft Word 2010 Quick Reference Summary *(continued)*

Task	Page Number	Mouse	Ribbon	Shortcut Menu	Keyboard Shortcut
Line Spacing, Change	WD 73		Line and Paragraph Spacing button (Home tab | Paragraph group)	Paragraph, Indents and Spacing tab (Paragraph dialog box)	CTRL+[number of desired line spacing, i.e., 2 for double-spacing]
Move Text	WD 47	Drag and drop selected text	Cut button (Home tab | Clipboard group); Paste button (Home tab | Clipboard group)	Cut; Paste	CTRL+X; CTRL+V
Normal Style, Apply	WD 106		Normal in Quick Style gallery (Home tab | Styles group)		CTRL+SHIFT+S
Normal Style, Modify	WD 71		Styles Dialog Box Launcher (Home tab | Styles group), style box arrow, Modify	Right-click style (Home tab | Styles group), Modify	
Open a Document	WD 45		Open (File tab)		CTRL+O
Page Border, Add	WD 41		Page Borders button (Page Layout tab | Page Background group)		
Page Break, Insert	WD 106		Page Break button (Insert tab | Pages group)		CTRL+ENTER
Page Number, Insert	WD 77		Insert Page Number button (Header & Footer Tools Design tab | Header & Footer group)		
Paste	WD 113		Paste button (Home tab | Clipboard group)	Paste	CTRL+V
Paste Options Menu, Display	WD 114	Paste Options button by moved/copied text			
Picture Style, Apply	WD 37		More button in Picture Styles gallery (Picture Tools Format tab | Picture Styles group)		
Picture Effects, Apply	WD 38		Picture Effects button (Picture Tools Format tab | Picture Styles group)	Format Picture	
Picture, Insert	WD 31		Insert Picture from File button (Insert tab | Illustrations group)		
Preview a Document	WD 124		File tab | Print tab, Next Page and Previous Page buttons		CTRL+P, ENTER
Print Document	WD 51		Print button (File tab | Print tab)		CTRL+P
Quit Word	WD 44	Close button on title bar	Exit (File tab)		ALT+F4
Redo	WD 23	Redo button on Quick Access Toolbar			CTRL+Y
Remove Character Formatting	WD 81				CTRL+SPACEBAR
Remove Paragraph Formatting	WD 81				CTRL+Q
Remove Space after Paragraph	WD 74		Line and Paragraph Spacing button (Home tab | Paragraph group)	Paragraph, Indents and Spacing tab (Paragraph dialog box)	CTRL+0 (zero)

Table 1: Microsoft Word 2010 Quick Reference Summary *(continued)*

Task	Page Number	Mouse	Ribbon	Shortcut Menu	Keyboard Shortcut
Replace Text	WD 116	Select Browse Object button on vertical scroll bar, Find button, Replace tab (Find and Replace dialog box)	Replace button (Home tab | Editing group)		CTRL+H
Research Task Pane, Look Up Information	WD 120	ALT+click desired word	Research button (Review tab | Proofing group)		
Right-Align	WD 76		Align Text Right button (Home tab | Paragraph group)	Paragraph, Indents and Spacing tab (Paragraph dialog box)	CTRL+R
Rulers, Display	WD 82	View Ruler button on vertical scroll bar	View Ruler check box (View tab | Show group)		
Save New Document	WD 12	Save button on Quick Access Toolbar	Save or Save As (File tab)		F12
Save Document, Same File Name	WD 30	Save button on Quick Access toolbar	Save (File tab)		CTRL+S
Scroll, Page by Page	WD 112	Previous Page/Next Page button on vertical scroll bar			CTRL+PAGE UP or CTRL+PAGE DOWN
Scroll, Up/Down One Line	WD 11	Click scroll arrow at top/bottom of vertical scroll bar			
Scroll, Up/Down One Screen	WD 11	Click above/below scroll box on vertical scroll bar			
Select Block of Text	WD 30	Click beginning, SHIFT-click end			
Select Character(s)	WD 30	Drag through characters			SHIFT+RIGHT ARROW or SHIFT+LEFT ARROW
Select Entire Document	WD 30	In left margin, triple-click	Select button arrow (Home tab | Editing group)		CTRL+A
Select Graphic	WD 30	Click graphic			
Select Group of Words	WD 27	Drag mouse pointer through words			CTRL+SHIFT+RIGHT ARROW
Select Line	WD 15	Click in left margin			SHIFT+DOWN ARROW
Select Multiple Lines	WD 21	Drag mouse pointer in left margin			SHIFT+DOWN ARROW
Select Nonadjacent Items	WD 15	Select first item, hold down CTRL key while selecting item(s)			
Select Paragraph	WD 30	Triple-click paragraph			CTRL+SHIFT+DOWN ARROW or CTRL+SHIFT+UP ARROW
Select Sentence	WD 30	CTRL-click			
Select Word	WD 30	Double-click word			CTRL+SHIFT+RIGHT ARROW or CTRL+SHIFT+LEFT ARROW
Shade Paragraph	WD 20		Shading button arrow (Home tab | Paragraph group)		

Table 1: Microsoft Word 2010 Quick Reference Summary *(continued)*

Task	Page Number	Mouse	Ribbon	Shortcut Menu	Keyboard Shortcut
Single-Space Lines	WD 81		Line and Paragraph Spacing button (Home tab | Paragraph group)	Paragraph, Indents and Spacing tab (Paragraph dialog box)	CTRL+1
Small Caps	WD 81		Font Dialog Box Launcher (Home Tab | Font group), Font tab (Font dialog box)		CTRL+SHIFT+K
Source, Edit	WD 97		Click citation, Citation Options box arrow, Edit Source		
Source, Modify	WD 109		Manage Sources button (References tab | Citations & Bibliography group), Edit button		
Spelling and Grammar, Check at Once	WD 118	Spelling and Grammar check icon on status bar, Spelling	Spelling & Grammar button (Review tab | Proofing group)	Spelling	F7
Spelling, Check as You Type	WD 9	Click word, Spelling and Grammar Check icon on status bar		Right-click error, click correct word on shortcut menu	
Style, Update to Match Selection	WD 74		Right-click style in Quick Style gallery (Home tab | Styles group)	Styles	
Subscript	WD 81		Subscript button (Home tab | Font group)	Font, Font tab (Font dialog box)	CTRL+EQUAL SIGN
Superscript	WD 81		Superscript button (Home tab | Font group)	Font, Font tab (Font dialog box)	CTRL+SHIFT+PLUS SIGN
Synonym, Find and Insert	WD 118		Thesaurus (Review tab | Proofing group)	Right-click word, click desired synonym on Synonym submenu	SHIFT+F7
Text Effect, Apply	WD 19		Text Effects button (Home tab | Font group)		
Theme Colors, Change	WD 28		Change Styles button (Home tab | Styles group)		
Underline	WD 27	Underline button on Mini toolbar	Underline button (Home tab | Font group)	Font, Font tab (Font dialog box)	CTRL+U
Underline Words, Not Spaces	WD 81		Font Dialog Box Launcher (Home tab | Font group), Font tab (Font dialog box), Underline style box arrow		CTRL+SHIFT+W
Undo	WD 23	Undo button on Quick Access Toolbar			CTRL+Z
Zoom Document	WD 33	Zoom Out or Zoom In button on status bar	Zoom button (View tab | Zoom group)		
Zoom One Page	WD 41		One Page button (View tab | Zoom group)		

Table 2: Microsoft PowerPoint 2010 Quick Reference Summary

Task	Page Number	Mouse	Ribbon	Shortcut Menu	Keyboard Shortcut
Clip Art, Insert	PPT 27	Clip Art icon in slide	Clip Art button (Insert tab | Images group)		
Clip Art, Photo, or Shape, Move	PPT 36	Drag			ARROW KEYS move selected image in small increments
Copy	PPT 108		Copy button (Home tab | Clipboard group)	Copy	CTRL+C
Document Properties, Change	PPT 46		Properties button (File tab | Info tab)		
Document Theme, Change Color	PPT 81		Colors button (Design tab | Themes group)		
Document Theme, Choose	PPT 5		More button (Design tab | Themes group)		
Font Size, Decrease	PPT 104	Decrease Font Size button or Font Size box arrow on Mini toolbar	Decrease Font Size button or Font Size box arrow (Home tab | Font group)		CTRL+SHIFT+<
Font Size, Increase	PPT 11	Increase Font Size button or Font Size box arrow on Mini toolbar	Increase Font Size button or Font Size box arrow (Home tab | Font group)		CTRL+SHIFT+>
Font, Change	PPT 102	Font box arrow on Mini toolbar	Font box arrow (Home tab | Font group)	Font, Font tab (Font dialog box)	CTRL+SHIFT+F
Font, Change Color	PPT 13	Font Color button or Font Color button arrow on Mini toolbar	Font Color button or Font Color button arrow (Home tab | Font group)	Font, Font tab (Font dialog box)	CTRL+SHIFT+F
Format Painter, Use	PPT 105	Format Painter button on Mini toolbar	Double-click Format Painter button (Home tab | Clipboard group), select text with format you want to copy, select text to apply previously selected format; press ESC to turn off Format Painter		
List Level, Increase	PPT 17	Increase List Level button on Mini toolbar	Increase List Level button (Home tab | Paragraph group)		TAB or ALT+SHIFT+RIGHT ARROW
List Level, Decrease	PPT 18	Decrease List Level button on Mini toolbar	Decrease List Level button (Home tab | Paragraph group)		SHIFT+TAB or ALT+SHIFT+LEFT ARROW
Next Slide	PPT 25	Next Slide button on vertical scroll bar or next slide thumbnail on Slides tab			PAGE DOWN
Open Presentation	PPT 50		Open (File tab)		CTRL+O
Paste	PPT 109		Paste button (Home tab | Clipboard group)	Paste	CTRL+V
Photo, Insert	PPT 32, 83	Insert Picture from File icon on slide or Insert Clip Art icon on slide	Picture button or Clip Art button (Insert tab | Images group)		
Picture, Add Border	PPT 91		Picture border button (Picture Tools Format tab | Picture Styles group)		

Table 2: Microsoft PowerPoint 2010 Quick Reference Summary *(continued)*

Task	Page Number	Mouse	Ribbon	Shortcut Menu	Keyboard Shortcut
Picture, Correct	PPT 87		Corrections button (Picture Tools Format tab | Adjust group)	Format Picture, Picture Corrections (Format Picture dialog box)	
Picture Border, Change Color	PPT 92		Picture border button (Picture Tools Format tab | Picture Styles group)		
Picture Effects, Apply	PPT 89		Picture Effects button (Picture Tools Format tab | Picture Styles group)	Format Picture	
Picture Style, Apply	PPT 87		More button (Picture Tools Format tab | Picture Styles group)		
Previous Slide	PPT 26	Previous Slide button on vertical scroll bar or click previous slide thumbnail on Slides tab			PAGE UP
Print a Presentation	PPT 51		Print button (File tab | Print tab)		CTRL+P
Quit PowerPoint	PPT 50	Close button on title bar	Exit (File tab)	Right-click Microsoft PowerPoint button on taskbar, click Close window	ALT+F4
Resize	PPT 33, 93	Drag sizing handles	Enter height and width values (Picture Tools Format tab | Size group or Drawing Tools Format tab | Size group)	Format Picture or Format Shape, Size tab; or enter height and width in Shape Height and Shape Width boxes	
Save a Presentation	PPT 14	Save button on Quick Access Toolbar	Save or Save As (File tab)		CTRL+S or F12
Shape, Apply Style	PPT 110		More button or Format Shape Dialog Box Launcher in Shapes Style gallery (Drawing Tools Format tab | Shape Styles group)	Format Shape	
Shape, Insert	PPT 106		Shapes button (Home tab | Drawing group); More button (Drawing Tools Format tab | Insert Shapes group)		
Slide, Add	PPT 14		New Slide button (Home tab | Slides group)		CTRL+M
Slide, Arrange	PPT 39	Drag slide in Slides tab or Outline tab to new position, or in Slide Sorter view drag to new position			
Slide, Duplicate	PPT 38		New Slide arrow (Home tab | Slides group), Duplicate Selected Slides		

Table 2: Microsoft PowerPoint 2010 Quick Reference Summary *(continued)*

Task	Page Number	Mouse	Ribbon	Shortcut Menu	Keyboard Shortcut
Slide, Format Background	PPT 95		Background Styles button (Design tab | Background group)	Format Background	
Slide, Insert Picture as Background	PPT 97		Background Styles button (Design tab | Background group)	Format Background, Picture or Texture Fill, Insert from File (Format Background dialog box)	
Slide, Select Layout	PPT 21		Layout button or New Slide arrow (Home tab | Slides group)		
Slide Show View	PPT 47	Slide Show button at lower-right PowerPoint window	Slide Show button (Slide Show tab | Start Slide Show group)		F5
Slide Show, End	PPT 49	Click black ending slide		End Show	ESC or HYPHEN
Text, Add Shadow	PPT 103		Text Shadow button (Home tab | Font group)		
Text, Bold	PPT 20	Bold button on Mini toolbar	Bold button (Home tab | Font group)	Font, Font tab (Font dialog box)	CTRL+B
Text, Change Color	PPT 13	Font Color button or Font Color button arrow on Mini toolbar	Font Color button or Font Color button arrow (Home tab | Font group)	Font, Font tab (Font dialog box)	
Text, Delete	PPT 41		Cut button (Home tab | Clipboard group)	Cut	DELETE or CTRL+X or BACKSPACE
Text, Italicize	PPT 11	Italic button on Mini toolbar	Italic button (Home tab | Font group)	Font, Font tab (Font dialog box)	CTRL+I
Text, Select Paragraph	PPT 10	Triple-click paragraph			SHIFT+DOWN ARROW or SHIFT+UP ARROW
Text, Select Word	PPT 12	Double-click word			CTRL+SHIFT+RIGHT ARROW or CTRL+SHIFT+LEFT ARROW
Transition, Add	PPT 43		Transitions tab | Transition to This Slide group		ALT+A , T
Transparency, Change	PPT 98		Background Styles button (Design tab | Background group), Format Background, move Transparency slider	Format Background, Transparency slider	
WordArt, Add Text Effects	PPT 115		Text Effects button (Drawing Tools Format tab | WordArt Styles group)		
WordArt, Insert	PPT 114		WordArt button (Insert tab | Text group)		

Table 3: Microsoft Excel 2010 Quick Reference Summary

Task	Page Number	Mouse	Ribbon	Shortcut Menu	Keyboard Shortcut
Accounting Number Format, Apply	EX 100		Accounting Number Format button (Home tab | Number group)		
All data in a cell, Select	EX 51	Double-click if there are no spaces in data			
Auto Fill	EX 18	Drag fill handle	Auto Fill Options button (Home tab | Editing group)		
AutoCalculate	EX 48	Select range | right-click AutoCalculate area | click calculation			
Average Function	EX 84	Insert Function box in formula bar | AVERAGE in Select a function list | OK | range | OK	Sum button arrow (Home tab | Editing group) or Sum button arrow (Formulas tab | Function Library)		Type =av | press DOWN ARROW | ENTER
Background Color, Change	EX 96		Format Cells Dialog Box Launcher (Home tab | Font group) | Fill tab | click color | click OK	Format Cells on shortcut menu	CTRL+1
Best Fit	EX 107	Select columns | point to boundary until arrow is split double arrow | double-click			
Bold	EX 25	Bold button on Mini toolbar	Bold button (Home tab | Font group)	Format Cells on shortcut menu | Font tab | Bold	CTRL+B
Cell Entries, Clear Selected	EX 52	Drag fill handle from empty cell through cells with entries	Clear button (Home tab | Editing group) | Clear Contents	Clear Contents on shortcut menu	DELETE
Cell Reference, Add	EX 78	Click cell			
Cell Style, Change	EX 52		Cell Styles button (Home tab | Styles group)		
Cell, Highlight	EX 19	Drag mouse pointer			
Cell, Select	EX 34	Click cell or click Name box, type cell reference, press ENTER			Use arrow keys
Cells, Merge and Center	EX 28	Merge & Center button on Mini toolbar	Merge & Center button (Home tab | Alignment group)	Format Cells on shortcut menu | Alignment tab	
Characters to left of insertion point, Delete	EX 50				BACKSPACE
Characters to right of insertion point, Delete	EX 50				DELETE
Characters, Highlight	EX 51	Drag through adjacent characters			SHIFT+RIGHT ARROW or SHIFT+LEFT ARROW
Chart, Add	EX 38		Charts group | Insert tab		
Color Text	EX 27	Font Color button on Mini toolbar	Font Color button arrow (Home tab | Font group)		
Column Width	EX 33	Drag column heading boundary		Column Width on shortcut menu	

Table 3: Microsoft Excel 2010 Quick Reference Summary *(continued)*

Task	Page Number	Mouse	Ribbon	Shortcut Menu	Keyboard Shortcut
Comma Style Format, Apply	EX 100		Comma Style button (Home tab | Number group)		
Complete an Entry	EX 8	Click Enter box			Press ENTER
Conditional Formatting	EX 104		Conditional Formatting button (Home tab | Styles group)		
Copy Range of Cells	EX 80	Select range | drag fill handle |	Copy button (Home tab | Clipboard group) |	Copy on shortcut menu	CTRL+C
Currency Style Format, Apply	EX 100		Format Cells: Number Dialog Box Launcher (Home tab | Number group)		CTRL+1 OR CTRL+SHIFT+ DOLLAR SIGN ($)
Date, Format	EX 98		Format Cells: Number Dialog Box Launcher on Home tab	Format Cells on shortcut menu | Number tab (Format Cells dialog box)	
Document Properties, Change	EX 43		Properties button (File tab | Info tab)		
Document Properties, Print	EX 45		File tab | Print tab, first box arrow (Settings area)		
Document Properties, Set or View	EX 43		File | Info tab		
Entry, Complete	EX 8	Click Enter box			Press ENTER
Font Color	EX 27	Font Color box arrow on Mini toolbar	Font Color button arrow (Home tab | Font group)	Format Cells on shortcut menu | Font tab	
Font Size, Decrease	EX 26	Font Size box arrow on Mini toolbar	Decrease Font Size button (Home tab | Font group)	Format Cells on shortcut menu | Font tab	
Font Size, Increase	EX 26	Font Size box arrow on Mini toolbar	Increase Font Size button (Home tab | Font group)	Format Cells | Font Tab	
Font Type	EX 24	Font box arrow on Mini toolbar	Font box (Home tab | Font group)	Format Cells | Font tab	
Font, Change	EX 24	Font Size box arrow on Mini toolbar	Font box arrow (Home tab | Font group)	Format Cells | Font tab	
Formulas Version	EX 119				CTRL+ACCENT MARK (`)
Highlight Cells	EX 18	Drag mouse pointer			SHIFT+ARROW KEY
In-Cell Editing	EX 50	Double-click cell			F2
Insert and Overtype modes, Toggle between	EX 50				INSERT
Insertion point, Move	EX 8	Click			Use arrow keys
Insertion point, move to beginning of data in cell	EX 51	Point to left of first character and click			HOME
Insertion point, move to ending of data in cell	EX 51	Point to right of last character and click			END
Margins, Change	EX 114	Page Layout button on status bar | Page Layout tab | Margins button	Page Setup Dialog Box Launcher | Margins tab (Page Layout tab | Page Setup group)		

Table 3: Microsoft Excel 2010 Quick Reference Summary (continued)

Task	Page Number	Mouse	Ribbon	Shortcut Menu	Keyboard Shortcut
Max Function	EX 86	Insert Function box in formula bar | MAX in Select a function list | OK | range | OK	Sum button arrow (Home tab | Editing group) or Sum button arrow (Formulas tab | Sum group)		
Min Function	EX 87	Insert Function box in the formula bar | MIN in Select a function list | OK | range | OK	Sum button arrow (Home tab | Editing group) or Sum button arrow (Formulas tab | Sum group)		
New Line in Cell, Start	EX 71				ALT+ENTER
Numbers, Format	EX 31	Accounting Number Format, Percent Style, or Comma Style button on Mini toolbar	Cell Styles button (Home tab | Styles group) or Accounting Number Format, Percent Style, or Comma Style button (Home tab | Number group), or Format Cells: Number dialog box launcher | Accounting, or Percentage or Number Format list arrow | Accounting or Percentage		
Open a Workbook	EX 48		Open or Recent (File tab)		CTRL+O
Percent style format	EX 103		Percent Style button (Home tab | Number group)	Format Cells on shortcut menu | Number tab | Percentage (Format Cells dialog box)	CTRL+SHIFT+ percent sign (%)
Print Scaling Option	EX 120		Page Setup Dialog Box Launcher (Page Layout tab | Page Setup group)		
Print Section of Worksheet	EX 118		File | Print tab | Print Active Sheets or Print Area button (Page Layout tab | Page Setup group)		
Print Worksheet	EX 46		File tab | Print tab		CTRL+P
Quit Excel	EX 47	Close button on right side of title bar	Exit (File tab)		
Range Finder	EX 91	Double-click cell			
Range, Deselect	EX 18	Click outside range			
Range, Select	EX 28	Drag fill handle through range			
Redo	EX 51	Redo button on Quick Access Toolbar			CTRL+Y
Row Height	EX 110	Drag row heading boundary		Row Height on shortcut menu	
Save Workbook	EX 20	Save button on Quick Access Toolbar	Save (File tab | Save button)		CTRL+S
Save Workbook, New Name	EX 20	Save button on Quick Access Toolbar			
Save Workbook, Same Name	EX 20	Save button on Quick Access Toolbar	Save (File tab | Save button)		CTRL+S

Table 3: Microsoft Excel 2010 Quick Reference Summary (continued)

Task	Page Number	Mouse	Ribbon	Shortcut Menu	Keyboard Shortcut
Select Cell	EX 7	Click cell or click Name box, type cell reference, press ENTER			Use arrow keys
Select Entire Worksheet	EX 52	Click Select All button			CTRL+A
Select Nonadjacent Cells	EX 100	Select first cell, hold down CTRL key while selecting second cell			
Selected characters, Delete	EX 50		Cut button (Home tab | Clipboard group)		DELETE
Selected Chart, Delete	EX 53				DELETE
Sheet Name, Change	EX 42	Double-click type name		Rename on shortcut menu	
Spelling	EX 112		Spelling button (Review tab | Proofing group)		F7
Sum	EX 15	Click Insert Function button in formula bar | SUM in Select a function list | OK | range | OK	Sum button (Home tab | Editing group)		ALT+EQUAL SIGN (=) twice
Text, Delete after typing but before pressing the ENTER key	EX 8	Click Cancel box in formula bar			Press ESC
Text, Delete while typing	EX 8				Press BACKSPACE
Undo	EX 51	Undo button on Quick Access Toolbar			CTRL+Z
Workbook Theme, Change	EX 94		Themes button (Page Layout tab | Themes group)		
Worksheet Name, Change	EX 42	Double-click sheet tab, type name		Rename on shortcut menu	
Worksheet, Clear	EX 52		Select All button | Clear button (Home tab | Editing group)		CTRL A, press DELETE
Worksheet, Preview	EX 46		File tab | Print tab		CTRL+P

Table 4: Microsoft Access 2010 Quick Reference Summary

Task	Page Number	Mouse	Ribbon	Shortcut Menu	Keyboard Shortcut
All Fields in Query, Include	AC 79, AC 80	Double-click asterisk			
Calculated Field in Query, Use	AC 116			Right-click field row, Zoom	
Caption, Change in Query	AC 118		Property Sheet button (Query Tools Design Tab | Show/Hide group), Caption box	Right-click field in design grid, click Properties on shortcut menu, Caption box	
Close Object	AC 23	Close button for object		Right-click item, Close	

Table 4: Microsoft Access 2010 Quick Reference Summary (continued)

Task	Page Number	Mouse	Ribbon	Shortcut Menu	Keyboard Shortcut
Column Headings, Modify	AC 54			Right-click field name, Rename Field	
Column, Resize	AC 54, AC 55	Double-click right boundary of field selector in datasheet		Right-click field name, Field Width	
Comparison Operator, Use	AC 91	Create query, enter comparison operator in criterion			
Compound Criterion Involving AND, Use	AC 92				Place criteria on same line
Compound Criterion Involving OR, Use	AC 93				Place criteria on separate lines
Criteria, Use in Calculating Statistics	AC 121		Totals button (Query Tools Design Tab | Show/Hide group), Total box arrow, click calculation		
Criterion, Use	AC 46	Right-click query, Design View, Criteria row			
Crosstab Query, Create	AC 124		Query Wizard button (Create tab | Queries group), Crosstab Query Wizard		
Data, Export to Excel	AC 111		Excel button (External Data tab | Export group)	Right-click object, click Excel on Export menu	
Data, Import	AC 38		Button for imported data format (External Data tab | Import & Link group)	Right-click object, click selected format on Import menu	
Data, Sort in Query	AC 96		Select field in design grid, click Sort row, click Sort row arrow, select order		
Database Properties, Change	AC 59		View and edit database properties link (File tab | Info tab)		
Database, Create	AC 13		Blank database button (File tab | New tab)		
Design Grid, Clear	AC 95	In Design view, select all columns, DELETE			
Duplicates, Omit	AC 97		In Design view, click first empty field, Property Sheet button (Query Tools Design tab | Show/Hide group), click Yes in Unique Values property box	Right-click first empty field, click Properties on shortcut menu, click Yes in Unique Values property box	
Field in Query, Add	AC 79	Double-click field in upper pane			
Form for Query, Create	AC 109		Select query, Form button (Create tab | Forms group)		
Form, Create	AC 48		Form button (Create tab | Forms group)		

Table 4: Microsoft Access 2010 Quick Reference Summary *(continued)*

Task	Page Number	Mouse	Ribbon	Shortcut Menu	Keyboard Shortcut
Grouping, Use	AC 122	Create query, select Group By in Total row, select field to group by			
Join Properties, Change	AC 105			In Design view, right-click join line	
Multiple Keys, Sort on	AC 98	Assign two sort keys in design grid			
Navigation Pane, Customize	AC 127	Navigation Pane arrow			
Number Criterion, Use	AC 90	Create query, select table, enter criterion in field grid			
Open Database	AC 27		Open button (File tab)		
Open Table	AC 24	Double-click table in Navigation Pane		Right-click table in Navigation Pane, click Open in shortcut menu	
Parameter Query, Create	AC 87		In Design view, type parameter in square brackets in criterion row of field grid, View button (Query Tools Design tab | Results group)		
Preview or Print Object	AC 31		Print or Print Preview button (File tab | Print tab)		CTRL+P, ENTER
Query, Create in Design View	AC 78		Query Design button (Create tab | Queries group)		
Query, Create using Simple Query Wizard	AC 43		Query Wizard button (Create tab | Queries group)		
Query, Export	AC 111, AC 113, AC 114		Select query in Navigation Pane, application button (External Data tab | Export group)	Right-click query in Navigation Pane, click Export	
Record, Add	AC 28	New (blank) record button in Navigation buttons	New button (Home tab | Records Group)		CTRL+PLUS SIGN (+)
Records in a Join, Restrict	AC 115	In Design view, enter criterion for query			
Remaining Fields in Table, Define	AC 19	In Datasheet view, click Click to Add field (Fields tab)			
Report, Create	AC 52		Report button (Create tab | Reports group)		
Report, Create Involving Join	AC 106		Select query, Report Wizard button (Create tab | Reports group)		
Save Object	AC 21	Save button on Quick Access Toolbar	File tab, Save		CTRL+S
Statistics, Calculate	AC 119		Create query, Totals button (Query Tools Design tab | Show/Hide group), click Total row in design grid, click Total box arrow, select calculation		

Table 4: Microsoft Access 2010 Quick Reference Summary (continued)

Task	Page Number	Mouse	Ribbon	Shortcut Menu	Keyboard Shortcut
Table, Create in Design View	AC 33		Table Design button (Create tab | Tables group)		
Table, View in Design View	AC 21		View button arrow (Table Tools Fields tab | Views group), Design View		
Tables, Join	AC 102		Query Design button (Create tab | Queries group), add field lists for tables to join, add desired fields to design grid, view query		
Text Data Criterion, Use	AC 80	Enter text as criterion in Criteria row of design grid			
Top Values Query, Create	AC 99		In Design view, Return box arrow (Query Tools Design tab | Query Setup group)		
Totals, Add to a Report	AC 57		Totals button (Report Layout Tools Design tab | Grouping & Totals group)		
Wildcard, Use	AC 83	In Design view, click Criteria row in design grid, type criterion including wildcard			